The Zinn Reader

The Zinn Reader

Writings on Disobedience and Democracy

Howard Zinn

Seven Stories Press/New York

In the U.K.:
Turnaround Publisher Services Ltd., Unit 3, Olympia Trading Estate, Coburg Road, Wood Green, London N22 6TZ U.K.

In Canada:
Hushion House, 36 Northline Road, Toronto, Ontario M4B 3E2, Canada

Library of Congress Cataloging-in-Publication Data

Zinn, Howard, 1922-
    [Essays. Selections]
    The Zinn reader: writings on disobedience and democracy / Howard Zinn—Seven Stories press 1st ed.
       p.   cm.
    ISBN 1-888363-53-3 (cloth). —ISBN 1-888363-54-1 (pbk.)
    1. United States—History. 2. United States—Politics and govern-
ment. 3. United States—Social conditions. I. Title.
E178.6.Z552 1997
973—dc21   97-24778
                                            CIP

Seven Stories Press
632 Broadway, 7th Floor
New York, NY 10012

9 8 7 6 5 4 3 2 1

Printed in the U.S.A.

To Noah, and his generation.

Contents

II. Class

III. War

V. History

VI. Means and Ends

Acknowledgments

I must first thank my editor and publisher, Dan Simon of Seven Stories Press, not just for initiating this project, but for carrying it through all the way with extraordinary intelligence and energy. He is an ideal editor, clear in his vision of what a book should be, firm in pursuing that vision, and still sensitive to the needs of the writer—altogether a pleasure to work with.

My wife Roslyn, as always, encouraged me to do what had to be done, providing wise counsel again and again.

Thanks also to HarperCollins for permission to use material from my book *Declarations of Independence*, to Beacon Press for permission to use material from my book *You Can't Be Neutral on a Moving Train*, to the University of Illinois Press for permission to use material from my book *The Politics of History.*

Introduction

This seems to me a big book to swallow, and I blame it on the fact that in 1978, when I was teaching in Paris, I looked up the son of friends back in the States, a young man of college age. He was working in a tiny restaurant in the Latin Quarter—indeed with only one table—Le Petit Vatel. This was the start of a friendship with Dan Simon, who went on to become the ingenious editor and publisher of the small, independent, much-respected Seven Stories Press, and who proposed the idea of a Zinn Reader.

I delayed my response for two years, to give the appearance of modesty, and then agreed. I wanted to think of it as a generous act—giving all those who know my biggest-selling book (*A People's History of the United States*) a chance to sample my other work: books out of print, books still in print, essays, articles, pamphlets, lectures, reviews, newspaper columns, written over the past thirty-five years or so, and often not easy to find. An opportunity, or a punishment? Only the reader can decide.

My first published writings came out of my seven years in the South, teaching at Spelman College, a college for black women in Atlanta, Georgia. I was finishing my Ph.D. in history at Columbia University, with the indispensable help of the GI Bill, after serving as a bombardier with the Eighth Air Force in World War II.

My years at Spelman were 1956 to 1963, and I became involved, with my students, in the Southern movement against racial segregation. My very first published article, in *Harper's Magazine* in 1959 ("A Fate Worse Than Integration"), became the basis for a larger essay "The Southern Mystique," which appeared in *The American Scholar.*

I was invited to become a member of the executive board (as an "adult adviser") of the Student Nonviolent Coordinating Committee (SNCC), which had come out of the sit-ins and was, I think it is fair to say, the leading edge of the Southern civil rights movement. In the next several years I became an observer-participant in demonstrations in Atlanta; in Albany, Georgia; Selma, Alabama; and Hattiesburg, Mississippi. I was now writing for *The Nation, The New Republic, The Crisis,* and other publications.

The historian Martin Duberman, whose documentary play, *In White America,* I had greatly admired, asked me to write an essay comparing the Civil War-era abolitionists with the activists of the Sixties. It appeared in a volume he edited called *The Anti-Slavery Vanguard,* and I called it "Abolitionists, Freedom Riders, and the Tactics of Agitation." It was an approach I was going to use again and again—to find wisdom and inspiration from the past for movements seeking social justice in our time.

There was never, for me as teacher and writer, an obsession with "objectivity," which I considered neither possible nor desirable. I understood early that what is presented as "history" or as "news" is inevitably a selection out of an infinite amount of information, and that what is selected depends on what the selector thinks is important.

Those who talk from high perches about the sanctity of "facts" are parroting Charles Dickens' stiff-backed pedant in *Hard Times,* Mr. Gradgrind, who insisted his students give him "facts, facts, nothing but facts." But behind any presented fact, I had come to believe, is a judgment—the judgment that *this* fact is important to put forward (and, by implication, other facts may be ignored). And any such judgment reflects the beliefs, the values of the historian, however he or she pretends to "objectivity."

I was relieved when I decided that keeping one's judgments out of historical narrative was impossible, because I had already determined that I would never do that. I had grown up amidst poverty, had been in a war, had witnessed the ugliness of race hatred, and I was not going to pretend to neutrality.

As I told my students at the start of my courses, "You can't be neutral on a moving train." That is, the world is already moving in certain directions—many of them horrifying. Children are going hungry, people are dying in wars. To be neutral in such a situation is to collaborate with what is going on. The word "collaborator" had a deadly meaning in the Nazi era. It should have that meaning still.

Therefore, I doubt you will find in the following pages any hint of "neutrality."

The GI Bill paid my way all through undergraduate and graduate school. While my wife, Roslyn, worked, and our two kids were in nursery school, we lived in a low-income housing project on the Lower East Side. I attended classes during the day and worked the four to midnight shift loading trucks at a Manhattan warehouse. It is hardly surprising that I was to have a persistent interest, as a historian, in the issue of economic justice.

For my doctoral thesis at Columbia University I chose as my subject Fiorello LaGuardia. He was known best as the feisty, rambunctious mayor of New York in the New Deal era, but before that, in the Twenties, he was in Congress, representing a district of poor people in East Harlem.

As I began reading through his papers, left to the Municipal Archives in New York by his widow, he spoke to my young radicalism. He was on his feet in the House of Representatives perhaps more often than any other member, demanding to be heard above the din of the Jazz Age, crying out to the nation about the reality of suffering underneath the spurious "prosperity" of the Twenties.

My thesis, "Conscience of the Jazz Age: LaGuardia in Congress," won a prize from the American Historical Association, which sponsored its publication by Cornell University Press. Out of that came an essay published in my book *The Politics of History*. It was a glimpse of LaGuardia at work against the hypocrisy of "a booming economy" which concealed distress. We see that today in the exultation accompanying every upward leap in the Dow Jones average, even while a quarter of the nation's children grow up in poverty.

Reading on my own, I became fascinated by the history of labor struggles in the United States, something that was absent in my courses in American history. Reaching back into that history (often disheartening, often inspiring), I began to look closely into the Colorado coal strike of 1913-14, and my essay "The Ludlow Massacre" comes out of that.

Later, when I was asked to edit a volume of writings on *New Deal Thought*, I found even the welcome reforms of the New Deal insufficient. My introduction to that volume, printed here as "The Limits of the New Deal," points to the inability of the Roosevelt reforms to cure the underlying sickness of a system which put business profit ahead of human need. There were thinkers in the Thirties who understood this, and I used the volume to present their ideas.

In 1963, Roz, our children, and I left Spelman College and Atlanta and headed to Boston. Although I was a full professor, with tenure, and head of the department at Spelman, I had been fired for "insubordination." I suppose the charge was accurate; I had supported the Spelman students in their revolt against a tyrannical and patronizing administration.

I continued to go back and forth to the South, participating (with Roz) in the Mississipi Freedom Summer of 1964, joining the Selma to Montgomery march, and writing about my experiences. That year in Boston I wrote two books about the South and the Movement: *SNCC: The New Abolitionists* (Beacon Press) and *The Southern Mystique* (Alfred Knopf).

An invitation came to join the department of political science at Boston University just about the time the United States was intensifying its military intervention in Vietnam. I became active in the movement against the war and began writing about it with the same sense of urgency that surrounded my writing on events in the South.

I reprint here some material from my book *Vietnam: The Logic of Withdrawal*, published in early 1967 by Beacon Press. There had been a number of books published on the war, but mine was the first, I believe, to call for an immediate withdrawal of U.S. troops from Vietnam. Its final chapter, which I include in this volume, is a speech I wrote "for Lyndon Johnson" (no, he didn't ask for it) in which I have him announcing such a withdrawal and explaining his reasons to the nation. This speech was reproduced in a number of newspapers around the country.

Even before American intervention in Vietnam, the problem of war was a central preoccuption for me. I had been a bombardier, an enthusiastic one, in the "good war," the war against Fascism, and yet, when the war was over, I began to rethink the question of whether there was such a thing as a good war, a just war. I explore that in the opening essay of the section on War in this reader.

I did a good deal of research on the atomic bombing of Hiroshima and Nagasaki while I was a Fellow in East Asian Studies at Harvard University in 1961, and wrote an article for the *Columbia University Forum* called "A Mess of Death and Documents." Later, I made a connection between the bombing of Hiroshima and a much smaller event of World War II, but one in which I had been a participant, the bizarre and deadly napalm bombing of the French town of Royan just before the war's end. In 1967, I visited the town which I had bombed, pored through its records, and wrote an essay which then appeared in my book *The Politics of History*, and which I reproduce here.

In the tumultuous years of the movement against the Vietnam War, the issue of civil disobedience, the role of law in society and its relation to justice, became for me important philosophical problems, as well as practical ones. (I was arrested myself a number of times for protesting the war.)

You will find reprinted here some of my writings on those issues, as well as descriptions of my experience as witness in the Pentagon Papers case and other trials of war protesters. In one essay, I examine critically the views of Plato on obligation to the state. This appeared as an essay in *Z Magazine* (a friendly venue for radical writers) and was reproduced in my book *Failure to Quit*.

In 1974, with the Vietnam war coming to a close, I was invited by the *Boston Globe* (along with a militant student activist named Eric Mann) to write a bi-weekly column. We did that for over a year, until our columns became a little hard to take. The liberalism of the *Globe* had its limits. I wrote an anti-war, anti-militarism column for Memorial Day, 1976 (reprinted here), and after it appeared I was informed that my column was no longer wanted.

I was by profession a historian, by choice an activist, and the tension between the two was something I thought about constantly. What was the proper (or improper) role of the historian in a time of crisis. That was the subject of my book *The Politics of History* (first published by Beacon Press in 1970, reissued later by the University of Illinois Press). I reprint here several essays illustrating my approach to history, as in the talk I gave at the University of Wisconsin during the 1992 quincentennial discussions of Columbus.

And what should be the function of a university when the world outside is in turmoil? At Boston University, faculty and students found themselves debating such questions, and I was very much in the midst of that. Once more, I was being "insubordinate" in my relations with the university administration, and several of the essays in this volume reflect that. One of these "A University Should Not Be A Democracy" (a quote from my university president) appeared in *The Progressive.*

Throughout my activity and my writings, questions arose, both practical and theoretical, of how injustice can be remedied. How does social change come about, and what tactics are both effective and morally acceptable in that process? And what reason do we have to be hopeful? The final set of essays, dealing with such issues, are drawn from *The Nation*, *Z Magazine*, *The Boston Globe*, from other periodicals, and from my memoir *You Can't Be Neutral on a Moving Train.*

I have certainly not been neutral. I have tried to keep moving. I hope a few readers will come along with me.

—Auburndale, MA
July 1997

PART ONE

RACE

1

The Southern Mystique

I did not deliberately seek employment in a black college. I was only vaguely aware that such an institution existed when, in 1956, about to get my doctorate at Columbia University, I was introduced to the president of Spelman College, a college for African-American women in Atlanta, Georgia. He offered me a tempting job—chair of Spelman's department of history and social science. My wife and I, with our young son and daughter, spent the next seven years living in Atlanta's black community, certainly the most interesting seven years of my life. I soon became involved, along with my students, in what came to be known affectionately as "the movement." I did not see how I could teach about liberty and democracy in the classroom and remain silent about their absence outside the classroom. I became both participant in and chronicler of the growing conflict between the old Southern order of racial segregation, and the increasingly vocal demands for freedom and equality by Southern blacks. Some long-held notions about the South, white people and black people, were powerfully challenged by what I observed. I sent an article to *Harper's Magazine*, and to my surprise they accepted it.

It was my first published article, and later became the basis for an essay I wrote for *The American Scholar* in the winter issue, 1963-64, and as the introductory chapter in my book *The Southern Mystique* (Alfred Knopf, 1964).

Do I stand by everything I wrote thirty years ago about the race question in the United States? That would mean I have learned nothing from all these years of turmoil. I undoubtedly would not write exactly the same way today. But I suppose I believe in the long-run validity of what I say in this essay, and so I unashamedly reproduce it here.

It has occurred to me only recently that perhaps the most striking development in the South is not that the process of desegregation is under way, but that the mystique with which Americans have always surrounded the South is beginning to vanish.

Driving into Atlanta in a heavy rain one hot August night six and a half years ago, my wife and two small children waking up to watch the shimmering wet lights on Ponce de Leon Avenue, I was as immersed in this mystique as anyone else. For the last full day of driving, the talk and the look of people were different. The trees and fields seemed different. The air itself smelled different. This was the mysterious and terrible South, the Deep South, soaked in blood and history, of which Faulkner wrote—and Margaret Mitchell, and Wilbur J. Cash. White Atlanta had been ravaged and still knew it. Negroes had been slaves and still remembered it. Northerners were strangers, no matter how long they stayed, and would never forget it.

There was something about Atlanta, about Georgia, the Carolinas, that marked them off as with a giant cleaver from the rest of the nation: the sun was hotter, the soil was redder, the people blacker and whiter, the air sweeter, heavier. But beyond the physical, beyond the strange look and smell of this country, was something more that went back to cotton and slavery, stretching into history as far as anyone could remember—an invisible mist over the entire Deep South, distorting justice, blurring perspective, and, most of all, indissoluble by reason.

It is six and a half years later. I have lived these years inside what is often thought to be the womb of the South's mystery: the Negro community of the Deep South. My time has been spent mostly with the remarkable young women in my classes at Spelman; but also with the earnest young men across the street at Morehouse, with the strangely mixed faculties of the Negro colleges (the white and the dark, the silent and the angry, the conservative and the radical), with the black *bourgeoisie* of college presidents and business executives, with the poor Negro families in frame houses across the street and their children playing with ours on the campus grass. From this, I have been able to wander out into the glare of the white South, or cross into those tiny circles of shadow, out of sight, where people of several colors meet and touch as human beings, inside the tranquil eye of the hurricane.

The Southern mystique hovered nearby even on yellow spring afternoons when we talked quietly to one another in the classroom. At times it grew suddenly dense, fierce, asphyxiating. My students and I were ordered out of the gallery of the Georgia General Assembly, the Speaker of the House shouting hoarsely at us. One nightmarish winter evening, I was arrested and put behind bars. Hundreds of us marched one day toward the State Capitol where helmeted soldiers with rifles and gas masks waited. A dozen of us "sat in" at a department store cafeteria, silent as the manager dimmed the lights, closed the counter and ordered chairs piled on top of tables all around. I drove four hours south to the Black Belt country of Albany, Georgia, to call through a barbed wire fence surrounding the County Jail to a student of mine who was invisible beyond a wire mesh window. It was in Albany also that I sat in the office of the Sheriff of Dougherty County who a month before had given a bloody beating with a cane to a young Negro lawyer. And nowhere was the mystique so real, so enveloping, as on a dirt road in the dusk, deep in the cotton and peanut land of Lee County, Georgia, where justice and reason had never been, and where the night before bullets had ripped into a farm house belonging to Negro farmer James Mays and exploded around the heads of sleeping children.

And yet, I can say now after living intensely in the deep South in exactly those six years when the South itself has lived most intensely, that the mystique is dissolving, for me, and for others. The South is still the most terrible place in America. Because it is, it is filled with heroes. The South is monstrous and marvelous at the same time. Every cliché ever uttered about the South, every stereotype attached to its people, white and Negro, is true; a thousand other characteristics, complex and subtle, are also true. The South has not lost its fascination. But it is no longer mysterious. And I want to explain this by talking about those two groups who have been at the center of this mystery, the whites and the Negroes of the Deep South.

Although the darkness of the Negro physically suggests mystery, it is the white Southerner, oddly enough, who has been presented as the great national enigma. This, despite the whiteness of his skin, against which flaws and blemishes show up more easily, a whiteness unsullied by that admixture of Slavic and Latin blood found in the North, and kept homogeneous by the simple expedient of tossing over the wall in the night all offspring from black-white sexual encounter. The mystery of the white Southerner comes from a trait that he is presumed to possess in quantity and quality sharply distinct from everyone else. That trait is race prejudice.

Other white people, it is acknowledged, are color-biased. There is considered to be, however, something special about the quality of the white Southerner's prejudice. The Yankee is rather businesslike in his mat-ter-of-fact exclusion of the Negro from certain spheres of ordinary living. The British imperialist was haughty and sure of himself. But the violence, the passion, the murderous quality of the white Southerner's feeling against the Negro has become a canon of American thought deep in our consciousness and our literature (and of European literature; see Sartre's *La Putain respectueuse*). And what is more significant, while the outward signs of this prejudice are clear enough, at its core, at the *why* of this crazy feeling, is a mystery.

When reporter John Bartlow Martin wrote, right after the Supreme Court decision, *The Deep South Says "Never,"* central to the book's thesis was the implication of some ineradicable mystical hatred, so deep and so invisible in the white Southerner, that no blasts of social change could touch it. When I had lived a year or so in the Deep South, talking to and living next door to the same white people described by the author of that book, I began to suspect he was wrong. Six years later, I knew he was. Prejudice, discrimination, race hatred are real problems, to the point of viciousness, even murder. But their mystery, for those who will look hard, is gone.

I will not tangle with *cause*, because once you acknowledge *cause* as the core of a problem, you have built something into it that not only baffles people, but, worse, immobilizes them. Causation is not merely complex—it may be impossible of solution (as some of the new philosophers say), one of those metaphysical conundrums created by our own disposition to set verbal obstacles between ourselves and reality. Why not ignore cause as a general philosophical problem and concentrate on *result?* The point is devilishly, irreverently simple: if you can get a desired result, the mystery is gone. Stop fumbling with the *cause* of prejudice except for those aspects on which we can operate. A physicist may still not know what really is behind the transformation of matter into energy, but if he has figured out how to release this energy, his achievement is stupendous.

Atlanta is in the Deep South. Atlanta has as many crackpots, KKK sympathizers, country wool-hats, white supremacists, barbershop lynchers, vicious policemen, as any Southern city. If the deep South said "Never," Atlanta, too, said "Never." In 1958 it was tightly segregated. By 1963: the buses had desegregated; so had the public libraries, the rail and bus terminals, a number of theaters and restaurants downtown, the department store cafeterias, the opera, the municipal auditorium, the legitimate theater, the public schools, the colleges (public and private), several hotels, the plainclothes squad of the Police Department, the Fire Department, the baseball team, the tennis courts, the parks, the golf courses, the Chamber of Commerce, several professional organizations, the county committee of the Democratic Party and even the Senate of the Georgia General Assembly!

Now that it is all done, there are obvious reasons, which can be advanced with great casualness: a flexible city administration, a layer of Negro intellectuals, a determined student movement, a band of white liberals giving cosmopolitan salting to the country-style Talmadge ham. But none of this takes account of the fact that all the above forces are a minority of the population, that most of Atlanta's population, the overwhelming majority of its 350,000 white people, still consider Negroes inferior, and prefer a segregated society, and that these people were numerous enough to have prevented most of the change—by riot, by election, by boycott—*if they cared enough.* They stood by passively and accepted, with the puniest of resistance, a series of fundamental changes in the sociolegal structure of the city.

There is, then, a key to the traditionally mysterious vault of prejudice locked inside the mind of the white Southerner. He cares, but not enough. Or, to put it another way, while he cares about segregation, there are things he cares about more. The white Southerner has a hierarchy of desires, in which many other things are rated higher than segregation: monetary profit, political power, staying out of jail, the approval of one's immediate peers, conforming to the dominant decision of the community. Desegregation has come in varying degrees, to Atlanta and a hundred other places in the Deep South, in the face of persistent anti-Negro feelings in the community, simply because one or another of these desires, which stand higher in the Southerner's value-scheme, was threatened if he did not surrender.

Except as an academic exercise, there is no need then to probe the fog that inescapably shrouds the philosophical question of causation in race prejudice. What needs to be done is to decide for each group of whites in the community which value is more important and to plan a web of multiple tactics—negotiation, boycott, lawsuit, voting, demonstration—that will effectively appeal to these priorities. In a rough semiconscious way, the actions of the federal courts and of Negro leaders in the South have aimed at this; a more deliberate use of the hierarchy-of-value concept would bring even more dramatic results.

The white man in the South is subject to the same simplicities and the same complexities that surround the human species of any color any place; he has certain biological needs, which he will try to satisfy whichever way he can; on top of this he has other wants which he has learned from his culture—and because these often conflict with one another he has an unconscious set of priorities that enables him to make choices. He is subject to economic pressure and ambition. Also, if Jungian theory is correct and the notions of modern role psychology valid (and I believe they are), he needs approval from certain people around him, and seeks to play out the role society has cast him in. Beyond all this, as beyond all the frontiers of human knowledge, there is mystery in the behavior of the human animal. But it's time to clear from our minds that artificial and special mystique, so firmly attached to the Southern white, that has too long served as a rationale for pessimism and inaction.

But what of the black man—or woman? There is a strange and damnable unanimity of segregationists, white liberals and Negroes on one fervent belief—the mystery of *négritude*—the irreducible kernel, after all sociological peelings, of race difference. The segregationist (White Citizen or Black Muslim) shouts this in all directions. The white liberal is subtle, sophisticated and ingenious in the various ways he can express this—he sweetens it with sympathy or admiration or affection—he delights in the sheer thrill of a mystery. He cherishes it as a secret shared with his fellow liberals: "Yes, yes—we can never know what it is to be a Negro. No, no—they will never trust a white man, and we can't blame them." The Negro, robbed of other protection, clings to it, plays with it, turns it to his advantage when he can. Even the most perceptive of his literary leaders (Baldwin, Ellison) use it in cunning, or in pride. And all of them, white liberal and Negro intellectual, fondle it, nurture it as men, having subdued a forest fire, might play with the last flames, too fascinated when in the midst of peril, to put them out for good.

Physical difference is so gross a stimulus to human beings, cursed as they are by the gift of vision, that once it is latched onto as explanation for difference in personality, intelligence, demeanor, it is terribly difficult to put aside. It becomes an easy substitute for the immensely difficult job of explaining personal and social behavior. Conservatives use it openly; liberals secretly, even unknowingly. It seems to be the hardest thing in the world to convince ourselves that once we've noted skin color, facial features and hair texture, we have exhausted the subject of race—that everything beyond that is in our heads, put there by others and kept there by ourselves, and all the brutal material consequences of centuries, from lynching to patronizing friendship, were spun from an original thread of falsehood.

The most vicious thing about segregation—more deadly than its immediate denial of certain goods and services—is its perpetuation of the mystery of racial difference. Because there is a magical and omnipotent dispeller of the mystery; it is *contact*. Contact—but it must be massive, unlike those "integrated" situations in the North, and it must be equal, thus excluding maid-lady relationships of the South—destroys the man-made link between physical difference and behavior explanation. Race consciousness is hollow, its formidable-looking exterior is membrane-thin and is worn away by simple acts of touch, the touching of human beings in contact that is massive, equal and prolonged. The brightness of the physical difference impression is relative; it stands out in that darkness created by segregated living, and is quickly lost in the galaxy of sense impressions that come from being with a person day-in, day-out.

In our country, the kind of contact that rubs away race consciousness is possible only in rare places, and intermittently. But it exists, in scattered underground pockets of resistance to the norm. One of them is the Negro college, where white people can become so immersed in a Negro environment that they are oblivious, at least temporarily, of race. The fact that they live on an island, against which waves of prejudice roll from time to time, means that they slide back and forth from over-consciousness on some days to a blissful racial amnesia on others.

A white student, after several months living, eating, studying, playing in a totally Negro college environment, visited a nearby white college and returned saying, "How pallid they all seemed—all those white faces and sharp noses!" This is a startling example of race consciousness in reverse, but it is encouraging to see how quickly one can change the temper of racial awareness by an inundation of sense experiences.

Once the superficiality of the physical is penetrated and seen for what it is, the puzzle of race loses itself in whatever puzzle there is to human behavior in general. Once you begin to look, in human clash, for explanations other than race, they suddenly become visible, and even where they remain out of sight, it is comforting to know that these non-racial explanations exist, as disease began to lose its eeriness with the discovery of bacteria, although the specific problem of identifying each bacterial group remained.

So long as evil exists—and it exists in poisonous heaps, South and North—the raw material for mystery is here. We can make the most—if we want to—of white mobs in Oxford, mass Negro indignation in Albany, blazing churches in Birmingham, gunfire on rural porches, and the sheer wonder of blackness and whiteness. But the specialness of the Southern mystique vanishes when one sees that whites and Negroes behave only like human beings, that the South is but a distorted mirror image of the North, and that we are powerful enough today, and free enough—to retain only as much of the past as we want. We are all magicians. We created the mystery of the South, and we can dissolve it.

2

A Quiet Case of Social Change

The history of that time usually records the dramatic moments—the Montgomery bus boycott, the sit-ins, the Freedom Rides, the marches in Birmingham. What is often omitted is what happened more quietly in between the great events, and it is one of those historical moments I wanted to record in this piece, which appeared in the NAACP publication The Crisis in October of 1959. I was the faculty adviser to Spelman College's Social Science Club, which undertook as a project the desegregation of the Atlanta public libraries. I appear in this piece anonymously as "a representative of Spelman's Social Science Club."

On the afternoon of May 22, 1959, Dr. Irene Dobbs Jackson, a professor of French at Spelman College, accompanied by a young white faculty wife from Spelman, walked through the electrically operated door of the marbled and modern Carnegie Library in downtown Atlanta, went to the front desk, and filled out a membership application. She turned it in, and the slim girl behind the desk handed her a new membership card. The girl's voice was calm, but her hand trembled slightly, perhaps because Dr. Jackson was the first Negro ever to receive a membership card at a "white" library in Atlanta.

At the same moment, on the second floor of the library, violinist and music professor Earl Sanders, a bespectacled, dark-skinned young man, whose outbursts of good humor were a counterpoint to a powerful indignation, was thumbing through stacks of records to find some chamber music he wanted. Exactly three weeks before, while looking at records in the same room, he had been asked to leave. Now, as he approached the check-out desk, the attractive girl sitting there noted his selections with a friendly smile, and he walked out.

The desegregation of the public library system in the city of Atlanta took place quietly. Not until after the fact did the newspapers announce to the community that the main library and its fourteen branches, formerly reserved for whites, were now open to all. Atlanta Negroes, as word spread slowly among them, were surprised and gratified. There had been no lawsuit, no headlines, no violence. To explain the event, we need to examine a number of intertwining threads which knotted together in May of 1959, and which when unraveled, afford a glimpse into the subsurface mechanics of peaceful, purposeful social change.

A handful of Spelman students and faculty members, conscious of the unplanned and violent cataclysms that have shaken the world in this century, had been talking about the idea of deliberate social change. In a seminar on the philosophy of history, we explored two approaches which have dominated intellectual speculation: first, the notion that some great force, inscrutable like God, or ascertainable like economic necessity, is working behind the scenes of the human drama; and second, the more recent empiricist attempt to attack problems piecemeal by scientific scrutiny of individual phenomena rather than by insight into some universal explanation. We found ourselves critical of both these approaches, because they implied a passivity on the part of the intellectual, whose eye was at the telescope or the microscope but whose hands were rather idle.

More provocative than these ideas was one expressed by Charles Frankel in *The Case for Modern Man*: man is not a feeble creature pecking with a tackhammer at an impenetrable steel fence, but a free and mighty agent who, while studying the determinants of social change, can become a chief determinant himself. The potency of this idea actually has already affected some of the traditional schools of thought: the church fosters more and more activists for social reform; and the Marxists have shifted the emphasis from "inevitability" and the strength of "material forces" to the will and power of the Communist Party. Perhaps the atom-splitting of scientists has invested both communists and clerics with a new sense of command.

In our discussions at Spelman we played with the notion that man can coolly and deliberately locate a particular problem, survey the forces standing in the way of a solution, and either skillfully navigate around obstacles or, when the balance of power is just right, bowl them over. Translated into action and applied on a very modest scale, this kind of thinking played a part in the peaceful desegregation of the Atlanta public-library system, which opened to 150,000 Negroes of that city a wealth of books, paintings, and recorded music.

My students were at that time feeling uncomfortable about confining their studies to books while the South was being shaken by ideological and political upheaval. Why not select, out of the mass of events in the integration crisis, a limited field of combat where the enemy was weak and the possibility of gaining allies strong, and set out deliberately to occupy a tiny bit of territory? Why not plan and carry through to victory a minor skirmish in the big battle, through purposeful and rational action? The tactics, not quite customary for young women from a decorous and conservative Negro college, were to be those of guerilla warfare.

The library system was singled out for attention because it was a situation small enough to be handled by our little group, yet significant in its importance for the entire community. The relationship of forces seemed favorable. Atlanta's city administration, which supervised the libraries, had been showing more flexibility as it watched the growing Negro vote. The policy of separate libraries was not written into law; it was simply an administrative rule of the library's Board of Trustees, and it could be changed by action of the Board, on which the Mayor was an important influence. At that time, various groups, particularly the interracial American Veterans Committee, had tried to get the Mayor to act.

Not the least of the factors we considered was that action to desegregate the Atlanta library system represented a genuine need of students and faculty in the Atlanta University Center and of the city's Negro community. Of the three city libraries built especially for Negroes, one was a newly erected showplace, part of the post-war rash of attempts to introduce a bit more equality into the "separate-but-equal" premise of Southern life. But the Carnegie Library had no match in the Negro community. Built in downtown Atlanta some thirty years before, it housed an impressive collection of books in all categories, as well as paintings and recordings, which were available for loan. The "for whites only" label on the world's great literature was not only a moral challenge but a practical obstacle to learning.

As a first step, it was decided that students and Negro faculty, heretofore reluctant in the face of certain rejection, should begin visiting the Carnegie Library whenever they needed books unavailable elsewhere. They expected to be rebuffed. But the visits would continue. So, the advance guard of the gradually increasing stream of Negro visitors began passing through the electric-eye entrance to the Carnegie Library. It was accidental irony that the first book sought in this campaign was John Locke's *An Essay Concerning Human Understanding*. The Spelman student who requested this was given the same treatment that subsequent Negro visitors were to receive: a courteous query as to whether the Negro branch had been tried, and then assurance that the book would be sent to the Negro branch and made available there. When a student said the book was needed immediately, she was told it could be studied right there in the library, in a special room downstairs, or in the office behind the main desk—anywhere, so long as there would be no contact with the white patrons.

Here was a typical Southern paradox: across the street from the library, in one of Atlanta's leading department stores, Negroes and whites could brush by each other at the counters, try on the same clothes, and, thanks to the irresistable impetus of the profit motive, be treated as near-equals. But nonsense has been uttered with aplomb for a long time in the South, and no one proved better at it than degree-encrusted library officials. Spelman and Morehouse College students visiting the Carnegie Library accepted whatever service was offered them, and left. Their purpose was simply to make the library aware that Negroes were in need of its facilities.

The Atlanta Council on Human Relations, meanwhile, had been working on the problem. This newly formed inter-racial group was headed by a white Unitarian minister, Edward Cahill, and the dynamic Whitney Young, then Dean of the Atlanta University School of Social Work. They began a sixteen-month campaign of persistent effort to convince the Library Board of Trustees, through detailed research and rational argument, that Atlanta libraries should be open to all. They collected statistics, made special maps, and referred the Library Director pointedly to the American Library Association's Bill of Rights, which says that "as a responsibility of Library service there should be no discrimination based on race or nationality." The Library Board remained unmoved, and the Council on Human Relations wearily announced this fact in February of 1959: "The Council urges all groups and individuals in the city to take such action as they deem appropriate to persuade the Library Board to desegregate the tax-supported facilities of the public library system."

With this, Spelman and Morehouse College students stepped up their visits to the Carnegie Library. In March, I paid a visit to the Director of the Atlanta Library systems, to probe the prospects for desegregation. He was discouraging. Of course, he assured me, the policy was not his desire, but a rule upheld by the Board which he was bound to enforce. No, he could not take the initiative in making a change. If Negroes began to use the library there would probably be violence. If this was his fear, I suggested, why not desegregate quietly, since there would otherwise be a lawsuit and the change would come anyway, with more publicity.

In the event of a court order to desegregate, the Director said matter-of-factly, he would close the libraries, as Governor Faubus had closed schools in Little Rock, to prevent violence. Surely, I said, white people who use your library would not riot over the use of the library by a few Negroes. You don't know these folks, he replied. The interview was over.

The library director's argument was the same one advanced so often in the South on the eve of change: there will be trouble. But in 90 percent of the cases where desegregation had already taken place in the South (though one would never know this from reading newspaper headlines), there had been no violent reaction at all, only quiet if grudging acceptance. And although there is never any way of guaranteeing an absence of trouble, the probabilities in a case like this were on the side of peaceful change. We proceeded therefore to prepare a suit in federal court, and Whitney Young and I took the responsibility for getting plaintiffs, money, and legal help.

Just a few months earlier, the federal courts in Atlanta had given two favorable decisions, one desegregating the city's transit system, the other barring discrimination on grounds of race in the admissions policy of the University of Georgia. Several years before, a lawsuit had forced the municipal golf courses at Atlanta to admit Negroes. And in one Virginia county the mere threat of a lawsuit had opened up libraries to Negroes.

Our first job was to find plaintiffs, and this was not easy. A number of students were anxious to file suit, but they were discouraged by the complications of obtaining parental consent and of meeting other technical requirements, such as residence. Many Negroes were subject to economic reprisal if they dared participate in court action. I began to appreciate the work of the NAACP in handling lawsuits when I saw how difficult it was to get plaintiffs, something I had always assumed was no problem. But finally, two people came forward.

One was a young minister named Otis Moss, who was doing advanced study in theology and had often suffered from the inadequacy of the library facilities available to him. Moss's wife was a student in my American History course, articulate and intelligent. Moss himself, slim and very quiet, hardly seemed a social activist. (I began to make out the depth of the man only a year later at a mass protest meeting in Atlanta when the apparently shy Reverend Moss lifted the crowd to a state of high emotion with a magnificent speech.)

The other plaintiff was Irene Dobbs Jackson, Professor of French at Spelman College, a friend and colleague, who said quietly as we sat having coffee in the Snack Shop on the campus, "It's what my husband would be doing if he were alive." Irene Jackson's rock-like strength had been put to its most severe test when her husband, a prominent Atlanta minister, died, leaving her with six growing children. She continued their education somehow, took four of them to France with her, where she studied for several years and received her doctorate at the University of Toulouse. Dr. Jackson came from a well-known Atlanta family. Her sister, Mattiwilda Dobbs, a Spelman college graduate, became famous because she was the first Negro to sing a starring role with the Metropolitan Opera company. Her father, John Wesley Dobbs, was one of Atlanta's most distinguished citizens, a militant battler for equal rights and a great orator in the old Southern tradition. I heard him keep a crowd of thousands in an uproar one night at the Wheat Street Baptist Church. "My Mattiwilda was asked to sing here in Atlanta," he thundered at one point, "but she said, 'No sir! Not while my daddy has to sit in the balcony!'" Irene Dobbs Jackson told me: "Why, I've passed by the Carnegie Library a hundred times, and always wanted to go in. I think it's time."

Student visits to the Carnegie Library were now stepped up. City officials were apparently becoming uneasy, because a high municipal officeholder telephoned an Atlanta University administrator to plead that legal action be held up until the adjournment of the state legislature, which was in constant battle with the city administration.

What happened shortly after this, on May 19, 1959, I will quote from the notes I made on that day:

> Tuesday, May 10th: made an appointment to see Whitney Young at 2 P.M., to discuss with him next moves in suit to desegregate library system. Whitney told of an interesting development which might change things. A member of the Library Board had called him that morning, said he was disturbed at hearing that lawsuit was pending on library situation, wanted very much to avoid lawsuit. Whitney told him there was long history of conferences, requests, etc., and we were going ahead, and as a matter of fact had appointment at 2 P.M. with the parties involved in the suit to discuss pending action. The Board member said don't do anything, call me at 2 P.M. before talking to parties involved, and meanwhile will try to get lunch meeting of Board together.
>
> We talked a few minutes, then the Board member called. Library Board had just met at Atlanta Athletic Club. Whole board was there. Mayor was there. Chief of Police, City Attorney there. Library Director was there. Decision was to change policy. Mayor told the Board they had been foolish long enough. The board member told Whitney hold off a few days, just long enough to allow Director to inform staff of change.
>
> Whitney and I agreed that we would give them Wednesday and Thursday, test it out Friday and for a week thereafter. Agreed I would go with Mrs. Jackson to Carnegie Library Friday.

So it was that Friday, May 22, 1959, four of us rode downtown to the Carnegie Library: Dr. Irene Jackson, Professor Earl Sanders, myself, and Pat West, the charming and spirited Alabama-born wife of a Spelman philosophy professor. Irene Jackson joined the library, and Earl Sanders took out his long-sought records. Later that week two Spelman students and one Morehouse student walked into a "white" branch library on Peachtree Street and gave it its initiation.

As predicted by all groups who had asked integration, the desegregation decision caused no great commotion. Not until five days after the Board action did the newspapers carry the story, and by then it was an accomplished fact. The library director received a few angry letters, Dr. Jackson was kept wake one night by nasty telephone calls: "You that integratin' nigger?" "This is the KKK." And as she sat at the library table reading, that first day, a man came by and slammed his books down hard on the table in voiceless protest. But the general reaction was an enormous silence. One white Atlantan said in a letter he sent to the *Atlanta Constitution* that he had lived in Atlanta all his life and never knew the libraries were segregated, and he felt ashamed.

At a press conference a few days later, Georgia Governor Ernest Vandiver predicted that voluntary segregation would continue at the library because integration "does not represent the thinking or the wishes of the vast rank and file of colored citizens who would prefer to use their own library facilities." He turned out to be wrong, for the Carnegie Library, in the several years since it was integrated, has been used constantly by Negroes, without any trouble from whites. Mayor William Hartsfield turned out to be a better prophet than the Governor, when he told reporters: "A public library is a symbol of literacy, education, and cultural progress. It does not attract troublemakers."

In the library episode, a number of our hypotheses were underlined: Negroes acted and whites reacted. The reaction of the whites was consistent with their particular value-schemes. The Mayor, dependent on Negro votes for election, saw a gain in popularity among Negroes which would not be offset by white disaffection, for the library was not, by its nature, an emotional issue; its users were not likely to be rabid on the race issue. Even if the library users were not delighted at the idea of Negroes using "their" library, they were not so unhappy as to cramp their own needs by staying away or by creating a scene in the genteel atmosphere of the reading room. The library Board did not gain any political advantage by changing its policy; but it also would not have gained anything by battling with the Mayor, whose favor it wanted. And behind all this was the impending lawsuit, which would undoubtedly result in a court desegregation order, with attendant publicity. So the choice was not between segregation and desegregation but between quiet and noisy desegregation. As for the library employees, like most employees, their supreme value was keeping their jobs; so, they were likely to carry out policy as directed from above, no matter what it was, and whatever their personal wishes.

This analysis of the advantages that were weighed does not take account of the element of genuine idealism present in the Mayor, in some Library Board members, in some library employees. But such idealism unfortunately is rarely preponderant enough to change a situation where one value clearly outweighs another. It can be important in circumstances where the advantages are so evenly balanced that even the feather-weight of social conviction may tip the decision-making scales. And for a small number of radical prime movers, idealism has become their greatest interest; it serves thus as an igniting spark for the self-interest of the mass.

3

Finishing School for Pickets

I was on the faculty of Spelman College in Atlanta, Georgia, for seven years, from 1956 to 1963, and was lucky enough to live in a black Southern community in the midst of the Civil Rights revolution. The sit-ins of February 1960, in Greensboro, North Carolina spread quickly through the South, and in May, the students of Spelman and Morehouse and other colleges in the Atlanta University Center quietly moved into ten public places downtown—historically segregated. They refused to leave, were arrested, and nothing was the same in Atlanta after that. The "young lady" who put up the dormitory notice was Marian Wright, later Marian Wright Edelman, founder of the Children's Defense Fund in Washington, D.C. Another of my students at Spelman was Alice Walker, for whom even the changed Spelman did not change enough. She left a year after I was fired by the college president for "insubordination." I had supported the Spelman students not only in their actions in the city, but in their rebellion against the old order on campus. In this article, which appeared in *The Nation* August 6, 1960, I try to convey what was happening to Spelman and that old order.

ATLANTA, GEORGIA.

One quiet afternoon some weeks ago, with the dogwood on the Spelman College campus newly bloomed and the grass close-cropped and fragrant, an attractive, tawny-skinned girl crossed the lawn to her dormitory to put a notice on the bulletin board. It read: Young Ladies Who Can Picket Please Sign Below.

The notice revealed, in its own quaint language, that within the dramatic revolt of Negro college students in the South today another phenomenon has been developing. This is the upsurge of the young, educated Negro woman against the generations-old advice of her elders: be nice, be well-mannered and ladylike, don't speak loudly, and don't get into trouble. On the campus of the nation's leading college for Negro young women—pious, sedate, encrusted with the traditions of gentility and moderation—these exhortations, for the first time, are being firmly rejected.

Spelman College girls are still "nice," but not enough to keep them from walking up and down, carrying picket signs, in front of two supermarkets in the heart of Atlanta. They are well-mannered, but this is somewhat tempered by a recent declaration that they will use every method short of violence to end segregation. As for staying out of trouble, they were doing fine until this spring, when fourteen of them were arrested and jailed by Atlanta police. The staid New England women missionaries who helped found Spelman College back in the 1880s would probably be distressed at this turn of events, and present-day conservatives in the administration and faculty are rather upset. But respectability is no longer respectable among young Negro women attending college today.

"You can always tell a Spelman girl," alumni and friends of the college have boasted for years. The "Spelman girl" walked gracefully, talked properly, went to church every Sunday, poured tea elegantly and, in general, had all the attributes of the product of a fine finishing school. If intellect and talent and social consciousness happened to develop also, they were, to an alarming extent, by-products.

This is changing. It would be an exaggeration to say: "You can always tell a Spelman girl—she's under arrest." But the statement has a measure of truth. Spelman girls have participated strongly in all of the major actions undertaken by students of the Atlanta University Center in recent months. They have also added a few touches of their own and made white Atlanta, long proud that its nice Negro college girls were staying "in their place," take startled notice. A few weeks ago a Spelman student, riding downtown on the bus, took a seat up front. (This is still a daring maneuver, for in spite of a court decision desegregating the buses, most Negroes stay in the rear.) The bus driver muttered something unpleasant, and a white woman sitting nearby waved her hand and said, "Oh, she's prob'ly goin' downtown to start another one o' them demonstrations."

The reputedly sweet and gentle Spelman girls were causing trouble even before the recent wave of sit-ins cracked the wall of legalism in the structure of desegregation strategy. Three years ago, they aroused the somnolent Georgia Legislature into near-panic by attempting to sit in the white section of the gallery. They were finally shunted into the colored area, but returned for the next legislative session. This time they refused to sit segregated and remained on their feet, in a pioneering show of nonviolent resistance, until ordered out of the chamber.

The massive, twelve-foot stone wall, barbed-wire fence and magnolia trees that encircle the Spelman campus have always formed a kind of chastity belt around the student body, not only confining young women to a semi-monastic life in order to uphold the ruling matriarchs' conception of Christian morality, but "protecting" the students from contact with the cruel outside world of segregation. Inside the domain of the Atlanta University Center, with its interracial faculty, occasional white students and frequent white visitors, there flourished a microcosm of the future, where racial barriers did not exist and one could almost forget this was the deep South. But this insulation, while protecting the University Center's island of integration, also kept the city of Atlanta for many years from feeling the barbed resentment of Negro students against segregation. Spelman girls, more sheltered than women at the other colleges, were among the first to leave the island and to begin causing little flurries of alarm in the segregated world outside.

Even before bus segregation in the city was declared illegal, some Spelman girls rode up front and withstood the glares and threats of fellow passengers and the abuse of the bus driver. Once, a white man pulled a knife from his pocket and waved it at a Spelman sophomore sitting opposite him in a front seat. She continued to sit there until she came to her stop, and then got off. Spelman students, along with others, showed up in the main Atlanta library in sufficient numbers last year to worry the city administration into a decision to admit Negroes there. The girls spent hours between classes at the county courthouse, urging Negroes to register for voting. They made a survey of the Atlanta airport in connection with a suit to desegregate the airport restaurant, and a Spelman student took the witness stand at the trial to help win the case.

Such activities may bring bewilderment to the conservative matriarchy which has played a dominant role in the college's history, but they are nothing short of infuriating to the officialdom of the State of Georgia, ensconced inside the gold-domed Capitol just a few minutes' drive from the Negro colleges of the Atlanta University Center. Georgia's bespectacled but still near-sighted Governor Vandiver, who resembles a pleasant and studious junior executive until he begins to speak, began his current burst of hysteria when student leaders at the six Negro colleges put their heads together and produced a remarkable document which was placed as a full-page ad in the Atlanta newspapers on March 9 (and reprinted by *The Nation* on April 2). The document, entitled "An Appeal for Human Rights," catalogued Negro grievances with irritating specificity and promised to "use every legal and non-violent means at our disposal" to end segregation. Vandiver's reaction was immediate: the appeal was "anti-American" and "obviously not written by students." Furthermore, the Governor said: "It did not sound like it was prepared in any Georgia school or college; nor, in fact, did it read like it was written in this country." Actually, a Spelman student had written the first rough draft, and student leaders from the other five colleges collaborated in preparing the finished product.

On the sixth day after publication of the appeal, at 11:30 on a Tuesday morning, several hundred students from the Atlanta University Center staged one of the South's most carefully planned and efficiently executed sit-in demonstrations at ten different eating places, including restaurants in the State Capitol, the county courthouse and City Hall. Among the demonstrators were several carloads of Spelman students, riding into town that morning without the knowledge of deans or presidents or faculty, to participate in the sit-ins, tangle with the police and end up in prison.

Of the seventy-seven students arrested, fourteen were Spelmanites; and all but one of the fourteen were girls from the deep South, from places like Bennettsville, South Carolina; Bainbridge, Georgia; Ocala, Florida— the Faulknerian small towns of traditional Negro submissiveness.

The Atlanta *Constitution* and the *Journal* noted the remarkable discipline and orderliness of the demonstration. Perhaps their training came in handy; in prison, Spelman girls were perfect ladies. A Spelman honor student sat behind bars quietly reading C.S. Lewis' *The Screwtape Letters*, while flashbulbs popped around her.

The State of Georgia, however, reacted with a special vindictiveness. To the seventy-seven sit-inners, the Fulton County prosecutor has added the names of the six students who wrote and signed "An Appeal for Human Rights." All eighty-three are facing triple charges of breaching the peace, intimidating restaurant owners and refusing to leave the premises, the penalties for which add up to nine years in prison and $6,000 in fines. The use of "conspiracy" charges to tie all eighty-three students to each of the ten eating places creates a theoretical possibility of ninety-year sentences. Nothing is fantastic in this state.

On May 17, to commemorate the 1954 Supreme Court decision, over a thousand students marched through downtown Atlanta to a mass meeting at the Wheat Street Baptist Church, while a hundred hastily summoned state troopers guarded the Capitol a few blocks away with guns, billy clubs and tear gas. The students were heavily armed with books and songs, and when they were assembled in the church sang, "That Old Ne-gro, He Ain't What He Used to Be!"

What is the source of this new spirit which has angered the state administration and unsettled the old guardians of genteel passivity? There is something fundamental at work which is setting free for the first time the anger pent up in generations of quiet, well-bred Negro college women, not only at Spelman College, but at Fisk, Bennett, Alabama State and other institutions throughout the South. The same warm currents which are loosening the ice-blocks of the *status quo* throughout the world are drifting into the South and mingling with local eddies of discontent. What has been called a global "revolution in expectations" rises also in the hearts and minds of Southern Negroes.

Expanding international contacts are reaching even into small Southern colleges. The arrested Spelman girl from Bennettsville, South

Carolina spent last year in Geneva studying international relations, and spent the summer in Soviet Russia. The Atlanta student who helped draft the Appeal had just returned from a year of studying music in Paris. Last September, two young African women, under the auspices of the militant Tom Mboya, flew in from Kenya to enroll at Spelman. The tame-sounding phrase "cultural exchange" may have revolutionary political implications.

Like many Negro campuses in the South, Spelman is losing its provincial air. This spring, the first white students came—five girls from Midwestern colleges who are the advance guard of a long-term exchange program. In the past few months there has been a sudden burgeoning of contact, both intellectual and social, with students from the half-dozen white colleges in Atlanta. Liberal Southern whites have joined the faculties of Spelman and Morehouse colleges. This growing inter-racial contact is helping to break down the mixture of awe-suspicion-hostility with which deep-South Negroes generally regard whites. And for Spelman, unexpressed but obvious pressure to adopt the manners and courtesies of white middle-class society breaks down as Spelman girls get a close look at how whites really behave.

The new Spelman girl is having an effect on faculty and administrators. Many who were distressed and critical when they first learned their sweet young things were sitting behind bars later joined in the applause of the Negro community and the nation at large. Spelman's President Albert Manley, who inherited the traditions of conservatism and moderation when he took the helm seven years ago, has responded with cautious but increasing encouragement to the boldness of his young women. At the college commencement exercises this year, Manley startled the audience by departing from the printed program and the parade of parting platitudes with a vigorous statement of congratulations to the senior class for breaking the "docile generation" label with its sit-ins, demonstrations and picketing.

Four years ago, a girl in my Western Civilization course spoke candidly and bitterly about her situation and that of her classmates. "When I was little," she said, "my mother told me: remember, you've got two strikes against you—you're colored, and you're a woman; one more strike and you're out—so be careful." The student continued: "That's the trouble with all these Spelman girls. They're careful. They hardly utter a peep. They do everything right, and obey the rules, and they'll be fine ladies some day. But I don't want to be that kind of a lady. I'm leaving at the end of the semester and going back up North."

I don't know where that student is today. She would have graduated with this class on Commencement Day, with students who marched and picketed and sat-in and were arrested, and will soon come up for trial. I wish she had stayed to see.

4

Out of the
Sit-ins

After a number of my articles on the Southern situation had appeared in *Harper's*, *The Nation*, and *The New Republic*, Beacon Press in Boston asked me to write a book on the NAACP. By this time I had been in various places in the South, participating and reporting on movement activity, and I responded to the editors at Beacon that the real story in the South was the work of the Student Nonviolent Coordinating Committee (SNCC). They agreed that my book, entitled *SNCC: The New Abolitionists*, should be about this remarkable group of young black militants. This chapter describes the emergence of SNCC in the spring of 1960, out of some of the most dramatic moments in the history of the civil rights movement.

"**M**y stomach always hurt a little on the way to a sit-in.... I guess it's the unexpected." Candie Anderson, a white girl attending Fisk University as an exchange student from Pomona college in California, had joined her Negro classmates to demonstrate against segregation in Nashville, Tennessee. It was the explosion of sit-ins throughout the South in early 1960 that led to the formation of the Student Nonviolent Coordinating committee.

On February 1, 1960, four freshmen at A & T College in Greensboro, North Carolina, took seats at a lunch counter downtown, not knowing they were starting a movement that would soon take on the proportions of a revolution. "For about a week, " David Richmond recalled later, "we four fellows sat around at A & T campus, talking about the integration movement. And we decided we ought to go down to Woolworth's and see what would happen." They spent an hour sitting at the Woolworth's counter, with no service. Then the counter was closed for the day, and they went home.

In a matter of days, the idea leaped to other cities in North Carolina. During the next two weeks, sit-ins spread to fifteen cities in five Southern states. Within the following year, over 50,000 people—most were Negroes, some were white—had participated in one kind of demonstration or another in a hundred cities, and over 3,600 demonstrators spent time in jail. But there were results to show: by the end of 1961, several hundred lunch counters had been desegregated in scores of cities—in Texas, Oklahoma, the border states of the South, and even as far as Atlanta, Georgia. A wall of resistance, however, apparently impenetrable, faced the student in the rest of Georgia, South Carolina, Alabama, Mississippi, Louisiana—and the hard-core Deep South.

It is hard to overestimate the electrical effect of that first sit-in in Greensboro, as the news reached the nation on television screens, over radios, in newspapers. In his Harlem apartment in New York City, Bob Moses, a former Harvard graduate student and mathematics teacher, saw a picture of the Greensboro sit-inners. "The students in that picture had a certain look on their faces, " he later told writer Ben Bagdikian, "sort of sullen, angry, determined. Before, the Negro in the South had always looked on the defensive, cringing. This time they were taking the initiative. They were kids my age, and I knew this had something to do with my own life..."

In Atlanta, Morehouse College student Julian Bond, who wrote poetry and thought about being a journalist, reacted quickly to the Greensboro sit-in. He and another student, discussing it in the Yates & Milton drug store across the street from the campus, decided to summon

Morehouse men to a meeting. Out of that grew the Atlanta student movement, which six weeks later erupted in one of the largest and best organized sit-in demonstrations of all.

Also in Atlanta, seventeen-year-old Ruby Doris Smith, a sophomore at Spelman College, heard about the Greensboro sit-in and ran home that evening to see it on television:

> I began to think right away about it happening in Atlanta, but I wasn't ready to act on my own. When the student committee was formed in the Atlanta University Center, I told my older sister, who was on the Student Council at Morris Brown College, to put me on the list. And when two hundred students were selected for the first demonstration, I was among them. I went through the food line in the restaurant at the State Capitol with six other students, but when we got to the cashier, she wouldn't take our money. She ran upstairs to get the Governor. The Lieutenant-Governor came down and told us to leave. We didn't, and went to the county jail.

Charles ("Chuck") McDew, a husky former athlete from Massilon, Ohio, was studying at South Carolina State College in Orangeburg. McDew had never adjusted to South Carolina; he had been arrested three times in his first three months there, and was struck by a policeman for trying to enter the main YMCA. When, during Religious Emphasis Week at the College, some visiting white Protestant ministers had responded negatively to his question about attending their churches, and a rabbi invited him to the temple, he converted to Judaism. With the news of Greensboro being discussed all around him, McDew read in the Talmud: "If I am not for myself, then who is for me? If I am for myself alone, then what am I? If not now, when?" He became a leader of the local sit-in movement.

To these young people, the Supreme Court decision of 1954 was a childhood memory. The Montgomery bus boycott of 1955, the first mass action by Southern Negroes, though also dimly remembered, was an inspiration. The trouble at Little Rock in 1957 was more vivid, with the unforgettable photos of the young Negro girl walking past screaming crowds towards Central High School. The Greensboro sit-ins struck a special chord of repressed emotion, and excitement raced across the Negro college campuses of the South.

Bob Moses, Julian Bond, Ruby Doris Smith, Chuck McDew: all were to become stalwarts in the Student Nonviolent Coordinating

Committee. And for so many others in SNCC, the Greensboro sit-in—
more than the Supreme Court decision, more than the Little Rock crisis,
more than the Montgomery bus boycott, more than the recent declarations of independence by a host of African nations, and yet, perhaps,
owing its galvanic force to the accumulation of all these events—was a
turning point in their lives. James Forman, studying French in graduate
school in the North, began turning his thoughts southward. Exactly what
was going on in the minds of so many other students, soon to leave school
for "The Movement," remains unknown.

Out of the Nashville, Tennessee, sit-ins, a battalion of future
SNCC people took shape. Tall, quiet, Marion Barry, a graduate student
in chemistry at Fisk University, who would later become the first chairman of SNCC, took a leading part in the Nashville sit-ins from the beginning. His father, a Mississippi farmer, migrated to Memphis, Tennessee,
and Barry went to school there. As an undergraduate at LeMoyne College
in Memphis, he publicly protested an anti-Negro remark made by a
prominent white trustee of the college, created an uproar in the city, and
barely avoided being expelled.

> I came to Fisk...inquired about forming a college chapter of the NAACP....
> But we didn't do much.... We had not at any time thought of direct
> action.... In the meantime in Greensboro, N.C., the student movement
> began February 1, 1960. So we in Nashville decided we wanted to do some-
> thing about it.... I remember the first time I was arrested, about February
> 27...I took a chance on losing a scholarship or not receiving my Master's
> degree. But to me, if I had received my scholarship and Master's degree, and
> still was not a free man, I was not a man at all.

John Lewis, short, fiery, from a small town in Alabama, was also
in Nashville as a seminary student when the sit-ins began. He immediately became involved and went to jail four times. "My mother wrote me
a letter and said 'Get out of the movement,' but I couldn't...I wrote her
and said, 'I have acted according to my convictions and according to my
Christian conscience.... My soul will not be satisfied until freedom, justice, and fair play become a reality for all people'"Lewis later followed
Marion Barry and Chuck McDew to become Chairman of SNCC.

"Do show yourself friendly at the counter at all times. Do sit
straight and always face the counter. Don't strike back, or curse back if
attacked. Don't laugh loud. Don't hold conversations. Don't block

entrances." These were the instructions to sit-in demonstrators in Nashville. They demanded a careful balance of quiet non-resistance and a determined militancy, and perhaps no one better expressed this than Diane Nash, a tiny, slender, campus beauty queen at Fisk, one of the pillars of the Nashville student movement and later a founder of SNCC. When students were being cross-examined at the trials that followed the Nashville demonstrations one of the standard questions was: "Do you know Diane Nash?" Friendship with her was apparently full of perils.

Twelve days after the Greensboro incident, forty students sat in at Woolworth's in Nashville. There was at first some discussion about whether the white exchange students should go along, but finally the prevailing opinion was in favor. Candie Anderson recalls:

> That first sit-in was easy.... It was a Thursday afternoon and it was snowing. There were not many people downtown. Store personnel ran around nervously.... My friends were determined to be courteous and well-behaved.... Most of them read or studied while they stayed at the counters, for three or four hours. I heard them remind each other not to leave cigarette ashes on the counter, to take off their hats, etc.... When the sit-in was over we all met in church. There must have been five hundred kids there, and we all sang together...

By the fourth sit-in, tension was mounting rapidly. There was violence that day. Lighted cigarettes were pushed against the backs of girls sitting at the counter. A white sit-inner, on a stool beside a Negro girl, became a special object of attention by the crowd nearby. Someone kept calling him a "nigger lover." When he didn't respond he was pulled off the stool, thrown to the floor, and kicked. At McClellan's variety store, a white man kept blowing cigar smoke into the face of a Negro sitting at the counter, a Fisk University student named Paul LePrad, who made no move. This infuriated the man. He pulled the student from his stool and hit him. LePrad got back on the stool. He was pulled off again and hit. The police came and arrested LePrad and the seventeen students sitting in with him.

The group at Woolworth's, where Candie Anderson was, heard about this incident. They decided to go McClellan's to protest.

> There was a rope around the stools, showing that the counter was closed. We climbed over the rope. A policeman stood there and said quite clearly, "do not sit down," and we sat down...I became suddenly aware of the crowd

of people standing behind us.... Young kids threw french fried potatoes at us, and gum, and cigarette butts. I looked down the counter at Barbara Crosby in a straight pink skirt and nice white blouse, and at Stephen in a dark suit, with a calculus book.... The policemen simply lined up behind us and peeled us two by two off the stools.... The crowd in the store...shouted out approval. They said about Barbara and me...Oh, white...WHITE, WHITE, WHITE! Three paddy wagons were blinking at us from the street. Once more we had to walk through those crowds. Someone spit right in front of me.... The TV cameras took lots of pictures, and we drove off to the Nashville city jail.

With seventy-six students in jail, a group of NAACP people in Nashville met the next day and pledged support. Fisk University President Stephen Wright said: "Students have been exposed all their lives to the teachings of the great American scriptures of democracy, freedom, and equality, and no literate person should be surprised that they reflect these teachings in their conduct."

But at white Vanderbilt University in Nashville, where a thirty-one-year-old Negro named James Lawson was enrolled in the Divinity School, it was different. Lawson, a conscientious objector and a pacifist, believed in nonviolent resistance. When the first mass arrests took place, newspapermen quoted him as saying he would advise students to violate the law. *The Nashville Banner* immediately called this "incitation to anarchy" and added: "There is no place in Nashville for flannel-mouthed agitators, white or colored—under whatever sponsorship, imported for preachment of mass disorder; self-supported vagrants, or paid agents of strife-breeding organizations." The Vanderbilt trustees, one of whom was the publisher of the *Nashville Banner*, another of whom was president of one of the large department stores where sit-ins had taken place, voted the next day to give Lawson the choice of withdrawing from the movement or dismissal from the University.

Charging the press with distorting his statements, Lawson refused to leave the movement, and in early March he was expelled, three months before his scheduled graduation. Most of the sixteen faculty members of the divinity school, all white, protested. By May, eleven of them, as well as Dean J. Robert Nelson, had resigned over the refusal of the school to re-admit Lawson, leaving four persons on the divinity school faculty. The *Richmond News Leader* commented: "Good riddance...Vanderbilt University will be better off..."

The Nashville sit-ins continued, with arrests, trials, and students deciding to stay in jail in protest rather than pay fines or put up bond. Chief defense lawyer for the students was sixty-two-year-old Z. Alexander Looby, a distinguished Negro attorney, born in Trinidad, and a member of the Nashville City Council.

On April 19, at five o'clock in the morning, while Looby and his wife were asleep in the backroom of their home, one block away from Fisk University's campus, a bomb exploded on his porch. In her dormitory room, Candie Anderson was awakened by the noise. "Only one time in my life have I heard a sound worse than the one when Mr. Looby's house was bombed," she wrote later. "That was when a girl fainted and I heard her head hit the floor: That's the kind of feeling it left when we heard the explosion.... It would have seemed unreal, I think, if the sirens had not kept insistently coming..."

One hundred and forty-seven windows were blown out in Meharry Medical School across the street, and the front part of the Looby's house was demolished, but the attorney and his wife were not hurt. Perhaps, as James Bevel (who married Diane Nash) said, "The Devil has got to come out of these people." For after the bombing, and after a protest march of 2000 Negroes on City Hall, negotiations for desegregation got under way in earnest. In early May, four theaters and six lunch counters downtown declared an end to the color line. In the meantime, the sit-ins had spread to Chattanooga, Knoxville, Memphis, and Oak Ridge. By late spring, seven Tennessee cities had desegregated some of their lunch counters.

CORE, with its long emphasis on nonviolent direct action, played an important part, once the sit-ins began, as an educational and organizing agent, Tom Gaither, of Claflin College in Orangeburg, South Carolina, tells of CORE classes which started there, inspired by the Rock Hill sit-ins. (Those, the first in South Carolina, took place even before the first Nashville sit-ins, with one hundred students from two Negro junior colleges sitting in.)

The Orangeburg students held classes in nonviolence over a period of three or four days for students from Claflin College and South Carolina State, both Negro colleges, and then picked forty students who felt confident in the use of nonviolent techniques. Here is a sample of the instructions to people being schooled in nonviolence:

You may choose to face physical assault without protecting yourself, hands at the sides, unclenched; or you may choose to protect yourself, making plain you do not intent to hit back. If you choose to protect yourself, you practice positions such as these:

To protect the skull, fold the hands over the head.

To prevent disfigurement of the face, bring the elbows together in front of the eyes.

For girls, to prevent internal injury from kicks, lie on the side and bring the knees upward to the chin; for boys, kneel down and arch over, with skull and face protected.

The Kress five and dime store in Orangeburg became the object of careful plans. Students checked the store entrances, counted the number of stools at the lunch counter, calculated exactly the number of minutes it took to walk from a central point on campus to the Kress store. On February 25, tie sit-ins began, and lunch counters closed in downtown Orangeburg. A thousand students were being trained meanwhile, and a mass march through the streets of the city took place, with no violence, no arrests.

When lunch counters reopened on March 14, followed by another great march designed to support a new wave of sit-ins, the police moved in with tear gas bombs and water hoses. The weather was subfreezing. Students were drenched and knocked off their feet by the water pressure. One of these was a blind girl. Over five hundred were arrested and, with the jails full, three hundred and fifty were jammed into a chicken coop and enclosed by a seven-foot wire fence. There was no shelter against the bitter cold.

Meanwhile, students crowded into the basement of the city jail were sweating in 90-degree temperatures from the nearby boiler room. One student, drenched from head to toe, was locked in solitary confinement with water three inches deep covering the cell floor. Requests for dry clothing were denied. A Claflin College nurse came to give first aid, and had to force her way inside. Two hundred students marched around the courthouse in protest. Tom Gaither, the movement's leader (and today a professional civil rights worker with CORE), was marching with them when he was seized and put into jail.

The sit-ins were spreading southward now. They were also becoming larger and better organized. In Atlanta, where they were preceded by many meetings and by a sensational full-page ad of eloquent protest in the *Atlanta Constitution* addressed to a startled white community, the sit-ins were planned like a military operation. On March 15, at exactly 11:00 A.M., two hundred students moved into ten downtown restaurants which had been carefully selected because they were connected with city or county or federal government, and were therefore subject to the Fourteenth Amendment's requirement that *public* places may not discriminate. Seventy-six students were arrested, and the city of Atlanta was never the same again.

There was some violence in those first months of the sit-ins. In Jacksonville, Florida, the city was in turmoil for three days: a white sit-in student was attacked in jail and his jaw was broken; a sixteen-year-old Negro boy was pistol-whipped by the Ku Klux Klan; a Negro man unconnected with the demonstrations who went through a police roadblock was shot to death by a white service station attendant. In Atlanta, acid was thrown at sit-in leader Lonnie King. In Frankfort, Kentucky, the gymnasium of a Negro college was set afire. In Columbia, South Carolina, a Negro sit-in student was stabbed. In Houston, Texas, a twenty-seven-year-old Negro was kidnapped and flogged with a chain, and the symbol KKK was carved on his chest.

Mississippi responded with a special savagery. When students marched down the street in Jackson, police used clubs, tear gas, and police dogs. Women, children, and a photographer were beaten by police and bystanders, and some demonstrators were bitten by dogs. In Biloxi, Mississippi, Negroes trying to use a public beach were attacked with clubs and chains by crowds of whites, and ten were wounded by gunfire.

Yet, considering the number of people involved in demonstrations and the intense psychological tremors accompanying this sudden attack by long-quiescent Negroes on the old way of life, violence was minimal. The restraint of the demonstrators themselves was one factor; they gave the least possible excuse for club-happy and trigger-happy policemen, and the most the police could justify, in most cases, was carting them off to jail. The ratio of social change, both immediate and long-term, to the resulting violence, was extremely high.

The sit-ins marked a turning point for the Negro American, subordinate for three hundred years. He was rebelling now, not with the blind, terrible, understandable hatred of the slave revolts, but with skill in organization, sophistication in tactics, and an unassailable moral position.

With these went a ferocious refusal to retreat. What had been an orderly, inch-by-inch advance via legal processes now became a revolution in which unarmed regiments marched from one objective to another with bewildering speed.

The idea so long cherished by Southern whites—and by many Northerners too—that the Southern Negro (whether through ignorance or intimidation or a shrewd recognition of reality) was content with the way things were, that only a handful of agitators opposed the system of segregation, was swept aside by the mass marches, demonstration, meetings. Montgomery had been the first sign of this, and now it was made clear beyond argument that Negroes all across the South had only been waiting for an opportunity to end their long silence.

Impatience was the mood of the young sit-in demonstrators: impatience with the courts, with national and local governments, with negotiation and conciliation, with the traditional Negro organizations and the old Negro leadership, with the unbearably slow pace of desegregation in a century of accelerated social change.

A Negro never before seen by white Americans was brought into the national view. The young educated Negro was raised inside a ghetto, then went off to a Negro college, where he or she was kept behind the ivy-colored walls by conservative Negro college administrators. Ostensibly this was to protect the sensitive Negro student, but as a by-product, it protected white society from the possibility of rebellion. And in addition, the separation left unmarred the images in white American minds of the faithful, hard-working Negro maid or handyman or the lazy drunk. In early 1960, the Negro student climbed over the wall and into view on millions of television screens all over the country. The picture was impressive, even to those not really convinced these youngsters were doing the right thing. The Richmond News Leader (the same paper which had declared "Good riddance" to Lawson, *et al.*) said in an editorial on February 22, 1960:

> Many a Virginian must have felt a tinge of wry regret at the state of things as they are, in reading of Saturday's "sit-downs" by Negro students in Richmond stores. Here were the colored students, in coats, white shirts, ties, and one of them was reading Goethe and one was taking notes from a biology text. And here, on the sidewalk outside, was a gang of white boys come to heckle, a ragtail rabble, slack-jawed, black-jacketed, grinning fit to

kill, and some of them, God save the mark, were waving the proud and honored flag of the Southern States in the last war fought by gentlemen. Eheu! It gives one pause.

Ralph McGill, long a believer—in the face of bitter attack by segregationists—in the deliberate processes of law to effect an equalitarian society, did not immediately endorse the sit-ins. But by the time he wrote his book, *The South and the Southerner*, he had come to a blunt conclusion:

> The sit-ins were, without question, productive of the most change.... No argument in a court of law could have dramatized the immorality and irrationality of such a custom as did the sit-ins.... The sit-ins reached far out into the back country. They inspired adult men and women, fathers, mothers, grandmothers, aunts and uncles, to support the young students in the cities. Not even the Supreme Court decision on the schools in 1954 had done this.... The central moral problem was enlarged.

Actually, the sit-ins represented an intricate union of economic and moral power. To the store owner, they meant a disruption of normal business; liberal and moderate people in the city and in the nation now, perhaps for the first time, faced their own status as a privileged group in American society.

The sit-ins were an important learning experience for white Southerners, and also for those Northerners who were convinced of some mystical irremovable germ of prejudice in the Southern mind: when the first lunch-counters were desegregated, the world did not come to an end. Whites and Negroes could use public facilities together, it was shown, without violent repercussions, without white withdrawal. Southern whites, once a new pattern became accepted and established in the community, would conform to it as they conformed to the old. Men and women seeking a sandwich at a lunch counter, as young Negroes could see readily in many of the sit-ins, were more interested in satisfying their hunger or their thirst than in who sat next to them. After two months of desegregation in Winston Salem, North Carolina, the manager of a large store said: "You would think it had been going on for fifty years. I am tickled to death over the situation."

There were potential repercussions on the American social structure of enormous scope, far beyond the problem of race. For what happened in the sit-ins is that Americans were resorting to civil disobedience on a national scale, ignoring local statutes, applying the direct pressure of masses of aggrieved people to the nerve centers of the opposition, without using the intermediary of normal political channels. To move outside the American governmental structure in order to effectuate social change, to assert the power of the popular demonstration as superior to that of the parliamentary process, was dangerously suggestive. And, in fact, civil disobedience as a technique spread in a matter of weeks from sit-ins in restaurants to stand-ins at movies, kneel-ins at churches, wade-ins at beaches, and a dozen different kinds of extra-legal demonstrations against segregation.

The sit-ins took the established Negro organizations by surprise. The NAACP had a large membership in the Southern states, had handled thousands of legal cases there, and was a long-established center for Negroes wanting to share their dissatisfactions. But it had not carried on any widespread campaigns of direct protest in the South. The Congress of Racial Equality, or CORE, was a Northern-based organization, with just a few staff members below the Mason-Dixon line. The Southern Christian Leadership Conference, which grew out of the Montgomery boycott and was led by Martin Luther King, Jr., had an office in Atlanta, and was planning various actions in the South, but had engaged in no large-scale movement since Montgomery. Spontaneity and self-sufficiency were the hallmarks of the sit-ins; without adult advice or consent, the students planned and carried them through.

What happened then was that the student movement galvanized the older organizations into a new dynamism, won the support of some of the established Negro leaders who quickly sensed that a new wind was blowing, and left far behind those leaders who could not break either old habits of thinking, or old ties with the white elite.

From the beginning, the students found strong backing in the generation just ahead of them—young Negro professionals in their thirties or early forties, who helped mobilize community support behind the young people. One thinks of Carl Holman, Dr. Clinton Warner, and Whitney Young in Atlanta; also of Dr. Anderson, Slater King and C.B. King in Albany; and of Martin Luther King himself.

On the other hand, the self-interest of some elements in the Negro community had long become enmeshed with that of the whites who held political and economic power, and even the explosive force of the sit-ins could not break that tie. Presidents of state-supported Negro colleges, with an eye on trustees, regents, and state legislatures, lashed out at their student rebels. Faculty members, fearful for their jobs, remained silent. At Southern University in Baton Rouge, whose 5,000 students made it the largest Negro institution in the nation, eighteen sit-in leaders were suspended. At Albany State College in Albany, Georgia, the president eventually got rid of forty student demonstrators. At Alabama State and Florida A & M, punishment was swift. Even at some private, church-supported institutions, like Benedict and Allen Colleges in South Carolina, college administrators threatened expulsion for students who joined the sit-in movement and fired the few faculty members who spoke their minds.

Between the unequivocal supporters and the conservative diehards in the adult Negro community was a third group, whose response to the new militancy of the college generation was complex and curious. These were Negroes ranking high in the social structure of the community, who were beset by a number of conflicting pressures: that of the white side of town, where they had some useful relationships; that of the Negro community at large, which embraced the sit-ins, and on which they were dependent socially and politically; that of their own long resentment against segregation; of a conservatism fundamental to their lofty position; of an uncomfortable feeling of being left in the shadows by the immature upstarts of the student movement. In this confusion of interests, the reaction of such people was often to support the movement publicly, and try privately to keep it within respectable limits.

Atlanta is a case in point. Here, a number of the college presidents in the Atlanta University Center, while publicly expressing their support, tried to discourage their students from direct action activities. Some ministers and businessmen reacted similarly. Jeremy Larner, writing in the *New Leader* at the time of the sit-ins, reports a meeting that spring of five student leaders summoned to a conference with the Negro old guard of Atlanta.

> While the students wore slacks and sport shirts, their elders were dressed like New York bankers. Their faces were somber and the atmosphere was somewhat like that of an emergency meeting of the General Motors board of directors. From a high table in front, the meeting was presided over by a man with a pleasant face and remarkably light skin who spoke and looked like President Eisenhower. He was flanked by an Episcopalian minister, a banker, a realtor, and a lawyer. One by one they rose and delivered sober, articulate speeches. I was impressed by the absence of Southern accents, and later discovered that they sent their own children to Northern universities.

Whether Larner's report of what these "elders" said to the sit-in leaders is an exact quote, or a paraphrase, it catches the spirit of what so many of the students heard from well-placed adults in those hectic days:

> So you see, kids, we've been in this a long time. We want the same things you do, but we know by now they can't be gotten overnight. It's our experience that you have to work slowly to get lasting results. We'd hate to see your movement backfire and spoil the things we've worked so hard for. You need guidance, and we hope you'll have the vision to accept it.

The response of the students was brief, unpolished, to the point. "We are continuing the movement as best we know how. We hope you will join us."

They did continue the movement, and the important men of the Negro community, whatever qualms they had, let it be known to the public that they had joined.

As pointed out earlier, there was no central direction to the sit-ins. The sparks from that first almost-innocent sit-in of four college freshmen in Greensboro showered the South and caught fire in a hundred localities. But hardly a month had passed before Ella Baker, in charge of the Southern Christian Leadership Conference office in Atlanta and observing the wild spread of the sit-ins, decided that something should be done to coordinate them.

Ella Baker, middle-aged, dark-skinned, beautiful, with a deep-throated voice that seemed suited for the stage, had grown up in a little town in North Carolina. As a girl, she had listened to stories of slave revolts told by her ninety-year-old grandmother, who as a slave had been whipped for refusing to marry the man picked out for her by her master. Miss Baker was a champion debater in high school and valedictorian of her graduating class at Shaw University in Raleigh. She wanted to go to medical school and become a medical missionary, then dreamed of teaching sociology at the University of Chicago. But family difficulties intervened. Instead, she went to New York.

There, she found that despite her college education, jobs were closed to her because of her color; she worked as a waitress, or found a job in a factory. She lived in Harlem in the 1930s worked for the WPA on consumer education, started consumers' cooperatives in Philadelphia and Chicago, and then in 1940 turned to the NAACP, spending six years with them as a field secretary. Then she worked for the Urban League and other groups.

When the Southern Christian Leadership Conference was organized by Martin Luther King, Bayard Rustin, and Stanley Levison in 1957, Ella Baker came South to organize a series of mass meetings for them. In early 1958, she set up the SCLC office in Atlanta and was its first full-time executive-secretary. Deciding, in late February of 1960, that the sit-in leaders should be brought together, she asked the SCLC to underwrite it financially. With $800 of SCLC money, the prestige of Martin Luther King, the organizing wisdom of Ella Baker, and the enthusiasm of the rare young people who were leading the new student movement, the Student Nonviolent Coordinating Committee was born.

Ella Baker went to Raleigh and got her Alma Mater, Shaw University, to provide facilities for a meeting of about a hundred students. But by the time of the conference on Easter weekend, April 15-17, 1960, demonstrations had spread so fast that there were sixty centers of sit-in activity. Also, nineteen northern colleges were interested enough to send delegates. The result was that over two hundred people came to the conference, one hundred twenty-six of them student delegates from fifty-eight different Southern communities in twelve states.

Jane Stembridge, from Virginia, later described her feelings that first night in Raleigh:

> The most inspiring moment for me was the first time I heard the students sing "We Shall Overcome".... It was hot that night upstairs in the auditorium. Students had just come in from all over the South, meeting for the first time. February 1 was not long past. There was no SNCC, no *ad hoc* committees, no funds, just people who did not know what to expect but who came and released the common vision in that song. I had just driven down from Union Seminary in New York—out of it, except that I cared, and that I was a Southerner.... It was inspiring because it was the beginning, and because, in a sense, it was the purest moment. I am a romantic. But I call this moment the one...

James Lawson, the divinity school student just expelled from Vanderbilt University, gave the keynote address. At the organizing sessions, there was some tension over whether to have an official connection with SCLC. It was finally decided to maintain a friendly relationship with SCLC and other organizations but to remain independent. This urge for

freedom from adult fetters and formal ties had marked the student movement from the beginning, so the decision was important, reflecting a
mood which has continued in SNCC to this day. The conference set up a
temporary committee, which would meet monthly through the spring and
summer, and would coordinate the various student movements around the
South. Ed King, who had ben a leader in the Frankfort, Kentucky sit-ins,
was asked to serve, at least temporarily, as administrative secretary.

The first meeting after the Raleigh Conference was held in May,
1960, on the campus of Atlanta University. About fifteen of the student
leaders were there, as were Martin Luther King, Jr. , James Lawson, Ella
Baker, Len Holt (a CORE lawyer from Norfolk, Virginia), and observers
from the National Student Association, the YWCA, the American Friends
Service Committee, and other groups. They now called themselves the
Temporary Student Nonviolent Coordinating Committee, and elected
Marion Barry, at this time doing graduate work at Fisk, as chairman. A
statement of purpose was adopted, of which the first paragraph states the
theme:

> We affirm the philosophical or religious ideal of non-violence as the foun-
> dation of our purpose, the pre-supposition of our faith, and the manner of
> our action. Nonviolence as it grows from Judaic-Christian traditions seeks
> a social order of justice permeated by love. Integration of human endeavor
> represents the first step towards such a society...

It was decided to set up an office, hire a secretary to man it over
the summer months, begin to raise money, plan non-violence institutes
for the summer, print a newsletter, and try to coordinate the various student activities throughout the South. Marion Barry told reporters that the
sit-in movement "demonstrates the rapidity with which mass action can
bring about social change. This is only the beginning."

They called Jane Stembridge at Union Theological Seminary in
New York and asked her if she would serve as SNCC's first office secretary. In early June, 1960, she arrived in Atlanta. Bob Moses, recalling his
first trip South that summer of 1960, described later how "SNCC and
Jane Stembridge were squeezed in one corner of the SCLC office.... I was
licking envelopes, one at a time, and talking—Niebuhr, Tillich and
Theos—with Jane, who was fresh from a year at Union.... Miss Ella Baker
was in another corner of the office."

In June, the first issue of *The Student Voice* appeared. Three years later it would be beautifully printed and designed (though still small, direct, terse) and illustrated by remarkable photos of SNCC in action. At this time it was crudely mimeographed, carrying news of the Raleigh Conference and the May meeting. It was not so intensely organizational that it could not find room for a poem, written by one of the founders of SNCC, later to be its chief writer of press releases and editor of *The Student Voice*, Julian Bond:

> I too, hear America singing
> But from where I stand
> I can only hear Little Richard
> And Fats Domino
> But sometimes,
> I hear Ray Charles
> Drowning in his own tears
>   or Bird
> Relaxing at Camarillo
> or Horace Silver doodling,
> Then I don't mind standing
>   a little longer.

The new SNCC organization, that summer and early fall of 1960, found that "coordinating" was not easy. Jane Stembridge later recalled:

> A great deal of time was spent trying to find out exactly what was going on in the protest centers.... Response was next to nil.... This was because the students were too busy protesting and because they did not understand the weight of the press release (thank God some still don't).... No one really needed "organization" because we then had a movement.... Members of the first SNCC were vague simply because they were right damn in the middle of directing sit-ins, being in jail, etc., and they did not know what was going on anywhere outside of their immediate downtown.... We had no one "in the field" either. SNCC called for demonstrations once or twice. The response was extremely spotty and then the news was not sent in. We could not afford phone calls and so it went. SNCC was not coordinating the movement.... I would say the main thing done then was to let people know we existed.... We were not sure, and still aren't, "what SNCC is"...

In July, in Los Angeles, where the National Democratic Convention was about to nominate John F. Kennedy and Lyndon Johnson, Marion Barry appeared for SNCC before the Platform Committee of the Convention, recommending strong federal action: to speed school desegregation, to enact a fair employment law, to assure the right to vote against Southern economic reprisal and violence, to protect demonstrators against false arrest and police repression by invoking that clause of the Fourteenth Amendment which says: "No state shall make or enforce any law which shall abridge the privileges and immunities of citizens of the United States."

The sit-ins Barry told the platform Committee, "in truth were peaceful petitions to the conscience of our fellow citizens for redress of the old grievances that stem from racial segregation and discrimination." Characteristically, the statement was not coldly organizational, but carried some of the poetic freshness of the new student movement:

> ...The ache of every man to touch his potential is the throb that beats out the truth of the American Declaration of Independence and the Constitution. America was founded because men were seeking room to become.... We are again seeking that room.... We want to walk into the sun and through the front door. For three hundred and fifty years, the American Negro has been sent to the back door.... We grow weary...

Barry spoke directly to the charge made by ex-President Harry Truman during the sit-ins, that the student movement was somehow connected with communism. He said:

> To label our goals, methods, and presuppositions 'communistic' is to credit Communism with an attempt to remove tyranny and to create an atmosphere where genuine communication can occur. Communism seeks power, ignores people, and thrives on social conflict. We seek a community in which man can realize the full meaning of the self which demands open relationship with others.

In October of 1960, at a conference of several hundred delegates in Atlanta, SNCC was put on a permanent basis. It was not (and never has become) a membership organization. This left the adhesion of individuals to the group fluid and functional, based simply on who was carrying on activity. The Student Nonviolent Coordinating Committee consisted of a delegate from each of sixteen Southern states and the District of Columbia, plus a few voting members and many observers from various national student and race relations organizations, such as CORE, SCLC, the YWCA, the National Student Association, the NAACP, the Southern Conference Educational Fund.

Again, the purpose was to coordinate the student movement. But the movement, still with a quality of abandon, still spontaneous and unstructured, refused to be put into a bureaucratic box. The twig was bent, and the tree grew that way. For SNCC, even after it had a large staff, its own office, and money for long-distance phone calls, managed to maintain an autonomy in the field, an unpredictability of action, a lack of overall planning which brought exasperation to some of its most ardent supporters, bewilderment to outside observers, and bemusement to the students themselves.

Throughout the winter of 1960-1961, sit-ins continued, linked only vaguely by SNCC, but creating a warmth of commitment, a solidarity of purpose which spurred awareness of SNCC by students all over the South. They also sustained a vision—or perhaps, knowing SNCC, a set of various visions, which kept Marion Barry, Jane Stembridge, Julian Bond, Diane Nash, Charles Sherrod, Charles Jones, and others, going.

When ten students were arrested in Rock Hill, South Carolina, in February, 1961, the SNCC steering committee, meeting in Atlanta, made its boldest organizational decision up to that date. Four people, it was agreed, would go to Rock Hill to sit in, would be arrested, and would refuse bail, as the first ten students had done, in order to dramatize the injustice to the nation. The Rock Hill action was the start of the jail-no bail policy.

Sit-in veterans Charles Sherrod (Petersburg, Virginia), Charles Jones (Charlotte, North Carolina) and Diane Nash were to go. The fourth person was a relative novice in the movement, Spelman College student Ruby Doris Smith, who talked her older sister out of the trip so she could go instead. "I went home that night to explain to my mother. She couldn't understand why I had to go away—why I had to go to Rock Hill."

Ruby Doris and the others spent thirty days in prison, the first time anyone had served full sentences in the sit-in movement. "I read a lot there: *The Ugly American, The Life of Mahatma Gandhi, Exodus, The Wall Between....* Every day at noon we sang 'We Shall Overcome'...." The fellows had been put on a road gang: Tom Gaither of CORE, Charles Sherrod and Charles Jones of SNCC, and nine others. The captain of the guards took their textbooks away, saying: "This is a prison—not a damned school." He turned out to be wrong.

"Jail-no bail" spread. In Atlanta, in February, 1961, eighty students from the Negro colleges went to jail and refused to come out. I knew some, but not all, of the participants from Spelman, where I taught history and political science. That fall, when a very bright student named Lana Taylor, fair-skinned, rather delicate looking, joined my course on Chinese Civilization, I learned she had been in jail. In early 1964 I came across a reminiscence of Jane Stembridge:

> ...the most honest moment—the one in which I saw the guts-type truth—stripped of anything but total fear and total courage...was one day during 1961 in Atlanta.... Hundreds went out that day and filled every lunch counter.... There was much humor—like A.D. King coordinating the whole damn thing with a walkie-talkie.... The moment: Lana Taylor from Spelman was sitting next to me. The manager walked up behind her, said something obscene, and grabbed her by the shoulders. "Get the hell out of here, nigger." Lana was not going. I do not know whether she should have collapsed in nonviolent manner. She probably did not know. She put her hands under the counter and held. He was rough and strong. She just held and I looked down at that moment at her hands...brown, strained...every muscle holding.... All of a sudden he let go and left. As though he knew he could not move that girl—ever..."

The sit-ins of 1960 were the beginning. They left not only excitement, but a taste of victory. The spring and summer of 1961 brought, for the youngsters in SNCC and for many others, an experience of a different kind: an ordeal by fire and club. These were the Freedom Rides.

5

Kennedy: The Reluctant Emancipator

This article, which appeared in *The Nation* on December 1, 1962, came out of an investigation I did for the Southern Regional Council in Atlanta of the mass demonstrations of that year in Albany, Georgia. My report focused on the failure of the federal government to enforce constitutional rights in Albany. It made national news, and when Martin Luther King, Jr. told reporters he agreed with my criticism of the FBI, he aroused the special anger of J. Edgar Hoover. My critique went beyond the FBI to the national administration, whose collaboration with the racist South—by inaction—was to become a persistent issue throughout the struggles of the movement for equal rights.

The dispatch of federal troops to Oxford, Mississippi, tends to obscure the true cautiousness of John F. Kennedy in the movement for Negro rights. Oxford diverted attention from Albany, Georgia. In the former, the national government moved boldly and with overwhelming force. In the latter, which twice this past year has been the scene of Negro demonstrations, mass arrests and official violence, the federal government showed cautiousness to the point of timidity. The two situations, occurring in comparable Black Belt areas, point up the ambiguous, uncomfortable role of the Administration in civil rights. Oxford is fresh in the memory today and was the object of an international uproar. Albany, now in the backwash of national attention, deserves to be brought forward for a good look.

I had the benefit of two such looks: last December, when that Black Belt city erupted with racial demonstrations for the first time in a long history going back to slavery days; and again last summer, when trouble burst out once more. Both times, the Southern Regional Council, which studies race matters throughout the South from its headquarters in Atlanta, had asked me to investigate and report. What I saw convinced me that the national government has an undeserved reputation, both among Southern opponents and Northern supporters, as a vigorous combatant for Negro rights.

To be fair, this much should be said at the outset in behalf of the Administration: fundamentally, it is behaving no differently from any of its predecessors. We have always lived in a white society, where even liberalism is tinged with whiteness. I am measuring the actions of the Kennedys not against past performances, but against the needs of our time. My object is not to denounce, but to clarify. It is important for American citizens to know exactly how far they can depend on the national government, and how much remains for them to do. In the field of racial equality, this government simply cannot be depended upon for vigorous initiatives. It will, however respond to popular indignation and pressure. When I say that it often responds slowly and reluctantly, my intention is not to vilify John F. Kennedy, but to light a flame under the rest of us.

The Kennedy Administration has set limits, never publicized but nevertheless implicit in its actions, to its own power in the field of desegregation. It will act to keep law and order in cases of extreme and admitted defiance of federal authority, as in Oxford. But it will not act against violation of federal law in other cases—in Albany, Georgia, for instance—where the circumstances are less stark.

There is a rough analogy between Lincoln's insistence (in that famous letter to Horace Greeley) that he was more concerned with *union* than with slavery, and Kennedy's unspoken but obvious preoccupation with *law and order* above either desegregation or the right of free assembly. This explains why the Justice Department, while over a period of nine months 1,000 Negroes were being jailed in Albany for peaceful demonstrations against racial discrimination, gave tacit support to the chief of police for maintaining "law and order." Only after eight months of pressure and complaint did it enter the picture as "friend of the court" in a defensive suit. But it never took the initiative in behalf of Albany Negroes.

The analogy with Lincoln is only a rough one because even the "law and order" principle is applied by Kennedy rather narrowly, with shadowy situations interpreted against the Negro rather than for him. In the case of Ole Miss, the law was unquestionably clear and the imminence of disorder equally clear. But in Albany, there was legal doubt. True, there was an Interstate Commerce Commission ruling and explicit court decisions calling for desegregation of the bus and train terminals. But did not the chief of police say on three successive occasions, when arresting young people who had used the "white" section of the terminal, that it was not a matter of race, but of keeping "order"? A forthright national government might have dismissed this argument as easily as it did Barnett's contention that race was not the basic reason for barring James Meredith from Ole Miss. But the Kennedy Administration chose not to challenge Albany's Chief Pritchett.

And when, last December, more than 700 Negro men, women and children were packed into jails in the Albany area for protesting segregation by marching through downtown streets and holding prayer meetings in front of City Hall, the government might have gone to court, on the basis of the First Amendment, to defend the right of free assembly. It might be contended, however, that with Negroes in jail, Albany had more "order." Also, constitutional lawyers disagree over the right of the government to take the initiative in enforcing the First Amendment. The Kennedy Administration has talked of the New Frontier, but perhaps this frontier does not extend into the South or into the field of constitutional law.

Albany is a quiet commercial town in southwest Georgia surrounded by farm land that, in pre-Civil War days, was slave plantation country. Negroes, once a majority in the community, now make up 40 percent of its population of 56,000. Interestingly enough, like many

Southern cities just beginning the process of desegregation, Albany has been free of white mob violence of the kind that made headlines at Oxford, Little Rock, and a few other places. When, last December, Negroes marched downtown in large but peaceful groups to sing and pray in front of City Hall, whites stood by and watched with curiosity—resentful, perhaps, but quiet. It was the city and county officials who, by jailing the peaceful demonstrators, repeatedly violated the Fourteenth Amendment, which not only prohibits the application of local law on the basis of color, but also—according to constitutional doctrine accepted since the 1920s—bars deprivation by local officials of the rights of free speech, assembly, and petition.

The fact that it was local police who violated constitutional doctrine is important because it is against local governments, rather than private persons, that the federal government has the clearest right to act in defense of the rights of citizens.

A shaky truce ended the December demonstrations, which had been provoked by arrests at the train terminal, but were rooted, of course, in the total segregation and white domination that make Albany, Georgia, such a hard place for Negroes to live in. By January, the truce began to fall apart. That month, an eighteen-year-old Negro girl named Ola Mae Quarterman sat in the front seat of an Albany bus, refused to move on the command of the driver, was arrested by a policeman and convicted in city court for using "obscene" language. The driver testified that she had told him: "I paid my damn twenty-cents, and I can sit where I want." Subsequently Miss Quarterman told a federal court, to which her case had gone on appeal, that she had used the word "damn" in relation to her twenty cents, not in relation to the driver. (Anywhere but the Deep South a judge might have thought it incredible that she should be forced to defend her words by making such a distinction.) The city's counsel insisted her race had nothing to do with her arrest, and in cross-examination asked if it were not true that the cause of her arrest was her "vulgar language." She replied softly, "That's what they said."

There followed several hundred arrests as the city police moved promptly against every Negro who in any way and under any circumstances, challenged segregation patterns: two young men who sat in the Trailways terminal restaurant; four men picketing a store down town; thirty youngsters asking service at a lunch counter; twenty-nine people praying in front of City Hall; 150 more on the way to City Hall; seven praying in front of City Hall; ten more; eighteen more; sixteen more; all praying in front of City Hall; fourteen praying at the Carnegie Library—all thrown into jail.

After a thousand arrests, Police Chief Laurie Pritchett emerged into national prominence as some sort of hero. He had kept the peace. Somehow, the standard for American democracy accepted by the Administration became the standard for the nation: the sole criterion was the prevention of violence. The fact that violence had at no time been imminent in the demonstrations was overlooked.

There is a statute in the U.S. Criminal Code, Section 242, going back to 1866, which makes it a crime for a local law-enforcement officer deliberately to subject "any inhabitant of any State...to the deprivation of any rights, privileges, or immunities secured or protected by the Constitution and laws of the United States..." Under any reasonable interpretation, this law was broken in Albany at least thirty times from November 1, 1961, when police for the first time ignored the ICC ruling desegregating the bus terminal, to the middle of August 1962, when three youngsters trying to attend services at a white church were arrested. To select one instance with at least fifty witnesses; a county judge watched quietly from his bench as deputy sheriffs dragged and pushed out of his courtroom five young people—one Negro and four whites—who had taken seats in the "wrong" section (by race). One was a young woman whom a deputy dragged over a row of seats and pushed through a revolving door.

The U.S. Department of Justice maintains an FBI office in Albany. Affidavits have flowed into that FBI office in a steady stream, attesting to violations by local officials of the constitutional rights of Negroes. But nothing was done. As recently as last week, the Rev. Martin Luther King, Jr. publicly charged that the FBI agents in Albany have been favoring the segregationists. [As to the role of the FBI in the investigation of complaints by Negroes in the South charging violations of civil rights, and of the attitude of Negroes toward the bureau, see Volume V of the 1961 *Report of the Civil Rights Commission,* particularly the notes on pages 211 and 219.—Ed]

The Department of Justice, citing a 1943 case in which the conviction of a Georgia sheriff in the brutal killing of a Negro named Bobby

Hall was overturned by a narrow Supreme Court interpretation of Section 242, takes the position that it should prosecute only in extreme cases of police brutality. This policy allows transgressors of Negro rights who stop short of premeditated murder to act with reasonable assurance that the federal government will not move. Last summer, as least three acts of brutality occurred in the Albany area, were duly reported to the FBI, and thus far have resulted in no federal action. I will describe these three in some detail as told to me by the principals.

On July 23, 1962, about 5:30 P.M., Mrs. Slater King, wife of a Negro leader in the Albany Movement, drove from Albany to the Camilla jail in neighboring Mitchell County, carrying food to a girl who had been arrested with a hundred other Negroes while on a march to City Hall. Mrs. King was in her sixth month of pregnancy, and had her three children along. "All you niggers get away from the fence," one of the deputies standing nearby called out as a group of visiting women approached the jailhouse. Mrs. King walked slowly towards her car. A deputy pointed her out, cursed her, threatened to arrest her if she didn't hurry. She turned and said, "If you want to arrest me, go ahead." She was then kicked, hit twice on the side of the head and was knocked unconscious.

Several days later, William Hansen, a twenty-year-old white field worker for the Student Non-Violent Coordinating Committee, and a veteran of jails in Mississippi and Maryland for participating in desegregation actions, was put in the Dougherty County jail in Albany after a prayer session in front of City Hall. A prison trusty, to whom the jailer had earlier suggested that Hansen needed to be "straightened out," beat the Cincinnati youth into senselessness as he sat on the floor reading. His jaw and several ribs were broken. Bleeding profusely from the mouth, he asked the jailer for medical aid, and was told that was not within the jailer's jurisdiction. Finally, a message shouted through the cell window brought about his transfer to the city jail, where he was hospitalized.

That same Saturday afternoon, C. D. King, thirty-six, the first and only Negro attorney in the city of Albany and the legal backbone of the Albany Movement, heard of Hansen's beating. He visited Sheriff Cull Campbell of Dougherty County to check on Hansen's condition. A Negro minister who was waiting to meet King in the Sheriff's office at the time later described what happened. Sheriff Campbell, seeing King in his office, said, "Nigger, haven't I told you to wait outside?" As King turned to reply, the Sheriff picked up a walking stick and hit him viciously on the head, breaking the cane. King staggered from the office, blood streaming from his head and crossed the street to City Hall, where Chief Pritchett had him taken to a hospital. Pritchett, who had just arrested twenty-eight Negroes for praying and singing in front of City Hall called the beating of King "very regrettable." The *New York Times* reporter, Claude Sitton, noted that "Chief Pritchett had more than 160 city, county and state law-enforcement officers standing by to prevent violence." Sheriff Campbell readily admitted the beating when I questioned him a month after the incident: "Yeah, I knocked hell out of him, and I'll do it again. I let him know I'm a white man and he's a damn nigger."

All of the above three incidents were reported to the FBI, which dutifully recorded them. Thus far, the federal government has taken no action.

The few things that the national government *did* do in Albany give a clue to the boundaries it has drawn for itself in the field of civil rights. It went into a frantic day of telephone calls when Martin Luther King, Jr., was jailed in Albany; King, of course, is a politically important symbol. President Kennedy, in answer to questions on Albany at two different press conferences, made two statements. In one, he criticized Albany officials for refusing to negotiate with Negroes; in the other, he denounced the burning of Negro churches that had been used for voter-registration activities in the Albany area. The President's plea for negotiation, like his careful speech on the eve of Meredith's registration at Ole Miss, carefully skirted the moral issue of racial equality and stuck to procedural questions: the law, negotiation. The President has still not followed the advice of his own Civil Rights Commission to give "moral leadership" and to use "education and persuasion." His statement on church-burning covered two points on which the Administration is especially sensitive: its antipathy to nationally publicized violence and its careful defense of voter-registration activity.

There is a plausible legal argument to the effect that voting rights are protected by specific legislation (the Civil Rights Acts of 1957 and 1960), while the First Amendment rights of free speech, assembly, etc., and the Fourteenth Amendment right to color-blind treatment by local officials, are not. However, a national administration less timorous than the present one could find solid legal sanction for the widespread use of injunctions to protect free assembly and to attack legal segregation. In the *Debs* case of 1895, the Supreme Court supported the issuance of injunctions without specific statutory basis, saying: "Every government has a right to apply to its own courts in matters which the Constitution has entrusted to the care of the national government." This ruling has never been overturned.

A truly bold national administration might do the following: (1) prosecute vigorously, under Sec. 242, violations of Negro rights by local officers; (2) create a corps of special agents-not encumbered, as is the FBI, by intimate relations with local police officers—to prevent, as well as to investigate, violations of constitutional rights; (3) use the power of injunction freely, both to prevent policemen from curtailing the right of assembly and petition and to break down legal enforcement of segregation; (4) tell the South and the nation frankly that racial discrimination is morally wrong as well as illegal, and that the nation intends to wipe it out.

At this moment, because of the limitations that the Administration has imposed upon itself, there is a vast no-man's-land for American Negroes into which they are invited by the Constitution, but where federal authority will not protect them. It was into this no-man's-land that the Negro population of Albany ventured, and found itself deserted. The future may bring one or two more Oxfords, but there are a hundred potential Albanys. Throughout the Deep South, Negroes are on the move towards dangerous territory. And so far, though these men, women and children live in a nation whose power encircles the globe and reaches into space, they are very much on their own.

6

Alabama: Freedom Day in Selma

The black young men and women who staged the sit-ins all over the South in early 1960 got together that Spring to form the Student Nonviolent Coordinating Committee (SNCC—to be known as Snick). Their spiritual and intellectual guide in this was an extraordinary black woman named Ella Baker, who had been a long-time activist in Harlem, an organizer for the NAACP, and aide to Martin Luther King. I was asked to join her in being an "adult advisor" to SNCC, serving on its executive committee. In October of 1963, SNCC decided to tackle one of the most dangerous of jobs, to register black voters in Dallas County, Alabama, by bringing hundreds of them into the county seat, the small city of Selma, for "Freedom Day." I went along as participant-writer, and then wrote an angry article for *The New Republic* (later enlarged as a chapter in my book *SNCC: The New Abolitionists*), and what follows this introduction is that chapter. I pointed to the failure of federal officials on the scene to prevent police brutality against SNCC workers helping people with voter registration. My article led to a sharp exchange with Burke Marshall, head of the Civil Rights Division of the Department of

Justice, who insisted the federal government did not have the power
to intercede. Shortly after this, he wrote a small book defending his
thesis, and when I read a review of it in a major law journal I was
happy to see his ideas demolished by Richard Wasserstrom, one of
the Department of Justice lawyers who had been on the scene in
Selma that day. Wasserstrom corroborated what I had found: that
statutes going far back in the history of the nation gave the federal
government clear power to enforce constitutional rights when local
officials failed to do so.

On the night of June 11, 1963, the Rev. Bernard Lafayette, ready to
park at his home, was approached by a man who told him that his car
had stalled across the street and he needed a push. "How much will you
charge me for a push?" the man asked. "Nothing," replied Lafayette, and
lined up his car behind the other one. It was a scene that has taken place
a thousand times in a thousand American towns. But this was different:
the town was Selma, Alabama; Bernard Lafayette was a former Freedom
Rider and a field secretary for SNCC; the man asking for help was white.
When Lafayette bent to see if the bumpers matched, he was clubbed on
the head, and he fell to the pavement, blood spurting over his clothes.
Then he was hit twice more on the head, and the man drove off. He got
to a doctor, who sewed up his wound with six stitches, and the next day
he was back at his job, registering voters in Selma.

Selma has an unreal air about it. It is as if a movie producer had
reconstructed a pre-Civil War Southern town—decaying buildings, the
muddy streets, the little cafes, and the huge red brick Hotel Albert, mod-
elled after a medieval Venetian palace. A mule draws a wagonload of cotton down the street. But cotton is just hanging on. At one time, 627,000
acres in the area grew cotton. Now it's down to 27,000 acres.

You walk into the Silver Moon Cafe. On the shelves facing you
there are bottles of whiskey and boxes of corn flakes. At your feet, running the length of the counter, is a tin channel spittoon. Past a swinging
door you can make out the murky interior of the Negro section of the
cafe. In the white section, in a booth, sits a Mexican family, eating in
silence (eighty-five Mexicans were brought in this year to pick cotton;
they pick more cotton for less money than Negroes do, say the local

whites). Two women sit at a table, drinking beer, looking up to curse the strangers sitting at the counter. You recall what *Newsweek* writer Karl Fleming was told in another Alabama city: "We killed two-year-old Indian babes to get this country, and you want to give it to the niggers."

Selma was a slave market before the Civil War. In one three-story house, still standing, four or five hundred Negroes were kept at one time to be exhibited and sold. The town became a military depot for the Confederacy. At the turn of the century, it was a lynching town. By the 1950s the lynching had stopped, but the threat of it remained. Selma became the birthplace of the Citizens Council in Alabama, wrapped tight in the rules of race.

A little south of the geographic center of Alabama, Selma is about fifty miles due west of Montgomery, and downstream from it on the Alabama River. It is the seat of Dallas County, where, in 1961, 57 percent of the population was Negro, but only about 1 percent of the eligible Negroes were registered to vote, while 64 percent of the eligible whites were registered. The median income for Negroes is about $28 a week. With several new government buildings in the center of town, Selma has a trace of the twentieth century; but beyond it the Alabama countryside is an unpenetrated social jungle. In neighboring Wilcox County, for instance, where Negroes are 78 percent of the population, not one of them is registered to vote; their median income is about $20 a week.

Bruce Boynton is a Negro attorney, now in Chattanooga, who grew up in Selma. (His mother, Mrs. Amelia Boynton, still lives there, a rock to whom the new freedom movement is anchored, a 1964 candidate for the U.S. Senate.) Mr. Boynton says:

> A Negro boy growing up in Selma lives a life that other Americans cannot easily understand. When he wakes up in the morning he looks outside the window and it is dusty, hot, wet, the street mired in mud. He is aware that his mother is away all the time, at work. He is aware of the jobs his mother and father have, how little they make, how much more the white folks make. Coming home from school he sees the sign on the bus directing him to the back. One of his first ideas is: I must get out of this town.

In February of 1963, Bernard Lafayette and his wife Colia came to Selma to begin a voter registration drive for SNCC. It was slow, hard going, One of the first consequences was that thirty-two schoolteachers who tried to register to vote were fired. Arrests mounted, for minor or

imaginary traffic offenses, for picketing at the county courthouse, for simply being seen downtown or riding in an automobile. Worth Long, a
SNCC man, was beaten by a deputy sheriff in the county jail. John Lewis
was arrested for leading a picket line at the courthouse. A nineteen-year
old girl was knocked off a stool in a store and prodded with a electric pole
as she lay on the floor unconscious.

Between September 15 and October 2, 1963, over three hundred
people were arrested in Selma in connection with voter registration activities. The Federal government filed suit, but its mild efforts left the constitutional liberties of Selma citizens in the hands of Sheriff Jim Clark.
Clark augmented his regular force of deputies with several hundred ordinary citizens, armed them with clubs and cattle prods, and stated that he
was convinced that all this voting activity was part of a world communist
conspiracy. In May, when Jim Forman came to Selma to address the first
mass meeting at the Tabernacle Baptist Church, the posse surrounded the
church. Those inside waited, long after the meeting was over, until they
felt it safe to go home.

"Do you know any white man in Selma—just one even—who is
sympathetic with your cause?" I asked three young Selma fellows as we
talked in Mrs. Boynton's home. "Not one," they said. "Well, maybe one,"
one of them added. There was a Jewish storekeeper for whom his mother worked, and the man would sit and talk with the boy in the back of the
store, telling him, "Keep up the good work." Later that night, I saw a list
of Citizens Council members who signed a proclamation in the local
paper; the storekeeper's name was near the top of the list. There are over
a hundred Jews in Selma, many of them businessmen, many of them—
through conviction or through fear—members of the Citizens Council.

The only white man who openly helped the Negro movement
was Father Maurice Ouillet, a thirty-seven-year old Catholic priest in
charge of St. Edmonds Mission in Selma. Father Ouillet was called in
once by a group of white leaders of the city and advised to leave town for
his own protection, told he might be killed. He received abusive phone
calls. Once, he told *Texas Observer* editor Ronnie Dugger, as he visited
demonstrators at the jail, someone called him an "adjective, adjective nig-
ger-lover."

With John Lewis and seven others still in jail in October, 1963,
with Sheriff Clark's posse armed and on the prowl, with people afraid to

go down to the courthouse, SNCC decided on a large-scale offensive. They had discovered elsewhere that fear decreased with numbers. It was decided to set October 7 as the day to bring hundreds to the county courthouse to register. As Freedom Day approached, mass meetings were held every night, and the churches were packed.

On October 5, Dick Gregory came to Selma. His wife, Lillian, had been jailed in Selma while demonstrating. He spoke to a crowded church meeting that evening. It was an incredible performance. With armed deputies ringing the church outside, and three local officials sitting in the audience taking notes, Gregory lashed out at white Southern society with a steely wit and a passion that sent his Negro listeners into delighted applause again and again. Never in the history of this area had a black man stood like this on a public platform, ridiculing and denouncing white officials to their faces. It was a historic coming of age for Selma, Alabama. It was also something of a miracle that Gregory was able to leave town alive. The local newspaper said that a "wildly applauding crowd" listened that night to "the most scathing attack unleashed here in current racial demonstrations."

Gregory told the audience that the Southern white man had nothing he could call his own, no real identity, except "segregated drinking fountains, segregated toilets, and the right to call me nigger." He added, "And when the white man is threatened with losing his *toilet*, he's ready to kill!" He wished, Gregory said, that the whole Negro race would disappear overnight. "They would go crazy looking for us!" The crowd roared and applauded. Gregory lowered his voice, and he was suddenly serious: "But it looks like we got to do it the hard way, and stay down here, and educate them."

He called the Southern police officials "peons, the idiots who do all the dirty work, the dogs who do all the biting." He went on for over two hours in that vein; essentially it was a lesson in economics and sociology, streaked with humor. "The white man starts all the wars, then he talks about you cuttin' somebody...They talk about our education. But the most important thing is to teach people how to live..."

Later, Jim Forman spoke to the crowd, making the last preparations for Freedom Day. "All right, let's go through the phone book. You'll know who's Negro, because they won't have Mr. or Mrs. in front of their names! You got to get on the phone tonight and call these people and tell them to come down to the courthouse tomorrow, that it's Freedom Day. You take a boloney sandwich and a glass of cool water and go down there and stay all day. Now get on that phone tonight. Who'll take the letter 'A'?..."

The Selma Freedom Chorus sang, the most beautiful singing I had heard since the mass meetings in Albany; among them there were some really small children, some teen-agers, a boy at the piano. There was a big sign up on the platform, "DO YOU WANT TO BE FREE." After the singing, everyone went home, through the doors out into the street, where two cars with white men inside had been parked all evening in the darkness outside the church.

Some of us waited that night at Mrs. Boynton's for James Baldwin to arrive. He was flying into Birmingham; some SNCC fellows would pick him up there and drive him to Selma. He was coming to observe Freedom Day. While waiting, we sat around in the kitchen and talked. Jim Forman expertly scrambled eggs in a frying pan with one hand, gesturing with the other to make a point. It was after midnight when Baldwin came in, his brother David with him. Everyone sat in the living-room and waited for him to say something. He smiled broadly: "You fellows talk. I'm new here. I'm trying to find out what's happening." Forman started off; there was a fast exchange of information and opinions, then everyone said goodnight. It was getting close to Freedom Day.

I made notes, almost minute by minute, that October 7, 1963:

9:30 A.M. It was sunny and pleasant in downtown Selma. I asked a Negro man on the corner the way to the county courthouse. He told me, looking at me just a little longer than a Negro looks at a white man in the South. The courthouse is green stone, quite modern looking compared to the rest of Selma. There was already a line of Negroes outside the door, on the steps of the courthouse, then running alongside the building, broken briefly to make room for people going in and out of an alley which ran along the courthouse, then continuing for another seventy-five feet. I counted over a hundred people on line. On the steps of the courthouse and down in the street stood a dozen or so deputy sheriffs and members of Sheriff Clark's special posse. They wore green helmets or white helmets, guns at their hips, long clubs. One young deputy, black-haired, with very long sideburns, swung a club as long as a baseball bat. A few newspapermen were already on the scene. The editor of the *Selma Times-Journal,*

Arthur Capell, quiet, thin, dark-haired, said: "Those people on line will never get registered. There are three members of the Board inside, and they spend quite some time on each registrant. There's never been more than thirty or forty registered in one day." The office would close at 4:30 P.M., and I realized now those people were going to wait on line eight hours, knowing they would not get inside the courthouse. I looked down the line. Middle-aged Negro men and women, some old folks, a few young ones, dressed not in their Sunday best, but neatly, standing close together in line.

In Alabama, as in Mississippi, one doesn't simply register to vote; one applies to register. This meant filling out a long form with twenty-one questions. Question 15: "Name some of the duties and obligations of citizenship." Question 15A: "Do you regard those duties and obligations as having priority over the duties and obligations you owe to any other secular organization when they are in conflict?" Then the registrar would ask oral questions, such as, "Summarize the Constitution of the United States." Three weeks later there would be a postcard: passed or failed. Another quaint thing about registration procedure in Dallas County was that applications were accepted only on the first and third Mondays of each month. Registering at the rate of thirty a day, even if all were passed, it would take ten years for Negroes to make up the 7,000 plurality held by white registrants in Dallas County.

9:45 A.M. The line now extended around the corner. I saw Sheriff Jim Clark for the first time, a six-footer with a big stomach, on his green helmet a gold medallion with an eagle, a big gold star on his shirt, the Confederate flag stamped on his helmet, an open collar, epaulets on his shoulders. Gun at his hip.

10:00 A.M. More posse members were arriving and taking up positions near the line. It was clear they hadn't expected so many Negroes to show up, so that they had to keep calling for reinforcements. I walked down the line counting—about twenty-five inside the door and on the steps, then one hundred down to the corner, then fifty around the corner—total, 175. It was clear and sunny. Cameramen from NBC and CBS were arriving. I noticed a scaffold up one story on the county courthouse; two young white men in painter's overalls were on the scaffold, puttying windows, suspended eerily over the events below.

10:45 A.M. The line of Negroes growing. Never in the history of Selma had so many Negroes showed up to register to vote. More members of the posse took up positions near the line; now there was an unbroken line of helmeted men in khakis or fatigues, carrying guns at their hips, clubs in their hands.

I wondered if Patti Hall would show up at the courthouse. She was a field secretary for SNCC, a pleasant, very intelligent young woman from Philadelphia, with a reputation for fervent oratory at mass meetings. She had gained her experience in the movement the preceding year in Terrae County, Georgia. Now she was directing the voter registration campaign in Selma. She'd been absent from the mass meeting Saturday night: word was out that a warrant had been issued for her arrest. Yesterday, Sunday, I had spoken to her at Mrs. Boynton's house and was going to interview her at length, but we delayed it so she could get some rest (our talk was not to take place, for she was arrested the next day).

10:25 A.M. Jim Forman was coming down the street. Walking alongside him was James Baldwin, in an open collar sportshirt and tan windbreaker, and next to him his brother David. I talked with one of the two Justice Department lawyers here to observe Freedom Day. I looked up and saw the American flag waving overhead; now I realized the new stone building directly across the street from the county courthouse was the federal building. Inside was the federal court; also, the social security office, the draft board, and the local offices of the FBI. I asked the Justice Department man, "How many lawyers are there now with the Civil Rights Division of the Justice Department?" "About forty," he said.

I went down the line again, counting, walking between the members of the posse and the Negroes on line. I counted over two hundred. Among them were about ten white people. It was voter registration day for everyone, and the line was integrated. Someone told me that the Citizens Council had put on a special drive to get white people to register today.

The Baldwin brothers walked with Jim Forman as he went down the line, saying hello, encouraging people to stay. "Now you just sit here," Forman said as he walked along, "just sit here and get some sunshine." Two posse men followed him. When Forman stopped, one of them said: "Get goin'! You're blockin' the sidewalk."

10:40 A.M. More posse arriving. Two posse members stood near me, munching peanuts. There were enough now to have them a few feet apart all along the line and around the corner. Nothing in the Deep South was more dangerous to public order, it seemed, than a line of Negro citizens trying to register to vote. Across the street was a police car with two loudspeakers on top. Two young police officers in white helmets were near it. Aside from the dozen or so news photographers and reporters, there were very few white people around—just a handful of onlookers standing at the corner.

11:00 A.M. More people joining the line. I counted again, thinking once more that these people coming on to the line knew they would never enter the courthouse that day. There were twenty on the steps and inside, fifty in the first section up to the alley, one hundred twenty in the second section down to the corner, one hundred around the corner—290 people altogether.

11:15 A.M. Jim Forman spoke to Bruce Gordon about its getting near lunch time, Bruce is a SNCC field secretary, originally from New York. I had talked with him when I arrived in Selma Saturday afternoon, at the First Baptist Church, and he was dressed now as then—he wore jeans and a T-shirt; a pack of cigarettes was stuck inside the shoulder of the T-shirt. He is slim, very dark, with a big head of curly hair, very articulate—a former actor and set man. "My father never taught hate...He encouraged me to go into the movement, said it's better to fail grandly than to succeed at piddling little things...I got out of the Army in March '62, got to Atlanta in June, got with SNCC...Julian said to me, 'how would you like a job with SNCC for ten dollars a week?' I said, 'Yes...'I haven't seen that money yet." He laughed. "I had a scholarship at Clark College for this fall, a job with Lockheed for $110 a week, and a chance to play a good role with an overseas troupe which is doing *Jamaica* in Europe in November. But I threw it all over for the movement. I was in Savannah for a while. Now I'm here." (The next day someone told me that Bruce had led a demonstration against police headquarters in Savannah, and had spent fifty-five days in jail.)

Forman told Bruce to get three big slabs of boloney and about ten to twelve loaves of bread, to feed the people on line.

11:20 A.M. Forman, Gordon, and I were talking near the side entrance of the County Courthouse, around the corner—no line there. Sheriff Clark came over, his eyes vacant, his voice rising: "All right, clear out of here, you're blocking the sidewalk!"

11:30 A.M. On the corner, in front of the courthouse door, a man with sound equipment spoke to James Baldwin. Baldwin's eyes looked enormous, fiery. He waved towards the line of helmeted troopers: "The federal government is not doing what it is supposed to do..."

11:40 A.M. Nobody up to this point could find a Negro who had come out of the courthouse who had actually gone through the registration procedure. But now a small group gathered around a Negro woman on the corner. "Yes, I went through, just finished. I believe twelve have gone through." Twelve, in three hours. And over three hundred people on line.

11:45 A.M. The two white men were still on the scaffold above the scene, calmly puttying windows.

11:50 A.M. Jim Forman told us Sheriff Clark and two deputies had just been to Mrs. Boynton's and arrested Prathia Hall. The charge was "contributing to the delinquency of a minor." Clark had just returned from this little mission, for he now appeared behind Forman. His mood was ugly. He poked his club again and again into Forman's side. "Get on! Get on!" Forman moved down the line towards the end. Ten Negro men were joining the line. We kept going, completely around the corner, Clark now far behind.

11:55 A.M. Forman mused about the problem of getting water to the people on line. The sun was beating down, I was in front of the courthouse door, the posse thicker now. I looked across the street to the federal building and saw there on the steps—standing so still that for a weird moment they looked like statues—two SNCC fellows, holding signs that faced the registration line. One, in overalls and a fedora, had a sign saying, REGISTER TO VOTE."

I moved across the street to get a better look. As I did so, Sheriff Clark and three helmeted deputies came walking fast across the street. They went past two Justice Department attorneys and two FBI men up the steps of the federal building and grabbed hold of the two SNCC fellows. Clark called out: "You're under arrest for unlawful assembly!" A small knot of white men on the corner were yelling: "Get 'em, Big Jim! Get 'em!" The deputies pulled the two fellows down the steps of the federal building and pushed them into a police car. One of the white men on the corner yelled, "You forgot one, Big Jim!" I looked around and saw a lone SNCC man around the corner, on the steps to the other entrance into the federal building, holding a Voter Registration sign. Clark mounted the steps, and reached the lone sign-carrier: "You're under arrest for unlawful assembly!" He too was pulled into the police car.

I had seen other instances of federal invisibility in Deep South crises, but this was too much. I turned to the Justice Department man near me. "Is that a *federal* building?" I asked. "Yes," he said, and turned away. The police car with the three SNCC men sped off.

12:10 P.M. Jim Forman walked over to Mrs. Boynton's office three blocks away to phone the Atlanta SNCC office about the arrests, and I walked with him. On the way, we intercepted six young SNCC fellows on the way to the county courthouse. Forman waved them back. "We need all of you today. We can't afford to have any of you arrested." In the office, before phoning, he sat down for a moment, reached into his overalls and pulled out his ulcer pills. In January, he had had to have surgery on a badly bleeding ulcer, requiring five blood transfusions. "How often do you take those?" I asked. He smiled. "Every two hours. But now, with what we have here, every twenty minutes." He told me that last night he had wired the Justice Department for federal marshals, sure there would be trouble. The Justice Department had not replied.

12:15 P.M. J. L. Chestnut, the one Negro lawyer in town, a slim, youthful man, came by. Forman said to him: "We've got to get Prathia out of jail *today*. We need her, man."

In the little room behind Mrs. Boynton's front office, James Baldwin sat with his brother David. A bottle of Ballantine Scotch was on the table in front of him and a few paper cups of water. He was writing in his notebook. Forman and the fellows in the office began discussing how to get the people on line fed. Many of them had been there since early in the morning with no food, no water. Someone suggested that there was a Community Center two blocks from the courthouse where food might be set up. People could leave the line in groups, get fed at the center, then return. They considered this idea for a while until someone said that it would be bad psychologically for people to leave the line; some might not return. Jim agreed. Food would either have to be brought to the line, or people would come across the street to a food station and then return.

In the front office, a young Negro woman, fair-skinned, her hair tinted lightly with red, was sitting at a desk going over the registration form with an old bent Negro woman who might have been seventy. She read off the questions, and with each one, asked, "Do you understand, mother?" The woman nodded her head calmly each time.

Word came back that the registrars had stopped registering for the lunch period. They would start again at two. Forman said, "We've got to keep those people in line." Again, the question of food and drink was discussed. More word from the courthouse: a caravan of automobiles with state troopers had arrived at the county courthouse. People counted 350 Negroes on the registration line.

I walked back alone to the courthouse. The state troopers' autos were lined up along the curb from one end of the street to the other— eleven long automobiles, searchlights mounted on top. The troopers themselves had now taken posts all along the registration line—about forty of them—with blue helmets, clubs, guns. A few of them, apparently in command, were bunched near the courthouse entrance. Their commander, Colonel Al Lingo, the veteran bully of Birmingham and the Freedom Walk, the man who had made infamous the use of electric prods in civil rights demonstrations, was not around. Taking his place was a hefty trooper with gold leaf insignia on his shoulders, Major Joe Smelley. I got up close to the troopers near the door. Several of them were holding cattle prods, squarish sticks with prongs at the end, the juice supplied by a battery and activated by a touch of the finger, burning the skin wherever it touched.

1:40 P.M. Jim Forman conferred briefly with a representative of the Department of Justice. The problem was the same: how to get the people fed. The word had gotten through the line that the troopers would not let anyone leave and return to the line. Joe Smelley stood there, near the head of the line, surrounded by a coterie of blue helmets, a cigar in his mouth. The sun was warmer; the hunger on the line was greater; Jim Forman's anger was increasing; the Justice Department lawyers were more nervous. Tension was building up on that normally quiet corner, now a blur of painted helmets and armed men. A SNCC car was parked in front of the federal building and in it were the sandwiches. The only problem was: how to get them to the people on line without breaking up the line.

1:45 P.M. A Negro lawyer, visiting Selma this day from Detroit, made no effort to contain his fury, as he spoke to me about the impotence of the federal government on that corner in Selma, Alabama: four FBI men ten feet away. He shook his head. "He's a real hot number, isn't he!

Boy, whenever anyone tells me about the FBI..." His own words seemed to build his anger, because he suddenly walked over to the FBI man and said "No comment," and walked away.

1:50 P.M. It was fairly clear by now that the sheriff, his posse, and the state troopers were determined that the people on line would not be fed or approached in any way. At this moment, a little old white man walked down the line of Negroes, unconcerned, and immune. He was selling newspapers, and doing very well; after all, he was the line's only direct contact with the outside world.

1:55 P.M. Word kept coming to Jim Forman, "People won't leave the line to get something to eat. They're afraid they won't be able to get back!"

Forman and Mrs. Boynton walked across the street from the federal building to the courthouse entrance to talk to Sheriff Jim Clark. The Sheriff seemed to be in a rage. The conversation went something like this (I was a few feet away and scribbled as fast as I could):

Forman: We'd like to bring food to these people on line. They've been waiting all day.
Clark: They will not be molested in any way.
Mrs. Boynton: Does giving them food mean molesting them?
Clark: They will not be molested in any way. If you do, you'll be arrested.
Forman: We'd like to talk to them; they're standing on line to register to vote, and we'd like to explain registration procedure to them.
Clark: They will not be molested in any way, and that includes talking to them.

2:00 P.M. A fragile thread was stretched taut, and everyone watched. Forman and Mrs. Boynton went back across the street. As they did, I heard a loud, creaking noise and looked up; it was the scaffold that had been suspended above the scene with the two window puttiers; it was coming down now. I looked closer at the windows of the courthouse and saw the faces of county employees jammed up against them.

I spoke briefly with Danny Lyon, the photographer who had been following "the movement" all over the South and taking pictures of it, a curly-haired fellow with a thick mustache, high-spirited, unafraid. We mused over the emblem on the door of the county courthouse. It said, "Dallas County, Alabama," and showed what looked like a figure bearing a set of scales. The scales were tipped sharply. "Justice?" Danny asked, smiling. A posse man near us was showing his electric cattle prod to a companion.

2:05 P.M. I spoke to the senior Justice Department attorney: "Is there any reason why a representative of the Justice Department can't go over and talk to the state troopers and say these people are entitled to food and water?" He was perturbed by the question. There was a long pause. Then he said, "I won't do it." He paused again. "I believe they do have the right to receive food and water. But I won't do it."

2:10 P.M. Forman was calling newsmen and photographers together to witness the next scene. All were gathered in the alley alongside the Federal Building, around a shopping cart which contained the uneaten sandwiches and the keg of water. Mrs. Boynton said: "We're determined to reach these people on line with food." Two SNCC field secretaries stood before the shopping cart and filled their arms with food. One of them was Avery Williams, Alabama-born. Another was Chico Neblett from Carbondale, Illinois. Both had left college to work for SNCC.

Chico gave his wallet to Forman, a final small gesture of acceptance of going to jail. He said to Avery, "Let's go, man." They walked down to the corner (a SNCC man never jaywalks in the South!) with all eyes on the street focused on them. They crossed at the corner. A group of us—photographers, newsmen, others—crossed the street at the same time. It was 2:20 P.M. As Chico and Avery came close to the line, the fat trooper with the cigar and the blue helmet, Major Smelley, barked at them, "Move on!" They kept going towards the line of registrants. He called out, "Get 'em!" The next thing I saw was Chico Neblett on the ground, troopers all around him. They poked at him with clubs and sticks. I heard him cry out and saw his body jump convulsively again and again; they were jabbing him with the cattle prods. Photographer were taking pictures, and the Major yelled, "Get in front of those cameramen!" Four troopers lifted Chico by his arms and legs, carried him to the corner, threw him into the green arrest truck that stood at the curb.

Now the troopers and posse men turned on the group of us who had followed all this; they pushed and shoved, ripped a photographer's shirt. A young reporter for the *Montomery Advertiser*, himself a native of Selma, had his camera smacked by a state trooper using his billyclub. Then the trooper pinned the reporter against a parked truck and ripped his shirt. When he walked to the sidewalk, a posse man back-handed him across the mouth.

We moved back across the street to the federal building. The Justice Department attorney was at the public telephone on the corner, making a call. He looked troubled. The green arrest truck pulled away. Chico and Avery waved. The Justice Department attorney took the name of the photographer who had been hit; several of us went into the FBI office and swore out statements on what had happened.

3:30 P.M. Four of us sat on the steps of the federal building and talked: the young Negro attorney from Detroit, James Baldwin, the white attorney from the Justice Department, and myself. The Detroit attorney said, "Those cops could have massacred all those three hundred Negroes on line, and still nothing would have been done." Baldwin was angry, upset. The Justice Department man was defensive. He asked Baldwin what he was working on now. Answer: a play. What was the title? *Blues for Mister Charlie*, Baldwin replied.

3:40 P.M. Still no food and no water for the people waiting. I walked down the street, checking the number of people, to see if the arrests and the excitement had diminished the line. It was longer than before.

3:55 P.M. Baldwin was talking to a newspaperman, "It cannot be true, it is impossible that the federal government cannot do anything."

A police loudspeaker boomed out into the street: "All you people who don't have business here get on. White and colored folks, move on." We gathered on the steps of the federal building, not sure it would prove a refuge. Jim Forman joined us.

4:30 P.M. The courthouse closed its doors. The line was breaking up. The Detroit lawyer watched men and women walk slowly away. His voice trembled, "Those people should be given medals." We made our way back to SNCC headquarters.

That night, there was a mass meeting at the church called for 8:00 P.M. At 7:00 P.M. fifteen people were there. I spoke to an old man. He was a veteran of World War I, seventy-three years old, had lived in Selma all his life. I asked him if, in his recollection, there had ever been any activity by Selma Negroes like this. He shook his head. "Nothing like this ever happened to Selma. Nothing, until SNCC came here."

At five minutes of eight, the church was packed, every seat taken, people standing along the walls. Father Ouillet and another Catholic priest sat in the audience. The Negro attorney from the Justice Department sat there also. The kids in the chorus were up front, singing: "Oh, that light of free-ee-dom, I'm gonna let it shine!" A chandelier hung way up in the domed ceiling, a circle of twenty-five bare light bulbs glowing. A Negro minister started the meeting with prayer, the local newspaper editor, a white man, bowing his head as the minister intoned: "Bless this wicked city in which we live, oh Lord, have mercy on us!"

Forman spoke. The emotion of the day was still inside him: part of it triumph because 350 Negroes had stood on line from morning to evening in full view of the armed men who ruled Dallas County; part of it bitterness that those people, defending the United States Constitution against Sheriff Jim Clark and his posse, had to do it alone. "We ought to be happy today," Forman told the crowd, "because we did something great..." Everyone applauded. Forman went on: "Jim Clark never saw that many niggers down there!" The audience laughed with him. "Yeah, there was Jim Clark, rubbin' his head and his big fat belly; he was shuffling today like *we* used to!" The crowd roared, needing release. When Forman finished, the Freedom Chorus sang: "If you miss me, can't find me nowhere, just come on over to the county jail, I'll be sittin' over there."

David Baldwin spoke, his voice choked: "Until you come down here, you don't believe it...I'm not going to lie and say I wish I was going to stay longer...It's an evil town." Just before he spoke, the Freedom Chorus sang the African folk song "Kumbaya," with their own words. One of the stanzas was: "Selma needs you, Lord, Kumbaya! Selma needs you, Lord, Kumbaya! Selma needs you, Lord, Kumbaya! Oh Lord, Kumbaya!"

Then James Baldwin stood at the rostrum, his huge eyes burning into the crowd: "The sheriff and his deputies...these ignorant people...were created by the good white people on the hill—and in Washington—and they've created a monster they can't control...It's not an act of God. It is deliberately done, deliberately created by the American Republic."

The meeting closed as always, with everyone linking arms and singing "We Shall Overcome," youngsters and old people and young women with babies in their arms, the SNCC people, the Catholic priests, the speakers on the platform. Over on the other side of the church I could see the young Negro attorney for the Justice Department, his arms crossed like everyone else, singing.

7

Mississippi:
Hattiesburg

Hattiesburg is a town in southern Mississippi, and this account of Freedom Day in January, 1964 appeared in my book *SNCC: The New Abolitionists*. The part of the story that deals with the jailhouse beating of Oscar Chase appeared in *The Nation* as "Incident in Hattiesburg." Mrs. Fannie Lou Hamer, a sharecropper from Sunflower County, who was evicted from her plantation, shot at, and beaten by police after she joined the Movement, would soon become nationally known. She led a delegation of black Mississippians to the Atlantic City convention of the Democratic Party that summer and the television cameras focused on her anguished plea for justice. "I'm sick an' tired o' bein' sick an' tired," she said.

It was a bumpy air ride going west out of Atlanta on the twin-engined Southern Airways DC-3. The tall, very friendly air stewardess was surprised to see the airplane crowded with clergymen from the North on their way to Hattiesburg, and joked with them all the way in her deep drawl. I was the only one in the group not a member of the clergy, but when they found that I was also going to Hattiesburg to be with SNCC for Freedom Day, I was almost ordained.

Driving from the airport to SNCC headquarters, we passed a huge sign: "In the Beginning, God Made Us Holy." Some months before, a SNCC Field secretary had written from Hattiesburg to the Atlanta office:

> We plan to let Guyot speak...We are going to announce an interdenominational Bible study course that will be dedicated to the proposition that religion doesn't have to be bullshit. We hope to tie in an active image of the Christ, and what would he have done had he been here, now...you see?

The ministers probably would have approved.

Hattiesburg, a short drive from the Gulf in Southern Mississippi, had been looked on by SNCC workers with some hope, ever since Curtis Hayes and Hollis Watkins left school in the spring of 1962 to start a voter registration campaign there, at the request of their McComb cellmate, Bob Moses, CORE man Dave Dennis had done some crucial ground-breaking work there. "Hattiesburg," one of the reports to Atlanta read, "is fantastic material for a beautifully organized shift from the old to the new...they are ready now..." Hattiesburg Negroes were not quite as poor as those in the Delta; police brutality seemed not quite as harsh there. As we drove into town, we passed the mansion of Paul Johnson, whose father had been governor himself. The radio was reporting Governor Johnson's inaugural address; it had a distinctly more moderate tone than his fierce campaign pronouncements on race.

In the rundown Negro section of Hattiesburg, on a cracked and crooked street filled with little cafes, was SNCC's Freedom House, owned by Mrs. Wood, a widow and a member of a prominent Negro family in Hattiesburg. (When John O'Neal, a SNCC worker from Southern Illinois University, arrived to work in Hattiesburg in the summer of 1963, he wrote to Moses: "Mrs. Wood received us late Wednesday night, and put a room open for us. She's a fine old warrior...." Outside the headquarters, a crowd of Negro youngsters milled around in the street, talking excitedly. Snatches of freedom songs rose here and there. This was Tuesday, January 21, 1964, and tomorrow was Freedom Day in Hattiesburg.

Inside the Freedom House, which was cluttered with typewriters, mimeograph machines, charts, photos, and notices, and was filled with people and incessant noise, the first person I saw was Mrs. Hamer sitting near the doorway. Upstairs, Bob Moses greeted me and took me past the big open parlor area where a meeting was going on planning strategy for the next day. He showed me into the room where he and his wife Dona were staying; only a few weeks before he had married Dona Richards, a diminutive, attractive University of Chicago graduate with a tough, quick mind, who had come to Mississippi to work with SNCC on a special education project. It was a combination bedroom and SNCC office, with a huge mirrored closet, carved mahogany bedstead, four typewriters, a gas heater, a suitcase, a wash basin, a map of Hattiesburg, and a vase of flowers.

Other SNCC people drifted into the room, and a session on Freedom Day strategy began. It was assumed that, as in every case where a picket line was set up in Mississippi, the pickets would be arrested. So a number of decisions had to be made. Some SNCC staff people would have to go to prison to keep up the morale of those who were not so experienced in Mississippi jails—Lawrence Guyot, Dona Moses, and five or six more; others would have to stay out to run the voter registration campaign after the jailings—Jesse Harris, MacArthur Cotton, Mrs. Hamer. Bob Moses, it was decided, would join the picket line, would go to jail, and would stay there, to dramatize to the nation that the basic right of protest did not exist in Mississippi.

The meeting moved outside into the hall, so that Dona Moses could begin packing the few little things they would need in jail. A wire was sent to Attorney General Robert Kennedy:

> Tomorrow morning, hundreds of Hattiesburg's citizens will attempt to register to vote. We request the presence of federal marshals to protect them. We also request that local police interfering with constitutional rights be arrested and prosecuted. Signed, Bob Moses.

The meeting was interrupted briefly as Ella Baker and John Lewis walked in, having just arrived from Atlanta after a long and wearing train ride. Plans for the summer of '64 were put forth. A thousand or two thousand people would be brought from all over the country to work in Mississippi during the summer months, to man newly set-up community centers, to teach in "freedom schools" for Mississippi youngsters, and to work on voter registration. The National Council of Churches was going to give massive help. Both CORE and SCLC would send more people in. As the group talked, you could hear the young kids outside singing: "We will go-o-o to jail...Don't need no bail...No, no, no...we won't come out...until our people vo-o-o-te!"

That night there was a mass meeting in a church, with every seat filled, every aisle packed, the doorways jammed; it was almost impossible to get in. The lights went out, and a buzz of excitement ran through the audience; there were a thousand people, massed tight in the blackness. Then, out of the dark, one person began singing, "We shall not, we shall not be moved..." and everyone took it up. Someone put a flashlight up on the speakers' stand, and the meeting began that way until after a while the lights came on.

Aaron Henry, for whom Hattiesburg Negroes had turned out en masse to vote in the Freedom Ballot (3,500 Negroes out of 7,400 of voting age in Forrest County cast Freedom Ballots) told the crowd that it was back in 1949 that the first affidavit had been filed in Hattiesburg with the Justice Department citing discrimination against Negroes trying to register, and here it was fifteen years later and the Federal government had not been able to make good. "We don't plan to leave Hattiesburg," Henry said, "until the Justice Department takes Registrar Lynd in hand. That's why we're here."

Henry introduced John Lewis, saying about SNCC: "If there is any group that has borne more the burden of the struggle, none of us know about it." After Lewis spoke, Annelle Ponder spoke for the Southern Christian Leadership Conference, and Dave Dennis for CORE. A lawyer from the National Council of Churches, John Pratt, pointed out that the Justice Department had just secured a final decision from the Supreme Court ordering Registrar Theron Lynd to stop discriminating and to stop picking out of the 285 sections of the Mississippi constitution different ones for Negroes to interpret than were given to whites: "We're here to prod the Justice Department a bit." A rabbi spoke, one of two in the delegation of fifty ministers who were ready to picket and go to jail the next day.

Then Ella Baker spoke, holding before the crowd, as she did so often, a vision beyond the immediate: "Even if segregation is gone, we will still need to be free; we will still have to see that everyone has a job. Even if we can all vote, but if people are still hungry, we will not be free... Singing alone is not enough; we need schools and learning... Remember, we are not fighting for the freedom of the Negro alone, but for the freedom of the human spirit, a larger freedom that encompasses all mankind."

Lawrence Guyot, who had come after his beating in Winona and his long prison term in Parchman to direct the operation in Hattiesburg, was introduced, and a great roar went up. Everyone in the church stood and applauded as he came down the aisle; it was a spontaneous expression of the kind of love SNCC organizers receive when they have become part of a community in the Deep South. Guyot combines a pensive intellectualism with a fierce and radical activism. He stood before the audience, his large frame trembling, raised a fist high over his head, and shouted, pronouncing slowly and carefully: "Immanuel Kant... " The church was hushed. "Immanuel Kant asks—Do you exist?" In the front row, teen-age boys and girls stared at Guyot; a young woman was holding two babies. Guyot paused. "Kant says, every speck of earth must be treated as important!" His audience waited, somewhat awed, and he went on to get very specific about instructions for Freedom Day at the county courthouse.

When Guyot finished, someone cried out: "Freedom!" And the audience responded: "Now!" Again and again: "Freedom!...Now!" The meeting was over, and everyone linked hands and sang "We Shall Overcome," then poured out into the darkness outside the church, still singing. It was almost midnight.

At the Freedom House, on Mobile Street, some people prepared to go to sleep; others stood around, talking. Mrs. Wood came down to the big cluttered open area where we were, anxious that we should all have a place to stay for the night. She took Mendy Samstein and me to a little room in the back and pointed out the cot she had just set up for both of us. We returned to the front and continued talking. The place began to empty as youngsters drifted out, or lay down to sleep on tables, benches, chairs, the floor. It was one in the morning; over on a long counter a half-dozen people, including Dona Moses, were lettering the picket signs to be carried seven hours later.

Lawrence Guyot sat wearily on a chair against the wall and we talked. He was born in a tiny coastal town in Mississippi, on the Gulf, named Pass Christian ("That town is the most complete mechanism of destruction I have seen"), the eldest of five brothers. His father was a cement finisher, now unemployed, his mother a housewife and a maid. When he graduated from Tougaloo College in 1963 he had already been a SNCC staff member for many months.

> Why did I join the movement? I was rebelling against everything. I still am. I think we need to change every institution we know. I came to that conclusion when I was seventeen years old. At first I thought of being a teacher, or a doctor; now I would like to get married, and do just what I'm doing now... I'm not satisfied with any condition that I'm aware of in America.

Mendy and I decided to hit the sack for the night, but when we went back we found a body snoring on our cot; it looked like Norris MacNamara, free-lance photographer and audio man who decided some time in 1963 to give his talents to SNCC. We decided to let him be, and went back into the front room. At 2:00 A.M. there were still a dozen people around; the signs were still being made; we talked some more. Guyot said someone was trying to find a place for us to stay; there were four of us now looking for a place to sleep. Besides me, there were Mendy Samstein, Brandeis graduate and University of Chicago doctoral candidate in history, a faculty member at Morehouse College, now a SNCC field man in Mississippi; Oscar Chase, Yale Law school graduate, now with SNCC; and Avery Williams, a cheerful SNCC man from Alabama State College. At 3:00 A.M. we began looking for a good spot on the floor, since all the benches and tables were taken, but then someone came along with a slip of paper and an address.

A cab let us out in front of a small frame house in the Negro part of town. It was about 3:30 A.M. The street was dark, and the house was dark inside. We hesitated, then Oscar approached and knocked cautiously on the front door. A Negro man opened the door and looked at us; he was in his pajamas. Here we were, three whites and a Negro, none of whom he had ever seen. Oscar said hesitantly, "They told us at headquarters..." The man smiled broadly, "Come on in!" He shouted through the darkness back into his bedroom, "Hey, honey, look who's here!" The lights were on now and his wife came out: "Can I fix something for you fellows?" We said no, and apologized for getting them up. The man waved his hand: "Oh, I was going to get up soon anyway."

The man disappeared and came back in a moment dragging a mattress onto the floor near the couch. "Here, two of you can sleep on the mattress, one on the couch, and we have a little cot inside." The lights went out soon after. There was a brief murmured conversation in the dark among us, and then we were asleep.

I awoke just as dawn was filtering through the windows, and in the semi-darkness I could see the forms of the other fellows near me, still asleep. I became aware of the sound that had awakened me; at first I had thought it part of a dream, but I heard it now still, a woman's voice pure and poignant. She was chanting softly. At first I thought it came from outside, then I realized it was coming from the bedroom of the Negro couple, that the man was gone from the house, and it was his wife, praying, intoning... "Oh, Lord, Jesus, Oh, let things go well today, Jesus... Oh, make them see, Jesus... Show your love today, Jesus... Oh, it's been a long, long time, oh, Jesus... Oh, Lord, Oh, Jesus..."

The chanting stopped. I heard Avery call from the next room: "Wake up, fellow, it's Freedom Day." A radio was turned on with dance music played loud. A light went on in the kitchen. As we dressed I looked through the open doorway into the Negro couple's bedroom and saw there was no mattress on their bed. They had led us to believe that they had brought out a spare mattress for us, but had given us theirs.

The woman came out of the kitchen and turned on the gas heater in the living room for us: "Come and get your breakfast, fellows." It was a feast—eggs and grits and bacon and hot biscuits and coffee. Her husband drove down to the Gulf every day to work on the fishing docks, and the woman was soon to be picked up in a truck and taken off to work as a maid; her daughter was a senior in high school. Her young son said: "Yesterday morning, when I woke up, the light from a police car was shining in the windows. Guess they know us." The woman, waiting outside for her ride, came in for a second to report to us what a neighbor had just told her. Downtown the streets were full of police, carrying clubs and sticks and guns, wearing helmets. She went off in the truck. We prepared to leave, and Avery Williams looked outside: "It's raining!"

At the headquarters were noise and confusion and great crowds of people—ministers, carrying signs, walking back and forth in front of the concrete steps leading up to the Forrest County Courthouse, employees staring out of the windows of the courthouse, a camera in a second story window focused on the scene.

About 9:30 A.M., there was the sound of marching feet on the wet pavement and two lines of policemen came down the street, heading for the courthouse, all traffic cleared in front of them. A police car swung to the curb, a loudspeaker on its roof, and then the announcement blared out into the street, harsh, hurting the ears: "This is the Hattiesburg Police Department. We're asking you to disperse. Clear the sidewalk!" There were thirty-two pickets on the line. John Lewis and I stood across the street in front of Sears Roebuck, on the sidewalk. No one made a move to leave. The marching policemen came up even with the county courthouse, in four squads, wearing yellow rain slickers, and blue or white or red helmets, carrying clubs. "First squad! Forward march!" The first line peeled off and came up on the sidewalk parallel to the picket line. "Squad halt!"

The loudspeaker rasped again: "People who wish to register, line up four at a time, and they will be accepted. All those not registering to vote move off. This is the Hattiesburg Police Department!" Fifty Negro youngsters came out of nowhere and formed a second picket line in front of the courthouse, near the line of ministers. All four squads of police had peeled off now and were facing the picket line, clubs in hand. It looked as if everything would go as predicted: an order to disperse, no one moving, everyone put under arrest. I could see Moses across the street, peering at the scene, hunched a little under the falling rain.

It was 9:40 A.M. Ten minutes had elapsed since the police had come marching in formation down the street. They were lined up now opposite the two picket lines, twenty-five helmets a few feet from the line and twenty-five more across the street. For the third time, from the police loudspeaker: "All those not registering to vote move off."

The line of black youngsters merged with the line of white ministers to form one long picket line in front of the courthouse, the messages on their signs clear even in the grayness of the day: ONE MAN, ONE VOTE; FREEDOM DAY IN HATTIESBURG. No one moved off the line. Police began clearing off the sidewalk across the street from the courthouse and we moved across to the steps of the courthouse. The picket line remained undisturbed. The scene was peaceful. There were virtually no white observers. If our senses did not deceive us, something unprecedented was taking place in the state of Mississippi: a black and white line of demonstrators was picketing a public building, allowed to do so by the police. In all of the demonstrations of the past two and one-half years, this had never happened.

Over a hundred pickets were walking now, the rain still coming down. A blond Episcopalian minister was carrying a picket sign with an inscription in Hebrew. A Negro schoolboy carried a sign: LET MY PARENTS VOTE. Jim Forman escorted a Negro woman across the street, through the rain, up the stairs. But they wouldn't let her in the courthouse. Voter registrants were lined up on the steps outside the glass door, which was guarded on the inside by the sheriff. Only four people were being allowed inside at a time, and it took about an hour for another four to be admitted, so the rest of the people formed a line down the steps, exposed to the rain. At ten o'clock what had been a medium drizzle became a downpour. No one left the line. Bob Moses escorted a Negro man across the street and up the steps.

I walked around the back, got inside the courthouse, and made my way to the registrar's office, just inside the glass door. Television cameras were focused on Theron Lynd, the three-hundred-pound Forrest County Registrar, who was now under final injunction by the Supreme Court to stop discriminating against Negroes under penalty of going to jail. Lynd was dressed in a black suit, his grey hair cut short, a stub of a cigar in his mouth, his manner affable. At a federal court hearing in March, 1962, the Justice Department pointed out that Lynd, who had never registered a single Negro, had allowed 1,836 whites to register without filling out the application form or interpreting a section of the constitution. Until January 30, 1961, no Negro had even been permitted to fill out a form. In early January, 1964, the Supreme Court had affirmed a Fifth Circuit Court decision that Lynd was guilty of civil contempt unless he complied with court orders not to discriminate.

Two Negro women were filling out blanks at the counter, and one Negro man was there, with a big SNCC button on his overalls. Lynd ambled around, apparently trying to be helpful, as newspapermen and photographers stood nearby. I spoke to him: "Mr. Lynd, is it to be assumed that all orders of the court are being followed now?" He turned to me: "Yes, indeed. I will treat all applicants alike, just as I have always done. To us this is no special day."

I went outside. It was still raining, coming down hard. Someone said that Bob Moses had just been taken off to jail. He'd been arrested for standing on the sidewalk opposite the courthouse and refusing to move on.

Jim Forman stood just outside the glass door of the courthouse, shirt collar open under his raincoat, pipe in his right hand, gesticulating with his left hand, Negro men and women bunched around him. He was calling to the sheriff and two well-dressed official-looking men who were holding the door shut from the inside: "Sheriff, it's raining out here, and these people would like to come into the courthouse. You seem to have plenty of room inside." No reply. Forman held the arm of an old Negro woman and called again through the glass door: "Sheriff, will you be a Christian and let this old lady inside, a lady who has toiled in the fields of Forrest County many years, an old lady who now must stand out in the rain because she wants to register to vote? Is there no compassion in Forrest County for a woman seventy-one years old, whose feet are wet as she waits, who has nursed white children in her time, who can't even get a chair so she can sit down, for whom there is no room in the county courthouse?" No reply. A newspaperman gestured to me: "Forman is really putting it on, isn't he?"

It was 11:15 A.M. and still raining. Forman motioned to the people standing in line on the steps. "Maybe if we get down on our knees and pray, someone will hear us." Twenty people knelt in the rain on the courthouse steps and an old Negro man prayed aloud. Below, in the long line of people with signs moving in front of the courthouse, someone was handing out little boxes of raisins and crackerjacks to sustain the energy of those who had been marching for three hours.

At noon the courthouse closed for lunch. Through the morning twelve people had gotten inside to fill out applications. I walked back with Forman to SNCC headquarters. He said: "Maybe it seems strange to make a fuss over standing in the rain, but it's exactly in all these little things that the Negro has been made to feel inferior over the centuries. And it's important educationally. To show the Negroes in Hattiesburg that it is possible to speak up loudly and firmly to a white sheriff as an equal—something they're not accustomed to doing."

The picket line continued all afternoon. Two white girls from Mississippi Southern University in Hattiesburg stood on the courthouse steps, watching, taking notes. They were from the University radio station. They would not oppose a Negro's admission to the University, they said. Lafayette Surney, a nineteen-year-old SNCC staff member from Ruleville, Mississippi, came over, and the three of them chatted amiably, about Mississippi, civil rights, voter registration, and college.

Down on the picket line, I could see the familiar form of Mrs. Hamer, moving along with her characteristic limp, holding a sign, her face wet with the rain and turned upwards, crying out her song against the sky: "Which Side Are You On?" A little later I took her picket sign from her and walked while she rested on the steps. At five the line disbanded, gathered briefly on the courthouse steps to bow in prayer, and marched back to headquarters. The policemen ended their vigil.

There was one more piece of news: Oscar Chase had been taken off to jail. His car had bumped a parked truck that morning, doing no damage, but a policeman had noted what happened, and about 4:00 P.M. he had been hustled into a police car and carted away. The charge: "Leaving the scene of an accident."

It had been a day of surprises. The picketing went on all day with no mass arrests. Perhaps this was due to the desire of the newly-elected Governor Paul Johnson to play the race issue slow; perhaps it was due to the presence of clergymen, TV cameras, newspapermen; or perhaps it was simply a tribute to the tirelessness of SNCC in putting people out in the streets again and again, until police and politicians got weary of trundling them off to jail. At any rate, over a hundred Negro men and women had come to register, though few got through the courthouse door, and only a handful were eventually declared to have passed the test

So, Freedom Day passed as a kind of quiet victory and everyone was commenting on how well things had gone. Nobody was aware, of course, that about six o'clock that evening, in his cell downtown, Oscar Chase, the SNCC man fresh out of Yale Law School, was being beaten bloody and unconscious by a fellow prisoner while policemen stood by watching.

No one knew until the next morning. I awoke at six on the narrow cot in the back of the Freedom House. Everyone around me was still asleep. Through the wall I could hear the faint sound of a typewriter and wondered who the heck was typing at six in the morning. I dressed and went into the next room. A Negro kid, about fifteen years old, was sitting at a typewriter, pecking slowly at the keys. He looked at me apologetically, seeing he had roused me: "Writing a letter to my sister."

I walked into the big front room, where in the darkness I could make out the forms of sleeping youngsters. One fellow was stretched out on a wooden table, one on the counter where the signs had been lettered, one on three chairs, using his jacket as a pillow, one leaning back in a chair, his head against the wall. Around a desk sat three teen-agers, as if holding a conference sound asleep in their chairs. The first rays of sunlight were coming in through the windows.

I walked outside to get some breakfast, and SNCC field secretary Milton Hancock joined me at a little cafe across the street. We sat at a table, ate and talked, and watched through a window as a man on the sidewalk unloaded a batch of fresh-caught sheepshead fish from a truck, just up from the gulf. Then someone came along to say that Oscar Chase had phoned in to headquarters that he had been beaten the night before, and he wanted to be bonded out. Two of the visiting ministers were going down to fetch him, and I went along.

The police dogs in their kennels were growling and barking as we entered the jailhouse. It was a few minutes before 8:00 A.M. The bond money was turned over. A moment later, Oscar came down the corridor, unescorted, not a soul around. A few moments before, the corridor had been full of policemen; it seemed now as if no one wanted to be around to look at him. Even the dogs had stopped growling. He was still wearing his badly worn corduroy pants, and his old boots, caked with mud. His blue workshirt was splattered with blood, and under it his T-shirt was very bloody. The right side of his face— his lips, his nose, his cheek— was swollen. His nose looked as if it were broken. Blood was caked over his eye.

We called for the police chief: "We want you to look at this man as he comes out of your jail, chief." The chief looked surprised, even concerned. He turned to Oscar, put his face close to his, "Tell them, tell them, didn't I take that fellow out of your cell when he was threatening you?" Oscar nodded. He told us the story.

The chief had removed one of the three prisoners in the cell early in the evening, when Oscar complained that he was being threatened. But shortly afterward they put in another prisoner, of even uglier disposition. And this was the one who a few hours later kicked and beat Oscar into insensibility in the presence of several policemen. He was not as drunk as the man who'd been taken out. But he was in a state of great agitation. He announced, first, that he could lick any man in the cell; there were Oscar and another prisoner. "He was very upset about the demonstration—wanted to know why the jail wasn't 'full of niggers.'" He had been a paratrooper in World War II, and told Oscar he "would rather kill a nigger lover than a Nazi or a Jap."

The third man in the cell proceeded to tell the former paratrooper that Oscar was an integrationist. Now he began a series of threatening moves. He pushed a cigarette near Oscar's face and said he would burn his eyes out. He said that first he would knock him unconscious and while he was out he would use a lighted cigarette on his eyes. Oscar called for the jailer. The jailer came. Oscar asked to be removed from the cell. The jailer didn't respond. The ex-paratrooper asked the jailer if Oscar was "one of them nigger-lovers." The jailer nodded.

What Oscar Chase remembers after that is that the prisoner said something close to "Now I know why I'm in this jail." Then:

> The next thing I can remember was lying on the floor, looking up. I could see the jailer and some other policemen looking at me and smiling. I could also see the other prisoner standing over me, kicking me. I began to get up, was knocked down again, and then heard the door of the cell open. The cops pulled me out and brought me into another cell, where I remained by myself for the rest of the night...I was still bleeding a couple of hours after the incident. Watching from the door of my new cell, I saw the trusty put a pack of cigarettes and some matches under the door of my attacker's cell. Later I heard the police come in and let him out. I could hear them laughing...

We went from the jailhouse to the home of one of the two Negro doctors in town and agreed to meet him at his clinic in a little while. Then we took Oscar to SNCC headquarters. Mrs. Wood kept pressing her hands together, in great distress. "Oh, my poor boy!" Jim Forman came out of his room sleepily, waking up quickly as he saw Oscar. He shook his head: "Jesus Christ!" The lawyers were summoned, and we prepared to go to the FBI.

There was one moment of sick humor as the incident came to a close. Four of us waited in the FBI office in Hattiesburg for the interrogating agent to come in to get the facts from Oscar Chase about his beating. John Pratt, attorney with the National Council of Churches, tall, blond, slender, was impeccably dressed in a dark suit with faint stripes. Robert Lunney, of the Lawyer's Committee on Civil Rights (set up as a volunteer group to aid in civil rights cases), dark-haired and clean-cut, was attired as befit an attorney with a leading Wall Street firm. I did not quite come up to their standards because I had left without my coat and tie, and my pants had lost their press from the rain the day before; but I was clean-shaven, and not too disreputable looking. Oscar sat in a corner, looking exactly as he had a few hours before when I saw him come down the corridor from his cell, his face swollen, his clothes bloody. The FBI agent came out from the inner office and closed the door behind him. He surveyed the four of us with a quick professional eye and then asked, "Who was it got the beating?"

At four that afternoon, the Hattiesburg Municipal Court convened to hear the case of Robert Moses, on trial for obstructing traffic by standing on the sidewalk and refusing to move on when ordered to by a policeman. Many of the white ministers went to the trial, and we had agreed that we would sit in the Negro section; so far, any attempt made in Mississippi to sit integrated in a local courtroom had ended in arrest. I entered the courtroom, sat down on the 'colored' side of the aisle, and noted that there were about ten white people on that side, and an equal number of Negroes on the "white" side. Nine marshals stood against the wall. The judge entered the chamber and everyone rose. To our surprise, it was a woman, Judge Mildred W. Norris, an attractive, gracious lady who smiled and posed for the photographers as she approached the bench, then nodded for everyone to be seated. She smiled pleasantly at the spectators, paused a moment, then said sweetly, "Will the marshals please segregate the courtroom?" Everything was quiet.

The marshals moved towards us. The lady judge said: "I will ask you to please move to the side of the courtroom where you belong, or leave. If you do not, you will be held in contempt of court and placed under arrest." No one moved. The marshals came up closer. As one approached me, I raised my hand. He stopped, and said, rather uncertainly, "Do you wish to make a statement?" I replied, "Yes." The judge said, "You may make a statement." I got to my feet and said, "Your Honor, the Supreme Court of the United States has ruled that segregated seating in a courtroom is unconstitutional. Will you please abide by that ruling?" The courtroom buzzed. The judge hesitated. John Pratt, who with Bob Lunney was acting as counsel for Moses, spoke up and asked for a recess of a few minutes, and the judge granted it. The courtroom became alive with conversation again.

During the recess, no one changed seats. The judge reconvened the court, and the room was absolutely silent. She said: "We here in Mississippi have had our way of life for hundreds of years, and I obey the laws of Mississippi. I have asked that you sit segregated or leave, or be placed under arrest. We would have appreciated your complying." She paused. "But since you do not, we will allow you to remain as you are, provided you do not create a disturbance." We sat there, astonished, but silent. And the court session began.

"Defendant Robert Moses, come right up." Bob Moses stood before the bench, in his blue overall jacket, corduroy pants, white shirt with open collar, while the charge was read: ."..with intent to provoke a breach of peace, did congregate on the sidewalk and did interfere with the passage of pedestrians and refused to move on when ordered to do so..." He pleaded not guilty.

Three policemen took the stand, the first one named John Quincy Adams. He testified that Moses had obstructed pedestrian traffic by standing on the sidewalk. The courtroom was hot, and the judge, smiling slightly, picked up a cardboard sign near her and began fanning herself with it. It was one of the exhibits, a picket sign with large letters: "FREEDOM NOW!" It showed a picture of two small Negro boys, and said "GIVE THEM A FUTURE IN MISSISSIPPI." The judge continued to fan herself with the sign.

Cross-examined by Bob Lunney, Patrolman John Quincy Adams admitted no other pedestrians had complained about the sidewalk being obstructed, and that he did not see anyone who did not have free access. The second policeman was shown a picket sign by the city attorney which said, "JOIN THE FREEDOM FITE." The attorney asked, "Do you understand what a fight is?" "Yes," the patrolman replied.

At about 7:00 P.M. Bob Moses took the stand, the only witness in his defense. After a series of questions by Robert Lunney, he was turned over for cross-examination to the attorney for the city, Francis Zachary, a large man with iron grey hair, a black suit, and horn-rimmed glasses. Zachary kept Moses on the stand for over an hour in the most fierce, pounding cross-examination I had ever seen. Zachary's voice was filled alternately with anger, contempt, disgust. He walked back and forth in front of the witness, using his voice like a whip, shaking papers in front of Moses' face, and moving up close and pointing his finger, the combination of voice and gestures and incessant pointless questions adding up to an assault on the senses, an attempt to break down the witness through emotional exhaustion. Through it all, Moses, a little tired from his day in jail, sat there on the witness stand, answering in the same quiet, even voice, pointing out patiently again and again where the prosecutor had misunderstood his reply, occasionally blinking his eyes under the glare of the lights in the courtroom, looking steadily, seriously at his questioner.

> Zachary: Let me ask you this: You knew there were 150 of you outsiders in this community demonstrating, didn't you?
> Moses: No, that is not true.
> Zachary: That is not true?
> Moses: That is not true.
> Zachary: (angrily): At the time you were arrested, there wasn't 150 of you walking around in front of the Court House?
> Moses: You said "outsiders." There were not 150 outsiders walking around the Court House.

Or again:

> Zachary: Where would this democracy be if everybody obeyed officers like you did?
> Moses: I think that it would be in very good shape. I...
> Zachary: Good, now, you've answered it, now let's move on...

Zachary held up a list of the ministers who had come down for Freedom Day and waved it in Moses' face. He went down the list, asking about the ministers and the organizations on it.

> Zachary: The (he paused, and stumbled over the word "Rabbinical") Rabbin-in-ical Assembly of America. Are you a member of that organization?
> Moses: (gently correcting him): Rabbinical Assembly. No. I am not.

At one point, the prosecutor, trying to hold in his rage against the quiet calm of the witness, broke out: "Moses! Let me tell you something..."

Again:

Zachary: Why didn't you mind this officer when he gave you an order?
Moses: I had a right to be there...
Zachary: What law school did you graduate from?
Lunney: Objection.
The Court: I will have to overrule you.
Zachary: (again to Moses): I want to know what you base this right on. Are you a legal student?
Moses: I base the right on the fact of the First Amendment....That is the whole point of democracy, that the citizens know what their rights are, and they don't have to go to law school to know what their rights are.

About 9:15 P.M., with the attorney's closing remarks over, the judge denied Lunney's motion to dismiss, and declared that the court found Robert Moses guilty, sentencing him to a fine of $200 and sixty days in jail. We all filed out of the courtroom into the night, and Patrolman John Quincy Adams took Bob Moses back to his cell.

A few days later Bob Moses was out on bail, once again directing the Mississippi voter registration drive for SNCC. Plans were being made for a big summer, with a thousand students coming into Mississippi for July and August of 1964. And, for the first time since Reconstruction, a group of Mississippi Negroes announced their candidacy for the U.S. Congress: Mrs. Fannie Hamer of Ruleville; Mrs. Victoria Gray of Hattiesburg; the Rev. John Cameron of Hattiesburg. Thus, a new native leadership was taking form, already beginning to unsettle the official hierarchy of the state by its challenge.

SNCC came out of McComb after the summer of 1961 battered and uncertain. It moved on to Greenwood and other towns in the Delta, grew in numbers, gathered thousands of supporters throughout the state. In places like Hattiesburg it took blows, but it left the town transformed, its black people—and possibly some white people—awakened. Most of all, for the Negroes of Mississippi, in the summer of 1964, as college students from all over America began to join them to help bring democracy to Mississippi and the nation, the long silence was over.

8

The Selma to Montgomery March

The summer of 1964 saw a massive effort against racial segregation in Mississippi, when a thousand people from all over the country, mostly white college students, joined local black Mississippians in Freedom Summer. Those weeks were filled with courageous attempts to break down racial barriers in what black people considered the most murderous of states. There were repeated acts of violence against the civil rights workers, culminating in the murder of one black and two white civil rights workers: James Chaney, Andrew Goodman, Michael Shwerner. Throughout, the federal government played its usual role of observing, but not acting, in effect abnegating its responsibility to enforce constitutional rights everywhere in the nation.

In early 1965, attempts at voter registration in Alabama resulted in repeated acts of violence by local officials against black people who dared to protest. A young black man named Jimmy Lee Jackson was beaten and shot to death by a state trooper. A column of black people, beginning to march from Selma to the state capital in Montgomery, were clubbed and gassed by state troopers. A white

minister from Boston, who had come to Selma to protest police brutality, was clubbed on a street and died. Now there were protests
and demonstrations world-wide. The federal government, speaking
through the Voice of America in thirty-eight languages, broadcast an
outrageous falsehood: that 'under the United States Constitution the
police powers belong to the states, not to the Federal Government.'
In fact, a federal law gave the national government absolute police
powers to protect the constitutional rights of citizens whenever a
state failed to do so. But the wave of protests had an effect.
President Lyndon Johnson now asked for a law to guarantee black
people the right to vote, which became the Voting Rights Act of
1965. And when a new march from Selma to Montgomery was organized, Johnson ordered several thousand National Guardsmen and
U.S. Army troops to protect the marchers. I was traveling through the
South to do an article for *The Nation* called "The South Revisited,"
and joined the march eighteen miles out of Montgomery.

MONTGOMERY, ALABAMA, MARCH 20-25, 1965

The march from Selma, a little over halfway along, turned into a field
a hundred yards off the main highway to Montgomery, deep in
Lowndes County ("a bad county") and settled down for the night. The
field was pure mud, so deep one's shoes went into it to the ankles, and
to pull out after each step was an effort. A chunk of moon shone, the sky
was crowded with stars, and yet the field was enveloped in blackness.
Two huge tents went up, one for men, one for women, and inside people spread plastic sheets over the mud, unrolled their sleeping bags, lay
down, weary.

There were three hundred of them, the "core" of the Long March,
mostly black people from Selma, Marion and other little towns in central
Alabama, but also young Negroes from the Southern Christian
Leadership Conference and the Student Nonviolent Coordinating
Committee, and some white people, young and old, from all over the
nation. Space under the tents was soon gone, so people sprawled outside
along the mired road that cut through the field.

At the edge of the field were gathered the jeeps and trucks of the
U.S. Army, soldiers in full battle dress, called out finally by Presidential

order after thirty days of murder and violence in Alabama and cries of
protest through the country.

Moving through the darkness in and out of sleeping forms on the
ground were men with white ragged emblems market "Security." They
carried walkie-talkies, the aerials glinting, and communicated with one
another across the encampment. There was a central transmitter in a
parked truck. People coming in off the main highway were checked at the
end of the mud road by two husky "Security" men, young Episcopalian
priests with turned-around collars. One of them said: "I don't really know
who to let in. If he's black I let him through."

Lying down in the darkness near the road, I could hear the hum
of the portable generators and an occasional burst of sound on a walkie-
talkie. The plastic sheet under me was soaked in mud and slime, but the
inside of the sleeping bag was dry. Two hundred feet away, in a great arc
around the field, were fires lit by soldiers on guard through the night.

I awoke just before dawn, with a half-moon pushing, flat side
first, through the clouds. The soldiers' fires at the perimeter were low now,
but still burning. Nearby, the forms of perhaps twenty people wrapped in
sleeping bags or blankets. The generator still whirred. Other clusters of
sleepers were now visible, beginning to awaken.

A line formed for oatmeal, hard-boiled eggs, coffee. Then everyone gathered to resume the march. A Negro girl washed her bare feet,
then her sneakers, in a stream alongside the road. Near her was a minister, his black coat streaked with mud. A Negro woman without shoes had
her feet wrapped in plastic. Andy Young was calling over the main transmitter to Montgomery: "Get us some shoes; we need forty pairs of shoes,
all sizes, for women and kids who have been walking barefoot the past 24
hours."

An old Negro man took his place beside me for the march. He
wore a shirt and tie under his overalls, also an overcoat and a fedora hat,
and used a walking stick to help him along. "Yes, I was in Marion the
night Jimmy Jackson was shot by the policeman. They got bullwhips and
sticks and shotguns, and they jab us with the electric poles."

At exactly 7 A.M. an Army helicopter fluttered overhead and the
march began, behind an American flag, down to the main highway and
on to Montgomery. The marchers sang: "FreeDOM! Freedom's Coming
and It Won't Be Long!"

It was seventeen miles to the edge of Montgomery, the original straggling line of three hundred thickening by the hour as thousands joined, whites and Negroes who had come from all over the country. There was sunshine most of the way, then three or four bursts of drenching rain. On the porch of a cabin set way back from the road, eight tiny Negro children stood in a line and waved, an old hobby horse in the front yard. A red-faced, portly Irishman, newly-arrived from Dublin, wearing a trench coat, held the hand of a little Negro boy who walked barefoot next to him. A Greyhound bus rode past with Negro kids on the way to school. They leaned out the window, shouting "Freedom!" A one-legged young white man on crutches, a black skullcap over red hair, marched along quickly with the rest. Two Negro boys with milky sun lotion smeared on their faces looked as if they had stepped off the stage in Genet's *The Blacks*. A group of white workingmen along the road watched silently. On the outskirts of Montgomery, students poured out of a Negro high school, lined the streets, waved and sang as the marchers went by. A jet plane zoomed close overhead and everyone stretched arms to the sky, shouting, 'FREEDOM! FREEDOM!"

9

Abolitionists, Freedom Riders and the Tactics of Agitation

As I studied the anti-slavery movement before the Civil War, and the freedom movement of the Sixties, I saw common issues, and I explore one of them in this essay. I wrote it for the collection of essays edited by Martin Duberman, called *The Anti-Slavery Vanguard* and published in 1965 by Princeton University Press. It also appeared in the *Columbia University Forum* as "Abolitionists and Freedom Riders."

Few groups in American history have taken as much abuse from professional historians as that mixed crew of editors, orators, run-away slaves, free Negro militants, and gun-toting preachers known as the abolitionists. Many laymen sympathetic to the Negro have been inspired by Garrison, Phillips, Douglass, and the rest. Scholars, on the other hand (with a few exceptions), have scolded the abolitionists for their immoderation, berated them for their emotionalism, denounced them for bringing on the Civil War, or psychoanalyzed them as emotional deviates in need of recognition.

It is tempting to join the psychological game and try to understand what it is about the lives of academic scholars which keeps them at arm's length from the moral fervor of one of history's most magnificent crusades. Instead, I want to examine in fact the actions of the abolitionists, to connect them with later agitators against racial exclusiveness and try to assess the value of "extremists," "radicals," and "agitators" in the bringing of desired social change.

At issue are a number of claims advanced by liberal-minded people who profess purposes similar to the radical reformers, but urge more moderate methods. To argue a case too heatedly, they point out, provokes the opponent to retaliation. To urge measures too extreme alienates possible allies. To ask for too much too soon results in getting nothing. To use vituperative language arouses emotions to a pitch which precludes rational consideration. To be dogmatic and inflexible prevents adjustment to rapidly changing situations. To set up a clash of extremes precipitates sharp conflict and violence.

All of these tactical sins, adding up to immoderation, extremism, impracticality, have been charged, at different times, by different people, to the American abolitionists. But the charges have not been carefully weighed or closely scrutinized as part of a discussion of preferable tactics of reform. I am claiming here only to initiate such a discussion.

Twentieth century man is marking the transition from chaotic and quite spontaneous renovation of the social fabric to purposeful and planned social change. In this transition, the tactics of such change need much more careful consideration than they have been given.

The Abolitionists

There is no denying the anger, the bitterness, the irascibility of the abolitionists. William Lloyd Garrison, dean of them all, wrote in blood in the columns of the *Liberator* and breathed fire from speakers' platforms all over New England. He shocked people: "I am ashamed of my country." He spoke abroad in brutal criticism of America: "I accuse the land of my nativity of insulting the majesty of Heaven with the greatest mockery that was ever exhibited to man." He burned the Constitution before several thousand witnesses on the lawn at Framingham, calling it "source and parent of all other atrocities—a covenant with death and an agreement with hell" and spurred the crowd to echo "Amen!"*

He provoked his opponents outrageously, and the South became apoplectic at the mention of his name.

South Carolina offered $1,500 for conviction of any white person circulating the *Liberator*, and the Georgia legislature offered $500 for the arrest and conviction of Garrison. Garrison's wife feared constantly that reward-seekers would lie in wait for her husband on his way back from a meeting and snatch him off to Georgia.

Wendell Phillips, richer, and from a distinguished Boston family, was no softer. "Don't shilly-shally, Wendell," his wife whispered to him as he mounted the speakers' platform, and he never did. The anger that rose in him one day in 1835 as he watched Boston bluebloods drag Garrison through the streets never left him, and it remained focused on what he considered America's unbearable evil—slavery. "The South is one great brothel," he proclaimed.

Gradualism was not for Phillips. "No sir, we may not trifle or dally...Revolution is the only thing, the only power, that ever worked out freedom for any people." The piety of New England did not intimidate him: "The American church—what is it? A synagogue of Satan." He scorned patriotic pride: "They sell a little image of us in the markets of Mexico, with a bowie knife in one side of the girdle, and a Colt's revolver in the other, a huge loaf of bread in the left hand, and a slave whip in the right. That is America!"

Phillips did not use the language of nonresistance as did Garrison. On that same green where Garrison burned the Constitution, Phillips said: "We are very small in numbers; we have got no wealth; we have got no public opinion behind us; the only thing that we can do is , like the eagle, simply to fly at our enemy, and pick out his eyes." And: "I want no man for President of these States...who has not got his hand half clenched, and means to close it on the jugular vein of the slave system the moment he reaches it, and has a double-edged dagger in the other hand, in case there is any missing in the strangulation."

But even Garrison and Phillips seem moderate against the figure

---

* I have not given citations for the more familiar of Garrison's and Phillips' statements, and a few other quotations which are easily found in the better-known studies of the leading abolitionists, in biographies of Lincoln, and in standard works on the pre-Civil War period.

of John Brown, lean and lusty, with two wives and twenty children, filled with enough anger for a regiment of agitators, declaring personal war on the institution of slavery. Speeches and articles were for others. The old man studied military strategy, pored over maps of the Southern terrain, raised money for arms and planned the forcible liberation of slaves through rebellion and guerrilla warfare. On Pottowattomie Creek in the bleeding Kansas of 1856, on the Sabbath, he had struck one night at an encampment of proslavery men, killing five with a cold ferocity. On his way to the gallows, after the raid on the Harpers Ferry arsenal in Virginia in the fall of 1859, he wrote: "I John Brown am now quite certain that the crimes of this guilty land will never be purged away; but with Blood."

The Negro abolitionist, Frederick Douglass, newly freed from slavery himself, and long a believer in "moral suasion" to free others, talked with John Brown at his home in 1847 and came away impressed by his arguments. Two years later, Douglass told a Boston audience; "I should welcome the intelligence tomorrow, should it come, that the slaves had risen in the South, and that the sable arms which had been engaged in beautifying and adorning the South, were engaged in spreading death and devastation." He thought the Harpers Ferry plan wild, and would not go along; yet, to the end, he maintained that John Brown at Harpers Ferry began the war that ended slavery. "Until this blow was struck, the prospect for freedom was dim, shadowy, and uncertain...When John Brown stretched forth his arm the sky was cleared."

These are the extremists. Did they hurt or help the cause of freedom? Or did they, if helping this cause, destroy some other value, like human life, lost in huge numbers in the Civil War? To put it another way, were they a hindrance rather than a help in abolishing slavery? Did their activities bring a solution at too great a cost? If we answer these questions, and others, we may throw light on the uses or disuses of modern-day agitators and immoderates, whose cries, if not as shrill as Garrison's are as unpleasant to some ears, and whose actions, if not as violent as John Brown's are just as distasteful to those who urge caution and moderation.

What is Extremism?

The first four pages of a well-known book on Civil War politics (T. Harry Williams's, *Lincoln and the Radicals*) refers to abolitionists, individually and collectively, in the following terms: "radical... zealous...

fiery... scornful... revolutionary... spirit of fanaticism... hasty... Jacobins... aggressive... vindictive... narrowly sectional... bitter... sputtering...fanatical... impractical... extreme."

Such words, in different degrees of concentration, are used by many historians in describing the abolitionists. Like other words of judgment frequently used in historical accounts, they have not been carefully dissected and analyzed, so that while they serve as useful approximations of a general attitude held by the writer (and transferred without question to the reader) they fail to make the kinds of distinctions necessary to move historical narrative closer to the area of social science. The word "extremist," used perhaps more often than any other in connection with the abolitionists, might serve as subject for inspection.

"Extremist" carries a psychological burden when attached to political movements, which it does not bear in other situations. A woman who is extremely beautiful, a man who is extremely kind, a mechanic who is extremely skillful, a child who is extremely healthy—these represent laudable ideals. In politics, however, the label "extremist" carries unfavorable implications. It may mean that the person desires a change in the status quo which is more sweeping than that requested by most people. For instance, in a period when most people are willing to free the slaves, but not to enfranchise them, one wanting to give them equal rights would be considered an extremist. Or it may mean someone who urges a more drastic action to attain a goal shared by most people; that is, someone who advocates slave revolts (like John Brown) rather than compensated emancipation followed by colonization abroad (like Lincoln).

Yet, in any given political situation, there is a very large number of possible alternatives, both in desired goals and in the means of achieving them. The actual alternatives put forward in any one situation are usually much fewer than the total range of possibilities. And the most extreme suggestion put forward at the time will be labeled "extremist" even though it may be far less sweeping than other possible courses of action.

For instance, William Lloyd Garrison, looked upon both by his antagonists and by modern historians as an "extremist," did not seek goals as far-reaching as he might have. He explained, around 1830, his stand for "immediate abolition" as follows: "Immediate abolition does not mean that the slaves shall immediately exercise the right of suffrage, or be eligible to any office, or be emancipated from law, or be free from the benevolent restraints of guardianship." Yet the ideas of suffrage and office-holding were not too much for Thaddeus Stevens and Charles Sumner—nor for Garrison—in 1865, when actual freedom had come for the slaves.

Wendell Phillips, another "extremist," opposed the use of violence to free the slaves. He said, in 1852: "On that point, I am willing to wait. I can be patient...The cause of three millions of slaves, the destruction of a great national institution, must proceed slowly, and like every other change in public sentiment, we must wait patiently for it." John Brown was not as patient.

Charles Sumner, the "radical" Republican in the Senate, did not urge going beyond the Constitution, which gave Southern states the right to maintain slavery if they chose. Garrison, burning the Constitution, was less restrained. The Anti-Slavery Society announced that "we will not operate on the existing relations of society by other than peaceful and lawful means, and that we will give no countenance to violence or insurrection." Yet, the Society was denounced as a hotbed of extremism, the public memory of Nat Turner's violent insurrection having been dimmed by just a few years of time.

The point is, that we are not precise in our standards for measuring "extremism." We do not take into account all possible alternatives, in either goal or method, which may be more extreme than the one we are so labeling. This leads writers to call "extreme" any proposal more drastic than that favored by the majority of articulate people at the time (or by the writer). In a society where the word "extreme" has a bad connotation, in a literate community enamored of the Aristotelian golden mean, we often hurl that word unjustifiably at some proposal which is extreme only in a context of limited alternatives.

Consider how movements denounced all over the South as virtually Communist, began to look respectable and legalistic when the sit-inners and Freedom Riders moved into mass, extra-legal action in 1960 and 1961. And the White Citizens Councils of the South could lay claim to being "moderate" segregationists so long as the KKK was around. (The *deliberate* creation of a new extremist group to make an old one more palatable is not yet a major tactic by either right or left; McCarthyism could have been, though it probably was not, the clever offspring of someone who wanted to make "normal" Communist-hunting in this country seem mild.)

With the criterion for extremism so flexible, with the limits constantly shifting, how can we decide the value or wrongness of a position by whether it is "extreme" or "moderate"? We accept these labels because they afford us a test simple enough to avoid mental strain. Also, it is easy and comfortable—especially for intellectuals who do not share the piercing problems of the hungry or helplessly diseased of the world (who, in other words, face no extreme problems)—to presume always that the "moderate" solution is the best.

To jump to the cry "extremism" at the first glimpse of the unfamiliar is like a boy with his little telescope peering into the heavens and announcing that the star he dimly perceives at his edge of vision is the farthest object in the universe. It was James Russell Lowell who said: ."..there is no cant more foolish or more common than theirs who under the mask of discretion, moderation, statesmanship, and what not, would fain convict of fanaticism all that transcends their own limits... From the zoophyte upward everything is *ultra* to something else..."

If the notion of "extremism" is too nebulous to sustain a firm judgment on a goal or a tactic, how do we judge? One point of reference might be the nature and severity of the problem. Even that moderate, Lao Tzu, said you use a boat for a stream and a litter for a mountain path; you adapt your means to your problem. While more modest evils might be dislodged by a few sharp words, the elimination of slavery clearly required more drastic action. The abolitionists did not deceive themselves that they were gentle and temperate; they quite consciously measured their words to the enormity of the evil.

Garrison said in 1833: "How, then, ought I to feel and speak and write, in view of a system which is red with innocent blood drawn from the bodies of millions of my countrymen by the scourge of brutal drivers... My soul should be, as it is, on fire. I should thunder, I should lighten, I should blow the trumpet of alarm long and loud. I should use just such language as is most descriptive of the crime."

How evil was slavery? It was a complex phenomenon, different in every individual instance, with the treatment of slaves varying widely. But the whole range of variation was in a general framework of unspeakable inhumanity. Even at its "best," slavery was a ferocious attack on man's dignity. It was described matter-of-factly by a supporter of the system, Judge Edmund Ruffin of North Carolina: "Such services can only be expected from one who has no will of his own; who surrenders his will in implicit obedience to another. Such obedience is the consequence only of uncontrolled authority over the body. There is no remedy. This discipline belongs to the state of slavery... It constitutes the curse of slavery to both the bond and the free portion of our population. But it is inherent in the relation of master and slave."

And at its worst, slavery was, as Allan Nevins has said: ."..the greatest misery, the greatest wrong, the greatest curse to white and black alike that America has ever known."

Ads for fugitive slaves in the Southern press (5,400 advertisements a year) contained descriptions like the following to aid apprehension: "...Stamped N.E. on the breast and having both small toes cut off... Has some scars on his back that show above the skin, caused by the whip... Has an iron band around his neck... Has a ring of iron on his left leg... Branded on the left cheek, thus 'R,' and a piece is taken off her left ear on the same side; the same letter is branded on the inside of both legs." One plantation diary read: "...whipped every field hand this evening."

A Natchez slave who attacked a white man was chained to a tree and burned alive.

Against this, how mild Garrison's words seem.

Emotionalism and Irrationality

In the 1820s, G. F. Milton wrote, in *The Eve of Conflict,* "a new and rival spirit welled up from the West... an emotional democracy, bottoming itself on Rousseau's mystic claims of innate rights, looking on Liberty as a spontaneous creation and asserting rights unconnected with responsibilities, among these the universal manhood competence for self-government... The Abolition movement... was a manifestation of emotional democracy." Milton talks further of "deep-seated passions" and "the emotional flood... psychic forces clamoring for expression... a drive for reform, change, agitation, which boded ill for any arbitrament of intelligence." Thoreau, Parker, and other reformers, he says, "showed a remarkably keen insight into latent mass emotions and did not hesitate to employ appropriate devices to mobilize the mob mind."

Fanaticism, irrationality, emotionalism—these are the qualities attributed again and again, in a mood of sharp criticism, to the aboli-

tionists; and, indeed, to radical reformers in general. How valid is the criticism?

If being "emotional" means creating a state of excitement, both
for oneself and for others, which intensifies the forms of already existent
behavior, or creates new, more energetic behavior patterns, then we need
not argue. The abolitionists were all, in varying degrees, emotional in
their response to situations and in the stimuli they projected into the
atmosphere. What is arguable is the notion that this "emotionalism" is to
be deplored.

The intellectual is taken aback by emotional display. It appears to
him an attack on that which he most reveres—reason. One of his favorite
terms of praise is "dis-passionate." The words "calm...judicious...reason-
able" seem to belong together. He points to evil rousers of emotion: the
Hitlers, the Southern demagogues of racism, the religious charlatans, and
faith healers. And yet, sitting in a Negro Baptist Church in the deep
South listening to the crowd sing "We shall overcome...we shall overcome..." and hearing it cry "Freedom! Freedom!" the intellectual may well
feel a surge of joy and love, damped only slightly by a twinge of uneasi-
ness at his spontaneous display of feeling.

He is uneasy, I would suggest, because of a failure to recognize several things: that emotion is a *morally neutral* instrument for a wide variety
of ends; that it serves a positive purpose when linked to laudable goals; that
it is not "irrational" but "nonrational" because, being merely an instrument, its rationality is derived only from the value with which it is linked.

When, at a high moment of tension in the battle over slavery,
William Lloyd Garrison first heard the freed Negro Frederick Douglass
speak, at a crowded meeting in Nantucket, he rose and cried out: "Have
we been listening to a man—or a thing?" The audience stirred. In this
flash of words and transferred emotion, a group of New England men and
women, far removed from the plantation and its daily reminders of
human debasement, were confronted with an experience from which they
were normally separated by space and social status. By this confrontation,
they became more ready to act against an evil which existed just as crassly before Garrison's words were spoken, but whose meaning now flooded
in on them for the first time.

The Horst Wessel Song drove Nazi myrmidons forward, but the
Battle Hymn of the Republic inspired anti-slavery fighters. Like music

and poetry, whose essence is the enlargement of sensuous experience, and whose potency can be focused in any ethical direction—or in none—the agitation of emotions by words or actions is an art. And as such, it is an instrument of whatever moral camp employs it.

What needs to be said, finally, to assuage the embarrassment of the emotionally aroused intellectual, is that there is no necessary connection between emotionalism and irrationality. A lie may be calmly uttered, and a truth may be charged with emotion. Emotion can be used to make more rational decisions, if by that we mean decisions based on greater knowledge, for greater knowledge involves not only extension but intensity. Who "knows" more about slavery—the man who has in his head all the available information (how many Negroes are enslaved, how much money is spent by the plantation for their upkeep, how many run away, how many revolt, how many are whipped and how many are given special privileges) and calmly goes about his business, or the man who has less data, but is moved by the book (Harriet Beecher Stowe's) or by an orator (Wendell Phillips) to *feel* the reality of slavery so intensely that he will set up a station on the underground railroad? Rationality is limited by time, space, and status, which intervene between the individual and the truth. Emotion can liberate it.

Does the Agitator Distort the Facts?

Abolitionist reformers, and those who supported them, historian Avery Craven wrote in *The Coming of the Civil War*, spread thousands of distortions about the South. The American people, he said, "permitted their short-sighted politicians, their overzealous editors, and their pious reformers to emotionalize real and potential differences and to conjure up distorted impressions of those who dwelt in other parts of the nation. For more than two decades, these molders of public opinion steadily created the fiction of two distinct peoples contending for the right to preserve and expand their sacred cultures... In time, a people came to believe... that the issues were between right and wrong; good and evil."

Craven's thesis is that the war was repressible, but abolitionist (and slaveholder) exaggerations brought it about.

A similar charge is made by T. Harry Williams in *Lincoln and the Radicals*: "Thirty years of abolitionist preachings had instilled in the popular mind definite thought patterns and reactions regarding the Southern

people and their social system. It was widely believed that slavery had brutalized the Southern character, that the owner of human chattels was a
dour, repulsive fiend, animated by feelings of savage hatred toward
Negroes and Northern whites."

Because the reformist agitator is so often charged with distortion
and exaggeration, and because thinkers with an abiding concern for the
truth are often led by such charges to keep a safe distance from such agitators, it is essential to discuss this point.

Distinctions ought first to be made between outright misstate-
ments of fact and personal slander on the one hand, and on the other,
exaggerations of the truth, and the singling out of those aspects of a complex truth which support the viewpoint of the reformer. It needs to be
acknowledged that false statements have at times been made by radical
reformers, and this is unpardonable, for if the reformer speaks the truth,
then material exists on all hands to support him, and he needs no falsification of the evidence to back his case. As for character-denigration, it is
not only repugnant to truth-seekers, but makes explanation embarrassing
when the attacked person is revealed as something different. Witness
Phillips' angry assault on Lincoln: "Who is this huckster in politics? Who
is this county court advocate?" And during the war: "...if he had been a
traitor, he could not have worked better to strengthen one side, and haz-
ard the success of the other." And again, in a *Liberator* article, Phillips'
headline: "Abraham Lincoln, the Slave-Hound of Illinois."

More serious, and more frequent, however, are charges of exaggeration and distortion, leveled at the radicals. At the root of this problem is that once we get past simple factual statements ("On March 3,
1851, field hand................................ was whipped by his master.") we
are in a realm where words like "true" and "false" cannot be applied so
simply. Slavery was a complex institution, and no one statement can
describe it fully. Slave-master relationships varied from kindness to cruelty and also defy generalization. We are here in that philosophical realm
dealing with the theory of knowledge, a field in which historians play all
the time, without paying any attention to the rules, while the philosophers sit in their studies discussing the rules and rarely look out the window to see how the game is played.

There is an answer to the problem of how to state simply a complex truth—but this requires an activist outlook rare among scholars. It

means deciding from a particular ethical base what is the action-need of the moment, and to concentrate on that aspect of the truth-complex which fulfills that need. If we start from the ethical assumption that it is fundamentally wrong to hold in bondage—whether kindly or cruelly—another human being, and that the freeing of such persons requires penetrating the moral sensibilities of a nation, then it is justifiable to focus on those aspects of the complexity which support this goal. When you teach a child to be careful crossing the street, and say, "You can be killed by an automobile," you are singling out of the totality of automobile behaviors that small percentage of incidents in which people are killed. You are not telling the whole truth about automobiles and traffic. But you are emphasizing that portion of the truth which supports a morally desirable action.

The complaint by T. Harry Williams that is a result of abolitionist agitation, "It was widely believed that slavery had brutalized the Southern character..." takes note of an abolitionist emphasis which does not photographically depict total reality. Not every white Southerner was brutalized by slavery. And yet, some were, and many others were affected—by the simple fact of learning to accept such a system without protest. These effects are so various and complicated that the word "brutalized" does not exactly fit, nor does any other word. But the focusing on this fact of brutalization points to a crucial aspect of slavery, and the recognition of that aspect may be decisive in overthrowing a terrible system. The scholar who accepts no harsh judgment because it does not do justice to the entire complex truth, can really accept no judgment about society, because all are simplifications of the complex. The result is scholarly detachment from the profound ethical conflicts of society, and from that human concern without which scholarship becomes a pretentious game.

Historical Perspective and the Radical

It is paradoxical that the historian, who is presumably blessed with historical perspective, should judge the radical from within the narrow moral base of the radical's period of activity, while the radical assesses his immediate society from the vantage point of some future, better era. If progress is desirable, and if escape from the bonds of the immediate is healthy, whose perspective is more accurate—that of the agitator, or that of the scolding historian?

James Russell Lowell wrote in 1849: "... the simple fact undoubtedly is that were the Abolitionists to go back to the position from which they started, they would find themselves less fanatical than a very respectable minority of the people. The public follows them step by step, occupying the positions they have successively fortified and quitted, and it is necessary that they should keep in advance in order that people may not be shocked by waking up and finding themselves Abolitionists."

Garrison himself took note of the profound change in the nation by 1860, thirty years from the time he had started his tiny, maligned newspaper. He spoke to the Massachusetts Anti-Slavery Society, shortly after John Brown's execution, which had brought shock and indignation throughout the North: "Whereas, ten years since, there were thousands who could not endure my lightest rebuke of the South, they can now swallow John Brown whole, and his rifle into the bargain."

The historian too often moves back a hundred years into a moral framework barbarian by modern standards and thinks inside it, while the radical shakes the rafters of this framework at the risk of his life. Wendell Phillips, speaking affectionately of the abolitionist leader Angelina Grimke, said: "Were I to single out the moral and intellectual trait which most won me, it was her serene indifference to the judgment of those about her." That kind of indifference (David Riesman calls it inner directedness) is hard to find in contemporary scholarship.

Compromise

The argument over the wisdom of radical agitation in the tactics of social reform was aptly expressed in Boston in pre-Civil War years by two leading figures. Samuel May, speaking of Garrison, said: "... he will shake our nation to its center, but he will shake slavery out of it." Reverend Lyman Beecher said: "True wisdom consists in advocating a cause only so far as the community will sustain the reformer." The agitator, declare the moderate reformers, shakes so hard that he makes compromise impossible, alienates friends, and delays rather than speeds the coming of reform.

Compromise was not disdained by the abolitionists, they were fully conscious of the fact that the outcome of any social struggle is almost always some form of compromise. But they were also aware of that which every intelligent radical knows: that to compromise in advance is to vitiate at the outset that power for progress which only the radical propels into the debate. Lowell put this most vividly, declaring that the abolitionists "are looked upon as peculiarly ungrateful and impracticable if they do not devote their entire energies to soliciting nothing, and express a thankfulness amounting almost to rapture when they get it."

The abolitionist took an advanced position so that even if pushed back by compromise, substantial progress would result. Garrison wrote: "Urge immediate abolition as earnestly as we may, it will be gradual abolition in the end." And Phillips said: "If we would get half a loaf, we must demand the whole of it." The Emancipation Proclamation itself was a compromise, the tortured product of a long battle between radicals and moderates in and out of the Lincoln administration, and only the compelling force of the abolitionist intransigeants made it come as soon as it did.

Two factors demand recognition by moderates who disdain "extreme" positions on the ground that compromise is necessary. One is the above-mentioned point that the early projection of an advanced position ensures a compromise on more favorable terms than would be the case where the timorous reformer compromises at the start (in which case the result is a compromise upon a compromise, since he will be forced to retreat even from his retreat after all the forces are calculated at the social weighing-in). The other is that there is a huge difference between the passive wisher-for-change who quietly adds up the vectors and makes a decision as to which is the composite of all existing forces, and the active reformer who pushes so hard *in the course of adding-up* that the composite itself is changed. The latter—the radical—is viewing compromise as a dynamic process, in which his own actions are part of the total force being calculated. He bases his estimate of what is possible on a graph in which his own action and its consequences are calculated from the first.

Moderation as a Tactic

Does the agitator alienate potential allies by the extremism of his demands, or the harshness of his language? Lewis Tappan, the wealthy New Yorker who financed many abolitionist activities, wrote anxiously to George Thompson, the British abolitionist: "The fact need not be concealed from you that several emancipationists so disapprove of the harsh, and, as they think, the unchristian language of *The Liberator,* that they do not feel justified in upholding it." This, in general, was the feeling of the Executive Committee of the American Anti-Slavery Society in the early years of the movement. Undoubtedly, the Society itself was not diverted from its aim of abolishing slavery because of Garrison's immoderation; they were concerned lest others be alienated.

But who? The slaveholder? The slave? The moderate reformer? The open-minded conservative? It needs to be acknowledged that different sections of the population will respond differently to the same appeal, and in judging the effect of bold words upon the population, this population must be broken up into parts, based on the varying degrees of receptivity to the ideas of the reformer. Why should the radical soften his language or his program to please that element of the population which cannot possibly be pleased by anything short of total surrender of principle, whose self-interest in fact dictates rejection of any reform? Lowell wrote: "The slaveholder, when Mr. Greeley would politely request him to state what method would be most consonant to his feelings, would answer, as did the...boy whose mother asked him what he would like for breakfast, 'Just what you ain't gut!'"

Only the hypothesis of common interest for the entire population can justify an appeal to the opponent on the basis of reason, asking him to perceive his interest more accurately. But if in fact there is a diversity of interest, then the lighting up of the truth can only bring out more sharply that conflict which stands in the way of agreement. The slaveholders themselves pointed to the impossibility of their being won over by moderate overtures. In 1854, the editor of the *Richmond Enquirer* wrote: "That man must be a veritable verdigreen who dreams of pleasing slaveholders, either in church or state, by any method but that of letting slavery alone."

William Ellery Channing tried such appeal and failed. One of his brochures against slavery was so mild that some described it as putting people to sleep, but he was abused so harshly it might as well have been one of Garrison's flame-breathing *Liberator* editorials.

With a population of diversified interests, tactics must be adapted and focused specially for each group, and for the group most inimical to reform, it is doubtful that moderation is effective. With the intransigeants, it may be only the most powerful action that impels change. It was Nat Turner's violent slave revolt in Virginia in 1831 that led the Virginia legislature into its famous series of discussions about the abolition of slavery. "For a while indeed," Ralph Korngold writes, "it seemed that what years of propaganda by the Quakers had failed to accomplish would come as a result of Turner's blood-letting."

When friends of the reformers rail against harsh words or strong action (as the American Anti-Slavery Society did against Garrison) it is clear that they themselves will not be put off from reform because of it, but fear the effects on others. And if neither extreme opposition nor hard-and-fast friends can be moved by tactics of moderation, this leaves, as a decisive group, that large part of the population which is at neither end of the ideological spectrum, which moves back and forth across the center line, depending on circumstances.

Garrison was quite aware that most of the American population to which he was appealing was not sympathetic with his views, and he was completely conscious of how distant were his own fiery convictions from those of the average American. But he was persuaded, as were Phillips and other leading abolitionists (John Brown felt it, and acted it, if he did not express it intellectually) that only powerful surges of words and feelings could move white people from their complacency about the slave question. He said once in Philadelphia: "Sir, slavery will not be overthrown without excitement, a most tremendous excitement." He must lash with words, he felt, those Americans who had never felt the whip of a slave-owner. To his friend Samuel May, who urged him to keep more cool, saying: "Why, you are all on fire," Garrison replied: "Brother May, I have need to be all on fire, for I have mountains of ice about me to melt."

We have the historical record as a check on whether the vituperative language of Garrison, the intemperate appeals of Wendell Phillips, hurt or advanced the popular sentiment against slavery. In the 1830s a handful of men cried out against slavery and were beaten, stoned, and shot to death by their Northern compatriots. By 1849, antislavery sentiment was clearly increasing, and some of the greatest minds and voices in America were speaking out for abolition. Lowell asked curtly of those who charged the abolitionists with retarding the movement: "... has there really been a change of public opinion for the worse, either at the North or the South, since the *Liberator* came into existence eighteen years ago?"

And by 1860, with millions of Americans convinced that slavery was an evil, open insurrection by John Brown brought more public support than had the mere words of Garrison thirty years before.

This is not to say that extremists may not drive possible allies from their movement. But this is generally not because of the ferocity of their attack on an institution which is the object of general dislike, but because of their insertion of other issues which do not touch public sensibilities as much. Theodore Weld, an effective Midwestern abolitionist, who was marvelous at organizing abolitionist societies in Ohio, criticized Garrison for his violent attacks on the clergy, for his anarchist utterances against government in general, and for his insistence on bringing many other issues—women's rights, pacifism, etc.—into the antislavery fight. For marginal supporters, such side issues may bring alienation. Whether such estrangement would be significant enough to offset the general social value of having one important issue ride on the back of another, is another question.

The Agitator and the Politician

The politician is annoyed and angry at the pushing of the radical reformer, and the moderate observer thinks the radical unfair and injudicious in making extreme demands of the man in office, but both critics fail to distinguish between the social role of the politician and that of the agitator. In general, this distinction is perceived more clearly by reformers than by office-holders. Wendell Phillips put it neatly: "The reformer is careless of numbers, disregards popularity, and deals only with ideas, conscience, and common sense.... He neither expects nor is overanxious for immediate success. The politician dwells in an everlasting now.... His office is not to instruct public opinion but to represent it."

James Russell Lowell expressed the idea in another way: "The Reformer must expect comparative isolation, and he must be strong enough to bear it. He cannot look for the sympathy and cooperation of popular majorities. Yet these are the tools of the politician.... All true Reformers are incendiaries. But it is the hearts, brains and souls of their fellow-men which they set on fire, and in so doing they perform the function appropriated to them in the wise order of Providence."

The observer who is critical of the radical may be subconsciously conjuring the picture of a world peopled only with radicals, a world of incessant shouting, lamenting, and denunciation. But it would be good for him to also imagine a world without any radicals—a placid, static, and evil-ridden world with victims of injustice left to their own devices, a world with the downtrodden friendless. In all ages, it has been first the radical, and only later the moderate, who has held out a hand to men knocked to the ground by the social order.

The moderate, whose sensitive ears are offended by the wild language of the radical, needs to consider the necessary division of labor in a world full of evil, a division in which agitators for reform play an indispensable role. When Horace Greeley charged Garrison with fanaticism, Lowell retorted: "Why God sent him into the world with that special mission and none other.... It is that which will make his name a part of our American history. He would not have all men fanatics, but let us be devoutly thankful for as many of that kind as we can get. They are by no means too common as yet."

In Abraham Lincoln we have the prototype of the political man in power, with views so moderate as to require the pressure of radicals to stimulate action. The politician, by the very nature of the electoral process, is a compromiser and a trimmer, who sets his sails by the prevailing breezes, and without the hard blowing of the radical reformer would either drift actionless or sail along with existing injustice. It is hard to find a set of statements more clearly expressive of the politician's ambivalence than those which Lincoln made during his 1858 race for the Senate against Douglass. At that time he told a Chicago audience in July: "Let us discard this quibbling about this man and the other man, this race and the other race being inferior, and therefore they must be placed in an inferior position." But in September he told an audience in southern Illinois:

> I am not, nor ever have been, in favor of bringing about in any way the social or political equality of the white and black races. I am not nor ever have been in favor of making voters of the free negroes, or jurors, or qualifying them to hold office, or having them marry with white people. I will say in addition that there is a physical difference between the white and black races which, I suppose, will forever forbid the two races living together upon terms of social and political equality; and in as much as they cannot so live, that while they do remain together, there must be the position of the superiors and the inferiors; and that I, as much as any other man, am in favor of the superior being assigned to the white man.

The most shocking statement about Lincoln—and all the more shocking when we realize its essential truth—was made by Frederick Douglass in 1876 at the unveiling of the Freedmen's Monument in Washington:

To protect, defend, and perpetuate slavery in the United States where it existed Abraham Lincoln was not less ready than any other President to draw the sword of the nation. He was ready to execute all the supposed constitutional guarantees of the United States Constitution in favor of the slave system anywhere inside the slave states. He was willing to pursue, recapture, and send back the fugitive slave to his master, and to suppress a slave rising for liberty, though his guilty master were already in arms against the Government. The race to which we belong were not the special objects of his consideration. Knowing this, I concede to you, my white fellow citizens, a pre-eminence in his worship at once full and supreme. First, midst, and last, you and yours were the objects of his deepest affection and his most earnest solicitude. You are the children of Abraham Lincoln. We are at best only his stepchildren, children by adoption, children by force of circumstances and necessity.

In the fascinating dialogue—sometimes articulated, sometimes unspoken—between Abraham Lincoln and the abolitionists, we have the classic situation of the politician vis-a-vis the radical reformer. It would be wrong to say that Lincoln was completely a politician—his fundamental humanitarianism did not allow that—and wrong to say that some of the abolitionists did not occasionally play politics—but on both sides the aberrations were slight, and they played their respective roles to perfection.

Albert Beveridge, in his biography of Lincoln, emphasized the fact that despite the influence of Herndon, his abolitionist law partner, Lincoln's early environment was powerfully affected by the Southern viewpoint. This accounted for "his speeches, his letters, his silence, his patience and mildness, his seeming hesitations, his immortal inaugural, his plans for reconstruction."

Beveridge saw Lincoln as a man who "almost perfectly reflected public opinion" in his stands. Lincoln opposed repeal of the Fugitive Slave Law, was silent on the violence in Kansas and the beating of Sumner, and followed the tactic of saying nothing except on issues most people agreed on—like stopping the extension of slavery.

During the secession crisis, and through most of the war, Lincoln's stand on slavery was so ambiguous and cautious as to make the British abolitionist George Thompson tell Garrison: "You know how impossible it is at this moment to vindicate, as one would wish, the course of Mr. Lincoln. In no one of his utterances is there an assertion of a great principle—no appeal to right or justice. In everything he does and says, affecting the slave, there is the alloy of expediency."

Lincoln made no move against slavery in those border states siding with the Union, except to offer them money as an inducement for gradual abolition, and when Generals David Hunter and John Fremont acted to free slaves under their command Lincoln revoked their orders. His position was quite clear (as both abolitionist-minded Ralph Korngold and conservative-minded Harry Williams agree in their historical studies); Lincoln's first desire was to save the Union; abolition was secondary and he would sacrifice it, if necessary, to maintain Republican rule over the entire nation.

While Lincoln kept reading the meter of public opinion, the abolitionists assaulted in massive ideological waves both the public and the meter-reader. In the winter of 1861-62, fifty thousand persons heard Wendell Phillips speak. Millions read his speeches. Petitions and delegations besieged Lincoln at the White House. Garrison went easy on Lincoln, but his own writings had created an army of impatients. Samuel Bowles, editor of the *Springfield Republican*, wrote that "a new crop of Radicals has sprung up, who are resisting the President and making mischief."

Evidence is that Lincoln, who had reflected public opinion well enough in 1860 to win the election, was not abreast of it in 1861 and 1862, on the issue of slavery. And this points to something with huge significance: that while both the politician and the agitator have their own specific roles to play in that fitful march toward utopia, which involves both surge and consolidation, the politician meter-reader is plagued by an inherent defect. His reading is a static one, not taking into account the going and imminent actions of the reformers, which change the balance of forces even while he is making the decision. The tendency, therefore, is for all political decisions to be conservative. Most of all, the politician is so preoccupied with evaluation of the existing forces that he leaves out of the account his own power, which is expended on *reading* public opinion rather than on *changing* it.

Where presidents have been more than reflectors of a static consensus, the exertion of their force into the balance of power has usually been in pursuit of nationalistic goals rather than reformist ones. The carrying out of any war requires the conscious shifting of the balance of public sentiment in support of the war, which is not likely to have enthusiastic and overwhelming support before its inception. (Even the supposed mass clamor for war in 1898 was an exaggerated image created in a rather placid pond by the heavy stones of Hearst and Pulitzer.) Lincoln, Wilson, Roosevelt, and Truman worked hard to create popular support for the wars they administered.

Andrew Jackson's dynamic action on the bank was a creator rather than a reflector of public opinion; but historians and economists are still puzzled over whether his policy was designed genuinely to broaden economic democracy to reach the lowest societal levels, or was on behalf of disgruntled small bankers and entrepreneurs hearkening for a laissez-faire which would increase their own share of national profit-taking. The reforms of Teddy Roosevelt and Wilson were largely diluted toasts to Populist and Progressive protest. Franklin D. Roosevelt's New Deal comes closest to a dynamic effort to push through a reform program while creating the sentiment to support it. Since Roosevelt, we have had no such phenomenon.

In the area of racial equality, from Lincoln to Kennedy, the man at the pinnacle of national political power has chosen to play the cautious game of responding, inch by inch, to the powerful push of "extremists," "trouble-makers," and "radicals." For Lincoln it was the abolitionists; for Kennedy the sit-inners and Freedom Riders. The man sitting in the White House has the inner mechanism of the public opinion meter in his lap; he can, by a direct manipulation of its gears, bring a transformation that otherwise requires a thousand times more energy directed from the outside by protest and outcry. So far, no one with presidential power has played such a dynamic role in the area of racial exclusiveness.

Agitators and War

A Tulane University professor of history wrote in the May 1962 issue of the *Journal of Southern History*:

> Eventually, however, the abolitionists reached a large Northern audience and thus brought on the bloodiest war in American history. Convinced that they had an exclusive line to God they determined to force their brand of morality on their Southern brethren. It is not surprising that many Southerners still regard this assumption of moral superiority by the New England Puritans—and by their pharisaical heirs the latter-day abolitionists—as obnoxious.

One of the standard arguments against the agitator is that his proddings and shoutings, his emotional denunciations, lead to violent conflict—that, in the case of the Civil War, it was the abolitionists who played a crucial role in bringing about the terrible bloodbath. Avery Craven, in *The Coming of the Civil War*, blames "shortsighted politicians...over-zealous editors...pious reformers" for emotionalizing and exaggerating sectional differences, for bringing people to believe the issue was between good and evil, thus creating mythical devils to be fought. It was, Craven says, a repressible conflict, made irrepressible by these forces.

It is clear that we cannot ascribe to the abolitionists the power to push moderates into action and at the same time deny that their words and actions have the effect of sharpening conflict over the social issue which concerns them. But the distinction between social conflict and war is overwhelmingly important. Agitators had the power to heighten feelings and tensions, but they are outside of the decision-making machinery which produces a war. It is strange that a society and a culture which are so resentful of "determinist" theories gave great credence to the idea that the Civil War was irrepressible, once given the conflict of ideas represented by slaveholders and abolitionists. This clash, however, existed in sharp form for thirty years without producing war. War became inevitable only with the simultaneous emergence of two factors: the determination of leading Southerners, holding state power, to create a separate nation; and the insistence of the Republicans, in possession of the national government, that no such separate nation must be permitted to exist. It was this issue which brought war, because only this, the issue of national sovereignty, constituted a direct attack on that group which ran the country and had the power to make war.

The institution of slavery did lie at the root of the economic and social schism between the sections. However, it was not the antihuman, immoral aspect of the institution which brought all the weight of national power against it; it was the antitariff, antibank, anticapitalist, antinational aspect of slavery which aroused the united opposition of the only groups in the country with the power to make war—the national political leaders and controllers of the national economy. Jefferson Davis' speech, April 29, 1861, before a special session of the Confederate Congress, saw the Northern motives not as humanitarian, but as based on a desire to control the Union.

The conflict between the slave states and the Northern politicians existed independently of the battle between slaveholders and abolitionists. The latter by itself could not lead to war because the abolitionists were not in charge of war-making machinery (and in fact, did not advocate war as a method of solving their problem). The former conflict by itself could have brought war and did bring it precisely because it brought into collision two forces in both sections of the country with the power to make war. What the abolitionists contributed to this conflict was that they gave Lincoln and the North a moral issue to sanctify and ennoble what was for many Republican leaders a struggle for national power and economic control. They could have waged war without such a moral issue, for politicians have shown the ability to create moral issues on the flimsiest of bases—witness Woodrow Wilson in 1917—but it was helpful to have one at hand.

What the abolitionists did was not to precipitate the war, nor even to cause the basic conflict, which led to war—but to ensure, by their kind of agitation, that in the course of the war, some social reform would take place. That this reform was drastically limited is shown by the feeble character of the Emancipation Proclamation (of which Richard Hofstadter has said: "It had all the moral grandeur of a bill of lading").

The Radical Reconstruction period rode along on a zooming moral momentum created by the Civil War, but crass political desires were in control; when these desires could no longer be filled by Negro suffrage, the Negro was sacrificed and Radical Reconstruction consigned to the ash heap. The abolitionists were not responsible for the war—they were responsible for sowing the seeds—with the Thirteenth, Fourteenth, and Fifteenth amendments—of an equalitarian society, seeds which their generation was unwilling to nurture, but which were to come to life after a century.

Agitators Today: The Sit-Inners of the South

There is no point—except for that abstract delight which accompanies historical study—in probing the role of the agitator in the historical process, unless we can learn something from it which is of use today. We have, after a hundred years, a successor to the abolitionist: the sit-in agitator, the boycotter, the Freedom Rider of the 1960s. Every objection—and every defense—applicable to the abolitionist is pertinent to his modern-day counterpart.

When the sit-in movement erupted through the South in the spring of 1960, it seemed a radical, extreme departure from the slow, law-court tactics of the NAACP, which had produced favorable court decisions but few real changes in the deep South. And it upset Southern white liberals sympathetic to the Negro and friendly to the 1954 Supreme Court school decision. This, they felt, was going too far. But the fact that "extremism" is a relative term, and the additional fact that the passage of time and the advance of social change make a formerly radical step seem less radical, became clear within a year.

For one thing, the increased frequency and widespread character of the sit-ins got people accustomed to them and they began to look less outrageously revolutionary. But more important, the advent of the Freedom Rides in 1961—busloads of integrated Northerners riding through the most backward areas of the deep South in direct and shocking violation of local law and custom—made the sit-ins seem a rather moderate affair. And, at the same time, the emergence of the Black Muslims as anti-white militants, with their claim of black superiority, put the integrationist advocates of nonviolence in the position of being more radical than the NAACP, but less so than the Black Muslims. Nonviolence itself, the accepted tactic of the sit-in and Freedom Ride people, was a rather moderate tactic in a century of violent upheaval throughout the world.

The old argument of Garrison that his racialism was pitched to the level of the evil he was fighting is directly applicable to the new young radicals of the American South. Is sitting at a lunch counter in a white restaurant, and refusing to leave, really a very extreme measure in relation to the evil of segregation? Is insisting on the right to sit side by side, regardless of race, in a bus or train or waiting room, a terribly radical move—in the face of a century of deep humiliation for one-tenth of a nation? By 1960 the NAACP, denounced in 1954 and 1955 as radical and Communistic, seemed remarkably mild next to the sit-in students. By 1961, the sit-in students seemed moderate against the Freedom Riders, and the Riders themselves even timid compared to the Muslims.

The element of emotionalism, present in any mass movement, has a special place in the movement for racial equality in the 1960s. Every important demonstration and action has been accompanied by church-meetings, singing, fiery oratory. But all of this has been an instrument designed to heighten a most rational objective: securing in fact as well as in theory the basic principles of the Declaration of Independence and the Fourteenth Amendment to the Constitution. The leadership of Martin Luther King, Jr. represents that new blending of emotional religion and intellectual sophistication which marks the current equal rights campaign. King plays upon the emotions and religious feelings of his people, but contains this within a controlled rationality which drives towards carefully defined goals.

Does the race agitator in the South today exaggerate the truth about conditions in that part of the country? "Don't believe all those stories you hear about us," a soft-voiced woman from South Carolina told me once. "We're not all that bad to our colored people." She was right, and wrong. The South is far better than most agitated Northerners imagine; and much worse than any white Northerner believes. It is a complexity of swift progress and deep-rooted evil. Dramatic and publicized progress in race relations is still only a thin veneer on a deep crust of degradation. To be a Negro in the South has, for most Negroes, most of the time, no drastic consequences like beatings or lynchings. But it has, for all Negroes in the South, all of the time, a fundamental hurt which cannot be put into words or statistics. No Negro, even in that minority of wealth and position, can escape the fact that he is a special person, that wherever he goes, whatever he does, he must be conscious of this fact, that his children will bear a special burden on their emotions from the moment they begin to make contact with the outside world. For the majority, their entire way of life is conditioned by it, the fact that the women must be office cleaners rather than stenographers, that the men must be porters rather than foremen; their children may have it better, but their own generation, their own lives, constitute a sacrifice offered to the future.

And for a certain minority of Negroes, there is police brutality, courtroom injustice, horrible conditions in Southern jails and work-gangs, the simple fact that capital punishment is much more likely to be invoked for a Negro criminal than for a white. The South is not one mad orgy of lynchings and brutality, as Communist propaganda might have it. But there is a kind of permanent brutality in the atmosphere, which nobody's propaganda has quite accurately described. Because of this, no accusation directed against the South is much of an exaggeration. Any emphasis upon the evil aspects of Southern life is a valuable prod to the movement for equality.

As for the moderate exhortation to compromise, the angry but cool Negro students in the South have learned that this is best left as the very last act in the succession of moves toward settlement of any issue. Department stores, before the sit-ins, were willing to compromise by adding more segregated eating facilities for Negroes. After the sit-ins, the only compromise which the students had to accept was to wait a few months in some cases, or to leave some restaurants out of the settlement, or to put up with inaction on connected issues like employment rights; but the lunch counters were fully integrated. The lesson has been well learned by now; throw the full weight of attack into the fray despite demands for prior concessions; then the final compromise will be at the highest possible level.

"You'll alienate the merchants if you sit-in, and they'll never agree to integrate," the students were told when they began their movement. But they know, through some semiconscious perception rather than by complex rational analysis, that certain antagonists in a social struggle cannot be won over by gentleness, only by pressure. The merchants were alienated, not only from the students, but from their customers. It was the latter effect which was most striking, and it led to their capitulation and the integration of lunch counters in leading Southern cities. On the other hand, students were careful to try not to alienate the ordinary Southern white, the customer, the observer. They were scrupulously polite, nonviolent, and impressive in their intelligence and deportment. With a precise instinct, they singled out of the complex of opponents which ones would have to be irritated, and which would need to be cajoled.

In spite of some fearful murmurs immediately after the 1954 Supreme Court Decision, there is no prospect of civil war in the United States over desegregation. And this points up the fact that the total collision between two power groups which is called war cannot come about through the action of radial reformers, who stand outside these power groupings. The movement for desegregation today has all the elements of the abolition movement: its moral fervor and excitement, its small group of martyrs and mass of passive supporters, its occasional explosions of mob scenes and violence. But there will be no war because there are no issues between the real power groups in society serious enough, deep enough, to necessitate war as a solution. War remains the instrument of the state. All that reformers can do is put some moral baggage on its train.

The role of the politicians vis-á-vis the agitator was revealed as clearly in the Kennedy Administration as it was under Lincoln. Like Lincoln, Kennedy read the meter of public concern and reacted to it, but never exerted the full force of his office to change the reading drastically. He too had a deeply ingrained humanitarianism, but it took the shock of Birmingham to bring from him his first clear moral appeal against segregation and his first move for civil rights legislation (the Civil Rights Act of 1964). Lyndon Johnson holding to the level created by the agitation of that Birmingham summer, still hesitated—even while modern-day abolitionists were being murdered in Mississippi—to revoke the Compromise of 1877 and decisively enforce federal law in that state.

Behind every one of the national government's moves toward racial equality lies the sweat and effort of boycotts, picketing, beatings, sit-ins, and mass demonstrations. All of our recent administrations have constituted a funnel into which gargantuan human effort—organized by radical agitators like Martin Luther King, Jr. and the young professional militants of the Student Non-Violent Coordinating Committee—is poured, only to emerge at the other end in slow dribbles of social progress. No American President, from Lincoln to Johnson, was able to see the immense possibilities for social change that lie in a *dynamic* reading of public opinion. Progress toward racial equality in the United States is certain, but this is because agitators, radicals and "extremists"—black and white together—are giving the United States its only living reminder that it was once a revolutionary nation.

10

When Will the Long Feud End?

I had argued in *The Southern Mystique* in 1964 that the South was not radically different than the North, that racism was a national phenomenon, not just a Southern one. In the Seventies, in northern cities, including my city of Boston, whites, usually in working-class districts, gathered in mobs to protest the busing of black children into their neighborhood schools. What follows is one of the bi-weekly columns I was writing in 1975 for the *Boston Globe*. It appeared in the September 19, 1975 issue.

"Despite considerable apprehension, violence failed to materialize. In September...Negro children entered Boston's white schools with little difficulty.... Although a few white parents withdrew their children and some Negroes suffered insults, integrated schools resulted in neither race violence nor amalgamation."

The year was 1855. The description is from Leon Litwack's book "North of Slavery." He tells about Sarah Roberts, who passed five white

elementary schools on the way to hers. Her father sued for her right to go
to a neighborhood school, and her lawyer, Charles Sumner, argued before
the Supreme Court of Massachusetts against the segregation rule of the
Primary School Committee: "On the one side is the city of Boston...on
the other side is a little child.... This little child asks, at your hands, her
personal rights."

The court upheld the School Committee, but the Legislature
then passed a law to integrate Boston schools. A pessimist, reviewing this
history, might say: We see now how far we have come in 120 years: three
inches. An optimist might point to how much has changed since then.
But it is hard to ignore the persistence, through three centuries, of race
hostility to the point of recurring violence.

Another fact is hard to ignore: it is the economically harassed
white people who have turned repeatedly in anger against blacks, thinking, "There is the cause of our misery, there is the threat to our jobs, our
safety, our children." My father was a slum-dwelling immigrant, and prejudiced against Negroes. I had an aunt who kept warning us kids not to
go under the El, where blacks lived in even more run-down tenements
than ours.

We need to pay attention to these people with lives of frustration
and unfulfilled dreams. Not to dismiss them if they are full of racial epi-
thets. Not to doubt them if they say: "I am not a racist, all I want is..." I
recall some lines from a book about street orphans in postwar Naples,
which apply to whites and blacks alike: "The cry of the poor is not always
just, but if you do not listen to it, you will never know what justice is."

It started early in our history. The first whites in Virginia were
stricken with hunger and sickness. In the heat of the first summer, every
other man died. They called it "The Starving Time." In 1618, they
begged King James for vagabonds and criminals to work in servitude. The
following year, came a solution: the first shipload of blacks. When it
docked, race prejudice began.

In the pre-Civil War South, there were 300,000 slave plantations,
but most of the five million whites were poor, and not slave-owners. They
were described by a Southern historian: "Uninspired, physically deficient,
occupying the pine barrens or the infertile back country, they lived a
hand-to-mouth existence, mere hangers-on of a regime in which they had
no determining part."

In New York, in the midst of the Civil War, during four hot days in July, poor Irish rioted against the draft. They were being sent to die for the freedom of black slaves they did not know, while the rich, making fortunes out of the war, could escape the draft by paying $300. Here is an account: "...another mob was sacking houses in Lexington avenue. Elegant furniture and silver plate were borne away by the crowd...and the whole block on Broadway, between 28th and 29th streets, was burned down...." Then they set out to destroy the Colored Orphan Asylum on Fifth Avenue and 44th street, which contained 200 children, from infants up to 12 years of age.

And so it continues. Hassled whites turn on blacks. Angry blacks retaliate.

Will this hostility ever end? Not until black and white people discover together, the source of their long feud—an economic system which has deprived them and their children for centuries, to the benefit of, first, the Founding Fathers, and lately, the hundred or so giant corporations that hog the resources of this bountiful country.

PART TWO

CLASS

1

Growing Up Class-Conscious

This is a chapter from my 1994 memoir, *You Can't Be Neutral on a Moving Train*, published by Beacon Press. In that book I write about my experiences in the South, as a bombardier in World War II, in the movement against the Vietnam War, my encounters with courtrooms and jails, my jousts with academic administrations. About three-quarters of the way through the book I go back to my early years to try to understand my path to radical thinking.

I was in my teens when I wrote this poem:

Go see your Uncle Phil
And say hello.
Who would walk a mile today
To say hello,
The city freezing in the snow?

Phil had a news stand
Under the black El.

He sat on a wooden box
In the cold and in the heat.
And three small rooms across the street.

Today the wooden box was gone,
On top the stand Uncle Phil was curled,
A skeleton inside an Army coat.
He smiled and gave me a stick of gum
With stiffened fingers, red and numb.

Go see your Uncle Phil today
My mother said again in June
I walked the mile to say hello
With the city smelling almost sweet
Brand new sneakers on my feet.

The stand was nailed and boarded tight
And quiet in the sun.
Uncle Phil lay cold, asleep,
Under the black El, in a wooden box
In three small rooms across the street.

I recall these lines, certainly not as an example of "poetry," but because they evoke something about my growing up in the slums of Brooklyn in the thirties, when my father and mother in desperate moments turned to saviors: the corner grocer, who gave credit by writing down the day's purchases on a roll of paper; the kind doctor who treated my rickets for years without charging; Uncle Phil, whose army service had earned him a newsstand license and who loaned us money when we had trouble paying the rent.

Phil and my father were two of four brothers, Jewish immigrants from Austria, who came to this country before the First World War and worked together in New York factories. Phil's fellow workers kept questioning him: "Zinn, Zinn—what kind of name is that? Did you change it? It's not a Jewish name." Phil told them no, the name had not been changed, it was Zinn and that's all there was to it. But he got tired of the interrogations and one day had his name legally changed to Weintraub, which from then on was the name of that branch of the family.

My father, looking to escape the factory, became a waiter, mostly at weddings, sometimes in restaurants, and a member of Local 2 of the Waiters Union. While the union tightly controlled its membership, on

New Year's Eve, when there was a need for extra waiters, the sons of the members, called juniors, would work alongside their fathers, and I did too.

I hated every moment of it: the ill-fitting waiter's tuxedo, borrowed from my father, on my lanky body, the sleeves absurdly short my father was five-foot-five and at sixteen I was a six-footer); the way the bosses treated the waiters, who were fed chicken wings just before they marched out to serve roast beef and filet mignon to the guests; everybody in their fancy dress, wearing silly hats, singing "Auld Lang Syne" as the New Year began and me standing there in my waiter's costume, watching my father, his face strained, clear his tables, feeling no joy at the coming of the New Year.

When I first came across a certain e.e. cummings poem, I didn't fully understand why it touched me so deeply, but I knew it connected with some hidden feeling.

> my father moved through dooms of love
> through sames of am through haves of give,
> singing each morning out of each night
> my father moved through depths of height

His name was Eddie. He was always physically affectionate to his four boys, and loved to laugh. He had a strong face, a muscular body, and flat feet(due, it was said, to long years as a waiter, but who could be sure?), and his waiter friends called him "Charlie Chaplin" because he walked with his feet splayed out—he claimed he could balance the trays better that way.

In the Depression years the weddings fell off, there was little work, and he got tired of hanging around the union hall, playing cards, waiting for a job. So he became at different times a window cleaner, a pushcart peddler, a street salesman of neckties, a WPA worker in Central Park. As a window cleaner, his supporting belt broke one day and he fell off the ladder onto the concrete steps of a subway entrance. I was perhaps twelve and I remember him being brought, bleeding, into our little flat. He had hurt himself badly. My mother would not let him clean windows again.

All his life he worked hard for very little. I've always resented the smug statements of politicians, media commentators, corporate executives

who talked of how, in America, if you worked hard you would become
rich. The meaning of that was if you were poor it was because you hadn't
worked hard enough. I knew this was a lie, about my father and millions
of others, men and women who worked harder than anyone, harder than
financiers and politicians, harder than *anybody* if you accept that when you
work at an unpleasant job that makes it very hard work indeed.

My mother worked and worked without getting paid at all. She
was a plump woman, with a sweet, oval Russian face—a beauty, in fact.
She had grown up in Irkutsk, in Siberia. While my father worked *his*
hours on the job, she worked all day and all night, managing the family,
finding the food, cooking and cleaning, taking the kids to the doctor or
the hospital clinic for measles and mumps and whooping cough and ton-
sillitis and whatever came up. And taking care of family finances. My
father had a fourth-grade education and could not read much or do much
arithmetic. My mother had gone as far as seventh grade, but her intelligence went far beyond that; she was the brains of the family. And the
strength of the family.

Her name was Jenny. Roz and I sat with her in our kitchen one
day when she was in her seventies and had her talk about her life, with a
tape recorder on the table. She told of her mother's arranged marriage in
Irkutsk, of how "they brought a boy home, a Jewish soldier stationed in
Irkutsk, and said, 'This is who you'll marry.'"

They emigrated to America. Jenny's mother died in her thirties,
having given birth to three boys and three girls, and her father—against
whom she boiled with indignation all her life—deserted the family. Jenny,
the eldest but only a teenager, became the mother of the family, took care
of the rest, working in factories, until they grew up and found jobs.

She met Eddie through his sister, who worked in her factory, and
it was a passionate marriage all the way. Eddie died at sixty-seven. To the
end he was carrying trays of food at weddings and in restaurants, never
having made enough money to retire. It was a sudden heart attack, and I
got the news in Atlanta, where Roz and I had just moved. I remembered
our last meeting, when my father was clearly upset about our little family moving south, so far away, but said nothing except "Good luck. Take
care of yourself."

My mother outlived him by many years. She lived by herself,
fiercely insisting on her independence, knitting sweaters for everybody,

saving her shopping coupons, playing bingo with her friends. But toward the end she suffered a stroke and entered a nursing home.

As a child, I was drawn to a framed photograph on the wall, of a delicate-faced little boy with soft brown eyes and a shock of brown hair, and one day my mother told me it was her firstborn, my older brother, who died of spinal meningitis as the age of five. In our tape recording she tells how and when he died, how they'd been in the country for a brief, cheap vacation, and how she and my father held the boy's body on the long train ride back to New York City.

We lived in a succession of tenements, sometimes four rooms, sometimes three. Some winters we lived in a building with central heating. Other times we lived in what was called a cold-water flat—no heat except from the coal cooking stove in the kitchen, no hot water except what we boiled on that same stove.

It was always a battle to pay the bills. I would come home from school in the winter, when the sun set at four, and find the house dark—the electric company had turned off the electricity, and my mother would be sitting there, knitting by candlelight.

There was no refrigerator, but an icebox, for which we would go to the "ice block" and buy a five-or-ten-cent chunk of ice. In the winter a wooden box rested on the sill just outside the window, using nature to keep things cold. There was no shower, but the washtub in the kitchen was our bathtub.

No radio for a long time, until one day my father took me on a long walk through the city to find a second-hand radio, and triumphantly brought it home on his shoulder, me trotting along by his side. No telephone. We could be called to the phone at the candy store down the block, and pay the kid who ran upstairs to get us two pennies or a nickel.

And yes, the roaches. Never absent, wherever we lived. We'd come home and they'd be all over the kitchen table and scatter when we turned on the light. I never got used to them.

I don't remember ever being hungry. The rent might not be paid (we moved often, a step ahead of eviction), no bills might be paid, the grocer might not be paid, but my mother was ingenious at making sure there was always food. Always hot cereal in the morning, always hot soup in the evening, always bread, butter, eggs, milk, noodles and cheese, sour cream, chicken fricassee.

My mother was not shy about using the English language, which she adapted to her purposes. We would hear her telling her friend about the problem she was having with "very close veins," or "a pain in my crutch." She would look in the dairy store for "monster cheese." She would say to my father if he forgot something, "Eddie, try to remember, wreck your brains."

My brothers—Bernie, Jerry, Shelly—and I had lots of fun over the years recalling her ways. She would sign her letters to us, "Your mother, Jenny Zinn." We laughed at those memories even while standing by in the hospital room where she lay in a coma, kept "alive" by a tangle of tubes, her brain already damaged beyond repair. We had signed that terrible order, "Do Not Resuscitate," shortly after which she coughed up her breathing tube and died. She was ninety.

We four boys grew up together—sleeping two or three to a bed, in rooms dark and uninviting. So I spent a lot of time in the street or the schoolyard, playing handball, football, softball, stickball, or taking boxing lessons from a guy in the neighborhood who had made the Golden Gloves and was our version of a celebrity.

In the time I did spend in the house I read. From the time I was eight I was reading whatever books I could find. The very first was one I picked up on the street. The beginning pages were torn out, but that didn't matter. It was *Tarzan and the Jewels of Opar* and from then on I was a fan of Edgar Rice Burroughs, not only his Tarzan books but his other fantasies: *The Chessmen of Mars*, about the way wars were fought by Martians, with warriors, on foot or on horses, playing out the chess moves; *The Earth's Core*, about a strange civilization in the center of the earth.

There were no books in our house. My father had never read a book. My mother read romance magazines. They both read the newspaper. They knew little about politics, except that Franklin Roosevelt was a good man because he helped the poor.

As a boy I read no children's books. My parents did not know about such books, but when I was ten, the *New York Post* offered a set of the complete works of Charles Dickens (of whom they had never heard, of course). By using coupons cut out of the newspaper, they could get a volume every week for a few pennies. They signed up because they knew I loved to read. And so I read Dickens in the order in which we received the books, starting with *David Copperfield, Oliver Twist, Great Expectations, The Pickwick Papers, Hard Times, A Tale of Two Cities*, and all the rest, until the coupons were exhausted and so was I.

I did not know where Dickens fitted into the history of modern literature because he was all I knew of that literature. I did not know that he was probably the most popular novelist in the English-speaking world (perhaps in any world) in the mid-nineteenth century, or that he was a great actor whose readings of his own work drew mobs of people, or that when he visited the United States in 1842 (he was thirty), landing first in Boston, some of his readers traveled two thousand miles from the Far West to see him.

What I did know was that he aroused in me tumultuous emotions. First, an anger at arbitrary power puffed up with wealth and kept in place by law. But most of all a profound compassion for the poor. I did not see myself as poor in the way Oliver Twist was poor. I didn't recognize that I was so moved by his story because his life touched chords in mine.

How wise Dickens was to make readers feel poverty and cruelty through the fate of children who had not reached the age where the righteous and comfortable classes could accuse them of being responsible for their own misery.

Today, reading pallid, cramped novels about "relationships," I recall Dickens' unashamed rousing of feeling, his uproariously funny characters, his epic settings—cities of hunger and degradation, countries in revolution, the stakes being life and death not just for one family but for thousands.

Dickens is sometimes criticized by literary snobs for sentimentality, melodrama, partisanship, exaggeration. But surely the state of the world makes fictional exaggeration unnecessary and partisanship vital. It was only many years after I read those Dickens novels that I understood his accomplishment.

For my thirteenth birthday, my parents, knowing that I was writing things in notebooks, bought me a rebuilt Underwood typewriter. It came with a practice book for learning the touch system, and soon I was typing book reviews for everything I read and keeping them in my drawer. I never showed them to anyone. It gave me joy and pride just to know that I had read these books and could write about them—on a typewriter.

From the age of fourteen I had after-school and summer jobs, delivering clothes for a dry cleaner, working as a caddy on a golf course in Queens. I also helped out in a succession of candy stores my parents bought in a desperate attempt to make enough money so my father could quit being a waiter. The stores all failed, but my three younger brothers and I had lots of milkshakes and ice cream and candy while they existed.

I remember the last of those candy store situations, and it was typical. The six of us lived above the store in a four-room flat in a dirty old five-story tenement on Bushwick Avenue in Brooklyn. The street s were always full of life, especially in spring and summer, when everyone seemed to be outside—old folks sitting on chairs, mothers holding their babies, teenagers playing ball, the older guys "throwing the bull," fooling with girls.

I especially remember that time because I was seventeen and had begun to be interested in world politics.

I was reading books about fascism in Europe. George Seldes' *Sawdust Caesar*, about Mussolini's seizure of power in Italy, fascinated me. I could not get out of my mind the courage of the Socialist deputy Matteotti, who defied Mussolini and was dragged from his home and killed by brown-shirted thugs.

I read something called *The Brown Book of the Nazi Terror*, which described what was happening in Germany under Hitler. It was a drama beyond anything a playwright or novelist could imagine. And now the Nazi war machine was beginning to move into the Rhineland, Austria, Czechoslovakia. The newspapers and radio were full of excitement: Chamberlain meeting Hitler at Munich, the sudden, astonishing nonaggression pact of the two archenemies, Soviet Russia and Nazi Germany. And finally, the invasion of Poland and the start of the Second World War.

The Civil War in Spain, just ended with victory for the Fascist general Franco, seemed the event closest to all of us because several thousand American radicals—Communists, socialists, anarchists—had crossed the Atlantic to fight with the democratic government of Spain. A young fellow who played street football with us—short and thin, the fastest runner in the neighborhood—disappeared. Months later the word came to us: Jerry has gone to Spain to fight against Franco.

There on Bushwick Avenue, among the basketball players and street talkers, were some young Communists, a few years older then me.

They had jobs, but after work and on weekends they distributed Marxist literature in the neighborhood and talked politics into the night with whomever was interested.

I was interested. I was reading about what was happening in the world. I argued with the Communist guys. Especially about the Russian invasion of Finland. They insisted it was necessary for the Soviet Union to protect itself against future attack, but to me it was a brutal act of aggression against a tiny country, and none of their carefully worked out justifications persuaded me.

Still, I agreed with them on lots of things. They were ferociously antifascist, indignant as I was about the contrasts of wealth and poverty in America. I admired them—they seemed to know so much about politics, economics, what was happening everywhere in the world. And they were courageous—I had seen them defy the local policeman, who tried to stop them from distributing literature on the street and to break up their knots of discussion. And besides, they were regular guys, good athletes.

One summer day they asked me if I wanted to go with them to "a demonstration" in Times Square that evening. I had never been to such a thing. I made some excuse to my parents, and a little bunch of us took the subway to Times Square.

When we arrived it was just a typical evening in Times Square—the streets crowded, the lights glittering. "Where's the demonstration?" I asked my friend Leon. He was tall, blond, the ideal "Aryan" type, but the son of German Communists who were also nature worshippers and part of a little colony of health-conscious German socialists out in the New Jersey countryside. "Wait," he said. "Ten o'clock." We continued to stroll.

As the clock on the Times tower struck ten, the scene changed. In the midst of the crowd, banners were unfurled, and people, perhaps a thousand or more, formed into lines carrying banners and signs and chanting slogans about peace and justice and a dozen other causes of the day. It was exciting. And non-threatening. All these people were keeping to the sidewalks, not blocking traffic, walking in orderly, nonviolent lines through Times Square. My friend and I were walking behind two women carrying a banner, and he said, "Let's relieve them." So we each took an end of the banner. I felt a bit like Charlie Chaplin in *Modern Times*, when he casually picks up a red signal flag and suddenly finds a thousand people marching behind him with raised fists.

We heard the sound of sirens and I thought there must be a fire somewhere, an accident of some kind. But then I heard screams and saw hundreds of policemen, mounted on horses and on foot, charging into the lines of marchers, smashing people with their clubs.

I was astonished, bewildered. This was America, a country where, whatever its faults, people could speak, write, assemble, demonstrate without fear. It was in the Constitution, the Bill of Rights. We were a *democracy*.

As I absorbed this, as my thoughts raced, all in a few seconds, I was spun around by a very large man, who seized my shoulder and hit me very hard. I only saw him as a blur. I didn't know if it was a club or a fist or a blackjack, but I was knocked unconscious.

I awoke in a doorway perhaps a half-hour later. I had no sense of how much time had elapsed, but it was an eerie scene I woke up to. There was no demonstration going on, no policemen in sight. My friend Leon was gone, and Times Square was filled with its usual Saturday night crowd—all as if nothing had happened, as if it were all a dream. But I knew it wasn't a dream; there was a painful lump on the side of my head.

More important, there was a very painful thought in my head: those young Communists on the block were right! The state and its police were not neutral referees in a society of contending interests. They were on the side of the rich and powerful. Free speech? Try it and the police will be there with their horses, their clubs, their guns, to stop you.

From that moment on, I was no longer a liberal, a believer in the self-correcting character of American democracy. I was a radical, believing that something fundamental was wrong in this country—not just the existence of poverty amidst great wealth, not just the horrible treatment of black people, but something rotten at the root. The situation required not just a new president or new laws, but an uprooting of the old order, the introduction of a new kind of society—cooperative, peaceful, egalitarian.

Perhaps I am exaggerating the importance of that one experience. But I think not. I have come to believe that our lives can be turned in a different direction, our minds adopt a different way of thinking, because of some significant though small event. That belief can be frightening or exhilarating, depending on whether you just contemplate the event or *do* something with it.

The years following that experience in Times Square might be called "my Communist years," but that phrase would be easy to misunderstand because the word "Communist" conjures up Joseph Stalin and the gulags of death and torture, the disappearance of free expression, the atmosphere of fear and trembling created in the Soviet Union, the ugly bureaucracy that lasted seventy years, pretending to be socialism.

None of that was in the minds or intentions of the young working-class people I knew who called themselves Communists. Certainly not in my mind. Little was known about the Soviet Union, except the romantic image, popularized by people like the English theologian Hewlitt Johnson, the Dean of Canterbury. In his book *The Soviet Power,* distributed widely by the Communist movement, he gave idealists disillusioned with capitalism the vision they longed for, of a place where the country belonged to "the people," where everyone had work and free health care, and women had equal opportunities with men, and a hundred different ethnic groups were treated with respect.

The Soviet Union was this romantic blur, far away. What was close at hand, visible, was that Communists were the leaders in organizing working people all over the country. They were the most daring, risking arrest and beatings to organize auto workers in Detroit, steel workers in Pittsburgh, textile workers in North Carolina, fur and leather workers in New York, longshoremen on the West Coast. They were the first to speak up, more than that, to demonstrate—to chain themselves to factory gates and White House fences—when blacks were lynched in the South, when the "Scottsboro Boys" were being railroaded to prison in Alabama.

My image of "a Communist" was not a Soviet bureaucrat but my friend Leon's father, a cabdriver who came home from work bruised and bloody one day, beaten up by his employer's goons (yes, that word was soon part of my vocabulary) for trying to organize his fellow cabdrivers into a union.

Everyone knew that the Communists were the first antifascists, protesting against Mussolini's invasion of Ethiopia and Hitler's persecution of the Jews. And, most impressive of all, it was the Communists, thousands of them, who volunteered to fight in Spain in the Abraham Lincoln Brigade, to join volunteers from all over the world to defend Madrid and the Spanish people against the army of Francisco Franco, which was given arms and airplanes by Germany and Italy.

Furthermore, some of the best people in the country were connected with the Communist movement in some way, heroes and heroines one could admire. There was Paul Robeson, the fabulous singer-actor-athlete whose magnificent voice could fill Madison Square Garden, crying out against racial injustice, against fascism. And literary figures (weren't Theodore Dreiser and W.E.B. DuBois Communists?), and talented, socially conscious Hollywood actors and writers and directors (yes, the Hollywood Ten, hauled before a congressional committee, defended by Humphrey Bogart and so may others).

True, in that movement, as in any other, you could see the righteousness leading to dogmatism, the closed circle of ideas impermeable to doubt, an intolerance of dissent by people who were the most persecuted of dissenters. But however imperfect, even repugnant, were particular policies, particular actions, there remained the purity of the ideal, represented in the theories of Karl Marx and the noble visions of many lesser thinkers and writers.

I remember my first reading of *The Communist Manifesto*, which Marx and Engels wrote when they too were young radicals; Marx was thirty, Engels twenty-eight. "The history of all hitherto existing society is the history of class struggle." That was undeniably true, verifiable in any reading of history. Certainly true for the United States, despite all the promises of the Constitution ("We the people of the United States..." and "No state shall deny...the equal protection of the laws").

The analysis of capitalism by Marx and Engels made sense: capitalism's history of exploitation, its creation of extremes of wealth and poverty, even in the liberal "democracy" of this country. And their socialist vision was not one of dictatorship or bureaucracy but of a free society. Their "dictatorship of the proletariat" was to be a transitional phase, the goal a classless society of true democracy, true freedom. A rational, just economic system would allow a short work day and leave everyone freedom and time to do as they liked—to write poetry, to be in nature, to play sports, to be truly human. Nationalism would be a thing of the past. People all over the world, of whatever race, of whatever continent, would live in peace and cooperation.

In my teenage reading, those ideas were kept alive by some of the finest writers in America. I read Upton Sinclair's *The Jungle*; work in the Chicago stockyards was the epitome of capitalist exploitation, and the vision of a new society in the last pages of the book was thrilling. John Steinbeck's *The Grapes of Wrath* was an eloquent cry against the conditions of life wherein the poor were expendable and any attempt on their part to change their lives was met with police clubs.

When I was eighteen, unemployed and my family desperate for help, I took a much-publicized Civil Service examination for a job in the Brooklyn Navy Yard. Thirty thousand young men (women applicants were unthinkable) took the exam, competing for a few hundred jobs. It was 1940, and New Deal programs had relieved but not ended the Depression. When the results were announced, four hundred applicants had gotten a score of 100 percent on the exam and would get jobs. I was one of them.

For me and my family it was a triumph. My salary would be $14.40 for a forty-hour week. I could give the family $10 a week and have the rest for lunch and spending money.

It was also an introduction into the world of heavy industry. I was to be an apprentice shipfitter for the next three years. I would work out on "the ways," a vast inclined surface at the edge of the harbor on which a battleship, the USS *Iowa*, was to be built. (Many years later, in the 1980s I was called to be a witness at the Staten Island trial of pacifists who had demonstrated against the placement of nuclear weapons on a battleship docked there—the USS *Iowa*.)

I have no idea of the dimensions of a battleship. Stood on end, it would have been almost as tall as the Empire State Building. The keel had just been laid, and our job—thousands of us—was to put together the steel body and inner framework of the ship. It was hard, dirty, malodorous work. The smell caused by cutting galvanized steel with an acetylene torch is indescribable—only years later did we learn that the zinc released in such burning also causes cancer.

In the winter, icy blasts blew from the sea, and we wore thick gloves and helmets, and got occasional relief around the little fires used by the riveters. They heated their rivets in these fires until the rivets were glowing globules which they then pulled from the fire and pounded into the steel plates of the hull with huge hammers driven by compressed air. The sound was deafening.

In the summer, we sweated under our overalls and in our steel-tipped boots, and swallowed salt pills to prevent heat exhaustion. We did a lot of crawling around inside the tiny steel compartments of the "inner bottom," where smells and sounds were magnified a hundred times. We measured and hammered, and cut and welded, using the service of "burners" and "chippers."

No women workers. The skilled jobs were held by white men, who were organized in A.F. of L. craft unions known to be inhospitable to blacks. The few blacks in the shipyard had the toughest, most physically demanding jobs, like riveting.

What made the job bearable was the steady pay and the accompanying dignity of being a workingman, bringing home money like my father. There was also the pride that we were doing something for the war effort. But most important for me was that I found a small group of friends, fellow apprentices—some of them shipfitters like myself, others shipwrights, machinists, pipefitters, sheetmetal workers—who were young radicals, determined to do something to change the world. No less.

We were excluded from the craft unions of the skilled workers, so we decided to organize the apprentices into a union, an association. We would act together to improve our working conditions, raise our pay, and create a camaraderie during and after working hours to add some fun to our workaday lives.

This we did, successfully, with three hundred young workers, and for me it was an introduction to actual participation in a labor movement. We were organizing a union and doing what working people had done through the centuries, creating little spaces of culture and friendship to make up for the dreariness of the work itself.

Four of us who were elected as officers of the Apprentice Association became special friends. We met one evening a week to read books on politics and economics and socialism, and talk about world affairs. These were years when some fellows our age were in college, but we felt we were getting a good education.

Still, I was glad to leave the shipyard and join the Air Force. And it was while flying combat missions in Europe that I began a sharp turn in my political thinking, away from the romanticization of the Soviet Union that enveloped many radicals (and others, too), especially in the atmosphere of World War II and the stunning successes of the Red Army against the Nazi invaders.

The reason for this turn was my encounter with an aerial gunner on another crew who questioned whether the aims of the Allies—England, France, the United States, the Soviet Union—were really antifascist and democratic.

One book he gave me shook forever ideas I had held for years. This was *The Yogi and the Commisar*, by Arthur Koestler. Koestler had been a Communist, had fought in Spain, but he had become convinced—and his factual evidence was powerful, his logic unshakable—that the Soviet Union, with its claim to be a socialist state, was a fraud. (After the war I read *The God That Failed*, in which writers whose integrity and dedication to justice I could not question—Richard Wright, André Gide, Ignazio Silone, and Koestler, too—describe their loss of faith in the Communist movement and the Soviet Union.)

But disillusionment with the Soviet Union did not diminish my belief in socialism, any more than disillusionment with the United States government lessened my belief in democracy. It certainly did not affect my consciousness of *class*, of the difference in the way rich and poor lived in the United States, of the failure of the society to provide the most basic biological necessities—food, housing, health care—to tens of millions of people.

Oddly enough, when I became a second lieutenant in the Army Air Corps I got a taste of what life was like for the privileged classes—for now I had better clothes, better food, more money, higher status than I had in civilian life.

After the war, with a few hundred dollars in mustering-out money, and my uniform and medals packed away, I rejoined Roz. We were a young, happy married couple. But we could find no other place to live but a rat-infested basement apartment in Bedford-Stuyvesant ("rat-infested" is not a figure of speech—there was that day I walked into the bathroom and saw a large rat scurry up the water pipe back into the ceiling).

I was back in the working class, but needing a job. I tried going back to the Brooklyn Navy Yard, but it was hateful work with none of the compensating features of that earlier time. I worked as a waiter, as a ditch-digger, as a brewery worker, and collected unemployment insurance in between jobs. (I can understand very well the feeling of veterans of the Vietnam War, who were *important* when soldiers, coming back home with no jobs, no prospects, and without the glow that surrounded the veterans of World War II—a diminishing of their selves.) In the meantime, our daughter, Myla, was born.

At the age of twenty-seven, with a second child on the way, I began college as a freshman at New York University, under the GI Bill of Rights. That gave me four years of free college education and $120 a month, so that with Roz working part-time, with Myla and Jeff in nursery, with me working a night shift after school, we could survive.

Whenever I hear that the government *must not* get involved in helping people, that this must be left to "private enterprise," I think of the GI Bill and its marvelous nonbureaucratic efficiency. There are certain necessities—housing, medical care, education—about which private enterprise gives not a hoot (supplying these to the poor is not profitable, and private enterprise won't act without *profit*).

Starting college coincided with a change in our lives: moving out of our miserable basement rooms into a low-income housing project in downtown Manhattan, on the East River. Four rooms, utilities included in the rent, no rats, no cockroaches, a few trees and a playground downstairs, a park along the river. We were happy.

While going to NYU and Columbia I worked the four-to-twelve shift in the basement of a Manhattan warehouse, loading heavy cartons of clothing onto trailer trucks which would carry them to cities all over the country.

We were an odd crew, we warehouse loaders—a black man, a Honduran immigrant, two men somewhat retarded mentally, another veteran of the war (married, with children, he sold his blood to supplement his small pay check). With us for a while was a young man named Jeff Lawson whose father was John Howard Lawson, a Hollywood writer, one of the Hollywood Ten. There was another young fellow, a Columbia College student who was named after his grandfather, the socialist labor leader Daniel DeLeon. (I encountered him many years later; he was in a bad way mentally, and then I got word that he had laid down under his car in the garage and breathed in enough carbon monoxide to kill himself.)

We were all members of the union (District 65), which had a reputation of being "left-wing." But we, the truck-loaders, were more left than the union, which seemed hesitant to interfere with the loading operation of this warehouse.

We were angry about our working conditions, having to load outside on the sidewalk in bad weather with no rain or snow gear available to us. We kept asking the company for gear, with no results. One night, late, the rain began pelting down. We stopped work, said we would not continue unless we had a binding promise of rain gear.

The supervisor was beside himself. That truck had to get out that night to meet the schedule, he told us. He had no authority to promise anything. We said, "Tough shit. We're not getting drenched for the damned schedule." He got on the phone, nervously called a company executive at his home, interrupting a dinner party. He came back from the phone. "Okay, you'll get your gear." The next workday we arrived at the warehouse and found a line of shiny new raincoats and rainhats.

That was my world for the first thirty-three years of my life—the world of unemployment and bad employment, of me and my wife leaving our two-and three-year-olds in the care of others while we went to school or to work, living most of that time in cramped and unpleasant places, hesitating to call the doctor when the children were sick because we couldn't afford to pay him, finally taking the children to hospital clinics where interns could take care of them. This is the way a large part of the population lives, even in this, the richest country in the world. And when, armed with the proper degrees, I began to move out of that world, becoming a college professor, I never forgot that. I never stopped being class-conscious.

I note how our political leaders step gingerly around such expressions, how it seems the worst accusation one politician can make about another is that "he appeals to class hostility...he is setting class against class." Well, class has been set against class in the realities of life for a very long time, and the words will disappear only when the realities of inequity disappear.

It would be foolish for me to claim that class consciousness was simply the result of growing up poor and living the life of a poor kid and then the life of a hard-pressed young husband and father. I've met many people with similar backgrounds who developed a very different set of ideas about society, and many others, whose early lives were much different from mine but whose world-view is similar.

When I was chair of the history department at Spelman and had the power (even a *little power* can make people heady!) to actually hire one or two people, I invited Staughton Lynd, a brilliant young historian, graduate of Harvard and Columbia, to join the Spelman faculty. (We were introduced at a historians' meeting in New York, where Staughton expressed a desire to teach at a black college.)

The summer before Staughton Lynd came south, we met in New England and decided to climb a New Hampshire mountain (Mt. Monadnock) together and get acquainted. My two children, Myla and Jeff, came with us. They were thirteen and eleven. When we reached the summit, tired and hungry, we found the remains of a pack of cigarettes, and the four of us—all nonsmokers, it is fair to say—sat down cross-legged and puffed silently, pretending we were characters in *Treasure of the Sierra Madre.*

That mountain-climbing conversation was illuminating. Straughton came from a background completely different from mine. His parents were quite famous professors at Columbia and Sarah Lawrence, Robert and Helen Lynd, authors of the sociological classic *Middletown.* Staughton had been raised in comfortable circumstances, had gone to Harvard and Columbia. And yet, as we went back and forth on every political issue under the sun—race, class, war, violence, nationalism, justice, fascism, capitalism, socialism, and more—it was clear that our social philosophies, our values, were extraordinarily similar.

In the light of such experiences, traditional dogmatic "class analysis" cannot remain intact. But as dogma disintegrates, hope appears. Because it seems that human beings, whatever their backgrounds, are more open than we think, that their behavior cannot be confidently predicted from their past, that we are all creatures vulnerable to new thoughts, new attitudes.

And while such vulnerability creates all sorts of possibilities, both good and bad, its very existence is exciting. It means that no human being should be written off, no change in thinking deemed impossible.

2

LaGuardia in
the Jazz Age

I had known Fiorello LaGuardia as the colorful mayor of New York during the Thirties. While looking for a subject for my doctoral dissertation at Columbia University, I was walking in downtown New York and happened to pass a rather decrepit building marked "Municipal Archives." I walked upstairs, asked what they had, and was told that LaGuardia's widow, Marie LaGuardia, had just deposited all his papers. Delving into the files of the 1920s, I discovered, to my delight, that LaGuardia, though a Republican, was the leading radical in Congress during the "Jazz Age." Indeed, once he ran on both Republican and Socialist tickets, and won. His Congressional career became the subject of my dissertation, which my adviser, Professor William Leuchtenburg of Columbia University, submitted to a committee of the American Historical Association. It was awarded a prize, which, I must confess, was named after Albert Beveridge, leading apologist in the U.S. Senate for American imperialism. It was then published by Cornell University Press as *La Guardia in Congress* in 1959. Out of that came this essay, which appeared first in my book *The Politics of History* (Beacon Press, 1970), and was reissued by Illinois University Press in 1990. The ideas for which LaGuardia fought, almost alone, in Congress in the Twenties and early Thirties—government responsibility for people in need, fundamental changes in the economic system—still remain relevant in our time.

There is an underside to every Age about which history does not often speak, because history is written from records left by the privileged. We learn about politics from the political leaders, about economics from the entrepreneurs, about slavery from the plantation owners, about the thinking of an age from its intellectual elite.

It is the victors who give names to the wars, and the satisfied who give labels to the ages. But what did the Crusades mean to the peasants who died in them, or the Renaissance to the vast majority who suffered while the Medicis financed art, or the Enlightenment to the unenlightened, or the Era of Good Feeling to the slaves in Virginia, or the Progressive Period to girls in the Lawrence textile mills, or the New Deal to blacks in Harlem?

Sometimes we search hard, and find the narratives of those in chains, or other bits and scraps of evidence showing all was not as we thought. And sometimes there are men or women on the border of their time or their class, who manage to save for us, by a great effort, the traces of what history tends to bury. Even then, we get only the faintest glimpse of what a war was to the wounded, or an epoch to the vast, silent numbers who populated it—like artifacts from a buried civilization, only hinting at what was endured.

In the United States, the twenties were the years of Prosperity, and Fiorello LaGuardia is one of its few public figures who suspected to what extent that label was a lie. The twenties were also, to later generations, a time of quiet isolation from foreign affairs. LaGuardia did not believe this. The twenties also became known as a time of national political consensus, when a general mood of well-being softened political combat. LaGuardia tried to speak for those left out of the consensus, those whose votes were tallied but whose condition was ignored.

Fiorello LaGuardia was elected to Congress in 1916, went off to fly on the Italian front for the American army, ran again successfully for

Congress in 1922. From then until 1933 he viewed the national scene from his seat in the House, and through the eyes of his constituents, looking out of their tenement windows in East Harlem.

From this vantage point, the "prosperity" of the twenties seemed a bitter joke; under the raucous cries of the Jazz Age, LaGuardia, listening closely, could hear the distinct sound of the blues. For many Americans, the high living of the twenties was only a spectacle seen from the cheap seats, and when they left the theater they went home, not to Babylon, but to what Robert and Helen Lynd have called "the long arm of the job." LaGuardia was one of a handful of men in Washington who recognized this fact, and acted upon it.

He set his stocky body and rasping voice against all the dominant political currents of his day. While the Klan membership soared into the millions, and nativists wrote their prejudices into the statute books, LaGuardia demanded the end of immigration restriction. When the marines were dispatched to make the Caribbean an American lake, LaGuardia demanded their recall. Above the jubilant message of the ticker tapes, LaGuardia tried to tell the nation about striking miners in Pennsylvania. As Democrats and Republicans lumbered like rehearsed wrestlers in the center of the political ring, LaGuardia stalked the front rows and bellowed for real action. He did not get it, but we need to listen for those echoes, to see what was then and still is undone, to look beneath the fogged membrane that hides the shame of our own age.

LaGuardia was born in a modest flat in Greenwich Village, of a Jewish mother from Trieste, and an Italian father who was a gifted musician, having come to America as arranger for the famous soprano Adelina Patti. His father joined the American army as bandmaster, and during the Spanish-American War died of food poisoning, one of the thousands of victims of the "embalmed beef" sold to the Quartermaster Corps by the big packinghouses. All his life, Fiorello LaGuardia would blame "profiteers" for his father's death.

He worked in the American consulates in Budapest and Fiume, then as an interpreter for immigrants on Ellis Island. He went to law school at night, walked the picket lines with striking garment workers in Manhattan and became attracted to the Progressive wing of the Republican party, surprising the machine men by his victory in 1916. In Congress, he introduced a bill (pigeonholed, as were virtually all his bills during his career) asking the death penalty for anyone selling inferior supplies to the armed forces in wartime. He denounced the Espionage Act of 1917 which forbade "scurrilous, abusive" criticism of the government. He fought to ease the tax burden on the poor, and urged that the national government regulate the food industry in peace as well as war. He supported World War I as meaning liberation for the millions of subjects of the Hapsburg Empire, and left Congress to fly bombing raids behind Austrian lines. But when the war ended and Wilson's "self-determination" was lost in the power struggles of the peace conferences, LaGuardia became bitter about the "war to make the world safe for democracy."

The Republican party kept trying to get LaGuardia out of the way, while using him to pick up immigrant votes. They eased him in as President of the New York City Board of Aldermen in 1920-21 (there were 100,000 Italian voters in New York City), but he became a political nuisance. He denounced the Republican legislature for ejecting five duly elected Socialist members, raged at the Republican governor for not restoring the five-cent fare, and went up to Albany to tell a cheering crowd of tenants demanding rent relief that he had come to the capitol "not to praise the landlord, but to bury him."

To get LaGuardia out of the way of a possible gubernatorial campaign in 1922, the Republican machine offered him the Congressional candidacy in East Harlem—a Jewish-Italian tenement district on the upper East Side of New York. He accepted and outlined his political philosophy for the New York *World*: "I stand for the Republicanism of Abraham Lincoln; and let me tell you that the average Republican leader east of the Mississippi doesn't know anything more about Abraham Lincoln than Henry Ford knows about the Talmud. I am a Progressive."

LaGuardia's Democratic opponent in the 1922 race was Herman Frank, whose backers grew desperate as polling time drew near, and sent out Rosh Hashonoh cards to every Jewish voter in the district, referring to "the Italian LaGuardia, who is a pronounced anti-Semite and Jew-hater," and appealing for support of Herman Frank, "a Jew with a Jewish heart."

LaGuardia was furious. He proceeded to dictate, in Yiddish, a letter which was distributed throughout the district, challenging Frank to debate the issues of the campaign, but in the Yiddish language. When Frank ignored this (he could not speak Yiddish) LaGuardia set out on a tour of the Jewish district, making three speeches in Yiddish. His opponent was seeking votes, LaGuardia asserted, on the ground that he was a Jew: "After all, is he looking for a job as a *schamas*, or does he want to be elected Congressman?" (A *schamas* is the caretaker of a synagogue.) LaGuardia won the election by 245 votes.

In Congress once again, LaGuardia continued to confound the Democrats, exasperate the Republicans, and confuse the Socialists. A New York Republican leader said of him: "He is no Republican at all. He is no more a Republican than the representatives of Soviet Russia are Republicans."

Aided by a small group of Congressmen from New York and Chicago, LaGuardia fought the mounting tide of nativism in the twenties. He denounced the drastic restriction of immigration, and particularly the "national origins" method of determining quotas which was designed to limit the number of immigrants from Southern and Eastern Europe. The floor of the House was the scene of bitter exchanges between the proponents of restriction and LaGuardia. "We have too many aliens in this country...we want more of the American stock," declared Elton Watkins of Oregon, "Education and environment do not fundamentally alter racial values," Michigan's Grant Hudson said. Tincher of Kansas drew loud applause by urging his colleagues to "think, act and do real Americanism" and warning that one day, if immigration continued as in the past, Congressmen would have to address the Speaker of the House "in Italian or some other language."

The restriction bills were "unscientific," LaGuardia retorted, the "result of narrow-mindedness and bigotry" and "inspired by influences who have a fixed obsession on Anglo-Saxon superiority." Angered by a reference to the "Italian bloc" from New York made by Kentucky's Fred Vinson, LaGuardia referred to the illiteracy of the Blue Ridge mountain folk. This drew a stirring response from another Kentuckian, who rose to his full height and declared that his constituents "suckle their Americanism and their patriotism from their mother's breast...and I resent the gentleman's insolent, infamous, contemptible slander against a great, honest, industrious, law-abiding, liberty-loving God-fearing, patriotic people."

Restriction became law, but the debate continued through the Twenties. LaGuardia exchanged arguments in a national magazine with a writer who insisted: "The time to gird our loins for battle is here and now," and cried for resistance against "the inroads of the degeneracy which arises from the mixture of unassimilable and disharmonic races." LaGuardia called the national origins plan "the creation of a narrow mind, nurtured by a hating heart." But the time was not right for his views. The Klan was never more powerful. (Vice-President Charles Dawes himself, as LaGuardia put it, had "praised them with faint damn.") The American Legion, the Harding, Coolidge, and Hoover administrations, and even "Progressives" from the Midwest like Norris and Borah and Johnson were on the other side. LaGuardia swam powerfully, but with increasing futility, against the nativist tidal wave of the Twenties.

LaGuardia's mightiest verbal barrages were to be aimed, however, at the myth of universal prosperity in the twenties. The riotous New Year celebrations that ushered in 1922 could barely be heard above the general din, for it was an era identified in terms of sound—the "Roaring Twenties," the "Jazz Age." The noise was, all agreed, simply the joyful gurgle of prosperity.*

Prosperity was real for substantial numbers of Americans.** Those who made more than two thousand dollars a year, 40 percent of all families, could buy a fair share, either in cash or on the installment plan, of the exciting new gadgets and machines crowding the show windows in every city and town. For the 305,000 people who received 15 percent of the total national income, there were more expensive autos, as well as jewels, furs, and endless amusements. Because spending is by its very nature a conspicuous activity, and because frolic is more newsworthy than a ten-hour day in a textile mill, the general aura of the Twenties—prosperity and well-being—was that given to it by its most economically active members.

Amid the general self-congratulation, however, amid the smug speeches of the business leaders, and the triumphant clatter of ticker-tape

---

* Part of it, however, was the sound of violence, which seems to scar every age of high living. F. Scott Fitzgerald wrote: "A classmate killed his wife and himself on Long Island, another tumbled 'accidentally' from a skyscraper in New York. One was killed in a speakeasy in Chicago; another was beaten to death in a speakeasy in New York and crawled home to the Princeton Club to die; still another had his skull crushed by a maniac's axe in an insane asylum where he was confined. These are not catastrophes that I went out of my way to look for—these were my friends; moreover, these things happened not during the depression but during the boom." From his article "Echoes of the Jazz Age," *Scribner's*, November 1931.

** Unemployment declined, 1921-27, from 4,270,000 to 2,055,000. Real wages rose. The number of prosperous farmers grew, so that by 1929, 25,000 farms had gross incomes over $20,000 a year. *Recent Social Trends: Report of the President's Research Committee on Social Trends*, McGraw-Hill, 1933, Vol. II, p. 820.

machines, millions of Americans worked all day in mines, factories, and on patches of rented or mortgaged land. In the evening they read the newspaper or listened to the not-yet-paid-for radio and looked forward to Saturday night, when they might hold their mouths under the national faucet for a few drops of the wild revelry that everyone spoke about. For the fact was that a large section of the American population was living sparely and precariously and, though not jobless and impoverished (as many would be a decade later), were shut out of the high, wild, and prosperous living that marked the upper half of the population.

After a detailed study of economic conditions in the twenties, George Soule concluded that while production and profits rocketed in bursts of happy speculation, "the American people did not all enjoy the ride." From 1919-28, productivity grew 40 percent, compared to a 26 percent rise in real earnings so that "business did not fully share its productive gains with earners and consumers by a combination of wage increases and price reduction." This led to a "tremendous growth of profits for the more fortunately situated sectors of business and for the big corporations that dominated them." From 1922-29, while real wages per capita in manufacturing advanced at a rate of 1.4 percent a year, common stockholders gained 16.4 percent a year.

The classic sociological study of the Twenties, that of Muncie, Indiana, in the Lynds' *Middletown*, shows graphically that ordinary working people did not share the prosperity of that time and went about their mundane lives day to day never free from "the long arm of the job." In Middletown, whose thirty thousand people lived much like people in the hundreds of other industrial towns scattered across the nation, there were two clearly defined groups: "the Working Class and the Business Class."

The Lynds reported: "As one prowls Middletown streets about six o'clock of a winter morning one notes two kinds of homes: the dark ones where the people still sleep, and the ones with a light in the kitchen where the adults of the household may be seen moving about, starting the business of the day." A speaker urging parents to help children by making a breakfast a "leisurely family reunion" did not realize that for two-thirds of the city's families "the father gets up in the dark in the winter, eats hastily in the kitchen in the gray dawn, and is at work from an hour to two and a quarter hours before his children have to be at school."

When some people looked behind the facade to catch a glimpse of suffering, their voices were either shouted down or ignored.*

Merle Curti wrote:

> It was, in fact, only the upper ten percent of the population that enjoyed a marked increase in real income. But the protests which such facts normally have evoked could not make themselves widely or effectively felt. This was in part the result of the grand strategy of the major political parties. In part it was the result of the fact that almost all the avenues to mass opinion were now controlled by large-scale publishing industries.

Not all voices were stilled. There were some too eloquent, too powerful, or simply too insistent to be ignored: Sinclair Lewis, Theodore Dreiser, John Dos Passos, H.L. Mencken, Oswald Garrison Villard, Lewis Mumford. They spoke to their generation with kindliness or with cynicism, with anger or with irony. They probed into the vitals of the social structure, sometimes crudely, sometimes delicately, but in any case deriding the cult of material wealth and the deification of orthodoxy.

And in Congress, a small group of Progressives and Socialists tried to jab at the conscience of their age. Among them the most vociferous, the most colorful, the most radical was Fiorello LaGuardia, the Congressman from East Harlem.

When the issue of extending the wartime rent controls rose, LaGuardia argued in Congress for the rights of tenants. Landlords had used college professors and legal experts to support their arguments, LaGuardia said:

> ...but gentlemen, with all of their experts, with all of their professors, with all of their legal talent, there is no argument that can prevail when a man with a weekly income and a family to support is compelled to pay out of his income such a large proportion that there is not sufficient left to properly care for and nourish his children. That is the condition in New York City; that is the condition in Washington, DC...

LaGuardia was aware that the farmer was getting little for his work, and the consumer was paying too much for his food. He told congress:

> Some of my friends sometimes refer to me as a radical. If by that they mean that I am seeking radical changes in the very conditions which brought

---

* F. Scott Fitzgerald wrote about this period: "It was borrowed time ... the whole upper tenth of a nation living with the insouciance of grand ducs and the casualness of chorus girls." *Op. cit*

about the disparity between the exorbitant retail prices of food and the starvation prices paid to the farmer, I am not at all shocked by being called a radical.... Something is radically wrong when a condition exists that permits the manipulation of prices, the creation of monopolies on food to the extent of driving the farmer off his farm by foreclosures and having thousands of underfed and ill-nourished children in the public schools of our cities.

What LaGuardia asked for was comprehensive legislation establishing national regulation of transportation, marketing, and money. "You have protected the dollar and disregarded the producers. You have protected property and forgotten the human being, with the result that we have legalized a cruel system of exploitation. Now we are approaching the time when a real change is necessary."

In early 1926, LaGuardia told the House about the rise in meat prices in New York City, and of his request for aid from the Department of Agriculture. "This is the help I got," he said, holding up a pamphlet on the economical use of meat. The Department had also sent him a pamphlet on "Lamb and Mutton and Their Uses in the Diet," despite the fact, he said, that 90 percent of the people in New York could not afford lamb chops.

"Why, I have right here with me..." LaGuardia said, and pulled out of his vest pocket a rather scrawny lamb chop. This had cost thirty cents in New York, he said. Then he reached into another pocket and pulled out a steak, saying: "There is $1.75 worth of steak." Then out of another pocket, a roast, commenting: "Now here is a roast—three dollars worth of roast. What working man's family can afford to pay three dollars for a roast that size?"

The cattle grazer, he noted, was getting two and one half to five cents a pound, while the consumer paid seventy-five to eighty cents a pound. This meant, he concluded, that the packinghouse monopolies were making unjustifiably large profits and could afford to cut prices substantially.

LaGuardia appeared on a dozen different sectors of the labor front throughout the Twenties, wherever he thought his voice could have some effect. He walked the picket line and then spoke at a Madison Square Garden meeting supporting the 1926 garment strike in New York, and several months later aided striking paper-box makers. He denounced the use of "kidnapped" Chinese strikebreakers to replace striking American sailors and attacked the Pullman Company for preventing the organization of twelve thousand Pullman porters. He fought for pay raises for government workers and even made the sports pages by denouncing "baseball slavery" and calling for the unionization of baseball players.

Testifying before the House Civil Service Committee, LaGuardia declared that women earning $1,200 a year in government service could not attend church on Sunday because they had to stay home to do their own washing. "They talk of Andrew Mellon being a great financier," he said, "Gentlemen, it is easy to play with hundreds of millions of dollars, but a woman who can keep her family clean and decent on $1,200 a year is a real financier."

When anthracite miners in eastern Pennsylvania went on strike in August 1925, LaGuardia called for government ownership of the mines:

> There seems to be one solution only. This country is blessed with a rich supply of coal. It is not the invention of any one man, it is God's gift to the people of America. It requires human labor to dig the coal, bring it back from the bowels of the earth so it may be used for the benefit of mankind. The American people all have an interest in this coal. The government should...take such actions as eventually will put the government in possession of the gift of God that surely was intended to be used for the benefit of all American people.

Two years later, when another strike, this time against a series of wage cuts, tied up the Pennsylvania coal fields, LaGuardia visited the strike area. He interviewed strikers, their wives, and children, and his anger reached the boiling point. Once again he saw the labor injunction in action when a group of men and women were arrested by state police for mass picketing in violation of a federal court injunction. He watched children hide under their beds in miners' shacks because the day before strikebreakers had poured volley after volley of bullets through the windows of the school at Broughton just before 350 children were to be dismissed. He told newspapermen:

> I have never seen such thought-out, deliberate cruelty in my life as that displayed against the unfortunate strikers by the coal operators and their army of coal and iron police. Imagine, gentlemen, a private army, with its private jail, where the miners are unlawfully detained and viciously assaulted!... I have been preaching Americanism as I understand it, where justice and freedom and law and order prevail, but these miners and their families don't

even get a shadow of it.... Asbestos will not hold the statements I shall make on the floor of the House.

Throughout the decade, LaGuardia clashed with the seventy-year-old Secretary of the Treasury, Andrew W. Mellon, the man described by Wiliam Allen White as the "guardian angel of all that the Chamber of Commerce held sacred in its white marble palace." The vast Mellon empire included coal, coke, gas, oil, and aluminum. "No other Croesus," a biographer of Mellon wrote, "had levied toll on so many articles and services." War contracts boosted the already considerable Mellon fortune, which one day would reach two billion dollars. One hundred Mellon companies were connected through a two hundred and fifty million-dollar banking institution, Union Trust.

Mellon's various tax proposals in the Twenties had one basic theme: to lower taxes on high incomes. For instance, his first report to Congress, in 1921, recommended tax cuts, but only on incomes over $66,000 a year. Attacked by Bob LaFollette of Wisconsin, Mellon replied:

> Any man of energy and initiative in this country can get what he wants out of life. But when that initiative is crippled by a tax system which denied him the right to receive a reasonable share of his earnings, then he will no longer exert himself, and the country will be deprived of the energy on which its continued greatness depends.

LaGuardia fought the Mellon Plan in Congress. When a stenographer wrote to him in complaint, he replied: "I readily understand your anxiety and that of your co-workers on the taxes over $200,000 a year. I was a stenographer once and I remember how much I had to worry about my income over $200,000 a year."

Despite LaGuardia and a few others, the Mellon principles won out in the tax bills passed by Congress, and the business community celebrated. The president of Columbia University, Nicholas Murray Butler wrote happily to a Republican leader: "I am just back from Pittsburgh where on Saturday night there took place at the Chamber of Commerce dinner the most magnificent demonstration in favor of Secretary Mellon that is possible to imagine.... It was really a great occasion."

The nation's economic nationalism—its insistence on war debt payments and towering tariff barriers—was a reflection, not of isolationism, but of an intervention in world affairs based on cash returns rather than democratic ideals. The State Department, throughout the Twenties, exercised strong influence on private loans to other nations, partly in order to ensure political "stability" in certain areas like the Caribbean. Herbert Feis writes that in this period: "We acted as banker to the whole needy world. Private capital provided the funds. But the American Government concerned itself with the lending operations."

Despite the Wilsonian cry for self-determination in the peace treaties, the United States was established as a dominant power in the Caribbean, having purchased the Virgin Islands during the war, possessing a naval base in Cuba, and exercising such control over the Republic of Panama, Nicaragua, Haiti, and the Dominican Republic as to make them "virtual protectorates." Furthermore, American influence in the Far East extended from the Aleutian Islands to Hawaii and across the western Pacific to the Philippines.

The United States was cautious about the League of Nations, but at the same time the Coolidge Administration was acting with force and determination to protect American investments and political power in the Caribbean area. By 1924 the finances of half of the twenty Latin American States were being directed to some extent by the United States. When other tactics did not work, marines were dispatched—to Haiti, the Dominican Republic, and Nicaragua. The realities did not match Coolidge's promise in his inaugural address: "America seeks no earthly empire built on blood and force.... The legions which she sends forth are armed, not with the sword, but with the cross."

Nicaragua was a vivid example of marine diplomacy at work. Her proximity to Panama, and the ever-present possibility of a trans-Nicaraguan canal, gave Nicaragua a special place in the plans of the State Department, while fruit and lumber investments gave American private business groups a sphere of interest there. Ever since 1909, when a United States-aided revolution had overthrown the Liberal Zelaya government, a pattern of Yankee intervention was established, with bank credits and marines standing guard alternately over shaky conservative governments.[*]

---

[*] Elihu Root said in 1915 that "the present government with which we are making this treaty is really maintained in office by the presence of the United States marines in Nicaragua." Council on Foreign Relations, *Survey of American Foreign Relations,* 1929, pp. 167-197.

On January 8, 1927, American marines were ordered to station themselves in Fort Loma, commanding the Nicaraguan capital, and two days later Coolidge sent a special message to Congress, saying:*

> I am sure it is not the desire of the United States to intervene in the internal affairs of Nicaragua or of any other Central American republic. Nevertheless, it must be said, that we have a very definite and special interest in the maintenance of order and good government in Nicaragua at the present time.

In the next six weeks, five thousand United States troops landed, and the United States gave the Nicaraguan government three thousand rifles, two hundred machine guns, and three million rounds of ammunition. Later, the State Department said:

> In entering into the transaction the United States government followed its customary policy of lending encouragement and moral support to constitutional governments beset by revolutionary movements intended to overthrow the established order. Secretary of State Frank Kellogg explained to the Senate Foreign Relations Committee that the threat of Communist influences in Nicaragua had brought on American intervention.

LaGuardia, asked to comment on Kellogg's statement, called it "aldermanic stuff." There was no proof of Communist activity in Nicaragua, he said, adding : "The protection of American life and property in Nicaragua does not require the formidable naval and marine forces operating there now. Give me fifty New York cops and I can guarantee full protection."

LaGuardia wrote a constituent that Kellogg, back in November, had planted the story of Communist activities in the press by asking various wire services to print such a story. The Associated Press had complied. When LaGuardia made this accusation publicly, the State Department denied it, and when LaGuardia said that he had conferred with Kellogg and had gotten the impression that no forces would be sent to Nicaragua, Kellogg denied the conference had taken place.

In April 1927, Coolidge, harassed by a nationwide barrage of criticism, ordered Colonel Henry L. Stimson to negotiate peace between the

---

* Ruhl J. Bartlett, *The Record of American Diplomacy*, p. 546. Graham H. Stuart, *Latin America and the United States*, Appleton-Century-Crofts. 1955, says: "The first landing of troops was declared to be solely for the protection of American lives and property, but there was little evidence that American lives and property were in jeopardy." p. 332.

rival factions in Nicaragua. Stimson reported later how he met rebel leader Moncada under "a large black thorn tree" and in thirty minutes reached an agreement on peace terms. This included American supervision of elections to be held in 1929, the appointment of Liberal governors in six of the country's thirteen departments, and the maintenance of marines in Nicaragua.*

LaGuardia kept up a constant stream of criticism. He wrote to Kellogg: "Permit me to state, Mr. Secretary, that universal suffrage and the secret ballot are absolutely inconsistent with uniformed marines and fixed bayonets. The two cannot be harmonized."

Stimson, on the other hand, felt that the United States had "no cause to be ashamed" of its effort "to do an unselfish service to a weak and sorely beset Central American State." His argument that the United States had not transgressed upon Nicaraguan sovereignty was based on his belief that every step taken was upon the request of the Nicaraguan government.

The arguments of the Twenties in connection with Nicaragua could be transplanted easily to the Sixties in connection with Vietnam. So could the arguments on poverty, prices, taxation made in that era be transferred to our own. If there is a persistence of policy and rhetoric in American history from that decade to this one (and beyond) we are helped to find it by those few who, like LaGuardia, dug beneath the surface and held up to public view that which had been hidden. This suggests, perhaps, what people with energy, with voices, sensing the suffering beneath the smugness of their age, might do in any time.

---

* Moncada's concession was born of a sense of futility in the face of overwhelming power. He said at the time of his acceptance: "I am not inhuman.... I cannot advise the nation to shed all its patriotic blood for our liberty, because in spite of this new sacrifice, this liberty would succumb before infinitely greater forces and the country would sink more deeply within the claws of the North American eagle." Council on Foreign Relations, op. cit., p. 195.

3

The
Wobbly
Spirit

I had become conscious, in the Southern movement for equal rights in the early Sixties, how much the struggles of ordinary people were ignored in the recording of history. So, when *The Nation* asked me, in the spring of 1965, to review Joyce L. Kornbluh's book *Rebel Voices: An IWW Anthology*, I happily agreed, realizing how little the general public knew of that extraordinary moment in American history when the Industrial Workers of the World were on the scene. The review appeared in the April 5, 1965 issue, under the title *The Wobbly Spirit*.

Do we see small signs these days—Selma, Berkeley, and who knows where tomorrow—of the Wobbly spirit, still alive? There is a stirring among the young, and talk of a "new radicalism." The timing could hardly be better then, for the publication of *Rebel Voices*.

This is a large, handsome, blazing-red book in which Joyce Kornbluh has assembled a treasury of articles, songs, poems, cartoons and photographs, from the Labadie Collection of IWW documents at the

University of Michigan. Those who at some point in their lives have been excited by the story of the Wobblies, and wished it might somehow be kept alive for the new generation, will be grateful to Mrs. Kornbluh for her work.

She introduces the collection with a description of a Chicago meeting hall one June morning in 1905, when the thirty-six-year-old former cowboy and miner, "Big Bill" Haywood, walked to the front, picked up a piece of loose board, hammered on the table for silence, and called out:

> Fellow Workers: This is the Continental Congress of the Working Class. We are here to confederate the workers of this country into a working-class movement in possession of the economic powers, the means of life, in control of the machinery of production and distribution without regard to capitalist masters.

On the speakers' platform with Haywood were two of the great figures of American radicalism: white-haired Mother Jones, the seventy-five-year-old organizer for the United Mine Workers of America; and Eugene Debs, leader of the Socialist Party. Also at the meeting was the sharp-tongued polemicist of the Socialist Labor Party, Daniel DeLeon; the renegade Catholic priest, black-bearded Father Hagerty; and Lucy Parsons, widow of the Haymarket Affair martyr, Albert Parsons. That day, the Industrial Workers of the World was formed, and for the next decade (until it was crushed in the repression of the war to make the world safe for democracy) gave the nation its first close look at a revolutionary movement.

In those years, the permanent characteristics of the United States in the twentieth century were being hardened. There was the growing power of giant corporations (United States Steel had been formed in 1901). A minority of the nation's workers were organized into an exclusive trade union with conservative leadership (the A.F. of L., under Samuel Gompers, had almost two million members). And this era saw the inauguration of benign governmental regulation of business, supported by a new consensus of businessmen, Presidents, and reformers, which traditional historians have called "the Progressive Era," but which Gabriel Kolko (in his book *The Triumph of Conservatism*) terms "political capitalism." In retrospect, the IWW appears to have been a desperate attempt to disrupt this structure before its rivets turned cold.

The IWW played for keeps. Where the A.F. of L. called for "a fair day's wage for a fair day's work," the Wobblies wrote, in the preamble to their constitution:

> The working class and the employing class have nothing in common. There can he no peace so long as hunger and want are found among millions of working people and the few, who make up the employing class, have all the good things of life. Between these two classes, a struggle must go on until the workers of the world organize as a class, take possession of the earth and the machinery of production, and abolish the wage system.

Against the craft union concept (what they called "The American Separation of Labor") the IWW set as their goal: "One Big Union," and in each industry organized the skilled and unskilled, foreign-born and native Americans, Negroes and whites, women and men. They were fiercely militant, opposed to contracts with employers, unyielding in retaining the right to strike at all times. They were suspicious of politics for, as Father Hagerty put it, "Dropping pieces of paper into a hole in a box never did achieve emancipation of the working class.... "The abolition of capitalism would come, they believed through a series of general strikes, after which workers would run the industries themselves. "By organizing industrially we are forming the structure of the new society within the shell of the old."

The IWW never gained a mass membership as did the A.F. of L. At its peak, it probably had 60,000 members: miners, lumberjacks, construction workers and migratory farm hands, with pockets of influence among steel and textile workers. But it shook up the nation as had no other organization of its time.

The Wobblies engaged in dozens of "free-speech fights" in places like Missoula, Montana and Spokane, Washington, to establish their right to speak on street corners to working people. *Rebel Voices* contains some of the eyewitness reports that came out of those campaigns. In Spokane, arrested one by one for mounting a soapbox, IWW men kept pouring into town, until 600 of them were crowded into the jails, and finally the city officials, after several deaths from brutal treatment in prison, gave in to the demand for free speech and assembly.

In 1912 and 1913, the strikes organized by the IWW reached a crescendo: lumbermen in Aberdeen, Washington, streetcar workers in

Portland, Oregon, dock workers in San Pedro, California. The high point of IWW organizing activity, and its greatest victory, came in the 1912 strike of textile workers in Lawrence, Massachusetts. *Rebel Voices* records the account of a strike meeting by journalist Ray Stannard Baker:

> It is the first strike I ever saw which sang. I shall not soon forget the curious lift, the strange sudden fire of the mingled nationalities at the strike meetings when they broke into the universal language of song...

The Lawrence textile strike lasted ten weeks, involved 25,000 men, women and children, and was watched with mounting tension by the entire nation. Paul Brissenden, in his classic history of the IWW, wrote: "Lawrence was not an ordinary strike. It was a social revolution. The section of *Rebel Voices* dealing with Lawrence is one of its best. There are the cartoons (a giant policeman raising a club over huddled women and children), photographs (a portrait of poet Arturo Giovanitti, IWW organizer in Lawrence), and page after page of personal recollections. A woman observer testified about what happened at the railroad station, where 150 strikers' children were preparing to leave, to stay with families in Philadelphia who had promised them shelter and food for the duration of the strike:

> When the time came to depart, the children, arranged in a long line, two by two... were about to make their way to the train when the police...closed in on us with their clubs, beating right and left.... The mothers and the children were thus hurled in a mass and bodily dragged to a military truck and even then clubbed...

There is the account of the strike by a fifteen-year-old textile worker in Lawrence, named Fred Beal:

> ...two Italian spinners came to me with a long white paper: *The Following People Working in the Spinning Room Will Go on Strike Friday, January 12 If Wages Are Cut.* Queenie read it over my shoulder "Don't sign it, Lobster," she cautioned. "Those wops'll get you in trouble."...But I signed it. So did Gyp and Lefty Louie.

There is the testimony before the Congressional committee investigating the Lawrence strike, by teen-ager Camella Teoli:

> Well, I used to go to school, and then a man came up to my house and asked my father why I didn't go to work, so my father says I don't know

whether she is 13 or 14 years old. So the man says you give me $4 and I will make the papers come from the old country saying you are 14. So my father gave him the $4 and in one month came the papers that I was 14. I went to work...

A parade of fascinating figures and historic events marches through the pages of *Rebel Voices*: the young, dark-haired Irish IWW organizer in Lawrence, Elizabeth Gurley Flynn; the pageant put on by John Reed at Madison Square Garden for the Paterson textile strikers of 1913; the songs of Joe Hill, the story of his death, and his last cry, "Don't mourn. Organize!" There are the lumberjacks and miners and harvest stiffs. Finally, there are the attacks on the IWW by the government after the nation went to war in 1917.

In 1914, the IWW had declared: "We as members of the industrial army will refuse to fight for any purpose except the realization of industrial freedom." A Wobbly orator said: "In the broad sense, there is no such thing as a foreigner. We are all native-born members of this planet.... We ought to have in the place of national patriotism, a broader concept—that of international solidarity." The IWW refused to call off strikes because the nation was at war, and a Tulsa, Oklahoma, newspaper wrote:

The first step in the whipping of Germany is to strangle the IWWs. Kill them, just as you would kill any other kind of a snake.... It is no time to waste money on trials.... All that is necessary is evidence and a firing squad.

The year 1918 brought mass arrests and mass trials of IWW members charged with interfering with the war effort in various ways. Judge Kenesaw Mountain Landis tried a hundred Wobblies in Chicago, and John Reed wrote: "Small on the huge bench sits a wasted man with untidy white hair, an emaciated face in which two burning eyes are set like jewels, parchment skin split by a crack for a mouth; the face of Andrew Jackson three years dead."

The Wobblies went to prison. Big Bill Haywood jumped bail and sailed to Russia, where he died in 1928. After the war was over, the IWW was not the same.. A photo in *Rebel Voices* speaks eloquently: it shows the shambles made of IWW headquarters in New York City, after a raid by federal agents in 1919.

Today, the Wobblies live, not so much in the embers of that once fiery organization but in the people whose lives they changed. They live also in that special way in which art and literature keep the past alive—in Mrs. Kornbluh's book, or in the autobiographies of Bill Haywood, Mother Jones, Ralph Chaplin, and in Wallace Stegner's novel *The Preacher and the Slave.* But when will some audacious American film maker match the Italian production *The Organizer* with a motion picture on the Lawrence textile strike of 1912, or the Ludlow, Colorado, massacre of 1914?

Half a century separates the IWW from the militant wing of the civil rights movement today, but the parallels are striking. One might see a sharp contrast in the attitudes toward violence, yet the popular image of the dynamite-carrying Wobbly was overdrawn. The IWW emphasis was on self-defense; the Wobblies' big weapons were the withholding of their labor, the power of their voices. Even their "sabotage" meant mostly slowing down on the job. Consider the other characteristics, however: the plunging into areas of maximum danger; the impatience with compromises and gradualist solutions; the deep suspicion of politics (even in the midst of so imaginative a use of politics as the Freedom Democratic Party); the emphasis on direct, militant, mass action; the establishment of pieces of the new world within the old (the Freedom Schools etc.); the migrant, shabby existence of the organizer (DeLeon reprimanded the Wobblies for their "bummery," their overalls and red neckerchiefs); the songs and humor; the dream of a new brotherhood.

Somehow, time and circumstance (or is it a feeling of security?) make the Wobblies and the Molly Maguires more palatable today to the country at large. Would those who think romantically of them now have befriended them in the days when they were hated and hunted? It does not hurt to suggest that historical perspective often shines a kindly light on those who disregard some of the proprieties of respectable liberalism in their passionate sweep toward justice. *Rebel Voices* provides such a reminder.

4

The Ludlow Massacre

There was not a word in any of the history texts or history courses I had, either as an undergraduate or a graduate student, about the Colorado Coal Strike of 1913-14. That extraordinary episode came to my attention in two ways, first in a song by Woodie Guthrie called "The Ludlow Massacre," then in a chapter of the book by Samuel Yellen, *American Labor Struggles*, written in 1936. I became fascinated with the event, went through five thick volumes of congressional reports and whatever else I could find, made it the subject of my Masters Essay at Columbia University, and later wrote this essay for my book *The Politics of History*.

In their scholarly history of the labor movement, we find this terse statement by Selig Perlman and Philip Taft: "On April 20, 1914, the Colorado coal strike was brought to the attention of the entire country by the gruesome burning of eleven children and two women in the Ludlow tent colony."

The event they describe became known as the Ludlow Massacre. it was the culminating act of perhaps the most violent struggle between corporate power and laboring men in American history.

I recall it now, but not for its dramatic particulars, which might, in their uniqueness, be seen as a set of events happily submerged in the new welfare state. Rather, I find in it a set of suggestions about the relations between people and government which, stripped of their particularity, are still alive (so that, in place of miners, we might see blacks; in place of unions we might see student movements or welfare rights organizations). I find, from 1914 to 1969, a continuity of governmental behavior which is easily forgotten if one is distracted by the intricately embroidered veil of words and gestures, or by the specificities of the Colorado countryside: the mining canyons, the strange and unrepeatable sounds, colors, tones, of that time, that place.

I would point to several elements in that continuity, and let the reader judge, from the facts of the Colorado events, from what we know of contemporary America, whether I am concluding too much from too little:

1. The firm connection between entrenched wealth and political power, manifested in the decisions of government, and in the machinery of law and justice.

2. The team play of the federal system, in which crass action by local police on behalf of the rich and powerful is modified—especially after resistance develops—with a more masked but still biased intervention by the national government.

3. The selective control of violence, in which government power is fumbling and incompetent in dealing with corporate and local police violence, sure and efficient in dealing with the violence of protest movements.

4. The somewhat different style of the national government (without difference in substance) in dealing with those outside its bounds who are helpless to resist and impotent as an internal political force—that is, with foreigners (Mexico, 1914; Dominican Republic, 1965). The style there is more like a local police force dealing with the locally powerless.

5. The opiate effect of commissions and investigations.

But let us turn to Colorado, 1913-14.

Formed under the enormous weight of the Rockies, soft coal was found in Southern Colorado not long after the Civil War. Railroads moved south from Denver, north from New Mexico. Settlers, coming down the old Santa Fe trail, converged on the banks of the Purgatory River, just east of the Rockies and about fifteen miles north of the New Mexican border, and built the town of Trinidad. The great Colorado Fuel and Iron Corporation, along with smaller companies, sank shafts into the hillsides, advertised for immigrant labor, and lowered workers into the earth to remove the coal.

In 1902, Colorado Fuel and Iron was purchased by John D. Rockefeller. Then, in 1911, he turned his interests (about 40 percent of the stock, more than enough to control) over to his son, John D. Rockefeller, Jr., who made major policy decisions from his office at 26 Broadway in New York City.

Two hundred and fifty feet, three hundred, four hundred feet below the surface—in blackness so complete it seemed alive, grotesque— men hacked away at the face of the coal seam with hand picks. Their helpers shoveled the coal into waiting railroad cars, which were drawn through tunnels by mules to the main shaft, and lifted to the surface to the top of the tipple, the coal then showering down through the sorting screens onto flat cars. The average coal seam was about three feet high, so the miner worked on his knees or on his side. The ventilation system depended on the manipulation of tunnel doors by "trapper boys"—often thirteen or fourteen-year-old children being initiated into mining.

At the edge of the mountains, in steep-walled canyons, were the camps where the miners lived, in sagging, wooden huts, with old newspapers nailed to the walls to keep out the cold. Nearby were the mine buildings and the coke ovens. with clouds of soot clogging the air. Behind the huts was a sluggish creek, dirty-yellow, laden with mine slag and camp refuse, alongside which the children played.

The mining camps were feudal kingdoms run by the coal corporation, which made the laws; curfews were imposed, suspicious strangers were not allowed to visit the homes, the company store must be patronized, the company doctor used. The laws were enforced by company-appointed marshals. The teachers and preachers were picked by the company. By 1914, Colorado Fuel and Iron owned twenty-seven mining camps, and all the land, the houses, the saloons, the schools, the churches, the stores. Company superintendents, in charge of the camps, were described once by a corporation employee as "uncouth, ignorant, immoral, and in many instances the most brutal set of men... Blasphemous bullies."*

At first the miners were Welshmen and Englishmen, who had gained experience in their home countries. But in the 1880s and 1890s, the new immigration brought Italians, Greeks, Poles, Hungarians. There were many Mexicans and Negroes.**

Colorado Fuel and Iron became unmistakably the major political force in Colorado. A letter from C.F. & I. Superintendent Bowers to the secretary of John D. Rockefeller, Jr., written in May 1913, summed up the situation:***

> The Colorado Fuel & Iron Company for many years were accused of being the political dictator of southern Colorado, and in fact were a mighty power in the whole state. When I came here it was said that the C.F. & I. Co. voted every man and woman in their employ without regard to their being naturalized or not; and even their mules, it used to be remarked, were registered, if they were fortunate enough to possess names.

Bowers told Rockefeller that the company, in the 1904 election campaign, had contributed $80,605, and that it "became notorious in many sections for their support of the liquor interests. They established saloons everywhere they possibly could." A sheriff elected with company support became a partner in sixteen liquor stores in the mining camps.

Apparently, Bowers' entrance onto this scene did not change the situation. Company officials continued to be appointed as election judges. Company-dominated coroners and judges prevented injured employees from collecting damages. Polling places were often on company property. In Las Animas County, John C. Baldwin, a gambler, bar-

---

* Statement by Rev. Eugene S. Gaddis, Superintendent of the Sociological Department of the Colorado Fuel and Iron Corporation during the strike, to the U.S. Commission on Industrial Relations, May 19, 1915. For descriptions of life in the mining camps see George Korson, *Coal Dust on the Fiddle*, Folklore, 1965, also McAlister Coleman, *Men and Coal*, Farrar & Rinehart, 1943.

** In 1901, out of 7500 employees of C.F. & I., 500 were Negroes. Sterling Spero and Abram Harris, *The Black Worker*, Atheneum, 1968.

*** George P. West, *Report on the Colorado Strike*, Government Printing Office, 1915, p. 46. This is the official summary of the report of the Commission on Industrial Relations.

tender, and friend of Colorado Fuel and Iron, was jury foreman in 80 percent of the county cases. During the strike, Governor Ammons was questioned about civil liberties in the state of which he was chief executive, and his interviewer, Rev. Atkinson, reported this exchange:

> Rev. Atkinson: Have you no constitutional law and government in Colorado?
> Gov. Ammons: Not a bit in those counties where the coal mines are located.
> Rev. Atkinson: Do you mean to say that in large sections of your state there is no constitutional liberty?
> Gov. Ammons: Absolutely none.

One Colorado official told the House Committee investigating the strike: "It's very seldom you can convict anyone in Huerfano County if he's got any friends. Jeff Farr, the sheriff, selects the jury and they're picked to convict or acquit as the case may be."

In early 1913, the United Mine Workers, which had unsuccessfully led a strike in the southern Colorado coal fields ten years before, began another organizing drive. It asked the mine operators to negotiate. The operators refused and hired the Baldwin-Felts Detective Agency. The governor sent his deputy labor commissioner to Trinidad to investigate what seemed a growing tension. Hundreds of deputies were sworn in by the sheriffs of Las Animas and Huerfano Counties.

On the evening of August 16, 1913, a young United Mine Workers organizer names Gerald Lippiatt arrived in Trinidad by train, walked down the main street through a Saturday night crowd, exchanged angry words with two Baldwin-Felts detectives who had recently been deputized, and was shot to death.

The two detectives, George Belcher and Walter Belk, were released on $10,000 bond, while a coroner's jury was formed. On it were six Trinidad men: the manager of the Wells Fargo Express company, the cashier of the Trinidad National Bank, the president of the Sherman-Cosmer Mercantile Company, the manager of the Columbia Hotel, the proprietor of a chain of mercantile stores, and John C. Baldwin, gambler and saloonkeeper, who acted as foreman.

There were conflicting reports to the jury on who fired first, how many shots were fired, and what was said between Lippiatt and the detectives. The only details on which all witnesses agreed was that Lippiatt walked down the street, encountered Belcher and Belk, exchanged gun-fire with Belcher, and was killed. The first man to reach Lippiatt, a miner named William Daselli, said Belk reached for his gun, Belcher pulled his gun and fired, and Lippiatt fell, fired from the ground, wounding Belcher in the thigh, then fell for the last time. When Daselli raised Lippiatt's head, he said, Belk's gun was still trained on him.*

The jury's verdict was: justifiable homicide.

The pace of union organizing in the mining canyons now quick-ened. Secret meetings were held, in churches, at picnics, in abandoned mine workings hidden in the mountains. A convention was called for mid-September in Trinidad, and delegates were elected at hundreds of meetings.

Meanwhile, the Baldwin-Felts Agency was importing hundreds of men, from the saloons and barrrelhouses of Denver, and from points out-side the state, to help break the impending strike. In Huerfano County, by September 1, 326 men were deputized by Sheriff Jeff Farr, all armed and paid by the coal companies.

The miners' convention, with 280 delegates, opened in the Great Opera House of Trinidad. For two days, rank-and-file miners registered their complaints: that they were robbed of from 400-800 pounds on each ton of coal, that they were paid in scrip worth ninety cents on the dollar (a violation of Colorado law), that the eight-hour law was not observed, that the law allowing miners to elect checkweighmen of their own choice was completely ignored, that their wages could only be spent in compa-ny stores and saloons (where prices were 25-40 percent higher), that they were forced to vote according to the wishes of the mine superintendent, that they were beaten and discharged for voicing complaints, that the armed mine guards conducted a reign of terror which kept the miners in subjection to the company. Their average daily wage was $1.68 for eight hours, $2.10 for ten hours. Casualty rates were twice as high in Colorado as in other mining states.

The high point of the Trinidad convention was the appearance of Mary Jones (the fabled Mother Jones), eighty-year-old organizer for the United Mine Workers, just back from a bitterly fought strike in the coal

* Accounts of the shooting are found in the *United Mine Workers Journal* for August 21 and August 28, 1913. Also in Michael Beshoar, *Out of the Depths*, Golden Bell, Denver, 1957 (a biography of strike leader John Lawson).

fields of West Virginia. Mother Jones represented a radical view (she had been one of the founders of the IWW) inside the rather conservative United Mine Workers (which had, for instance, supported Governor Ammons and the Democratic Party in 1912 against Progressive and Socialist candidates).* Mother Jones' speech deserves to be quoted at length:

The question that arises today in the nation is an industrial oligarchy.... What would the coal in these mines and in these hills be worth unless you put your strength and muscle in to bring them?

I went into the state of West Virginia.... There I saw women that had been beaten to death and a babe of the coming generation was beaten to death and murdered by the Baldwin-Felts thugs in the womb of her mother. That is in America, my friends, and I said, "I will never leave the state until the Baldwin thugs leave too" and I didn't...

Three thousand men assembled in Charlestown and we marched up with banners, with demands upon those banners, and we walked into the state house grounds, for they are ours, and we have a right to take possession of them if we want to... I called a committee and I said, "Here, take this document into the governor's office and present it to him. Now don't get on your knees. We have got no kings in America. Stand on both your feet with your head erect," said I, and present that document to the governor, and they said "Will we wait?" and I said, "No, don't wait, and don't say your honor," said I, because very few of those fellows have any honor...

And there was that meeting. I would give the United States Treasury if I had it, boys, if there had been someone there with a pen who grasped the sociology of that meeting—he would have paralyzed the world with it.... Men came from the mountains with toes out of their shoes, with stomachs empty.... Fifteen hundred men came there, the militia was there, the Baldwin thugs came there.... When I was about to close the meeting I said, "Boys, let Mother tell you one thing." And they said, "What, Mother?" And I said, "Liberty is not dead, she is only quietly resting, waiting only for you to call" and that voice of fifteen hundred men rang the air, reached to Heaven, and they said, "Oh God, Mother, call her, call her now!"

Sure we'll get in the bullpen. There is nothing about that. I was in jail. God Almighty, what if you do, you build the jail! I was jailed...and tried in Federal court and the old judge said, "Did you read my injunction?" I said I did. "Did you notice that that injunction told you not to look at the mines and did you look at them?" "Certainly," I said. "Why did you do it?" the judge said. "Because there was a judge bigger than you, and he gave me my eyesight, and I am going to look at whatever I want to."

---

* Michael Beshoar wrote: "John Lawson and his miners were naive on the subject of politics. They invariably regarded the Democratic Party as the champion of the downtrodden, a position that could not have been sustained had they had the experience to draw obvious conclusions from the party's record in the state" (*Out of the Depths*). Beshoar was a grandson of Dr. Michael Beshoar, a physician friendly to the miners in early Colorado history.

A lickspittle of the court comes up, and he says, "You must say your Honor, this is the court, His Honor on the bench." Yes, that was His Honor on the bench, the fellow behind the counter with the mustache... You have collected more wealth, created more wealth, than they in a thousand years of the Roman Republic, and yet you have not any...

When I get Colorado, Kansas, and Alabama organized, I will tell God Almighty to take me to my rest. But not before then!

The convention, rebuffed by the company again on requests to negotiate, voted to call a strike for September 23, 1913.

On that day, an epic scene took place in the coal districts of Southern Colorado. Eleven thousand miners, about 90 percent of the workers in the mines, gathered their families and their belongings on carts and mules and on their backs, and marched out of the mining camps to tent colonies set up in the countryside by the union.* One observer wrote:

All the tents had not yet arrived and the elements seemed to be in league with the operators. For two days it rained and snowed. There was never a more pitiful sight than the exodus of those miners fortunate enough to get wagons for their household goods. It rained all day Tuesday, and there streamed into Trinidad from every road miners with their wives and kids, crowded up on top of pitifully few household things.

Mother Jones testified later that twenty-eight wagonloads of personal belongings came into the Ludlow tent colony that day, on roads deep in mud, with the horses weary, and mothers carrying tiny babies in their arms. Tents and mattresses were wet, and the children had to sleep on those mattresses that night.

The largest of the tent colonies was at Ludlow, a railroad depot eighteen miles north of Trinidad, on a direct line to Walsenburg, at the edge of Colorado Fuel and Iron property. There were four hundred tents here, for a thousand people, including 271 children. In the course of the strike, twenty-one babies were born in this colony. Later a National Guard officer, reporting to the governor, said of the Ludlow colony: "The colony numbered hundreds of people of whom only a few families were Americans. The rest were for the most part Greeks, Montenegrins, Bulgars, Servians, Italians, Mexicans, Tyroleans, Croatians, Austrians,

---

* President Welborn of C.F. & I. estimated 70 percent of C.F. & I. struck. West, *Report on the Colorado Strike*.

Savoyards, and other aliens from the Southern countries of Europe."*

Violence began immediately. The Baldwin-Felts Agency constructed a special auto, steel-armored, with a Gatling gun mounted on top, which became known as the Death Special. It roamed the countryside, and on October 17, attacked the tent colony at Forbes, killing one man, leaving a ten-year-old boy with nine bullets in his leg. Around the same time, two rows of armed guards marched forty-nine miners to Trinidad, with the Death Special crawling along to the rear, its guns trained on the strikers' backs. When G.E. Jones, a member of the Western Federation of Miners (the militant miners' union which helped form the IWW) tried to photograph the armored car, Albert Felts, manager of the Baldwin-Felts Agency, beat him unconscious with the butt of his pistol. Jones was then arrested for disturbing the peace.

That same month, a steel-clad train manned by 190 guards with machine guns and rifles, headed for the Ludlow colony. It was intercepted by a detachment of armed miners, and a battle took place in which one mine guard was killed. The *New York Times* commented, after this first small victory for the union: "The situation is extremely critical tonight. More than 700 armed strikers are reported to be in the field against the mine guards."

By this time there had been at least four battles between strikers and guards, and at least nine men had been killed—mostly strikers. The tent colonies were in a state of siege, with machine guns and high-powered searchlights perched on inaccessible ridges, constantly aimed at the tents.

On October 28, 1913, Governor Ammons declared martial law, issued an order forbidding the import of strikebreakers from outside the state, and ordered General Chase of the Colorado National Guard, to move his troops into the strike district. It was one of those "balanced" political moves, in which the concession to one side (the ban on imported strikebreakers) is unenforced, and that to the other side (the reinforcement of the mine guards by government troops) effectively carried out. Some of the pressures behind Ammons' calling of the Guard are explained in a letter written by Vice-President Bowers of C.F. & I. to John D. Rockefeller, Jr., in New York:

---

* Edward Broughton, *Report to the Governor* (Denver, 1914). Boughton headed a military commission asked to report to the governor on the events of April 20, 1914.

You will be interested to know that we have been able to secure the cooperation of all the bankers of the city, who have had three or four interviews
with our little cowboy governor, agreeing to back the State and lend it all
funds necessary to maintain the militia and afford ample protection so our
miners could return to work.... Besides the bankers, the chambers of commerce, the real estate exchange, together with a great many of the best business men, have been urging the governor to take steps to drive these vicious
agitators out of the state. Another mighty power has been rounded up on
behalf of the operators by the getting together of fourteen of the editors of
the most important newspapers in the state.

After five weeks of terror organized by the mine operators' private
army, the striking miners were ready to believe that the National Guard, representing the government of the United States, had come to restore order.
At the Ludlow tent colony, pennies and nickels were collected to buy a large
American flag to greet the Guard. A thousand men, women, children, gaunt
from lack of food, lined up on the road from the railroad station to the
Ludlow colony, dressed in their Sunday best, the children in white, waving
little American flags, a hastily assembled band, dressed in faded Greek and
Servian army uniforms, playing "The Union Forever." From the station
marched the first troop of cavalry, with General Chase himself on a pranc-
ing white stallion, then a small detachment of field artillery, then two regiments of infantrymen, in wide-brimmed hats and yellow leggings. The miners and their wives and children shouted greetings and sang until the last
troops had disappeared past the colony, down Berwind Canyon.

But the National Guard turned out to be no different than the
Baldwin-Felts men, during that cold, hungry winter of 1913-14. In
December, a teen-ager was accosted on the road near the Ludlow colony
by Lieutenant Linderfeldt, a stocky, beribboned veteran of the Spanish-
American War, and knocked unconscious by the lieutenant's fists. A
women's parade in Trinidad in January was attacked by cavalry, and a
frightened sixteen-year-old girl, trying to get away, was kicked in the chest
by a man on a rearing white horse—General Chase. The leader of the
Ludlow colony, a college-educated Greek man named Lou Tikas, was
beaten by Linderfeldt and dragged off to jail.[*]

---

[*] These and the other instances of National Guard brutality cited in this essay are part of a
600-page compilation of eyewitness reports by the Colorado State Federation of Labor, which
were the basis for a short report, *Militarism in Colorado* (published in Denver, 1914), by
William Brewster of the Yale Law School.

The National Guard made 172 arrests that winter. A Welsh woman named Mary M. Thomas, mother of two, was held for three weeks in a vermin-ridden cell. One striker, forced to sleep on an icy cement floor, died after twenty-five days. A nineteen-year-old-girl, pregnant, was dragged through an alley by National Guardsmen one night until she lost consciousness. One miner's wife, Mrs. Yankinski, was home with four children when militia men broke into her home, robbed her money, and broke her little girl's nose with a kick. In the town of Segundo, a group of drunken Guardsmen forced some children to march about the city for two hours, prodding them with bayonets.

There was violence by the strikers. Strikebreaker Pedro Armijo was murdered near the Aguilar tent colony. A mine clerk named Herbert Smith, scabbing in a Colorado Fuel and Iron mine, was brutally beaten near Trinidad. Strikers fired on the Forbes mining camp, where strikebreakers were living, and were dispersed by an infantry company. Four mine guards were killed at La Veta while escorting a scab. And on November 20, 1913, George Belcher, the killer of Lippiatt, was leaving a Trinidad drug store, stopped on the corner to light a cigar, and was killed by a single rifle shot by an unseen gunman.[*]

Governor Ammons rescinded his order against out-of-state strikebreakers, and the National Guard began escorting strikebreakers to the mines. A trainload of such men from St. Louis, disembarking in the mine area, were protected by militiamen with unsheathed bayonets. A House committee heard testimony on the violation of federal peonage laws. Salvatore Valentin, a Sicilian, told the committee that he had been brought from Pittsburgh through deception, and forced to work in the Delagua mine. One of his fellow strikebreakers, he said, was shot and killed in the mines by an unknown person.[**]

Early in January 1914, Mother Jones came back to Trinidad, "to help my boys," and was immediately deported by the National Guard. Eluding three detectives, she returned, but over a hundred militiamen

---

[*] The instances of miners' violence are reported in *The Military Occupation of the Coal Strike Zone of Colorado*, a report to the Governor by the Adjutant-General's office, 1914. The killing of Belcher was reported in the *International Socialist Review*, February 1914.

[**] *New York Times*, February 11. 1914. Dozens of accusations of peonage appear in House Mines and Mining Committee, *Conditions in the Coal Mines of Colorado*, pp. 749, 1239, 1363, 1374, 1407, and other places in the hearings.

stormed the Toltec Hotel in Walsenburg, and took her prisoner. She was held in prison for twenty days, with two armed sentinels outside her door. When women paraded in Trinidad to protest her arrest, eighteen were jailed. When General Chase reported later to the governor on the conduct of the National Guard, he wrote: "It is hoped that a just and discriminating public will in the end come to realize the disinterested service of these champions of the state's integrity and honor."

As spring approached in 1914, funds for the Guard began to run out. The payroll alone was $30,000 a month, and critics pointed to the disproportionate number of officers: 397 officers to 695 privates. The state was heavily in debt to the bankers. As it became unable to pay salaries, the regular enlisted militia dropped out, and their places were taken by mine guards of Colorado Fuel and Iron, now in Guard uniforms, drawing their pay from the company.

In early April, 1914, Governor Ammons recalled all but two companies of the National Guard, consisting now mostly of mine guards, in the pay of C. F. & I. and under the command of Major Pat Hamrock, a local saloonkeeper, and Lieutenant Linderfeldt. They were stationed on a rocky ridge overlooking the thousand men, women, and children who lived in the tent colony at Ludlow.

On Monday morning, April 20, two dynamite bombs were exploded in the hills above Ludlow by Major Hamrock's men—a signal for operations to begin. At 9 A.M. a machine gun began firing into the tents, and then others joined. Women, holding children, ran from tent to tent, seeking shelter, crying out wildly. Some managed to escape into the hills. Others crawled into the dark pits and caves which had been dug under a few of the tents. Miners left the tents to draw off the fire, flung themselves into deep arroyos (gashes left by old creek beds) and fired back. One eyewitness reported later:

> The firing of the machine guns was awful. They fired thousands and thousands of shots. There were very few guns in the tent colony. Not over fifty, including shotguns. Women an children were afraid to crawl out of the shallow pits under the tents. Several men were killed trying to get to them. The soldiers and mine guards tried to kill everybody; anything they saw move, even a dog, they shot at.

The old feud between strike leader Tikas and Lieutenant Linderfeldt came to its end that afternoon. Tikas was in the big tent, finding shelter for women and children, helping the wounded, when a telephone, its wires amazingly intact, started ringing. It was Linderfeldt, up on the ridge. He wanted to see Tikas—it was urgent, he said. Tikas refused. The phone rang again and again. Tikas answered, said he would come.

Carrying a white flag, Tikas met Linderfeldt on the hill. The Lieutenant was surrounded by militiamen. The only eyewitness report is from a young engineer visiting Colorado with a friend, who saw the scene from a nearby cliff. They saw the two men talking, then Linderfeldt raised his rifle and brought the stock down with all his strength on Tikas' skull. The rifle broke in two as Tikas fell, face downward. "As he lay there, we saw the militiamen fall back. Then they aimed their rifles and fired into the unconscious man's body. It was the first murder I had ever seen..."

Two other strikers, unarmed and under guard, met their deaths on the hill in a similar manner. The machine guns continued firing into the tents, and five people died in their fire. One of them was Frank Snyder, ten yours old. His father told about it:

> Frank was sitting on the floor...and he was in the act of stooping to kiss or caress his sister.... I was standing near the front door of my tent and I heard the impact of the bullet striking the boy's head and the crack...as it exploded inside of his brain.

As the sun fell behind the Black Hills, the firing lessened. Now soldiers moved down the slopes into the shadows alongside the tents, drenched the canvas with coal oil, and set the tents afire. The visiting engineer later described the scene:

> We watched from our rock shelter while the militia dragged up their machine guns and poured a murderous fire into the arroyos from a height by Water Tank Hill above the Ludlow depot. Then came the firing of the tents. I am positive that by no possible chance could they have been set ablaze accidentally. The militiamen were thick about the northern corner of the colony where the fire started, and we could see distinctly from our lofty observation place what looked like a blazing torch waved in the midst of the militia a few seconds before the general conflagration swept through the place.

While bullets whistled through the flaming canvas, people fled in panic from their tents and from the caves beneath. A dispatch to the *New York Times* reported some of the results:

A seven-year-old girl dashed from under a blazing tent and heard the scream of bullets about her ears. Insane from fright, she ran into a tent again and fell into the hole with the remainder of her family to die with them. The child is said to have been a daughter of Charles Costa, a union leader at Aguilar, who perished with his wife and another child.... James Fyler, financial secretary of the Trinidad local, died with a bullet in his forehead as he was attempting to rescue his wife from the flames.... Mrs. Marcelina Pedragon, her skirt ablaze, carried her youngest child from the flames, leaving two others behind.... An unidentified man, driving a horse attached to a light buggy, dashed from the tents waving a white flag, just after the fire started. When ordered to halt he opened fire with a revolver and was killed by a return volley from the militia.

The tents became crackling torches, and for hours the countryside shone in a ghastly light, while men, women, and children roamed through the hills, looking for others in their families. At 8:30 P.M. the militia "captured" the Ludlow tent colony, now a smoldering pile of ashes.

It was on the following day, April 21, that a telephone linesman, going through the ruins, lifted a twisted iron cot that covered one of the pits dug beneath the tents for shelter. There he found the mangled, charred bodies of two women and eleven children, heaped together in what had been a desperate struggle to escape.

Funerals for the dead were held in Trinidad; according to the Trinidad Red Cross, twenty-six bodies of strikers had been found at Ludlow. Then the miners turned from the coffins of the dead and took up arms, joined by union miners from a dozen neighboring camps, who left wives and children behind, and swarmed over the hills, carrying arms and ammunition. From Denver, the day after the discovery of the Ludlow death pit, United Mine Workers' officials issued a "Call to Arms":*

Organize the men in your community in companies of volunteers to protect the workers of Colorado against the murder and cremation of men, women, and children by armed assassins in the employ of coal corporations, serving under the guise of state militiamen.

Gather together for defensive propose all arms and ammunition legally available...

The state is furnishing no protection to us and we must protect ourselves.... We intend to exercise our lawful right as citizens to defend our homes and our constitutional rights.

---

* House Mines and Mining Committee, *Conditions in the Coal Mines of Colorado*, Vol. II, Appendix. The call was signed by John Lawson and other U.M.W. officials, and by Ernest Mills, secretary-treasurer of the Western Federation of Miners.

Three hundred armed strikers marched from tent colonies in neighboring Fremont County to help. Others came overland in the dark, carrying guns and ammunition. The press reported a series of encounters between soldiers and strikers in an area of three square miles south of Ludlow, the battlefield isolated by the cutting of telephone and telegraph wires. Four train crews of the Colorado and Southern Railroad refused to take soldiers and ammunition from Trinidad to Ludlow. There was talk of a general strike in Colorado.

Near Aguilar, the Empire mine was besieged, the tipple burned, the mouth of the slope caved in by dynamite explosions. Three mine guards were reported dead there, two mine shafts were in ashes, and the press reported that "the hills in every direction seem suddenly to be alive with men." Two hundred militia and company guards along the tracks at Ludlow were cut off from the rest of the district by "armed bands of strikers whose ranks are swelled constantly by men who swarm over the hills from all directions." At Colorado Springs, three hundred union miners quit work to go to the Trinidad district, carrying revolvers, rifles, and shotguns.

The first legal move came from Pueblo, where a federal grand jury returned indictments against eight striking miners on charges of attacking the company post office at Higgins, Colorado.

Governor Ammons reported an attack on Delagua and Hastings by the miners. An attack on Berwind mine was expected momentarily. Now the Trinidad mayor and Chamber of Commerce appealed to President Woodrow Wilson to intervene.

President Wilson was busy at this time with Mexico. Several American sailors from a vessel which was blockading Mexico as an act of pressure against the Huerta regime on April 9, 1914, went ashore at Tampico and were arrested. The American admiral demanded that Mexico apologize, hoist the American flag, and give it a twenty-one-gun salute. Wilson gave Mexico until April 9 to act. Meanwhile, twenty-two thousand men and fifty-two ships were ready.* The Mexican foreign minister responded that Mexico would exchange salutes with the United States, would even salute first, but would not salute unconditionally. The officer who had arrested the American sailors was under arrest, he said,

---

* *New York Times*, April 20, 1914. The headline read: "Campaign Worked Out by Naval Experts in Recent Months Now Being Carried Out in Detail."

and the Americans had been freed even before investigation. "Mexico had yielded," he said, "as much as her dignity will permit. Mexico trusts to the fairmindedness and spirit of justice of the American people."

On April 20, Wilson asked Congress for the right to use armed force: "There can in what we do be no thought of aggression or selfish aggrandizement. We seek to maintain the dignity and authority of the United States only because we wish always to keep our great influence unimpaired for the uses of liberty, both in the United States, and wherever else it may be employed for the benefit of mankind."

The *New York Times* carried an editorial on the Mexican affair:

> Just as when we went to war with Spain there were those who insisted that we should ignore the destruction of the Maine...so there are now those who hold that Huerta is in the right and that he had given us no cause of offense. As to that, we may trust the just mind, the sound judgment, and the peaceful temper of President Wilson. There is not the slightest occasion for popular excitement over the Mexican affair; there is no reason why anybody should get nervous either about the stock market or about his business.

Without waiting for Congress, Wilson ordered American naval forces to act. On April 21, the day of the discovery of the death pit at Ludlow, American ships bombarded Vera Cruz, landed ten boatloads of marines, and occupied the city. Over a hundred Mexicans were killed.

Business men had been asking for intervention in Mexico ever since the Mexican Revolution of 1910 created a threat to American investments in Mexican oil, mines, land, and railroad—which totaled a billion dollars by 1913. Now there was enthusiasm for Wilson's move. The *Times* reported:[*]

> The five hundred or more business men who attended the luncheon of the Members Council of the Merchants Association of New York, jumped to their feet yesterday when William C. Breed, the toastmaster, called upon those present to express their loyalty to President Wilson "to whatever course he shall determine necessary to restore peace, order and a stable government in the Republic of Mexico."

It took President Wilson several days to turn his attention to Colorado. Meanwhile, the armed revolt of the miners was growing there.

---

[*] *New York Times*, April 23, 1914. By July, Huerta was forced out of office. In November, the U.S. occupation forces withdrew from Vera Cruz.

A troop train leaving Denver to carry soldiers to the strike zone ran into trouble. Eighty-two men in Company C mutinied and refused to go to the district. "The men declared they would not engage in the shooting of women and children. They hissed the 350 men who did start and shouted imprecations at them."

Five thousand people demonstrated in Denver, standing in a pouring rain on the lawn in front of the capitol. A resolution was read, asking that Hamrock, Linderfeldt, and other National Guard officers be tried for murder, that the state seize the mines and operate them. Governor Ammons was denounced as a traitor and accessory to the murder, and Colorado citizens were asked to arm themselves for self-protection. The Denver Cigar Makers Union voted to send five hundred armed men to Ludlow and Trinidad in the morning, and women of the United Garment Workers Union in Denver announced that four hundred of their members had volunteered as nurses to aid the Colorado strikers.

All over the country meetings and demonstrations took place in support of the Colorado miners. Upton Sinclair and others picketed Rockefeller's office at 26 Broadway, in funeral garb. In front of the church where Rockefeller sometimes preached Sunday sermons, a minister was clubbed by police while protesting the Massacre. The usually mild Eugene Debs, angered by the Colorado events, wrote:

> The time has come for the United Mine Workers and the Western Federation of Miners to levy a special monthly assessment to create a Gunmen Defense Fund. This Fund should be sufficient to provide each member with the latest high power rifles, the same ones used by the corporation gunmen, and 500 rounds of cartridges. In addition to this, every district should purchase and equip and man enough Gatling and machine guns to match the equipment of Rockefeller's private army of assassins. This suggestion is made advisedly, and I hold myself responsible for every word of it.

With the National Guard in Colorado unable to control the marauding miners, with damages amounting to millions of dollars, and over twenty killed since the Massacre, pressure grew for President Wilson to restore order with federal troops. The formal request was made by Governor Ammons, but a powerful informal signal was flashed by the *New York Times*, whose reaction, representing important elements in business and political circles, deserves a moment's attention.

The *Times'* first account of the Ludlow Massacre was an inaccurate one. Its headline read: "Women and Children Roasted in Pits of Tent Colony as Flames Destroy It. Miners Store of Ammunition and Dynamite Exploded, Scattering Death and Ruin." The *Times* had been unsympathetic to the miners throughout the strike; now it expressed horror at the killing of women and children. However, it seemed to be most angry that the militia and the authorities had been stupid enough to create a situation on which the strikers might capitalize to their advantage. Here is the *Times* editorial following the Massacre:

> Somebody blundered. Worse than the order that sent the Light Brigade into the jaws of death, worse in its effect than the Black Hole of Calcutta, was the order that trained the machine guns of the state militia of Colorado upon the strikers' camp at Ludlow, burned its tents, and suffocated to death the scores of women and children who had taken refuge in the rifle pits and trenches.... Strike organizers cannot escape full measure of blame for the labor war.... But no situation can justify the acts of a militia that compels women and babes to lie in ditches and cellars twenty-four hours without food or water, exposes them to cannon and rifle fire, and lets them die like trapped animals in the flames of their camp...when a sovereign State employs such horrible means, what may not be expected from the anarchy that ensues?

Two days later, when the miners had taken up arms against the militia, the *Times* ran another editorial:

> With the deadliest weapons of civilization in the hands of savage-minded men, there can be no telling to what lengths the war in Colorado will go unless it is quelled by force. The President should turn his attention from Mexico long enough to take stern measures in Colorado.

The indignation at the militia, such as it was, had lasted about a day. The *Times* had never, in the course of the long violent series of attacks on the miners, called for federal intervention to stop that. Once the miners took up arms, it became concerned for order. A week after the Massacre, another *Times* editorial criticized two clergymen, Rev. Percy Stickney Grant of Manhattan, and Rev. John Howard Melish of Brooklyn, who had denounced from their pulpits the actions of the National Guard against the strikers.

The *Times* said about the sermons:

> These are sympathetic utterances and differ from cold impartiality.... There are those who think that infamy in Colorado consists in the fact that the

militia are shooting workers. It may be contended that there is something like infamy in the opposition of workers to society and order. The militia are as impersonal and impartial as the law.

On April 29, Woodrow Wilson sent federal troops into Colorado to bring order. Secretary of War Garrison asked everyone to surrender their arms to federal troops. The commander of the federal forces prohibited the import of strikebreakers from other states, banned picketing, and protected scabs.

For the next seven months, the air was filled with talk of negotiations, peace offers, mediation plans. The governor appointed an investigating commission. The Mines and Mining Committee of the House and the Industrial Relations Commission of the Senate held hearings, while federal troops patrolled the strike area. Testimony for House and Senate added up to over five thousand pages. The strike petered out, was officially called off in December 1914. The Union had not won recognition. Sixty-six men, women and children had been killed. Not one militiaman or mine guard had been indicted for crime.* Under the weight of volumes of words, suspended from the tips of bayonets, the miners' resistance was crushed.

How shall we read the story of the Ludlow Massacre? As another "interesting" event of the past? Or as supporting evidence for an analysis of that long *present* which spans 1914 and 1970. If it is read narrowly, as an incident in the history of the trade union movement and the coal industry, then it is an angry splotch in the past, fading rapidly amidst new events. If it is read as a commentary on a larger question—the relationship of government to corporate power and of both to movements of social protest—then we are dealing with the present. Then we see a set of characteristics which have persisted, not only in American history, but in the history of all nations, although the forms vary. Then we see the complex alternating techniques of brute force and innocent solicitude, and the rain of investigations, words, negotiations, commissions, denunciations—all adding up to inches of progress and the basic retention of

---

* On the contrary, John Lawson, the strike leader, was, a year later, tried and convicted of murder. He was accused of murdering John Nimmo, one of the army of deputies paid by the companies. No effort was made to prove Lawson fired the fatal shot; he was held responsible because he led the strike, was at the Ludlow tent colony the day of the battle. The judge, Granby Hillyer, was a former attorney for Colorado Fuel and Iron and had helped prepare cases against the strikers. The jury was chosen by a panel selected by the sheriff of Las Animan County. Lawson's conviction was later overturned. West, *Report on the Colorado Strike*, p. 22.

power and wealth where it now resides. Of course things have changed; there are now larger portions of material benefits meted out to the under-dog; there are now more subtle methods used by both government and business in dealing with resistance* and more modern weapons (gas, planes)** when other methods fail. And one set of victims exchanged for others of different color, nationality, geography as tolerance runs dry.

The story can be read as a problem in personal responsibility, which leads to a continuing, inane argument about blame. Shall we blame John D. Rockefeller, Jr., who testified after the Massacre that he and his company had been fighting to defend the workers' right to work? (A Congressman had asked him: "You'll do that, even if you lose all your money, and have all your employees killed?" And Rockefeller answered: "It's a great principle. It's a national issue.") Or should we blame his managers, or the Governor, or the President? Or Lieutenant Linderfeldt?

Or—shall we look beyond blame? In that case, we might see a similarity in behavior among the privileged (and their followers) in all times, all countries: the willingness to kill for a great principle—the word "principle" a euphemism for keeping the fruits of the earth divided according to present rules. Then, we might see that the killing is not the result of an elitist conspiracy, but of a social structure larger than the con-sciousness of any of its parts. With such a vision, we might conclude that the responsibility belongs to no one in the past, but to us today to figure out—by acts as much as by thought—how to dismantle that structure, while constructing one which does not require as its indispensable work force a team comprised of executioners and victims.

---

* Note the bewildering variety of government agencies and commissions to represent welfare and beneficence; note that Rockefeller, after the Colorado strike, hired Ivy Lee, the nation's leading public relations man, and how public relations has become a vital part of government and business operations; note that the Rockefeller Foundation, new at the time of the strike, stepped up its activities, and that foundations in general multiplied.

** I write this shortly after police in Berkeley, California, carried out the first aerial gas attack on a domestic demonstration (May 1969).

5

The Limits
of the
New Deal

In the early Sixties, historians Leonard Levy and Alfred Young were editing for Bobbs-Merrill the multi-volume "American Heritage Series," consisting of collections of documents ranging all through United States history. They knew of my book on LaGuardia, and asked me to do a volume of readings on the New Deal. President Franklin D. Roosevelt was a hero to my family in the depression years of the Thirties. And yet, my experience in the South, and my work on LaGuardia, had taught me to doubt that important social change came from the top. I put together writings by John Dewey, Charles Beard, Heywood Broun, W.E.B. Dubois, and other thinkers whose ideas went beyond Roosevelt's political boundaries. The book was called *New Deal Thought*. It came out in 1965 and what follows is my introduction to it.

When we compel the past to speak, we want neither the gibberish of total recall nor the nostalgia of find memories; we would like the past to speak wisely to our present needs. And so we have a good reason for trying to recapture some of the lost dialogue of the New Deal years—that which was carried on, with varying degrees of tension, inside and outside the Roosevelt circle.

The New Dealers themselves were articulate, humane, and on occasion profound. Among them were the "brains trust" (Adolf A. Berle, Raymond Moley, Rexford Guy Tugwell), the cabinet members (Henry Wallace, Frances Perkins, Harold Ickes, and others), the administrators of the alphebetic agencies (Harry Hopkins, David Lilienthal and others), the Congressional spokesmen (Robert F. Wagner, Hugo Black, and others). And above them all was Franklin D. Roosevelt himself. They had no clearly defined set of goals, beyond that of extricating the nation from the depression of 1929-1932. In the course of easing the crisis, however, they found themselves—pushed partly by the cries of alarm on all sides, partly by inner humanitarian impulses—creating new laws and institutions like the Tennessee Valley Authority, the social security system, farm subsidies, minimum wage standards, the National Labor Relations Board, and public housing.

These accomplishments were considerable enough to give many Americans the feeling they were going through a revolution, while they successfully evaded any one of a number of totalitarian abysses into which they might have fallen. So it is not surprising that the New Deal left a glow of enthusiasm, even adoration, in the nation at large.

Yet, when it was over, the fundamental problem remained—and still remains unsolved—how to bring the blessings of immense natural wealth and staggering productive potential to every person in the land. Also unsolved was the political corollary of that problem; how to organize ordinary people to convey to national leadership something more subtle than the wail of crisis (which speaks for itself); how to communicate the day-to-day pains felt, between emergencies, in garbage-strewn slums, crowded schools, grimy bus stations, inadequate hospital wards, Negro ghettos, and rural shacks—the environment of millions of Americans clawing for subsistence in the richest country in the world.

When the reform energies of the New Deal began to wane around 1939 and the depression was over, the nation was back to its normal state: a permanent army of unemployed; twenty or thirty million poverty-ridden people effectively blocked from public view by a huge, prosperous, and fervently consuming middle class; a tremendously efficient yet wasteful productive apparatus that was efficient because it could produce limitless supplies of what it decided to produce, and wasteful because what it decided to produce was not based on what was most needed by society but on what was most profitable to business.

What the New Deal did was to refurbish middle-class America, which had taken a dizzying fall in the depression, to restore jobs to half the jobless, and to give just enough to the lowest classes (a layer of public housing, a minimum of social security) to create an aura of good will. Through it all, the New Dealers moved in an atmosphere thick with suggestions, but they accepted only enough of these to get the traditional social mechanism moving again, plus just enough more to give a taste of what a truly far-reaching reconstruction might be.

This harsh estimate of New Deal achievements derives from the belief that the historian discussing the past is always commenting—whether he realizes it or not—on the present; and that because he is part of a morally responsible public, his commentary should consider present needs at the expense, if necessary, of old attachments. It is fruitless today to debate "interpretations" of the New Deal. We can no longer vote for or against Roosevelt. We can only affect the world around us. And although this is the 1960s, not the 1930s, some among us live very high, and some live very low, and a chronic malaise of lost opportunities and wasted wealth pervades the economic air.

It is for today, then, that we turn to the thinking of the New Deal period. Although the New Deal gave us only fragments of solutions, it did leave us—perhaps because those were desperate years, and desperation stimulates innovation—with a public discussion more intense and more sweeping than any we have had before or since. People outside the New Deal entourage, invited or not, joined that discussion and extended the boundaries of political and economic imagination beyond those of the New Dealers—sometimes to the left, sometimes to the right, sometimes in directions hard to plot.

Among these were philosophers, writers, critics, lawyers, poets, college professors, journalists, dissident politicians, or commentators without special portfolio. Their names are still known today; John Dewey, Charles Beard, Reinhold Niebuhr, Paul Douglas, Stuart Chase, John Maynard Keynes, Norman Thomas, Oswald Garrison Villard, Heywood

Broun, Max Lerner, Morris Cohen, Walter White, Edmund Wilson, Felix
Frankfurter, John Steinbeck, John L. Lewis, Upton Sinclair.

Their thinking does not give us facile solutions, but if history has
uses beyond that of reminiscence, one of them is to nourish lean ideological times with the nectars of other years. And although the present shape
of the world was hardly discernible in 1939, certain crucial social issues
persist in both eras. Somehow, in the interaction between the ideas of the
New Dealers themselves and those of social critics who gathered in various stances and at various distances around the Roosevelt fire, we may
find suggestions or approaches that are relevant today.

I.

The word "pragmatic" has been used, more often perhaps than
any other, to describe the thinking of the New Dealers. It refers to the
experimental method of the Roosevelt administration, the improvisation
from one step to the next, the lack of system or long-range program or
theoretical commitment. Richard Hofstadter, in fact, says that the only
important contribution to political theory to come out of the Roosevelt
administration was made by Thurman Arnold, particularly in his two
books, *The Symbols of Government* and *The Folklore of Capitalism.*
Hofstadter describes Arnold's writing as "the theoretical equivalent of
FDR's opportunistic virtuosity in practical politics—a theory that
attacks theories." As the chief expression of Roosevelt's "ideology,"
Arnold's work deserves some attention.

All through both his books, in a style of cool irony, Arnold cuts
away at "preconceived faiths," "preconceived principles," "theories and
symbols of government," "high-sounding prejudices," "traditional ideals,"
"moral ideals," "permanent cures." In the last paragraphs of T*he Symbols
of Government*, he writes:

> So long as the public hold preconceived faiths about the fundamental princi-
> ples of government, they will persecute and denounce new ideas in that sci-
> ence, and orators will prevail over technicians. So long as preconceived prin-
> ciples are considered more important than practical results, the practical alle-
> viation of human distress and the distribution of available comforts will be
> paralyzed.... The writer has faith that a new public attitude toward the ideals
> of law and economics is slowly appearing to create an atmosphere where the
> fanatical alignments between opposing political principles may disappear and
> a competent, practical, opportunistic governing class may rise to power...

Because the Roosevelt administration did, in fact, experiment and improvise without a total plan, FDR's "pragmatism" has come, for many, to be the most important statement about the thinking of the New Dealers. This emphasis on the method rather than on the substance of that thinking tends to obscure what may be its greatest significance.

Most statesmen experiment: Tsar Nicholas instituted a Duma, Lenin encouraged private enterprise for several years, Bismarck sponsored social welfare measures, Mao Tse-tung introduced back-yard steel furnaces, and George Washington supported a national bank. These examples show that experimentation can be linked to a variety of social ideals. Some statesmen engage in more experiments than others, and in a time of crisis one who is willing to undertake a vast number of them deserves commendation, as Roosevelt does. The truly important question that can be asked about the thinking of any government is: in what direction, and how far, is it willing to experiment? What goals, what ideals, what expectations direct that experimentation?

Thurman Arnold himself contributed to this misplaced emphasis on method rather than substance. He was so anxious to demolish old myths that stood in the way of the welfare measures of the New Deal that mythology itself became his chief concern. He was so intent on sweeping away old debris, that he became obsessed, ironically, with a folklore of his own, in which the idea of debris-clearing crowded out the concept of what he wanted to plant in the cleared area.

Examining Arnold's *The Symbols of Government*, one sees that what started him on a crusade against myths was that he sought to expose the symbolism that stood in the way of bringing cheap electric power to people and of instituting relief, public works, social security. His strongest expression on social justice was his statement that: "Those who rule our great industrial feudalism still believe inalterably the old axioms that man works efficiently only for personal profit; that humanitarian ideals are unworkable as the principal aim of government or business organization; that control of national resources, elimination of waste, and a planned destruction of goods would destroy both freedom and efficiency."

As was true of his associate, Thurman Arnold, FDR's experimentalism and iconoclasm were not devoid of standards and ideals. They had a certain direction, which was toward governmental intervention in the economy to prevent depression, to help the poor, and to curb ruthless practices in big business. Roosevelt's speeches had the flavor of a moral crusade. Accepting the nomination at the Democratic Convention of 1932, he said that "the Federal Government has always had and still has a continuing responsibility for the broader public welfare," and pledged "a new deal for the American people." In a campaign speech that year at the Commonwealth Club in San Francisco, he said: "Our government...owes to every one an avenue to possess himself of a portion of that plenty sufficient for his needs, through his own work." In his 1936 speech accepting the nomination, he spoke of the power of the "economic royalists" and said: "Our allegiance to American institutions requires the overthrow of this kind of power."

But FDR's ideas did not have enough clarity to avoid stumbling from one approach to another: from constant promises to balance the budget, to large-scale spending in emergencies; from an attempt to reconcile big business interests and labor interests (as in the National Recovery Act), to belated support for a pro-labor National Labor Relations Act; from special concern for the tenant farmer (in the Resettlement Administration), to a stress on generous price supports for the large commercial farmer (in the Agricultural Adjustment Act of 1938).

His ideas on political leadership showed the same indecision, the same constriction of boundaries, as did his ideas about economic reform. Roosevelt was cautious about supporting the kind of candidates in 1934 (Socialist Upton Sinclair in California, Progressive Gifford Pinchot in Pennsylvania) who represented bold approaches to economic and social change; and when he did decide to take vigorous action against conservative Congressional candidates in 1938, he did so too late and too timorously. He often attempted to lead Congress in a forceful way to support his economic program; yet his leadership was confined to working with the existing Congressional leadership, including many Southern conservatives who ruled important committees. Roosevelt's political daring did not extend to building new political forces among the poor, the unemployed, the tenant farmers, and other disadvantaged groups, with whose support he might have given the country a bolder economic program.

The circle of men around Roosevelt, the cabinet members and administrators, was an odd mixture of liberals and conservatives who often worked at cross-purposes. Rexford Guy Tugwell, a bold advocate of national planning to help the lower-income groups, was close to Roosevelt for several years; but so was Raymond Moley, who believed in a kind of planning more beneficial to business interests. Even the liberal New Dealers, with rare exceptions, hesitated to carry their general concern for the underprivileged too far. Frances Perkins, the Secretary of Labor, had the humanitarian instincts of a first-rate social worker, but she seemed often to be trailing behind the labor movement, rather than helping to give it direction. (The most advanced piece of New Deal labor legislation was the Wagner Act, but Secretary Perkins wrote later: "I myself, had very little sympathy with the bill.") Progressive Secretary of the Interior Harold Ickes was offset by conservative Secretary of Commerce Daniel Roper. And although Roper was succeeded in 1939 by Harry Hopkins, there remained in the cabinet a powerful force for fiscal conservatism and budget-balancing—Secretary of the Treasury Henry Morgenthau.

The experimentalism of the New Deal, in short, had its limits: up to these limits, Roosevelt's social concern was genuinely warm, his political courage huge, his humanitarian spirit unfailing; beyond them, his driving force weakened. Thus, by 1938, with the nation out of the worst of the depression, with a skeletal structure of social reform in the statute books, and with that year's Congressional elections showing a sudden waning of political approbation, the Roosevelt program began to bog down. As it slid to its close, it left behind a mountain of accomplishment, and ahead, mountains still unclimbed. Many millions—businessmen, professionals, unionized workingmen, commercial farmers—had been given substantial help. Many millions more—sharecroppers, slum-dwellers, Negroes of north and South, the unemployed—still awaited a genuine "New Deal."

II.

Why did the New Deal sputter out around 1938-1939? One important factor seems to be that the urgency of 1933-1935 was gone. By 1939, although there were still nine million unemployed, the sense of panic was over. After all, unemployment was normal in America. Harry Hopkins had said in 1937 that even in prosperity it was "reasonable to expect a probable minimum of 4,000,000 to 5,000,000 unemployed." The American nation had developed over the years a set of expectations as to what constituted "normal" times, and by 1938 it was approaching these.

Hopkins' statement and the administration's inaction indicate that the ideals of the New Dealers did not extend very far beyond the traditional structure of the American economy. They had wanted to get out of the terrible economic despair of 1932 and 1933 and to establish certain moderate reforms. These aims had been accomplished. True, some of the New Dealers, including FDR himself, did speak of what still remained to be done. But once the nation was restored to close to the old balance—even if income was still distributed with gross inequality, even if rural and urban slums crisscrossed the land, even if most workingmen were still unorganized and underpaid, and a third of the nation still, in FDR's words, "ill-nourished, ill-clad, ill-housed"—the driving force of the New Deal was gone.

Why were the expectations and ideals of the New Deal (its folklore, its symbols, according to Thurman Arnold) so limited? Why did the New Dealers not declare that the government would continue spending, experimenting, and expanding governmental enterprises—until no one was unemployed, and all slums were gone from the cities, until no family received below-subsistence incomes and adequate medical care was available to everyone, until anyone who wanted a college education could get one? True, there were political obstacles to realizing such objectives, but to state them as goals would itself have constituted the first step toward overcoming those obstacles. For this might have enabled FDR to do what political scientist James MacGregor Burns asserts was not done: to build "a solid, organized mass base" among labor and other underprivileged groups.

Humanitarianism pure and simple can go only so far, and self-interest must carry it further. Beyond the solicitude felt by the New Dealers for the distressed, beyond the occasionally bold rhetoric, there was not enough motive power to create a radically new economic equilibrium; this would have to be supplied by the groups concerned themselves; by the tenant farmers, the aged, the unemployed, the lowest-paid workers in the economy. Those who did organize—the larger farm operators, the several million industrial workers who joined the CIO—improved their position significantly. But as Paul Douglas, then an economics professor at the University of Chicago and now a United States Senator, wrote in 1933:

Along with the Rooseveltian program must go...the organization of those who are at present weak and who need to acquire that which the world respects, namely, power.... Unless these things are done, we are likely to find the permanent benefits of Rooseveltian liberalism to be as illusory as are those of the Wilsonian era.

Many organized movements sprang up in the 1930s, spurred by need and encouraged by the new atmosphere of innovation. The Townsend Movement sought $200 a month pensions for the aged. Father Charles Coughlin's panacea of "Social Justice" was heard by millions of radio listeners. Huey Long, the Louisiana Senator, excited many others with his "Share the Wealth" plan. The National Negro Congress, the Farmers Union, the American Youth Congress all represented special needs and all hurled their energies into the boiling political pot in Washington.

But there was no political program around which these disparate groups could effectively unite. And many of them began to lose their thrust when their demands were partially met. Even the Congress of Industrial Organizations, the latest and most successful of those mass movements born in the depression and stimulated by New Deal legislation, came eventually to represent a special interest of its own.

The Madisonian argument that political stability would be assured in a federal republic of many states, because an uprising in one would die for lack of support, applied also in the economic sphere, where no single economic interest, fierce as it might be in its own domain, ever developed a concern wide enough to embrace society at large. Perhaps one reason is that in the United States every little rebellion, every crisis, has been met with enough concessions to keep general resentment below the combustible level, while isolated aggrieved groups fought their way up to the point of complacency.

But if—as Paul Douglas forecasts—the underprivileged are the only ones who can supply the driving force for a sharp change in their condition, then it is probably the intellectuals of society who will furnish the theories, state the ideals, define the expectations. And so it is from those thinkers who clustered, half-friendly, half-reproachful, around the New Deal, their ideological reach less restrained, perhaps, by the holding of power, that our generation may find suggestions.

III.

Almost immediately, with John Dewey, we are brought face to face with the proof that it is not the fact of experimentalism but the definition of its boundaries, that is of supreme significance. He was one of the fathers of American pragmatism, the theoretician par excellence of the experimental method. In an article of 1918, he expressed the view of pragmatic experimentation that he held to the end of his life in 1952.

> The question is whether society...will learn to utilize the intelligence, the insight and foresight which are available, in order to take hold of the problem and to go at it, step by step, on the basis of an intelligent program—a program which is not too rigid, which is not a program in the sense of having every item definitely scheduled in advance, but which represents an outlook on the future of the things which most immediately require doing, trusting to the experience which is got in doing them to reveal the next things needed and the next steps to be taken.

Roosevelt and Dewey were both experimentalists and they both operated within a range of ideals; but that range, for John Dewey, involved goals that went well beyond Roosevelt's farthest bounds. Roosevelt wrote to newspaper publisher Roy Howard on September 2, 1935, that his legislation was "remedial," described the New Deal program as involving "modifications in the conditions and rules of economic enterprise" and said that: "This basic program, however, has now reached substantial completion." Undoubtedly he was bending over backward to satisfy an anxious and influential citizen. And his program did go on to embrace a minimum wage law, public housing, and other measures. But that was largely because of the momentum already created for reform and because of pressures among the public. The Roosevelt vision had been stretched almost to its limits.

In Dewey's 1935 lectures at the University of Virginia, he said:

> The only form of enduring social organization that is now possible is one in which the new forces of productivity are cooperatively controlled and used in the interest of the effective liberty, and the cultural development of the individuals that constitute society. Such a social order cannot be established by an unplanned and external convergence of the actions of separate individuals, each of whom is bent on personal private advantage.... Organized social planning, put into effect for the creation of an order in which industry and finance are socially directed...is now the sole method of social action by which liberalism can realize its professed aims.

Both Roosevelt and Dewey believed in moving step by step. But FDR wanted to preserve the profit system. Dewey was willing to reshape it drastically. Because Dewey's aim was larger, his steps were longer ones, taken two or three at a time, and were less haphazard. "In short," he said, "liberalism must now become radical.... For the gulf between what the actual situation makes possible and the actual state itself is so great that it cannot be bridged by piecemeal policies undertaken *ad hoc*. "Dewey was very conscious of the dangers of totalitarianism, but he believed that the spirit of free expression could remain alive, even while liberalism went on to "socialize the forces of production." Among pragmatists, apparently, crucial distinctions exist.

Part of Roosevelt's "pragmatism" was his rejection of doctrinaire ideas of the left. Marxism was in the air all around him. Many intellectuals were enthusiastic about the Five Year Plans of Soviet Russia. British Marxists were influential: Harold J. Laski lectured and wrote extensively in the United States: John Strachey popularized the concepts of socialism in *The Nature of Capitalist Crisis* (1935) and other works. Some in depression-ridden America were attracted to Marxism's claims that society could be analyzed "scientifically": that economic crisis was inevitable where production was complex and gigantic, yet unplanned; that exploitation of working people was built into a system where private profit was the chief motive; that the state was not neutral but an instrument of those who held economic power; that only the working class could be depended on to take over society and move it towards a classless, strifeless commonwealth. A true pragmatist might at least have explored some of the suggestions of Marxist thought. Roosevelt's thinking, however, remained in a kind of airtight chamber that allowed him to regulate what currents he would permit inside—and Marxism was not one of them.

Nevertheless, to steer clear of the theories of the Marxists, as of the Hooverian folklore of "free enterprise," "thrift," and "laissez-faire," left a vast middle ground of which Roosevelt explored only one sector. Edmund Wilson, for instance, a social critic and essayist, also rejected Marxian dialectics; yet he tried to extract from it some truths. He wrote with apparent warmth of the idea that (as he put it, in an imaginary restatement of a more acceptable Marxism): "...if society is to survive at all, it must be reorganized on new principles of equality." Others, not

Marxists, but more demanding in their notion of reform than was the New Deal, reconnoitered beyond its ideological fences.

Reinhold Niebuhr, a theologian and social philosopher who carried the Social Gospel to new borders in the 1930s urged that "private ownership of the productive processes" be abandoned, yet he hoped that through an alliance among farmers, industrial workers, and the lower income classes, the transition to a new order could be accomplished without violence. Stuart Chase, an economist who wrote a series of widely selling books in the 1930s, suggested that old alternatives had been swept aside by the onrush of technology, that the choice was no longer between capitalism and socialism; there was a need, he said, for some uncategorizable collectivist society whose "general objective will be the distribution of the surplus, rather than a wrangling over the ownership of a productive plant which has lost its scarcity position."

William Ernest Hocking, a Harvard philosopher, asked for "collectivism of a sort," but neither the collectivism of a "headless Liberalism" or of a "heady" Communism or Fascism. He wrote: "What the State has to do with production is to drive into economic practice the truth that there is little or no capital whose use is not 'affected by a public interest.'" Hocking said: "Economic processes constitute a single and healthy organism only when the totality of persons in a community who have a right to consume *determine what is produced....*" Hocking was setting goals quite beyond the Rooseveltian ones.

Upton Sinclair, a muckraker since the early part of the century, preached a non-Marxist, home-grown socialism that attracted enough adherents to bring him very close to winning the gubernatorial election in California in 1934. Sinclair prophesied that "in a cooperative society every man, woman, and child would have the equivalent of $5000 a year income from labor of the able-bodied young men for three or four hours per day." This prophesy was certainly utopian in 1933, but such vision, even if it were going to be bent and modified in practice, might carry a program of social reform much further—and perhaps win more powerful blocs of electoral support—than did the more moderate goals of the New Deal.

A program may be pragmatic in its willingness to explore various means, yet be certain of its goals; it may be limited in how far it is willing to go, and yet be clear about the direction of its thrust. There is a difference between experimentation and vacillation. Robert MacIver, a distinguished social scientist, was impressed in 1934 by the variety of new institutions created under Roosevelt, but wondered if they meant "the inauguration of a period of social and cultural reformation." He asked: "The new institutions are here, but the essential point is—Who shall control them?" There was uncertainty about the New Deal, particularly in its first two years, when the National Recovery Act set out to create large planning organizations for industry in which big business seemed to be making the important decisions. It led some liberals and radicals to see in it possible Fascist aims, led some important businessmen to support it, and kept political loyalties crisscrossed in a happy chaos.

After 1935 (although ambiguity remained in specific areas like trust-busting), the over-all direction of the New Deal became clear: it was sympathetic to the underprivileged, and to organized labor, and it was pervaded by a general spirit of liberal, humanitarian reform. But also the scope of the New Deal became clear. This limitation is shown in a number of issues that the New Deal faced, or sometimes tried to avoid facing, between 1933 and 1939: the problem of planning; the question of how to deal with monopolistic business; the controversy over deficit financing and the extension of public enterprise; the creation of an adequate system of social security.

IV.

When Roosevelt told students at Ogelthorpe University during his 1932 campaign that he was in favor of a "larger measure of social planning," it was not clear how large this measure was. Was he willing to go as far as his own advisor, Columbia professor Rexford Guy Tugwell? Tugwell attacked the profit motive, said that "planning for production means planning for consumption too," declared that "profits must be limited and their uses controlled," and said he meant by planning "something not unlike an integrated group of enterprises run for its consumers rather than for its owners." The statement, he said, that "business will logically be required to disappear" is "literally meant" because: "Planning also implies adjustment of production to consumption; and there is no way of accomplishing this except through a control of prices and of profit margins. To limit business in all these ways, he said, meant in effect "to destroy it as business and to make of it something else."

Raymond Moley, who played a direct role in shaping Roosevelt's early legislation, also deplored the lack of planning in the New Deal. But Moley was interested in planning for quite different groups. Tugwell was concerned with the lower classes' lack of purchasing power. Moley, although he too was moved by a measure of genuine concern for deprived people, was most worried about "the narrow margin of profit" and "business confidence." In the end, Roosevelt rejected both ideas. Whatever planning he would do would try to help the lower classes, for example, the Tennessee Valley Authority. On the other hand, the planning would not be national; nor would it interfere with the fundamental character of the American economy, based as it was on corporate profit; nor would it attempt any fundamental redistribution of wealth in the nation. And the TVA embodied these too because it represented *piecemeal* planning.

David Lilienthal's defense of this method, in his book on the TVA, comes closest to the New Deal approach. "We move step by step—from where we are," wrote Lilienthal. Not only was any notion of national economic planning never seriously considered, but after the TVA, the moving "step by step" did not carry very far. Housing developments and several planned communities were inspiring, but came nowhere near matching the enormity of the national need.

Ambiguity persisted longest in the policy towards monopoly and oligopoly. The NRA was a frank recognition of the usefulness—or at least, the inevitability—of large enterprise, when ordered by codes. The Securities Exchange Commission and the Public Utilities Holding Company Act moved back (but weakly, as William O. Douglas recognized at the time) to the Brandeis idea of trying to curb the size and strength of large enterprises. Roosevelt's basic policy towards giantism in business, although he vigorously attacked "economic royalists" in 1936, remained undetermined until 1938, when he asked Congress for a sweeping investigation of monopoly. And although he was clearly returning to the idea of restraining the power of big business, one sentence in his message to Congress reveals his continuing uncertainty: "The power of the few to manage the economic life of the Nation must be diffused among the many or be transferred to the public and its democratically responsible government."

The first alternative was an obviously romantic notion; the second was really much farther than either Congress or FDR was prepared to go. Hence, the Temporary National Economic Committee, after hearing enough testimony to fill thirty-one volumes and forty-three monographs, was unwilling, as William Leuchtenburg writes, "to tackle the more difficult problems or to make recommendations which might disturb vested interests." Roosevelt had come close to expressing, but he still did not possess, nor did he communicate to the nation, a clear, resolute goal of transferring giant and irresponsible economic power "to the public and its democratically responsible government." The restraints on the New Dealers' thinking is shown best perhaps by Adolf A. Berle, who said that prosperity depended on either a gigantic expansion of private activity or nationalization of key industries. Yet, knowing private industry was not going to fill the need, he did not advocate nationalization—nor did any other New Dealer.

Roosevelt was experimental, shifting, and opportunistic in his espousal of public enterprise and the spending that had to accompany such governmental activity. As James MacGregor Burns says: "Roosevelt had tried rigid economy, then heady spending, then restriction of spending again. He had shifted back and forth from spending on direct relief to spending on public works." The significant measure, however, was not the swings of the pendulum, but the width of the arcs. When FDR went all-out for spending, it was still only a fraction of what the British economist John Maynard Keynes was urging as a way of bringing recovery. An American Keynesian, Professor Alvin Hansen, was arguing that the economy was "mature" and therefore required much more continuous and powerful injections of governmental spending than was being given.

Roosevelt himself had introduced into public discussion the idea of a "yardstick," which the Tennessee Valley Authority represented—a public enterprise that would, by competing with private producers, force them to bend more towards the needs of the consumer. (Later FDR tried, unsuccessfully, to get Congress to introduce "seven little TVAs" in other river valleys.) But the vast implications of the concept were left unexplored. When political scientist Max Lerner called for government-owned radio stations and government-subsidized newspapers to break into the growing monopolization of public opinion by giant chains, there was no response. TVA, a brief golden period of federal theater, a thin spread of public housing, and a public works program called into play only at times of desperation, represented the New Deal's ideological and emotional limits in the creation of public enterprise.

It is one thing to experiment to discover the best means of achieving a certain objective; it is quite another thing to fail to recognize that objective. The Social Security System, as set up, was not an experiment to find the best type of system. Roosevelt knew from the beginning that it was not the most effective way to handle the problems of poverty for the aged, the unemployed, and the helpless. Behind the basic political problem of getting the bill passed lay fundamental narrowness of vision. Social security expert Abraham Epstein pointed this out at the time, and it was noted on the floor of Congress. Henry E. Sigerist, a physician and student of welfare medicine in other countries, wrote patiently and clearly about the need for socialized medicine, answered the arguments against it, and explained how it might operate.

Thus, if the concept of New Deal thought is widened to include a large circle of thinkers—some close to the administration itself, others at varying distances from it—we get not panaceas, or infallible schemes but larger commitments, bolder goals, and greater expectations of what "equality" and "justice" and "security" meant.

V.

For our view of the New Deal as a particularly energetic gyroscopic motion putting the traditional structure aright again, we have what the natural scientists might call a set of "controls"—a way of checking up on the hypothesis—one in the area of race relations, another in the experience of war.

In the field of racial equality, where there was no crisis as in economics, where the gyroscope did not confront a sharply titled mechanism, there was no "new deal." The special encumbrances of the depression were lifted for Negroes as for many other Americans, but the permanent caste structure remained unaltered by the kind of innovations that at least threatened the traditional edifice in economics. The white South was left, as it had been since the Compromise of 1877, to deal with Negroes as it chose—by murder, by beatings, by ruthless exclusion from political and economic life; the Fourteenth Amendment waited as fruitlessly for executive enforcement as it had in all earlier administrations since Grant. Washington, D.C., itself remained a tightly segregated city. And the Harlems of the North continued as great symbols of national failure.

The warm belief in equal rights held by Eleanor Roosevelt, as well as by FDR himself, the appointments of Mary McLeod Bethune, Robert Weaver, and others to important secondary posts in the government, even the wide distribution of relief and WPA jobs, were not enough to alter the fundamental injustice attached to being a Negro in the United States. The disposition of the New Deal to experiment could have led to important accomplishments, but the clear goal of ending segregation, as with comparable objectives in economics, was never established.

With the coming of World War II, economic and social experimentation blossomed under Roosevelt's leadership and involved a good measure of national planning, jobs for everyone, and a vast system of post war educational benefits to eighteen million veterans. There was little inhibition; new, radically different national goals were not required for the traditional objective of winning at war. With such an aim, policy could be fearless and far-reaching.

Some coming generation perhaps, while paying proper respects to the spirit of the New Deal, may find, as William James put it, "the moral equivalent of war"—in new social goals, new expectations, with imaginative, undoctrinaire experimentation to attain them. If, in such an adventure, the thought of the past can help, it should be put to work.

6

Who Owns
the Sun?

I take this title from a 1996 book by Daniel Berman and John O'Connor (*Who Owns the Sun? People, Politics, and the Struggle for a Solar Economy*), in which they make out a powerful case for the control of solar energy by the citizenry instead of by the corporate utilities. The article here that I wrote twenty years ago for the *Boston Globe* (February 28, 1975) may be out of date in its specific proposals for action, but it suggests that problems of class, of poverty and deprivation, were as true in the Seventies (a decade often presented as a prosperous one) as any other time. The spirit of the article, I believe, is still pertinent today.

As kids, we never came straight home from school. Those were the depression years, and I was growing up in New York. The sun set early on winter evenings, and I remember coming home to find my father, who had walked the streets all day looking for work (he was a waiter and a window-washer, a hard-working man who never finished elementary school) sitting with my mother and three brothers in the darkness, in our four-room flat, because we hadn't paid our electric bill. It happened more than once.

When I learned that Boston Edison had shut off the electricity in over 1200 homes last month because people did not pay their bills, an old anger returned.

Why should rich corporations have the right to deprive families of electricity, of gas to cook with, of fuel to heat their homes. These are life's necessities, like food, air, water. They should not be the private property of corporations, which use them to hold us hostage to the dark, to the cold, until we pay their price.

It is as if, all over this country, families lived in intensive-care units, with the dials controlling their supply of precious life fluids manipulated in some office far away, turned on or off, depending on the payment of a fee.

Legally, that is not extortion. But I think it is. Officially, it does not lead to loss of life. But then we have to find some way to describe the act of the Massachusetts Electric Company, cutting off power to that family in Athol earlier this month because a bill was not paid, forcing it to rely on a makeshift kerosene stove for heat, resulting in a fire that killed six children and a woman.

How many families in Dorchester and Roxbury and Somerville are freezing this winter, how many eating cold suppers, how many living by candlelight, because they didn't pass the supreme test of worth in our society, the test of money?

The anger against this is growing. The helplessness, the frustration are turning into action:

1. A consumer group called Fair Share walked into a Boston Edison stockholders' meeting last week trying to present proposals against shutoffs and high rates. But there is as much democracy in stockholders' meetings as in an army regiment, and the chairman hurriedly adjourned the session.

2. In the Massachusetts Legislature, a bill supported by the signatures of 97,000 voters would put all new electric power production in the hands of the state, and possibly take existing plants away from the power companies. With publicly owned power, our bills would be much lower. The Federal Power Commission reported in 1970 that municipal

electrical systems charged about 40 percent less than private companies.

3. If you think your electric bill is too high, you can appeal to the state Department of Public Utilities. Then your service cannot be shut off and you don't have to pay your bill until you get a hearing, which can take months. A group called CAP-Energy (Citizens Action Program on Energy, 129 South St. Boston) is trying to get at least 20,000 customers of Boston Edison to pledge to withhold payment of exorbitant bills, through this legal method, until rates come down.

Shouldn't it be an elementary rule of civilization that no human being should be deprived of heat or light or cooking fuel because of lack of money? Where does all that gas and electricity come from anyway? From coal, from oil, from the earth, from the stored energy of the sun, shining down for a billion years. Who took it on themselves, in some distant past, to sell the sun to Boston Edison? And what must the public do to get it back?

7

The
Secret
Word

This article appeared in the *Boston Globe* January 24, 1976. Twenty years later, the Soviet Union and other countries in Eastern Europe which called themselves "socialist" have overturned their governments and do not call themselves that any more. This is just as well for those of us who think socialism is an honorable idea, and that it was badly tainted by those ugly dictatorships. With those governments fallen, and capitalism failing to solve basic problems of human rights (an equal right to life, liberty and the pursuit of happiness, as stated in the Declaration of Independence) this may be a good time to revive the word and the idea.

Do you remember the old Groucho Marx quiz program where, if a contestant happened to mention a certain secret word, the word dropped down and he or she won a big prize?

Well, there's a secret word I've been waiting many years for someone on TV to say—some news commentator, political figure, panelist, entertainer, anyone.

Lately, I've been especially careful in listening for it. On news programs, I've seen lines of unemployed people getting longer and longer. I've seen a movie made inside a welfare office, where old people were shunted around like cattle.

I've seen a program about citrus-fruit pickers in Florida, forced to take their little kids out of school to pick oranges with them so they could pay the rent. Meanwhile, the citrus owners were celebrating their prosperity with champagne and making speeches about how wonderful life was for everybody in the citrus industry.

I've watched the President at news conferences and his economic advisers at other news conferences, all pretending that things were going to be all right, but obviously bumbling and incapable of dealing with rising food prices, spreading unemployment, high rents, impossible medical costs and the shameful fact of a fabulously rich country unable to take care of the most basic needs of its people.

Not one of these people, on network programs watched by millions, mentioned the word which, with the obvious failure of our economic system, I thought someone was bound to blurt out.

The word? Socialism.

Of course, it's not just saying the word that is important. It's the idea of it— an idea too threatening to those who profit from the present system to be allowed adequate exploration on TV, radio, the newspapers, the motion pictures.

Let's hasten to say: I don't mean the "socialism" of Soviet Russia or any other oppressive regime claiming to be socialist. Rather, a genuine socialism which not only distributes the wealth but maintains liberty.

That may not exist anywhere in its best form, but the idea has caught the imagination of many people in world history, famous and obscure, who were sensitive to poverty and injustice and wanted a truly democratic world society, without war, without hunger, without discrimination.

There were Karl Marx and Rosa Luxemburg. Also, George Bernard Shaw, Helen Keller, Albert Einstein, W.E.B. DuBois.

Socialism was once an important movement in the United States. There was Eugene Debs, who organized the railroad workers in the big strike of 1894, went to prison for that, and there, reading and thinking, became a socialist: "While there is a lower class I am in it; while there is a criminal element I am of it; while there is a soul in prison I am not free."

There was Mother Jones, who at 82 fought alongside the coal miners against the Rockefeller interests in Colorado. There was Jack London, the adventure writer. And Heywood Broun, who organized newspapermen into a union and defended Sacco and Vanzetti against the cold authority of the governor of Massachusetts and the presidents of MIT and Harvard. And Elizabeth Gurley Flynn, who as an Irish rebel girl, helped the women textile workers of Lawrence in their successful strike of 1912. Socialists all.

In 1776, the time was right for Tom Paine to speak "Common Sense" about Independence, and the idea spread through the country. (It has just reached Gerald Ford.) Isn't the time right, in 1976, for us to begin discussing the idea of socialism?

To break the hold of corporations over our food, our rent, our work, our lives—to produce things people need, and give everyone useful work to do and distribute the wealth of the country with approximate equality—whether you call it socialism or not, isn't it common sense?

W A R

1

Just and Unjust War

I enlisted in the Army Air Corps in World War II and was an eager bombardier, determined to do everything I could to help defeat Fascism. Yet, at the end of the war, when I collected my little mementos—my photos, logs of some of my missions—I wrote on the folder, without really thinking, and surprising myself: "Never Again." In the years after the war, I began to plumb the reasons for that spontaneous reaction, and came to the conclusions which I describe in the following essay, published as a chapter in my book *Declarations of Independence* (HarperCollins, 1990).

Years before (in *Postwar America*, Bobbs Merrill, 1973), I had written an essay called "The Best of Wars," in which I questioned—I was unaware of anyone else asking the same question—the total acceptance of World War II. After my own experience in that war, I had moved away from my own rather orthodox view that there are just wars and unjust wars, to a universal rejection of war as a solution to any human problem. Of all the positions I have taken over the years on questions of history and politics, this has undoubtedly aroused the most controversy. It is obviously a difficult viewpoint to present persuasively. I try to do that here, and leave it to the reader to judge whether I have succeeded.

There are some people who do not question war. In 1972, the general who was head of the U.S. Strategic Air Command told an interviewer, "I've been asked often about my moral scruples if I had to send the planes out with hydrogen bombs. My answer is always the same. I would be concerned only with my professional responsibility."

It was a Machiavellian reply. Machiavelli did not ask if making war was right or wrong. He just wrote about the best way to wage it so as to conquer the enemy. One of his books is called *The Art of War*.

That title might make artists uneasy. Indeed, artists—poets, novelists, and playwrights as well as musicians, painters, and actors—have shown a special aversion to war. Perhaps because, as the playwright Arthur Miller once said, "When the guns boom, the arts die." But that would make their interest too self-centered; they have always been sensitive to the fate of the larger society round them. They have questioned war, whether in the fifth century before Christ, with the plays of Euripedes, or in modern times, with the paintings of Goya and Picasso.

Machiavelli was being *realistic*. Wars were going to be fought. The only question was how to win them.

Some people have believed that war is not just inevitable but desirable: "It is adventure and excitement, it brings out the best qualities in men—courage, comradeship, and sacrifice. It gives respect and glory to a country. In 1897, Theodore Roosevelt wrote to a friend, "In strict confidence...I should welcome almost any war, for I think this country needs one."

In our time, fascist regimes have glorified war as heroic and ennobling. Bombing Ethiopia in 1935, Mussolini's son-in-law Count Ciano described the explosions as an aesthetic thrill, as having the beauty of a flower unfolding.

In the 1980s two writers of a book on war see it as an effective instrument of national policy and say that even nuclear war can, under certain circumstances, be justified. They are contemptuous of "the pacifist passions: self-indulgence and fear," and of "American statesmen, who believe victory is an archaic concept." They say, "The bottom line in war and hence in political warfare is who gets buried and who gets to walk in the sun."

Most people are not that enamored of war. They see it as bad, but also as a possible means to something good. And so they distinguish between wars that are just and those that are unjust. The religions of the West and Middle East—Judaism, Christianity, and Islam—approve of violence and war under certain circumstances. The Catholic church has a specific doctrine of "just" and "unjust" war, worked out in some detail. Political philosophers today argue about which wars, or which actions in wars, may be considered just or unjust.

Beyond both viewpoints—the glorification of war and the weighing of good and bad wars—there is a third: that war is too evil to ever be just. The monk Erasmus, writing in the early sixteenth century, was repelled by war of any kind. One of his pupils was killed in battle and he reacted with anguish:

> Tell me, what had you to do with Mars, the stupidest of all the poet's gods, you who were consecrated to the Muses, nay to Christ? Your youth, your beauty, your gentle nature, your honest mind—what had they to do with the flourishing of trumpets, the bombards, the swords?

Erasmus described war: "There is nothing more wicked, more disastrous, more widely destructive, more deeply tenacious, more loathsome." He said this was repugnant to nature: "Whoever heard of a hundred thousand animals rushing together to butcher each other, as men do everywhere?"

Erasmus saw war as useful to governments, for it enabled them to enhance their power over their subjects: "...once war has been declared, then all the affairs of the State are at the mercy of the appetites of a few."

This absolute aversion to war of any kind is outside the orthodoxy of modern thinking. In a series of lectures at Oxford University in the 1970s, English scholar Michael Howard talked disparagingly about Erasmus. He called him simplistic, unsophisticated, and someone who did not see beyond the "surface manifestations" of war. He said,

> With all [Erasmus's] genius he was not a profound political analyst, nor did he ever have to exercise the responsibilities of power. Rather he was the first in that long line of humanitarian thinkers for whom it was enough to chronicle the horrors of war in order to condemn it.

Howard had praise for Thomas More: "Very different was the approach of Erasmus's friend, Thomas More; a man who had exercised political responsibility and, perhaps in consequence, saw the problem in all its complexity." More was a realist; Howard says,

> He accepted, as thinkers for the next two hundred years were to accept, that European society was organized in a system of states in which war was an inescapable process for the settlement of differences in the absence of any higher common jurisdiction. That being the case, it was a requirement of humanity, of religion and of common sense alike that those wars should be fought in such a manner as to cause as little damage as possible.... For better or worse war was an institution which could not be eliminated from the international system. All that could be done about it was, so far as possible, to codify its rationale and to civilize its means.

Thus, Machiavelli said: Don't question the ends of the prince, just tell him how best to do what he wants to do, make the means more *efficient*. Thomas More said: You can't do anything about the ends, but try to make the means more *moral*.

In the 400 years following the era of Machiavelli and More, making war more humane became the preoccupation of certain liberal "realists." Hugo Grotius, writing a century after More, proposed laws to govern the waging of war (*Concerning the Law of War and Peace*). The beginning of the twentieth century saw international conferences at The Hague in the Netherlands and at Geneva in Switzerland which drew up agreements on how to wage war.

These realistic approaches however, had little effect on the reality of war. Rather than becoming more controlled, war became more uncontrolled and more deadly, using more horrible means and killing more noncombatants than ever before in the history of mankind. We note the use of poison gas in World War I, the bombardment of cities in World War II, the atomic destruction of Hiroshima and Nagasaki near the end of that war, the use of napalm in Vietnam, and the chemical warfare in the Iran-Iraq war of the early 1980s.

Albert Einstein, observing the effects of attempts to "humanize" wars, became more and more anguished. In 1932, he attended a conference of sixty nations in Geneva and listened to the lengthy discussions of which weapons were acceptable and which were not, which forms of killing were legitimate and which were not.

Einstein was a shy, private person, but he did something extraordinary for him: he called a press conference in Geneva. The international press turned out in force to hear Einstein, already world famous for his theories of relativity. Einstein told the assembled reporters, "One does not make wars less likely by formulating rules of warfare...War cannot be humanized. It can only be abolished." But the Geneva conference went on, working out rules for "humane" warfare, rules that were repeatedly ignored in the world war soon to come, a war of endless atrocities.

In early 1990 President George Bush, while approving new weapons systems for nuclear warheads (of which the United States had about 30,000) and refusing to join the Soviet Union in stopping nuclear testing, was willing to agree to destroy chemical weapons, but only over a ten-year period. Such are the absurdities of "humanizing" war.

Liberal States and Just Wars: Athens

The argument that there are just wars often rests on the social system of the nation engaging in war. It is supposed that if a "liberal" state is at war with a "totalitarian" state, then the war is justified. The beneficent nature of a government is assumed to give rightness to the wars it wages.

Ancient Athens has been one of the most admired of all societies, praised for its democratic institutions and its magnificent cultural achievements. It had enlightened statesmen (Solon and Pericles), pioneer historians (Herodotus and Thucydides), great philosophers (Plato and Aristotle), and an extraordinary quartet of playwrights (Aeschylus, Sophocles, Euripides, and Aristphanes). When it went to war in 431 B.C. against its rival power, the city-state of Sparta, the war seemed to be between a democratic society and a military dictatorship.

The great qualities of Athens were described early in that war by the Athenian leader Pericles at a public celebration for the warriors, dead or alive. The bones of the dead were placed in chests; there was an empty litter for the missing. There was a procession, a burial, and then Pericles spoke. Thucydides recorded Pericles' speech in his *History of the Peloponnesian War.*

> Before I praise the dead, I should like to point out by what principles of action we rose to power, and under what institutions and through what manner of life our empire became great. Our form of government does not

enter into rivalry with the institutions of others... It is true that we are called a democracy, for the administration is in the hands of the many and not of the few.... The law secures equal justice to all alike.... Neither is poverty a bar.... There is no exclusiveness in our public life.... At home the style of our life is refined.... Because of the greatness of our city the fruits of the whole earth flow in upon us.... And although our opponents are fighting for their homes and we on foreign soil, we seldom have any difficulty in overcoming them.... I have dwelt upon the greatness of Athens because I want to show you that we are contending for a higher prize than those who enjoy none of these privileges.

Similarly, American presidents in time of war have pointed to the qualities of the American system as evidence for the justness of the cause. Woodrow Wilson and Franklin Roosevelt were liberals, which gave credence to their words exalting the two world wars, just as the liberalism of Truman made going into Korea more acceptable and the idealism of Kennedy's New Frontier and Johnson's Great Society gave an early glow of righteousness to the war in Vietnam.

But we should take a closer look at the claim that liberalism at home carries over into military actions abroad.

The tendency, especially in time of war, is to exaggerate the difference between oneself and the opponent, to assume the conflict is between total good and total evil. It was true that Athens had certain features of political democracy. Each of ten tribes selected 50 representatives, by lot, to make a governing council of 500. Trial juries were large, from 100 to 1,000 people, with no judge and no professional lawyers; the cases were handled by the people involved.

Yet, these democratic institutions only applied to a minority of the population. A majority of the people—125,000 out off 225,000—were slaves. Even among the free people, only males were considered citizens with the right to participate in the political process.

Of the slaves, 50,000 worked in industry (this is as if, in the United States in 1990, 50 million people worked in industry as slaves) and 10,000 worked in the mines. H.D. Kitto, a leading scholar on Greek civilization and a great admirer of Athens, wrote: "The treatment of the miners was callous in the extreme, the only serious blot on the general humanity of the Athenians.... Slaves were often worked until they died." (To Kitto and others, slavery was only a "blot" on an otherwise wonderful society.)

The jury system in Athens was certainly preferable to summary executions by tyrants. Nevertheless, it put Socrates to death for speaking his mind to young people.

Athens was more democratic than Sparta, but this did not affect its addiction to warfare, to expansion into other territories, to the ruthless conduct of war against helpless peoples. In modern times we have seen the ease with which parliamentary democracies and constitutional republics have been among the most ferocious of imperialists. We recall the British and French empires of the nineteenth century and the United States as a world imperial power in this century.

Throughout the long war with Sparta, Athens' democratic institutions and artistic achievements continued. But the death toll was enormous. Pericles, on the eve of war, refused to make concessions that might have prevented it. In the second year of war, with the casualties mounting quickly, Pericles urged his fellow citizens not to weaken: "You have a great polis, and a great reputation; you must be worthy of them. Half the world is yours—the sea. For you the alternative to empire is slavery."

Pericles' kind of argument ("Ours is a great nation. It is worth dying for.") has persisted and been admired down to the present. Kitto, commenting on that speech by Pericles, again overcome by admiration, wrote,

> When we reflect that this plague was as awful as the Plague of London, and that the Athenians had the additional horror of being cooped up inside their fortifications by the enemy without, we must admire the greatness of the man who could talk to his fellow citizens like this, and the greatness of the people who could not only listen to such a speech at such a time but actually be substantially persuaded by it.

They were enough persuaded by it so that the war with Sparta lasted twenty-seven years. Athens lost through plague and war (according to Kitto's own estimate) perhaps one-fourth of its population.

However liberal it was for its free male citizens at home, Athens became more and more cruel to its victims in war, not just to its enemy Sparta, but to every one caught in the crossfire of the two antagonists. As the war went on, Kitto himself says, "a certain irresponsibility grew."

Could the treatment of the inhabitants of the island of Melos be best described as "a certain irresponsibility"? Athens demanded that the

Melians submit to its rule. The Melians, however, argued (as reported by Thucydides), "It may be to your interest to be our masters, but how can it be ours to be your slaves?" The Melians would not submit. They fought and were defeated. Thucydides wrote, "The Athenians thereupon put to death all who were of military age, and made slaves of the women and children." (It was shortly after this event that Euripides wrote his great antiwar play, *The Trojan Women*).

What the experience of Athens suggests is that a nation may be relatively liberal at home and yet totally ruthless abroad. Indeed, it may more easily enlist its population in cruelty to others by pointing to the advantages at home. An entire nation is made into mercenaries, being paid with a bit of democracy at home for participating in the destruction of life abroad.

Liberalism at War

Liberalism at home, however, seems to become corrupted by war waged abroad. French philosopher Jean Jacques Rousseau noted that conquering nations "make war at least as much on their subjects as on their enemies." Tom Paine, in America, saw war as the creature of governments, serving their own interests, not the interests of justice for their citizens. "Man is not the enemy of man but through the medium of a false system of government." In our time, George Orwell has written that wars are mainly "internal."

One certain effect of war is to diminish freedom of expression. Patriotism becomes the order of the day, and those who question the war are seen as traitors, to be silenced and imprisoned.

Mark Twain, observing the United States at the turn of the century, its wars in Cuba and the Philippines, described in *The Mysterious Stranger* the process by which wars that are at first seen as unnecessary by the mass of the people become converted into "just" wars:

> The loud little handful will shout for war. The pulpit will warily and cautiously protest at first.... The great mass of the nation will rub its sleepy eyes, and will try to make out why there should be a war, and they will say earnestly and indignantly: "It is unjust and dishonorable and there is no need for war."
>
> Then the few will shout even louder.... Before long you will see a curious thing: anti-war speakers will be stoned from the platform, and free

speech will be strangled by hordes of furious men who still agree with the speakers but dare not admit it...

Next, the statesmen will invent cheap lies...and each man will be glad of these lies and will study them because they soothe his conscience; and thus he will bye and bye convince himself that the war is just and he will thank God for a better sleep he enjoys by his self-deception.

Mark Twain died in 1910. In 1917, the United States entered the slaughterhouse of the European war, and the process of silencing dissent and converting a butchery into a just war took place as he had predicted.

President Woodrow Wilson tried to rouse the nation, using the language of a crusade. It was a war, he said, "to end all wars." but large numbers of Americans were reluctant to join. A million men were needed, yet in the first six weeks after the declaration of war only 73,000 volunteered. It seemed that men would have to be compelled to fight by fear of prison, so Congress enacted a draft law.

The Socialist Party at the time was a formidable influence in the country. It had perhaps 100,000 members, and more than a thousand Socialists had been elected to office in 340 towns and cities. Probably a million Americans read Socialist newspapers. There were fifty-five weekly Socialist newspapers in Oklahoma, Texas, Louisiana, and Arkansas alone; over a hundred Socialists were elected to office in Oklahoma. The Socialist party candidate for president, Eugene Debs, got 900,000 votes in 1912 (Wilson won with 6 million).

A year before the United States entered the European war, Helen Keller, blind and deaf and a committed Socialist, told an audience at Carnegie Hall:

Strike against war, for without you no battles can be fought! Strike against manufacturing shrapnel and gas bombs and all other tools of murder! Strike against preparedness that means death and misery to millions of human beings! Be not dumb, obedient slaves in an army of destruction! Be heroes in an army of construction!

The day after Congress declared war, the Socialist party met in an emergency convention and called the declaration "a crime against the American people." Antiwar meetings took place all over the country. In the local elections of 1917, Socialists made great gains. Ten Socialists were elected to the New York State legislature. In Chicago the Socialist party had won 3.6 percent of the vote in 1915 and it got 34.7 percent in 1917. But with the advent of war, speaking against it became a crime; Debs and hundreds of other Socialists were imprisoned.

When that war ended, 10 million men of various countries had died on the battlefields of Europe, and millions more had been blinded, maimed, gassed, shell-shocked, and driven mad. It was hard to find in that war any gain for the human race to justify that suffering, that death.

Indeed, when the war was studied years later, it was clear that no rational decision based on any moral principle had led the nations into war. Rather, there were imperial rivalries, greed for more territory, a lusting for national prestige, and the stupidity of revenge. And at the last moment, there was a reckless plunge by governments caught up in a series of threats and counterthreats, mobilizations and countermobilizations, ultimatums and counterultimatums, creating a momentum that mediocre leaders had neither the courage nor the will to stop. As described by Barbara Tuchman in her book *The Guns of August*:

> War pressed against every frontier. Suddenly dismayed, governments strug-
> gled and twisted to fend it off. It was no use. Agents at frontiers were
> reporting every cavalry patrol as a deployment to beat the mobilization
> gun. General staffs, goaded by their relentless timetables, were pounding
> the table for the signal to move lest their opponents gain an hour's head
> start. Appalled upon the brink, the chiefs of state who would be ultimate-
> ly responsible for their country's fare attempted to back away, but the pull
> of military schedules dragged them forward.

Bitterness and disillusion followed the end of the war, and this was reflected in the literature of those years: Ernest Hemingway's *A Farewell to Arms*, John Dos Passo's *U.S.A.*, and Ford Madox Ford's *No More Parades*. In Europe, German war veteran Erich Maria Remarque wrote the bitter antiwar novel *All Quiet on the Western Front*.

In 1935 French playwright Jean Giradoux wrote *La guerre de Troi n'aura pas lieu (The Trojan War WIll Not Take Place*; the English transla-
tion was retitled *Tiger at the Gates*). The war of the Greeks against Troy, more than a thousand years before Christ, was provoked, according to legend, by the kidnapping of the beautiful Helen by the Trojans. Giraudoux at one point uses Hecuba, an old woman, and Demokos, a Trojan soldier, to show how the ugliness of war is masked by attractive causes, as in this case, the recapture of Helen.

Demokos: Tell us before you go, Hecuba, what it is you think war looks like.

Hecuba: Like the bottom of a baboon. When the baboon is up in a tree, with its hind end facing us, there is the face of war exactly; scarlet, scaly, glazed, framed in a clotted filthy wig.

Demokos: So war has two faces: this you describe, and Helen's.

An Eager Bombardier

My own first impressions of something called war had come at the age of ten, when I read with excitement a series of books about "the boy allies"—A French boy, an English boy, an American boy, and a Russian boy, who became friends, united in the wonderful cause to defeat Germany in World War I. It was an adventure, a romance, told in a group of stories about comradeship and heroism. It was war cleansed of death and suffering.

If anything was left of that romantic view of war, it was totally extinguished when, at eighteen, I read a book by a Hollywood screen-writer named Dalton Trumbo (jailed in the 1950s for refusing to talk to the House Committee on Un-American Activities about his political affiliations). The book was called *Johnny Got His Gun*. It is perhaps, the most powerful antiwar novel ever written.

Here was war in its ultimate horror. A slab of flesh in an American uniform had been found on the battlefield, still alive, with no legs, no arms, no face, blind, deaf, unable to speak, but the heart still beating, the brain still functioning, able to think about his past, ponder his present condition, and wonder if he will ever be able to communicate with the world outside.

For him, the oratory of the politicians who sent him off to war—the language of freedom, democracy, and justice—is now seen as the ultimate hypocrisy. A mute, thinking torso on a hospital bed, he finds a way to communicate with a kindly nurse, and when a visiting delegation of military brass comes by to pin a medal on his body, he taps out a message. He says: Take me into the workplaces, into the schools, show me to the little children and to the college students, let them see what war is like.

Take me wherever there are parliaments and diets and congresses and chambers of statesmen. I want to be there when they talk about honor and justice and making the world safe for democracy and fourteen points and the self determination of peoples.... Put my glass case upon the speaker's desk and every time the gavel descends let me feel its vibration.... Then let them speak of trade policies and embargoes and new colonies and old grudges. Let them debate the menace of the yellow race and the white man's burden and the course of empire and why should we take all this crap off Germany or whoever the next Germany is.... Let them talk more munitions and airplanes and battleships and tanks and gases and why of course we've got to have them we can't get along without them how in the world could we protect the peace if we didn't have them...

But before they vote on them before they give the order for all the little guys to start killing each other let the main guy rap his gavel on my case and point down at me and say here gentleman is the only issue before this house and that is are you for this thing here or are you against it.

Johnny Got His Gun had a shattering effect on me when I read it. It left me with a bone-deep hatred of war.

Around the same time I read a book by Walter Millis, *The Road to War,* which was an account of how the United States had been led into World War I by a series of lies and deceptions. Afterward I would learn more about those lies. For instance, the sinking of the ship *Lusitania* by German submarines was presented as a brutal, unprovoked act against a harmless passenger vessel. It was later revealed that the *Lusitania* was loaded with munitions, intended for use against Germany; the ship's manifest had been falsified to hide that. This didn't lessen the ugliness of the sinking, but did show something about the ways in which nations are lured into war.

Class consciousness accounted for some of my feeling about war. I agreed with the judgment of the Roman biographer Plutarch, who said, "The poor go to war, to fight and die for the delights, riches, and superfluities of others."

And yet, in early 1943, at the age of twenty-one, I enlisted in the U.S. Army Air Force. American troops were already in North Africa, Italy, and England; there was fierce fighting on the Russian front and the United States and Britain were preparing for the invasion of Western Europe. Bombing raids were taking place daily on the continent, U.S. planes bombing during the day, British planes bombing at night. I was so anxious to get overseas and start dropping bombs that after my training in gunnery school and bombing school I traded places with another man who was scheduled to go overseas sooner than me.

I had learned to hate war. But this war was different. It was not for profit or empire, it was a people's war, a war against the unspeakable brutality of fascism. I had been reading about Italian fascism in a book about Mussolini by journalist George Seldes called *Sawdust Caesar*. I was inspired by his account of the Socialist Matteotti, who stood up in the Italian Chamber of Deputies to denounce the establishment of a dictatorship. The black-shirted thugs of Mussolini's party picked up Matteotti outside his home one morning and shot him to death. That was fascism.

Mussolini's Italy, deciding to restore the glory of the old Roman Empire, invaded the East African country of Ethiopia, a pitifully poor country. Its people, armed with spears and muskets, tried to fight off an Italian army equipped with the most modern weapons and with an air force that, unopposed, dropped bombs on the civilian populations of Ethiopian towns and villages. The Ethiopians who resisted were slaughtered, and finally surrendered.

American black poet Langston Hughes wrote,

The little fox is still—
The dogs of war have made their kill.

I was thirteen when this happened and was only vaguely aware of headlines: "Italian Planes Bomb Addis Ababa." But later I read about it and also about German Nazism. John Gunther's *Inside Europe* introduced me to the rise of Hitler, the SA, the SS, the attacks on the Jews, the shrill oratory of the little man with the mustache, and the monster rallies of Germans in sports stadia who shouted in unison: "Heil Hitler! Heil Hitler!" Opponents were beaten and murdered. I learned the phrase *concentration camp*.

I came across a book called *The Brown Book of the Nazi Terror*. It told in detail about the burning of the German Reichstag shortly after Hitler came to power and the arrest of Communists accused of setting the fire, clearly a frame-up. It told also of the extraordinary courage of the defendants, led by the remarkable Bulgarian Communist George Dimitrov, who rose in the courtroom to point an accusing finger at Hermann Goering, Hitler's lieutenant. Dimitrov tore the prosecution's case to shreds and denounced the Nazi regime. The defendants were acquitted by the court. It was an amazing moment, which would never be repeated under Hitler.

In 1936 Hitler and Mussolini sent their troops and planes to support the Spanish Fascist Franco, who had plunged his country into civil war to overthrow the mildly socialist Spanish government. The Spanish Civil War became the symbol all over the world of resistance to fascism, and young men—many of them socialists, Communists and anarchists—volunteered from a dozen countries, forming brigades (from the United States, the Abraham Lincoln Brigade), going immediately into battle against the better-equipped army of Franco. They fought heroically and died in great numbers. The Fascists won.

Then came the Hitler onslaught in Europe—Austria, Czechoslovakia, and Poland. France and England entered the war, and, a year after the quick defeat of France, three million German soldiers supported by tanks, artillery, and dive bombers turned eastward to attack the Soviet Union ("Operation Barbarossa") along a thousand-mile front.

Fascism had to be resisted and defeated. I had no doubts. This was a just war.

I was stationed at an airfield out in the countryside of East Anglia (between the towns of Diss and Eye), that part of England that bulges eastward toward the Continent. East Anglia was crowded with military airfields, from which hundreds of bombers went out every day across the Channel.

Our little airfield housed the 490th Bomb Group. Its job was to make sure that every morning twelve B17s—splendid-looking, low-winged, four-engined heavy bombers—each with a crew of nine, wearing sheepskin jackets and fur-lined boots over electrically heated suits and equipped with oxygen masks and throat mikes—were ready to fly. We would take off around dawn and assemble with other groups of twelve, and then these huge flotillas would make their way east. Our bomb bay was full; our fifty-caliber machine guns (four in the nose, one in the upper turret, one in the ball turret, two in the waist, and one in the tail) were loaded and ready for attacking fighter planes.

I remember one morning standing out on that airfield, arguing with another bombardier over who was scheduled to fly that morning's mission. The target was Regensburg, and Intelligence reported that it was heavily defended by antiaircraft guns, but the two of us argued heatedly over who was going to fly that mission. I wonder today, was his motive like mine—wanting to fly another mission to bring closer the defeat of fascism. Or was it because we had all been awakened at one A.M. in the cold dark of England in March, loaded onto trucks, taken to hours of briefings and breakfast, weighed down with equipment, and after going through all that, he did not want to be deprived of another step toward his air medal, another mission. Even though he might be killed.

Maybe that was partly my motive too, I can't be sure. But for me, it was also a war of high principle, and each bombing mission was a mission of high principle. The moral issue could hardly be clearer. The enemy could not be more obviously evil—openly espousing the superiority of the white Aryan, fanatically violent and murderous toward other nations, herding its own people into concentration camps, executing them if they dared dissent. The Nazis were pathological killers. They had to be stopped, and there seemed no other way but by force.

If there was such a thing as a just war, this was it. Even Dalton Trumbo, who had written *Johnny Got His Gun*, did not want his book to be reprinted, did not want that overpowering antiwar message to reach the American public, when a war had to be fought against fascism.

If, therefore, anyone wants to argue (as I am about to do) that there is no such thing as a just war, then World War II is the supreme test.

I flew the last bombing missions of the war, got my Air Medal and my battle stars. I was quietly proud of my participation in the great war to defeat fascism. But when I packed up my things at the end of the war and put my old navigation logs and snapshots and other mementos in a folder, I marked that folder, almost without thinking, "Never Again."

I'm still not sure why I did that, because it was not until years later that I began consciously to question the motives, the conduct, and the consequences of that crusade against fascism. The point was not that my abhorrence of fascism was in any way diminished. I still believed something had to be done to stop fascism. But that clear certainty of moral rightness that propelled me into the Air Force as an enthusiastic bombardier was now clouded over by many thoughts.

Perhaps my conversations with that gunner on the other crew, the one who loaned me *The Yogi and the Commisar*, gave me the first flickers of doubt. He spoke of the war as "an imperialist war," fought on both sides for national power. Britain and the United States opposed fascism only because it threatened their own control over resources and people. Yes, Hitler was a maniacal dictator and invader of other countries. But what of the British Empire and its long history of wars against native peoples to subdue them for the profit and glory of the empire? And the Soviet Union—was it not also a brutal dictatorship, concerned not with the working classes of the world but with its own national power?

I was puzzled. "Why," I asked my friend, "are you flying missions, risking your life, in a war you don't believe in?" His answer astonished me. "I'm here to speak to people like you."

I found out later he was a member of the Socialist Workers party; they opposed the war but believed that instead of evading military service they should enter it and propagandize against the war every moment they could. I couldn't understand this, but I was impressed by it. Two weeks after that conversation with him, he was killed on a mission over Germany.

After the war, my doubts grew. I was reading history. Had the United States fought in World War II for the rights of nations to independence and self-determination? What of its own history of expansion through war and conquest? It had waged a hundred-year war against the native Americans, driving them off their ancestral lands. The United States had instigated a war with Mexico and taken almost half its land, had sent marines at least twenty times into the countries of the Caribbean for power and profit, had seized Hawaii, had fought a brutal war to subjugate the Filipinos, and had sent 5,000 marines into Nicaragua in 1926. Our nation could hardly claim it believed in the right of self-determination unless it believed in it selectively.

Indeed, the United States had observed Fascist expansion without any strong reactions. When Italy invaded Ethiopia, the United States, while declaring an embargo on munitions, allowed American businesses to send oil to Italy, which was crucial for carrying on the war against Ethiopia. An official of the U.S. State Department, James E. Miller, reviewing a book on the relations between the United States and Mussolini, acknowledged that "American aid certainly reinforced the hold of Fascism."

During the Spanish Civil War, while the Fascist side was receiving arms from Hitler and Mussolini, Roosevelt's administration sponsored a Neutrality Act that shut off help to the Spanish government fighting Franco.

Neither the invasion of Austria nor Czechoslovakia nor Poland brought the United States into armed collision with fascism. We went to war only when our possession Hawaii was attacked and when our navy was disabled by Japanese bombs. There was no reason to think that it was Japan's bombing of civilians at Pearl Harbor that caused us to declare war. Japan's attack on China in 1937, her massacre of civilians at Nanking, and her bombardments of helpless Chinese cities had not provoked the United States to war.

The sudden indignation against Japan contained a good deal of hypocrisy. The United States, along with Japan and the great European powers, had participated in the exploitation of China. Our Open Door Policy of 1901 accepted that ganging up of the great powers on China. The United States had exchanged notes with Japan in 1917 saying, "the Government of the United States recognizes that Japan has special interests in China," and in 1928, American consuls in China supported the coming of Japanese troops.

It was only when Japan threatened potential U.S. markets by its attempted takeover of China, but especially as it moved toward the tin, rubber, and oil of Southeast Asia, that the United States became alarmed and took those measures that led to the Japanese attack: a total embargo on scrap iron and a total embargo on oil in the summer of 1941.

A State Department memorandum on Japanese expansion, a year before Pearl Harbor, did not talk of the independence of China or the principle of self-determination. It said,

> Our general diplomatic and strategic position would be considerably weakened—by our loss of Chinese, Indian and South Seas markets (and by our loss of much of the Japanese market for our goods, as Japan would become more and more self-sufficient) as well as by insurmountable restrictions upon our access to the rubber, tin jute, and other vital materials of the Asian and Oceanic regions.

A War to Save the Jews

Did the United States enter the war because of its indignation at Hitler's treatment of the Jews? Hitler had been in power a year, and his campaign against the Jews had already begun when, in January 1934, a resolution was introduced into the Senate expressing "surprise and pain" at what the Germans were doing and asking for a restoration of Jewish rights. The State Department used its influence to get the resolution buried in committee.

Even after we were in the war against Germany (it should be noted that after Pearl Harbor Germany declared war on the United States, not vice versa) and reports began to arrive that Hitler was planning the annihilation of the Jews, Roosevelt's administration failed to take steps that might have saved thousands of lives.

Goebbels, minister of propaganda for Hitler's Germany, wrote in his diary on December 13, 1942: "At bottom, however, I believe both the English and the Americans are happy we are exterminating the Jewish riffraff." Goebbels was undoubtedly engaging in wishful thinking, but in fact, the English and American governments had not shown by their actions that they were terribly concerned about the Jews. As for Roosevelt, he shunted the problem to the State Department, where it did not become a matter of high priority.

As an example of this failure to treat the situation as an emergency, Raul Hilberg, a leading scholar of the Holocaust, points to an event that took place in 1942. Early in August of that year, with 1,500,000 Jews already dead, the Jewish leader Stephen Wise was informed indirectly through a German industrialist that there was a plan in Hitler's headquarters for the extermination of all Jews; Wise brought the information to Under Secretary of State Sumner Welles. Welles asked him not to release the story until it was investigated for confirmation. Three months were spent checking the report. During that time a million Jews were killed in Europe.

It is doubtful that all those Jews could have been saved. But thousands could have been rescued. All the entrenched governments and organizations were negligent.

The British were slow and cautious. In March 1943, in the presence of Franklin D. Roosevelt, Secretary of State Hull pressed British Foreign Minister Anthony Eden on plans to rescue the 60,000 Jews in Bulgaria threatened with death. According to a memo by Roosevelt aide Harry Hopkins who was at that meeting, Eden worried that Polish and German Jews might then also ask to be rescued. "Hitler might well take us up on any such offer and there simply are not enough ships and means of transportation in the world to handle them." When there was a possibility of bombing the railroad lines leading into the murder chambers of Auschwitz, to stop further transportation of Jews there, the opportunity was ignored.

It should be noted that the Jewish organizations themselves behaved shamefully. In 1984, the American Jewish Commission on the Holocaust reviewed the historical record. It found that the American Jewish Joint Distribution Committee, a relief agency set up during World War II by the various Jewish groups, "was dominated by the wealthier and more 'American' elements of U.S. Jewry.... Thus, its policy was to do nothing in wartime that the U.S. government would not officially contenance."

Raul Hilberg points out that the Hungarian Jews might have been saved by a bargain: the Allies would not make air raids on Hungary if the Jews would be kept in the cities and not sent away. But "the Jews could not think in terms of interfering with the war effort, and the Allies on their part could not conceive of such a promise.... The Allied bombers roared over Hungary at will, killing Hungarians and Jews alike."

As I read this I recalled that one of the bombing raids I had done was on a town in Hungary.

Not only did waging war against Hitler fail to save the Jews, it may be that the war itself brought on the Final Solution of genocide. This is not to remove the responsibility from Hitler and the Nazis, but there is much evidence that Germany's anti-Semitic actions, cruel as they were, would not have turned to mass murder were it not for the psychic distortions of war, acting on already distorted minds. Hitler's early aim was forced emigration, not extermination, but the frenzy of it created an atmosphere in which the policy turned to genocide. This is the view of Princteton historian Arno Mayer, in his book *Why Did the Heavens Not Darken*, and it is supported by the chronology—that not until Germany was at war was the Final Solution adopted.

Hilberg, in his classic work on the Holocaust, says, "From 1938 to 1940, Hitler made extraordinary and unusual attempts to bring about a vast emigration scheme.... The Jews were not killed before the emigration policy was literally exhausted." The Nazis found that the Western powers were not anxious to cooperate in emigration and that no one wanted the Jews.

A War for Self-Determination?

We should examine another claim, that World War II was fought for the right of nations to determine their own destiny. This was declared with great fanfare by Winston Churchill and Franklin Roosevelt when they met off the coast of Newfoundland in August 1941 and announced the Atlantic Charter, saying their countries, looking to the postwar world, respected "the right of all peoples to choose the form of government under which they will live." This was a direct appeal to the dependent countries of the world, especially the colonies of Britain, France, Holland, and Belgium, that their rights of self-determination would be upheld after the war. The support of the nonwhite colonial world was seen as crucial to the defeat of fascism.

However, two weeks before the Atlantic Charter, with the long-time French colony of Indochina very much in mind, acting Secretary of State Sumner Welles had given quiet assurances to the French: "This Government, mindful of its traditional friendship for France, has deeply sympathized with the desire of the French people to maintain their territories and to preserve them intact." And in late 1942, Roosevelt's personal representative told French General Henri Giraud, "It is thoroughly understood that French sovereignty will be reestablished as soon as possible throughout all the territory; metropolitan or colonial, over which flew the French flag in 1939." (These assurances of the United States are especially interesting in view of the claims of the United States during the Vietnam War, that the United States was fighting for the right of the Vietnamese to rule themselves.)

If neither saving the Jews nor guaranteeing the principle of self-determination was the war aim of the United States (and there is no evidence that either was the aim of Britain or the Soviet Union), then what *were* the principal motives? Overthrowing the governments of Hitler, Mussolini, and Tojo was certainly one of them. But was this desired on humanitarian grounds or because these regimes threatened the *positions* of the Allies in the world?

The rhetoric of morality—the language of freedom and democracy—had some substance to it, in that it represented the war aims of many ordinary citizens. However, it was not the citizenry but the governments who decided how the war was fought and who had the power to shape the world afterward.

Behind the halo of righteousness that surrounded the war against fascism, the usual motives of governments, repeatedly shown in history, were operating: the aggrandizement of the nation, more profit for its wealthy elite, and more power to its political leaders.

One of the most distinguished of British historians, A.J.P. Taylor, commented on World War II that "the British and American governments wanted no change in Europe except that Hitler should disappear." At the end of the war, novelist George Orwell, always conscious of class, wrote, "I see the railings [which enclosed the parks and had been torn up so the metal could be used in war production] are returning in one London park after another, so the lawful denizens of the squares can make use of their keys again, and the children of the poor can be kept out."

World War II was an opportunity for United States business to penetrate areas that up to that time had been dominated by England. Secretary of State Hull said early in the war,

> Leadership toward a new system of international relationships in trade and other economic affairs will devolve very largely upon the United States because of our great economic strength. We should assume this leadership, and the responsibility that goes with it, primarily for reasons of pure national self-interest.

Henry Luce, who owned three of the most influential magazines in the United States—*Life, Time,* and *Fortune*—and had powerful connections in Washington, wrote a famous editorial for *Life* in 1941 called "The American Century." This was the time, he said, "to accept wholeheartedly our duty and our opportunity as the most powerful and vital nation in the world and in consequence to exert upon the world the full impact of our influence, for such purposes as we see fit and by such means as we see fit."

The British, weakened by war, clearly could not maintain their old empire. In 1944 England and the United States signed a pact on oil agreeing on "the principle of equal opportunity." This meant the United States was muscling in on England's traditional domination of Middle East oil. A study of the international oil business by the English writer Anthony Sampson concluded,

> By the end of the war the dominant influence in Saudi Arabia was unquestionably the United States. King Ibn Saud was regarded no longer as a wild desert warrior, but as a key piece in the power-game, to be wooed by the West. Roosevelt, on his way back from Yalta in February, 1945, entertained the King on the cruiser Quincy, together with his entourage of fifty, including two sons, a prime minister, an astrologer and flocks of sheep for slaughter.

There was a critic inside the American government, not a politician but poet Archibald MacLeish, who briefly served as assistant secretary of state. He worried about the postwar world: "As things are now going the peace we will make, the peace we seem to be making, will be a peace of oil, a peace of gold, a peace of shipping, a peace, in brief...without moral purpose or human interest."

A War Against Racism?

If the war was truly a war of moral purpose, against the Nazi idea of superior and inferior races, then we might have seen action by the U.S. government to eliminate racial segregation. Such segregation had been declared lawful by the Supreme Court in 1896 and existed in both South and North, accepted by both state and national governments.

The armed forces were segregated by race. When I was in basic training at Jefferson Barracks, Missouri, in 1943, it did not occur to me, so typical an American white was I, that there were no black men in training with us. But it was a huge base, and one day, taking a long walk to the other end of it, I was suddenly aware that all the GIs around me were black. There was a squad of blacks taking a ten-minute break from hiking in the sun, lying on a small grassy incline, and singing a hymn that surprised me at the moment, but that I realized later was quite appropriate to their situation: "Ain't Gonna Study War No More."

My air crew sailed to England on the *Queen Mary*. That elegant passenger liner had been converted into a troop ship. There were 16,000 men aboard, and 4,000 of them were black. The whites had quarters on deck and just below deck. The blacks were housed separately, deep in the hold of the ship, around the engine room, in the darkest, dirtiest sections. Meals were taken in four shifts (except for the officers, who ate in prewar *Queen Mary* style in a chandeliered ballroom—the war was not being fought to disturb class privilege), and the blacks had to wait until three shifts of whites had finished eating.

On the home front, racial discrimination in employment continued, and it was not until A. Philip Randolph, head of the Brotherhood of Sleeping Car Porters, a union of black workers, threatened to organize a march on Washington during the war and embarrass the Roosevelt administration before the world that the president signed an order setting up a Fair Employment Practices Commission. But its orders were not enforced and job discrimination continued. A spokesman for a West Coast aviation plant said, "The Negro will be considered only as janitors and in other similar capacities.... Regardless of their training as aircraft workers, we will not employ them."

There was no organized black opposition to the war, but there were many signs of bitterness at the hypocrisy of a war against fascism that did nothing about American racism. One black journalist wrote: "The Negro...is angry, resentful, and utterly apathetic about the war. 'Fight for what?' he is asking. 'This war doesn't mean a thing to me. If we win I lose, so what?'"

A student at a black college told his teacher: "The Army jim-crows us. The Navy lets us serve only as messmen. The Red Cross refuses our blood. Employers and labor unions shut us out. Lynchings continue. We are disenfranchised, jim-crowed, spat upon. What more could Hitler do than that?" That student's statement was repeated by Walter White, a leader of the National Association for the Advancement of Colored People (NAACP), to an audience of several thousand black people in the Midwest, expecting that they would disapprove. Instead, as he recalled, "To my surprise and dismay the audience burst into such applause that it took me some thirty or forty seconds to quiet it."

In January 1943, there appeared in a Negro newspaper a "Draftee's Prayer":

Dear Lord, today
I go to war:
To fight, to die.
Tell me, what for?
Dear Lord, I'll fight,
I do not fear,
Germans or Japs
My fears are here
America!

In one little-known incident of World War II, two transport ships being loaded with ammunition by U.S. sailors at the Port Chicago naval base in California suddenly blew up on the night of July 17, 1944. It was an enormous explosion, and its glare could be seen in San Francisco, thirty-five miles away. More than 300 sailors were killed, two-thirds of them black, because blacks were given the hard jobs of ammunition loaders. "It was the worst home front disaster of World War II," historian Robert Allen writes in his book *The Port Chicago Mutiny.*

Three weeks later 328 of the survivors were asked to load ammunition again; 258 of them refused, citing unsafe conditions. They were immediately jailed. Fifty of them were then court-martialed on a charge of mutiny, and received sentences ranging from eight to fifteen years imprisonment. It took a massive campaign by the NAACP and its counsel, Thurgood Marshall, to get the sentences reduced.

To the Japanese who lived on the West Coast of the United States, it quickly became clear that the war against Hitler was not accompanied by a spirit of racial equality. After the attack by Japan on Pearl Harbor, anger rose against all people of Japanese ancestry. One Congressman said, "I'm for catching every Japanese in America, Alaska and Hawaii now and putting them in concentration camps.... Damn them! Let's get rid of them now!"

Hysteria grew. Roosevelt, persuaded by racists in the military that the Japanese on the West Coast constituted a threat to the security of the country, signed Executive Order 9066 in February 1942. This empowered the army, without warrants or indictments or hearings, to arrest every Japanese-American on the West Coast—110,000 men, women and children—to take them from their homes, to transport them to camps far in the interior, and to keep them there under prison conditions.

Three-fourths of the Japanese so removed from their homes were Nisei—children born in the United States of Japanese parents and, therefore American citizens. The other fourth—the Issei, born in Japan—were barred by law from becoming citizens. In 1944 the United States Supreme Court upheld the forced evacuation on the grounds of military necesssity.

Data uncovered in the 1980s by legal historian Peter Irons showed that the army falsified material in its brief to the Supreme Court. When Congress in 1983 was considering financial compensation to the Japanese who had been removed from their homes and lost their possessions during the war, John J. McCloy wrote an article in the *New York Times* opposing such compensation, defending the action as necessary. As Peter Irons discovered in his research, it was McCloy, then assistant secretary of war, who had ordered the deletion of a critical footnote in the Justice Department brief to the Supreme Court, a footnote that cast great doubt on the army's assertions that the Japanese living on the West Coast were a threat to American security.

Michi Weglyn was a young girl when her family experienced evacuation and detention. She tells in her book *Years of Infamy* of bungling in the evacuation; of misery, confusion, and anger; but also of Japanese-American dignity and of fighting back. There were strikes, petitions, mass meetings, refusals to sign loyalty oaths, and riots against the camp authorities.

Only a few Americans protested publicly. The press often helped to feed racism. Reporting the bloody battle of Iwo Jima in the Pacific, *Time* magazine said, "The ordinary unreasoning Jap is ignorant. Perhaps he is human. Nothing...indicates it."

In the 1970s, Peter Ota, then fifty-seven, was interviewed by Studs Terkel. His parents had come from Japan in 1904, and became respected members of the Los Angeles community. Ota was born in the United States. He remembered what had happened in the war:

> On the evening of December 7, 1941, my father was at a wedding. He was dressed in a tuxedo. When the reception was over, the FBI agents were waiting. They rounded up at least a dozen wedding guests and took 'em to county jail.
>
> For a few days we didn't know what happened. We heard nothing. When we found out, my mother, my sister and myself went to jail.... When my father walked through the door my mother was so humiliated.... She cried. He was in prisoner's clothing, with a denim jacket and a number on the back. The shame and humiliation just broke her down.... Right after that day she got very ill and contracted tuberculosis. She had to be sent to a sanitarium.... She was there till she died...
>
> My father was transferred to Missoula, Montana. We got letters from him—censored, of course.... It was just my sister and myself. I was fifteen, she was twelve.... School in camp was a joke.... One of our basic subjects was American history. They talked about freedom all the time. (Laughs.)

In England there was similar hysteria. People with German-sounding names were picked up and interned. In the panic, a number of Jewish refugees who had German names were arrested and thrown into the same camps. There were thousands of Italians who were living in England, and when Italy entered World War II in June of 1940, Winston Churchill gave the order: "Collar the lot." Italians were picked up and interned, the windows of Italian shops and restaurants were smashed by patriotic mobs. A British ship carrying Italian internees to Canada was sunk by a German submarine and everyone drowned.

A War for Democracy?

It was supposed to be a war for freedom. But in the United States, when Trotskyists and members of the Socialist Workers Party spoke out in criticism of the war, eighteen of them were prosecuted in 1943 in Minneapolis. The Smith Act, passed in 1940, extended the anti-free-speech provisions of the World War I Espionage Act to peacetime. It prohibited joining any group or publishing any material that advocated revolution or that might lead to refusal of military service. The Trotskyists were sentenced to prison terms, and the Supreme Court refused to review their case.

Fortunes were made during the war, and wealth was concentrated in fewer and fewer hands. By 1941 three-fourths of the value of military contracts were handled by fifty-six large corporations. Pressure was put on the labor unions to pledge they would not strike. But they saw their wages frozen, and profits of corporations rising, and so strikes went on. There were 14,000 strikes during the war, involving over 6 million workers, more than in any comparable period in American history.

An insight into what great profits were made during the war came years later, when the mulitmillionaire John McCone was nominted by President John F. Kennedy to head the CIA. The Sentate Armed Services Committee, considering the nomination, was informed that in World War II, McCone and associates in a shipbuilding company had made $44 million on an investment of $100,000. Reacting indignantly to criticism of McCone, one of his supporters on the Senate committee asked him:

> Sen. Symington: Now, it is still legal in America, if not to make a profit, at
>   least to try to make a profit, is it not?
> McCone: That is my understanding.

Bruce Catton, a writer and historian working in Washington during the war, commented bitingly on the retention of wealth and power in the same hands, despite a war that seemed to promise a new world of social reform. He wrote:

> We were committed to a defeat of the Axis but to nothing else... It was
> solemnly decided that the war effort must not be used to bring about social
> or economic reform and to him that hath shall be given...
>   And through it all... the people were not trusted with the facts or relied
> on to display that intelligence, sanity, and innate decency of spirit, upon

which democracy...finally rests. In a very real sense, our government spent the war years looking desperately for some safe middle ground between Hitler and Abraham Lincoln.

Dresden and Hiroshima

It becomes difficult to sustain the claim that a war is just when both sides commit atrocities, unless one wants to argue that their atrocities are worse than ours. True, nothing done by the Allied Powers in World War II matches in utter viciousness the deliberate gassing, shooting, and burning of six million Jews and four million others by the Nazis. The deaths caused by the Allies were less, but still so massive as to throw doubt on the justice of a war that includes such acts.

Early in the war, various world leaders condemned the indescriminate bombing of city populations. Italy had bombed civilians in Ethiopia; Japan, in China; Germany and Italy, in the Spanish Civil War. Germany had dropped bombs on Rotterdam in Holland, on Coventry in England, and other places. Roosevelt described these bombings as "inhuman barbarism that has profoundly shocked the conscience of humanity."

But very soon, the United States and Britain were doing the same thing and on a far larger scale. When the Allied leaders met at Casablanca in January 1943, they agreed on massive air attacks to achieve "the destruction and dislocation of the German military, industrial and economic system and the undermining of the morale of the German people to the point where their capacity for armed resistance is fatally weakened." Churchill and his advisers had decided that bombing working-class districts of German cities would accomplish just that, "the undermining of the morale of the German people."

The saturation bombing of the German cities began. There were raids of a thousand planes on Cologne, Essen, Frankfurt, and Hamburg.

The British flew at night and did "area bombing" with no pretense of aiming at specific military targets.

The Americans flew in the daytime, pretending to precision, but bombing from high altitudes made that impossible. When I was doing my practice bombing in Deming, New Mexico, before going overseas, our egos were built up by having us fly at 4,000 feet and drop a bomb within twenty feet of the target. But at 11,000 feet, we were more likely to be 200 feet away. And when we flew combat missions, we did it from

30,000 feet, and might miss by a quarter of a mile. Hardly "precision bombing."

There was huge self-deception. We had been angered when the Germans bombed cities and killed several hundred or a thousand people. But now the British and Americans were killing tens of thousands in a single air strike. Michael Sherry, in his study of aerial bombing, notes that "so few in the air force asked questions." Sherry says there was no clear thinking about the effects of the bombing. Some generals objected, but were overruled by civilians. The technology crowded out moral considerations. Once the planes existed, targets had to be found.

It was terror bombing, and the German city of Dresden was the extreme example. (The city and the event are immortalized in fiction by Kurt Vonnegut's comic, bitter novel, *Slaughterhouse Five*.) It was February, 1945, the Red Army was eighty miles to the east and it was clear that Germany was on the way to defeat. In one day and one night of bombing, by American and British planes, the tremendous heat generated by the bombs created a vacuum, and an enomous firestorm swept the city, which was full of refugees at the time, increasing the population to a million. More than 100,000 people died.

The British pilot of a Lancaster bomber recalled, "There was a sea of fire covering in my estimation some forty square miles. We were so aghast at the awesome blaze that although alone over the city, we flew around in a stand-off position for many minutes before turning for home, quite subdued by our imagination of the horror that must be below."

One incident remembered by survivors is that on the afternoon of February 14, 1945, American fighter planes machine-gunned clusters of refugees on the banks of the Elbe. A German woman told of this years later: "We ran along the Elbe stepping over the bodies."

Winston Churchill, who seemed to have no moral qualms about his policy of indiscriminate bombing, described the annihilation of Dresden in his wartime memoirs with a simple statement: "We made a heavy raid in the latter month on Dresden, then a centre of communication of Germany's Eastern Front."

At one point in the war Churchill ordered thousands of anthrax bombs from a plant that was secretly producing them in the United States. His chief science adviser, Lord Cherwell, had informed him in February 1944: "Any animal breathing in minute quantities of these N (anthrax) spores is extremely likely to die suddenly but peacefully within the week. There is no known cure and no effective prophylaxis. There is little doubt that it is equally lethal to human beings." He told Churchill that a half dozen bombers could carry enough four-pound anthrax bombs to kill everyone within a square mile. However, production delays got in the way of this plan.

The actor Richard Burton once wrote an article for the *New York Times* about his experience playing the role of Winston Churchill in a television drama:

> In the course of preparing myself...I realized afresh that I hate Churchill and all of his kind. I hate them virulently. They have stalked down the corridors of endless power all through history.... What man of sanity would say on hearing of the atrocities committed by the Japanese against British and Anzac prisoners of war, 'We shall wipe them out, everyone of them, men, women, and children. There shall not be a Japanese left on the face of the earth? Such simple-minded cravings for revenge leave me with a horrified but reluctant awe for such single-minded and merciless ferocity.

When Burton's statement appeared in the "Arts and Leisure" section of the *New York Times*, he was banned from future BBC productions. The supervisor of drama productions for BBC said, "As far as I am concerned, he will never work for us again.... Burton acted in an unprofessional way."

It seems that however moral is the cause that initiates a war (in the minds of the public, in the mouths of the politicians), it is in the nature of war to corrupt that morality until the rule becomes "An eye for an eye, a tooth for a tooth," and soon it is not a matter of equivalence, but indescriminate revenge.

The policy of saturation bombing became even more brutal when B29s, with carried twice the bombload as the planes we flew in Europe, attacked Japanese cities with incendiaries, turning them into infernos.

In one raid on Tokyo, after midnight on March 10, 1945, 300 B29s left the city in flames, fanned by a strong northwest wind. The fires could be seen by pilots 150 miles out in the Pacific Ocean. A million people were left homeless. It is estimated that 100,000 people died that night. Many of them attempting to escape leaped into the Sumida River and drowned. A Japanese novelist who was twelve years old at the time, described the scene years later: "The fire was like a living thing. It ran, just like a creature, chasing us."

By the time the atomic bomb was dropped on Hiroshima (August 6, 1945) and another on Nagasaki (three days later), the moral line had been crossed psychologically by the massive bombings in Europe and by the fire bombings of Tokyo and other cities.

The bomb on Hiroshima left perhaps 140,000 dead; the one on Nagasaki, 70,000 dead. Another 130,000 died in the next five years. Hundreds of thousands of others were left radiated and maimed. These numbers are based on the most detailed report that exists on the effects of the bombings; it was compiled by thirty-four Japanese specialists and was published in 1981.

The deception and self-deception that accompanied these atrocities was remarkable. Truman told the public, "The world will note that the first atomic bomb was dropped on Hiroshima, a military base. That was because we wished in this first attack to avoid, insofar as possible, the killing of civilians."

Even the possibility that American prisoners of war would be killed in these bombings did not have any effect on the plans. On July 31, nine days before Nagasaki was bombed, the headquarters of the U.S. Army Strategic Air Forces on Guam (the take-off airfield for the atomic bombings) sent a message to the War Department:

> Reports prisoner of war sources not verified by photo give location of Allied prisoner-of-war camp, one mile north of center of city of Nagasaki. Does this influence the choice of this target for initial Centerboard operation? Request immediate reply.

The reply came, "Targets previously assigned for Centerboard remain unchanged."

The terrible momentum of war continued even after the bombings of Hiroshima and Nagasaki. The end of the war was a few days away, yet B29s continued their missions. On August 14, five days after the Nagasaki bombing and the day before the actual acceptance of surrender terms, 449 B29s went out from the Marianas for a daylight strike and 372 more went out that night. Altogether, more than 1,000 planes were sent to bomb Japanese cities. There were no American losses. The last plane had not yet returned when Truman announced the Japanese had surrendered.

Japanese writer Oda Makoto describes that August 14 in Osaka, where he lived. He was a boy. He went out into the streets and found in the midst of the corpses American leaflets written in Japanese, which had been dropped with the bombs: Your government has surrendered; the war is over."

The American public, already conditioned to massive bombing, accepted the atomic bombings with equanimity, indeed with joy. I remember my own reaction. When the war ended in Europe, my crew flew our plane back to the United States. We were given a thirty-day furlough and then had to report for duty to be sent to Japan to continue bombing. My wife and I decided to spend that time in the countryside. Waiting for the bus to take us, I picked up the morning newspaper, August 7, 1945. The headline was "Atomic Bomb Dropped on Hiroshima." My immediate reaction was elation: "The war will end. I won't have to go to the Pacific."

I had no idea what the explosion of the atomic bomb had done to the men, women, and children of Hiroshima. It was abstract and distant, as were the deaths of the people from the bombs I had dropped in Europe from a height of six miles; I was unable to see anything below, there was no visible blood, and there were no audible screams. And I knew nothing of the imminence of a Japanese surrender. It was only later when I read John Hersey's *Hiroshima*, when I read the testimony of Japanese survivors, and when I studied the history of the decision to drop the bomb that I was outraged by what had been done.

It seems that once an initial judgment has been made that a war is just, there is a tendency to stop thinking, to assume then that everything done on behalf of victory is morally acceptable. I had myself participated in the bombing of cities, without even considering whether there was any relationship between what I was doing and the elimination of fascism in the world. Thus a war that apparently begins with a "good" cause—stopping aggression, helping victims, or punishing brutality—ends with its own aggression, creates more victims than before, and brings out more brutality than before, on both sides. The Holocaust, a plan made and executed in the ferocious atmosphere of war, and the saturation bombings, also created in the frenzy of war, are evidence of this.

The good cause in World War II was the defeat of fascism. And, in fact, it ended with that defeat: the corpse of Mussolini hanging in the public square in Milan; Hitler burned to death in his underground bunker; Tojo, captured and sentenced to death by an international tribunal. But forty million people were dead, and the elements of fascism—militarism, racism, imperialism, dictatorship, ferocious nationalism, and war—were still at large in the postwar world.

Two of those forty million were my closest Air Force friends, Joe Perry and Ed Plotkin. We had suffered through basic training and rode horses and flew Piper Cubs in Burlington, Vermont, and played basketball at Santa Ana before going our own ways to different combat zones. Both were killed in the final weeks of the war. For years afterward, they appeared in my dreams. In my waking hours, the question grew: What did they really die for?

We were victorious over fascism, but this left two superpowers dominating the world, vying for control of other nations, carving out new spheres of influence, on a scale even larger than that attempted by the Fascist powers. Both superpowers supported dictatorships all over the world: the Soviet Union in Eastern Europe and the United States in Latin America, Korea, and the Philippines.

The war machines of the Axis powers were destroyed, but the Soviet Union and the United States were bulding military machines greater than the world had ever seen, piling up frightful numbers of nuclear weapons, soon equivalent to a million Hiroshima-type bombs. They were preparing for a war to keep the peace, they said (this had also been said before World War I) but those preparations were such that if war took place (by accident? by miscalculation?) it would make the Holocaust look puny.

Hitler's aggression was over but wars continued, which the superpowers either initiated or fed with military aid or observed without attempting to halt them. Two million people died in Korea; two to five million in Vietnam, Cambodia, and Laos; one million in Indonesia; perhaps two million in the Nigerian civil war; one million in the Iran-Iraq War; and many more in Latin America, Africa, and the Middle East. It is estimated that, in the forty years after 1945, there were 150 wars, with twenty million casualties.

The victorious and morally righteous superpowers stood by in the postwar world while millions—more than had died in Hitler's Holocaust—starved to death. They made gestures, but allowed national ambitions and interpower rivalries to stand in the way of saving the hungry. A United Nations official reported, with great bitterness that

> in pursuit of political objectives in the Nigerian Civil War, a number of great and small nations, including Britain and the United States, worked to prevent supplies of food and medicine from reaching the starving children of rebel Biafra.

Swept up in the obvious rightness of a crusade to rid the world of fascism, most people supported or participated in that crusade, to the point of risking their lives. But there were skeptics, especially among the nonwhite peoples of the world—blacks in the United States and the colonized millions of the British Empire (Gandhi withheld his support).

The extraordinary black writer Zora Neale Hurston wrote her memoir, *Dust Tracks on a Road,* at the start of World War II. Just before it was to come out, the Japanese attacked Pearl Harbor, and her publisher, Lippincott, removed a section of the book in which she wrote bitterly about the "democracies" of the West and their hypocrisy. She said:

> All around me, bitter tears are being shed over the fate of Holland, Belgium, France and England. I must confess to being a little dry around the eyes. I hear people shaking with shudders at the thought of Germany collecting taxes in Holland. I have not heard a word against Holland collecting one twelfth of poor people's wages in Asia. Hitler's crime is that he is actually doing a thing like that to his own kind...
>
> As I see it, the doctrines of democracy deal with the aspirations of men's souls, but the application deals with things. One hand in somebody else's pocket and one on your gun, and you are highly civilized.... Desire enough for your own use only, and you are a heathen. Civilized people have things to show to their neighbors.

The editor at Lippincott wrote on her manuscript, "Suggest eliminating international opinions as irrelevant to autobiography." Only when the book was reissued in 1984 did the censored passages appear.

Hurston, in a letter she wrote to a journalist friend in 1946, showed her indignation at the hypocrisy that accompanied the war:

> I am amazed at the complacency of Negro press and public. Truman is a monster. I can think of him as nothing else but the Butcher of Asia. Of his grin of triumph on giving the order to drop the Atom bombs on Japan. Of his maintaining troops in China who are shooting the starving Chinese for stealing a handful of food.

Some white writers were resistant to the fanaticism of war. After it was over, Joseph Heller wrote his biting, brilliant satire *Catch-22* and Kurt Vonnegut wrote *Slaughterhouse Five*. In the 1957 film *Bridge on the River Kwai*, the Japanese military is obsessed with building a bridge, and the British are obsessed with destroying it. At the end it is blown up and a British lieutenant, barely surviving, looks around at the river strewn with corpses and mutters: "Madness. Madness."

There were pacifists in the United States who went to prison rather than participate in World War II. There were 350,000 draft evaders in the United States. Six thousand men went to prison as conscientious objectors; one out of every six inmates in U.S. federal prisons was a conscientious objector to the war.

But the general mood in the United States was support. Liberals, conservatives, and Communists agreed that it was a just war. Only a few voices were raised publicly in Europe and the United States to question the motives of the participants, the means by which the war was being conducted, and the ends that would be achieved. Very few tried to stand back from the battle and take a long view. One was the French worker-philosopher Simone Weil. Early in 1945 she wrote in a new magazine called *Politics*:

> Whether the mask is labelled Fascism, Democracy, or Dictatorship or the Proletariat, our great adversary remains the Apparatus—the bureaucracy, the police, the military.... No matter what the circumstances, the worst betrayal will always be to subordinate ourselves to this Apparatus, and to trample underfoot, in its service, all human values in ourselves and in others.

The editor of *Politics* was an extraordinary American intellectual named Dwight MacDonald, who with his wife, Nancy, produced the magazine as an outlet for unorthodox points of view. After the bombing of Hiroshima, MacDonald refused to join in the general jubilation. He wrote with a fury:

> The CONCEPTS "WAR" AND "PROGRESS" ARE NOW OBSOLETE...THE FUTILITY OF MODERN WARFARE SHOULD NOW BE CLEAR. Must we not now conclude, with Simone Weil, that the technical aspect of war today is the evil, regardless of political factors? Can one imagine that the atomic bomb could ever be used "in a good cause"?

But what was the alternative to war, with Germany on the march in Europe, Japan on its rampage through Asia, and Italy looking for empire? This is the toughest possible question. Once the history of an epoch has run its course, it is very difficult to imagine an alternate set of events, to imagine that some act or acts might set in motion a whole new train of circumstances, leading in a different direction.

Would it have been possible to trade time and territory for human life? Was there an alternative preferable to using the most modern weapons of destruction for mass annihilation? Can we try to imagine instead of a six-year war a ten-year or twenty-year period of resistance; of guerilla warfare, strikes, and noncooperation; of underground movements, sabotage, and paralysis of vital communication and transportation; and of clandestine propaganda for the organization of a larger and larger opposition?

Even in the midst of war, some nations occupied by the Nazis were able to resist: the Danes, the Norweigians, and the Bulgarians refused to give up their Jews. Gene Sharp, on the basis of his study of resistance movements in World War II, writes:

> During the second World War—in such occupied countries as the Netherlands, Norway and Denmark—patriots resisted their Nazi overlords and internal puppets by such weapons as underground newspapers, labor slowdowns, general strikes, refusal of collaboration, special boycotts of German troops and quislings, and noncooperation with fascist controls and efforts to restructure their societies' institutions.

Guerrilla warfare is more selective, its violence more limited and more discriminate, than conventional war. It is less centralized and more democratic by nature, requiring the commitment, the initiative, and the cooperation of ordinary people who do not need to be conscripted, but who are motivated by their desire for freedom and justice.

History is full of instances of successful resistance (although we are not informed very much about this) without violence and against tyranny, by people using strikes, boycotts, propaganda, and a dozen different ingenious forms of struggle. Gene Sharp, in his book *The Politics of Non-Violent Action*, records hundreds of instances and dozens of methods of action.

Since the end of World War II, we have seen dictatorships overthrown by mass movements that mobilized so much popular opposition that the tyrant finally had to flee in Iran, in Nicaragua, in the Philippines, and in Haiti. Granted, the Nazi machine was formidable, efficient, and ruthless. But there are limits to conquest. A point is reached where the conquerer has swallowed too much territory, has to control too many people. Great empires have fallen when it was thought they would last forever.

We have seen, in the Eighties, mass movements of protest arise in the tightly controlled Communist countries of Eastern Europe, forcing dramatic changes in Hungary, Czechoslovakia, Poland, Bulgaria, Rumania, and East Germnay. The Spanish people, having lost a million lives in their civil war, waited out Franco. He died, as all men do, and the dictatorship was over. For Portugal, the resistance in its outlying African Empire weakened control; corruption grew and the long dictatorship of Salazar was overthrown—without a bloodbath.

There is a fable written by German playwright Bertolt Brecht that goes roughly like this: A man living alone answers a knock at the door. When he opens it, he sees in the doorway the powerful body, the cruel face, of The Tyrant. The Tyrant asks, "Will you submit?" The man does not reply. He steps aside. The Tyrant enters and establishes himself in the man's house. The man serves him for years. Then The Tyrant becomes sick from food poisoning. He dies. The man wraps the body, opens the door, gets rids of the body, comes back to his house, closes the door behind him, and says, firmly, "No."

Violence is not the only form of power. Sometimes it is the least effective. Always it is the most vicious, for the perpetrator as well as for the victim. And it is corrupting.

Immediately after the war, Albert Camus, the great French writer who fought in the underground against the Nazis, wrote in *Combat*, the daily newspaper of the French Resistance. In his essay called "Neither Victims Nor Executioners," he considered the tens of millions of dead caused by the war and asked that the world reconsider fanaticism and violence:

> All I ask is that, in the midst of a murderous world, we agree to reflect on murder and to make a choice.... Over the expanse of five continents throughout the comng years an endless struggle is going to be pursued between violence and friendly persuasion, a struggle in which, granted, the former has a thousand times the chances of success than has the latter. But I have always held that, if he who bases his hopes on human nature is a fool,

he who gives up in the face of circumstances is a coward. And henceforth, the only honorable course will be to stake everything on a formidable gamble: that words are more powerful than munitions.

Whatever alternative scenarios we can imagine to replace World War II and its mountain of corpses, it really doesn't matter any more. That was is over. The practical effect of declaring World War II just is not for that war, but for the wars that follow. And that effect has been a dangerous one, because the glow of rightness that accompanied that war has been transferred, by false analogy and emotional carryover, to other wars. To put it another way, perhaps the worst consequence of World War II is that it kept alive the idea that war could be just.

Looking at World War II in perspective, looking at the world it created and the terror that grips our century, should we not bury for all time the idea of just war?

Some of the participants in that "good war" had second thoughts. Former GI Tommy Bridges, who after the war became a policeman in Michigan, expressed his feelings to Studs Terkel:

> It was a useless war, as every war is.... How gaddamn foolish it is, the war. They's no war in the world that's worth fighting for, I don't care where it is. They can't tell me any different. Money, money is the thing that causes it all. I wouldn't be a bit surprised that the people that start wars and promote 'em are the men that make the money, make the ammunition, make the clothing and so forth. Just think of the poor kids that are starvin' to death in Asia and so forth that could be fed with how much you make one big shell out of.

Higher up in the military ranks was Admiral Gene LaRocque, who also spoke to Studs Terkel about the war:

> I had been in thirteen battle engagements, had sunk a submarine, and was the first man ashore in the landing at Roi. In that four years, I thought, What a hell of a waste of a man's life. I lost a lot of friends. I had the task of telling my roommate's parents about our last days together. You lose limbs, sight, part of your life—for what? Old men send young men to war. Flag, banners, and patriotic sayings...
>
> We've institutionalized militarism. This came out of World War Two... It gave us the National Security Council. It gave us the CIA, that is able to spy on you and me this very moment. For the first time in the history of man, a country has divided up the world into military districts.... You could argue World War Two had to be fought. Hitler had to be stopped. Unfortunately, we translate it unchanged to the situation today...

I hate it when they say, "He gave his life for his country." Nobody gives their life for anything. We steal the lives of these kids. We take it away from them. They don't die for the honor and glory of their country. We kill them.

Granted that we have started in this century with the notion of just war, we don't have to keep it. Perhaps the change in our thinking can be as dramatic, as clear, as that in the life of a French general, whose obituary in 1986 was headed: "Gen. Jacques Paris de Bollardiere, War Hero Who Became a Pacifist, Dead at the age of 78."

He had served in the Free French Forces in Africa during World War II, later parachuted into France and Holland to organize the Resistance, and commanded an airborne unit in Indochina from 1946 to 1953. But in 1957, according to the obituary, he "caused an uproar in the French army when he asked to be relieved of his command in Algeria to protest the torture of Algerian rebels. In 1961 he began to speak out against militarism and nuclear weapons. He created an organization called The Alternative Movement for Non-Violence and in 1973 participated in a protest expedition to France's South Pacific nuclear testing site.

It remains to be seen how many people in our time will make that journey from war to nonviolent action against war. It is the great challenge or our time: How to achieve justice, with struggle, but without war.

2

The Bombing of Royan

In mid-April of 1945, a combined air-ground attack completed the destruction of the French seaside resort of Royan, a town of ancient chateaux and lovely beaches (a favorite spot of Picasso), on the Atlantic coast near Bordeaux. It was ten months after D-day, the invasion of Western Europe by Allied Forces—and three weeks before the final surrender of Germany. The official history of the U.S. Army Air Forces in World War II refers briefly to the attack on Royan:

> On the 14 through 16 April more than 1,200 American heavies went out each day to drop incendiaries, napalm bombs, and 2,000-pound demolition bombs on stubborn German garrisons still holding out around Bordeaux. The bombing was effective, and French forces soon occupied the region.

According to the official history those bombs were dropped "on stubborn German garrisons." This is misleading. The bombs were dropped in the general vicinity of Royan, where there were German garrisons (mostly outside the town) and where there were also civilian occupants of the town. It was my participation in this mission, as a bombardier with the 490th Bomb Group, that prompted me, after the war, to inquire into the bombing of Royan. At the time, it seemed just another bombing mission, with a slightly different target, and a slightly different cargo of bombs. We were awakened in the early hours of morning, went to the briefing, where we were told our job was to bomb pockets of German troops remaining in and around Royan, and that in our bomb bays were thirty 100-pound bombs containing "jellied gasoline," a new substance (now known as napalm). Our bombs were not precisely directed at German installations but were dropped by toggle switch over the Royan area, on seeing the bombs of the lead ship leave the bomb bay—a device good for saturation bombing, not pinpoint bombing (aside from the fact that the Norden bombsight, which we were trained to use, could not be counted on to hit enemy installations and miss nearby civilians from a height of 25,000 feet). The toggle switch was connected to an intervalometer which automatically dropped the bombs, after the first fell, in a timed sequence. I remember distinctly seeing, from our great height, the bombs explode in the town, flaring like matches struck in fog. I was completely unaware of the human chaos below.

In 1966, I spent some time in Royan and found in the town library most of the material on which this essay is based.

A letter from Colonel H. A. Schmidt, of the Office of the Chief of Military History, Department of the Army, responding to my request for information on the bombing of Royan, stated:

> The liberation of the port of Bordeaux required the reduction of the bridgeheads of Royan, la Pointe, de Grave and Oléron. The Royan sector was the principal German garrison holding out in the Bordeaux area, and first priority in the operations. The Eighth U.S. Air Force paved the way of the Allied ground forces by massive bombing.

The quick, casual description of potentially embarrassing episodes is common in histories written by men in government. Winston Churchill, who was Prime Minister when the city of Dresden was indiscriminately saturated with fire-bombs in February 1945, leaving 135,000 dead, and who had approved the general strategy of bombing urban areas, confined himself to this comment in his memoirs: "We made a heavy raid in the latter month on Dresden, then a centre of communications of Germany's Eastern front."[*]

Strenuous arguments were made for the bombing attacks on Hiroshima and Dresden on the basis of military necessity, although ultimately the evidence was overwhelmingly against such arguments. In the case of Royan, it was virtually impossible to even launch a defense of the attack on grounds of military need. It was a small town on the Atlantic coast, far from the fighting front. True, it commanded the sea entrance to Bordeaux, a great port. But this was not crucially needed. Without Bordeaux, and later without its port facilities, the Allies had invaded Normandy, taken Paris, crossed the Rhine, and were now well into Germany. Furthermore, the general air-ground assault on Royan took place three weeks before the end of the war in Europe, at a time when everyone knew it would all soon be over and all one had to do for the surrender of the German garrisons in the area was to wait.[**]

Nevertheless, on April 14, 1945, the attack on Royan began, reported as follows in a dispatch from London the next day to the *New York Times*:

> The full weight of the United States Eighth Air Force was hurled yesterday against one of Europe's forgotten fronts, the German-held pocket in the Gironde Estuary commanding the great southwestern French port of Bordeaux. The blow by 1,150 Flying Fortresses and Liberators, without fighter escort, preceded a limited land attack by French troops...
> Some 30,000 to 40,000 Nazi troops have been holed up in the Gironde Estuary pocket since the tides of war swept around and past them last summer.... The striking force was probably the biggest heavy bombing fleet ever sent out from Britain in daylight without escorting fighters. Five of the big planes failed to return.

Was the air raid worth even the loss of only five air crews—forty-five men? That was just the tip of the tragedy, counted in lives lost, homes destroyed, persons wounded and burned. For the next day, April 15, the

---

[*] David Irving, *The Destruction of Dresden*, Part II, esp. Ch. II, "Thunderclap," which shows the part Churchill played in pushing the massive raids on cities in Eastern Germany; and Part V, Ch. II, where Churchill later seems to be trying to put the blame on the Bomber Command.

[**] Also, in a remark I must confine to a footnote as a gesture to the equality of all victims: there was something to distinguish Royan from both Hiroshima and Dresden; its population was, at least officially, friend, not foe.

attack was heavier, and the airplanes had a new weapon. A front-page dispatch in the *New York Times* from Paris reported "two days of shattering aerial bombardment and savage ground attacks in the drive to open the port of Bordeaux." It went on:

> More than 1300 Flying Fortresses and Liberators of the United States Eighth Air Force prepared the way for today's successful assault by drenching the enemy's positions on both sides of the Gironde controlling the route to Bordeaux with about 460,000 gallons of liquid fire that bathed in flames the German positions and strong points...
>
> It was the first time that the Eighth Air Force had employed its new bomb. The inflammable substance is dropped in tanks that are exploded on impact by detonators that ignite the fuel, splashing the flaming contents of each tank over an area of approximately sixty square yards.

The liquid fire was napalm, used for the first time in warfare. The following day, there was another bombing, with high explosive bombs, and further ground assaults. Altogether, it took three days of bombing and land attacks to bring the Germans in the area to surrender. The French ground forces suffered about two hundred dead; the Germans lost several hundred. There is no accurate count on the civilian dead resulting from those attacks, but the *New York Times* dispatch by a correspondent in the area reported:

> French troops mopped up most of Royan, on the north side of the river's mouth.... Royan, a town of 20,000, once was a vacation spot. About 350 civilians, dazed or bruised by two terrific air bombings in forty-eight hours, crawled from the ruins and said the air attacks had been "such hell as we never believed possible."

In a few weeks, the war was over in Europe. The town of Royan, "liberated," was totally in ruins.

That eve-of-victory attack in mid-April 1945 was the second disaster suffered by Royan at the hands of the Allied forces. On January 5, 1945, in the darkness before dawn, two waves of heavy British bombers, about an hour apart, flew over Royan, which was still inhabited, despite a voluntary evacuation in the preceding months, by about two thousand persons. There was no warning, there were no shelters. The bombs were dropped in the heart of the city (completely missing the German troops, who were outside) within a rectangle marked out by flares dropped by one of the planes. Over a thousand people were killed (some of the estimates are twelve hundred, others fourteen hundred). Several hundred people were wounded. Almost every building in Royan was demolished. The later attack in April, came therefore, on the ruins of buildings and the remnants of families, and made the annihilation of the city complete.

That January bombing has never been adequately explained. One phrase recurs in all the accounts—"*une tragique erreur.*" The explanation given by military officials at the time was that the bombers were originally scheduled to bomb in Germany, but because of bad weather there, were rerouted to Royan without a map of the German positions. French planes from nearby Cognac were supposed to mark the positions with flares but this was either not done, or done badly, or the flares were carried away by the wind.*

A dispatch written by a local person soon after that bombing, entitled "La Nuit Tragique," contained this description:**

> Under the German occupation. It is night, calm reigns over the sleeping town, Midnight sounds in the Royan church. Then one o'clock, then two.... The Royannais sleep, muffled against the chill. Three, four o'clock. A humming is heard in the distance. Rockets light up the sky. The inhabitants are not afraid; they are tranquil, because they know that Allied airplanes, if these are such, will aim at the German fortifications, and besides, is this not the evening when German supply planes come in? The clock sounds five. Then follows the catastrophe, brutal, horrible, implacable. A deluge of steel and fire descended on Royan; a wave of 350 planes lets go 800 tons of bombs on the town. Some seconds later, the survivors are calling for aid to the wounded. Cries, death rattles... A woman appeals for help, her head appears alone, her body crushed under an enormous beam.
>
> ...A whole family is imprisoned in a cave, the water mounts. The rescuers lift their heads—this humming, yet, it is another wave of planes. This achieves the complete destruction of Royan and its inhabitants. Royan has gone down with the civilized world, by the error, the bestiality, the folly of

---

* This is repeated as late as 1965 in Dr. J.R. Colle's book, *Royan, son passé, ses environs* (La Rochelle, 1965), who summarizes the incident in his chapter, "La Résistance et La Libération."

** The periodical in which the article appeared is no longer available, but the article, along with many others to which I will refer, was collected in a remarkable little book, produced by a printer in Royan, a former member of the Resistance (Botton, Père et fils) in 1965, entitled: *Royan—Ville Martyre.* The translations are mine. A bitter introductory note by Ulysse Botton speaks of "*la tuerie*" (the slaughter) of January 5, 1945. There is a picture of the rebuilt Royan, modern buildings instead of ancient châteaux. "Our visitors, French and foreign vacationers, should thus learn, if they do not know it, that this new town and this modern architecture proceed from a murder, to this day neither admitted nor penalized..."

man. (Royan a sombré en même temps que le monde civillisé, par l'erreur, la bêtise et la folie des hommes.)

Eight days after the attack, an article appeared in *La Libération* appealing for help: "American friends, you whose Florida beaches have never known such hours, take charge of the reconstruction of Royan!"

In 1948, General de Larminat, who was in charge of French forces in the West (that is, the Bordeaux region) for the last six months of the war, broke a long silence to reply to bitter criticism of both the January and April bombings by local leaders. He exonerated the French military command at Cognac, saying they were not responsible for directing the English planes to Royan. It was, rather, a "tragic error" by the Allied Command; the whole episode was one of the unfortunate consequences of war:*

> Will we draw from this an excuse to attack our Allies, who gave countless lives to liberate our country? That would be profoundly unjust. All wars carry these painful errors. Where is the infantryman of 1914-18, and of this war, who has not received friendly shells, badly aimed? How many French towns, how many combat units, have suffered bombings by mistake at the hands of allied planes? This is the painful ransom, the inevitable ransom of war, against which it is vain to protest, about which it is vain to quarrel. We pay homage to those who died in the war, we help the survivors and repair the ruins; but we do not linger on the causes of these unfortunate events because, in truth there is only a single cause: War, and the only ones truly responsible are those who wanted war.

(Compare this with the explanation of the Dresden bombing given by Air Marshal Sir Robert Saundby:

> It was one of those terrible things that sometimes happen in wartime, brought about by an unfortunate combination of circumstances. Those who approved it were neither wicked nor cruel, though it may well be that they were too remote from the harsh realities of war to understand fully the appalling destructive power of air bombardment in the spring of 1945...
>
> It is not so much this or the other means of making war that is immoral or inhumane. What is immoral is war itself. Once full-scale war has broken out it can never be humanized or civilized, and if one side

---

*Botton collection. This is of course, a widely held view: "c'est la guerre" —a resigned, unhappy surrender to inevitability. We find it again in *Le Pays d'Ouest*, a postwar periodical, now defunct, which published an article, "Le Siège et Attaque de Royan," saying: "Whatever the reason, the bombardment of Royan on January 5, 1945, must be considered among the regrettable errors that unfortunately it is hard to avoid in the course of the extremely complicated operations of modern war."

attempted to do so it would be most likely to be defeated. So long as we resort to war to settle differences between nations, so long will we have to endure the horrors, the barbarities and excesses that war brings with it. That, to me, is the lesson of Dresden.)

Some important evidence on the January bombing appeared in 1966 with the publication of the memoirs of Admiral Hubert Meyer, French commander in the Rochefort-La Rochelle area (the two Atlantic ports just north of Royan). Meyer, in September and October 1944, when the Germans, having fled west from the Allied invasion in northern France, were consolidating their pockets on the Atlantic coast, had begun negotiation with the German commander of La Rochelle-Rochefort, Admiral Schirlitz. In effect, they agreed that the Germans would not blow up the port installations, and in return the French would not attack the Germans. Then the Germans evacuated Rochefort, moving north into the La Rochelle area, to lines both sides agreed on.

In late December 1944, Meyer was asked to travel south along the coast from Rochefort to Royan, where the second German coastal pocket was under the command of Admiral Michahelles, to negotiate a prisoner exchange. In the course of these talks, he was told that the German admiral was disposed to sign an agreement to hold the military *status quo* around Royan, as had been done by Schirlitz at Rochefort-La Rochelle. Meyer pointed out that Royan was different, that the Allies might have to attack the Germans there because Royan commanded Bordeaux, where free passage of goods was needed to supply the Southwest. The Germans, to Meyer's surprise, replied that they might agree to open Bordeaux to all but military supplies.

Conveying this offer to the French military headquarters at Saintes and Cognac, Meyer received a cool response. The French generals could not give a sound military reason for insisting on an attack, but pointed to "*l'aspect moral.*" It would be hard, said General d'Anselme, "to frustrate an ardent desire for battle—a battle where victory was certain—by the army of the Southwest, which had been champing at the bit for months."*

---

* This is Meyer's recollection of the conversation, in his chapter "Royan, Ville Détruite par erreur." Meyer tends to glorify his own activities in this book, but his account fits the other evidence.

Meyer said the morale of the troops was not worth the sacrifice of a town and hundreds of lives for a limited objective, when the war was virtually won, that they did not have the right to kill a single man when the adversary had offered a truce.[*]

Further discussion, he was told, would have to await the return of General de Larminat, who was away.

Meyer left that meeting with the distinct impression that the die was cast for the attack (*"l'impression tres nette que les jeux etaient faits, que Royan serait attaquée"*). This was January 2. Three days later, sleeping at Rochefort, he was awakened by the sound of airplanes flying south toward Royan. Those were the British Lancasters, three hundred and fifty of them, each carrying seven tons of bombs.

Meyer adds another piece of information: that about a month before the January 5 bombing, an American General, Commander of the Ninth Tactical Air Force, came to Cognac to offer the Southwest forces powerful bombing support, and suggested softening the Atlantic pockets by massive aerial bombardment. He proposed that since the Germans did not have aerial defenses for Royan, here were good targets for bomber-crew trainees in England. The French agreed, but insisted the targets be at two points which formed clear enclaves on the ocean, easily distin-guishable from the city itself. No more was heard from the Americans, however, until the bombing itself.[**]

As it turned out, not trainees, but experienced pilots did the bombing, and Meyer concludes that even the American general (sent back to the U.S. after this, as a scapegoat, Meyer suggests) was not completely responsible.

---

[*] Three other pieces of evidence support Meyer's claim of German readiness to surrender:

A. A dispatch in *Samedi-Soir* in May, 1948 (reproduced in part in the Botton col-lection) tells a strange story which goes even further than Meyer. It reports, on the basis of a document it clams to have found in the Ministry of the Armed Forces, that a British agent, with the code name of "Aristede," parachuted into France to join the Resistance, reported later to his government in London that the Germans in the Royan area had offered to sur-render if they would be given the honors of war, but that the French General Bertin said a surrender to the British would create a "diplomatic incident." This was, allegedly, September 8, 1944.

B. An open letter to General de Larminat by Dr. Veyssière Pierre, a former leader of the Royan Resistance (reproduced in the Botton collection) says: "Now we are sure that in August and September, 1944, the German high command—the commander of the fortress of Royan—made proposals of surrender that, if they had come about, would have prevented the worst; we know that on two occasions, he made contact with Colonel Cominetti, called Charly, commander of the Medoc groups; we know also that these attempts at negotiations

Some blame devolved, he says, on the British Bomber Command, and some on the French generals, for not insisting on a point DeGaulle had made when he visited the area in September—that aerial attacks should only be undertaken here in coordination with ground assaults. Meyer concludes, however, that the real responsibility did not rest with the local military commanders. "To wipe out such a city is beyond military decision. It is a serious political act. It is impossible that the Supreme Command [he refers to Eisenhower and his staff] had not been at least consulted." In the event, he says, that the Allies are shocked by his accusations, they should open their military dossiers and, for the first time, reveal the truth.

If by January 1945 (despite von Rundstedt's Christmas counter-offensive in the Ardennes), it seemed clear that the Allies, well into France, and the Russians, having the Germans on the run, were on the way toward victory—then by April 1945 there was little doubt that the war was near its end. The Berlin radio announced on April 15 that the Russians and Americans were about to join forces around the Elbe, and that two zones were being set up for a Germany cut in two. Nevertheless, a major land-air operation was launched April 14 against the Royan pocket, with over a thousand planes dropping bombs on a German force of 5,500 men, on a town containing at the time probably less than a thousand people.[***]

An article written in the summer of 1946 by a local writer commented on the mid-April assault:

> These last acts left great bitterness in the hearts of the Royannais, because the Armistice followed soon after, an Armistice foreseen by all. For the Royannais, this liberation by force was useless since Royan would have been, like La Rochelle, liberated normally some days later, without new damage, without

---

were purely and simply repulsed by the French headquarters at Bordeaux, in order, no doubt, to add to the grandeur of military prestige."

    C. The article of Paul Metadier (reprinted in a pamphlet, available in the library of Royan) in *La Lettre Medicale,* February 1948, gives Sir Samuel Hoare, former British Ambassador to France, as a source of the fact that the French military command had opposed the surrender of the German General to the British.

[**] This story appears also in Robert Aron's *Histoire de la Libération de la France,* June, 1944-May, 1945 (Librarie Artheme Fayard, 1959). Aron adds the point that the American general spent some time on this visit with and FFI (French Forces of the Interior) journalist who called the inhabitants of Royan "collaborators."

[***] Colle, *Royan, son passé, ses environs.* He reports the Germans, under Admiral Michahelles had 5,500 men, 150 cannon, four anti-aircraft batteries. They were well entrenched in concrete bunkers and surrounded by fields of land mines.

new deaths, without new ruins. Only those who have visited Royan can give
an account of the disaster. No report, no picture or drawing can convey it.

Another local person wrote:[*]

> Surely the destruction of Royan, on January 5, 1945, was an error and a
> crime: but what put the finishing touches on this folly was the final air raid
> on the ruins, on the buildings partially damaged, and on others remarkably
> spared on the periphery, with that infernal cargo of incendiary bombs.
> Thus was accomplished a deadly work of obvious uselessness, and thus was
> revealed to the world the powerful destructiveness of napalm.

The evidence seems overwhelming that factors of pride, military
ambition, glory, honor were powerful motives in producing an unnecessary
military operation. One of the local commanders wrote later: "It would
have been more logical to wait for the surrender of Germany and thus to
avoid new human and material losses" but one could not "ignore important
factors of morale" (*"faire abstraction de facteurs essentiels d'ordre moral"*).[**]

In 1947, a delegation of five leaders of Royan met with General
de Larminat. After the war, the citizens of Royan had barred de Larminat
from the town, in anger at the military operations under his command
which had destroyed it, and at the widespread looting of the Royan
homes by French soldiers after "liberation." He hoped now to persuade
the Royannais that they had made a mistake. The meeting is described by
Dr. Veyssière Pierre, former leader of the Resistance in Royan, and a hold-
er of the Croix de Guerre, who says he hoped to get an explanation of the
"useless sacrifice" of the population of the town, but "my self-deception
was total, absolute." He quotes de Larminat saying the French military
did not want the enemy "to surrender of his own accord; that would give
the impression the Germans were unconquered."[***]

---

* "Les Préparatifs de l'Attaque" in Botton collection. The same writer claims (on the basis of
a historical work by J. Mortin, *Au carrefour de l'Histoire*) that the formula for napalm was
found in the eighteenth century by a Grenoblois goldsmith, who demonstrated it to the minister of war, after which Louis XV was so horrified he ordered the documents burned, saying
that such a terrifying force must remain unknown for the good of man.

** *Revue Historique de l'armee*, January, 1946. An article in a regional journal after the war
commented on those engaged in the April attacks: "Thanks to them, one could not say that
the French army remained impotent before the German redoubts on the Atlantic wall." *Le
Pays d'Ouest*, copy in the library at Royan.

*** Open letter to General de Larminat, caustically addressing him as "Liberateur" de Royan.
Reproduced in the Botton collection.

Another member of the French delegation, Dr. Domecq, a former Mayor and Resistance leader, responded to General de Larminat also:

> Royan was destroyed by mistake, you say, my general.... Those responsible have been punished, the order to attack, a few days before liberation, could not be questioned by the military.... The Germans had to feel our power! Permit me, my general, to tell you, once and for all, in the name of those who paid the cost: "La Victoire de Royan" does not exist, except for you.

General de Larminat responded to the criticism in the letter addressed to Paul Métadier.* Pride and military ambition, he pointed out, were not sufficient explanations for such a huge operation; one had to seek a larger source: "This pride, this ambition, did not have the power to manufacture the shells which were used, to create the units which were sent, to divert the important aerial and naval forces that participated." De Larminat said that he had prepared the necessary plans for liquidating "*les poches d'Atlantique*" but that he did not judge the date. The date was fixed for him, and he executed the plans.

He ended his reply with an appeal to patriotism: "Must we therefore, throw opprobrium on old combatants because some isolated ones committed acts, unhappily inevitable in wartime? This is how it has been in all the wars of all time. No one ever, that I know, used this as a pretext to reduce the glory and the valour of the sacrifices made by the combatants." He spoke of the "simple, brave people" who will put "glory and national independence" before "material losses" and give "the respect due to those who fell, and for which many sacrificed their lives, to a patriotic ideal that the malcontents ("*les attentistes*") have always ignored."

Admiral Meyer, who is more sympathetic to de Larminat than most of the general's critics, had watched the attack on Royan from the heights of Medis, and described the scene:

> The weather was clear, the warmth oppressive. Under a fantastic concentration of fire, the enemy positions, the woods, and the ruins of Royan flamed. The countryside and the sky were thick with powder and yellow smoke. One could with difficulty distinguish the mutilated silhouette of

---

* The exchange between Métadier and de Larminat is in a pamphlet in the possession of the library in Royan. The original Royan library was destroyed during the bombings, and in 1957, after twelve years, a new library was built.

the clock of Saint-Pierre, which burned like a torch. I knew that the allied planes were using for the first time, a new kind of incendiary explosive, a kind of jellied gasoline, known as napalm.

Larminat, he said, had good days and bad days, for in the evening after Royan was taken, and Meyer went to see the General: "He was visibly satisfied with having achieved this brilliant revenge.... Without saying that he was intoxicated with success, the General seemed to me however to have his appetite stimulated..."

That exultation was felt at all levels. A press correspondent on the scene described the very heavy artillery bombardment which prepared the attack on the Royan area: 27,000 shells. Then the first aerial bombing on Saturday, April 14, with high explosives. Then the bombing all Sunday morning with napalm. By seven that evening they were in Royan. It was a blazing furnace. ("*La ville est un brasier.*") The next morning, they could still hear the clatter of machine guns in the woods nearby. Royan was still burning. ("*Royan brule encore.*") The dispatch ends: "It is a beautiful spring."

With Royan taken, they decided to attack the island of Oléron, opposite Rochefort. As Meyer says:

> The new victory had inflamed the passions of our soldiers, giving them the idea that nothing could resist them. News from the German front forecast a quick end to the war. Each one wanted a last moment to distinguish himself and get a bit of glory; moderation was scorned, prudence was seen as cowardice.

Meyer did not believe the attack on Oléron was necessary. But he participated assiduously in planning and executing it, happy to be once again involved in a naval operation, and convinced that his duty was only to carry out orders from above.

> The attack on Oléron was disputable from the point of view of general strategy. It was a costly luxury, a conquest without military value, on the eve of the war's end. But this was not for me to judge. My duty was limited to doing my best in making those military decisions which would fulfil my orders.

Meyer blames the political leaders above. Yet *blame* seems the wrong word, because Meyer believes it honorable to follow orders, whatever they are, against whatever adversary is chosen for him: "*Quant au sol-*

dat, depuis des millénaires, ce n'est plus lui qui forge ses armes et qui choisit son adversaire. Il n'a que le devoir d'obeir dans la pleine mesure de sa foi, de son courage, de sa resistance." *

One can see in the destruction of Royan that infinite chain of causes, that infinite dispersion of responsibility, which can give infinite work to historical scholarship and sociological speculation, and bring an infinitely pleasurable paralysis of the will. What a complex of motives! In the Supreme Allied Command, the simple momentum of the war, the pull of prior commitments and preparations, the need to fill out the circle, to pile up the victories as high as possible. At the local military level, the ambitions, petty and large, the tug of glory, the ardent need to participate in a grand communal effort by soldiers of all ranks. On the part of the American Air Force, the urge to try out a newly developed weapon. (Paul Métadier wrote: "In effect, the operation was above all characterized by the dropping of new incendiary bombs which the Air Force had just been supplied with. According to the famous formulation of one general: 'They were marvelous!') And among all participants, high and low, French and American, the most powerful motive of all: The habit of obedience, the universal teaching of all cultures, not to get out of line, not even to think about that which one has not been assigned to think about, the negative motive of not having either a reason or a will to intercede.

Everyone can point, rightly, to someone else as being responsible. In that remarkable film *King and Country*, a simple-minded British country boy in the trenches of World War I walks away one day from the slaughter and is condemned to death in a two-step process where no one thinks he really should be executed but the officers in each step can blame those in the other. The original court sentences him to death thinking to make a strong point and then have the appeals tribunal overturn the verdict. The appeals board, upholding the verdict, can argue that the execution was not its decision. The man is shot. That procedure, one recalls, goes back to the Inquisition, when the church only conducted the trial,

---

* At one point, Meyer quotes Bismarck, who made German students write: "Man was not put in the world to be happy, but to do his duty!" In another frightening glimpse of what a well-trained military man of our century can believe, Meyer talks fondly of that special bond of the sea (*"une commune maitresse: la mer"*) which unites sailors of different nations in their patriotic duty, and points, as an example of such laudable unity in action, to the landing of European troops in China in 1900 to crush the Boxer uprising.

and the state carried out the execution, thus confusing both God and the people about the source of the decision.

More and more in our time, the mass production of massive evil requires an enormously complicated division of labor. No one is positively responsible for the horror that ensues. But every one is negatively responsible, because anyone can throw a wrench into the machinery. Not quite, of course—because only a few people have wrenches. The rest have only their hands and feet. That is, the power to interfere with the terrible progression is distributed unevenly, and therefore the sacrifice required varies, according to one's means. In that odd perversion of the natural which we call society (that is, nature seems to equip each species for its special needs) the greater one's capability for interference, the less urgent is the need to interfere.

It is the immediate victims—or tomorrow's—who have the greatest need, and the fewest wrenches. They must use their bodies (which may explain why rebellion is a rare phenomenon). This may suggest to those of us who have a bit more than our bare hands, and at least a small interest in stopping the machine, that we might play a peculiar role in breaking the social stalemate.

This may require resisting a false crusade—or refusing one or another expedition in a true one. But always, it means refusing to be transfixed by the actions of other people, the truths of other times. It means acting on what we feel and think, here, now, for human flesh and sense, against the abstractions of duty and obedience.

3

Vietnam: A
Matter of
Perspective

Those of us who had been involved in the Southern movement were not likely to accept, without deep suspicion, that the United States government—so loath to protect equal rights in its own country—was dropping bombs in Vietnam on behalf of democracy or liberty or self-determination or any other noble principle. In August 1964, the bodies of civil rights workers Chaney, Goodman and Schwerner were discovered in Neshoba County, Mississippi, shot to death. Earlier in the summer, a delegation of black Mississippians had traveled to Washington to plead with the national government for federal protection, and was received with silence. At a memorial service for the three young men, Bob Moses, SNCC organizer in Mississippi, held up a copy of that morning's newspaper which headlined LBJ SAYS SHOOT TO KILL IN THE GULF OF TONKIN. The United States had been conducting secret naval operations off the coast of North Vietnam and now claimed U.S. destroyers, on "routine patrol" had been fired on—a claim full of deceptions and outright lies, it turned out. Moses commented bitterly on the fact that the federal government refused protection for civil rights workers but was ready to send its armed forces halfway around the world for a cause no one could reasonably explain. I became involved in the anti-war movement very soon after that summer, spoke at the first anti-war rally on the Boston Common in the spring of 1965, and began writing about the war. In 1967 Beacon Press published my book *Vietnam: The Logic of Withdrawal*, which immediately went through eight printings. Reprinted here is the introductory chapter to that book.

Vietnam, it seems to me, has become a theater of the absurd.

1. By late 1966, the United States was spending for the Vietnam war at an annual rate of twenty billion dollars, enough to give every family in South Vietnam (whose normal annual income is not more than several hundred dollars) about $5,000 for the year. Our monthly expentiture for the war exceeds our annual expenditure for the Great Society's poverty program.

2. Early in 1966, a new pacification technique was developed by American soldiers. It involved surrounding a village, killing as many young men as could be found, and then taking away the women and children by helicopter. The Americans called this procedure "Operation County Fair."

3. The Pentagon disclosed in 1966 that it had paid to relatives an average of $34 in condolence money for each Vietnamese killed accidentally in American air strikes during that summer. At the same time, according to reports from Saigon, the Air Force was paying $87 for each rubber tree destroyed accidentally by bombs.

4. A *New York Times* dispatch from Saigon, June 21, 1966:

> The United States Air Force turned its attention yesterday to a column of 10 water buffalos sighted along a road just north of the Mugia Pass on the Laotian-North Vietnamese border.
> The spokesman said the buffalos were heavily laden with what was suspected to be enemy ammunition. The animals died under fire from F105 Thunderchief jets. The spokesman said, "There were no secondary explosions."
> United States Marine pilots also strafed a column of 11 pack elephants in the mountains 35 miles southwest of Danang in South Vietnam yesterday. Five of the animals were killed and five others seen to fall. Again there were no secondary explosions.

5. A Chicago newspaper, asked by a reader if it were true that for every enemy soldier it killed in Vietnam the United States was killing six civilians, replied that this was not true; we were killing only four civilians for every soldier.

6. Covering the Buddhist revolt against the Ky government in early 1966, *Life* magazine showed a photo of a South Vietnamese soldier coming up behind an unarmed, gowned Buddhist monk and clubbing him unconscious. No comment was made by *Life*.

7. At his press conference on March 22, 1966, at a time of expanding warfare and growing casualties in Vietnam, President Johnson said, among other things: "If I get real depressed when I read how everything has gone bad here, I just ask for the letters from Vietnam so I can cheer up."

8. The January 16, 1965 *Milwaukee Journal* reported that a young man who had studied agricultural economics at the University of Minnesota, learning to aid underdeveloped countries improve their yields, was now an Air Force captain and was using his knowledge to point out productive rice fields in Vietnam, so that United States planes could destroy them with bombs and chemicals.

9. In the spring of 1966, a journalist interviewed an Air Force general in Saigon:

> Journalist: Let me ask you a philosophical question. What is your reply to those who say we ought to stop our bombing—both North and South—and that would bring us closer to negotiating an end to this war?
> General: Well, we were sent out here to do a job, and we're doing it, and we'll stay here until it's done.
> Journalist: Thank you.

10. In March 1966, President Johnson, talking about Vietnam with Columbia University historian Henry Graff, said "proudly" (as Graff reported it): "I wanted to leave the footprints of America there."

Isolated oddities can, on investigation, prove to be deviations from an otherwise healthy set of circumstances. Or they may turn out to be small symptoms of a more generalized malady. In such a case, investigation may disclose larger absurdities:

1. The most powerful nation in the world, producing 60 percent of the world's wealth, using the most advanced weapons known to mili-

tary science short of atomic bombs, has been unable to defeat an army of peasants, at first armed with homemade and captured weapons, then with modern firearms supplied from outside, but still without an air force, navy, or heavy artillery.

2. Declaring its intent to preserve freedom, the United States has supported a succession of military dictatorships in South Vietnam.

3. Again and again President Johnson has insisted that American forces are in Vietnam to repel "aggression" and that "if they'll go home tomorrow, we'll go home." Our actions in South Vietnam have been conducted against a force of which 80 percent to 90 percent are already home (that is, in South Vietnam, where they are from) with the rest from North Vietnam, which is not very far from home. Indeed, if the Geneva Accords are to be taken as a basis (as the United States itself agrees), it is all one country, and all our opponents are home. The main fighting against these Vietnamese is conducted now by 350,000 Americans, all of whom are quite far from home, plus 40,000 Koreans, who also are definitely not home. In bombing North Vietnam, our fliers who are not home, are killing people who are.

4. Government officials have declared that we are at war in Vietnam to stop Chinese "expansion." Available evidence is that there are no Chinese troops in Vietnam, nor anywhere else outside of China. China is, indeed, half encircled by American military bases in Korea, Japan, the Philippines, Formosa, Okinawa, and Thailand—with about 250,000 United States soldiers, sailors, and airmen at those bases.

5. The United States maintains it must continue fighting in Vietnam so as not to lose prestige among its allies. As the war has continued, the prestige of the United States in Japan (its most important ally in Asia) and in England, France, and West Germany (its most important allies in Europe) has seriously declined.

"Absurdity" is in the mind of the viewer; it involves a simple mental operation. We come across what in itself seems an ordinary fact, but when we place it alongside another fact, we find an incongruity. That other fact may come out of the common pile which most people share or it may come out of the viewer's own life experience. Thus to see a situation as absurd does not depend on the number of facts we know about a situation, but on the way we relate the facts we know—on what we pull out of our memories when a fact presents itself.

Likewise, making moral judgments—as on the war in Vietnam—does not depend mainly on the volume of our knowledge. We find, indeed, that the experts in each field disagree sharply on the most fundamental questions. This is because ethical decisions depend on the relationships in which we place the facts we know.

Therefore what we bring to the common body of evidence in Vietnam—the *perspective* we have—is crucial. It determines what we choose to see or not to see. It determines how we relate the things we see. This perspective varies from one person to another. I think we get closer to wisdom, and also to democracy, when we add the perspectives of other people to our own.

What I want to do in this book is to focus my vision, coming from my own set of experiences, on the data of public record: government documents, newspaper reports, the published work of scholars. To begin, then, I should say a little about the biases that affect my view of the war in Vietnam.

In the midst of World War II, I enlisted in the United States Air Force and flew as a bombardier in the European theater of operations. From beginning to end, I believed fervently that Hitler's force had to be met with force. But when I was packing and labeling my folder of war days and mementos to go home, I impulsively marked it "Never Again." I had participated in a least one atrocity, and I came away from the war with several conclusions:

(1) that innocent and well-meaning people—of whom I considered myself one—are capable of the most brutal acts and the most self-righteous excuses, whether they be Germans, Japanese, Russians, or Americans;

(2) that one of the guiding rules for an Air Force in possession of large quantities of bombs is: "Get rid of them—anywhere";

(3) that the claims of statesmen and military men to be bombing only "military targets" should not be taken seriously;

(4) that war is a monstrously wasteful way of achieving a social objective, always involving indiscriminate mass slaughter unconnected with that objective; that even World War II, with its stark moral issues—the "best" of all wars—presented agonizing moral questions; and that any situation where right and wrong were *not* so clear, and where human life was being sacrificed, should be regarded with deep suspicion.

Later I was trained as a historian and learned that our country is capable of moral absurdities. There was the Spanish-American War, described by an American diplomat as a "splendid little war," though it reeked of corpses on Cuban hillsides and rotten meat fed to soldiers—thousands of whom died of food poisoning.

There were our warships cannonading Vera Cruz in 1914, with hundreds of Mexican civilians killed, because the Mexicans refused to give a twenty-one-gun salute to the American flag.

There was Haiti in 1915, where United States Marines brought "order" by shooting 2,000 Haitians, with an Admiral wiring the Secretary of the Navy: "Next Thursday...I will permit Congress to elect a President."

There was President McKinley's decision to "civilize" the Filipinos, and Andrew Carnegie's subsequent message to a friend who defended our crushing of the Filipino rebellion: "It is a matter of congratulaton that you seem to have about finished your work of civilizing the Filipinos. It is thought that about 8000 of them have been completely civilized and sent to Heaven."

My conclusion was not that the United States was more evil than other nations, only that she was just as evil (although she sometimes had more finesse). It does not take too much study of modern history to conclude that nations as a lot tend to be vicious.

My work in American history led to another idea: that there is no necessary relationship between liberalism in domestic policy and humaneness in foreign policy. Some of our most grotesquely immoral deeds have been committed by "liberals." Take Andrew Jackson's murderous attitude toward the Indians (whom we treated, ironically, as a foreign nation) in the bloody Trail of Tears, or Progressive Theodore Roosevelt's bullying activities in the Caribbean. Take Woodrow Wilson's behavior towards Haiti and Mexico and his carrying the nation, for reasons still inexplicable, into the pointless savagery of the First World War.

During a year off from teaching, I did research on modern Chinese history as a Fellow at the Harvard Center for East Asian Studies. I soon became aware of a great gap between the findings of scholars and the policy of the United States. Official policy seemed to be derived more from lurid headlines in the press than from the balanced findings of the academicians. It was not that the reports of "thought control" in China were wrong; it was that so much else that China had accomplished was ignored. It was not that the Chinese were not aggressive in their statements about the United States; it was that their foreign policy was quite restrained for a proud nation with a new regime. It was not that there was not much that was wrong in Communist China; it was that American policy-makers acted as if there was not much that was wrong with the United States.

This last point was important; the moral failures of other nations had to be seen not in isolation, but against our own failures. It was in this connection that another part of my life influenced my perspective on the problem of Vietnam: my years of living and teaching in a Negro community in the deep South and my involvement in some of the civil rights struggles of the early 1960s. That experience has given me a glimpse of American foreign policy from a special standpoint, one which I will try to explain in the third chapter of this book.

There is one final influence on my thinking which I should mention: the perspective of geographical distance, beginning to see American policy as people in a far-off country saw it. There are many Americans in recent years—Peace Corpsmen, travelers, students—who have been startled by a sudden awareness of how other people see us. My own recent experience was with Japan, and I want to discuss this in the next chapter.

On the basis of these angles of vision, brought to bear on the historical record of the Vietnam war, I am going to argue in the following pages that the United States should withdraw its military forces from Vietnam.

Thus far almost all of the nationally known critics of our Vietnam policy—perceptive as they are—have been reluctant to call for the withdrawal of the United States from Vietnam. Sometimes this is for substantive reasons, which I will discuss later on. But often, I believe, it is because these critics consider total military withdrawal, while logical and right, "too extreme" as a tactical position, and therefore unpalatable to the public and unlikely to be adopted as national policy.

Scholars, who pride themselves on speaking their minds, often engage in a form of self-censorship which is called "realism." To be "realistic" in dealing with a problem is to work only among the alternatives which the most powerful in society put forth. It is as if we are all confined to a, b, c, or d in the multiple choice test, when we know there is another possible answer. American society, although it has more freedom of expression than most societies in the world, thus sets limits beyond which respectable people are not supposed to think or speak. So far, too much of the debate on Vietnam has observed these limits.

To me this is a surrender of the role of the citizen in a democracy. The citizen's job, I believe, is to declare firmly what he thinks is right. To compromise with politicians from the very start is to end with a compromise of a compromise. This weakens the moral force of a citizenry which has little enough strength in the shaping of governmental policy. Machiavelli cautioned the prince not to adopt the ethics of the citizen. It is appropriate now to suggest to the Citizen that he cannot, without sacrificing both integrity and power, adopt the ethics of the Prince.

4

Of Fish and Fishermen

In June of 1966 I was invited to Japan, along with Ralph Featherstone, a black SNCC worker I knew from Mississippi. Our hosts were members of Beheiren, a Japanese group organized around opposition to the American war in Vietnam—they were journalists, novelists, poets, philosophers, movie-makers. Ralph and I traveled north to south through Japan, from Hokkaido to Hiroshima and Fukuoka, and across the East China Sea to Okinawa. We spoke at fourteen universities in nine different cities, at big meetings and small ones, at tea gatherings and beer sessions, with trade unionists and housewives. We found them virtually unanimous in their belief that the United States policy in Vietnam was not just a bit awry, but profoundly wrong. When I returned, wanting people in the United States to get a Japanese perspective on the war, I wrote an article for *Ramparts* magazine, which appeared in 1967 under the title "Of Fish and Fishermen," and then, in another form, as a chapter in *Vietnam: The Logic of Withdrawal*. (A tragic note: not long after our return from Japan, my companion on that trip, Ralph Featherstone, newly married, still involved with SNCC and the Movement, was killed when a bomb of unknown origin exploded in a car he was driving.)

There is an eerie ten minute motion picture called *The Fisherman*, in which a happy American angler hauls sleek, fat leaping fish out of the ocean and piles them lifeless on the beach, meanwhile devouring candy bars from his lunchbox. He finally runs out of food. Restless, unhappy, he sees a paper sack nearby with a sandwich in it, bites into the sandwich, and is hooked. He digs his feet frantically into the sand, but he is dragged, twisting and struggling at the end of a line, into the sea. The effect on the viewer is a sudden reverse of perspective, both horrifying and healthful, in which, for the first time he sees himself, the Fisherman, from the standpoint of the Fish.

Something like that happens when you spend time in Japan talking to the Japanese about American policy in Vietnam. The brutality of the war we are waging, no matter how sharply we feel it on occasion, has the quality of fiction as it appears on television screens or in news columns. Always at hand to "explain" the bombing of villages, the death toll of civilians, the crushing of Buddhist dissidents, are earnest "liberals" (Humphrey and Goldberg), "realistic" experts (Rostow), genial spokesmen for the Administration (Rusk and McNamara). We listen with the languor of a people who have never been bombed, who have only been the bombardiers. So even our flickers of protest somehow end up muted and polite.

The Japanese have had a more intimate association with death, both as killers and as victims. We in America still cling to the romance of war that is not really war, but Terry and the Pirates, Defending the Free World, or LBJ in a Green Beret. For the Japanese, the recollection of themselves as kamikaze pilots, and then the turn-about-Hiroshima and Nagasaki, wore off all the sheen. Out of their experience, the Japanese want desperately to speak to us.

In Tokyo, rain cascading down outside, the auditorium at Meiji University filled, popular novelist Kaiko Ken told about his four months of note-taking on the front lines in Vietnam, much of the time spent with American soldiers. Kaiko, who is thirty-six, wore a sporty tan suit with open shirt collar, and tan suede shoes. "It used to be said in Vietnam that it is disastrous to be born a man, for you are drafted and killed; it is better to be a woman. But in South Vietnam today, a woman has a child at each side and one in her belly, and still must flee the American bombs."

He had seen it himself, he said, that the Americans could not distinguish the Viet Cong from the air—no matter what the official assurances were—so they simply killed whomever they could find in the target area.

If this talk had been given in the United States, in any large gathering of students, one or more would have risen at some point in the discussion to challenge Kaiko's accusation—either to deny it, or to explain why the bombings were needed. In Japan, it is hard to find any defenders of American policy.

It was Kaiko, not a very political person, who last year collected money throughout Japan for a full-page ad which appeared in the *New York Times* as a plea to Americans: "The Japanese learned a bitter lesson from fifteen years of fighting on the Chinese mainland: weapons alone are of no avail in winning the minds and allegiance of any people.... America's conduct of the war in Vietnam is alienating the sympathy of the Japanese." Corroboration of this last statement came from a journalist of long experience with a leading conservative newspaper in Japan, who said to me: "The polls show 80 percent of the Japanese opposed to U.S. policy in Vietnam. Emotionally, it is closer to 100 percent."

This was confirmed again and again as we talked with Japanese students and professors in 14 different universities along the 1500 mile journey from Hokkaido to Okinawa. In Kyoto, a pediatrician spoke up from the audience. (Our interpreter—a poet and former Fulbright scholar in America—explained who the speaker was: "Dr. Matsuda's books on child care have sold in the millions; he is known as the Benjamin Spock of Japan.") Matsuda said: "What the United States does not understand is that communism is one of the effective ways in which underdeveloped countries become organized. Its reaction to this phenomenon in the world is neurotic." Matsuda, a vigorous man in his fifties, added: "Perhaps it needs..." Our interpreter hesitated at this point, and then translated the ending as "... a laxative." Then he corrected himself: "...a sedative."

At that meeting in Kyoto, a mountain-rimmed city of temples and pagodas, over a thousand people—students, faculty, town residents— came to talk about Vietnam. A ninety-two-year-old man, dean of the Buddhist priests in this holy city, spoke: "The American concept of freedom violates the principles of self-determination. It is the kind of liberalism that expresses only the purpose of the American state." And a Zen

Buddhist, head shaven, in black robes and white scarf, said, "There is a major law in Buddhism—not to kill. Mass killing should not go on; that is the simple slogan that binds Japanese Buddhists with Buddhists in North and South Vietnam. And this should be brought to America."

It was in Kyoto that a young professor of astronomy spoke, with great feeling: "As a child, I was machine-gunned by an American plane. And at that moment there came a shock of realization that it was a human being who pulled the trigger. I wanted so much to have been able to say to him 'Please—don't pull the trigger!'"

You find many men in Japanese universities who spent time in jail for opposing Japanese aggression in the '30s. At Nagoya—sprawling, smoky, the Detroit of Japan—we were met by Professor Shinmura, who in 1936-37 put out a humanist magazine called *Sekai Bunka* (World Culture) until he was seized by the police. Shinmura, quiet, gray-haired with a slight stoop, is a specialist in French literature, and after release from prison made a living by anonymously translating the writings of Rolland, Diderot and others. I asked how many members of his faculty supported American policy in Vietnam. There were 600 on the faculty, including graduate asistants. No one knew of any who supported American policy.

To the Japanese we met, America was so clearly in the wrong, that it was incomprehensible to them why anyone believed Johnson and his cabinet members. "No country should be permitted—as the U.S. is doing—to smuggle counter-revolution to another country," a professor of literature at Hosei University in Tokyo said.

After a four hour discussion session at Tohoku University in Sendai, a quiet town in northern Honshu, I was met by fifty students waiting eagerly to continue the discussion. We trooped off to the park. There in the cool darkness of Sendai, I wondered why fifty Japanese kids would stay out after midnight to discuss the war in Vietnam, when Japan was only a minor accessory to American action. When the U.S. was helping the French crush the Algerian revolt, did any group of American students ever gather in the park at midnight to brood over this? Did a thousand ever meet to protest it? By the end of our trip I thought I had found the answer. It lay in the Japanese people's piercing consciousness of their own recent history. Again and again, at virtually every meeting, there arose the accusation, directed at the Japanese past and the American present: "You are behaving in Asia as we once did."

There is widespread and vocal recognition of Japan's own sins, from the Manchurian invasion of 1931, to Pearl Harbor. Japanese scholars have done much research on those years, and see in American actions in Vietnam many of the same characteristics displayed by Japan in the '30s. Unlike the Nazis, the Japanese did not abruptly replace parliamentary democracy with authoritarian dictatorship. Rather, there was an almost imperceptible growth of the power of the military within the outwardly parliamentary system. When the Japanese took Manchuria in 1931, then attacked China proper in 1937 and moved into Sougheast Asia in 1940, they did not crassly declaim of world conquest like Hitler, but spoke of a "co-prosperity sphere" which they were creating in Asia for the benefit of all.

I asked one of Japan's most disginguished scholars about this analogy. This was Professor Maruyama of Tokyo University, a political scientist and prolific author, who five years ago was a visiting professor at Harvard. "There are many differences," Maruyama said, "but one crucial element is quite the same: the apologies and justification created by both governments for what is basically an attempt by a strong nation to establish a base of power inside a weaker one. Both Japan and the U.S. had difficulties and made excuses. The U.S. blames its difficulties in winning the Vietnamese war on China and North Vietnam. Japan attributed her failures not to the stubborn resistance of the Chinese, but to the aid of Great Britain and the United States. Japan declared that its aim was to emancipate the people of Southeast Asia and to bring them economic development. Just as the U.S. speaks not about economic and social reform while it carries on an essentially military action in Vietnam."

American commentators have a habit of dismissing Japanese criticism of our foreign policy as the work of communists, or—more vaguely—"leftists." This is comforting at first, but not after one reflects that most public opinion in the world, even in countries allied to us, is to the left of ours. We have become, since that period when Europe's monarchs feared we would spread the doctrine of revolution everywhere, a conservative nation. Even our "liberals" are conservative by global standards. Professor Maruyama said: "I am a liberal, not a radical. So I am concerned with what liberals in the States are doing. And I am very disappointed."

Our companions and interpreters in Japan were young intellectuals—two journalists, three novelists, a film producer, a poet, a philosopher—who last year decided to cross the maze of radical party lines in Japan
and form a group (called Beheiren) dedicated to ending the war in
Vietnam. Their chairman, Oda Makoto (family name first), is a wry thirty-
four-year-old novelist who refuses to wear a tie no matter how formal the
occasion. Oda started our meeting with students at Hokkaido University as
follows: "You know, I got the idea for this tour of conscience while in the
toilet. (Laughter) This is not strange. The peace movement starts like that,
from the most common behavior of human life, from the elemental."

Oda, like most Japanese intellectuals, is critical of Communist
China, but with no more heat than he is critical of Japan or America. He
sees it as a new society, with the spit and fire that other new nations show,
but not as a threat to the rest of Asia. It shows no signs of wanting to gob-
ble up Southeast Asia; it maintains pacific relations with Burma, which is
defenseless along a very long border—and with Cambodia. And, in contrast to the United States, China does not have a single soldier stationed
outside its borders. Japanese intellectuals do not doubt that, in view of
China's behavior, the U.S. is acting hysterically, and that people in
Vietnam are dying unnecessarily because of it.

The United States keeps saying its aim is a free and prosperous
Asia, but the Asians themselves, including the Vietnamese, are far from
ardent about this war, and the only countries giving substantial aid to the
American military effort (Korea and Thailand) are those which are economically dependent on th U.S., under its military occupation, and controlled by elites which can ignore popular desire. Japan is also a station for
American troops (under the much-resented Security Treaty of 1960) and
its former territory, Okinawa, has been taken away by the U.S. and converted into one of the most powerful military bases in the world. ("Please
inform your fellow Americans," a Tokyo University student sociologist
said, "that the majority of Japanese do not think these military bases protect Japan's security—in fact they feel endangered by them.")
Nevertheless, the government of Premier Sato, while nodding and bowing to the U.S. Department of State, keeps a wary eye on the Japanese
public, knowing their feelings.

Our envoy to Japan, Edwin Reischauer, an astute scholar of Asian
affairs before his appointment, now lives in a comfortable bubble of his

own in the Embassy, quietly ignoring Japanese disapproval of this country's actions. My last hour in Tokyo was spent in rapid-fire dialogue with him, trying to penetrate that bubble. But, except for Reischauer's personal charm, it was like listening to an LBJ press conference, or a McNamara briefing.

Reischauer thought differently in 1954 when, as a Harvard expert on Japan, he wrote *Wanted: an Asian Policy*. In it, he described the French suppression of the Viet Minh, with American aid, as "a sobering example of the weakness of defending the status quo." He found the main reason for the effectiveness of the Communists "in the realm of ideas" and because they "carried out much needed land reform for the peasants." He wishes the U.S. "had the foresight and the courage in the early postwar years to persuade the French to extricate themselves soon enough from their untenable position in Indochina." And, he said a policy based largely on stopping communism was "a dangerous oversimplification of our Asian problem." In his book, he accused American policy-makers of "frenzied emotionalism" and "dangerous inflexibility." But now he is the ambassador.

Japan is an embarrassment, because it was under our post-war tutelage that she put into her 1947 Constitution the statement: "...never again shall we be visited with the horrors of war through the action of government." And Article 9 contains a silent reproach to what the United States is doing in Vietnam: "... the Japanese people forever rennounce war as a sovereign right of the nation and the threat or use of force as a means of settling international disputes." It is the old human story, the little boy nurtured by his family on the Biblical exhortation Thou Shalt Not Kill, watching his father return, gun still smoking from a mission of murder.

The Japanese are trying to speak to us, but we will not listen. They have been both Fish and Fisherman, in a short space of time. We in the United States have never had to struggle at the end of the hook—and lose. We have no Hiroshima, no city of the blind and maimed, no professors still haggard from long terms in jail. And while, on a numbr of occasions, we have been the Fisherman, we have never been forced, as the Japanese have, to recognize our deeds, to bow, to apologize, to promise a life of peace. We have, in other words, never been caught.

5

A Speech
for LBJ

It is a common occurrence in American politics that critics of a certain policy, while fervently declaring their allegiance to moral principle, nevertheless say they can "understand" the reluctance of the President to act on such principle because of the "realities" of politics, that he cannot "afford" (a word I always associated with dire poverty and not with the occupant of the White House) to go against "public opinion." This is almost always a feeble rationalization for a deep lack of principle, and when the same argument for "realism" was put forth against the idea of withdrawal from Vietnam, I decided to challenge it. It seemed to me that public opinion was usually ahead of the national government on moral issues, that in any case such opinion was extremely volatile and movable by reasonable argument. My method was to write a speech for Lyndon Johnson which would persuasively explain to Ameircans more than ready for such an explanation, indeed eager for it as the bodybags of their sons were returning home in great numbers, why he was immediately withdrawing our military machine from Vietnam. I ended my book *Vietnam: The Logic of Withdrawal* with that speech. A busi-

296

nessman bought six hundred copies of the book and sent it to every member of Congress. The speech was reprinted in full-page ads in newspapers in various parts of the country. The *Cleveland Plain Dealer* ran simultaneous articles by Congressman Mendel Rivers of South Carolina, urging escalation of the war, by Senator William Fulbright, calling for gradual de-escalation and negotiations, and by me, agruing for immediate withdrawal. The paper then took a poll of its readers and 63% voted for immediate withdrawal. A columnist for the *Plain Dealer* wrote: "Howard Zinn, a professor of government at Boston University, who served as a bombardier in World War II, has written a speech for Lyndon Johnson which, if he delivered it, would make the President one of the great men of history in my opinion." But Johnson did not deliver that speech. He did start negotiations with the Vietnamese in Paris, and announced he would not run for President in 1968. The war continued, and the anti-war movement grew, and in 1973 the United States finally withdrew; 55,000 Americans had lost their lives, Vietnam was devastated, and two million of its people, mostly civilians, were dead. Here is the speech I wrote in 1967.

M y Fellow Americans:

Not long ago I received a letter from my fourth-grade school teacher who still lives back in the little town where I grew up. She is of advanced age now, but still as she was when I sat in her class, a kindly and wise woman. She had been through depression and war, through sickness and the death of loved ones, more than most of us. Let me share her letter with you; I am sure she will not mind.

> Dear Lyndon: You know I have always had faith in you and knew you would do what is right. And you have been trying your best on this Vietnam situation. But nothing seems to be going right. So many people are getting killed. Not only our boys, but all those poor people over there. You have tried talking peace. And you have tried bombing, and what not. But there is no end in sight. I hear people in town sayng: "We should never have gotten in, but now that we are in, we don't seem able to get out." Lyndon, can't you get us out? I am getting on now in years and would like to see peace gain. God Bless you. Sincerely, Mrs. Annie Mae Lindley

Now let me read just one more letter to you. It came to me from a young man fighting with the First Marine Division in South Vietnam:

Dear Mr. President: I am twenty years old and enlisted in the Marines as soon as I left high school in Massilon, Ohio. I have been in Vietnam six months now, and I have seen a lot. Three days ago my closest buddy was killed. Yesterday our outfit destroyed a hamlet that Intelligence said had been used by the VC as a base. We burned the huts and threw grenades down the tunnels. But there were no VC there. In one of the tunnels there were two women and three kids. We didn't know that. One of the kids was killed and one of the women lost an eye. We rounded up all the villagers and they stood around—children, old folks, women—crying and afraid. Of course we didn't mean to kill any kids. But we did. And that's war. I know you need sometimes to do nasty things for an important cause. The trouble is—there doesn't seem much of a cause left here in Vietnam. We're supposed to be defending these people against the VC. But they don't want us to defend them. They don't care about Communism or politics or anything like that. They just want to be left in peace. So, more and more, my buddies and I wonder—what are we doing here? We're not afraid. We've been sticking it out, in the mud and in the jungle. And we'll go on like this if you ask us to. But somehow it seems wrong. I don't know what we should do, but I just thought I'd let you know how soome of us feel. Sincerely, James Dixon, Corporal 1st Marine Division.

My fellow Americans, let me tell you, I have read and reread these two letters, and they have been on my mind. You all know how my administration has been concerned with the war in Vietnam. Night after night I have sat up thinking, and sometimes—I don't mind telling you—praying, that we would find a way to end this terrible war, which has cost tens of thousands of lives, American and Vietnamese, and which has caused so much pain and suffering to millions of people in that unfortunate little country.

What have been our objectives in Vietnam? I have said many times that what we wanted was for Vietnam to be free to determine its own affairs—that this is why we were fighting. We have tried every possible way to gain this objective. We have offered negotiations. And we have fought—hard, and courageously, on unfamiliar territory—with an increasing commitment of planes, ships and ground forces, all designed to bring the war to an end with honor.

I don't need to tell you that we have not been successful. We have not destroyed the Vietcong's will to fight. This is not a pleasant fact to report, but it is a fact.

There is another unpleasant fact to report. The government we have been supporting in Vietnam has not succeeded in gaining the respect of its own people there. No matter how valiant our men are, they cannot fight a war that is not supported by the people of the country we committed ourselves to defend. Always implied in our commitment was that if the war threatened to become our war, rather than a war by and for the Vietnamese, we would reconsider our position. That time has now come.

We have tried force, and we have offered negotiations. Neither has worked. Some have criticized us for not trying even more force. Of course we could do this. No one in the world needs to be told how powerful we are. We can stay in Vietnam as long as we like. We can reduce the whole country to ashes. We are powerful enough to do this. But we are not cruel enough to do this. I, as your president, am not willing to engage in a war without end that would destroy the youth of this nation and the people of Vietnam.

We had hoped this war could end by negotiations. But this has not worked. Pride and self-respect have often stood in the way for both sides. We are not willing to beg for negotiations. And we have too much compassion for those dying each day in Vietnam to let the war continue. In Korea, you may remember, the war dragged on, while the negotiators tried to agree on terms. The diplomats talked, while men died. For two years they talked, and for two years the corpses piled up in that unfortunate land. We do not want that kind of negotiation in Vietnam.

The American people have the courage to fight. We have shown this a dozen times in the past, from Bunker Hill to Gettysburg, from Normandy to Guadalcanal. We also have the courage to stop fighting, not when someone else decides for us, but when we decide for ourselves.

As commander-in-chief of the armed forces, I have ordered that, as of midnight tonight, our Air Force and our Navy will halt the bombings in North and South Vietnam. We have not run out of planes, nor have we run out of bombs, nor have we run out of the determination to use them when it is wise. What we have run out of is the willingness to see more people die under our bombs. Too many have died. Too many have suffered. It is time to call a halt.

Also, I have given orders to General Westmoreland, the capable and courageous Commander of our forces in Vietnam, to halt offensive operations and to begin the orderly withdrawal of our armed forces from that country.

Let us speak frankly now about the consequences of this decision.

We may see a period of turmoil and conflict in Vietnam. But that was true before we arrived. That is the nature of the world. It is hard to imagine, however, any conflict that will be more destructive than what is going on now. Our departure will inevitably diminish the fighting. It may end it.

There are many places in the world where people are going through the disorder and the violence of social change. The United States cannot interfere in every one of those instances. We do not intend to do so. To the extent that the United Nations can mediate in helping to bring tranquility to Vietnam, we will happily lend our moral and financial support.

Vietnam may become a Communist nation. The northern half of that country has been Communist for some time, and a good part of the population in the South has been sympathetic to the Vietcong. Desperate people often turn to Communism. But we have shown that we can live in peace with Communist nations, if there is mutual respect. Despite our many disagreements, we have maintained peaceful relations with the Soviet Union, with Yugoslavia, with Poland, with other Communist nations. We can certainly live in peace with Vietnam.

Everyone knows that behind our military activity in Vietnam has been our concern that Communist China shall not press its weght on other countries. Many experts on China have told us that much of China's belligerent attitude has been due to nationalistic feeling and to her fear that we intend to attack her. I hereby give my pledge that the United States will never initiate a war with China, and we will begin soon to seek ways and means of coming to a more amicable relationshp with her.

I have often said that the most effective means of maintaining a free society does not consist of armed might, but of economic development and prosperity. That will be our aim now in Asia.

To this end, I am going to ask Congress to take half of the $20 billion allocated for the Vietnam War this year and to put it into a fund—an international fund, if the United Nations will set this up—for the economic development of Vietnam and other countries in Southeast Asia. We will not force our favors upon these countries. But we will stand ready to help—with no political strings attached—on the basis of their own declarations, their own needs.

The war in Vietnam was beginnng to slow down many of our plans for the Great Society—plans to end poverty, to build homes and schools, to rebuild our cities, to eliminate the slums which have been at the root of unrest in various parts of the country. There will be $10 billion left unused from the war. I will ask Congress to redirect that money for purposes which I will outline in a special message next week.

We have made an important decision. It is a decision based on a fundamental American belief that human life is sacred, that peace is precious, and that true power does not consist in the brute force of guns and bombs, but in the economic well-being of a free people.

The dream I have always had since I was a boy in Texas, I still have—and I want to fulfill it for America. We are about to embark on a venture far more glorious, far more bold, requiring far more courage—than war. Our aim is to build a society which will set an example for the rest of mankind. I am happy to stand before you tonight and to say that we will now build this Great Society in earnest.

I need not tell you how long I have waited for this moment—and how happy I am to be able to say that now, after so much pain, after so much sacrifice, our boys will be coming home.

My fellow Americans, good night and sleep well. We are no longer at war in Vietnam.

6

Dow Shalt
Not Kill

The protest against the war took may forms. Violence was rare, engaged in by a small number of individuals on the fringe of the movement and generally disapproved by the movement as a whole. The general spirit of the movement was to follow the lead of the civil rights movement, to base its actions on the principle of non-violent direct action. This often meant confrontations with authority on many levels, including blocking streets and corporate offices, invading draft boards and destroying draft records (destruction of property, especially property that was an instrument of war, was not, unlike action against people, considered an act of violence). For instance, there were many demonstrations in Minneapolis against Minneapolis-Honeywell Corporation, which was manufacturing "cluster bombs," deadly packages of exploding pellets which left machines untouched, but people—mostly civilians—severely wounded and in agony. There were liberals who were made nervous by acts of trespassing, blockading, obstruction, arguing that they constituted violations of civil liberties. I did not think so, and used the occasion of a demonstration in which I participated, against the Dow Chemical Company, manufacturer of the deadly napalm, to make an argument defending such actions on both constitutional and moral grounds. My essay appeared in *The New South Student* in December 1967, and was reprinted in a number of other periodicals.

Many faculty members and students, being passionate opponents of American violence in Vietnam, and also insistent civil libertarians, are troubled by the recent demonstrations against Dow Chemical. No dilemma exists where the action is merely protest—by picketing, leafleting, speaking—against Dow, napalm, and the war. That is a plain exercise of free speech, press, and assembly.

But physical interposition, where Dow recruiters are blocked from carrying on their recruiting, opens puzzling questions. As one concerned both with civil liberties and the war, I would like to think aloud for a while, in print, and try to reach some conclusions.

First, it seems to me that the "civil liberties" of Dow Chemical are not in question. "Civil liberties" encompass various forms of freedom of expression, as well as certain procedural guarantees against arbitrary police or judicial action, and are fairly well covered by the First, Eighth, and Fourteenth Amendments. No one is abrogating Dow's right to express its views: indeed, the recent demonstrators in this area invited the Dow representative to state his case publicly, and gave him a platform for this purpose. If Dow wanted to set up a table, or hold a meeting, to declare its views, any interference would be a violation of civil liberties.

However, the *actions* of an individual or group which (unlike even the most malicious or slanderous speech) have immediate and irremediable effects on the lives and liberties of others, must sometimes be restricted for the health and safety of the public. Thus, we pass laws against murder, rape, arson. Thus, we regulate the sale and manufacture of harmful products. We even restrict the restaurant owner's freedom to choose his customers by racial standards. To put it more broadly: the whole body of criminal and social legislation is designed to restrict some people's freedom of action (not their civil liberties) in order to safeguard the health and happiness of others. Therefore, a *law* which prevented Dow Chemical Company from recruiting people who might be engaged in the manufacture, sale or promotion of a substance to be dropped on men, women, and children in order to burn them to death would be easily as justifiable as the Meat Inspection Act of 1906. It would (unlike a law interfering with talk for or against such a substance) no more be an infringement of civil liberties than a law barring the indiscriminate sale of deadly poisons at the corner grocery.

Robber Barons

The doctrine that the "civil liberties" of corporations are violated by regulatory laws was predominant in this country during the age of the "Robber Barons," and was constitutionally sanctioned for about fifty years, until 1938. Then, a sharply-worded opinion by Justice Black (*Connecticut General Life Insurance Co. v. Johnson*) declared that corporations should no longer be considered "persons" to be protected by the due process clause of the 14th Amendment. It soon became established in constitutional law that the regulation of business was not a deprivation of a civil liberty, that what is known as "substantive due process" would apply only to cases where real persons were being deprived of their rights of free expression. Today, it is well-established constitutionally that the U.S. government could make illegal the manufacture of napalm, and charge any persons recruiting for a napalm-manufacturing company with conspiring to violate the law.

But: there is no such law. Indeed, the government itself has ordered the napalm manufactured by Dow, and is using it to burn and kill Vietnamese peasants. Should private citizens (students and faculty—in this instance) act themselves, by physical interposition, against Dow Chemical's business activities?

To do so would be to "take the law into your own hands." That is exactly what civil disobedience is: the temporary taking of the law into one's own hands, in order to declare what the law *should* be. It is a declaration that there is an incongruence between the law and humane values, and that sometimes this can only be publicized by breaking the law.

Civil disobedience can take two forms: violating a law which is obnoxious; or symbolically enacting a law which is urgently needed. When Negroes sat-in at lunch counters, they were engaging in both forms: they violated state laws on segregation and trespassing; they were also symbolically enacting a public accommodations law even before it was written into the Civil Rights Act of 1964.

Most of us, I assume, would support civil disobedience under *some* circumstances: we would commend those who defied the Fugitive Slave Act by harboring a Negro slave, and those who symbolically enacted emancipation by trying to prevent soldiers in Boston from returning Anthony Burns to his master. Otherwise, to declare that the law in *all* circumstances is to be obeyed, is to suppress the very spirit of democracy, to surrender individual conscience to an omnipotent state. Thus, the issue becomes: under what circumstances is civil disobedience justified and is the Dow Chemical situation one of those circumstances?

It seems to me there are two essential conditions for the right to civil disobedience. One is that the human value at stake must involve fundamental rights, like life, health, and liberty. There is no real cause, for instance, to disobey a traffic light because it is inconveniently long. But human slavery, or racism, or war—these are overwhelmingly important. Thus, the argument "what if everyone disobeyed the law every time it displeased them" falls before the observable fact that those who engage in civil disobedience are almost always law-abiding citizens who on certain very important issues deliberately, openly, temporarily violate the law to communicate a vital message to their fellow citizens.

What of Dow Chemical and napalm? Four American physicians, in a report, "Medical Problems of South Vietnam," have written: "Napalm is a highly sticky inflammable jelly which clings to anything it touches and burns with such heat that all oxygen in the area is exhausted within moments. Death is either by roasting or by suffocation. Napalm wounds are often fatal (estimates are 90 percent). Those who survive face a living death. The victims are frequently children." Napalm is dropped daily on the villages, the forests, the people of Vietnam by American bombers; the saturation bombing of that tiny country is one of the cruelest acts perpetrated by any nation in modern history; it ranks with the destruction of Lidice by the Germans, the crushing of the Hungarian rebellion by the Russians, or the recent mass slaughter in Indonesia. Dr. Richard E. Perry, an American physician, wrote in *Redbook* in January 1967, on his return from Vietnam: "I have been an orthopedic surgeon for a good number of years, with rather a wide range of medical experience. But nothing could have prepared me for my encounters with Vietnamese women and children burned by napalm. It was shocking and sickening, even for a physician, to see and smell the blackened flesh."

We are not, then, dealing with trivialities, but with monstrous deeds. This fact somehow becomes lost in the bland, reasoned talk of businessmen and university officials, who speak as if Dow were just another business firm, recruiting for some innocuous purpose, making radios or toothpaste.

The root issue, it should be clear, is not simply napalm; it is the Vietnam war as a whole, in which a far-off country is being systematical-ly destroyed, and its population decimated, by the greatest military power on earth. The war itself is the object of the civil disobedience; the use of napalm is one particularly bestial tactic in this war.

This brings us to the second condition for civil disobedience: the inadequacy of legal channels for redressing the grievance. This is manifest-ly true in the case of the Vietnam war, which is being waged completely outside the American constitutional process, by the President and a hand-ful of advisers. Congress is troubled, but follows sheep-like what the White House decrees. The Supreme Court, by tradition, leaves foreign policy questions to the "political" branches of government (the President and Congress) but recently one of its more conservative members, Justice Potter Stewart, said that perhaps the Court should review the constitutionality of the war. This, after 100,000 American casualties! Citizens have taken to the auditoriums and to the streets precisely because they have no other way to protest; yet both President and Vice-President declare with the brazenness of petty dictators that no civic outcry will change their policy. If ever there was an issue which called for civil disoberience, it is this run-away war.

Then why do we become uneasy when students interfere with Dow Chemical? Occasionally, we read of housewives blocking off a busy inter-section because children have been killed there as a result of a lack of traf-fic lights. These housewives thereby interfere with the freedom of automo-biles and of pedestrians, in order to temporarily regulate, or even disrupt, traffic, on behalf of the lives of children—hoping this will lead to the per-manent regulation of traffic by government. (Those are not *the* automobiles that killed the child, anymore than *this* Dow Chemical representative, or the student he is recruiting, is actually dropping the napalm bomb.)

Why do we so easily sympathize with actions like that, where per-haps one child was killed, and not with actions against Dow Chemical, where countless children have been victims? Is it possible that we sub-consciously distinguish between the identifiable children down the street (who move us), and the faceless children of that remote Asian land (who do not)? It is possible also that the well-dressed, harassed representative of Dow Chemical is more human, therefore more an object of sympathy, to the well-dressed, harassed officials of the University (and to us), than the burning, bleeding, blurred faces of the Vietnamese?

There is a common argument which says: but where will these student actions lead? If we justify one act of civil disobedience, must we not justify them all? Do they then have a right to disobey the Civil Rights Acts? Where does it stop? That argument withers away, however, once we recognize the distinction between free speech, where absolute toleration is a social good, and free action, where the existence of values other than free speech demands that we *choose* right over wrong—and respond accordingly. We should remember that the social utility of free speech is in giving us the informational base from which we can then make social choices. To refrain from making choices is to say that beyond the issue of free speech we have no substantive values which we will express in action. If we do not discriminate in the actions we support or oppose, we cannot rectify the terrible injustices of the present world

Whether the issue of the Vietnam war is more effectively presented by protest and demonstration (that is, the exercise of speech, press, assembly) rather than by civil disobedience, is a question of tactic, and varies with each specific situation. Different student groups (at Harvard and MIT, for instance) have used one or another against Dow recruitment, and each tactic has its own advantages. I tend to favor the protest tactic as keeping the central issue of the war clearer. But, if students or faculty engaged in civil disobedience, I would consider that morally defensible.

So much for student-faculty action—but what of the University administration? The University's acceptance of Dow Chemical recruiting as just another business transaction is especially disheartening, because it is the University which tells students repeatedly on ceremonial occasions that it hopes students will be more than fact-absorbing automatons, that they will choose humane values, and stand up for them courageously. For the University to sponsor Dow Chemical activities as a protective civil liberty means that the University (despite its courses in Constitutional Law) still accepts the nineteenth century definition of substantive due process as defending corporations against regulation, that (despite a library with books on civil liberties) the University still does not understand what civil liberties are, that (despite its entrance requirement of literacy) the University has not read in the newspapers of the terrible damage our napalm bombs have done to innocent people.

The fact that there is only an indirect connection between Dow recruiting students and napalm dropped on Vietnamese villages, does not vitiate the moral issue. It is precisely the nature of modern mass murder that it is not visibly direct like individual murder, but takes on a corporate character, where every participant has limited liability. The total effect, however, is a thousand times more pernicious, than that of the individual entrepreneur of violence. If the world is destroyed, it will be a white-collar crime, done in a business-like way, by large numbers of individuals involved in a chain of actions, each one having a touch of innocence.

Sometimes the University speaks of the "right of recruitment." There is no absolute right of recruitment, however, because (beyond the package of civil liberties connected with free expression and procedural guarantees, which are the closest we can get to "absolute" right) all rights are relative. I doubt that Boston University would open its offices to the Ku Klux Klan for recruiting, or that it would apply an absolute right of private enterprise to peddlers selling poisonous food on campus. When the University of Pennsylvania announced it would end its germ-warfare research project, it was saying that there is no absolute right to do research on *anything*, for *any* purpose.

The existence of University "security" men (once known as campus police) testifies that all actions on campus are not equally tolerable. The University makes moral choices all the time. If it can regulate the movement of men into women's dormitories (in a firm stand for chastity), then why cannot it regulate the coming and going of corporations into the university, where the value is human life, and the issue is human suffering?

And if students are willing to take the risks of civil disobedience, to declare themselves for the dying people of Vietnam, cannot the University take a milder step, but one which makes the same declaration—and cancel the invitation to Dow Chemcal? Why cannot the University—so much more secure—show a measure of social commitment, a bit of moral courage? Should not the University, which speaks so often about students having "values," declare some of its own? It is written on no tablets handed down from heaven that the officials of a University may not express themselves on public issues. It is time (if not now, when? asks the Old Testament) for a University to forsake the neutrality of the IBM machines, and join the human race.

7

Aggressive Liberalism

For me, as for many others, the Vietnam war became an occasion for examining larger questions about the historical role of the United States in the world, particularly its record of expansion, both on the continent and overseas. As part of such an examination I wrote this essay, which appeared in *The Politics of History* (Beacon Press, 1970; Illinois University Press, 1990).

The concept of paradox is useful to our innocence. We keep it as a last defense, first erecting two other barriers. The first is not to look for, or not to see, those facts that challenge our deepest beliefs. The second is (when the world will not tolerate our ignorance) to keep separate in our consciousness those elements which, brought together, would explode the myths of our culture. When both those restraining walls collapse, we fall back, as an emergency measure, on the explanation: It's one of those paradoxes—an incredible but true combination.

With this triple defense, the liberal democracy of the Western world, bedecked with universal suffrage, parliamentary representation, technological progresss, mass education, Bills of Rights, social welfare, has managed to maintain its reputation for beneficence—despite its record of imperialism, war, racism, and exploitation. The unpleasant facts are first ignored (or made pallid by judicious juxtaposition with the more blatant sins of others). Then they are kept in a different compartment of the brain. Then, when the brain is so jostled that separation becomes impossible, the essential goodness of what we call Western Civilization is kept intact by the concept of paradox. Thus, liberalism can remain unscratched by the most prurient of juxtapositions, and the entire social system for which it is the shorthand symbol—the bad as well as the good—can remain unquestioned.

It is the first line of defense that this essay will deal with—the forgetting of discomfiting facts. The myth that refuses to be discomfited is that the United States, as might be expected from its behavior at home, is a peculiarly decent nation abroad.

Perhaps we took the myth, along with mother's milk, from British liberalism. A British historian, Geoffrey Barraclough, writing of German expansionism at the time of the First World War, says: "Easy though it is to criticize the imperialism of the French and British in Africa or China, their worst enormities simply do not compare. For all its faults, British imperialism had a genuine idealistic component, a sense of service and mission expressed in India by Curzon and in Egypt by Cromer."

"Idealistic components" have always been handy in aggressive international behavior. The chastity of Helen in the Trojan Wars, the sanctity of Christ's birthplace in the Crusades—and one can multiply the components indefinitely—no more altered the basic fact of conquest, murder, exploitation than did the more sophisticated rationale of the British liberals in the Boer War. As D.A.N. Jones has written about Winston Churchill's role at the time:

> Churchill lent an air of nobility to ugly realities. He had come to Parliament in 1901 as the war correspondent from South Africa, able to present the Boer War as a grand duel between blood-brothers. Some, he said, in his maiden speech, were prepared to "stigmatize this as a war of greed.... This war from beginning to end has only been a war of duty."

Churchill praised the white enemy for not arming the black population: "The Black Peril...is the one bond of union between the

European races." In a letter to his wife in 1907, Churchill, a junior Minister in the Liberal Government, talks of "...150,000 more natives under our direct control.... There will not, I think, be any bloodshed.... Thus the Empire grows under Radical Administration!"

Was this a "paradox" of British liberalism? Only if one ignores parallel features of liberalism at home which cast doubt on the total appraisal traditionally made of liberal democracy in the West. For instance, Churchill is "all for government intervention to assist the poor, to take the trailways and canals into public ownership, to establish a national minimum wage. It was all talk." He was also saying: "As for tramps and wastrels, there ought to be proper Labour Colonies where they could be... made to realise their duty to the State..." And in 1911, as Home Secretary, he accompanied the police who were after some foreign-born burglars alleged to be anarchists. The suspects' house was burned down; two corpses were found, and Churchill wrote to the Prime Minister.

> I thought it better to let the house burn down rather than spend good British lives in rescuing those ferocious rascals. I think I shall have to stiffen the administration of the Aliens Act a little...

To reply to the claim of "paradox" in American liberalism, we would have to place its external conduct alongside the facts of its domestic policies. But first, the external conduct itself requires a more scrupulous examination than is usually given: whether in the elementary school textbooks which glorify America's wars, or in the more sophisticated academic circles where benign motives and other "idealistic components" are thought to make American foreign policy notably more admirable than that of other nations.*

A quick survey of American foreign policy shows that aggressiveness, violence, and deception accompanied, from our first years as a nation, the development of those domestic attributes which (seen in isolation from other domestic traits) made us the prototype of Western liberal democracy. This survey is of course a selective one, but for purposes

---

* This insistence on our purity reaches absurd lengths. In 1968, *Life* magazine carried a picture of a Vietnamese girl whose leg was amputated after she was shot down by a United States helicopter. Dr. Howard Rusk, President of the World Rehabilitation Fund, wrote: "I think the readers of *Life* should know that young Tran would not have had an artificial limb had it not been for the American people working through the U.S. Agency for International Development."

of taking a hard look at our nation in a time of social crisis, it is a useful corrective to more orthodox selection. I suspect there is an important difference between individuals and nations which supports the idea of a critical selection. For a person, the overlooking of past miscreancy may have a positive effect on future conduct, as a psychological spur to change. For nations, there is not that sensitivity. A hardened, mindless mechanism requires not psychological encouragement but a taking apart and reassembling by its citizens—a task so arduous as to be spurred only by a sense of great peril, reinforced by a concentrated recollection of the number of times the mechanism has failed.

It was in our first diplomatic efforts as a new nation—the making of the peace treaty with England—that, despite the nobility of sentiment that accompanied a war for independence and the goals of the Declaration of Independence, we began to show the cupidity of our elders. Bradford Perkins, in his review of Richard B. Morris' *The Peacemakers*, makes the point as precisely as one could make it:

> ...like most American historians, Richard Morris seems to assume that, because the envoys served a noble people, their cynical and even dishonest efforts are to be excused, whereas their European counterparts are to be condemned because they served less enlightened states. In fact Jay, Franklin, and Adams triumphed precisely because they adopted the brutal morality of their contemporaries. They betrayed their instructions and the spirit of the alliance with France to obtain great benefits for their country. They cannot, as Morris seems to imply, be defended on moral grounds. They initiated, their contemporaries echoed, and their countrymen since have reaffirmed the false claim that Americans normally act with a morality superior to that of statesmen of other nations.

The peace that followed the Revolutionary War was a nervous one, accompanied by the first waves of post-independence nationalist passion. The British were holding on to their military and trading posts on the northern frontier, the Spanish were in the Floridas to the south, the French soon in possession of New Orleans and the vast Louisiana territory to the north, and the Indians everywhere. War fever rose and fell in those years, against the British under Washington, against the French under Adams (intensified by the French Revolution), against also (ironically—but irony is normal in international affairs) those Irish revolutionaries who came to this country with the same fierce anti-British feeling that we held in our Revolution.

From the first, aggressive expansion was a constant of national ideology and policy, whether the administration was "liberal" or "conservative"—that is, Federalist or Republican, Whig or Democrat, Democrat or Republican. The first and greatest act of territorial expansion was taken by Jefferson, in a legally dubious purchase, the President conveniently overlooking the fact that he was receiving, in effect, stolen goods (for Napoleon was violating a treaty with Spain by selling Louisiana).

Expansionism was given a moral justification; the nation had a "natural right" to security in the West, it was said. This was the customary jump in modern history, from an idealistic nationalism invoked to justify independence from colonial rule, to the stretching out over others' territory by a new nation. "The very peoples who had drunk most deeply of the new humanitarian nationalism succumbed most rapidly to the expansionist intoxication which led into the age of imperialism," writes Arthur K. Weinberg, in his classic study, *Manifest Destiny*.

France had leaped from Rousseau to Napoleon, and the United States from the Declaration of Independence to (as Weinberg puts it) "the extension of its rule over an alien people—Indians—without their consent." And it was the author of the phrase "consent of the governed," Jefferson himself, who sent troops into the Louisiana Territory to guard against Indian outbreaks at the time of purchase. He had written in 1787 that "it may be taken for a certainty that not a foot of land will ever be taken from the Indians without their own consent." The argument now used to justify taking this land from the Indians was that they were not cultivating it. But a score of years later, when the Indians began to settle down in the South and to cultivate the land, they were driven out (by Andrew Jackson, Jefferson's descendant in the "liberal" tradition).*

Expansionism, with its accompanying excuses, seems to be a constant characteristic of the nation-state, whether liberal or conservative, socialist or capitalist. I am not trying to argue that the liberal-democratic state is especially culpable, only that it is not less so than other nations. Russian expansionism into Eastern Europe, the Chinese moving into Tibet and battling with India over border territories—seem as belligerent as the pushings of that earlier revolutionary upstart, the United States.

---

* For an account of the long, murderous battle against the Indians see John Tebbel and Keith Jennison, *The American Indian Wars*, Harper & Row, 1960.

And in these cases, the initial revolution followed by others, led to a paranoid fear of revolution beyond the real potential.

Thus, six years after the American Revolution, France was convulsed in hers. After the turn of the century, Latin America caught fire: Haiti the first, suspiciously close to the American shore, then Venezuela, Argentina, Chile, and the rest. Europe's despots pointed accusingly at the United States, much as we now point to Soviet Russia (or more lately to China or Cuba) whenever there are rumblings of change anywhere in the world. The philosophy of Manifest Destiny in America was not far from the Soviet rationale today, that (in Weinberg's words) "one nation has a preeminent social worth, a distinctively lofty mission, and consequently unique rights in the application of moral principles." Socialism and liberalism both have advantages over feudal monarchies in their ability to throw a benign light over vicious actions.

On the eve of the war of 1812, the Madison administration, by a combination of subversive agitation and deception, took from under the nose of Spain the territory of West Florida, a strip of land along the Gulf of Mexico reaching as far west as Baton Rouge. Expansionist elements in the Southern states, encouraged and perhaps helped materially by the Madison administration, revolted against Spanish authority, set up a Lone Star Republic, and asked to join the United States. It was a preview in certain respects of the later annexation of Texas. According to Thomas A. Bailey, Secretary of State James Monroe "went so far as to falsify the dates of certain important documents" to show that the territory belonged to the United States as part of the Louisiana Purchase. Spain was too heavily involved in war with Napoleon to do much about it, but several years later, the London *Times* said: "Mr. Madison's dirty, swindling manoeuvres in respect to Louisiana and the Floridas remain to be punished."

A century and a half of historical research have not solved the question of exactly why the United States went to war with England in 1812. The grievance concerning British impressment of American seamen seems hopelessly knotted with expansionist aims. But, whatever the complex of actual reasons, there is no doubt about the powerful generation of expansionist sentiment at this point in American history. Congressman John Randolph of Virginia, suspicious of the imperial designs of John Calhoun and Henry Clay, told the House of Representatives that the impressment issue was false. "Agrarian cupidity, not maritime right, urges the war," he said. "Ever since the report of the Committee...we have heard but one word—like a whip-poor-will, but one eternal monotonous tone—Canada! Canada! Canada!"

As if to corroborate this accusation, the *Nashville Clarion* asked: "Where is it written in the book of fate that the American Republic shall not stretch her limits from the Capes of the Chesapeake to Nootka Sound, from the isthmus of Panama to Hudson Bay?" The entire North American continent lay waiting.

The war of 1812 ended too indecisively for the United States to extend her territorial possessions at the expense of Britain. But there was Spain, controlling Florida. In 1817, Andrew Jackson went into action. Given the right by the American Government to cross the Florida border in pursuit of pillagers—Seminole Indians, runaway slaves, white renegades—he did just that, and then more. He seized most of the important Florida posts, confiscated the royal Spanish archives, replaced the Spanish governor with an American, executed two Englishmen, and declared that United States tax laws would operate in Florida. For this, he became a national hero.

This led to what appears benignly in our textbook charts as "The Florida Purchase." Secretary of State John Quincy Adams insisted that Spain cede Florida, and promised to take care of American citizens' claims against Spain, amounting to five million dollars, but not a cent went to Spain for the Florida territory. As Bailey sums up:

> However much we may applaud the masterly diplomacy of Adams, there are features of the negotiation that are not altogether savory. Spain, to be sure, was shuffling, dilatory, and irresponsible; the United States was rough, highhanded and arrogant. Some writers have called the acquisition of Florida a case of international bullying. Others have called it Manifest Destiny—the falling of ripe fruit.

The Monroe Doctrine has been vested with a good deal of patriotic sentiment, accompanied by only a vague sense of what it was all about. In the 1920s, Christian Science leader Mary Baker Eddy took a full-page ad in the *New York Times*, heading it: "I believe strictly in the Monroe Doctrine, in our Constitution, and in the laws of God."

As we look into it, the Monroe Doctrine begins to look like the common tendency of all new nations to build a *cordon sanitaire* around themselves, and indeed to stretch that far beyond the needs of self-defense. Russia in Eastern Europe, China in South Asia, Egypt in the Middle East, have all showed the same behavior. And in August of 1960, the prime Minister of Ghana, Kwame Nkrumah, told his National Assembly that he "would not be so presumptuous as to put forward a Monroe Doctrine for Africa" but that he thought African problems should be settled by African states. His statement had just the tone of righteousness and just the tone of paternal supervision that marked the United States in 1823, when James Monroe's presidential message to Congress promised that the United States would not interfere in the internal concerns of European countries, but also warned that "we should consider any attempt on their part to extend their system to any portion of this hemisphere as dangerous to our peace and safety."

There is considerable doubt that the Monroe Doctrine saved either independence or democracy in Latin America, but there is little doubt that it served as a justification, by President Polk and later by Theodore Roosevelt, for the expansion of American influence in Latin America. Interestingly, Metternich in central Europe saw this common-place action of modern nationalism with the same ideological phobia that the United States sees the Soviet Union and other Communist nations. He responded to the Monroe Doctrine as follows: "These United States of America...lend new strength to the apostles of sedition and reanimate the courage of every conspirator. If this flood of evil doctrines and perni-cious examples should extend over the whole of America, what would become of our religious and political institutions..."

The spirit of Manifest Destiny was strong in those very decades of the early nineteenth century when the nation was creating institutions marking it as liberal and democratic: the extension of suffrage, the popu-lar election of the President, the spread of public education, the flowering of literature. One of the nation's leading orators, Edward Everett, in an ora-tion commemorating the battle of Bunker Hill in 1836, told his audience:

> ...wherever there are men living, laboring, suffering, enjoying—there are our brothers. Look then still further abroad, honored friends and patriots! Behold in distant countries, in other quarters of the globe, the influence of your example and achievements in stimulating the progress of social improvement. Behold the mighty spirit of Reform striding like a giant through the civilized world and trampling down established abuses at every

step!.... Behold him working out his miracles in France, knocking off the shackles of neighboring nations in Spanish America, pursuing his course, sometimes triumphant, sometimes temporarily trodden under foot, betrayed by false friends, overwhelmed by superior force, but still in the main, forward and onward over Spain, Portugal, Italy, Germany, Greece!

The liberal West, now fat, rich, and spread-eagled over the world, points with alarm at the upstart righteousness of the Communist states, the messianic fervor of the new nationalism in Asia and Africa. But liberalism, at a similar state in its development, showed the same character. Tocqueville wrote in the 1830s: "Nothing is more embarrassing in the ordinary intercourse of life, than this irritable patriotism of the Americans."

In the same period the most popular American historian was George Bancroft, who saw American democracy as God's special gift to the universe. His historical study of the United States, Bancroft said, aimed "to follow the steps by which a favoring Providence, calling our institutions into being, has conducted the nation to its present happiness and glory." Shall we rest on the explanation of "paradox" when we recall that at this same time, the nation was putting people in prison for debt, herding free men into labor gangs, under the most brutal conditions, and enslaving that one-sixth of its population which was black?

The administration of Andrew Jackson, who is seen sometimes as an early New Dealer, a conveyer of the liberal Jeffersonian tradition, was a particularly truculent one. The Cherokees were established in the South as a separate nation, by treaty after treaty which they signed with the United States. They were industrious, progressive, and peaceful. Their government was more democratic and their educational system more advanced than those of Georgia, North Carolina, and Tennessee, in whose mountain fastnesses the Cherokees maintained their society. When Georgia in 1832 defied a Supreme Court ruling that only the national government had jurisdiction over Cherokee territory, Andrew Jackson supported Georgia with his famous statement: "John Marshall has made his decision, now let him enforce it."

Jackson, after all, was an old Indian fighter, and he pushed through Congress an Indian Removal Act to force the Cherokees out. A few years later, General Winfield Scott invaded with 7000 troops. The Cherokees were put in concentration camps, their homes burned, and

14,000 of them herded onto the long trek westward, the "Trail of Tears," during which 4000 men, women and children died.

Any confidence in the special benignity of a "democratic" nation's foreign policy is shaken, at the least, by this episode. Four years after the crushing of the Hungarian revolt, Premier Khrushchev of the Soviet Union declared that the Hungarian situation was now settled to everyone's satisfaction. Andrew Jackson's handpicked successor, President Martin Van Buren, said about the Cherokee removal operation: "The measures authorized by Congress at its last session have had the happiest effects.... The Cherokees have emigrated without any apparent reluctance."

It was an aggressive war against Mexico that extended the nation's boundaries to the Pacific. In the 1819 treaty with Spain the United States had given up any claim to Texas. But this did not stop it from trying to bribe Mexican officials to sell Texas, as by United States Minister Anthony Butler in Jackson's administration. This failing, it gave active support to the revolution which separated Texas from Mexico and made it, for ten years, the Lone Star State. The United States had its eye not only on Texas, but on California and all the land between-about half of what was then Mexico. After Texas was annexed in 1845, President Polk sent secret instructions to his confidential agent in California, Thomas O. Larkin, to work for annexation.

Polk first tried to buy California and New Mexico, but Mexico refused, whereupon he sent troops into the disputed territory between the Nueces River and the Rio Grande, which both Texas and Mexico claimed. When Polk took the question of war to his cabinet, the suggestion was made that it would be better for Mexico to start the war. By some remarkable coincidence, a dispatch that same night reported Mexicans coming into the disputed area, and a battle ensued, with sixteen American casualties. Polk asked Congress to declare war, saying that Mexico "has invaded territory and shed American blood upon the American soil." Polk's claim to be protecting Texas was rather weak, in view of the fact that in nine years Mexico had made no effort to retake Texas.

The war was won without difficulty, and the 1848 Treaty of Guadalupe Hidalgo gave the United States what it wanted: New Mexico, California, and the disputed territory in Texas—altogether, half of Mexico. The States could even point to its restraint in not taking all of

Mexico. During the war, that thought had been widespread. At a Jackson Day dinner, Senator Dickinson of New York had offered a toast to "a more perfect Union, embracing the whole of the North American continent." The liberal *New York Evening Post* urged America not to withdraw from Mexico, saying:

> Now we ask, whether any man can coolly contemplate the idea of recalling our troops from the territory we at present occupy and... resign this beautiful country to the custody of the ignorant cowards and profligate ruffians who have ruled it for the last 25 years? Why, humanity cries out against it. Civilization and Christianity protest.

Expansionism was neither liberal nor conservative, Southern or Northern. It was a trait of the American nation, as of other nations, as of any unit bursting with power and privilege in a competitive, lawless world. The sentiment of the *New York Post* was not much different from that of Jefferson Davis, the Senator from Mississippi, who wrote just before the Civil War:

> We may expand so as to include the whole world. Mexico, Central America, South America, Cuba, the West India Islands, and even England and France we might annex without inconvenience...allowing them with their local legislatures to regulate their local affairs in their own way. And this sir, is the mission of this Republic and its ultimate destiny.

It was, indeed, in the direction of worldwide power, that the United States Government moved. It expanded, in the years between the Revolution and the Civil War, from a thin strip along the Atlantic to a huge continental power fronting the oceans. It did this by purchase and by pressure, by aggression, by deceit, and by war. It used these varied weapons against Spaniards, Frenchmen, Indians, Mexicans—and all with an air of arrogant righteousness, with the idea that to spread the American flag far and wide was to confer on other peoples the greatest gift in the world.

After 1890, we moved out into the Caribbean and the Pacific, as far as the coastal waters of China. That story is too well known to recount in detail: the "splendid little war" with Spain; the annexation of Hawaii, and the Philippines and the ugly war of extermination against the Filipino rebels; the taking of Puerto Rico and the establishment of a protectorate over Cuba; the shrewd creation of a Republic of Panama, pulling the site for a canal from under Colombia; the waves of marines into the

Caribbean—Haiti, the Dominican Republic, Nicaragua; the bombardment and occupation of Vera Cruz; in the meantime the concern with profit and influence in China and Japan by the judicious use of gunboats, dollars, and diplomacy. With World War I we became a banker of the world; with World War II we spread military bases onto every land mass, every ocean in the world, intervened openly or stealthily in Greece, Lebanon, Guatemala, Cuba, the Dominican Republic, Korea, Vietnam. By 1969, the Japanese had to protest the use of their former island, Okinawa, to store deadly nerve gas for American military use.

These, in terse summary, are the facts we tend either to ignore or to so mix into the rich potpourri of American history as to obscure them. Extricated, they force us to deal with them alongside the kindly view of our society as a summit of liberal, democratic achievement in world history. Refusing to simply separate "liberalism" at home from aggression abroad, refusing also to end the discussion by speaking of "paradox," we can attempt a reconciliation from one or another direction.

That is, we can find that our behavior abroad is not as bad as it seems on first look, that it is indeed invested with some of the saving characteristics we find in domestic liberalism. For instance, Frederick Merk, in *Manifest Destiny and Mission in American History, a Reinterpretation*, is unhappy with the idea that manifest destiny and imperialism represent the actual American spirit. He finds they are exceptions, and that the true American mood was that of "mission," of liberating other peoples, that the United States has been, in the main, "idealistic, self-denying, hopeful of divine favor for national aspirations, though not sure of it."

I would suggest another way of looking at the facts: that there is a similar principle, operating in domestic affairs and foreign affairs—for presumably liberal states as for other kinds of states: that in a world which has not yet developed either the mind or the mechanism for humane cooperation, power and privilege tend to be as rapacious as the degree of resistance by the victims will permit. That aggression at home is more disguised, more sporadic, more controlled than aggression abroad, comes from the development of countervailing forces at home, while those abroad have usually been helpless before the marauding foreign power. Where internal groups have been similarly helpless they have been treated as ruthlessly as enemies in wartime: the blacks, the Indians, the workingmen before they organized, the students when they dared to challenge authority.

All this suggests that we need to stop looking with special fondness on that group of Western states which represent, in those millions of textbooks distributed in high schools and colleges "Western civilization." Their external behavior is not an unfortunate departure from character. It is what their internal behavior would be if undeterred by a population whose greater literacy and greater activity (a necessity of modern industrial development) enabled them to at least partially resist.

The idealist rhetoric surrounding the foreign policies of liberal states is only a variant on the historic use of rhetoric by aggressive civilizations in the past: the Greeks had their noble excuses for destroying the people of Melos: the Popes drove Christian armies forward with words of holy purity; the socialist states invent socialist excuses for their assaults. A bit of historical perspective may help us to deal, in our own time, with the missionary-soldiers of other nations and of ours.

8

The Curious
Chronology
of the
Mayaguez
Incident

Vietnam was the first situation in which it could be said the United States had lost a war. And when the North Vietnamese army rolled into Saigon in 1975, ending the rule of the government favored by the U.S., putting all of Vietnam under Communist control, there was gloom in the higher circles of Washington. President Gerald Ford had taken over the presidency after Richard Nixon resigned in disgrace over the Watergate scandals. His Secretary of Defense, James Schlesinger, was reported as saying that "the world no longer regarded American military power as awesome." There was general public distrust of the government. In one survey of public opinion, 83% agreed with the statement, "The people running this country...don't tell us the truth."

In April of 1975, Secretary of State Henry Kissinger was quoted in the *Washington Post* as follows: "The U.S. must carry out some act somewhere in the world which shows its determination to continue to be a world power." The following month came the "Mayaguez Incident." The *Mayaguez* was an American cargo ship sailing from South Vietnam to Thailand in mid-May 1975, just three weeks after the defeat of the United States in Vietnam. When it came close to an island in Cambodia, where a revolutionary regime had just taken power, the ship was stopped by the Cambodians, taken to a port at a nearby island, and the crew removed to the mainland. President Ford demanded the release of the crew, and when thirty-six hours passed without their release (though it was not clear his demand had been received by the Cambodians), he began military operations. It was bizarre that the United States should use this situation to try to re-establish its reputation as the foremost military power in the world. As a columnist for the *Boston Globe* at this time, I wrote the following piece, which appeared in the May 23, 1975 issue.

It was a small incident, they say. Restraint was used. No B52s. Only 15 or 18 of our men died, by gunfire or drowning. Add 23 killed in a hushed-up helicopter crash over Thailand. Only 50 wounded.

So the Mayaguez affair is hardly worth mentioning. Unless, as some think, every human life is precious.

Let us agree first, the Cambodians did not behave wisely. It is unwise to take even a single marble from the neighborhood bully—he might smash your head in. And even if you bloody his nose a bit, he will prance all over the block, claiming a huge victory, confident now that no others will dare steal a marble, since they might have an eye gouged out just to teach them a lesson.

The Cambodians were unwise. But courteous. "A man who spoke English greeted us with a handshake and welcomed us to Cambodia," the crew said. "Capt. Miller and his men all said they were never abused by the captors. There were even accounts of kind treatment—of Cambodian soldiers feeding them first and eating what the Americans left, of the soldiers giving the seamen the mattresses off their beds." So reported the press.

The Cambodians asked the crew about spying and the CIA. Absurd questions of course; we never spy, and the CIA is a research group. Apparently persuaded of the ship's innocent intent after a half-day's discussion, they agreed to release the crew, and put them on a fishing boat headed for the American fleet (about 6:15 P.M., Wednesday, May 14, our time). At 7 P.M., Phnom Penh radio, heard in Bangkok, announced release of the Mayaguez.

Meanwhile, the American government, with no evidence that the men were being harmed, with no indication that the Cambodians had rejected or even received its messages, not waiting even 48 hours to work things out peacefully (the crew was detained early Monday morning; by Tuesday evening we were bombing ships), began military operations.

The chronology of those operations is curious, as one pieces it together:

Curiosity No. 1: On Tuesday evening, the boat taking the crew from Tang Island to the mainland had been flown over and strafed by American jets in such a way as to indicate they knew the crew was aboard. Indeed, President Ford told the Senate that crewmen were thought to be on a boat that left Tang. Yet, Wednesday afternoon, Mr. Ford ordered an attack on Tang Island.

Curiosity No. 2: The marine assault on Tang Island began about 7:15 P.M. Wednesday. But an hour earlier, the crewmen had already been released by the Cambodians and were on their way back. They were sighted at 10:45 P.M. and the captain said it was a four and a half hour trip, so they must have started out around 6:15 P.M. Furthermore, a U.S. recon plane circled and signaled that it had spotted them. Surely it would then have radioed headquarters. Then why the attack on Tang, with all the ensuing dead and wounded?

Curiosity No. 3: Why, with crew and ship recovered, did U.S. planes bomb the Cambodian mainland, twice? To protect Marines still on Tang? With total sea and air control, the United States could easily have intercepted any Cambodian force moving towards Tang.

The *New York Times* talked about the "admirable efficiency" of the operation. Efficient? It was a military disaster: Five of 11 helicopters, in the invasion force blown up or disabled, and no provision made for replacements to lift Marines off the island. One-third of the landing force was soon dead or wounded (65 out of 200). That exceeds the casualty rate in the World War II invasion of Iwo Jima.

How to explain all this? Blundering? Addiction in Washington to violent solutions? A brutal disregard of Cambodian and American lives to score points for Mr. Ford's nomination and Kissinger's prestige? The "tin, rubber, and oil" listed in the Pentagon Papers to explain U.S. interest in Southeast Asia? Or all of the above?

9

The CIA, Rockefeller, and the Boys in the Club

The CIA, it is generally understood by now (1996), has a long and dirty record of violating, again and again, norms of moral behavior: overthrowing governments, installing military dictatorships, planning the assassinations of foreign leaders, spying on American citizens, interfering in foreign elections, causing the deaths of large numbers of innocent people. In 1975, at the end of the Vietnam War, some of its activities were just coming to the fore, and to quiet further inquiry an investigating commission was set up under Nelson Rockefeller. When the commission released its report, I wrote a column (June 7, 1975) for the *Boston Globe*.

"Rockefeller Inquiry Clears CIA of Major Violations" was the headline in the *New York Times*. Now we can relax. Except for one troubling question: who will clear Rockefeller?

All these fellows go around clearing one another. It seems that only at the top levels of government is serious attention paid to the principle that criminals should be tried by juries of their peers. What would be the public reaction to the headline: "Boston Strangler Clears Cambridge Mugger"? Is that more shocking than: "Attica Massacre Chief Clears Assassination Plotters"?

Rockefeller was the perfect choice to head a commission investigating the CIA. Questioned during his nomination hearing last fall by Sen. Hatfield: "Do you believe that the Central Intelligence Agency should ever actively participate in the internal affairs of another sovereign country, such as in the case of Chile?" Rockefeller replied, "I assume they were done in the best national interest."

According to CIA head William Colby's testimony, the CIA tried—with $8 million—to change the election results in Chile when it seemed a Marxist, Allende, would win. American corporations didn't like Allende because he stood for nationalization of Anaconda Copper and other businesses. Anaconda Copper owed a quarter of a billion dollars to a group of banks led by Chase Manhattan, whose chairman is David Rockefeller, Nelson's brother. Now we are catching on to the meaning of "national interest."

But the circle is still not closed. The CIA action to overthrow Allende was approved by the Forty Committee, whose chairman is Henry Kissinger. And it was Kissinger who recommended that Rockefeller head the commission to investigate the CIA.

Rockefeller summed up the commission report: "There are things that have been done which are in contradiction to the statutes, but in comparison to the total effort, they are not major."

The same report can be made on the Corleone family, after studying them in the motion picture *The Godfather*. True, they murdered people who challenged their power, but in comparison to all the harmless things they did, like drinking espresso, going to weddings and christenings, and bouncing grandchildren on their knees, it was nothing to get excited about.

Yes, the CIA had its little faults. For instance:

It kept secret files on 10,000 American citizens. It engaged in domestic wiretapping, breaking and entering, and opening people's mail. It approved Mr. Nixon's "dirty tricks" plan, and abetted Howard Hunt's burglarizing. All this was illegal. And its director, Richard Helms, lied about it to the Senate Foreign Relations Committee.

The CIA plotted to overthrow various governments: successfully in Iran and Guatemala, unsuccessfully in Cuba. It discussed assassinating Fidel Castro, with the Kennedys' approval, Gen. Lansdale has testified.

The CIA ran a program of assassination, torture and imprisonment in Vietnam between 1967 and 1971, called Operation Phoenix, headed by the present CIA director William Colby, who admitted over 20,000 Vietnamese civilians were executed without trial. That is a bloodbath, by any definition.

One more fact: no President, no Congress, no Supreme Court, for 25 years, has done anything to stop these activities.

There is murder and deceit on the record of the CIA. But we mustn't abolish it, because we need it to fight Communism. Why do we need to fight Communism? Because Communism roams the earth, conspiring to overthrow other governments. And because we don't want to live in a society where secret police tap our wires, open our mail, and have the power to quietly eliminate anyone they decide will hurt "national security." Once, there was the Stone Age. Now, the Age of Irony.

It is only fitting that Rockefeller and his commission should befriend the CIA. It would confuse us if they denounced members of their own club. The Rockefeller report clears the air; our problem is not the CIA, but the club itself.

10

Whom Will We Honor Memorial Day?

In 1974, I was invited by Tom Winship, the editor of the *Boston Globe*, who had been bold enough in 1971 to print part of the top-secret Pentagon Papers on the history of the Vietnam War, to write a bi-weekly column for the op-ed page of the newspaper. I did that for about a year and a half. The column below appeared June 2, 1976, in connection with that year's Memorial Day. After it appeared, my column was cancelled.

Memorial Day will be celebrated as usual, by high-speed collisions of automobiles and bodies strewn on highways and the sound of ambulance sirens throughout the land.

It will also be celebrated by the display of flags, the sound of bugles and drums, by parades and speeches and unthinking applause.

It will be celebrated by giant corporations, which make guns, bombs, fighter planes, aircraft carriers and an endless assortment of military junk and which await the $100 billion in contracts to be approved soon by Congress and the President.

Memorial Day will be celebrated in other words, by the usual betrayal of the dead, by the hypocritical patriotism of the politicians and contractors preparing for more wars, more graves to receive more flowers on future Memorial Days.

The memory of the dead deserves a different dedication. To peace, to defiance of governments.

There was a young woman in New Hampshire who refused to allow her husband, killed in Vietnam, to be given a military burial. She rejected the hollow ceremony ordered by those who sent him and 50,000 others to their deaths. Her courage should be cherished on Memorial Day.

There were the B52 pilots who refused to fly those last vicious raids of Nixon's and Kissinger's war. Have any of the great universities, so quick to give honorary degrees to God-knows-whom, thought to honor those men at this Commencement time, on this Memorial Day?

No politician who voted funds for war, no business contractor for the military, no general who ordered young men into battle, no FBI man who spied on anti-war activities, should be invited to public ceremonies on this sacred day. Let the dead of past wars he honored. Let those who live pledge themselves never to embark on mass slaughter again.

"The shell had his number on it. The blood ran into the ground...Where his chest ought to have been they pinned the Congressional Medal, the DSC, the Medaille Militaire, the Belgian Croix de Guerre, the Italian gold medal, The Vitutea Militara sent by Queen Marie of Rumania. All the Washingtonians brought flowers .. Woodrow Wilson brought a bouquet of poppies."

Those are the concluding lines of John Dos Passos angry novel *1919*. Let us honor him on Memorial Day.

And also Thoreau, who went to jail to protest the Mexican War.

And Mark Twain, who denounced our war against the Filipinos at the turn of the century.

And I.F. Stone, who virtually alone among newspaper editors exposed the fraud and brutality of the Korean War.

Let us honor Martin Luther King, who refused the enticements of the White House, and the cautions of associates, and thundered against the war in Vietnam.

Memorial Day should be a day for putting flowers on graves and planting trees. Also, for destroying the weapons of death that endanger us more than they protect us, that waste our resources and threaten our children and grandchildren.

On Memorial Day we should take note that, in the name of "defense," our taxes have been used to spend a quarter of a billion dollars on a helicopter assault ship called "the biggest floating lemon," which was accepted by the Navy although it had over 2,000 major defects at the time of its trial cruise.

Meanwhile, there is such a shortage of housing that millions live in dilapidated sections of our cities and millions more are forced to pay high rents or high interest rates on their mortgages.

There's 90 billion for the B1 bomber, but people don't have money to pay hospital bills.

We must be practical, say those whose practicality has consisted of a war every generation. We mustn't deplete our defenses. Say those who have depleted our youth, stolen our resources.

In the end, it is living people, not corpses, creative energy, not destructive rage, which are our only real defense, not just against other governments trying to kill us, but against our own, also trying to kill us.

Let us not set out, this Memorial Day, on the same old drunken ride to death.

11

What Did Richard Nixon Learn?

No one American president can be blamed wholly for the disastrous U.S. military assault on Vietnam. The long line of blame, if we really stretch, can go as far back as Franklin D. Roosevelt, who spoke to the world of self determination but gave the French secret assurances that they would not be expelled from their colony in Indochina, comprising Vietnam, Laos, and Cambodia. Presidents Harry Truman and Dwight Eisenhower gave massive military aid to the French in their war against the Vietnamese independence movement. John F. Kennedy began the military escalation by sending the first large contingents of American troops and using U.S. warplanes to bomb Vietnam. Lyndon Johnson then carried on the major escalation of the war, with all-out bombing, and 525,000 troops. Nixon extended the war to Laos and Cambodia, but finally saw the need to sign a peace treaty which called for U.S. withdrawal. Ten years after the end of the war he wrote about his role in a memoir: *No More Vietnams*. I reviewed his book, as follows, in the Madison, Wisconsin *Capital Times* in May of 1985.

Richard Nixon has learned nothing from the Vietnam experience. And now he wants to teach us what he has learned. Let's examine his strange analysis.

Trying to persuade a public made skeptical by decades of lies, Nixon repeats a much-used formula to justify our war in Vietnam: "Events since 1975 have proved..."

The argument goes like this: Vietnam is now a dictatorial country, run by communists, from which a million people have fled due to political repression and economic disorder. That proves we were right to turn that country into a wasteland, to denude its forests, ruin its crop land, and kill over a million people, by raining millions of tons of bombs, napalm, Agent Orange, and various terror devices on peasant men, women and children.

Let's see where such logic takes us. Suppose the United States had "won," which, as Nixon tells us, would have required even more violence (killing another million people, destroying another thousand villages, leaving another thousand children without arms and legs, killing another 10,000 and 20,000 GIs and adding to the number of Americans who now wear artificial limbs?).

How would that have ensured a democratic and economically sound, independent Vietnam, when the government in Saigon that we supported was itself a brutal dictatorship, totally dependent on the U.S. military, abhorred by most Vietnamese? In Korea we "saved" South Korea, and we ended up as we had started, with a dictatorship in North Korea, a dictatorship in South Korea, but with one difference: two million people were dead.

Perhaps we should look at other situations where the U.S., intervening in another country to "stop communism," did indeed "win."

Take Guatemala, where the CIA in 1954 successfully overthrew a left-leaning government that had dared to take back the huge estates of the United Fruit Corporation. What was the result? One of the most ugly military dictatorships in the world has ruled Guatemala since that "victory"—death squads, mass executions of peasants, miserable conditions for the Indians who are a majority of that country.

Or, take another case where we "won"—Chile, where, with the help of the CIA and IT&T, the Marxist Allende was overthrown. (Both

Allende in Chile and Arbenz in Guatemala became president through remarkably democratic elections.) The result of that "victory" was the horror of General Pinochet, of which we get a glimpse in the film *Missing*—the disappearance of thousands of people, the streets patrolled by soldiers with machine guns, the atmosphere and reality of fascism.

There is not much to choose between the results of military interventions whether by the United States or the Soviet Union. The logic of military interventions is that they produce tyrannies, but that is considered a "victory" if the tyranny is friendly to the intervening power.

If the Soviets are forced to beat a retreat from Afghanistan, perhaps some Soviet Nixon will write a book explaining why they should have used more force, and how things would have been much better if they had won.

Nixon's "history" of the Vietnam War is a desperate attempt to make a silk purse out of a sow's behind. There is room to note only a few of his falsehoods and omissions.

War is war, he says, so why get excited over a million or two million deaths? Especially since it was "a cause that was worth fighting for."

Ask the veterans of Vietnam. Ask the families of the dead. Ask the amputees and walking wounded. Yes, some will insist it was a good cause; who wants to think lives were lost for nothing? But most are bitter and angry.

Hundreds of thousands of GIs gave their commentary on that "cause" by walking away from the war: desertions, AWOLs, mutinous behavior, leading to 250,000 undesirable, bad conduct, or dishonorable discharges, and 300,000 more less-than-honorable discharges.

There was a powerful anti-war movement among GIs, even extending to pilots who refused to fly those last vicious raids on the residential areas and hospitals of Hanoi and Haiphong.

Read *Bloods* by *Time* reporter Wallace Terry, with its oral histories of black GIs, who died at twice the rate of whites. See if they thought it "a cause worth fighting for." Consider also the 570,000 draft refusers, of whom very few were peace activists. Most of them were poor white and black kids who just didn't register or didn't show up for induction, so little heart did they have for a heartless war.

"Excessive casualties" among civilians? Oh, no! Nixon says. That is "bizarre," he says, because our forces "operated under strict rules of engagement," Nixon is bizarre (I speak as an ex-Air Force bombardier). Can jet planes, flying a high altitudes, dropping seven million tons of bombs (three times the total tonnage dropped in WW II), possibly operate under "strict rules of engagement"?

Hasn't Nixon read the Pentagon Papers, the official top secret Defense Department history of the Vietnam War, where it is clear that bombing was undertaken to destroy the morale of the population? Was the massacre of terrified women holding babies in their arms in the village of My Lai an "isolated incident"?

Col. Oran Henderson, charged with covering up My Lai, told reporters: "Every unit of brigade size has its My Lai hidden someplace."

Surely Nixon has read the book that fearlessly tries to justify U.S. policy in Vietnam, Guenter Lewy's *America in Vietnam*, where Lewy himself admits that the Vietnamese were "subjected to random bombardment by artillery and aircraft" and "indiscriminate killings" in the populated Delta area which "took a heavy toll of essentially men, women and children."

We tried to save South Vietnam from invasion by the North, Nixon repeats. The evidence against this, from the government's own records, is mountainous.

"South Vietnam was essentially the creation of the United States," the Pentagon historians wrote, not knowing their words would be released to the public. How can it possibly be argued that the U.S. cared about self determination for the Vietnamese when it did everything it could (and even proposed atomic bombing) to have the French retain control of their colony?

Nixon falsifies the record:

Despite his public statements, President Franklin Roosevelt privately assured the French they could retain control of Vietnam; the documentation is in the Pentagon Papers.

Invasion from the North? Most of the southern countryside was in rebellion against Diem, whom the United States had installed in power, flying him in from New Jersey! These southern rebels in the National Liberation Front had developed what Douglas Pike (a U.S. government analyst) admitted was the most popular mass organization in the history of the country. And the Pentagon historians wrote:

"Only the Viet Cong had any real support and influence on a broad base in the countryside."

Did we intervene only after there was invasion from the North? The first battalion of 500 North Vietnamese, according to U.S. Intelligence data, did not arrive until late 1964 or early 1965. By then there were 40,000 U.S. troops and thousands of bombing sorties had been flown by American pilots, as early as 1962 and 1963.

There was one foreign invader in Vietnam—the U.S. Army.

Congress—with its traditional cowardice, and based on lies told by President Lyndon Johnson, Secretary of State Dean Rusk and Secretary of Defense Robert McNamara about the supposed attacks on American vessels in the Gulf of Tonkin in 1964—had given LBJ a blank check for mass murder.

It was not Congress that stopped the war, though Nixon blames them. It was the American people, who by 1969 overwhelmingly rejected the war and wanted out.

Why is Nixon writing all this nonsense now? What he seems to want is to persuade us that we didn't kill enough GIs and Vietnamese in Vietnam. If we had killed more, we might have "won." Therefore, we must not be so hesitant in Central America.

But before we rush to send the boys and drop the bombs in Central America, or even just to supply our unsavory allies there, so Latins can kill Latins while the Dow Jones average goes up, we might reconsider the "cause that was worth fighting for." That cause has something to do with stopping Communism.

Before we get intoxicated, as Nixon and Reagan seem to be, on this anticommunist whiskey that has led to so much drunken driving in the world, such huge death tolls, we ought to stop and think.

It is useful to have Nixon back. He reminds us that he and Reagan are one—the discredited ex-president and the credited new president—brandishing a shining credit card for war that he wants to flash all over the world.

But the bill will be sent to us, not just in dollars, but in human lives. These blokes mean no good for the people of the United States, not for this generation, not for our children or our grandchildren.

12

Machiavellian Realism and U.S. Foreign Policy: Means and Ends

While teaching courses in political theory at Boston University, and fascinated by the figure of Machiavelli, I came across the remarkable volume by Ralph Roeder, *The Man of the Rennaisance*, with its brilliant portraits of the dissident Savonarola and the toady Machiavelli. At the same time I noted the respect with which Machiavelli was treated by people on all parts of the political spectrum. The Vietnam War led many people, including myself, to look more closely at the history of United States foreign policy, and to me there was a distinct Machiavellian thread running through that history. This essay appeared in my book *Declarations of Independence* (HarperCollins,1991).

Interests: The Prince and the Citizen

About 500 years ago modern political thinking began. Its enticing surface was the idea of "realism." Its ruthless center was the idea that with a worthwhile end one could justify any means. Its spokesman was Nicolo Machiavelli.

In the year 1498 Machiavelli became adviser on foreign and military affairs to the government of Florence, one of the great Italian cities of that time. After fourteen years of service, a change of government led to his dismissal, and he spent the rest of his life in exile in the countryside outside of Florence. During that time he wrote, among other things, a little book called *The Prince*, which became the world's most famous handbook of political wisdom for governments and their advisers.

Four weeks before Machiavelli took office, something happened in Florence that made a profound impression on him. It was a public hanging. The victim was a monk named Savonarola, who preached that people could be guided by their "natural reason." This threatened to diminish the importance of the Church fathers, who then showed their importance by having Savonarola arrested. His hands were bound behind his back and he was taken through the streets in the night, the crowds swinging lanterns near his face, peering for the signs of his dangerousness.

Savonarola was interrogated and tortured for ten days. They wanted to extract a confession, but he was stubborn. The Pope, who kept in touch with the torturers, complained that they were not getting results quickly enough. Finally the right words came, and Savonarola was sentenced to death. As his body swung in the air, boys from the neighborhood stoned it. The corpse was set afire, and when the fire had done its work, the ashes were strewn in the river Arno.

In *The Prince*, Machiavelli refers to Savonarola and says, "Thus it comes about that all armed prophets have conquered and unarmed ones failed."

Political ideas are centered on the issue of *ends* (What kind of society do we want?) and *means* (How will we get it?). In that one sentence about unarmed prophets Machiavelli settled for modern governments the question of ends: conquest. And the question of means: force.

Machiavelli refused to be deflected by utopian dreams or romantic hopes and by questions of right and wrong or good and bad. He is the father of modern political realism, or what has been called *realpolitik*: "It appears to me more proper to go to the truth of the matter than to its imagination...for how we live is so far removed from how we ought to live, that he who abandons what is done for what ought to be done, will rather learn to bring about his own ruin than his preservation."

It is one of the most seductive ideas of our time. We hear on all sides the cry of "be realistic...you're living in the real world," from political platforms, in the press, and at home. The insistence on building more nuclear weapons, when we already possess more than enough to destroy the world, is based on "realism." The *Wall Street Journal*, approving a Washington, D.C., ordinance allowing the police to arrest any person on the street refusing to move on when ordered, wrote, "D.C.'s action is born of living in the real world." And consider how often a parent (usually a father) has said to a son or daughter: "It's good to have idealistic visions of a better world, but you're living in the real world, so act accordingly."

How many times have the dreams of young people—the desire to help others; to devote their lives to the sick or the poor; or to poetry, music, or drama—been demeaned as foolish romanticism, impractical in a world where one must "make a living"? Indeed, the economic system reinforces the same idea by rewarding those who spend their lives on "practical" pursuits—while making life difficult for the artist, poets, nurses, teachers, and social workers.

Realism is seductive because once you have accepted the reasonable notion that you should base your actions on reality, you are too often led to accept, without much questioning, someone else's version of what that reality is. It is a crucial act of independent thinking to be skeptical of someone else's description of reality.

When Machiavelli claims to "go to the truth of the matter," he is making the frequent claim of important people (writers, political leaders) who press their ideas on others: that their account is "the truth," that they are being "objective."

But his reality may not be our reality; his truth may not be our truth. The real world is infinitely complex. Any description of it must be a partial description, so a choice is made about what part of reality to describe, and behind that choice is often a definite interest, in the sense of something useful for a particular individual or group. Behind the claim of someone giving us an objective picture of the real world is the assumption that we all have the same interests, and so we can trust the one who describes the world for us, because that person has our interests at heart.

It is very important to know if our interests are the same, because a description is never simply neutral and innocent; it has consequences. No description is merely that. Every description is in some way a prescription. If you describe human nature as Machiavelli does, as basically immoral, it suggests that it is realistic, indeed only human, that you should behave that way too.

The notion that all our interests are the same (the political leaders and the citizens, the millionaire and the homeless person) deceives us. It is a deception useful to those who run modern societies, where the support of the population is necessary for the smooth operation of the machinery of everyday life and the perpetuation of the present arrangements of wealth and power.

When the Founding Fathers of the United States wrote the Preamble to the Constitution, their first words were, "We the People of the United States, in order to form a more perfect union, establish justice..." The Constitution thus looked as if it were written by all the people, representing their interests.

In fact, the Constitution was drawn up by fifty-five men, all white and mostly rich, who represented a certain elite group in the new nation. The document itself accepted slavery as legitimate, and at that time about one of every five persons in the population was a black slave. The conflicts between rich and poor and black and white, the dozens of riots and rebellions in the century before the Revolution, and a major uprising in western Massachusetts just before the convening of the Constitutional Convention (Shays' Rebellion) were all covered over by the phrase "We the people."

Machiavelli did not pretend to a common interest. He talked about what "is necessary for a prince." He dedicated *The Prince* to the rich and powerful Lorenzo di Medici, whose family ruled Florence and included popes and monarchs. (*The Columbia Encyclopedia* has this intriguing description of the Medici: "The genealogy of the family is complicated by the numerous illegitimate offspring and by the tendency of some of the members to dispose of each other by assassination.")

In exile, writing his handbook of advice for the Medici, Machiavelli ached to be called back to the city to take his place in the inner circle. He wanted nothing more than to serve the prince.

In our time we find greater hypocrisy. Our Machiavellis, our presidential advisers, our assistants for national security, and our secretaries of state insist they serve "the national interest," "national security," and "national defense." These phrases put everyone in the country under one enormous blanket, camouflaging the differences between the interest of those who run the government and the interest of the average citizen.

The American Declaration of Independence, however, clearly understood that difference of interest between government and citizen. It says that the purpose of government is to secure certain rights for its citizens—life, liberty, equality, and the pursuit of happiness. But governments may not fulfill these purposes and so "whenever any form of government becomes destructive of these ends, it is the right of the people to alter or abolish it, and to institute new government."

The end of Machiavelli's *The Prince* is clearly different. It is not the welfare of the citizenry, but national power, conquest, and control. All is done in order "to maintain the state."

In the United States today, the Declaration of Independence hangs on schoolroom walls, but foreign policy follows Machiavelli. Our language is more deceptive than his; the purpose of foreign policy, our leaders say, is to serve the "national interest," fulfill our "world responsibility." In 1986 General William Westmoreland said that during World War II the United States "inherited the mantle of leadership of the free world" and "became the international champions of liberty." This, from the man who, as chief of military operations in the Vietnam War, conducted a brutal campaign that resulted in the deaths of hundreds of thousands of Vietnamese noncombatants.

Sometimes, the language is more direct, as when President Lyndon Johnson, speaking to the nation during the Vietnam War, talked of the United States as being "number one." Or, when he said, "Make no mistake about it, we will prevail."

Even more blunt was a 1980 article in the influential *Foreign Affairs* by Johns Hopkins political scientist Robert W. Tucker; in regard to Central America, he wrote, "We have regularly played a determining role in making and in unmaking governments, and we have defined what we have considered to be the acceptable behavior of governments." Tucker urged "a policy of a resurgent America to prevent the coming to power of radical regimes in Central America" and asked, "Would a return to a policy of the past work in Central America?... There is no persuasive reason for believing it would not.... Right-wing governments will have to be given steady outside support, even, if necessary, by sending in American forces."

Tucker's suggestion became the Central America policy of the Reagan administration, as it came into office in early 1981. His "sending in American forces" was too drastic a step for an American public that clearly opposed another Vietnam (unless done on a small scale, like Reagan's invasion of Grenada, and Bush's invasion of Panama). But for the following eight years, the aims of the United States were clear; to overthrow the left-wing government of Nicaragua and to keep in place the right-wing government of El Salvador.

Two Americans who visited El Salvador in 1983 for the New York City Bar Association described for the *New York Times* a massacre of eighteen peasants by local troops in Sonsonate province:

> Ten military advisers are attached to the Sonsonate armed forces... The episode contains all the unchanging elements of the Salvadoran tragedy— uncontrolled military violence against civilians, the apparent ability of the wealthy to procure official violence...and the presence of United States military advisers, working with the Salvadoran military responsible for these monstrous practices... after 30,000 unpunished murders by security and military forces and over 10,000 "disappearances" of civilians in custody, the root causes of the killings remain in place, and the killing goes on.

The purpose of its policy in Central America, said the U.S. government, was to protect the country from the Soviet threat: a Soviet base in Nicaragua and a possible Soviet base in El Salvador. This was not quite believable. Was the Soviet Union prepared to launch an invasion of the United States from Central America? Was a nation that could not win a war on its borders with Afghanistan going to send an army across the Atlantic Ocean to Nicaragua? And what then? Would that army then march up through Honduras into Guatemala, then through all of Mexico, into Texas, and then...?

It was as absurd as the domino theory of the Vietnam War, in which the falling dominos of Southeast Asia would have had to swim the Pacific to get to San Francisco. Did the Soviet Union, with intercontinental ballistic missiles, with submarines off the coast of Long Island, need Central America as a base for attacking the United States?

Nevertheless, the Kissinger Commission, set up by President Reagan to advise him on Central American policy, warned in its report that our "southern flank" was in danger—a biological reference designed to make all of us nervous.

Even a brief look at history was enough to make one skeptical. How could we explain our frequent interventions in Central America *before* 1917, before the Bolshevik Revolution? How could we explain our taking control of Cuba and Puerto Rico in 1898; our seizure of the Canal Zone in 1903; our dispatch of marines to Honduras, Nicaragua, Panama, and Guatemala in the early 1900s; our bombardment of a Mexican town in 1914; and our long military occupation of Haiti and the Dominican Republic starting in 1915 and 1916? All this before the Soviet Union existed.

There was another official reason given for U.S. intervention in Central America in the 1980s: to "restore democracy." This, too, was hardly believable. Throughout the period after World War II our government had supported undemocratic governments, indeed vicious military dictatorships; in Batista's Cuba, Somoza's Nicaragua, Armas's Guatemala, Pinoche's Chile, and Duvalier's Haiti as well as in El Salvador and other countries of Latin America.

The actual purpose of U.S. policy in Central America was expressed by Tucker in the most clear Machiavellian terms: "The great object of American foreign policy ought to be the restoration of a more normal political world, a world in which those states possessing the elements of great power once again play the role their power entitles them to play."

Undoubtedly, there are Americans who respond favorably to this idea, that the United States should be a "great power" in the world, should dominate other countries, should be number one. Perhaps the assumption is that our domination is benign and that our power is used for kindly purposes. The history of our relations with Latin America does not suggest this. Besides, is it really in keeping with the American ideal of equality of all peoples to insist that we have the right to control the affairs of other countries? Are we the only country entitled to a Declaration of Independence?

Means: The Lion and the Fox

There should be clues to the rightness of the ends we pursue by examining the means we use to achieve those ends. I am assuming there is always some connection between ends and means. All means become ends in the sense that they have immediate consequences apart from the ends they are supposed to achieve. And all ends are themselves means to other ends. Was there not a link, for Machiavelli, between his crass end—power for the prince—and the various means he found acceptable?

For a year Machiavelli was ambassador to Cesare Borgia, conqueror of Rome. He describes one event that "is worthy of note and of imitation by others." Rome had been disorderly, and Cesare Borgia decided he needed to make the people "peaceful and obedient to his rule." Therefore, "he appointed Messer Remirro de Orco, a cruel and able man, to whom he gave the fullest authority" and who, in a short time, made Rome "orderly and united." But Cesare Borgia knew his policies had aroused hatred, so,

> in order to purge the minds of the people and to win them over completely, he resolved to show that if any cruelty had taken place it was not by his orders, but through the harsh disposition of his minister. And having found the opportunity he had him cut in half and placed one morning in the public square at Cesena with a piece of wood and blood-stained knife by his side.

In recent American history, we have become familiar with the technique of rulers letting subordinates do the dirty work, which they can later disclaim. As a result of the Watergate scandals in the Nixon administration (a series of crimes committed by underlings in his behalf), a number of his people (former CIA agents, White House aides, and even the attorney-general) were sent to prison. But Nixon himself, although he was forced to resign his office, escaped criminal prosecution, arranging to be pardoned when his vice-president, Gerald Ford, became president. Nixon retired in prosperity and, in a few years, became a kind of elder statesman, a Godfather of politics, looked to for sage advice.

Perhaps as a way of calming the public in that heated time of disillusionment with the government because of Vietnam and Watergate, a Senate committee in 1974-1975 conducted an investigation of the intelligence agencies. It discovered that the CIA and the FBI had violated the law countless times (opening mail, breaking into homes and offices, etc.). In the course of that investigation, it was also revealed that the CIA, going back to the Kennedy administration, had plotted the assassination of a number of foreign rulers, including Cuba's Fidel Castro. But the president himself, who clearly was in favor of such actions, was not to be directly involved, so that he could deny knowledge of it. This was given the term *plausible denial.*

As the committee reported:

> Non-attribution to the United States for covert operations was the original
> and principal purpose of the so-called doctrine of "plausible denial."
> Evidence before the Committee clearly demonstrates that this concept,
> designed to protect the United States and its operatives from the conse-
> quences of disclosures, has been expanded to mask decisions of the presi-
> dent and his senior staff members.

In 1988, a story in a Beirut magazine led to information that
Ronald Reagan's administration had been secretly selling arms to Iran, the
declared enemy of the United States, and using the proceeds to give military aid to counterrevolutionaries (the "contras") in Nicaragua, thus violating an act passed by Congress. Reagan and Vice President Bush denied
involvement, although the evidence pointed very strongly to their participation. Instead of impeaching them, however, congress put their emis-
saries on the witness stand, and later several of them were indicted. One
of them (Robert McFarland) tried to commit suicide. Another, Colonel
Oliver North, stood trial for lying to Congress, was found guilty, but was
not sentenced to prison. Reagan was not compelled to testify about what
he had done. He retired in peace and Bush became the next president of
the United States, both beneficiaries of plausible denial. Machiavelli
would have admired the operation.

A prince, Machiavelli suggested, should emulate both the lion
and the fox. The lion uses force. "The character of peoples varies, and it
is easy to persuade them of a thing, but difficult to keep them in that persuasion. And so it is necessary to order things so that when they no longer
believe, they can be made to believe by force.... Fortune is a woman, and
it is necessary, if you wish to master her, to conquer her by force." The fox
uses deception.

> If all men were good, this would not be good advice, but since they are dis-
> honest and do not keep faith with you, you, in return, need not keep faith
> with them; and no prince was ever at a loss for plausible reasons to cloak a
> breach of faith.... The experience of our times shows those princes to have
> done great things who have had little regard for good faith, and have been
> able by astuteness to confuse men's brains.

This advice for the prince has been followed in our time by all
sorts of dictators and generalissimos. Hitler kept a copy of *The Prince* at his

bedside, it is said. (Who says? How do they know?) Mussolini used Machiavelli for his doctoral dissertation. Lenin and Stalin are also supposed to have read Machiavelli. Certainly the Italian Communist Gramsci wrote favorably about Machiavelli, claiming that Machiavelli was not really giving advice to princes, who knew all that already, but to "those who do not know," thus educating "those who must recognize certain necessary means, even if those of tyrants, because they want certain ends."

The prime ministers and presidents of modern democratic states, despite their pretensions, have also admired and followed Machiavelli. Max Lerner, a prominent liberal commentator on the post-World War II period, in his introduction to Machiavelli's writings, says of him: "The common meaning he has for democrats and dictators alike is that, whatever your ends, you must be clear-eyed and unsentimental in pursuit of them." Lerner finds in Machiavelli's *Discourses* that one of his important ideas is "the need in the conduct even of a democratic state for the will to survive and therefore for ruthless instead of half-hearted measures."

Thus the democratic state, behaving like the lion, uses force when persuasion does not work. It uses it against its own citizens when they cannot be persuaded to obey the laws. It uses it against other peoples in the act of war, not always in self-defense, but often when it cannot persuade other nations to do its bidding.

For example, at the start of the twentieth century, although Colombia was willing to sell the rights to the Panama Canal to the United States, it wanted more money than the United States was willing to pay. So the warships were sent on their way, a little revolution was instigated in Panama, and soon the Canal Zone was in the hands of the United States. As one U.S. Senator described the operation, "We stole it fair and square."

The modern liberal state, like Machiavelli's fox, often uses deception to gain its ends—not so much deception of the foreign enemy (which, after all, has little faith in its adversaries), but of its own citizens, who have been taught to trust their leaders.

One of the important biographies of President Franklin D. Roosevelt is titled *Roosevelt: The Lion and the Fox*. Roosevelt deceived the American public at the start of World War II, in September and October 1941, misstating the facts about two instances involving German submarines and American destroyers (claiming the destroyer *Greer*, which was attacked by a German submarine, was on an innocent mission when in fact it was tracking the sub for the British Navy). A historian sympathetic to him wrote, "Franklin Roosevelt repeatedly deceived the American people during the period before Pearl Harbor... He was like the physician who must tell the patient lies for the patient's own good."

Then there were the lies of President John Kennedy and Secretary of State Dean Rusk when they told the public the United States was not responsible for the 1961 invasion of Cuba, although in fact the invasion had been organized by the CIA.

The escalation of the war in Vietnam started with a set of lies— in August 1964—about incidents in the Gulf of Tonkin. The United States announced two "unprovoked" attacks on U.S. destroyers by North Vietnamese boats. One of them almost certainly did not take place. The other was undoubtedly provoked by the proximity (ten miles) of the destroyer to the Vietnamese coast and by a series of CIA-organized raids on the coast.

The lies then multiplied. One of them was President Johnson's statement that the U.S. Air Force was only bombing "military targets." Another was a deception by President Richard Nixon; he concealed from the American public the 1969-1970 massive bombing of Cambodia, a country with which we were supposed to be at peace.

The Advisers

Advisers and assistants to presidents, however committed they are in their rhetoric to the values of modern liberalism, have again and again participated in acts of deception that would have brought praise from Machiavelli. His goal was to serve the prince and national power. So was theirs. Because they were advisers to a liberal democratic state, they assumed that advancing the power of such a state was a moral end, which then justified both force and deception. But cannot a liberal state carry out immoral policies? Then the adviser (deceiving himself this time) would consider that his closeness to the highest circles of power put him in a position to affect, even reverse, such policies.

It was a contemporary of Machiavelli, Thomas More, who warned intellectuals about being trapped into service to the state and about the self-deception in which the adviser believes he will be a good influence in the higher councils of the government. In More's book

Utopia, spokesperson Raphael is offered the advice commonly given today to young people who want to be social critics, prodding the government from outside, like Martin Luther King or Ralph Nader. The advice is to get on the *inside*. Raphael is told, "I still think that if you could overcome the aversion you have to the courts of princes, you might do a great deal of good to mankind by the advice that you would give."

Raphael replies, "If I were at the court of some king and proposed wise laws to him and tried to root out of him the dangerous seeds of evil, do you not think I would either be thrown out of his court or held in scorn?" He goes on,

> Imagine me at the court of the King of France. Suppose I were sitting in his council with the King himself presiding, and that the wisest men were earnestly discussing by what methods and intrigues the King might keep Milan, recover Naples so often lost, then overthrow the Venetians and subdue all Italy, and add Flanders, Brabant, and even all Burgundy to his realm, besides some other nations he had planned to invade. Now in all this great ferment, with so many brilliant men planning together how to carry on war, imagine so modest a man as myself standing up and urging them to change all their plans.

More might have been describing the historian Arthur Schlesinger, Jr., adviser to President Kennedy, who thought it was "a terrible idea" to go ahead with the CIA Bay of Pigs invasion of Cuba in 1961, two years after the revolution there. But he did not raise his voice in protest, because, as he later admitted, he was intimidated by the presence of "such august figures as the Secretaries of State and Defense and the Joint Chiefs of Staff." He wrote, "In the months after the Bay of Pigs I bitterly reproached myself for having kept so silent during those crucial discussions in the Cabinet room."

But the intimidation of Schlesinger-as-adviser went beyond silencing him in the cabinet room—it led him to produce a nine-page memorandum to President Kennedy, written shortly before the invasion of Cuba, in which he is as blunt as Machiavelli himself in urging deception of the public to conceal the U.S. role in the invasion. This would be necessary because "a great many people simply do not at this moment see that Cuba presents so grave and compelling a threat to our national security as to justify a course of action which much of the world will interpret as calculated aggression against a small nation."

The memorandum goes on, "The character and repute of President Kennedy constitute one of our greatest national resources. Nothing should be done to jeopardize this invaluable asset. When lies must be told, they should be told by subordinate officials." It goes on to suggest "that someone other than the President make the final decision and do so in his absence—someone whose head can later be placed on the block if things go terribly wrong." (Cesare Borgia again, only lacking the bloodstained knife.)

Schlesinger included in his memo sample questions and lying answers in case the issue of the invasion came up in a press conference:

Q. Mr. President, is CIA involved in this affair?
A. I can assure you that the United States has no intention of using force to overthrow the Castro regime.

The scenario was followed. Four days before the invasion President Kennedy told a press conference, "There will not be, under any conditions, any intervention in Cuba by U.S. armed forces."

Schlesinger was just one of dozens of presidential advisers who behaved like little Machiavellis in the years when revolutions in Vietnam and Latin America brought hysterical responses on the part of the U.S. government. These intellectuals could see no better role for themselves than to serve national power.

Kissinger, secretary of state to Nixon, did not even have the mild qualms of Schlesinger. He surrendered himself with ease to the princes of war and destruction. In private discussions with old colleagues from Harvard who thought the Vietnam War immoral, he presented himself as someone trying to bring it to an end, but in his official capacity he was the willing intellectual tool of a policy that involved the massive killing of civilians in Vietnam.

Kissinger approved the bombing and invasion of Cambodia, an act so disruptive of the delicate Cambodian society that it can be considered an important factor in the rise of the murderous Pol Pot regime in that country. After he and the representatives of North Vietnam had negotiated a peace agreement to end the war in late 1972, he approved the breaking off of the talks and the brutal bombardment of residential districts in Hanoi by the most ferocious bombing plane of the time, the B52.

Kissinger's biographers describe his role: "If he had disapproved of Nixon's policy, he could have argued against the Cambodia attack. But there is no sign that he ever mustered his considerable influence to persuade the president to hold his fire. Or that he ever considered resigning in protest. Quite the contrary, Kissinger supported the policy."

During the Christmas 1972 bombings *New York Times* columnist James Reston wrote,

> It may be and probably is true, that Mr. Kissinger as well as Secretary of State Rogers and most of the senior officers in the State Department are opposed to the President's bombing offensive in North Vietnam.... But Mr. Kissinger is too much a scholar, with too good a sense of humor and history, to put his own thoughts ahead of the president's.

It seems that journalists too, can be Machiavellian.

Serving National Powers

Machiavelli never questioned that national power and the position of the prince were proper ends: "And it must be understood that a prince...cannot observe all those things which are considered good in men, being often obliged, in order to maintain the state, to act against faith, against charity, against humanity, and against religion."

The end of national power may be beneficial to the prince, and even to the prince's advisers, an ambitious lot. But why should it be assumed as a good end for the average citizen? Why should the citizen tie his or her fate to the nation-state, which is perfectly willing to sacrifice the lives and liberties of its own citizens for the power, the profit, and the glory of politicians or corporate executives or generals?

For a prince, a dictator, or a tyrant national power is an end unquestioned. A democratic state, however, substituting an elected president for a prince, must present national power as benign, serving the interests of liberty, justice, and humanity. If such a state, which is surrounded with the rhetoric of democracy and liberty and, in truth, has some measure of both, engages in a war that is clearly against a vicious and demonstrably evil enemy, then the end seems so clean and clear that any means to defeat that enemy may seem justified.

Such a state was the United States and such an enemy was fascism, represented by Germany, Italy, and Japan. Therefore, when the atomic bomb appeared to be the means for a quicker victory, there was little hesitation to use it.

Very few of us can imagine ourselves as presidential advisers, having to deal with their moral dilemmas (if, indeed, they retain enough integrity to consider them dilemmas). It is much easier, I think, for average citizens to see themselves in the position of the scientists who were secretly assembled in New Mexico during World War II to make the atomic bomb. We may be able to imagine our own trade or profession, our particular skills, called on to serve the policies of the nation. The scientists who served Hitler, like the rocket expert Werner von Braun, could be as cool as Machiavelli in their subservience; they would serve national power without asking questions. They were professionals, totally consumed with doing "a good job" and they would do that job for whoever happened to be in power. So, when Hitler was defeated and von Braun was brought by military intelligence agents to the United States, he cheerfully went ahead and worked on rockets for the United States, as he had done for Hitler.

As one satirical songwriter put it:

Once the rockets are up,
Who cares where they come down?
That's not our department,
Says Werner von Braun.

The scientists who worked on the Manhattan Project were not like that. One cannot imagine them turning to Hitler and working for him if he were victorious. They were conscious, in varying degrees, that this was a war against fascism and that it was invested with a powerful moral cause. Therefore, to build this incredibly powerful weapon was to use a terrible means, but for a noble end.

And yet there was one element these scientists had in common with Werner von Braun: the sheer pleasure of doing a job well, of professional competence, and of scientific discovery, all of which could make one forget, or at least put in the background, the question of human consequences.

After the war, when the making of a thermonuclear bomb was proposed, a bomb a thousand times more destructive that the one dropped on Hiroshima, J. Robert Oppenheimer, personally horrified by the idea, was still moved to pronounce the scheme of Edward Teller and Stanislaw Ulam for producing it as "technically sweet." Teller, defending the project against scientists who saw it as genocidal, said, "The important thing in any science is to do the things that can be done." And, whatever Enrico Fermi's moral scruples were (he was one of the top scientists in the Manhattan Project), he pronounced the plan for making the bombs "superb physics."

Robert Jungk, a German researcher who interviewed many of the scientists involved in the making of the bomb, tried to understand their lack of resistance to dropping the bomb on Hiroshima. "They felt themselves caught in a vast machinery and they certainly were inadequately informed as to the true political and strategic situation." But he does not excuse their inaction. "If at any time they had had the moral strength to protest on purely humane grounds against the dropping of the bomb, their attitude would no doubt have deeply impressed the president, the Cabinet and the generals."

Using the atomic bombs on populated cities was justified in moral terms by American political leaders. Henry Stimson, whose Interim Committee had the job of deciding whether or not to use the atomic bomb, said later it was done "to end the war in victory with the least possible cost in the lives of the men in the armies." This was based on the assumption that without atomic bombs, an invasion of Japan would be necessary, which would cost many American lives.

It was a morality limited by nationalism, perhaps even racism. The saving of American lives was considered far more important than the saving of Japanese lives. Numbers were wildly thrown into the air (for example, Secretary of State James Byrnes talked of "a million casualties" resulting from an invasion), but there was no attempt to seriously estimate American casualties and weigh that against the consequences for Japanese men and women, old people and babies. (The closest to such an attempt was a military estimate that an invasion of the southernmost island of Japan would cause 30,000 American dead and wounded.)

The evidence today is overwhelming that an invasion of Japan was not necessary to bring the war to an end. Japan was defeated, in disarray, and ready to surrender. The U.S. Strategic Bombing Survey, which interviewed 700 Japanese military and political officials after the war, came to this conclusion:

Based on a detailed investigation of all the facts and supported by the testimony of the surviving Japanese leaders involved, it is the Survey's opinion
that certainly prior to 31 December 1945, and in all probability prior to 1
November 1945, Japan would have surrendered even if the atomic bombs
had not been dropped, even if Russia had not entered the war, and even if
no invasion had been planned or contemplated.

After the war American scholar Robert Butow went through the
papers of the Japanese Ministry of Foreign Affairs, the records of the
International Military Tribunal of the Far East (which tried Japanese leaders as war criminals), and the interrogation files of the U.S. Army. He also
interviewed many of the Japanese principals and came to this conclusion:
"Had the Allies given the Prince (Prince Konoye, special emissary to
Moscow, who was working on Russian intercession for peace) a week of
grace in which to obtain his Government's support for the acceptance of
the proposals, the war might have ended toward the latter part of July or
the very beginning of the month of August, without the atomic bomb
and without Soviet participation in the conflict."

On July 13, 1945, three days before the successful explosion of
the first atomic bomb in New Mexico, the United States intercepted
Japanese Foreign Minister Togo's secret cable to Ambassador Sato in
Moscow, asking that he get the Soviets to intercede and indicating that
Japan was ready to end the war, so long as it was not unconditional sur-
render.

On August 2, the Japanese foreign office sent a message to the
Japanese ambassador in Moscow, "There are only a few days left in which
to make arrangements to end the war.... As for the definite terms... it is
our intention to make the Potsdam Three-Power Declaration [which
called for unconditional surrender] the basis of the study regarding these
terms."

Barton Bernstein, a Stanford historian who has studied the official documents closely, wrote,

This message, like earlier ones, was probably intercepted by American intelligence and decoded. It had no effect on American policy. There is not evidence that the message was sent to Truman and Byrnes [secretary of state],
nor any evidence that they followed the intercepted messages during the
Potsdam conference. They were unwilling to take risks in order to save
Japanese lives.

In his detailed and eloquent history of the making of the bomb, Richard Rhodes says, "The bombs were authorized not because the Japanese refused to surrender but because they refused to surrender unconditionally."

The one condition necessary for Japan to end the war was an agreement to maintain the sanctity of the Japanese emperor, who was a holy figure to the Japanese people. Former ambassador to Japan Joseph Grew, based on his knowledge of Japanese culture, had been trying to persuade the U.S. government of the importance of allowing the emperor to remain in place.

Herbert Feis, who had unique access to State Department files and the records on the Manhattan Project, noted that in the end the United States did give the assurances the Japanese wanted on the emperor. He writes, "The curious mind lingers over the reasons why the American government waited so long before offering the Japanese those various assurances which it did extend later."

Why was the United States in a rush to drop the bomb, if the reason of saving lives turns out to be empty, if the probability was that the Japanese would have surrendered even without an invasion? Historian Gar Alperovitz, after going through the papers of the American officials closest to Truman and most influential in the final decision, and especially the diaries of Henry Stimson, concludes that the atomic bombs were dropped to impress the Soviet Union, as a first act in establishing American power in the postwar world. He points out that the Soviet Union had promised to enter the war against Japan on August 8. The bomb was dropped on August 6.

The scientist Leo Szilard had met with Truman's main policy adviser in May 1945 and reported later: "Byrnes did not argue that it was necessary to use the bomb against the cities of Japan in order to win the war.... Mr. Byrnes' view was that our possessing and demonstrating the bomb would make Russia more manageable."

The *end* of dropping the bomb seems, from the evidence, to have been not winning the war, which was already assured, not saving lives, for it was highly probably no American invasion would be necessary, but the aggrandizement of American national power at the moment and in the postwar period. For this end, the means were among the most awful yet devised by human beings—burning people alive, maiming them horribly, and leaving them with radiation sickness, which would kill them slowly and with great pain.

I remember my junior-high-school social studies teacher telling the class that the difference between a democracy like the United States and the "totalitarian states" was the "they believe that the end justifies any means, and we do not." But this was before Hiroshima and Nagasaki.

To make a proper moral judgment, we would have to put into the balancing the testimony of the victims. Here are the words of three survivors, which would have to be multiplied by tens of thousands to gie a fuller picture.

A thirty-five-year-old man: "A woman with her jaw missing and her tongue hanging out of her mouth was wandering around the area of Shinsho-machi in the heavy, black rain. She was heading toward the north crying for help."

A seventeen-year-old girl: "I walked past Hiroshima Station...and saw people with their bowels and brains coming out.... I saw an old lady carrying a suckling infant in her arms...I saw many children...with dead mothers...I just cannot put into words the horror I felt."

A fifth-grade girl: "Everybody in the shelter was crying out loud. Those voices...they aren't cries, they are moans that penetrate to the marrow of your bones and make your hair stand on end... I do not know how many times I called begging that they would cut off my burned arms and legs."

In the summer of 1966 my wife and I were invited to an international gathering in Hiroshima to commemorate the dropping of the bomb and to dedicate ourselves to a world free of warfare. On the morning of August 6, tens of thousands of people gathered in a park in Hiroshima and stood in total, almost unbearable, silence, awaiting the exact moment—8:16 A.M.—when on August 6, 1945, the bomb had been dropped. When the moment came, the silence was broken by a sudden roaring sound in the air, eerie and frightening until we realized it was the sound of the beating of wings of thousands of doves, which had been released at that moment to declare the aim of a peaceful world.

A few days later, some of us were invited to a house in Hiroshima that had been established as a center for victims of the bomb to spend time with one another and discuss common problems. We were asked to speak to the group. When my turn came, I stood up and felt I must get something off my conscience. I wanted to say that I had been an air force bombardier in Europe, that I had dropped bombs that killed and maimed people, and that until this moment I had not seen the human results of such bombs, and that I was ashamed of what I had done and wanted to help make sure things like that never happened again.

I never got the words out, because as I started to speak I looked out at the Japanese men and women sitting on the floor in front of me, without arms, or without legs, but all quietly waiting for me to speak. I choked on my words, could not say anything for a moment, fighting for control, finally managed to thank them for inviting me and sat down.

For the idea that any means—mass murder, the misuse of science, the corruption of professionalism—are acceptable to achieve the end of national power, the ultimate example of our time is Hiroshima. For us, as citizens, the experience of Hiroshima and Nagasaki suggests that we reject Machiavelli, that we do not accept subservience, whether to princes or presidents, and that we examine for ourselves the ends of public policy to determine whose interests they really serve. We must examine the means used to achieve those ends to decide if they are compatible with equal justice for all human beings on earth.

The Anti-Machiavellians

There have always been people who did things for themselves, against the dominant ideology, and when there were enough of them history had its splendid moments: a war was called to a halt, a tyrant was overthrown, an enslaved people won its freedom, the poor won a small victory. Even some people close to the circles of power, in the fade of overwhelming pressure to conform have summoned the moral strength to dissent, ignoring the Machiavellian advice to leave the end unquestioned and the means unexamined.

Not all the atomic scientists rushed into the excitement of building the bomb. When Oppenheimer was recruiting for the project, as he later told the Atomic Energy Commission, most people accepted. "This sense of excitement, of devotion and of patriotism in the end prevailed." However, the physicist I.I. Rabi, asked by Oppenheimer to be his associate director at Los Alamos, refused to join. He was heavily involved in developing radar, which he thought important for the war, but he found it abhorrent, as Oppenheimer reported, that "the culmination of three centuries of physics" should be a weapon of mass destruction.

Just before the bomb was tested and used, Rabi worried about the role of scientists in war:

> If we take the stand that our object is merely to see that the next war is bigger and better, we will ultimately lose the respect of the public.... We will become the unpaid servants of the munitions makers and mere technicians rather than the self-sacrificing public-spirited citizens which we feel ourselves to be.

Nobel Prize-winning physical chemist James Franck, working with the University of Chicago metallurgical laboratory on problems of building the bomb, headed a committee on social and political implications of the new weapon. In June 1945, the Franck Committee wrote a report advising against a surprise atomic bombing of Japan: "If we consider international agreement on total prevention of nuclear warfare as a paramount objective...this kind of introduction of atomic weapons to the world may easily destroy all our chances of success." Dropping the bomb "will mean a flying start toward an unlimited armaments race," the report said.

The committee went to Washington to deliver the report personally to Henry Stimson, but were told, falsely, that he was out of the city. Neither Stimson nor the scientific panel advising him was in a mood to accept the argument of the Franck Report.

Scientist Leo Szilard, who had been responsible for the letter from Albert Einstein to Franklin Roosevelt suggesting a project to develop an atomic bomb, also fought a hard but futile battle against the bomb being dropped on a Japanese city. The same month that the bomb was successfully tested in New Mexico, July 1945, Szilard circulated a petition among the scientists, protesting in advance against the dropping of the bomb, arguing that "a nation which sets the precedent of using these newly liberated forces of nature for purposes of destruction may have to bear the responsibility of opening the door to an era of devastation on an unimaginable scale." Determined to do what he could to stop the momentum toward using the bomb, Szilard asked his friend Einstein to give him a letter of introduction to President Roosevelt. But just as the meeting was being arranged, an announcement came over the radio that Roosevelt was dead.

Would Einstein's great prestige have swayed the decision? It is doubtful. Einstein, known to be sympathetic to socialism and pacifism, was excluded from the Manhattan Project and did not know about the momentous decisions being made to drop the bombs on Hiroshima and Nagasaki.

One adviser to Harry Truman took a strong position against the atomic bombing of Japan: Undersecretary of the Navy Ralph Bard. As a member of Stimson's Interim Committee, at first he agreed with the decision to use the bomb on a Japanese city, but then changed his mind. He wrote a memorandum to the committee talking about the reputation of the United States "as a great humanitarian nation" and suggesting the Japanese be warned and that some assurance about the treatment of the emperor might induce the Japanese to surrender. It had no effect.

A few military men of high rank also opposed the decision. General Dwight Eisenhower, fresh from leading the Allied armies to victory in Europe, met with Stimson just after the successful test of the bomb in Los Alamos. He told Stimson he opposed use of the bomb because the Japanese were ready to surrender. Eisenhower later recalled, "I hated to see our country be the first to use such a weapon." General Hap Arnold, head of the army air force, believed Japan could be brought to surrender without the bomb. The fact that important military leaders saw no need for the bomb lends weight to the idea that the reasons for bombing Hiroshima and Nagasaki were political.

In the operations of U.S. foreign policy after World War II, there were a few bold people who rejected Machiavellian subservience and refused to accept the going orthodoxies. Senator William Fulbright of Arkansas was at the crucial meeting of advisers when President Kennedy was deciding whether to proceed with plans to invade Cuba. Arthur Schlesinger, who was there, wrote later that "Fulbright, speaking in an emphatic and incredulous way, denounced the whole idea."

During the Vietnam War, advisers from MIT and Harvard were among the fiercest advocates of ruthless bombing , but a few rebelled. One of the earliest was James Thomson, a Far East expert in the State Department who resigned his post and wrote an eloquent article in the *Atlantic Monthly* criticizing the U.S. presence in Vietnam.

While Henry Kissinger was playing Machiavelli to Nixon's prince, at least three of his aides objected to his support for an invasion of Cambodia in 1970. William Watts, asked to coordinate the White House announcement on the invasion of Cambodia, declined and wrote a letter of resignation. He was confronted by Kissinger aide General Al Haig, who told him, "You have an order from your Commander in Chief." He, therefore, could not resign, Haig said, Watts replied, "Oh yes I can—and I have!" Roger Morris and Anthony Lake, asked to write the speech for President Nixon justifying the invasion, refused and instead wrote a joint letter of resignation.

The most dramatic action of dissent during the war in Vietnam came from Daniel Ellsberg, a Ph.D. in economics from Harvard who had served in the Marines and held important posts in the Department of Defense, the Department of State, and the embassy in Saigon. He had been a special assistant to Henry Kissinger and then worked for the Rand Corporation a private "think tank" of brainy people who contracted to do top-secret research for the U.S. government. When the Rand Corporation was asked to assemble a history of the Vietnam War, based on secret documents, Ellsberg was appointed as one of the leaders of the project. But he had already begun to feel pangs of conscience about the brutality of the war being waged by his government. He had been out in the field with the military, and what he saw persuaded him that the United States did not belong in Vietnam. Then, reading the documents and helping to put together the history, he saw how many lies had been told to the public and was reinforced in his feelings.

With the help of a former Rand employee he had met in Vietnam, Anthony Russo, Ellsberg secretly photocopied the entire 7,000-page history—the "Pentagon Papers" as they came to be called—and distributed them to certain members of Congress as well as to the *New York Times*. When the *Times*, in a journalistic sensation, began printing this "top-secret" document, Ellsberg was arrested and put on trial. The counts against him could have brought a prison sentence of 130 years. But while the jury deliberated the judge learned, through the Watergate scandal, that Nixon's "plumbers" had tried to break into Ellsberg's psychiatrist's office to find damaging material and he declared the case tainted and called off the trial.

Ellsberg's was only one of a series of resignations from government that took place during and after the Vietnam War. A number of operatives of the CIA quit their jobs in the late sixties and early seventies and began to write and speak about the secret activities of the agency—for example, Victor Marchetti, Philip Agee, John Stockwell, Frank Snepp, and Ralph McGehee.

For the United States, as for others countries, Machiavellianism dominates foreign policy, but the courage of a small number of dissenters suggests the possibility that some day the larger public will no longer accept that kind of "realism." Machiavelli himself might have smiled imperiously at this suggestion, and said, "You're wasting your time. Nothing will change. It's human nature."

That claim is worth exploring.

13

Terrorism
Over Tripoli

In April of 1986, a bomb exploded in a discotheque in West Berlin, killing two people, one an American soldier. It was unquestionably an act of terrorism. Libya's tyrannical leader, Muammar Khadafi, had a record of involvement in terrorism, although in this case there seemed to be no clear evidence of who was responsible. Nevertheless, President Reagan ordered that bombers be sent over Libya's capital of Tripoli, killing perhaps a hundred people, almost all civilians. I wrote this piece, which could not find publication in the press, to argue against the principle of retaliation. I am always furious at the killing of innocent people for some political cause, but I wanted to broaden the definition of terrorism to include governments, which are guilty of terrorism far more often, and on an infinitely larger scale, than bands of revolutionaries or nationalists. The essay became part of a collection of my writings entitled *Failure to Quit*, published in 1993 by Common Courage Press.

"Indeed, I tremble for my country when I reflect that God is just." Thomas Jefferson wrote that in *Notes from Virginia.*

Those words came to mind as I listened to the announcement from our government that it had bombed the city of Tripoli.

We live in a world in which we are asked to make a moral choice between one kind of terrorism and another. The government, the press, the politicians, are trying to convince us that Ronald Reagan's terrorism is morally superior to Muommar Khadafi's terrorism.

Of course, we don't call our actions that, but if terrorism is the deliberate killing of innocent people to make a political point, then our bombing a crowded city in Libya fits the definition as well as the bombing—by whoever did it—of a crowded discotheque in Berlin.

Perhaps the word deliberate shows the difference: when you plant a bomb in a discotheque, the death of bystanders is deliberate; when you drop bombs on a city, it is accidental. We can ease our conscience that way, but only by lying to ourselves. Because, when you bomb a city from the air, you know, absolutely know, that innocent people will die.

That's why Defense Secretary Weinberger, reaching for morality (his reach will never be long enough, given where he stands) talked of the air raid being organized in such a way as to "minimize" civilian casualties. That meant there would inevitably be civilian casualties, and Weinberger, Schultz and Reagan were willing to have that happen, to make their point, as the discotheque terrorists were willing to have that happen, to make theirs.

In this case, the word "minimize" meant only about a hundred dead (the estimate of foreign diplomats in Tripoli), including infants and children, an eighteen-year old college girl home for a visit, an unknown number of elderly people. None of these were terrorists, just as none of the people in the discotheque were responsible for whatever grievances are felt by Libyans or Palestinians.

Even if we assume that Khadafi was behind the discotheque bombing (and there is no evidence for this), and Reagan behind the Tripoli bombing (the evidence for this is absolute), then both are terrorists, but Reagan is capable of killing far more people than Khadafi. And he has.

Reagan, and Weinberger, and Secretary of State Schultz, and their admirers in the press and in Congress are congratulating themselves that the world's most heavily-armed nation can bomb with impunity (only two U.S. fliers dead, a small price to pay for psychic satisfaction) a fourth-rate nation like Libya.

Modern technology has outdistanced the Bible. "An eye for an eye" has become a hundred eyes for an eye, a hundred babies for a baby. The tough-guy columnists and anonymous editorial writers (there were a few courageous exceptions) who defended this, tried to wrap their moral nakedness in the American flag. But it dishonors the flag to wave it proudly over the killing of a college student, or a child sleeping in a crib.

There is no flag large enough to cover the shame of killing innocent people for a purpose which is unattainable. If the purpose is to stop terrorism, even the supporters of the bombing say it won't work; if the purpose is to gain respect for the United States, the result is the opposite: all over the world there is anger and indignation at Reagan's mindless, pointless, soulless violence. We have had presidents just as violent. We have rarely had one so full of hypocritical pieties about "the right to life."

In this endless exchange of terrorist acts, each side claims it is "retaliating." We bombed Tripoli to retaliate for the discotheque. The discotheque may have been bombed to retaliate for our killing 35 Libyan seamen who were on a patrol boat in the Gulf of Sidra—in international waters, just as we were.

We were in the Gulf of Sidra supposedly to show Libya it must not engage in terrorism. And Libya says—indeed it is telling the truth in this instance—that the United States is an old hand at terrorism, having subsidized terrorist governments in Chile, Guatemala, and El Salvador, and right now subsidizing the terrorism of the contras against farmers, their wives and children, in Nicaragua.

Does a Western democracy have a better right to kill innocent people than a Middle Eastern dictatorship? Even if we were a perfect democracy that would not give us such a license. But the most cherished element of our democracy—the pluralism of dissenting voices, the marketplace of contending ideas—seems to disappear at a time like this, when the bombs fall, the flag waves, and everyone scurries, as Ted Kennedy did, to fall meekly behind "our commander-in-chief." We waited for moral leadership. But Gary Hart, John Kerry, Michael Dukakis and Tip O'Neill all muttered their support. No wonder the Democratic Party is in such pathetic shape.

Where in national politics are the emulators of those two courageous voices at the time of the Gulf of Tonkin incident in Vietnam—

Wayne Morse and Ernest Gruening—who alone in the Senate refused to go along with "our commander-in-chief" in that first big military strike that launched the ten-year shame of Vietnam?

And where was our vaunted "free press"? After the bombing, a beaming Schultz held a press conference for a group of obsequious reporters in Washington who buttered him up, who licked at his flanks, who didn't ask a single question about the morality of our action, about the civilians killed by our bombs in Tripoli. Where are the likes of I.F Stone, who did in his little newsletter for so many years what no big American daily would do—raise hard questions? Why did Anthony Lewis and Tom Wicker, who sometimes raise such questions—melt away?

Terrorism now has two names, world-wide. One is Khadafi. One is Reagan. In fact, that is a gross simplification. If Khadafi were gone, if Reagan were gone, terrorism would continue—it is a very old weapon of fanatics, whether they operate from secret underground headquarters, or from ornate offices in the capitols of the superpowers.

Too bad Khadafi's infant daughter died, one columnist wrote. Too bad, he said, but that's the game of war. Well, if that's the game, then let's get the hell out of it, because it is poisoning us morally, and not solving any problem. It is only continuing and escalating the endless cycle of retaliation which will one day, if we don't kick our habits, kill us all.

Let us hope that, even if this generation, its politicians, its reporters, its flag-wavers and fanatics, cannot change its ways, the children of the next generation will know better, having observed our stupidity. Perhaps they will understand that the violence running wild in the world cannot be stopped by more violence, that someone must say: we refuse to retaliate, the cycle of terrorism stops here.

LAW

1

Law and
Justice

I had not thought seriously about the problem of civil disobedience (that is, not seen the real problem as civil obedience) until I became involved in the Southern movement against racial segregation. As black people were arrested again and again for violation of various local laws, the distinction between law and justice became starkly clear. One of the courses I taught at Spelman College was "Constitutional Law." It was soon evident to me that to teach that course in the traditional way—to study what the law said, whether in the Constitution or in statutes, or in Supreme Court interpretations of the law—was to violate the most important principle in education: that all premises must be examined. And here, the unspoken and unexamined premise was that the law was right, and by implication, just, and even moral. I soon changed the name of the course to "Civil Liberties," to enable me to broaden the discussion, to consider the complex relationship between law and justice. What follows is an essay on the subject written after the experience of the civil rights movement and the protests against the war in Vietnam. It appears as a chapter in my book *Declarations of Independence* (HarperCollins,1990).

In 1978 I was teaching a class called "Law and Justice in America," and on the first day I handed out the course outline. At the end of the hour one of the students came up to the desk. He was a little older than the others. He said, "I notice in your course outline you will be discussing the case of *U.S. vs. O'Brien*. When we come to that I would like to say something about it."

I was a bit surprised but glad that a student would take such initiative. I said, "Sure. What's your name?"

He said, "O'Brien. David O'Brien."

It was, indeed, his case. On the morning of March 31, 1966, while American troops were pouring into Vietnam and U.S. planes were bombing day and night, David O'Brien and three friends climbed the steps of the courthouse in South Boston where they lived—a mostly Irish, working-class neighborhood—held up their draft registration cards before a crowd that had assembled, and set the cards afire.

According to Chief Justice Earl Warren, who rendered the Supreme Court decision in the case: "Immediately after the burning, members of the crowd began attacking O'Brien," and he was ushered to safety by an FBI agent. As O'Brien told the story to my class, FBI agents pulled him into the courthouse, threw him into a closet, and gave him a few blows as they arrested him.

Chief Justice Warren's decision said, "O'Brien stated to FBI agents that he had burned his registration certificate because of his beliefs, knowing that he was violating federal law." His intention was clear. He wanted to express to the community his strong feelings about the war in Vietnam, trying to call attention, by a dramatic act, to the mass killing our government was engaged in there. The burning of his draft card would get special attention precisely because it was against the law, and so he would risk imprisonment to make his statement.

O'Brien claimed in court that his act, although in violation of the draft law, was protected by the free speech provision of the Constitution. But the Supreme Court decided that the government's need to regulate the draft overcame his right to free expression, and he went to prison.

O'Brien had engaged in an act of civil disobedience—the deliberate violation of a law for a social purpose. To violate a law for individual gain, for a private purpose, is an ordinary criminal act; it is not civil disobedience. Some acts fall in both categories, as in the case of a mother stealing bread to feed her children, or neighbors stopping the eviction of a family that hadn't been able to pay the rent. Although limited to one family's need, they carry a larger message to the society about its failures.

In either instance, the law is being disobeyed, which sets up strong emotional currents in a population that has been taught obedience from childhood.

Obedience and Disobedience

"Obey the law." That is a powerful teaching, often powerful enough to overcome deep feelings of right and wrong, even to override the fundamental instinct for personal survival. We learn very early (it's not in our genes) that we must obey "the law of the land." Tommy Trantino, a poet and artist, sitting on death row in Trenton State Prison, wrote (in his book *Lock the Lock*) a short piece called "The Lore of the Lamb":

> i was in prison long ago and it was the first grade and i have to take a shit and...the law says you must first raise your hand and ask the teacher for permission so i obeyer of the lore of the lamb am therefore busy raising my hand to the fuhrer who says yes thomas what is it? and i thomas say I have to take a i mean may i go to the bathroom please? didn't you go to the bathroom yesterday thomas she says and i say yes ma'am mrs parsley sir but i have to go again today but she says NO...And I say eh...I GOTTA TAKE A SHIT DAMMIT and again she says NO but I go anyway except that it was not out but in my pants that is to say right in my corduroy knickers goddamm...
> i was about six years old at the time and yet i guess that even then i knew without cerebration that if one obeys and follows orders and adheres to all the rules and regulations of the lore of the lamb one is going to shit in one's pants and one's mother is going to have to clean up afterwards ya see?

Surely not all rules and regulations are wrong. One must have complicated feelings about the obligation to obey the law. Obeying the law when it sends you to war seems wrong. Obeying the law against murder seems absolutely right. To *really* obey that law, you should refuse to obey the law that sends you to war.

But the dominant ideology leaves no room for making intelligent and humane distinctions about the obligation to obey the law. It is stern and absolute. It is the unbending rule of every government, whether Fascist, Communist, or liberal capitalist. Gertrude Scholtz-Klink, chief of the Women's Bureau under Hitler, explained to an interviewer after the war the Jewish policy of the Nazis, "We always obeyed the law. Isn't that what you do in America? Even if you don't agree with a law personally, you still obey it. Otherwise life would be chaos."

"Life would be chaos." If we allow disobedience to law we will have anarchy. That idea is inculcated in the population of every country. The accepted phrase is "law and order." It is a phrase that sends police and the military to break up demonstrations everywhere, whether in Moscow or Chicago. It was behind the killing of four students at Kent State University in 1970 by National Guardsmen. It was the reason given by Chinese authorities in 1989 when they killed hundreds of demonstrating students in Beijing.

It is a phrase that has appeal for most citizens, who, unless they themselves have a powerful grievance against authority, are afraid of disorder. In the 1960s, a student at Harvard Law School addressed parents and alumni with these words:

> The streets of our country are in turmoil. The universities are filled with students rebelling and rioting. Communists are seeking to destroy our country. Russia is threatening us with her might. And the republic is in danger. Yes! danger from within and without. We need law and order! Without law and order our nation cannot survive.

There was prolonged applause. When the applause died down, the student quietly told his listeners: "These words were spoken in 1932 by Adolph Hitler."

Surely, peace, stability, and order are desirable. Chaos and violence are not. But stability and order are not the only desirable conditions of social life. There is also justice, meaning the fair treatment of all human beings, the equal right of all people to freedom and prosperity. Absolute obedience to law may bring order temporarily, but it may not bring justice. And when it does not, those treated unjustly may protest, may rebel, may cause disorder, as the American revolutionaries did in the eighteenth century, as antislavery people did in the nineteenth century, as Chinese students did in this century, and as working people going on strike have done in every country, across the centuries.

Are we not more obligated to achieve justice than to obey the law? The law may serve justice, as when it forbids rape and murder or requires a school to admit all students regardless of race or nationality. But when it sends young men to war, when it protects the rich and punishes the poor, then law and justice are opposed to one another. In that case, where is our greater obligation: to law or to justice?

The answer is given in democratic theory at its best, in the words of Jefferson and his colleagues in the Declaration of Independence. Law is only a means. Government is only a means. "Life, Liberty, and the pursuit of Happiness"—these are the ends. And "whenever any Form of Government becomes destructive of these ends, it is the Right of the People to alter or to abolish it, and to institute new government."

True, the disorder itself may become unjust if it involves indiscriminate violence against people, as the Cultural Revolution in China in the period 1966-1976 started out with the aim of equality but became vengeful and murderous. But that danger should not lead us back to the old injustices to have stability. It should only lead us to seek methods of achieving justice that, although disorderly and upsetting, avoid massive violence to human rights.

Should we worry that disobedience to law will lead to anarchy? The answer is best given by historical experience. Did the mass demonstrations of the black movement in the American South, in the early Sixties, lead to anarchy? True, they disrupted the order of racial segregation. They created scenes of disorder in hundreds of towns and cities in the country (although it might be argued that the police, responding to nonviolent protest, were the chief creators of that disorder). But the result of all that tumult was not general lawlessness. Rather the result was a healthy reconstitution of the social order toward greater justice and a healthy new understanding among Americans (not all, of course) about the need for racial equality.

The orthodox notion is that law and order are inseparable. However, absolute obedience to all laws will violate justice and sooner or later lead to enormous disorder. Hitler, calling for law and order, threw Europe into the hellish disorder of war. Every nation uses the power of law to keep its population obedient and to mobilize acquiescent armies, threatening punishment for those who refuse. Thus the law that inside each nation creates conscript armies leads to the unspeakable disorder of war, to the bloody chaos of the battlefield, and to international turmoil.

If law and order are only ways of making injustice legitimate, then the "order" on the surface of everyday life may conceal deep mental and emotional disorder among the victims of injustice. This is also true for the powerful beneficiaries of the system, in the way that slavery distorts the psyches of both slave and master. In such a case, the order will only be temporary; when it is broken, it may be accompanied by a bloodbath of disorder—as in the United States, when the tightly controlled order of slavery ended in civil war and 600,000 men died in a country of 35 million people.

The Modern Era of Law

We take much pride in the phrase of John Adams, second president of the United States, when he spoke of the "rule of law" replacing the "rule of men." In ancient societies, in feudal society, there were no clear rules, written in statute books, accompanied by constitutions. Everyone was subject to the whims of powerful men, whether the feudal lord, the tribal chief, or the king.

But, as societies evolved, modern times brought big cities, international trade, widespread literacy, and parliamentary government. With all that came the rule of law, no longer personal and arbitrary, but written down. It claimed to be impersonal, neutral, apply equally to all, and, therefore, democratic.

We profess great reverence for certain symbols of the modern rule of law: the Magna Carta, which set forth what are men's rights as against the king; the American Constitution, which is supposed to limit the powers of government and provide a Bill of Rights; the Napoleonic Code, which introduced uniformity into the French legal system. But we might get uneasy about the connection between law and democracy when we read the comment of two historians (Robert Palmer and Joel Colton) on Napoleon: "Man on horseback though he was, he believed firmly in the rule of law."

I don't want to deny the benefits of the modern era: the advance of science, the improvements in health, the spread of literacy and art beyond tiny elites, and the value of even an imperfect representative system over a monarchy. But those advantages lead us to overlook the fact that the modern era, replacing the arbitrary rule of men with the impartial rule of law, has not brought any fundamental change in the facts of unequal wealth and unequal power. What was done before—exploiting the poor, sending the young to war, and putting troublesome people in dungeons—is still done, except that this no longer seems to be the arbitrary action of the feudal lord or the king; it now has the authority of neutral, impersonal law.

The law appears impersonal. It is on paper, and who can trace it back to what men? And because it has the look of neutrality, its injustices are made legitimate. It was not easy to hold onto the "divine right" of kings—everyone could see that kings and queens were human beings. A code of law is more easily deified than a flesh-and-blood ruler.

Under the rule of men, the oppressor was identifiable, and so peasant rebels hunted down the lords, slaves killed plantation owners, and revolutionaries assassinated monarchs. In the era of a corporate bureaucracies, representative assemblies, and the rule of law, the enemy is elusive and unidentifiable. In John Steinbeck's depression-era novel *The Grapes of Wrath* a farmer having his land taken away from him confronts the tractor driver who is knocking down his house. He aims a gun at him, but is confused when the driver tells him that he takes his orders from a banker in Oklahoma City, who takes his orders from a banker in New York. The farmer cries out: "Then who can I shoot?"

The rule of law does not do away with the unequal distribution of wealth and power, but reinforces that inequality with the authority of law. It allocates wealth and poverty (through taxes and appropriations) but in such complicated and indirect ways as to leave the victim bewildered.

Exploitation was obvious when the peasant gave half his produce to the lord. It still exists, but inside the complexity of a market society and enforced by a library of statutes. A mine owner in Appalachia was asked, some years ago, why the coal companies paid so little taxes and kept so much of the wealth from the coal fields, while local people starved. The owner replied: "I pay exactly what the law asks me to pay."

There is a huge interest in the United States in crime and corruption as ways of acquiring wealth. But the greatest wealth, the largest fortunes, are acquired legally, aided by the laws of contract and property, enforced in the courts by friendly judges, handled by shrewd corporation lawyers, figured out by well-paid accountants. When our history books get to the 1920s, they dwell on the Teapot Dome scandals of the Harding administration, while ignoring the far greater reallocations of wealth that took place legally, through the tax laws proposed by Secretary of the Treasury Andrew Mellon (a very rich man, through oil and aluminum), and passed by Congress in the Coolidge Administration.

How can this be? Didn't the modern era bring us democracy? Who drew up the Constitution? Wasn't it all of us, getting together to draw up the rules by which we would live, a "social contract"? Doesn't the Preamble to the Constitution start with the words: "We the People, in order to...etc., etc."?

In fact, while the Constitution was certainly an improvement over the royal charters of England, it was still a document drawn up by rich men, merchants, and slaveowners who wanted a bit of political democracy, but had no sympathy for economic democracy. It was designed to set up a "rule of law," which would efficiently prevent rebellion by dissatisfied elements in the population. As the Founding Fathers assembled in Philadelphia, they still had in mind farmers who had recently taken up arms in western Massachusetts (Shays' Rebellion) against unjust treatment by the wealth-controlled legislature.

It is a deception of the citizenry to claim that the "rule of law" has replaced the "rule of men." It is still men (women are mostly kept out of the process) who enact the laws, who sit on the bench and interpret them, who occupy the White House or the Governor's mansion, and have the job of enforcing them.

These men have enormous powers of discretion. The legislators decide which laws to put on the books. The president and his attorney-general decide which laws to enforce. The judges decide who has a right to sue in court, what instructions to give to juries, what rules of law apply, and what evidence should not be allowed in the courtroom.

The lawyers, to whom ordinary people must turn for help in making their way through the court system, are trained and selected in such a way as to ensure their conservatism. The exceptions, when they appear, are noble and welcome, but too many lawyers are more concerned about being "good professionals" than achieving justice. As one student of the world of lawyers put it: "It is of the essence of the professionalization process to divorce law from politics, to elevate technique and craft over power, to search for 'neutral principles,' and to deny ideological purpose."

Equal Justice Under Law is the slogan one sees on the marble pillars of the courthouse. And there is nothing in the words of the Constitution or the laws to indicate that anyone gets special treatment. They look as if they apply to everyone. But in the actual administration of the laws are rich and poor treated equally? Blacks and whites? Foreign born and natives? Conservatives and radicals? Private citizens and government officials?

There is a mountain of evidence on this: a CIA official (Richard Helms) commits perjury and gets off with a fine. Alger Hiss spent four years in jail for perjury. A president (Nixon) is pardoned in advance of prosecution for acts against the law, and Oliver North and other Reagan administration officials are found guilty of violating the law in the Iran-Contra affair, but none go to prison.

Still, the system of laws, to maintain its standing in the eyes of the citizenry and to provide safety valves by which the discontented can let off steam, must keep up the appearance of fairness. And so the law itself provides for change. When the pressure of discontentment becomes great, laws are passed to satisfy some part of the grievance. Presidents, when pushed by social movements, may enforce good laws. Judges, observing a changing temper in the society, may come forth with humane decisions.

Thus we have alternating currents of progress and paralysis. Periods of war alternate with periods of peace. There are times of witch-hunts for dissenters and times of apologies for the witch-hunts. We have "conservative" presidents giving way to liberal presidents and back again. The Supreme Court makes decisions one week on behalf of civil liberties and the next week curtails them. No one can get a clear fix on the system that way.

The modern system of the rule of law is something like roulette. Sometimes you win and sometimes you lose. No one can predict in any one instance whether the little ball will fall into the red or the black, and no one is really responsible. You win, you lose. But as in roulette, in the end you almost always lose. In roulette the results are fixed by the structure of the wheel, the laws of mathematical probability, and the rules of "the house." In society, the rich and strong get what they want by the law of contract, the rules of the market, and the power of the authorities to change the rules or violate them at will.

What is the structure of society's roulette wheel that ensures you will, in the end, lose? It is, first of all, the great disparities in wealth that give a tremendous advantage to those who can buy and sell industries, buy and sell people's labor and services, buy and sell the means of communication, subsidize the educational system, and buy and sell the political candidates themselves. Second, it is the system of "checks and balances," in which bold new reforms (try free medical care for all or sweeping protections of the environment) can be buried in committee, vetoed by one legislative chamber or by the president, interpreted to death by the Supreme Court, or passed by Congress and unenforced by the president.

In this system, the occasional victories may ease some of the pain of economic injustice. They also reveal the usefulness of protest and pressure, suggest even greater possibilities for the future. And they keep you in the game, giving you the feeling of fairness, preventing you from getting angry and upsetting the wheel. It is a system ingeniously devised for maintaining things as they are, while allowing for limited reform.

Obligation to the State

Despite all I have said about the gap between law and justice and despite the fact that this gap is visible to many people in the society, the idea of obligation to law, obligation to government, remains powerful. President Jimmy Carter reinstated the draft of young men for military service in 1979, and when television reporters asked the men why they were complying with the law (about ten percent were not), the most common answer was "I owe it to my country."

The obligation that people feel to one another goes back to the very beginning of human history, as a natural, spontaneous act in human relations. Obligation to government, however, is not natural. It must be taught to every generation.

Who can teach this lesson of obligation with more authority than the great Plato?

In Plato's dialogue *Crito*, Socrates, in prison and facing death for speaking his mind to the young, is urged by his friend Crito to escape. Socrates refuses, arguing that he must obey the decision of the state. Plato has Socrates saying (we have no way of knowing if these are Socrates' words or if Plato is putting his favorite ideas into Socrates' mouth, for Plato wrote this dialogue decades after Socrates' death): "In war, and in the court of justice, and everywhere, you must do whatever your state and your country tell you to do, or you must persuade them that their commands are unjust."

There is no equality in Plato's scheme: the citizen may use persuasion, but no more; the state may use force. Why not insist that the *state* persuade *us* to do its bidding?

It is curious that Socrates (according to Plato in his dialogue *The Apology*) was willing to disobey the authorities by preaching as he chose, by telling the young what he saw as the truth, even if that meant going against the laws of Athens. Yet, when he was sentenced to death, and by a divided jury (the vote was 281 to 220), he meekly accepted the verdict, saying he owed Athens obedience to its laws, giving that puny 56 percent majority vote an absolute right to take his life.

It seems that the idea of owing, of obligation, is strongly felt by almost everyone. But what does one owe the government? Granted, the government may do useful things for its citizens: help farmers, administer old-age pensions and health benefits, regulate the use of drugs, apprehend criminals, etc. But because the government administers these programs (for which the citizens pay taxes, and for which the government officials draw salaries), does this mean that you owe the government your life?

Plato is enticing us to confuse the country with the government. The Declaration of Independence tried to make clear that the people of the country set up the government, to achieve the aims of equality and justice; and when a government no longer pursues those aims of equality and justice it loses its legitimacy, it has violated its obligation to the citizens, and deserves no more respect or obedience.

We are intimidated by the word patriotism, afraid to be called unpatriotic. Early in the twentieth century, the Russian-American anarchist and feminist Emma Goldman lectured on patriotism. She said,

> Conceit, arrogance and egotism are the essentials of patriotism.... Patriotism assumes that our globe is divided into little spots, each one surrounded by an iron gate. Those who had the fortune of being born on some particular spot, consider themselves better, nobler, grander, more intelligent than the living beings inhabiting any other spot. It is, therefore, the duty of everyone living on that chosen spot to fight, kill, and die in the attempt to impose his superiority upon all others.

Even the symbols of patriotism—the flag, the national anthem—become objects of worship, and those who refuse to worship are treated as heretics. When in 1989 the U.S. Supreme Court decided that a citizen has a right to express himself or herself by burning the American flag, there was an uproar in the White House and in Congress. President Bush, almost in tears, began speaking of a Constitutional amendment to make flag burning a crime. Congress, with its customary sheepishness, rushed to pass a law providing a year in prison for anyone hurting the flag.

The humorist Garrison Keillor responded to the president with some seriousness:

> Flag-burning is a minor insult compared to George Bush's cynical use of the flag for political advantage. Any decent law to protect the flag ought to prohibit politicians from wrapping it around themselves! Flag-burning is an impulsive act by a powerless individual—but the cool pinstripe demagoguery of this powerful preppie is a real and present threat to freedom.

If patriotism were defined, not as blind obedience to government, not as submissive worship to flags and anthems, but rather as love of one's country, one's fellow citizens (all over the world), as loyalty to the principles of justice and democracy, then patriotism would require us to disobey our government, when it violated those principles.

Accept Your Punishment!

Socrates's position—that he must accept death for his disobedience—has become one of the cardinal principles in the liberal philosophy of civil disobedience and part of the dominant American orthodoxy in the United States, for both conservatives and liberals. It is usually stated this way: it's your right to break the law when your conscience is offended; but then you must accept your punishment.

Why? Why agree to be punished when you think you have acted rightly, and the law, punishing you for that, has acted wrongly? Why is it all right to disobey the law in the first instance, but then, when you are sentenced to prison, start obeying it?

Some people, to support the idea of accepting punishment, like to quote Martin Luther King, Jr., one of the great apostles of civil disobedience in this century. In his "Letter from Birmingham City Jail," written in the spring of 1963, in the midst of tumultuous demonstrations against racial segregation, he said, "I submit that an individual who breaks a law that conscience tells him is unjust, and willingly accepts the penalty by staying in jail to arouse the conscience of the community over its injustices is in reality expressing the very highest respect for the law."

King was writing in answer to pleas by some white church leaders that he stop the demonstrations. They urged him to take his cause to the courts but "not in the streets." I believe King's reply has been seriously misinterpreted. It was an impassioned defense of nonviolent direct action, but it is obvious that he wanted to persuade those conservative church leaders of his moderation. He was anxious to show that, while committing civil disobedience he was "expressing the very highest respect for law."

The "law" that King respected, we know unquestionably from his life, his work, and his philosophy, was not man-made law, neither segregation laws nor even laws approved by the Supreme Court, nor decisions of the courts nor sentences meted out by judges. He meant respect for the higher law, the law of morality, of justice.

To be "one who willingly accepts" punishment is not the same as thinking it *right* to be punished for an act of conscience. If this were so, why would King agree to be released from jail by behind-the-scenes pressure, as he did in 1960 when a mysterious benefactor in a high position (someone close to President-elect Kennedy) pulled strings to get him out of prison? The meaning of "willingly accepts" is that you know you are risking jail and are willing to take that risk, but it doesn't mean it is morally right for you to be punished.

King talks about "staying in jail to arouse the conscience of the community over its injustice." He does not speak of staying in jail because he owes that to the government and that (as Plato argues) he has a duty to obey whatever the government tells him to do. Not at all. He remains in jail not for philosophical or moral reasons, but for a practical purpose, to continue his struggle "to arouse the conscience of the community over its injustice."

Knowing King's life and thought, we can safely say that if the circumstances had been different, he might well have agreed (unlike Socrates) to escape from jail. What if he had been sentenced, not to six months in a Georgia prison, but to death? Would he have "accepted" this?

Would King have condemned those black slaves who were tried under the Fugitive Slave Act of 1850 and ordered to return to slavery, but who refused to give themselves up and ran away from their sentence? Would he have criticized Angela Davis, the black militant who, after she had participated in a daring rescue of a black prisoner from a courtroom, refused to stand trial and went underground?

We can imagine another test of King's attitude toward "accepting" punishment. During the Vietnam War, which King powerfully opposed ("The long night of war must be stopped," he said in 1965), the Catholic priest-poet Daniel Berrigan committed an act of civil disobedience. He and other men and women of the "Catonsville Nine," entered a draft board in Catonsville, Maryland, removed draft records, and set them afire in a public "ceremony." Father Berrigan delivered a meditation:

> Our apologies, good friends, for the fracture of good order, the burning of paper instead of children.... We could not, so help us God, do otherwise...We say: killing is disorder, life and gentleness and community and unselfishness is the only order we recognize. For the sake of that order we risk our liberty, our good name. The time is past when good men can remain silent, when obedience can segregate men from public risk, when the poor can die without defense.

Although he used the term *men,* one of the Catonsville Nine was a woman, Mary Moylan. When the Nine were found guilty, sentenced to jail terms, and lost their appeals, she and Daniel Berrigan refused to turn themselves in, going "underground." Berrigan was found after four months, Mary Moylan was never apprehended. She wrote from underground: "I don't want to see people marching off to jail with smiles on their faces. I just don't want them going...I don't want to waste the sisters and brothers we have by marching them off to jail."

Berrigan and Moylan thought the war was wrong and thought their going to jail for opposing it was wrong. If, like King, they felt it would serve some practical use, they probably would have accepted it. Going to jail can make a certain kind of statement to the public: "Yes, I feel so strongly about what is happening in the world that I am willing to risk jail to express my feelings."

Refusing to go to jail makes a different kind of statement: "The system that sentenced me is the same foul system that is carrying on this war. I will defy it to the end. It does not deserve my allegiance." As Daniel Berrigan said, yes, we respect the order of "gentleness and community" but not the "order" of making war on children.

Daniel Berrigan and I had traveled together in early 1968 to Hanoi to pick up three American pilots released from prison by the North Vietnamese. We became good friends, and I was soon in close contact with the extraordinary Catholic resistance movement against the Vietnam War.

In early 1970 his last appeal was turned down; facing several years in prison, he "disappeared," sending the FBI into a frantic effort to find him. They had caught sight of him at a huge student rally in the Cornell University gymnasium, then the lights went out and before they could make their way through the crowd he was spirited away inside a huge puppet, to a nearby farmhouse.

A few days after his disappearance, I received a phone call at my home in Boston. I was being invited to speak at a Catholic church on the Upper West Side of Manhattan, on the issues of the war and the Berrigans. Philip Berrigan, Daniel's brother, a priest and one of the Catonsville Nine, was also living underground and had just been found by the FBI in a tiny apartment of the church's pastor.

The church was packed with perhaps 500 people. FBI agents mingled with the crowd, alerted that Daniel Berrigan might show up. I made a brief speech. Another friend of Daniel's spoke. As the two of us sat on the platform, a note was passed to us, to meet two nuns at a Spanish-Chinese restaurant farther up Broadway, near Columbia University. There we were given directions to New Jersey, to the house where Daniel was hiding out.

The next morning we rented a car, drove to New Jersey, and met him. The house he was staying in was not secure (in fact, an FBI agent lived across the street!). We arranged a trip to Boston, a car, a driver, and a destination. From that point on, for the next four months, he eluded and exasperated the FBI, staying underground, but surfacing from time to time, to deliver a sermon at a church in Philadelphia, to be interviewed on national television, to make public statements about the war, to make a film (*The Holy Outlaw*) about his actions against the war, both overt and underground.

During those four months, while helping take care of Dan Berrigan, I was teaching my course at Boston University in political theory. My students were reading the *Crito*, and I asked them to analyze reasons for going underground. They did not know, of course, that Berrigan was right there in Boston, living out his ideas.

I think it is a good guess, despite those often-quoted words of his on "accepting" punishment, that Martin Luther King, Jr., would have supported Berrigan's actions. The principle is clear. If it is right to disobey unjust laws, it is right to disobey unjust punishment for breaking those laws.

The idea behind "accept your punishment" (advanced often by "liberals" sympathetic with dissent) is that whatever your disagreement with some specific law or some particular policy, you should not spread disrespect for the law *in general*, because we need respect for the law to keep society intact.

This is like saying because apples are good for children, we must insist that they not refuse the rotten ones, because that might lead them to reject all apples. Well, good apples are good for your health, and rotten apples are bad. Bad laws and bad policies endanger our lives and our freedoms. Why can't we trust human intelligence to make the proper distinctions—among laws as among apples?

The domino theory is in people's minds: Let one domino fall and they will all go. It is a psychology of absolute control, in which the need for total security brings an end to freedom. Let anyone evade punishment and the whole social structure will come down.

We must ask, however: Can a decent society exist (*that* is our concern, not the *state*), if people humbly obey all laws, even those that violate human rights? And when unjust laws and unjust policies become the rule, should not the state (in Plato's words) "be overthrown"?

Most people quickly accept the idea of disobedience in a totalitarian society or in a blatantly undemocratic situation as in the American South with its racial segregation. But they look differently on breaking the law in a liberal society, where parties compete for the votes of citizens, where laws are passed by bodies of elected representatives, and where people have some opportunities for free expression of their ideas.

What this argument misses is that civil disobedience gives an *intensity* to expression by its dramatic violation of law, which other means—voting, speaking, and writing—do not possess. If we are to avoid majority tyranny over oppressed minorities, we must give a dissident minority a way of expressing the fullness of its grievance.

The fiery editor of the abolitionist newspaper in Boston, William Lloyd Garrison, understood the need. Criticized by another antislavery person for his strong language ("I will not hesitate, I will not equivocate, I will not retreat a single inch, and I will be heard") and his dramatic actions (he set a copy of the United States Constitution afire at a public gathering, to call attention to the Constitution's support of slavery), Garrison replied, "Sir, slavery will not be overthrown without excitement, a most tremendous excitement."

Several of Garrison's contemporaries understood his role. One said that Garrison had roused the country from a sleep so deep "nothing but a rude and almost ruffian-like shake could rouse her." Another said, "he will shake our nation to its center, but he will shake slavery out of it."

Protest beyond the law is not a departure from democracy; it is absolutely essential to it. It is a corrective to the sluggishness of "the proper channels," a way of breaking through passages blocked by tradition and prejudice. It is disruptive and troublesome, but it is a necessary disruption, a healthy troublesomeness.

Disobedience and Foreign Policy

In a little book he wrote in the 1960s, Supreme Court justice Abe Fortas worried about all the civil disobedience taking place and spoke of "the all-important access to the ballot box."

In later chapters I discuss the insufficiency of the ballot box to deal with racial discrimination or with economic justice. But probably the most clear-cut illustration of the inadequacy of that "all-important access to the ballot box" is in the area of foreign policy.

In foreign policy, access to the ballot box means very little. Foreign policy is made by the president and a small circle of people around him, his appointed advisers. Again and again, Americans have voted for a president to keep them out of a war, only to see the "peace" candidate elected who then brings the nation into war.

Woodrow Wilson was elected in 1916 on a peace platform: "There is such a thing as a nation being too proud to fight." The next year he asked Congress to declare war. Franklin Roosevelt was elected in 1940 with a pledge to keep the United States out of the war, yet his policies were more and more designed to bring the United States into the war.

In 1964, the situation in Vietnam was tense. Lyndon Johnson ran for president on a platform opposing military intervention in Southeast Asia, while his opponent, Barry Goldwater, urged such action. The voters chose Johnson, but they got Goldwater's policy: escalation and intervention.

The Constitution says it is up to Congress to declare war. James Madison, who presided over the Constitutional Convention in 1787, explained the reasoning of the Founding Fathers in a letter to Thomas

Jefferson written years later: "The constitution supposes, what the history of all Govts demonstrates, that the Executive is the branch of power most interested in war and most prone to it. It has accordingly with studied care vested the question of war in the legislature."

However, again and again, the president has made the decision to go to war, and Congress has obsequiously gone along. In the two most recent American wars, the Korean War and the Vietnam War, Congress, while ignored, nevertheless appropriated the money asked by the president to carry on the war. When it comes to making war, we might just as well have a monarchy as a constitutional government.

It seems that the closer we get to matters of life and death—war and peace—the most undemocratic is our so-called democratic system. Once the government, ignoring democratic procedures, gets the nation into war, it creates an atmosphere in which criticism of the war may be punished by imprisonment—as happened in the Civil War and in both world wars. Thus democracy gets a double defeat in matters of war and peace.

The Supreme Court itself, which (we were told back in junior-high-school civics class) is supposed to interpret the Constitution, presumably in the interests of democracy (checks and balances and all that), has interpreted it in such a way as to eliminate democracy in foreign policy. In a decision it made in 1936 (*U.S. v. Curtiss-Wright Export Corp.*), the Court gave the president total power over foreign policy, including the right to ignore the Constitution:

> The broad statement that the federal government can exercise no powers except those specifically enumerated in the Constitution, and such implied powers as are necessary and proper to carry into effect the enumerated powers, is categorically true only in respect of our internal affairs.

This is a shocking statement to any American who learned in school that the powers of government are limited to what the Constitution allows. But that decision has never been overturned. And all through the history of the United States we find Congress behaving like a flock of sheep when the president decides on war.

President Polk in 1846 (coveting California and other Mexican land) provoked a war with Mexico by sending troops into a disputed area. A battle took place, and when he asked Congress to declare war, they rushed to comply, the Senate spending just one day on debating the war resolution, the House of Representatives allowing two hours.

A century later in the summer of 1964 President Lyndon Johnson reported attacks on U.S. naval vessels off the coast of Vietnam in the Gulf of Tonkin. Congress took the president's account as truth (it turned out to be full of deceptions) and voted overwhelmingly (unanimously in the House, two dissenting votes in the Senate) to give the president blanket power to take whatever military action he wanted.

There was no declaration of war, as the Constitution required, but when citizens challenged this, the Supreme Court acted as timidly as Congress. The court never decided on the constitutionality of the Vietnam War. It would not even agree to discuss the issue.

For instance, in 1972 a man named Ernest Da Costa brought his case to the Supreme Court. He had been conscripted into the U.S. Army, but when ordered to go to Vietnam he refused, arguing that the American war in Vietnam had not been authorized by Congress, and, therefore, Congress could not draft him for overseas service. The Court refused even to hear his case. It takes the assent of four Supreme Court Justices to bring a case before the Court; only two wanted to hear Da Costa's argument. The Supreme Court's claim was that such questions are "political"— meaning that they are too important to be decided by the nonelected Supreme Court and should be decided by the "political" branches of government, those subject to election, namely the president and Congress.

But we have seen that Congress has never had the boldness to challenge a president's call for war. So much for those checks and balances that, we learned in school, would save us from one-man rule. It turns out that the much-praised "proper channels" are not channels at all, but mazes, into which we are invited, like experimental animals, to get lost.

The concentration of dictatorial power in the hands of the president, in regard to military actions, was underlined when Secretary of State Dean Rusk testified before Congress in 1962. He was explaining the attempt to invade Cuba the year before, an action planned secretly by the CIA and the White House without the involvement of Congress. You shouldn't get upset over being ignored on this, Rusk assured Congress, because it's been done lots of times. He then gave them a list compiled by the State Department called "Instances of the Use of United States Armed Forces Abroad 1798-1945," describing 127 military actions by the

United States, carried out by presidential order. A small sample of that list includes (in the language of the State Department):

> 1852-53—Argentine—Marines were landed and maintained in Buenos Aires to protect American interests during a revolution.
> 1854—Nicaragua—San Juan del Norte [Greytown] was destroyed to avenge an insult to the American Minister to Nicaragua.
> 1855—Uruguay—U.S. and European naval forces landed to protect American interests during an attempted revolution in Montevideo.

When U.S. troops were finally withdrawn from Vietnam in 1973, over 50,000 American men were dead after a war begun by the president, aided by a submissive Congress and a hands-off Supreme Court. Now Congress, mustering a bit of courage, passed a War Powers Act, intended to limit the power of the president in sending the American military into warlike situations. The act declared, among other provisions, "The President, in every possible instance, shall consult with Congress before introducing United States Armed Forces into hostilities or into situations where imminent involvement in hostilities is clearly indicated by the circumstances."

This War Powers Act has been ignored again and again, by various presidents. President Ford invaded a Cambodian island and bombed a Cambodian town in the spring of 1975 after the crew of an American merchant ship, the *Mayaguez*, was detained, but not harmed, by Cambodian authorities. According to the War Powers Act, Ford should have consulted with Congress. Senator Mike Mansfield, the Democratic leader of the Senate, said "I was not consulted, but notified after the fact."

President Ronald Reagan in the fall of 1982 sent troops into a dangerous situation in Lebanon, again without following the requirements of the War Powers Act, and soon after that over 200 marines were killed in Lebanon by a bomb that exploded in their barracks. In the spring of 1983, Reagan sent U.S. forces to invade the Caribbean island of Grenada, again only notifying Congress, not consulting them. And in 1986, U.S. planes bombed the capital of Libya, again without consulting Congress. In 1989, President Bush launched an invasion of Panama (he called it Operation Just Cause), again without consulting Congress.

We have been speaking of open military actions undertaken by the president, uncontrolled by Congress. But the absence of democracy in foreign policy is even more obvious when you consider how much is done secretly by the president and his advisers, behind the backs of the American public, as well as behind the backs of their elected representatives.

The list of secret actions includes the CIA's overthrow of the government of Iran in 1953, restoring the Shah to the throne; the 1954 invasion of Guatemala and the ousting of its democratically elected president; the invasion of Cuba in 1961; and the wide range of covert operations in Indochina in the 1950s and 1960s, including the secret bombing of Cambodia. More recently, we find the series of attempts to overthrow the Sandinista government in Nicaragua by arming a counterrevolutionary force (the "contras") across the border in Honduras, and mining Nicaragua's harbors, as well as the secret transfer of arms to the contras in violation of a law passed by Congress.

When the "Iran-Contra" scandal became public in 1986-1987, President Reagan feigned innocence—the doctrine of "plausible denial" again. With astounding hypocrisy, Reagan said in his State of the Union Address at the beginning of 1987 (the bicentennial of the Constitution), "In those other constitutions, the government tells the people what they are allowed to do. In our Constitution, we the people tell the government what it can do and that it can do only those things listed in that document and no other."

These actions (the word *covert* is used officially, perhaps it sounds more respectable than secret) are fundamentally undemocratic; they take place behind the backs of the American people. The people who carry them out are, therefore, not accountable to any democratic process. The government has bypassed its own channels. For the citizens to stop this, civil disobedience may be needed.

Is Civil Disobedience Always Right?

There is a common argument against civil disobedience that goes like this: If I approve your act of civil disobedience, am I not honor bound to approve *anyone's* civil disobedience? If I approve Martin Luther King's violations of law, must I not also approve the Ku Klux Klan's illegal activities?

This argument comes from a mistaken idea about civil disobedience. The violation of law for the purpose of committing an injustice (like the Governor of Alabama preventing a black student from entering a public school or Colonel Oliver North buying arms for terrorists in Central America) is not defensible. Whether it was *legal* (as it was until 1954) or illegal (after 1954) to prevent black children from entering a school, it would still be wrong. The test of justification for an act is not its legality but its morality.

The principle I am suggesting for civil disobedience is not that we must tolerate all disobedience to law, but that we refuse an absolute *obedience* to law. The ultimate test is not law, but justice.

This troubles many people, because it gives them a heavy responsibility, to weigh social acts by their moral consequences. This can get complicated and requires a never-ending set of judgments about practices and policies. It is much easier to lie back and let the law make out moral judgments for us, whatever the law happens to say at the moment, whatever politicians have made into law on the basis of *their* interests, however the Supreme Court interprets the law at the moment. Yes, easier. But recall Jefferson's words: "Eternal vigilance is the price of liberty."

There is fear that this kind of citizens' judgments about when to obey and when to disobey the law will lead to terrible consequences. In the summer of 1968 four people who called for resistance to the draft as a way of halting the war in Vietnam—Dr. Benjamin Spock, Reverend William Sloane Coffin, writer Mitchell Goodman, and Harvard student Michael Ferber—were sentenced to prison by Judge Francis Ford in Boston, who said, "Where law and order stops, obviously anarchy begins."

That is the same basically conservative impulse that once saw minimum wage laws as leading to Bolshevism, or bus desegregation leading to intermarriage, or communism in Vietnam leading to world communism. It assumes that all actions in a given direction rush toward the extreme, as if all social change takes place at the top of a steep, smooth hill, where the first push ensures a plunge to the bottom.

In fact an act of civil disobedience, like any move for reform, is more like the first push *up* a hill. Society's tendency is to maintain what has been. Rebellion is only an occasional reaction to suffering in human history; we have infinitely more instances of submission to authority than we have examples of revolt. What we should be most concerned about is not some natural tendency toward violent uprising, but rather the inclination of people faced with an overwhelming environment of injustice to submit to it.

Historically, the most terrible things—war, genocide, and slavery—have resulted not from disobedience, but from obedience.

Vietnam and Obedience

There are rare moments in the history of nations when citizens, their indignation overflowing, begin to refuse obedience to the authorities. Such a moment in the history of the United States was the war in Vietnam. When Americans saw their nation, which they had been taught to believe was civilized and humane, killing Vietnamese peasants with napalm, fragmentation bombs, and other horrible instruments of modern war, they refused to stay inside the polite and accepted channels of expression.

Most of the actions taken against the war were not acts of civil disobedience. They were not illegal, but extra-legal—outside the regular procedures of government: rallies, petitions, picketing, and lobbying. A national network of educational activities spontaneously grew: alternative newspapers, campus teach-ins, church gatherings, and community meetings.

When the supposed clash between U.S. naval vessels and North Vietnamese patrol boats took place in the Gulf of Tonkin during the summer of 1964, I was teaching in a Freedom School in Jackson, Mississippi. In August, the bodies of three missing civil rights workers, shot to death, were found near Philadelphia, Mississippi, and many of us working in the movement drove up to attend a memorial meeting held outdoors not far from where they had been killed.

At the meeting, one of the organizers of the Mississippi movement, Bob Moses, stood up to speak. He held aloft the morning newspaper from Jackson. The headline was "LBJ Says Shoot to Kill in Gulf of Tonkin." Moses spoke with a quiet bitterness (this is a rough recollection of his words): "The president wants to send soldiers to kill people on the other side of the world, people we know nothing about, while here in Mississippi he refuses to send anyone to protect black people against murderous violence."

That fall, as the U.S. involvement in Vietnam began to grow, I was starting to teach at Boston University and became immediately involved in the movement against the war. It was at first a puny movement, which seemed to have no hope of prevailing against the enormous power of the government. But as the war in Vietnam became more vicious and as it became clear that noncombatants were being killed in large numbers; that the Saigon government was corrupt, unpopular, and under the control of our own government; and that the American public was being told lies about the war by our highest officials, the movement grew with amazing speed.

In the spring of 1965, I and some others spoke against the war on the Boston Common to perhaps a hundred people. In October 1969 when antiwar meetings took place in hundreds of towns and cities around the country, there was another rally on the Boston Common, and 100,000 people were there. As the American involvement escalated—to 500,000 troops, to millions of tons of bombs dropped—the antiwar movement also escalated.

Young black civil rights workers connected with Student Nonviolent Coordinating Committee (SNCC) were among the first to resist the war. In mid-1965 in McComb, Mississippi, young blacks who had just learned that a classmate of theirs was killed in Vietnam distributed a leaflet:

> No Mississippi Negroes should be fighting in Viet Nam for the White man's freedom, until all the Negro people are free in Mississippi.
> Negro boys should not honor the draft here in Mississippi. Mothers should encourage their sons not to go.

In the summer of 1966, six young black men, members of SNCC, invaded an induction center to protest the war. They were arrested and sentenced to prison. Julian Bond, another SNCC member, who had just been elected to the Georgia House of Representatives, spoke out against the war and the draft, and the House voted that he not be seated. (The Supreme Court later restored his seat, saying his First Amendment right to free speech had been violated.)

Martin Luther King, Jr., spoke out publicly against the war, ignoring the advice of some other civil rights leaders, who feared that criticism might weaken Johnson's program of domestic reform. King refused to be silenced:

> Somehow this madness must cease. We must stop now. I speak as a child of

God and brother to the suffering poor of Vietnam. I speak for those whose land is being laid waste, whose homes are being destroyed, whose culture is being subverted. I speak for the poor of America who are paying the double price of smashed hopes at home and death and corruption in Vietnam. I speak as a citizen of the world as it stands aghast at the path we have taken. I speak as an American to the leaders of my own nation. The great initiative in this war is ours. The initiative to stop it must be ours.

Young men began to refuse to register for the draft or to refuse induction if called. Students signed petitions headed We Won't Go. Over a half million men, resisted the draft. About 200,000 were prosecuted, 3,000 became fugitives. There were too many cases to pursue and most were dropped. Finally, 8,750 men were convicted of draft evasion.

A student of mine, Philip Supina, wrote to his draft board in Tucson, Arizona, on May 1, 1968: "I am enclosing the order for me to report for my pre-induction physical exam for the armed forces. I have absolutely no intention to report for that exam, or for induction, or to aid in any way the American war effort against the people of Vietnam." He was sentenced to four years in prison.

In previous wars, there had been opposition within the armed forces, but the Vietnam War produced open protests and silent desertions on a scale never seen before. As early as June 1965, West Point graduate Richard Steinke refused to board an aircraft taking him to a remote Vietnamese village. He said, "The Vietnamese war is not worth a single American life."

There were many individual acts of disobedience. A black private in Oakland refused to board a troop plane to Vietnam. A navy nurse was court-martialed for marching in a peace demonstration while in uniform and for dropping antiwar leaflets from a plane onto navy installations. In Norfolk, Virginia, a sailor refused to train fighter pilots because he thought the war was immoral. An army lieutenant was arrested in Washington, D.C., in early 1968 for picketing the White House with a sign that said "120,000 American casualties—Why?" Two black marines were given prison sentences of six and ten years, respectively, for talking to other black marines against the war.

Desertions from the armed forces multiplied. We can't be sure of the exact number, but there may have been 100,000. Thousands went to Western Europe—France, Sweden, and Holland. Most deserters crossed the border into Canada; 34,000 were court-martialed and imprisoned. There were over a half million less-than-honorable discharges.

The GI movement against the war became organized. Antiwar coffeehouses were set up near military bases around the country, where GIs could come to meet others who were opposed to what was going on in Vietnam. Underground newspapers sprang up at military bases across the country—fifty of them by 1970. These newspapers printed antiwar articles, gave news about the harassment of GIs, and gave practical advice on the legal rights of people in the military.

The dissidence spread to the war front itself. When antiwar demonstrations were taking place in October 1969 all over the United States, some GIs in Vietnam wore arm bands to show their support. One soldier stationed at Cu Chi wrote to a friend on October 26, 1970, that separate companies had been set up for men refusing to go into the field to fight. He said, "It's no big thing here anymore to refuse to go." A news dispatch in April 1972 reported that 50 infantrymen of a company of 142 refused for an hour and a half to go out on patrol round Phu Bai. They shouted, "We're not going! This isn't our war." Others comment-ed, "Why the hell are we fighting for something we don't believe in?" One army sergeant, captured by the Vietnamese, told later about his march to the prisoner-or-war camp, "Until we got to the first camp, we didn't see a village intact; they were all destroyed. I sat down and put myself in the middle and asked myself: Is this right or wrong? Is it right to destroy villages? Is it right to kill people en masse? After a while it just got to me."

The French newspaper *Le Monde* reported that in four months, 109 soldiers of the first air cavalry division were charged with refusal to fight. "A common sight," the correspondent for *Le Monde* wrote, "is the black soldier, with his left fist clenched in defiance of a war he has never considered his own."

In the summer of 1970, 28 commissioned officers of the military, including some veterans of Vietnam, said they represented about 250 other officers and announced the formation of the Concerned Officers Movement Against the War. In mid-1973, it was reported there were drop-outs among West Point cadets. A reporter wrote that West Point officials attributed this to "an affluent, less disciplined, skeptical and ques-tioning generation and to the anti-military mood that a small radical minority and the Vietnam war had created."

There is probably no more disciplined, obedient, highly trained element of the armed forces than the fliers of the air force. But when the ferocious bombings of civilians in Hanoi and Haiphong was ordered by the Nixon administration around Christmas 1972, several B52 pilots refused to fly.

The massive civil disobedience against the Vietnam War—by men in the military, by draftees, and by civilians—cannot be justified simply because it was civil disobedience, but because it was disobedience on behalf of a human right—the right of millions of people in Vietnam not to be killed because the United States saw in Southeast Asia (as president John F. Kennedy put it), "an important piece of real estate."

Actions outside the law or against the law must be judged by their human consequences. That is why the civil disobedience of Colonel Oliver North, illegally sending military aid to the contras in Central America who committed acts of terrorism against Nicaraguan farmers cannot be justified. But the civil disobedience of those who wanted to stop the killing in Vietnam was necessary and right.

The congressional committee that interrogated Oliver North in 1987 as part of the Iran-Contra hearings did not ask him about the innocent people killed in Nicaragua because of what he had done. They concentrated, as the American court system generally does, on the technical question of *whether* he had violated the law, not on the more important question: for what *purpose* did he violate the law.

It is interesting to note that North did not hold to the rule of law over the rule of men. He was willing to break the law to obey the president. He told the hearing committee, "And if the Commander-in-Chief tells this Lieutenant Colonel to go sit in the corner and stand on his head I will do so."

Justice in the Courts

Those who run the legal system in the United States do not want the public to accept the idea of civil disobedience—even though it rests on the Declaration of Independence, even though it has the approval of some of the great minds of human history, even though some of the great achievements for equality and liberty in the United States have been the result of movements outside of and against the law. They are afraid that the idea will take hold, and they are right, because the common sense belief of most people, I think, is that justice is more important than law.

During the Vietnam War, not long after I got back from Hanoi, where I had visited villages devastated by American bombs, I was asked to testify at a trial in Milwaukee. Fourteen people, many of them Catholic priests and nuns, had invaded a draft board and destroyed documents to protest the war.

I was to testify as a so-called expert witness, to tell the judge and jury about the history of civil disobedience in the United States, to show its honorable roots in the American Revolution, and its achievements for economic justice and for racial equality.

I started out talking about the Declaration of Independence, and then about Thoreau's civil disobedience, and then gave a brief history of civil disobedience in the United States. The judge pounded his gavel and said, "Stop! You can't discuss that. This is getting to the heart of the matter."

The defense attorney asked me, "What is the difference between law and justice?" The prosecution objected, and the judge said, "Sustained." More questions about civil disobedience. More objections, all sustained. I turned to the judge (something a witness is not supposed to do) and asked, in a voice loud enough for the courtroom to hear, "Why can't I say something important? Why can't the jury hear something important?"

The judge was angry. He replied, "You are not permitted to speak out like that. If you do that once more I will have you put in jail for contempt of court." Later I felt I should have been more courageous and jointed my act of civil disobedience to that of the defendants.

What the judge wanted to hear about in his courtroom was merely the technical violations of law committed by the defendants—breaking and entering, destroying government documents, and trespassing. "This is a case about arson and theft." He did not want to hear *why* these usually upright and law-abiding citizens were breaking the law. He did not want to hear about the war in Vietnam. He did not want to hear about the tradition of civil disobedience.

To have the mechanical requirements of "due process"—a trial, contending arguments, and decision by a jury of citizens—is insufficient if the arguments are not fully made, if the jury does not know what is at stake, and if it cannot make a decision on the *justice* of the defendants' action, regardless of legality. Supposedly, it is the judge who sees to it that the law is made clear to the jury, but then it is up to the jury to see that justice is done. However, if the judge prevents the jury from hearing testimony about the issues, the jury is being compelled to stay within the narrow, technical confines of the law, and the democratic purpose of a jury trial is extinguished.

The courtroom, one of the supposed bastions of democracy, is essentially a tyranny. The judge is monarch. He is in control of the evidence, the witnesses, the questions, and the interpretation of law. In the mid-1980s I was called as a witness by some people in Providence, Rhode Island, who had done some small symbolic damage at the launching of a nuclear-armed submarine, in protest against the huge expenditure of money for deadly weapons and the escalation of the arms race. I was to tell the jury about the importance of civil disobedience for American democracy.

The judge would not let me speak. From the very first question—"Can you tell us about the history of civil disobedience in the United States?"—as I began to answer, the judge stopped me. "Objection sustained," he said loudly. I had not heard any objection from the prosecuting attorney.

Indeed, at this point the prosecuting attorney, a young man, spoke up, "Your honor, I did not object."

"Well," said the judge, "why didn't you?"

"Because," the prosecutor said, "I thought the question was relevant."

"I disagree," the judge said, with finality.

I was not able to say anything to the jury. It was clear that the judge was furious at these antimilitary protesters and was determined to send them to prison. They were facing a felony charge, calling for ten years in prison, and a misdemeanor, calling for one year in prison. The prosecutor, obviously not convinced that these defendants were dangerous criminals, perhaps a bit sympathetic to their cause, dropped the felony charge, telling the defendants, confidentially, that he did that because he was sure the judge would give the defendants the full ten year sentence.

The quality of justice in the United States is strained through the sieve of the power and prejudice of judges. Free speech in the courtroom does not exist, because the judge decides what can and cannot be said. In 1980, a New York City judge dropped a case against fifteen people who protested at a research facility for nuclear weapons on the advice of the prosecutor, who told him, "We want to prevent these defendants from using the Criminal Court as a forum for their views."

Judges are, for the most part, creatures of comfort—that is, they come from the affluent classes and tend to be conservative and hostile toward radicals, demonstrators, protesters, and violators of "law and order." They are also creatures of the American environment, subject to the dominant ideology.

But when the national mood changes, when the political atmosphere becomes differently charged, judges may be affected by that. If they then allow juries to hear the reasons why protesters acted, the common sense of juries comes into play. They may vote to acquit the defendants even if they have broken the law. Given the opportunity, when not bullied by judges, juries may choose justice before law.

By 1967 there was a formidable movement all across the country against the war in Vietnam. In Oakland, California, demonstrations that disrupted the normal operations of the Induction Center resulted in the prosecution of the Oakland Seven, charged with conspiracy to trespass, create a public nuisance and resist arrest. The judge permitted the defendants to tell the jury about their belief in the illegality of the war and told the jury they should take that belief into consideration in determining whether there was criminal intent in the defendants' actions. The jury acquitted all of the Seven. One of the jury members said later, "I'm not a puppet. I'm a free thinker."

Jury Nullification

The Camden jury had exercised a right that judges never tell juries about: the right to come to a verdict following their conscience rather than the strict requirements of the law—to choose justice over law.

That right of "jury nullification" goes back to eighteenth-century Britain, when jurors, despite being fined and jailed, refused to convict two Englishmen for speaking to a street crowd. A plaque in the famous Old Bailey courthouse in London commemorates the courage of these jurors and records the final opinion of the Chief Justice, "which established the Right of Juries to give their Verdict according to their conviction."

In America the principle of jury nullification was affirmed in 1735 when John Peter Zenger, a New York printer who was charged with seditious libel for printing material not authorized by the British mayor, was acquitted by a jury that ignored the instructions of the judge. The jury apparently followed the advice of the defense attorney to "see with their own eyes, to hear with their own ears and to make use of their consciences."

The antislavery preacher Theodore Parker, after the passage of the Fugitive Slave Act of 1850, spoke in New England about what he would do if a slave escaped from South Carolina to Massachusetts and "a Mr. Greatheart" helped her to escape, harbored and concealed her, and was then prosecuted, and he, Parker, was on the jury. He declared:

> I may take the juror's oath to give a verdict according to the law and the testimony. The law is plain, let us suppose and the testimony conclusive.
> ... If I have extinguished my manhood by my juror's oath, then I shall do my official business and find Greatheart guilty, and I shall seem to be a true man; but if I value my manhood, I shall answer after my natural duty to love a man and not hate him, to do him justice, not injustice, to allow him the natural rights he has not alienated, and shall say, "Not guilty."

Around the middle of the nineteenth century, however, the courts began to rule that juries did not have the right to decide the law, only the facts, that they had to obey the judge's instructions as to the law. This does not really settle the matter. The jury may not have the right to rule on questions of law, but they don't have to write legal opinions when they give their verdict; they can vote their consciences, regardless of the law explained to them by the judge. A distinguished legal scholar, Wigmore, wrote in 1929 about the importance of jury nullification to achieve justice.

> Law and Justice are from time to time inevitably in conflict. That is because law is a general rule;...The jury, in the privacy of its retirement, adjusts the general rule of law to the justice of the particular case...The jury, and the secrecy of the jury room, are the indispensable elements in popular justice.

Another famous legal scholar, Roscoe Pound, had written back in 1910 that "jury lawlessness is the great corrective in legal proceedings.

In other words, the jury must match the defendants' civil disobedience with its own disobedience of law, if, as a matter of conscience, it believes the defendants did the right thing. When it is submissive before the overbearing authority of a judge, it surrenders its own conscience. In the case of Dr. Spock and his other antiwar defendants who were found guilty by the jury, one of the jury members said later, "I was in full agreement with the defendants until we were charged by the judge. That was the kiss of death!"

Another juror in the *Spock* case, Frank Tarbi, wrote in the *Boston Globe* about his anguish:

> How and why did I find four men guilty? All men of courage and individuals whom I grew to admire as the trial developed...As the father of three teen-aged sons, two eligible for draft, and a veteran myself, my abhorrence of war is understandable...Was I ready to commit my sons?...Rev. Coffin's thought-provoking argument struck home—"Isn't the Cross higher than the flag? Must we not obey God before we obey man?..." The paradox was that I agreed wholeheartedly with these defendants, but...I felt that technically they did break the law...
>
> I departed to the waiting car and then to home. There I was embraced by my loved ones and I began to think and try to explain.... These four men were trying to save my sons whom I love dearly. Yet I found them guilty. To hell with my ulcer. After four or five stiff hookers (I lost count) I began to cry bitterly.

In the case of the Catonsville Nine draft board invaders, the Circuit Court of Appeals, while affirming their convictions, made a remarkable statement in support of jury nullification:

> We recognize...the undisputed power of the jury to acquit, even if its verdict is contrary to the law as given by the judge and contrary to the evidence.... If the jury feels that the law under which the defendant is accused is unjust, or that exigent circumstances justified the actions of the accused, or for any reason which appeals to their logic or passion, the jury has the power to acquit, and the courts must abide by that decision.

Nevertheless, it is always a struggle in the courtroom to get the judge to agree to admit into evidence those things that will allow the jury to vote its conscience. In the period since the Vietnam War, political protesters against the arms race, or against military intervention in Central America, have tried to introduce the defense of "necessity," or "justification." This defense is based on the idea that while a technical violation of law has taken place, it was necessary to prevent a greater harm to the community.

In 1980, the "Plowshares Eight" invaded a General Electric plant in King of Prussia, Pennsylvania, and did some minor damage to nuclear nose cones, as a protest against the arms race. They were charged with trespassing and destroying property. The judge would not allow a necessity defense, and when the jury was out for eight hours, the judge speeded up their decision by threatening to sequester them overnight. The jury then came in with a verdict of guilty. Juror Michael de Rosa said later, "I didn't think they really went to commit a crime. They went to protest... We really didn't want to convict them on anything. But we had to because of the way the judge said the only thing you can use is what you get under the law."

When juries have been allowed to hear the evidence of "necessity," the results may be startling. In Burlington, Vermont, in 1984 "The Winooski Forty-four" were arrested for refusing to leave the hallway outside of a senator's office. They were protesting his votes to give arms to the contras across the Nicaraguan border. The judge accepted the defendants' right to a necessity defense. He allowed them to call various expert witnesses: a refugee from Central America, who told the jury about the terror caused by American military intervention; a former leader of the contras, who explained that he had left their ranks after he realized they were organized and financed by the CIA and were committing atrocities against the people of Nicaragua. I testified about the history of civil disobedience in the United States and its usefulness in bringing about healthy social change.

The prosecuting attorney told the jury to disregard all that testimony. He pointed to a large chart on the stand facing the jury—one of the exhibits, which was a map of the senator's offices where the defendants had crowded into the corridor and refused to leave. He said, "The issue is not Nicaragua, not American foreign policy. *This* is the issue— trespassing."

When he had finished, a woman lawyer for the defendants rose for her summation. She walked over to the chart of the senator's office and folded it back, to reveal something underneath—a large map of Central America. She pointed and said, "*This* is the issue." They voted to acquit.

At another trial shortly after, in western Massachusetts, a number of people (including activist Abbie Hoffman and Amy Carter, daughter of an ex-president) were charged with blocking recruiters for the Central Intelligence Agency who had shown up at the University of Massachusetts in Amherst. Witnesses were called, including ex-CIA agents who told the jury that the CIA had engaged in illegal and murderous activities all around the world. The jury listened and voted to acquit.

One juror, a hospital worker named Ann Gaffney, said later, "I was not that familiar with the CIA's activities. I was surprised. I was shocked...I was kind of proud of the students." Another juror, Donna Moody, said, "All the expert testimony against the CIA was alarming. It was very educational." The county district attorney himself, Michael Ryan, had this reaction: "If there is a message, it was that this jury was composed of middle America.... Middle America doesn't want the CIA doing what they are doing."

In this case the judge allowed the defense of necessity and gave the green light to the jury in considering human rights more important than a technical violation of law. But the courts will continue to remain barricades against change, stiff upholders of the prevailing order, unless juries defy conservative judges and vote their consciences, commit their own civil disobedience in the courtroom, and ignore the law to achieve justice.

Or perhaps we should say "ignore man-made law, the law of the politicians" to obey the higher law—what Reverend Coffin and Father Berrigan would call "the law of God" and what others might call the law of human rights, the principles of peace, freedom, and justice. (Daniel Berrigan's elderly mother was asked by a reporter, when Dan went underground, how she felt about her son defying the law; she responded quietly, "It's not God's law.")

The truth is so often the total reverse of what has been told us by our culture that we cannot turn our heads far enough around to see it. Surely, it is obedience to governments, in their appeals to patriotism, their calls for war, that is responsible for the terrible violence of our century. The disobedience of conscientious citizens, for the most part nonviolent, has been directed to stopping the violence of war. The psychologist Erich Fromm, thinking about nuclear war, once referred to the biblical Genesis of the human race and the bite into the forbidden apple: "Human history began with an act of disobedience and it is not unlikely that it will be terminated by an act of obedience."

Does Protest Matter?

It is not easy to prove that protest changes policy. But in the case of the Vietnam War, there is powerful evidence. In the government's own top-secret documents, the "Pentagon Papers," we find anxious government memos about "public opinion...increasing pressure to stop the bombing...the breadth and intensity of public unrest and dissatisfaction with the war...especially with young people, the underprivileged, the intelligentsia and the women...a limit beyond which many Americans and much of the world will not permit the United States to go."

And in the spring of 1968, with over half a million troops in Vietnam and General Westmoreland asking President Johnson for 200,000 more, he was advised by a small study group in the Pentagon not to escalate the war further. There would be more U.S. casualties, the group said, more taxes needed. And

> The growing disaffection accompanied as it certainly will be, by increased defiance of the draft and growing unrest in the cities because of the belief that we are neglecting domestic problems, runs great risks of provoking a domestic crisis of unprecedented proportions.

Johnson, right after this report, refused Westmoreland's request, announced a limitation on the bombing of North Vietnam, and agreed to go to the peace table in Paris to negotiate with the North Vietnamese.

Even President Nixon, who had said of the growing antiwar activity that "under no circumstance will I be affected whatever by it," confessed in his memoirs, nine years later,

> Although publicly I continued to ignore the raging antiwar controversy,...I knew, however, that after all the protests and the Moratorium [the nationwide protests of October 1969], American public opinion would be seriously divided by any military escalation of the war.

Thoreau, Jefferson, and Tolstoy

The great artists and writers of the world, from Sophocles in the fifth century B.C. to Tolstoy in the modern era, have understood the difference between law and justice. They have known that, just as imagination is necessary to go outside the traditional boundaries to find and to create beauty and to touch human sensibility, so it is necessary to go out-side the rules and regulations of the state to achieve happiness for oneself and others.

Henry David Thoreau, in his famous essay "Civil Disobedience," wrote,

> A common and natural result of an undue respect for law is, that you may see a file of soldiers, colonels, captains, corporals, privates, powder-monkeys, and all, marching in admirable order over hill and dale to the wars, against their wills, ay, against their common sense and consciences, which makes it very steep marching indeed, and produces a palpitation of the heart.

When farmers rebelled in western Massachusetts in 1786 (Shays' Rebellion), Thomas Jefferson was not sympathetic to their action. But he hoped the government would pardon them. He wrote to Abigail Adams:

> The spirit of resistance to government is so valuable on certain occasions that I wish it to be always kept alive. It will often be exercised when wrong, but better so than not to be exercised at all. I like a little rebellion now and then. It is like a storm in the atmosphere.

What kind of person can we admire, can we ask young people of the next generation to emulate—the strict follower of law or the dissident who struggles, sometimes within, sometimes outside, sometimes against the law, but always for justice? What life is best worth living—the life of the proper, obedient, dutiful follower of law and order or the life of the independent thinker, the rebel?

Leo Tolstoy, in his story, "The Death of Ivan Illyich," tells of a proper, successful magistrate, who on his deathbed wonders why he sud-denly feels that his life has been horrible and senseless. "'Maybe I did not live as I ought to have done…But how can that be, when I did everything properly?'…and he remembered all the legality, correctitude and propriety of this life."

2

The Problem is Civil Obedience

By the latter part of May, 1970, feelings about the war in Vietnam had become almost unbearably intense. In Boston, about a hundred of us decided to sit down at the Boston Army Base and block the road used by buses carrying draftees off to military duty. We were not so daft that we thought we were stopping the flow of soldiers to Vietnam; it was a symbolic act, a statement, a piece of guerrilla theater. We were all arrested and charged, in the quaint language of an old statute, with "sauntering and loitering" in such a way as to obstruct traffic. Eight of us refused to plead guilty, insisting on trial by jury, hoping we could persuade the members of the jury that ours was a justified act of civil disobedience. We did not persuade them. We were found guilty, chose jail instead of paying a fine, but the judge, apparently reluctant to have us in jail, gave us forty-eight hours to change our minds, after which we should show up in court to either pay the fine or be jailed. In the meantime, I had been invited to go to Johns Hopkins University to debate with the philosopher Charles Frankel on the issue of civil disobedience. I decided it would be hypocritical for me, an advocate of civil disobedience, to submit dutifully to the court and thereby skip out on an opportunity to speak to hundreds of students about civil disobedience. So, on the day I was supposed to show up in court in Boston I flew to Baltimore and that evening debated with Charles Frankel. Returning to Boston I decided to meet my morning class, but two detectives were waiting for me, and I was hustled before the court and then spent a couple of days in jail. What follows is the transcript of my opening statement in the debate at Johns Hopkins. It was included in a book published by Johns Hopkins Press in 1972, entitled *Violence: The Crisis of American Confidence*.

I start from the supposition that the world is topsy-turvy, that things are all wrong, that the wrong people are in jail and the wrong people are out of jail, that the wrong people are in power and the wrong people are out of power, that the wealth is distributed in this country and the world in such a way as not simply to require small reform but to require a drastic reallocation of wealth. I start from the supposition that we don't have to say too much about this because all we have to do is think about the state of the world today and realize that things are all upside down. Daniel Berrigan is in jail—A Catholic priest, a poet who opposes the war—and J. Edgar Hoover is free, you see. David Dellinger, who has opposed war ever since he was this high and who has used all of his energy and passion against it, is in danger of going to jail. The men who are responsible for the My Lai massacre are not on trial; they are in Washington serving various functions, primary and subordinate, that have to do with the unleashing of massacres, which surprise them when they occur. At Kent State University four students were killed by the National Guard and students were indicted. In every city in this country, when demonstrations take place, the protestors, whether they have demonstrated or not, whatever they have done, are assaulted and clubbed by police, and then they are arrested for assaulting a police officer.

Now, I have been studying very closely what happens every day in the courts in Boston, Massachusetts. You would be astounded—maybe you wouldn't, maybe you have been around, maybe you have lived, maybe you have thought, maybe you have been hit—at how the daily rounds of injustice make their way through this marvelous thing that we call due process. Well, that is my premise.

All you have to do is read the Soledad letters of George Jackson, who was sentenced to one year to life, of which he spent ten years, for a seventy-dollar robbery of a filling station. And then there is the U.S. Senator who is alleged to keep 185,000 dollars a year, or something like that, on the oil depletion allowance. One is theft; the other is legislation. Something is wrong, something is terribly wrong when we ship 10,000 bombs full of nerve gas across the country, and drop them in somebody else's swimming pool so as not to trouble our own. So you lose your perspective after a while. If you don't think, if you just listen to TV and read scholarly things, you actually begin to think that things are not so bad, or that just little things are wrong. But you have to get a little detached, and then come back and look at the world, and you are horrified. So we have to start from that supposition—that things are really topsy-turvy.

And our topic is topsy-turvy: civil disobedience. As soon as you say the topic is civil disobedience, you are saying our *problem* is civil disobedience. That is *not* our problem.... Our problem is civil *obedience.* Our problem is the numbers of people all over the world who have obeyed the dictates of the leaders of their government and have gone to war, and millions have been killed because of this obedience. And our problem is that scene in *All Quiet on the Western Front* where the schoolboys march off dutifully in a line to war. Our problem is that people are obedient all over the world, in the face of poverty and starvation and stupidity, and war and cruelty. Our problem is that people are obedient while the jails are full of petty thieves, and all the while the grand thieves are running the country. That's our problem. We recognize this for Nazi Germany. We know that the problem there was obedience, that the people obeyed Hitler. People obeyed; that was wrong. They should have challenged, and they should have resisted; and if we were only there, we would have showed them. Even in Stalin's Russia we can understand that; people are obedient, all these herdlike people.

But America is different. That is what we've all been brought up on. From the time we are this high—and I still hear it resounding in Mr. Frankel's statement—you tick off, one, two, three, four, five lovely things about America that we don't want disturbed very much.

But if we have learned anything in the past ten years, it is that these lovely things about America were never lovely. We have been expansionist and aggressive and mean to other people from the beginning. And we've been aggressive and mean to people in this country, and we've allocated the wealth of this country in a very unjust way. We've never had justice in the courts for the poor people, for black people, for radicals. Now how can we boast that America is a very special place? It is not that special. It really isn't.

Well, that is our topic, that is our problem: civil obedience. Law is very important. We are talking about obedience to law—law, this marvelous invention of modern times, which we attribute to Western civilization, and which we talk about proudly. The rule of law, oh, how wonderful, all these courses in Western civilization all over the land. Remember those bad old days when people were exploited by feudalism? Everything was terrible in the Middle Ages—but now we have Western civilization, the rule of law. *The rule of law has regularized and maximized the injustice that existed before the rule of law, that is what the rule of law has done.* Let us start looking at the rule of law realistically, not with that metaphysical complacency with which we always examined it before.

When in all the nations of the world the rule of law is the darling of the leaders and the plague of the people, we ought to begin to recognize this. We have to transcend these national boundaries in our thinking. Nixon and Brezhnev have much more in common with one another than we have with Nixon. J. Edgar Hoover has far more in common with the head of the Soviet secret police than he has with us. It's the international dedication to law and order that binds the leaders of all countries in a comradely bond. That's why we are always surprised when they get together—they smile, they shake hands, they smoke cigars, they really like one another no matter what they say. It's like the Republican and Democratic parties, who claim that it's going to make a terrible difference if one or the other wins, yet they are all the same. Basically, it is us against them.

Yossarian was right, remember, in *Catch-22*? He had been accused of giving aid and comfort to the enemy, which nobody should ever be accused of, and Yossarian said to his friend Clevinger: "The enemy is whoever is going to get you killed, whichever side they are on." But that didn't sink in, so he said to Clevinger: "Now you remember that, or one of these days you'll be dead." And remember? Clevinger, after a while, was dead. And we must remember that our enemies are not divided along national lines, that enemies are not just people who speak different languages and occupy different territories. Enemies are people who want to get us killed.

We are asked, "What if everyone disobeyed the law?" But a better question is, "What if everyone obeyed the law?" And the answer to that question is much easier to come by, because we have a lot of empirical evidence about what happens if everyone obeys the law, or if even most people obey the law. What happens is what has happened, what is happening. Why do people revere the law? And we all do; even I have to fight it, for it was put into my bones at an early age when I was a Cub Scout. One reason we revere the law is its ambivalence. In the modern world we deal with phrases and words that have multiple meanings, like "national security." Oh, yes, we must do this for national security! Well, what does that mean? Whose national security? Where? When? Why? We don't bother to answer those questions, or even to ask them.

The law conceals many things. The law is the Bill of Rights. In fact, that is what we think of when we develop our reverence for the law. The law is something that protects us; the law is our right—the law is the Constitution. Bill of Rights Day, essay contests sponsored by the American Legion on our Bill of Rights, that is the law. And that is good.

But there is another part of the law that doesn't get ballyhooed—the legislation that has gone through month after month, year after year, from the beginning of the Republic, which allocates the resources of the country in such a way as to leave some people very rich and other people very poor, and still others scrambling like mad for what little is left. That is the law. If you go to law school you will see this. You can quantify it by counting the big, heavy law books that people carry around with them and see how many law books you count that say "Constitutional Rights" on them and how many that say "Property," "Contracts," "Torts," "Corporation Law." That is what the law is mostly about. The law is the oil depletion allowance—although we don't have Oil Depletion Allowance Day, we don't have essays written on behalf of the oil depletion allowance. So there are parts of the law that are publicized and played up to us—oh, this is the law, the Bill of Rights. And there are other parts of the law that just do their quiet work, and nobody says anything about them.

It started way back. When the Bill of Rights was first passed, remember, in the first administration of Washington? Great thing. Bill of Rights passed! Big ballyhoo. At the same time Hamilton's economic program was passed. Nice, quiet, money to the rich—I'm simplifying it a little, but not too much. Hamilton's economic program started it off. You can draw a straight line from Hamilton's economic program to the oil depletion allowance to the tax write-offs for corporations. All the way through—that is the history. The Bill of Rights publicized; economic legislation unpublicized.

You know the enforcement of different parts of the law is as important as the publicity attached to the different parts of the law. The Bill of Rights, is it enforced? Not very well. You'll find that freedom of speech in constitutional law is a very difficult, ambiguous, troubled concept. Nobody really knows when you can get up and speak and when you can't. Just check all of the Supreme Court decisions. Talk about predictability in a system—you can't predict what will happen to you when you get up on the street corner and speak. See if you can tell the difference between the *Terminiello* case and the *Feiner* case, and see if you can figure out what is going to happen. By the way, there is one part of the law that is not very vague, and that involves the right to distribute leaflets on the street. The Supreme Court has been very clear on that. In decision after decision we are affirmed an absolute right to distribute leaflets on the street. Try it. Just go out on the street and start distributing leaflets. And a policeman comes up to you and he says, "Get out of here." And you say, "Aha! Do you know *Marsh v. Alabama*, 1946?" That is the reality of the Bill of Rights. That's the reality of the Constitution, that part of the law which is portrayed to us as a beautiful and marvelous thing. And seven years after the Bill of Rights was passed, which said that "Congress shall make no law abridging the freedom of speech," Congress made a law abridging the freedom of speech. Remember? The Sedition Act of 1798.

So the Bill of Rights was not enforced. Hamilton's program was enforced, because when the whisky farmers went out and rebelled you remember, in 1794 in Pennsylvania, Hamilton himself got on his horse and went out there to suppress the rebellion to make sure that the revenue tax was enforced. And you can trace the story right down to the present day, what laws are enforced, what laws are not enforced. So you have to be careful when you say, "I'm for the law, I revere the law." What part of the law are you talking about? I'm not against all law. But I think we ought to begin to make very important distinctions about what laws do what things to what people.

And there are other problems with the law. It's a strange thing, we think that law brings order. Law doesn't. How do we know that law does not bring order? Look around us. We live under the rules of law. Notice how much order we have? People say we have to worry about civil disobedience because it will lead to anarchy. Take a look at the present world in which the rule of law obtains. This is the closest to what is called anarchy in the popular mind—confusion, chaos, international banditry. The only order that is really worth anything does not come through the enforcement of law, it comes through the establishment of a society which is just and in which harmonious relationships are established and in which you need a minimum of regulation to create decent sets of arrangements among people. But the order based on law and on the *force* of law is the order of the totalitarian state, and it inevitably leads either to total injustice or to rebellion—eventually, in other words, to very great disorder.

We all grow up with the notion that the law is holy. They asked Daniel Berrigan's mother what she thought of her son's breaking the law. He burned draft records—one of the most violent acts of this century—to protest the war, for which he was sentenced to prison, as criminals should be. They asked his mother who is in her eighties, what she thought of her son's breaking the law. And she looked straight into the interviewer's face, and she said, "It's not God's law." Now we forget that. There is nothing sacred about the law. Think of who makes laws. The law is not made by God, it is made by Strom Thurmond. If you nave any notion about the sanctity and loveliness and reverence for the law, look at the legislators around the country who make the laws. Sit in on the sessions of the state legislatures. Sit in on Congress, for these are the people who make the laws which we are then supposed to revere.

All of this is done with such propriety as to fool us. This is the problem. In the old days, things were confused; you didn't know. Now you know. It is all down there in the books. Now we go through due process. Now the same things happen as happened before, except that we've gone through the right procedures. In Boston a policeman walked into a hospital ward and fired five times at a black man who had snapped a towel at his arm—and killed him. A hearing was held. The judge decided that the policeman was justified because if he didn't do it, he would lose the respect of his fellow officers. Well, that is what is known as due process—that is, the guy didn't get away with it. We went through the proper procedures, and everything was set up. The decorum, the propriety of the law fools us.

The nation then, was founded on disrespect for the law, and then came the Constitution and the notion of stability which Madison and Hamilton liked. But then we found in certain crucial times in our history that the legal framework did not suffice, and in order to end slavery we had to go outside the legal framework, as we had to do at the time of the American Revolution or the Civil War. The union had to go outside the legal framework in order to establish certain rights in the 1930s. And in this time, which may be more critical than the Revolution or the Civil War, the problems are so horrendous as to require us to go outside the legal framework in order to make a statement, to resist, to begin to establish the kind of institutions and relationships which a decent society should have. No, not just tearing things down; building things up. But even if you build things up that you are not supposed to build up—you try to build up a people's park, that's not tearing down a system; you are building something up, but you are doing it illegally—the militia comes in and drives you out. That is the form that civil disobedience is going to take more and more, people trying to build a new society in the midst of the old.

But what about voting and elections? Civil disobedience—we don't need that much of it, we are told, because we can go through the electoral system. And by now we should have learned, but maybe we haven't, for we grew up with the notion that the voting booth is a sacred place, almost like a confessional. You walk into the voting booth and you come out and they snap your picture and then put it in the papers with a beatific smile on your face. You've just voted; that is democracy. But if you even read what the political scientists say—although who can?—about the voting process, you find that the voting process is a sham. Totalitarian states love voting. You get people to the polls and they register their approval. I know there is a difference—they have one party and we have two parties. We have one more party than they have, you see.

What we are trying to do, I assume, is really to get back to the principles and aims and spirit of the Declaration of Independence. This spirit is resistance to illegitimate authority and to forces that deprive people of their life and liberty and right to pursue happiness, and therefore under these conditions, it urges the right to alter or abolish their current form of government—and the stress had been on abolish. But to establish the principles of the Declaration of Independence, we are going to need to go outside the law, to stop obeying the laws that demand killing or that allocate wealth the way it has been done, or that put people in jail for petty technical offenses and keep other people out of jail for enormous crimes. My hope is that this kind of spirit will take place not just in this country but in other countries because they all need it. People in all countries need the spirit of disobedience to the state, which is not a metaphysical thing but a thing of force and wealth. And we need a kind of declaration of interdependence among people in all countries of the world who are striving for the same thing.

3

The Bill
of Rights

I was one of the speakers at historic Faneuil Hall in Boston (though named after an early slave trader, it was the scene of many meetings of anti-slavery groups before the Civil War) in 1991, when the Civil Liberties Union of Massachusetts organized a celebration of the Bicentennial of the Bill of Rights. I wanted to use the opportunity to make clear that whatever freedoms we have in the United States— of speech, of the press, of assembly, and more—do not come simply from the existence on paper of the first ten Amendments to the Constitution, but from the struggles of citizens to bring those Amendments alive in reality. My talk was reprinted in the book *Failure to Quit: Reflections of an Optimistic Historian* (Common Courage Press,1993).

A few years back, a man high up in the CIA named Ray Cline was asked if the CIA, by its surveillance of protest organizations in the United States, was violating the free speech provision of the First Amendment. He smiled and said: "It's only an Amendment."

And when it was disclosed that the FBI was violating citizens' rights repeatedly, a high official of the FBI was asked if anybody in the FBI questioned the legality of what they were doing. He replied: "No, we never gave it a thought."

We clearly cannot expect the Bill of Rights to be defended by government officials. So it will have to be defended by the people.

If you do a bit of research into the origins of the Bill of Rights—and I had to do some because it is a job requirement of the historical profession—you will find that when the new government of the United States adopted the Bill of Rights in 1791, it did not do so with enthusiasm. The Bill of Rights was a political tool to quiet down critics of the Constitution. A Bill of Rights on paper comforts people. You don't have to take it seriously. Like that CIA man, you can smile, and say, they're only Amendments.

Well, in 1791, the first ten Amendments—the Bill of Rights—were added to the Constitution, and the First Amendment says, among other things: "Congress shall make no law...abridging the freedom of speech, or of the press..." Seven years later, in 1798, Congress passed a law abridging the freedom of speech and the press. It was the Sedition Act of 1798, and it provided jail sentences for people who criticized the government. A number of writers and speakers were imprisoned. They appealed to the court. Now we all learned in junior high school about checks and balances and how if Congress passes a law violating the Constitution, we are very lucky to have the Supreme Court to check that and declare the law null and void. (I was always proud to know such a fancy phrase, "null and void.")

Well, the members of the Supreme Court, apparently having skipped junior high school, or perhaps understanding that the phrase "checks and balances" is just intended to satisfy schoolchildren—did not declare the Sedition Act null and void. Not at all. They said it was constitutional. You may ask: by what legal philosophy can Supreme Court justices explain how Congress can pass a law abridging the freedom of speech when the Constitution says Congress shall make no law abridging the freedom of speech? I could tell you how they did that; but it would take a while and cause indigestion. Let us just say that legal training is a wonderful thing, it enables you to explain the unexplainable, defend the indefensible, and rationalize the irrational.

It seems that especially in time of war or near-war (and in 1798 it was such a time), the First Amendment is ignored. You may have noticed that the year 1991 did not start with a celebration of the Bill of Rights, but with a war. And that the government established control over information and the mass media became tongue-tied with patriotic fervor, and the First Amendment was bombed into oblivion. It is a truism of our political culture: if you are at war for freedom and democracy, you can't have freedom and democracy. So, exactly when free speech is most needed, that is, when it is a matter of life and death for the young people about to be sent to the battlefield—exactly at such a moment the government declares it can be suspended.

In 1917, as armies of young men in Europe were slaughtering one another in the first World War, and the United States decided to send its own young men into the butchery, Congress passed the Espionage Act, and the Sedition Act, providing heavy sentences for those criticizing the war. The Supreme Court again put our junior high school lesson to shame: checks and balances? Not in wartime. Not when you need them. The great liberal Oliver Wendell Holmes himself wrote the opinions affirming the constitutionality of the Espionage Act, sending a man named Schenck to jail for distributing a leaflet criticizing the war and the draft. Two thousand people were prosecuted for speaking or writing against the war, including Eugene Debs, the great labor leader and Socialist.

There were ludicrous episodes in all that. A filmmaker who made a movie about the American Revolution was sent to prison for ten years because the movie portrayed the British as the enemy in the American Revolution, and now the British were our allies in the war. The name of the movie was *The Spirit of '76* and the title of the court case against the filmmaker was *U.S. v. Spirit of '76*.

And that case sums up the relationship of the government to the Bill of Rights: *U.S. v. Spirit of '76*. It was the President of the United States, Harry Truman, who instituted loyalty oaths even before Joseph McCarthy waved his lists of Communists in the State Department. It was the Congress of the United States, Democrats as well as Republicans, that set up the House Un-American Activities Committee, and voted contempt citations against people who refused to bow down to that Committee. It was the Supreme Court that affirmed the convictions of the Hollywood Ten for invoking the First Amendment. It was Republicans and Democrats, it was all three branches of government, all of them swearing to uphold the Constitution of the United States, and all of them violating that oath.

A word about the Supreme Court. We now have nine conservative justices, including one conservative woman and one conservative black man. It's called American pluralism. Many people have been depressed over this. Frankly, I tried to get depressed, but didn't succeed. Sure, it's better to have a liberal Supreme Court. But the Supreme Court at its most liberal has never been a dependable protector of people's rights. One year it will say you have a constitutional right to distribute leaflets in front of a supermarket. Another year it will say you can go to jail for that. One year it will say: high school students have a right to wear black armbands to protest a war. Another year it will say: high school students don't have the right to put out their own newspapers without censorship by the school authorities. The Supreme Court, when it was liberal, affirmed that Japanese-Americans could be put in concentration camps because we were at war. The Supreme Court, liberal or conservative, sworn to defend the Constitution, has never been a bulwark against unconstitutional wars.

If it were left to the institutions of government, the Bill of Rights would be left for dead. But someone breathed life into the Bill of Rights. Ordinary people did it, by doing extraordinary things. The editors and speakers who, in spite of the Sedition Act of 1798, continued to criticize the government. The black and white abolitionists who defied the Fugitive Slave Law, defied the Supreme Court's *Dred Scott* decision, who insisted that black people were human beings, not property, and who broke into courtrooms and police stations to rescue them, to prevent their return to slavery.

Women, who were arrested again and again as they spoke out for their right to control their own bodies, or the right to vote. Members of the Industrial Workers of the World, anarchists, radicals, who filled the jails in California and Idaho and Montana until they were finally allowed to speak to working people. Socialists and pacifists and anarchists like Helen Keller and Rose Pastor Stokes, and Kate O'Hare and Emma Goldman, who defied the government and denounced war in 1917 and 1918. The artists and writers and labor organizers and Communists— Dalton Trumbo and Pete Seeger, and W.E.B. Du Bois and Paul Robeson, who challenged the congressional committees of the 1950s, challenged the FBI, at the risk of their freedom and their careers.

In the 1960s, the students of Kent State and Jackson State and hundreds of other campuses, the draft resisters and deserters, the priests and nuns and lay people, all the marchers and demonstrators and trespassers who demanded that the killing in Vietnam stop, the GIs in the Mekong Delta who refused to go out on patrol, the B52 pilots who refused to fly in the Christmas bombing of 1972, the Vietnam veterans who gathered in Washington and threw their Purple Hearts and other medals over a fence in protest against the war.

And after the war, in the '70s and '80s, those courageous few who carried on, the Berrigans and all like them who continued to demonstrate against the war machine, the Seabrook fence climbers, the signers of the Pledge of Resistance against U.S. military action in Central America, the gays and lesbians who marched in the streets for the first time, challenging the country to recognize their humanity, the disabled people who spoke up, after a long silence, demanding their rights. The Indians, supposed to be annihilated and gone from the scene, emerging ghostlike, to occupy a tiny portion of the land that was taken from them, Wounded Knee, South Dakota. Saying: we're not gone, we're here, and we want you to listen to us.

These are the people, men, women, children, of all colors and national origins, who gave life to the Bill of Rights.

The Bill of Rights was expanded after the Civil War, with the passage of the 13th, 14th, and 15th Amendments, to apply to the states, to prevent them from keeping slavery, to require that they give all people, regardless of race or color, the equal protection of the laws. But these amendments were soon ignored, as blacks were kept in semi-slavery in the South, segregated, humiliated, beaten, lynched by mobs, unprotected by either the local police or the national government. For almost a hundred years after the 14th Amendment became law, every President, whether liberal or conservative, Republican or Democrat, violated his oath of office, his pledge to uphold the Constitution, by failing to enforce those Amendments. And the Supreme Court interpreted them so as to make them useless.

And so black people in the South, in the most dangerous towns and cities in the country, decided to give life to the 14th Amendment, at the risk of their own. They boycotted the buses in Montgomery, Alabama, they sat in at segregated lunch counters, they rode the buses as Freedom Riders, they marched through the streets of Albany, Georgia and Birmingham, demonstrated in Alabama, were arrested, set upon by dogs, knocked down by water hoses, beaten bloody by state troopers, and murdered. There were protests in 800 cities in the year 1963. And then the President acted, then Congress acted, then the Supreme Court acted. The 15th Amendment was now being enforced, only a hundred years late.

It is good to have a Bill of Rights, good to have a 14th and 15th Amendment. They are useful as standards. But it is disastrous to depend on them. Words have never been enough. Ask the authors of the Ten Commandments.

For many people there were not even words—not for working people, women, gays and lesbians, disabled people. The Bill of Rights says nothing about the right to work, to a decent wage, to housing, to health care, to the rights of women, to the right of privacy in sexual preference, to the rights of people with disabilities.

But we don't need permission from on high, words approved by the authorities, to tell us that certain truths are self-evident, as the Declaration of Independence put it. That we are all created equal, that we all have rights that cannot be taken from us, the rights to life, liberty, and the pursuit of happiness. And so working people went on strike thousands of times, were beaten and killed on the picket line, until they won an eight-hour day, and a bit of economic security. Women created a national movement that changed the consciousness of millions of people. Gays and lesbians, disabled people, organized, spoke up, declared: we exist, we must be paid attention to. And people began to pay attention.

We should look beyond the Bill of Rights to the UN's Universal Declaration of Human Rights, which says that all people, everywhere in the world, are entitled to work and decent wages, to holidays and vacations, to food and clothing and housing and medical care, to education, to child care and maternal care.

The guarantees of the Bill of Rights have little meaning so long as we have a class society with enormous differences of wealth and income. The rights of free speech and press depend on having the resources to use them. The right to legal counsel is different for rich and poor. The right to be free from unreasonable searches and seizures is dif-

ferent for a family living in a mansion and another living in a housing
project, or out on the street.

In the real world, the fate of human beings is decided every day
not by the courts, but out of court, in the streets, in the workplace, by
whoever has the wealth and power. The redistribution of that wealth
and power is necessary if the Bill of Rights, if any rights, are to have
meaning.

The novelist Aldous Huxley once said: "Liberties are not given;
they are taken." We are not given our liberties by the Bill of Rights, certainly not by the government which either violates or ignores those rights.
We take our rights, as thinking, acting citizens.

And so we should celebrate today, not the words of the Bill of
Rights, certainly not the political leaders who utter those words and violate them every day. We should celebrate, honor, all those people who
risked their jobs, their freedom, sometimes their lives, to affirm the rights
we all have, rights not limited to some document, but rights our common
sense tells us we should all have as human beings. Who should, for example, we celebrate?

I think of Lillian Gobitis, from Lynn, Massachusetts, a seventh-
grade student who, back in 1935, because of her religious convictions,
refused to salute the American flag even when she was suspended from
school.

And Mary Beth Tinker, a thirteen-year-old girl in Des Moines,
Iowa, who in 1965 went to school wearing a black armband in protest
against the killing of people in Vietnam, and defied the school authorities
even when they suspended her.

An unnamed black boy, nine years old, arrested in Albany,
Georgia, in 1961 for marching in a parade against racial segregation after
the police said this was unlawful. He stood in line to be booked by the
police chief, who was startled to see this little boy and asked him: "What's
your name?" And he replied: "Freedom, freedom."

I think of Gordon Hirabayashi, born in Seattle of Japanese parents, who, at the start of the war between Japan and the United States,
refused to obey the curfew directed against all of Japanese ancestry, and
refused to be evacuated to a detention camp, and insisted on his freedom,
despite an executive order by the President and a decision of the Supreme
Court.

Demetrio Rodriguez of San Antonio, who in 1968 spoke up and said his child, living in a poor county, had a right to a good education equal to that of a child living in a rich county.

All those alternative newspapers and alternative radio stations and struggling organizations that have tried to give meaning to free speech by giving information that the mass media will not give, revealing information that the government wants kept secret.

All those whistleblowers, who risked their jobs, risked prison, defying their employers, whether the government or corporations, to tell the truth about nuclear weapons, or chemical poisoning.

Randy Kehler and Betsy Corner, who have refused to pay taxes to support the war machine, and all their neighbors who, when the government decided to seize and auction their house, refused to bid, and so they are still defending their right.

The 550 people who occupied the JFK Federal Building in Boston in protest when President Reagan declared a blockade of Nicaragua. I was in that group—I don't mind getting arrested when I have company—and the official charge against us used the language of the old trespass law: "failure to quit the premises." On the letter I got dropping the case (because there were too many of us to deal with), they shortened that charge to "failure to quit."

I think that sums up what it is that has kept the Bill of Rights alive. Not the President or Congress, or the Supreme Court, or the wealthy media. But all those people who have refused to quit, who have insisted on their rights and the rights of others, the rights of all human beings everywhere, whether Americans or Haitians or Chinese or Russians or Iraqis or Israelis or Palestinians, to equality, to life, liberty, and the pursuit of happiness. That is the spirit of the Bill of Rights, and beyond that, the spirit of the Declaration of Independence, yes, the spirit of '76: refusal to quit.

4

Testifying at the Ellsberg Trial

In the summer of 1971, the *New York Times* created a sensation by beginning the publication of excerpts from a 7,000-page top-secret history of the Vietnam War, compiled for the Department of Defense by the Rand corporation. The *Times* had received the document, which came to be known as the Pentagon Papers, from one of the people who worked on it, Daniel Ellsberg. Ellsberg was a former Harvard scholar who had held a number of important government posts, and also served as a Marine in Vietnam. He and Anthony Russo, a former colleague at the Rand Corporation, both of whom had turned against the war, decided to secretly photocopy the Pentagon Papers and release them to the public, to expose the lies of the U.S. government about the war. They were eventually arrested and put on trial in Los Angeles on charges of violating the Espionage Act, which made it a crime to make public information that might do injury to the national defense. The multiple indictments added up to over a hundred years in prison for Ellsberg, forty years for Russo. Ellsberg and I had become friends, and he had given me some of the Papers to read before they became public. I went to Los

420

Angeles to testify in his trial, and wrote the following story for an alternative newspaper in Boston called *The Real Paper* (April 11, 1973). While the case was before the jury, the Watergate affair exploded into national attention. It was discovered that the Nixon administration had planned a break-in at the office of Daniel Ellsberg's psychiatrist, to find information that might discredit him, and the judge in the Pentagon Papers case then declared a mistrial.

I have just come back from testifying in the trial of Anthony Russo and Daniel Ellsberg in Los Angeles. It is a trial whose historic importance has been smothered under a double weight—the procedures of the judicial system, and the gleeful stomping of liberals and radicals who find the defendants an amusing target. It is not the first time in history that right-wing executioners and left-wing dilettantes combined in an unconscious conspiracy to knock down someone who did not fit either of their scrupulous standards.

We live in an age where issues are too gigantic to be hidden away, but they can be covered up. And, conveniently, it is also an age whose gross national product of trivia is so enormous that a little skillful shoveling can do the job. The shovelers from the left and those from the right can remain invisible to one another, and even snarl at each other from time to time, while burying the same target.

It works like this in the Pentagon Papers case, as I saw it in Los Angeles last week. The trial procedures—what we fondly call due process—successfully enshroud, in tedious routine and properly executed interruptions ("I object" and "objection overruled" and "let the clerk have Exhibit A-3" and "would the stenographer please repeat the last four sentences" and "let us confer at the side-bench" and "that is not relevant to the case") the matters of life and death, the cries and whispers of war and treachery, that led Ellsberg and Russo to spend a year of surreptitious evenings Xeroxing 7000 pages of secret government documents.

And, from the other side (I exempt a huge number of sympathizers—radical, liberal, and uncategorizable folk of heart) we have the journalistic taunters and chucklers and revolutionary purists who find (since today's reality is a super-supermarket in which one can find anything) something salable for good money or good political grades. What do they find? A post million-dollar defense, easing the late-night strategy meetings with morning swims in Olympic pools and weekends at Malibu Beach. A defendant (Dan Ellsberg) vulnerable to the fatuous observations of pretentious portraitists who manage to agree on three devastating facts: he and his wife have money; he was an enthusiastic Marine, Harvard Fellow, Defense Department analyst, and Rand Corporation whiz-kid; and he is, above all, *intense.*

As for Tony Russo, he gets less attention, because it would take too much imagination to find something to poke at in this ex-student of aeronautical engineering and physics, son of an Italian man and a Virginia woman, who worked with a Rand research team in Vietnam, and now doodles poems in the courtroom during the many gaps in intelligibility. Tony wrote one for me while I was testifying, and gave it to me, with his great broad smile, when I came off the stand. He is always thinking beyond that courtroom.

Fly face on.
Pan American wounds,
Wounded heart,
Wounded Knee,
Right the Arm of Lady,
Liberty.

There are two kinds of witnesses in the case, from a legal standpoint. There are the "fact" witnesses, who testify, if they are government witnesses, that the defendants stole the documents, and try to explain why it really was a theft even though Ellsberg worked for Rand, was entitled to have the documents, and returned them to the office each morning after his Xerox operation at night. And there are the "expert" witnesses, who testify for the government that they have read the 18 volumes of the Pentagon Papers picked out for indictment purposes (less than half of the total reproduced by Ellsberg and Russo) and that, if given to the public in 1969 (the year of the Xeroxing), the Papers would have done injury to the national defense or been of advantage to a foreign power. And then there are the "fact" and "expert" witnesses for the defense, who say the opposite.

Called in as an "expert," I was "the first radical witness," the *New York Times* reporter wrote on the first day of my testimony. I "made a good impression on the jury," he said, there would be more radical witnesses.

There was a wrangle in the defense team, he wrote, between Ellsberg and Russo, over whether there should be "radical" witnesses. The reporter was about as far off on this as when he referred to me as "the six foot six educator, towering over the courtroom." That is, about four inches off.

In fact, both Ellsberg and Russo, and just about everybody on the defense team, agreed that their first witnesses (Schlesinger, Sorenson, Bundy, Galbraith) may have performed a useful function in saying that what they read of the Pentagon Papers clearly did not relate to national defense, and could not be injurious to the United States. But they also agreed that these witnesses did not place before the jury and the public those clear and burning facts about this vicious war of white Westerners against Asian peasants, which alone could make the Ellsberg-Russo behavior morally understandable.

And while they want legal acquittal, there is something more important to the defendants: the American public should learn from those cold official memoranda what really went on inside the closed doors and closed minds of the plotters of mass murder in Washington and Saigon. And so, they agreed that the White House witnesses would have to be followed by people who had worked against the war and could speak a bit of their thoughts and feelings to the jury; people like Noam Chomsky, Tom Hayden, Ernest Gruening, Wayne Morse, Don Luce, Richard Falk, and the defendants themselves. The only disagreement was on the number of such witnesses, and on exactly which of the radical and near-radical antiwar people should be invited. They agreed to start with me.

On the stand, I had before me five of the 18 volumes cited in the indictment. "Will you tell the court what is in those volumes?" said Leonard Weinglass, one of the five defense-team lawyers. The jury was a few feet away from me: ten of the twelve are women, of whom at least three are black and one an emigrant from Australia. One of the two men is a black local official of an auto union; another is a wounded Marine veteran of Vietnam. The prosecutor sits and takes notes. The judge, Matthew Byrne, is youngish, smooth, a consummate dispenser of "fair" decisions in a trial whose very existence is a monstrosity of injustice: Ellsberg and Russo face 130 years and 40 years for revealing to the American people what the government was doing behind their backs. At the defense table, lawyers and defendants sit a little forward in their seats, like rooters in the bleachers trying to push a line drive into the stands.

I turn to the jury and start telling what is in those five volumes, quoting occasionally. How the Vietnamese movement rose in World War II, after 80 years of French colonial rule in which the peasants starved eight months out of the year. How Ho Chi Minh came to lead this movement, and everyone (even French and Americans) said he was an intelligent, dedicated, charming, gentle man, loved by the people of Vietnam. And how in spite of the noble words of Roosevelt and Churchill in the Atlantic Charter, promising freedom to colonial peoples after Hitler was defeated, the United States, when World War II was won, helped the French back into control in Vietnam. And what a blow this was to the Vietnamese, who on September 2, 1945 had adopted a Declaration of Independence which said "All men are created equal, etc., etc."

And how Ho Chi Minh wrote letter after letter to the White House, asking that the pledges be kept, that the French be kept out of Indochina, that the Vietnamese be allowed to rule themselves. And how not one of these letters—14 communications in all—was answered by the United States. I read to the jury from one of those letters, in which Ho wrote Truman and said: there is drought and famine, and the French have taken away the rice, and two million Vietnamese have died, and won't the American people help? No reply.

Then came the war, from 1946 to 1954, the French against the Viet Minh, which was a coalition of Vietnamese for independence, led by Ho Chi Minh and other communists. And the United States, by the end of that war, was supplying most of the guns and money for the French. And when the French were defeated, and had to sign a peace in Geneva, promising a united Vietnam in two years based on elections, the United States stepped in, propping up as head of state in Saigon Mr. Ngo Dinh Diem (the volumes refer to his "mandarin style") who refused to hold those elections.

The early volumes of the Pentagon Papers say why the United States intervened in Vietnam, why we had eased the French back in, why we opposed self-determination and the Atlantic Charter, why we replaced the French in 1954 with ourselves, through our man Diem, fresh from his stay in New Jersey. They say why Indochina was so important to us. There it is, again and again, in the official memoranda. Rubber, tin, oil, rice. We need that. Japan needs that, and we don't want Japan to have to turn to a Communist country instead of to us. Oh yes, and there is the matter of security. If Indochina falls, then the other dominoes will fall: Malaya, Indonesia, the Philippines, Japan. And...

I was able to point out to the jury that those in the higher circles of government never did explain, even to one another, how one country going Communist would lead to another country going Communist, and how any country going Communist would affect the national defense of the United States. And that the idea of containment, which started presumably, as preventing Russian aggression against her neighbors, ended as justifying American aggression against any country in the world that decided to be Communist.

Finally, the coup against the Diem regime, by his own generals, with the connivance of the United States. After nine years of collaboration, Diem counted on the U.S. for support. But he was not keeping order. He was attacking the pagodas, putting people in jail. And monks were burning themselves to death in downtown Saigon in protest against the cruelty of the regime. And the Vietcong were popular and winning.

The CIA met with the Saigon generals. The White House watched coolly, with Kennedy saying: let's not do anything openly, but covert stuff is okay. And Henry Cabot Lodge, our new Ambassador, enthusiastic for the coup, and in touch with the plotters. Lodge, who, between contacts with the plotters, accepted an invitation to spend a holiday weekend with Diem, a week before the attack on the palace and the execution of Diem and his brother Nhu. Lodge, who later told the *New York Times*: "We had nothing whatsoever to do with it."

So, I was able to give, without interruption, a brief history of the first 20 years of the war, in a one-hour presentation to the jury on Friday afternoon, and another hour the following Monday morning. This is very rare in a political case, but it would have been hard, legally, to stop this, since I was just saying—in my own words, and sometimes in the words of the documents—what was in those papers that were supposed to be the materials of a terrible crime.

"Are you finished?" Len Weinglass asked.

"Yes." Now the big question.

"Having read those volumes, would you say that, if made known to the public in 1969, they would have injured the national defense?"

"No."

"And what is the basis of your opinion?"

THE ZINN READER

Four points. One, there is no military information in these volumes; what we have here is political history, period. Two, if there were military information, we would have to distinguish: there are military activities for the defense of the country; there are others which are acts of intervention in the affairs of other countries, having nothing to do with defending ours, and such was the war in Vietnam.

Point three. A country's national defense rests partly on military strength, but mostly on the health of its society, the confidence of the people in the government, the sense of community, the belief that the principles of the nation are being fulfilled. All this adds up to the morale of the people, crucial in national defense. History has shown us nations whose main strength in self-defense was their morale, not their weapons. What was the morale of the American people in 1969? Very poor. Thirty thousand dead. Our soldiers destroying peasant villages, to our shame. Anti-war feeling growing. A hundred billion dollars spent for war, and the cities so neglected that blacks rose all over in 1967 and 1968. (I was going too far now, and the judge stopped me: "Mr. Weinglass, ask the witness a question.")

Point four. National defense means defense of the nation, of all the people, not defense of special interests. Secrets disclosed in 1969 might hurt special interests, might embarrass politicians, might hurt the profits of corporations wanting tin, rubber, oil in far-off places. But this is not the same as hurting the nation, which is the people.

My testimony was over. The prosecutor decided not to cross-examine me on the documents. He asked how I came to know Dan Ellsberg and Tony Russo and flashed a police photo of Ellsberg and me in a demonstration at the federal building in Boston, May 6, 1971. And then: "No more questions."

There will be more said about the war from the witness stand in the weeks to come. The mass media will minimize the trial of Anthony Russo and Daniel Ellsberg. And some people will deride it. But these men did a remarkable thing. And they did it, as we all do what we feel we must, amidst all the old and silly furniture of this world. And that's all right, as a beginning.

5

Amazing Grace: The Movement Wins in Camden

Again and again, determined anti-war activists, often priests and nuns joined by lay people, invaded draft boards and destroyed draft records as symbolic acts of protest against the Vietnam War. Philip and Daniel Berrigan, Catholic priests, were probably the most famous of these protesters, who became known by the number of participants; the Baltimore Four, the Catonsville Nine, the Milwaukee 14, and so on. One of the last of these trials was that of the Camden 28. I had testified in a number of these trials, and had just come from testifying in the Pentagon Papers case. Now one of the Camden defendants, a working-class young woman from Philadelphia named Kathleen (Cookie) Ridolfi, called on me to be a witness. It turned out to be a different experience from my other courtroom appearances, and I wrote about it for *Liberation* magazine, in its July-August 1973 issue.

There is much to learn from the trial of the Camden draft-board raiders which ended last week (May 20) with total acquittal and a happy courtroom standing and singing "Amazing Grace."

First, that it pays to struggle, that we must not listen to the wailers who point to the power of the Establishment, the impotence of the Movement, and how little has basically changed. The Camden "28" did in August, 1971, essentially what the Baltimore Four had done in 1967—they entered a draft board illegally to destroy or damage draft records, as a protest against the forced recruiting of young men to kill peasants in Indochina. But out of that first action, Phil Berrigan got six years in jail. In many trials of other draft board raiders in between, the sentences kept going down. And finally, with Camden, acquittal on all counts.

What can that clear progression toward exoneration be attributed to, except that the antiwar movement—and of course, events themselves—created an ever-stronger climate of opposition to the war which affected judges, juries, and public, and made possible the bold defiance of government that the Camden jury showed? True, the jurors had good legal ground to stand on for their verdict—an FBI informer, infiltrating the group, had made the raid possible by supplying equipment and expertise that the group lacked, and the judge told the jury that it could acquit if the government, in helping set up the raid, had gone to "intolerable" lengths that were "offensive to the basic standards of decency and shocking to the universal sense of justice."

But the jury would not have searched for that legal ground if it did not believe the defendants were right in opposing the war. One of the jurors, a fifty-three-year-old black taxi driver from Atlantic City named Samuel Braithwaite, who had spent 11 years in the Army, left a letter for the defendants when the verdict was in and the jury broke up to go home. His letter began:

> To you, the clerical physicians with your God-given talents, I say, well done. Well done for trying to heal the sick irresponsible men, men who were chosen by the people to govern and lead them. These men, who failed the people, by raining death and destruction on a hapless country, a country who was trying to govern their own country and lives, sans our interference.... You went out to do your part while your brothers remained in their ivory towers watching, waiting and criticizing your actions.... The two greatest commandments, to love God and to love your neighbor was shown

by you and your community. Keep up the good work and hopefully some day in the near future, peace and harmony may reign to people of all nations.

Braithwaite was a remarkable juror. He left a list of questions directed to "all men of the clergy," which included: "Didn't God make the Vietnamese? Was God prejudiced and only made American people?" Throughout the trial, Braithwaite did something the defendants urged jurors to do when the trial started, to take advantage of a right that juries have but never exercise: to question witnesses. He would send up questions to the judge for witnesses. The day I was in Camden to testify, Phil Berrigan was on the stand, and when he finished, Braithwaite sent up several questions. One of them was: "If, when a citizen violates the law, he is punished by the government, who does the punishing when the government violates the law?"

Braithwaite's bold sympathy for the Camden defendants was a product of this own past as a black man in America, of the black struggle of these 15 years (he often referred to Martin Luther King), and probably of the antiwar movement. But he, as well as other antiwar jurors, might never have gotten onto the jury if not for the fact that the Camden defendants, aided by a group of "movement social scientists," worked enormously hard at the start of the trial to figure out which jurors would be most likely to support them, and to handle the jury selection accordingly.

That worked, and it helps to answer a question often pondered by radicals in the political trial: isn't the whole trial procedure stacked against the defendants, even when it is "fair," and aren't we playing the system's game when we work with its rules, trying to use them instead of ignoring them, defying them, overthrowing them? The jury selection process—it's designed to produce middle-American people who won't like blacks, radicals, oddballs. The judge—he's a tool of the system; no point trying to be nice, or persuasive with him, only to fight him. The witnesses for the other side—especially the informer—they are enemies.

The experience of the Camden trial suggests that we must grasp the protuberances of the system as handles, knowing that they may fall off in our hands, but also knowing we need every advantage we can get hold of. We must, guerilla-fashion, pick up the implements of the other side and use them without naivete, but also without embarrassment.

The Camden experience suggests something else: that while people do tend to behave according to their class background and social role, it would be simplistic (we might call it a mechanical approach to the materialistic interpretation of history) to ignore the fact that individuals diverge from their social role under certain circumstances. And it is the job of conscious radicals to try to create the conditions under which that can happen, without the expectation that it will happen.

In Camden, people behaved in unanticipated ways. The jurors, first of all. But also the judge, a Nixon-appointed federal judge who had no reputation as a liberal, but who conducted the trial without the monarchical trappings of most courtrooms. He did not require people to stand when he came and left; the procedure was informal and relaxed; the court officers did not behave like cops; the judge was available to defendants in his chambers to talk over matters with him in a pleasant way. This came I think, out of the defendants' attitude toward him. They were strong, even fierce, in defending their rights in court, in fighting for the admission of evidence and witnesses, but they acted as if they expected the judge to be a human being. They didn't write him off from the start, and he came through.

Then there was the informer, Robert Hardy, who had been part of the group that planned the raid, then went to the FBI to tell them about it, and returned to take a leading part in the action. When the Camden people entered the draft board in the federal building (upstairs from where their trial was to be held), the FBI was waiting for them a hundred strong. But, in the ensuing weeks, Hardy did a turn-about. The FBI had deceived him, he said. They promised him his information would only be used to stop the defendants before they could carry out the raid, that the antiwar people were not really to be considered criminals, that they would be charged with, at most, a conspiracy count. Instead, they were allowed to carry the action through and were charged on seven counts, adding up to possible sentences of forty years in jail. Hardy was indignant and became a witness for the defense and a strong factor in their acquittal.

This might not have happened if the defendants had given up on Hardy immediately after he was revealed as an informer. He had once been their friend, and although they were angry, at least some of them maintained human relations with him. When in the midst of all this, his child was killed in an accident, they came to the wake. Human contact was maintained.

There were witnesses, called by the defense, who turned surprisingly from their traditional roles. One was Major Clement St. Martin, who was commander of the state induction center in Newark, New Jersey from 1968 to 1971. St. Martin described in detail how the draft system discriminated systematically against the poor, the black and the uneducated and how it regularly gave medical exemptions to the sons of the wealthy. He said he thought all draft files should be destroyed. He had tried, as commander, to speak out against some the draft's inequities, and one high official of the Selective Service System had told him: "Mind your business, we have 20 million animals to choose from." Under cross-examination, St. Martin was asked if he thought private citizens had the right to break into buildings to destroy draft files. He replied: "Probably today, if they plan another raid, I might join them."

What made all this possible, I think—this extraordinarily bold, imaginative defense, this creation of an atmosphere which brought out the best in the judge, the jury and the witnesses—was one fact I have omitted in the story so far, and which I think is the most important fact about the Camden trial: the seventeen defendants (of the original twenty-eight, a number of defendants' trials were severed) had decided to act as their own attorneys, to defend themselves. The Camden experience is the most powerful argument yet for the idea of self-defense in court. They worked harder to prepare their case than even the most dedicated movement lawyers. During the proceedings they would ask the judge to call a halt while they gathered in a football huddle to make collective decisions. In the courtroom they were a force, outnumbering, out-thinking, out-maneuvering the prosecution, letting the judge know they could not be tampered with, that while they were well mannered, there was the ever-present possibility of rebellion. Three young movement lawyers stood by as consultants, and wisely deferred to the defendants' wishes.

They called witnesses that are not usually called to the stand and fought to get the testimony allowed. One of these was a Vietnamese woman, Tran Tuyet, who described her life in South Vietnam and told a hushed courtroom: "In the name of liberty, you have destroyed our country." Mothers and fathers of the defendants took the stand and made emotional pleas for actions of conscience against the war taken by their sons and daughters. Phil Berrigan came and spoke about how he had come to his views about war and resistance. And the defendants themselves took the stand, telling about their lives, their thoughts, their anguish as they contemplated the bombs falling on the villages of Indochina while they and other Americans did nothing out of line. And how, one day, they decided to do something extraordinary, to awaken their neighbors to an emergency, and to awaken themselves.

It was a remarkable trial. It was only a moment in the long struggle. But the Camden defendants made the most of their moment—and thereby suggested to us how we might make the most of ours.

6

Punishment

When I wrote the following piece, for a book entitled *Justice in Everyday Life* (Morrow, 1974), I had spent just enough time in jail (it takes only twenty-four hours) to understand why Karl Menninger, a psychiatrist who worked for years with prisoners, spoke of "the crime of punishment." By this time I knew some prisoners, and had spent time observing conditions at Walpole State Prison in Massachusetts and at the Charles Street jail in Boston. I remembered what John Boone, a black prison guard in Atlanta (later to have his tenure as Commissioner of Corrections in Massachusetts cut short because he was too enlightened for the politicians of the state) told me. He said that while a small percentage of prisoners were dangerous to society, most could be given freedom—with help—and society would be better off. Keeping people in prison was cruel to the inmates and dangerous for the rest of us. Today, the United States, with one and a half million people in prison, has the highest rate of incarceration in the world. The state of California spends more money for prisons than for higher education. The situation cries out for change. I think you can hear those cries in what follows.

Excessive bail shall not be required, nor excessive fines imposed, nor cruel
and unusual punishments inflicted.
—EIGHTH AMENDMENT TO THE CONSTITUTION

If, as Dostoevski said, "The degree of civilization in a society can
be judged by entering its prisons," then it seems reasonable to say that the
degree of justice in a society can be judged the same way. And if prisons
are *in themselves*, monstrously inhuman and cruel (even if not unusual),
then as long as we have prisons, we live in an unjust society.

It is the courts that send people into prison, and it may be expecting too much that the courts should stop this practice, but long ago, the
Supreme Court made a statement which, if carefully observed today,
would end the practice of imprisonment. In 1879, in the case of
Wilkerson v. Utah, the Court, interpreting the Eighth Amendment to the
Constitution, said it was "safe to affirm that punishment of torture...and
all others in the same line of unnecessary cruelty, are forbidden by that
Amendment." All we need then, is general recognition that to imprison a
person inside a cage, to deprive that person of human companionship, of
mother and father and wife and children and friends, to treat that person
as a subordinate creature, to subject that person to daily humiliation and
reminders of his or her own powerlessness in the face of authority, to put
that person's daily wants in the hands of others who have total control
over his life, is indeed *torture*, and thus falls within the decision of the
Supreme Court a hundred years ago.

We need then to ask one more question: to decide if a practice is
torture, shall we ask the torturers or shall we ask the tortured? Are not certain conditions, by their nature, definable only by the people who suffer
them? Who but a black person can decide of he is being humiliated? Who
but a woman can decide if she has been sexually abused? And so, we will
have to listen to the prisoners to decide if what they are living with is torture, and if therefore, not just because the Supreme Court once said it,
but because human compassion demands it, the practice of imprisoning
people to punish them for past actions must end.

"We have been kidnapped from reality and subjected to life in a
vacuum," a prisoner in Massachusetts wrote.

"If we are what we are being treated as, then we should be shot,"
wrote another.

Timothy Currier was sent to Deer Island House of Correction September 30, 1970, escaped October 16, and turned himself in November 2. He wrote a statement:

"OK, I'm an escaped prisoner from Deer Island and I'm a felon, and to some, that's all there is to it. Yet that's far from just it. I'm a man, a human being with feelings, wants, needs, and desires as all of us have. Prison life, especially prison life at Deer Island, is a useless and fruitless one. Wasted are long, long hours of my life, wasted are time, money, and effort—all of which are expended to solely maintain the prison and the prisoner. I don't want to be maintained or supported, and I don't want someone to pay my way. I do, however need support. I need the opportunity to get myself together, to concentrate on changing some of my attitudes, hang-ups and such, and I try, I try daily, seeing change as I go on. But I don't need to waste years solely trying to cope with the hassles, frustrations, and restrictions that are so abundant in our prisons. That is 95 percent of an existence in prison—trying to cope with incarceration. It leaves little room for constructive and meaningful things that help me along toward rehabilitation.

"I left prison because I couldn't stand the nothingness—the loneliness each and every day, every hour, every minute. I'm returning because there is nothing to be accomplished 'on the run.' I'm returning now because eventually I would anyway and I choose now. The 'criminal justice' machine is determined that I pay. It cares little of what seems most important to me, and this is my rehabilitation—my ability to reenter society and lead an in-the-bounds productive existence. I feel the people want this. They want their prisons, their correctional institutions to be corrective; they want prisoners to be released ready, willing, and able to settle down into an acceptable lifestyle. They want this, yet sometimes fail to see what that takes, and what it does not take. Simply, some things are inducive to change, positive change, and others are not. What causes change in me is similar to, if not the exact same things, that cause change in everyone. Allowing an existence that has me staring out of a window for eight hours and laying in my cell for the other sixteen, causes me to be stagnant, depressed, and bitter.

"Right now I'd like to plead with the people, to try and cast aside any misconceptions they have about the convict, the ex-convict, the prisons. Try to understand that some of your impressions may be wrong. I would, I am, pleading with you to become aware, to become involved with prisons, with their administration, with their inmates, and with ex-inmates. I pray you let yourselves be heard. You have a lot to say about how our prisons are to be run. Your city and state government represents you. If you are apathetic, unaware, they are apathetic and unaware.

"It's not easy doing this, but I feel it's best. As I was out two weeks I hurt no one, stole nothing, and in answer to District Attorney of Middlesex County, Mr. Droney's statement that I and the majority of men in prison are animals—that was a very irrational statement—I question his sanity. I wonder how it is possible for a man in his social position to harbor feelings such as those about human beings. As is the case so often, he does not know the man, just a record that says very little; and it is easy to classify and categorize, but Mr. Droney could never ever justify.

"We are not animals, we are human beings subjected to a great deal of degradation that makes our attempts to 'get it together' sometimes impossible. We need your help. In a sense I'm asking you to set us free. Help us change such despicable places as Charles St. Jail and Deer Island. Listen if you will, though distasteful at times, to the convict, to the ex-convict. Who knows more about his needs than himself? Please listen..."

Who are the people who end up in prison in Massachusetts? Timothy Currier talks above about "such despicable places" as Charles Street Jail and Deer Island. In Charles Street, 60 percent of the inmates are black, in Deer Island, 68 percent. In Boston, 16 percent of the city is black.

But blackness is only part of the story. The poor are the ones who inhabit the jails. Is it because they commit the most crimes? They are the ones who most often *get caught* committing crimes, because they have the least resources for getting away with their crimes, for covering up their deeds, the least resources for paying fines, arranging bail, hiring first-class counsel, making the right contacts.

Consider these statistics about crimes of the rich and crimes of the poor, given by the President's Crime Commission and a 1969 study done in California:

Only 14 percent of the prison population consists of people who have committed "white collar crimes" (embezzling, fraud, tax fraud, forgery). Yet their thievery adds up to $1.7 billion in one recent year, while the crimes of the poor for the same year (robbery, burglary, auto theft, etc.) added up to $608 million, less than half.

In 1969, there were 502 convictions for tax fraud, each case averaging $190,000. Burglaries that year averaged $321 and car thefts averaged $992. But of the 502 businessmen and clerks convicted of fraud, only 20 percent ended up in jail, with sentences averaging seven months. For burglary and auto theft, 60 percent of those convicted ended up in prison, with sentences averaging eighteen months for auto theft, thirty-three months for burglary.

In the Boston area, people from poor neighborhoods are far more likely to go to jail. People with money enough to go to college don't end up in jail as often. In 1969, of prisoners sent to Walpole, Concord, Framingham, and Bridgewater, only 1 percent were college graduates; 73 percent had received an education from the sixth to the eleventh grade.

Anthony Marino writes about being a prisoner at Deer Island, which he calls "Devil's Island."

"I was sent here two months ago by Roxbury District Court to serve a two-year sentence for possession of drugs and drug-related thefts. A rehabilitation program person was in court in my behalf but the Judge listened to his pleas with deaf ears and told me I would get all the rehabilitation I needed here.

"Well I can't buy this kind of so-called rehabilitation.

"We get up about 7:30 A.M. and are herded to eat a cold breakfast and a cup of lukewarm coffee. Then we proceed to various shops—paint shop, machine shop, electrical shop, cutting room, and construction. These are nothing but handouts where the cons stay during the day. There is no machinery of any kind in these shops, no work or job training unless you happen to be one of the select inmates who work in the officers' mess, administration building, or work release. These inmates are predominately white and conformed to the ideas of the administrators in return for good food (officers' chow), cigarettes, and other special favors the guards give to 'good' cons.

"When I get to my shop along with twenty-seven cons, I can either watch cartoons or various TV quiz shows on the boob tube, play cards, or just bounce off the walls, which I usually do anyway. I cannot leave the shop until lunchtime, when the special today is spaghetti balls and meatballs. Yeah! That's right, spaghetti balls the size of a grapefruit

which you can only get at Deer Island because the spaghetti is so starchy
it sticks in big lump balls. It really is a task sitting down and trying to
make a meal of it.

"Then you have to fight for a spoon because of the spoon shortage. I have seen an inmate eat with his hands because he didn't want to
hassle waiting for another inmate to finish with his spoon, then having to
wash it, only to be rushed out of the chow hall because it was time to go
back to his cell. The other night I saw a kid eat jello out of his hands.

"After lunch it is back to the shop for a repeat of the morning's
activities. At 3:30 everyone goes back to the chow hall for the final meal
which might be cold soup; but by the time your turn comes up on the
line, they are out of metal bowls. So you either take your soup in a small
metal cup or on a flat metal tray.

"After supper you go back to your cell, which is approximately
five by eight feet with a tiny cold-water sink, a commode, and an old
army bed and if you're lucky a wooden chair or table. Then you get to
amuse yourself somehow because you are in that cell until 7:30 next
morning (fourteen hours) unless you happen to sleep in the dormitory.
About 30 percent of the population is allowed to sleep in the dormitory,
but the first openings go to the 'good' cons who are also the ones with the
good jobs.

"There is hardly any rehabilitation here unless you like to play
horseshoes.

"The administration encourages friction among the cons. Many
cons use dope (snuck in through visits or corrupt screws). There are frequent fights between cons over dope. Recently a con got stabbed and
another bashed in the head with a chair leg, all of this relating to a dope
incident. The administration does not care if the cons kill each other—it
makes it easier for them to run the joint. Cons should channel their hostilities in the right direction and stop this foolishness.

"Relations between black and white cons are uptight. White
racist guards favor white cons and encourage racist attitudes in white
cons. For instance, there is a lot of noise going on in my block on a certain night. A white guard comes by my cell and says, 'They're noisy bastards, aren't they?' nodding his head toward the cell next to me, which is
occupied by a black brother. I'm supposed to say, 'Yeah. They sure are and
they stink too.' etc., by this making friends with the screw. Now when he

sees me he might acknowledge my existence and say hi or put in a good word to the deputy for me so that I might get a good job, etc. But instead, I give him a look like he just crawled out of the nearest pigsty and he will probably call me a punk nigger lover to the other screws and racist white cons. I have heard racist conversations among the screws and racist cons about blacks and Puerto Ricans often. The administration is racist and there are three black guards representing a black inmate population of over 50 percent. These black guards have little or no voice in the administration and have it hard bidding for good jobs in the institution...

"I was locked up in 1969 (a previous commitment) for supposedly laughing at an officer. My sentence was 'five days on the boards.' The boards means that you are put in a cell on a segregated tier, with no clothes, no books, no smokes, no lights. You get a filthy mattress and an equally filthy blanket (no sheets, and a pillow is absurd). You are allowed one meal a day, and water. (You used to sleep on a board, that is where the name originated.) If this does not 'straighten you out,' you can be sent to Bridgewater. All cons fear Bridgewater, especially DSU—Departmental Segregation Unit, MCI Bridgewater..."

A woman whose husband was in prison wrote about the ordeal of visiting him. She called it "The Crime of Loving." Her name is Linda Camisa:

"I write this in order to give you a brief look at the agony caused by loving a man in prison. It is hard to face the reality that the man you love is for some reason put in prison. Even harder is the visit, because of the rules imposed by the prison system itself. Because then you are also treated as a prisoner when the only crime you have committed is loving this man. And that, to me, is no crime.

"The major problem is the guards. They are the ones who dictate the do's and don'ts. I know that on many occasions visiting my husband at Norfolk, I've been told by guards not to hold his hand, not to put my arms around him, not to even sit in certain parts of the visiting room because actually they didn't want to have to turn their heads to keep their eye on you. You are watched constantly.

"You are always aware of their eyes checking you out; now and then a wise one will even proposition you.

"You also have problems such as, if you don't smile in a certain manner, or if you comment on something, then you may even wait an hour before you get to see your husband. Does anyone realize what it's like sitting in a crowded (or empty) visiting room for sixty minutes, waiting? Well, I do, and when it happened to me I also had my two children with me, ages four and five. Let me say that after riding one hour up there on a hot summer afternoon, sitting for another hour in a crowded hot visiting room with my children was very nerve-racking and upsetting to the children and me. Finally, by the time I saw my husband, I felt so uptight I wasn't much good for his morale...

"Plus there is a hassle of getting there. I'm lucky enough to have access to a car; some people don't. Imagine being broke and wanting, needing, desperately to see the man you love. I've seen days when I was terribly depressed over matters ar home, the house, the kids, and mainly welfare. When the car was broken down, I was broke and had no way to see my husband. It hurts deep down when you can't visit the one you love, the only one who might make you feel alive, and make you realize you're loved and that better days are in the future (hopefully!)."

What happens when prisoners, feeling alone and incapable of getting even the smallest of reforms connected with visiting hours or food, or medical treatment, decide to organize? Norfolk and Walpole are the two maximum security institutions in Massachusetts, and in 1971, Norfolk prisoners began to organize, tried to negotiate with prison officials to get changes. The guards union was angry at this, and insisted that certain prisoners be shipped out of Norfolk to other institutions, or they would strike. On November 8, 1971, armed guards and state troopers, in a surprise raid, moved into cells at Norfolk, pulled out sixteen men, and shipped them out. One observer tells about it:

"By the time I finish this letter, maybe it will hurt less inside. But right now I feel drained, hurt, betrayed, and filled with a sickening anger. I wish there were some pay-back, but I can't think of one. It seems that they have all the cards. All the time, and it really sucks.

"All through the demonstration, committee meetings, negotiations, etc., there was one overriding theme. Amnesty... In spite of all the reassurances by more experienced cons that the kinds of changes that we have been initiating would not go down without some kind of retaliation, I believed. Foolish youth.

"Between one and two last night I was awakened (I've been a light sleeper since Vietnam), and I looked out my window. There were troopers. And screws. Lots. Armed with sidearms, and big clubs. They were going into dorms and taking people, all kinds of people.

"The only man I saw who had pants and a jacket on was Mike Riley. All the rest were near naked, and nearly all were barefoot. It was cold last night. Damn cold. In some houses guys did give the screws and troopers arguments. A lot of people are locked in isolation here in the camp. But over sixteen guys were shipped. Some natural leaders, some friends, and a few that just have big mouths...

"They took a friend of mine and it wasn't till late this afternoon that he could talk about it. He was able to tell it, because they decided, after getting him all the way out front, that they didn't want him. Being pulled outside in your underwear, at 1:30, in bare feet by two troopers and a house screw. Looking at those troops, with guns, and masks and clubs, with the moon shining off the helmets and the hate that you could see in their faces. Thinking that this is where these guys live, with the guns and the hate, and the helmets and masks, and you, you're trying to wake up, flashing on Kent State and Jackson, and Chicago. And Attica. Most of all Attica..."

At Concord Prison, a medium-security institution, leaders and organizers were also shipped out, November 11, 1971, and one of those men tells about it:

"I and five others like me were awakened by six screws in my room about 1:00 Monday morning. I was told nothing but to dress. They all wore helmets and face shields and carried clubs. One screw said that if I didn't hurry up and dress he would drive his club through my head. I was then handcuffed.

"I was taken outside my unit where numerous state police stood at attention with very large clubs. Again I asked what was going on and was told the club through the head story again.

"I was brought through the trap and was being pushed through to an awaiting van. There a screw with a list said I was to go to Walpole, no Concord. I mean Walpole, no Concord, and while he was struggling to read his list and stammer he rammed his club into my throat. Like it was my fault he couldn't read his list.

"I then entered the van to see a friend of mine already there. He knew as little of what was happening as I.

"Upon arrival here we were released from the van two at a time. I was the last man out of the van and the guard that struck me with his club was standing outside the van, with a carbine on his hip (like he must have seen *Cool Hand Luke* twelve times). Out of the side of his mouth he said, 'Go ahead. Make a move.' He was intimidating me to move so that he could blow me away..."

One of the young leaders of the prison reform movement at Concord was Jerry Sousa, who, with others, was taken out of Concord in the night and dumped into Walpole, where he was immediately put into one of the segregation units, Block Nine (this means twenty-four hours a day alone in a cell). Sousa had been in Walpole only a short time when he got a report out:

"We are writing with a somber report regarding the circumstances and events leading up to and surrounding the death of prisoner Joseph Chesnulavich which occurred here an hour ago in Nine Block.

"Since Christmas eve, vicious prison guards here in Nine Block have created a reign of terror directed toward us prisoners. Four of us have been beaten, one who was prisoner Donald King.

"Other prisoners tried to escape constant harassment and inhuman treatment. Prisoner George Hayes ate razor blades and prisoner Fred Ahern swallowed a needle...they both were rushed to Mass General Hospital.

"This evening at 6 P.M. prison guards Baptist, Sainsbury, and Montiega turned a fire extinguisher containing a chemical foam on Joe then slammed the solid steel door sealing him in his cell and walked away, voicing threats of , 'We'll get that punk.'

"At 9:25 P.M. Joe was found dead. Another human life snuffed out by the system. Twenty-six-year old Joe, who had served seven years of a life sentence at Walpole until the toll...the final payment...was extracted here tonight, by a cruel society that has turned her back on her brothers and sisters and children in prisons. Forced to serve part or all of their lives in cages, constantly in fear of being snatched from their bed in the middle of the night by blackjack-wielding prison guards, who stalk the corridors and cell blocks, seeking to vent their hostilities on some hapless prisoner. Prison authorities as well as news media will label little Joe's death a suicide, but the men here in Block Nine who witnessed this murder know. But are we next?"

An inmate named Don Sylvia wrote a poem: "The Man With No Identity."

When I was two years old
    my mother divorced my father for "cruelty.":
When I was five, ten years old, I went to school, and the kids
    called me "*bastard.*"
I went to court when I was thirteen (for breaking windows) and
    the "good judge" called me a "THUG."
When I was eighteen I got in a car accident
    (received some everlasting wounds on my head and face)
    and the "community" called me "*scarface.*"
I grew a beard when I was twenty-eight, and
    society called me a "*hippy.*"
I'm thirty-six, doing seven to twelve in society's prison, and the
    "District Attorney" calls me an "*animal.*"
When I leave this prison and settle down,
    I'll be titled "*Ex-Convict.*"
And when I'm dead, and laid to rest,
    I'll be an "*unknown soldier.*"

7

Attica

In September of 1971, Tom Wicker, *New York Times* columnist, was asked to serve on a committee of observers to go into Attica Prison in New York after prisoners there had rebelled, taken over a prison yard, and held prison guards as hostages, asking for various changes in their living conditions. They set up a community and organized their daily activities. More than half of the inmates were black, and Wicker later reported: "The racial harmony that prevailed among the prisoners—it was absolutely astonishing..." But after five days of stalled negotiations, Governor Nelson Rockefeller ordered an all-out military attack by state troopers, who used automatic rifles, carbines, and submachine guns. The prisoners had no guns. Thirty one prisoners were shot to death. So were nine of the hostages. In the following days there were protests around the country, some of the protesters carrying signs which read: "Ludlow, 1914. Attica, 1971," recalling the Ludlow massacre in Colorado, when John D. Rockefeller, Jr. declared, as his son did at Attica, that a military attack was necessary to defend "a great principle." What follows is my review of Tom Wicker's book *A Time to Die*, which appeared in

444

the *Saturday Review*, March 22, 1975, under the title "They Were Expendable."

O urs is a time of place names that need no explanation. To sound them is to stop the heart a fraction of a second. Auschwitz. Hiroshima. My Lai. Kent State. Attica.

Attica. An eerie camp of war inside a stone wall 30 feet high, with prisoners as guards and guards as prisoners, and then the guns, roaring, the chaos of slaughter, a moving circle of survivors stripped naked, disappearing behind enormous steel doors that clang shut, reverberating to infinity, behind which we faintly hear the methodical fall of clubs on flesh, and then a silence, signaling the restoration of law and order.

Tom Wicker's book on Attica is a tense narrative—told in the third person—about that week in September 1971, a week that was brought to a climax when the Governor of New York, now our Vice-President, spoke the words that turned D-yard into a slime of blood. But the book is more. It is the tough self-examination of a noted columnist, whose profession nervously stands watch over the passivity of its members, but whose own sensibilities demanded—almost before he could think about it—that he cross into the forbidden zone of commitment. The mood is fascination, growing ashamed of itself, turning to anger.

As Wicker left Washington for Attica, his name on a small list the prisoners had requested as observers, he made a simple pledge to himself: *Nobody gets killed.* It came from deep down, perhaps from his plain, morally scrupulous family in Hamlet, North Carolina; it was a simple idea that somehow stayed alive even inside the sophisticated journalistic world Wicker inhabited in Washington, D.C. When that pledge was shattered by the guns of the troopers at Attica, a back-home naivete, which had held its breath an unreasonably long time inside Wicker, collapsed.

You realize, reading this book, that Wicker is an incorrigible novelist, unrehabilitated by all his time in press clubs. You also learn, in compact digressions, about the prison system in America—enough to persuade you, if you need it, that prisons should not be reformed and prettied up, but should be dismantled, brick by brick, leaving to our grandchildren no physical reminder of our barbarity. Wicker skillfully sketches the evidence that prisons do not help fight crime, and that they probably make things worse—thus removing any justification for a system of unspeakable cruelty.

He might also have said (we always want the author to consult us before writing his book) that the huge proportion of poor people in jail for crimes against property suggests that prisons are inevitable counterparts of banks. And that so long as we have a system that breeds fierce and unequal competition for scarce resources (although it is not the only system that requires imprisonment), some steel bars will be needed to protect money, and others to confine human beings.

But mostly the book is those six days at Attica, Wicker and his fellow observers filing back and forth between a sullen, impatient army outside and the fragile friendship of the besieged inside. Wicker's honesty is as impressive as his prose. He gives a quick portrait of a white inmate who admits the observers to D-yard:

> The man did not look directly at him, but in the weak, yellow light, like that in a medieval painting, there was something—so it seemed to Wicker in his nervousness—hard and desperate about the white face, the tattooed arm, the rigid intensity with which the man's body seemed to be charged, as if he were about to spring from the darkness and strike right through the mask of affluence and ease and order that shielded the faces of men like Tom Wicker from the hardest weathers of human existence.

The inmates created their own community inside the yard—hardly ideal, inescapably violent, unexpectedly humane, but considering the circumstances, an astonishing testament to the human potential for self-rule, and far superior, ethically, both to the slave world they had just sundered and to the free world outside the walls, now getting ready to kill them. Wicker sketches the leaders and orators, almost all black: Herbert X. Blyden, eloquent, angry; Roger Champen, almost seven feet tall, cool; L.D. Barkley, bespectacled, precise, uncompromising (he was 21, in Attica for driving without a license, and had but a few days to live). He finds solidarity between black and white unbroken, from the seizure of the yard to the re-occupation.

There is diversity in the bureaucracy: the ruthless conservative, Warden Mancusi (the inmates, he said, were destroying "their home"); the rueful liberal, Commissioner Oswald; and the whole spectrum from itchy-fingered guards to manicured gubernatorial assistants. In the end, all differences in personal morality were ground into homogeneity by the work ethic and its chief rule: Obey the boss. The boss was Nelson Rockefeller, whose powers so transcended liberalism and conservatism that it would take a stronger stance than the mild reformism of an Oswald to resist the deadly suction that drew the cold and the compassionate alike into the vortex of the murderous. Rebellion was unthinkable inside the bureaucracy.

And in the end, even the observers—good men all, intelligent, brave—could only weep with despair and anger, sealed off in the Stewards' Room of the prison while the massacre proceeded a few hundred yards away. They had been more than observers: Wicker, Arthur Eve, Herman Badillo, William Kunstler, Lewis Steel, Clarence Jones, Jaybarr Kenyatta, and the rest. They had tried to mediate, tried to stall for time. They had, in the end, developed an agonized comradeship with the insurrectionists.

But the observers' powerlessness was ensured by adherence (though some of them knew better) to the "rationality" that is crucial to our higher learning. Only an "irrational" act (perhaps refusing to move from D-yard, thus forcing the authorities to reckon with killing not just obscure guards and worthless prisoners, but journalists and legislators as well) had even a chance of preventing or delaying the attack. The observers were not lacking in courage, but, as Wicker writes, "Wicker... was a middle-class product of a system he regarded as fundamentally rational. He took it for granted that no one wanted the irrationality of bloodshed and death." And while not all the observers believed this—certainly not Kunstler and Steel, not Herman Badillo, and probably no black among them—as a group they were trapped inside the Stewards' Room of our Machiavellian culture, where we are all taught to stay within the rules of rationality and civility by those who break the rules at will.

That the powerless can expect rational compromise from the powerful, that rulers and ruled share common values in the modern liberal state, is a seductive idea, mangled by history but kept alive by incessant transfusions. At Ludlow, Colorado in 1914, strike leader Lou Tikas went up the hill with a white flag to negotiate with the National Guard, which was being paid by John D. Rockefeller, Jr., to crush a miners' strike in his coalfields. Tikas was executed on the spot, and then the tent colony where the strikers' families lived was attacked. That was the Ludlow Massacre, John D.'s legacy to his sons.

At Attica, Herman Badillo said, "There's always time to die. I don't know what the rush was." It was a momentary of forgetting of the madness of those who ask for rationality.

The negotiations had broken down over the issue of amnesty, where—with the inequality in weaponry—no compromise was possible. To give amnesty would be to violate the Rockefeller Principle—the principle of Establishments everywhere: Don't let them think rebellion works.

And so the attack was ordered. Then came the official lies about the killing of the hostages, repeated in the press ("...convicts slashed their throats with knives, the *New York Times* said). The politicos were not anxious to have the remaining guards begin to think—that when the government is uptight, we are all as expendable as the prisoners.

Tom Wicker began to see that and more. A Time to Die is a meteor, following the unfinished trajectory of his thought, while illuminating D-yard in Attica, September 1971. With the Attica survivors now on trial in Buffalo, facing multiple life sentences (no amnesty, no pardons, no deals; they never held public office), Wicker's book is also a friend's powerful, passionate response to a call for help.

8

The
Biggest
Secret

In 1975, after Vietnam and Watergate, with public opinion surveys showing a general distrust by Americans of their government, including the once-admired FBI, the House and Senate set up committees to investigate the FBI and the CIA. Both agencies had broken the laws they were sworn to uphold, and valuable information about this came out of the Congressional investigations. But the revelations went just far enough, and in just the right way—moderate press coverage, little television coverage, thick books of reports with limited readership—to give the impression of an honest society correcting itself. I expressed my skepticism in a column I wrote for the *Boston Globe* (December 2, 1975), entitled "After the FBI and CIA Secrets Come Out, Very Little Will Change."

Secrets are coming out of the Senate committee probing the FBI and CIA. But the biggest secrets, I suspect will remain untouched.

Yes, we learn that the FBI tapped wires illegally, kept lists of people to be put in concentration camps, wrote fake letters to destroy personal lives and used dirty tricks to disrupt organizations it didn't like. The CIA opened mail illegally, plotted the murder of foreign leaders and conspired to overthrow a democratically elected government in Chile.

It is the habit of governments everywhere, including ours, when caught lying, stealing or murdering, to murmur a few words of confession, find a scapegoat to punish and go right on doing its dirty work in more subtle ways.

Recall: Families were burned to death in Vietnam, babies were shot in their mothers' arms, Cambodia was bombed secretly and Laos openly, the land and culture of 40 million people in Southeast Asia were laid waste. And then what? Instead of trying Mr. Nixon and Kissinger for mass murder by terror bombing, we scolded their flunkies for breaking-and-entering and gave them a little time in jail. Instead of trying the generals for the massacre at My Lai, we tried Calley and put him under house arrest.

What will happen now with these revelations on the CIA and FBI? The usual. A few changes in personnel, a few new laws. But the same exclusive club of corporate billionaires, with their teams of lawyers, accountants, politicians and intellectual advisers hoping to become Secretary of State, will remain in power.

For profound changes to come about in this country, we will have to start revealing to the American public, and especially to the school kids of the coming generation, the really big secrets, which no congressional committee will touch.

First, that there is little difference between Them (the enemy—Communism) and Us (the West, American, "democracy") when it comes to a reckless disregard for human lives in pursuit of something called "national interest." That "national interest," it usually turns out, is the interest, over there, of the Kremlin bureaucracy, and here, the interest of the oil companies, the banks, the military-industrial-political complex. When we were told in grade school that the difference between Them and Us is "they believe in any means to gain their ends and we don't"—we were lied to.

People are beginning to catch on. *The Spy Who Came in From the Cold* was the first best-selling novel to boldly make that point: "Our side" would use ex-Nazis, would sacrifice the lives of its own people, to score points in a game whose concern was not humanity but power.

The current movie, *Three Days of the Condor*, is even more explicit. The CIA is portrayed as a group of sophisticated men using dazzling scientific techniques to ruthlessly exterminate anyone, including their own employees, who stood in the way of control of oil in the Middle East and Venezuela.

Even the fantasies of movie scripts can't match the reality. There is evidence now that the FBI was involved in the planned murder of two black leaders in Chicago on December 4, 1969. A gang of police, armed with shotguns, pistols, rifles and submachine guns, and a plan of the house furnished by an FBI informant, attacked an apartment occupied by Black Panthers, at four in the morning, and executed Fred Hampton as he lay asleep in his bed.

The biggest secret of all is beginning to emerge: That "the enemy" of this government is anyone, here or abroad, who won't put up with control of the world by Chase Manhattan, Exxon, General Motors, I.T. & T. It is chilling but suddenly believable that a government willing to kill Vietnamese peasants and put Asian protesters in tiger cages will also assassinate native Americans and put citizens here in concentration camps.

That's a heavy secret for us to carry in our heads. But we need to know it, if we are going to figure out how to defend our lives and our liberties from those who have occupied America.

9

Where to Look for a Communist

Now that the Soviet Union has fallen apart and the other countries of the "Eastern bloc" have gone through radical changes in leadership, the word "communist" does not seem very threatening. But for forty-five years after the end of World War II, fear of a "Communist threat" distorted American public life, in a thousand ways. In the fall of 1988, a two-day conference was held at Harvard University to examine "Anti-Communism" and its effects. I was invited to give a talk to open the meetings. The editors of *Newsday* asked me to write a column for them based on the talk, and it appeared on January 22, 1989, under the title "Scare Words Leave Scars On Everyone." Another version was printed that month in *Z Magazine*.

In 1948, a series of pamphlets were distributed by the House Committee on Un-American Activities, entitled "100 Things You Should Know About Communism." When I came across this in my files (they have files on me, I have files on them), I was impressed that this committee knew 100 things about communism. The pamphlets had questions and answers:

Question 1: "What is communism?" (The idea is to start with something easy.) Answer: "A system by which one small group seeks to rule the world."

Question 76: "Where can a Communist be found in everyday life?" (This question interested me because there had been times when I was in need of a Communist and didn't know where to find one.) Answer: "Look for him in your school, your labor union, your church, or your civic club."

Question 86: "Is the YMCA a Communist target?" (This really worried me. I had always wondered why there was so much chlorine in the YMCA pool.) Answer: "Yes, so is the YWCA."

In 1950, Rep. Harold Velde of Illinois, a former FBI man, later chairman of HUAC, spoke in Congress to oppose mobile library service in rural areas because, he said, "Educating Americans through the means of the library service could bring about a change of their political attitude quicker than any other method. The basis of communism and socialistic influence is education of the people."

Let's skip to 1987, the year of the Contragate investigation, to Robert McFarlane, who conspired with John Poindexter, William Casey, Oliver North, Richard Secord, and almost certainly George Bush to violate the laws and the Constitution to give weapons to terrorists in Central America. McFarlane later said he knew the policy of getting arms to the contras would not work (not that it was wrong, but it would not work.) He said: "Where I went wrong was not having the guts to stand up and tell the president that. To tell you the truth, probably the reason I didn't is because if I'd done that, Bill Casey, Jeane Kirkpatrick and Cap Weinberger would have said I was some kind of Commie, you know."

Our bizarre preoccupation with communism, which mystifies most people in other countries, has lasted a long time. Ronald Reagan, in his first presidential campaign, said, "Let us not delude ourselves. The Soviet Union underlies all the unrest that is going on. If they weren't engaged in this game of dominoes, there wouldn't be any hot spots in the world,"

These are absurdities. But they represent something terribly serious. Because there are certain words calculated to stop thinking, end rational discourse, arouse hatred—words that are murderous. In our time, we have seen words used that way. The words "nigger" and "Jew" have led to lynchings, to mass murder. The word "Communist" has been used to justify the support of dictatorships (in Chile, the Philippines, Iran), the attempted invasion of other countries (Cuba), the bombing of peasant villages (in Vietnam, Laos, Cambodia, El Salvador), the destruction of the economy of a small, poor country (Nicaragua). The word also has been used to justify taxing the hard-earned salaries of the American people to finance billions of dollars worth of stupid weapons.

Is it an exaggeration to call such words "murderous"? A dispatch from Seattle, Washington, June 10, 1986, said: "A self-proclaimed soldier against communism faces a death sentence after a verdict today by a jury that found him guilty of murdering four members of the Charles Goldmark family. Rice has said he killed the Goldmark family because he thought they were part of an international conspiracy among Communists, Jews and the Federal Reserve Board."

Defense lawyers said this belief was evidence of the killer's mental illness. But the only thing that would cause me to think he was mentally ill was his accusation against the Federal Reserve Board. Otherwise, he belongs in the White House, certainly during the Nixon years, when "communism" was a reason for killing peasants in Southeast Asia, and when the president queried H.R. Haldeman (source: the Watergate tapes) on how many members of the Chicago Eight were Jews.

The word "Communist" used as an epithet, as an inducer of fear and trembling, is calculated to stop rational discussion of communism itself. We do need a sober critique of the Soviet Union, whose policies have given socialism a bad name. For me, reading Karl Marx, Eugene Debs, Helen Keller (how many of her admirers know she was a socialist?), and Emma Goldman, socialism had a good name. Any true socialist must feel anger and indignation at what has been done to human beings in the USSR. But there is a difference between such indignation and a hysterical, indiscriminate hatred that causes us to threaten to obliterate a nation of 280 million people—the very people we say are suffering under communism. There is a difference between a reasoned criticism of socialism and the use of deadly weapons by us, or by our mercenaries, to prevent change in countries that desperately need change.

In Vietnam, inflammatory words led to unspeakable atrocities. Charles Hutto, a GI, told the Army's Criminal Investigation Division: "I remember the unit's combat assault on My Lai Four.... The night before the mission we had a briefing by Capt. [Ernest] Medina.... He said everything in the village was Communist.... We shot men, women, and children."

Hutto, who now lives in Monroe, Louisiana, with his wife and two children, says, "I was nineteen years old and I'd always been told to do what the grown-ups told me to do. But now I'll tell my sons, if the government calls, to use their own judgment.... Now I don't even think there should be a thing called war...because it messes up a person's mind."

The change in Hutto's thinking is instructive. This country is not the same after the Vietnam War as it was before. Millions of Americans have learned to think twice when someone yells "Communist." That's why, as all the public opinion surveys show, they are not ready to launch an invasion of Nicaragua.

This country is not the same after the lessons of the civil rights movement. That movement, at its grass roots—at the level of the Student Nonviolent Coordinating Committee, and Rosa Parks and Ella Baker and Martin Luther King, Jr., and the black people of Montgomery and Selma—was not deflected from its work by the charges of communism. Harry Truman called the 1960s sit-ins inspired by Communists. When asked for proof, Truman said he had none. "But I know that usually when trouble hits the country the Kremlin is behind it." The FBI tried to link Martin Luther King to communism. The movement was not deterred.

In the '50s the House Un-American Activities Committee had been powerful. By the '60s, the American public was having doubts about it. In 1970, discredited and ludicrous, HUAC was abolished. Its interrogations now seemed laughable, as in this 1958 exchange between the committee and Joseph Papp, director of the New York Shakespeare Festival. Papp was asked: "Do you have the opportunity to inject into your plays any propaganda which would influence others to be sympathetic with the Communist philosophy?"

Papp replied, "Sir, the plays we do are Shakespeare's plays. Shakespeare said, 'To thine own self be true...'"

Richard Arens, staff director for the committee, said, "There is no suggestion here by this chairman or anyone else that Shakespeare was a Communist. That is ludicrous and absurd. That is the Commie line."

The use of scare words is profoundly undemocratic. It stifles debate; it creates an atmosphere in which people are afraid to speak their minds honestly, afraid to examine all ideas. This has been true in the Soviet Union as well, where words such as counter-revolutionary, bourgeois and Trotskyite have been used to stifle discussion, weed out heretics, send people to Siberia. Perhaps now Mikhail Gorbachev understands that the Soviet Union must get beyond its murderous words because it has serious problems it must solve.

For us, in the United States, there is too much to do for us to bankrupt ourselves for fear of communism. There are people without a place to live this winter, and others who can't pay their rent, and elderly people in nursing homes who can't go down to the dining room because there's no money to pay someone to push their wheelchair. But there's money for the B1 bombers and the Stealth fighter and the Trident submarines. With hungry children all over the world, we need to stop spending $300 billion a year for military junk, and use the money for human needs.

To do all this, we need bold solutions, and therefore we need an open debate not limited by fear that names will be called: Communist, socialist, anarchist, even liberal. We should not be afraid to talk about redistributing wealth and a world community, or to renounce the nationalism that insists on being Number One.

Bertolt Brecht, the German playwright, was never allowed to read his statement when called before the HUAC. Here is part of it: "We are living in a dangerous world. Our state of civilization is such that mankind already is capable of becoming enormously wealthy but as a whole is still poverty-ridden. Great wars have been suffered. Greater ones are imminent, we're told. Do you not think that in such a predicament every new idea should be examined carefully and freely?"

10

Plato:
Fallen Idol

In a course I taught for many years at Boston University, called "Law and Justice in America," I had fun with Plato, one of the gods of Western intellectual thought. I.F. Stone was long one of my heroes for his refusal to be bullied by authority, political or intellectual. So when I saw that he, retired from his remarkable *I.F. Stone's Weekly*, had written a book on Plato and Socrates, I was happy to review it for *Z Magazine*, where it appeared in April 1988 under the title *Perils of Plato*. The piece was then reprinted in a collection of my essays, *Failure to Quit* (Common Courage Press).

I once heard I.F. Stone, queried about his extraordinary investigative reporting, say: "I'm having so much fun, I should be arrested." After reading his new book *The Trial of Socrates*, I am willing to testify against him. He is clearly having too much fun.

He is also (though classical scholarship seems far removed from journalism) carrying on the work he did in his famous *Weekly*. He has lowered himself (secretly, guilty of trespass) into the mineshaft, with his lamp, his pick and shovel, dug deep into the documents kept by the authorities, and emerged at the end of a long day with some brilliant nuggets, which he offers to the world, and which damn the authorities.

He shows us that the usefulness of history does not depend on its newness. Events of two thousand years ago can be as illuminating as those of yesterday; the ideas of people in ancient Athens are as familiar as those we read in the daily newspaper.

Stone, who once annoyed presidents and FBI directors, is now irritating professional philosophers. He has moved into their territory, into the house they considered a private dwelling, indeed, into the best room, the one with Plato's *Complete Works*, in the original Greek. Lacking J. Edgar Hoover's resources, the philosophers are unable to let out a contract on I.F. Stone except to book reviewers.

One of these, in the *New York Times*, said that Stone is "determinedly unsympathetic" (to Socrates, to Plato), full of "misconceptions," and perhaps even "anti-intellectual prejudice."

For a long time Plato has been one of the untouchables of modern culture, his reputation that of an awesome mind, a brilliant writer of dialogue; his work the greatest of the Great Books. You don't criticize Plato without a risk of being called anti-intellectual.

I can't get excited, I confess, about the scholarly disputations in *The Trial of Socrates*. Like: should you trust Plutarch's or Diodorus Siculus' claim that the philosopher Anaxagoras was also the object of a political trial in Athens, when neither Thucydides nor Xenophon nor Plato mentioned it? Let I.F. Stone have his fun.

What is important is that Stone challenges the intellectual authorities of modern Western culture as brazenly as he has done with the political authorities.

It is easy for liberals and radicals to expose the Best and the Brightest as political advisers, like those Phi Beta Kissingers who gave Machiavellian advice to the warmakers of Vietnam. It seems harder to escape the thrall of the intellectual advisers, the Great Names and the Great Books. And even when we manage to do that, we may substitute our own, the Great Names and Great Books of the Left, thus replacing one cultural hegemony with another.

Surely we need more practice in challenging intellectual authority of all kinds. I.F. Stone sets a good example. And he picks the most formidable of targets, the great Plato.

If you have read Allan Bloom's book, *The Closing of the American Mind*, you will notice that it was written in a state of shock and fear caused by the tumults of the Sixties. There is no evidence of shock at the war in Vietnam, or at police dogs attacking blacks in Bull Connor's Birmingham, but there is hysteria over the fact that his Plato seminar was threatened with interruption by students demonstrating on the Cornell campus where he taught. In page after page, Bloom swoons over Plato.

He and his fellow conservatives have good reason to do so. And Western culture has good reason for making Plato a demi-God, required reading for every educated person who will take his or her proper place in society. It is good to see that I.F. Stone, characteristically, refuses to be intimidated.

Socrates left no writings that we know of. (Maybe that's why he was executed. Publish or perish.) So Plato put words in his mouth. This was shrewd, to *create* a character (we don't *really* know what Socrates was like) who could charm us, a wise, gentle man put to death by the government in Athens because he spoke his mind. The words coming from such a man will be especially persuasive.

But they are Plato's words, Plato's ideas. All we know of Socrates is what Plato tells us. Or, what we read in recollections of another contemporary of his, Xenophon. Or, what we can believe about him from reading his friend Aristophanes' spoof on Socrates in his play, *The Clouds*.

So we can't know for sure what Socrates really said to his friend Crito, who visited him in jail, after he had been condemned to death. But we do know that what Plato has him say, in the dialogue *Crito* (written many years after Socrates' execution in 399 B.C.), has been impressed, with or without attribution, on the minds of many generations, down to the present day, with deadly effect.

Plato's message is presented appealingly by a man calmly facing death. It is made even more appealing by the fact that it follows another dialogue, the *Apology*, in which Socrates addresses the jury in an eloquent defense of free speech, saying: "The unexamined life is not worth living."

Plato then unashamedly (lesson one in intellectual bullying: speak with utter confidence) presents us with some unexamined ideas. Having established Socrates' credentials as a martyr for independent thought, he proceeds in the *Crito* to put into Socrates' mouth an argument for blind obedience to government.

It is hardly a dialogue. Poor Crito is reduced to saying, to every one of Socrates' little speeches: "Yes...of course...clearly...I agree...Yes...I think that you are right.... True..." And Socrates is going on and on, like the good trouper that he is, saying Plato's lines, making Plato's argument for him. We can't be sure these are Socrates ideas. But we know they are Plato's because he makes an even more extended case for a totalitarian state in his famous *Republic.*

Crito offers to help Socrates escape from prison. Socrates replies: "No, I must obey the law. True, Athens has committed an injustice against me by ordering me to die for speaking my mind. But if I complained about this injustice, Athens could rightly say: 'We brought you into the world, we raised you, we educated you, we gave you and every other citizen a share of all the good things we could.'" Socrates accepts this, saying: "By not leaving Athens, I agreed to obey its laws. And so I will go to my death."

It is Plato's bumper-sticker: "Love it or leave it." Plato was the apostle of civil obedience. He did not live long enough to encounter the argument of Thoreau, who wrote a famous essay on civil disobedience. Thoreau said that whatever good things we have were not given us by the state, but by the energies and talents of the people of the country. And he would be damned if he would pay taxes to support a war against Mexico based on such a paltry argument.

Plato, the Western world's star intellectual, makes a number of paltry arguments in this so-called dialogue. He has the state say to Socrates (and Socrates accepts this so humbly one cannot believe this is the defiant orator of the *Apology*): "What complaint have you against us and the state, that you are trying to destroy us? Are we not, first of all, your parents? Through us your father took your mother and brought you into the world."

What complaint? Only that they are putting him to death! The state as parents? Now we understand those words: The Motherland, or The Fatherland, or The Founding Fathers, or Uncle Sam. It's not some little junta of military men and politicians who are sending you to die in some muddy field in Asia or Central America; it's your mother, your father, or your father's favorite brother. How can you say no?

Socrates listens meekly to the words of The Law: "Are you too wise to see your country is worthier, more to be revered, more sacred, and held in higher honor both by the gods and by all men of understanding, than your father and your mother and all your other ancestors; that you ought to reverence it and to submit to it...and to obey in silence if it orders you to endure flogging or imprisonment or if it send you to battle to be wounded or to die?"

Crito is virtually mute, a sad sack of a debater. You would think that Plato, just to maintain his reputation for good dialogue, would give Crito some better lines. But he took no chances. And so the admirable obligation one feels to one's neighbors, one's family, one's principles, indeed to other human beings wherever they reside on the planet, becomes confused with blind obedience to that disreputable artifice called government. And in that confusion, young men, going off to war in some part of the world they never heard of, for some cause that cannot be rationally explained, would say: "I owe it to my country."

These arguments are important, not because we want to make a judgment about Socrates or Plato or ancient Athens (it is too late for that), but because they are a way of thinking which every nation-state drums into the heads of its citizens from the time they are old enough to go to school. And because they show the perils of placing our trust, and the lives of our children, in the hands of the Experts, whether in politics or philosophy. It is not too late to try to overcome that.

And I was provoked to all of this by I.F. Stone, who was just having fun.

11

Upton Sinclair and Sacco & Vanzetti

As a teen-ager starting to read serious books, I became a fan of Upton Sinclair, the socialist muckraker who wrote with the kind of clarity and passion that appeals to young readers. After reading *The Brass Check*, *The Jungle*, *Oil*, and several other books, I came across one of his lesser-known novels, *Boston*, which was about the famous case of Sacco and Vanzetti. I had already become interested in that extraordinary, tragic episode in American history, and I just devoured the novel. It remained out of print for a long time, but a small publisher in Boston, Robert Bentley, also an admirer of Upton Sinclair, decided to re-issue it in a new, handsome edition in 1978, and asked me to write an Introduction, which is reprinted here.

Upton Sinclair's novel, *Boston*, long unavailable, is being reprinted, and it is a gift to have it back. Fifty years have passed since Nicola Sacco and Bartolomeo Vanzetti were strapped into a chair at Charlestown Prison, near Boston, and electrocuted. There is a need to recall what happened, and to understand why *Boston*, classified as fiction, is so true an account of that case, that time, and so unsettling in its closeness to our case, our time.

The story of Sacco and Vanzetti, whenever revived, even after half a century, awakens deep feelings. In the summer of 1977, Governor Michael Dukakis of Massachusetts officially pronounced that the two men had not had a fair trial, and immediately there were outcries in the state legislature, letters to the newspapers.

One citizen wrote: "By what incredible arrogance do Governor Dukakis and Daniel A. Taylor, his legal adviser, dare to put themselves above Gov. Alvin T. Fuller of Massachusetts, who declared that Sacco and Vanzetti had a fair trial, were fairly convicted and fairly punished for their crime?"

Another, signing his letter "John M. Cabot, U.S. Ambassador, Retired," expressed his "great indignation" and noted that Governor Fuller's affirmation of the death sentence was made after a special review by "three of Massachusetts's most distinguished and respected citizens—President Lowell of Harvard, President Stratton of MIT and retired Judge Grant."

Heywood Broun put it a bit differently, in his column in the *New York World* fifty years ago: "It is not every prisoner who has a President of Harvard University throw on the switch for him.... If this is a lynching, at least the fish peddler and his friend the factory hand may take unction to their souls that they will die at the hands of men in dinner jackets or academic gowns..."

Governor Fuller's son, Peter Fuller, Boston's leading Cadillac dealer, as well as a racer of thoroughbred horses, called Dukakis' statement "an attempt to besmirch a guy's record that we believe in and love, whose memory we cherish." He added: "We're sitting here in the last building my father built, and it's the most beautiful car agency on the Eastern Coast and perhaps in the United States."

In New York, a few days before August 23, 1977, the fiftieth anniversary of the execution, the *New York Times* reported: "Plans by Mayor Beame to proclaim next Tuesday 'Sacco and Vanzetti Day' have been canceled in an effort to avoid controversy, a City Hall spokesman said yesterday."

There must be good reason why a case fifty years old, its principals dead, arouses such emotion. It is not the kind of history that can be handled comfortably, in harmless ceremonies, like the Bicentennial cele-brations of 1976, in which the revolutionary doctrines of the Declaration of Independence were lost in a Disneyland of pageantry. Sacco and Vanzetti were not Washington and Jefferson, not wealthy insurgents mak-ing a half-revolution to replace a foreign ruling class with a native one, to exchange a limited monarchy for a limited democracy. They were (as Upton Sinclair reminds us, using the harsh word so often as to irritate us, to make us feel the insult ourselves) "wops," foreigners, poor working-men.

Worst of all, Sacco and Vanzetti were anarchists, meaning they had some crazy notion of a full democracy in which neither foreignness nor poverty would exit, and thought that without those provocations, war among nations would end for all time. But to do this, the rich would have to be fought and their riches confiscated. This is not like killing to rob a payroll. It is a crime much worse, and the story of two such men cannot be recalled without trouble.

Therefore, let us recall it. But let us not concentrate on that ques-tion which is the center of most discussion of the Sacco-Vanzetti case: were they guilty of the robbery committed April 15, 1920, at the Slater & Morrill shoe factory in South Braintree, Massachusetts, and the mur-der of the paymaster Frederick Parmewnter, and the guard, Alessandro Berardelli? Let us go beyond that question to ask others, more important, more dangerous. That is what *Boston* does.

Not that we can neglect the question of guilt or innocence: the trial, the witnesses, the defendants, the judge, the jury, the lawyers, and all those appeals to the higher courts, the governor, the presidents of Harvard and MIT, to the Supreme Court of the United States. It is, indeed, the suspiciousness surrounding all that which leads us further.

Why, three weeks after the holdup at South Braintree, were Sacco and Vanzetti arrested on a streetcar in Brockton? True, they had been at a garage to pick up a friend's car, and a getaway car had been used in the robbery, but no one knew what kind of car that was. True, they were both armed when picked up, but they had some reason to be worried for their safety. They were aliens and anarchists, and for months there had been raids carried out by order of Attorney General A. Mitchell Palmer, in which Department of Justice agents all over the country invaded meetings of suspected radicals, broke into homes in the middle of the night, held people incommunicado and without warrants, beat them with clubs and blackjacks.

In Boston, five hundred were arrested, chained together, and marched through the streets. Luigi Galleani, editor of the anarchist paper *Cronaca Sovversiva*, to which Sacco and Vanzetti subscribed, was picked up in Boston and quickly deported.

Something even more frightening had happened. A fellow anarchist of Sacco and Vanzetti, also a follower of Galleani, a typesetter named Andrea Salsedo, who lived in New York, was kidnapped (the proper word for illegal seizure of a person) by members of the Federal Bureau of Investigation, and held in their offices on the fourteenth floor of the Park Row Building. He was not allowed to call his family, friends, or a lawyer, was questioned and beaten, according to a fellow prisoner. During the eighth week of his imprisonment, on May 3, 1920, the body of Salsedo, smashed to a pulp, was found on the pavement near the Park Row Building, and the Bureau announced that he had committed suicide by jumping from the fourteenth floor window of the room in which they had kept him. (In 1977, one recalls an incident of the 1950s, disclosed recently: the mysterious death-fall of a scientist named Frank Olson from a sixteenth story hotel window in New York, after being surreptitiously dosed with LSD by the Central Intelligence Agency.)

It was May 5, 1920, having just learned of Salsedo's death, that Sacco and Vanzetti were found, armed, on a Brockton street car, arrested, and interrogated. They responded to police questions with lies, and these would later, at the trial, be considered as "consciousness of guilt," and form an important part of the evidence that would send them to the electric chair.

What did the police question them about, and why would they lie? Here is a sample:

Police: Are you a citizen?
Sacco: No
Police: Are you a Communist?
Sacco: No.
Police: Anarchist?
Sacco: No
Police: Do you believe in this government of ours?
Sacco: Yes. Some things I like different.
Police: Do you subscribe for literature of the Anarchist party?

Vanzetti: Sometimes I read them.
Police: How do you get them, through the mail?
Vanzetti: A man gave one to me in Boston.
Police: Who was that man?
Vanzetti: I don't know him.

Were the police intent on finding two robbers, who then turned out to be anarchists? Or two anarchists, who turned out to have enough that was suspicious about their behavior—carrying guns, lying to the police—to make them vulnerable? Conviction would be easy if they were Italians, and almost everyone who placed them far from the scene of the crime on that day—six of seven who testified they saw Sacco in Boston, all of the five who testified they saw Vanzetti in Plymouth—were Italians, speaking in broken English to a totally Anglo-Saxon jury, before an Anglo-Saxon judge who declared his hatred for radicals several times during the trial, outside the courtroom.

It would be helpful too, if the judge kept overruling the defense and supporting the prosecution, and if he mis-stated the evidence in summing up the case for the jury, especially on so crucial a question as: did the fatal bullets come from Sacco's gun? Felix Frankfurter, then a professor at Harvard Law School, would describe one of Judge Webster Thayer's opinions as "a farrago of misquotations, misrepresentations, suppressions, and mutilations."

The trial began immediately after Memorial Day, a year and a half after the end of that orgy of death and patriotism that was World War I, the newspapers still vibrating with the roll of drums, the jingo rhetoric. Twelve days into the trial, the press reported the bodies of three soldiers transferred from France to Brockton, the whole town turning out for a patriotic ceremony, and all of this in newspapers which the jury could read, only the reports on the trial having been cut out. On the fourth of July, in the midst of the trial, the papers reported a gathering of 5,000 veterans of the Yankee Division, in Plymouth.

This mood would be sustained during the cross-examinations of Sacco and Vanzetti by prosecutor Katzmann:

Katzmann (to Sacco): Did you love this country in the last week of May, 1917?
Sacco: That is pretty hard for me to say in one word, Mr. Katzmann.

Katzmann: There are two words you can use, Mr. Sacco, yes or no. Which one is it?

Sacco: Yes.

Katzmann: And in order to show your love for this United States of America when she was about to call upon you to become a soldier you ran away to Mexico?

At no point in the trial did the prosecution establish any motive that Sacco and Vanzetti may have had for the robbery. Neither had any record of criminal activity. The stolen money was never found.

It is not hard, however, to establish a motive for the prosecution. After the trial two long-time agents of the Department of Justice, Weyand and Letherman, gave affidavits saying: "The names of Sacco and Vanzetti were on the files of the Department of Justice as 'radicals to be watched'...the Department was eager for their deportation...the case against Sacco and Vanzetti for murder was part of a collusive effort between the District Attorney and agents of the Department of Justice to rid the county of these Italians because of their Red activities.... For it was the opinion of the Department of Justice agents that a conviction of Sacco and Vanzetti for murder would be one way of disposing of these men."

The affidavit said a deal was made: federal agents were to help the prosecutor get evidence on the criminal charge, and the prosecutor in turn would try to get information from Sacco and Vanzetti which might help deport their associates. Twelve agents were at one time assigned to the case, and an informer was placed inside of the Sacco-Vanzetti Defense Committee.

All of this rings even more true in the 1970s than in the 1920s. We know now, on the basis of FBI records disclosed reluctantly in recent aggressive lawsuits by black and radical groups, that the FBI, in its war on radicalism, has resorted to informers and spies, forged letters, and murder. We know that the FBI collaborated with a local District Attorney in 1969 in planning an armed attack on a Chicago apartment, in which police shot to death two black militant leaders.

Too many defenders of Sacco and Vanzetti are embarrassed by their radicalism and concentrate on the "who-done-it?" of the robbery-murder. But the determination to get rid of them was too persistently fanatical to be an oddity of Boston or Harvard, an unfortunate judicial slip, a prejudice of one person or another. It is best explained by the powerful resolve of the American capitalist system after World War I to eliminate all radical threats on the eve of a new and uncertain era in world history. This fear of opposition seems exaggerated, knowing the weakness of revolutionary movements in America, but there is considerable historical evidence that the American ruling class, with so much at stake—control of the greatest aggregate of wealth in the world—takes no chances.

Consider the situation in the United States in 1920, when Sacco and Vanzetti were first arrested on that streetcar in Brockton. Between 1877 and 1914, the nation had experienced the most violent rebellions of working people in the history of the modern state: the railroad uprisings of 1877 (including a take-over of the city of St. Louis), the anarchist-led demonstrations in Chicago in 1886, the Homestead steel strike of 1892, the nationwide Pullman strike of 1894, the victorious Lawrence textile strike of 1912, and, finally, the bloody warfare in the Colorado mine districts in 1914, where federal troops had to be called in after the Ludlow Massacre to control a state-wide insurrection of armed, angry miners.

In the years before the first World War, the Industrial Workers of the World was born—militant, revolutionary, uniting all sorts of workers the system had worked so hard to separate (skilled and unskilled, black and white, native and foreign), resisting vigilantes and police, arousing nationwide attention with its work in the Lawrence strike. In the electoral counterpart of those labor struggles, the Socialist Party, its magazine *Appeal to Reason* read by 500,000 people, was winning a million votes for Eugene Debs as president, and electing socialist officials in hundreds of towns throughout the country. Miners in the Far West, farmers in Oklahoma, and clothing workers in New York City were showing a class consciousness that might spread in a country so crassly dominated by Morgan, Rockefeller, Carnegie, Mellon, Armour, and the other robber barons.

The war in Europe created an opportunity for a patriotic assault on radical movements. Congress legislated, President Wilson signed, the Supreme Court sanctioned, the Justice Department moved, and two thousand dissenters from the war were prosecuted, nine hundred sent to prison. Virtually the entire leadership of the IWW was put on trial and jailed; the Socialist and anarchist movements were crippled by jailings and deportations.

With the war over, the repression did not end; indeed, it intensified, for in the meantime the Bolsheviks had taken power in Russia. It is hard for us today to understand fully the fright of the American capitalist class at that event. But if the American government, so powerful in the 1960s, could be driven to a frenzy of mass bombardment by the prospect of a small Asian country turning Communist, it becomes easier to understand the reactions to the Russian and Chinese revolutions. Indeed, the trial of Sacco and Vanzetti bears the same chronological and psychological connection to the Russian Revolution, as the trial of Julius and Ethel Rosenberg in 1951 does to the Chinese Communist victory two years earlier.

Had not this atmosphere cooled between 1920 (the trial of Sacco and Vanzetti) and 1927 (their execution)? Somewhat. But by now the case was a national cause, an international issue. It had become a test of will, of class strength. We'll show them! "Did you see what I did with those anarchist bastards the other day. That will hold them for a while?" (The words of Judge Thayer, spoken at a Dartmouth football game after he had turned down a defense motion for a new trial, quoted in an affidavit by Dartmouth Professor James Richardson.)

The American system keeps control not only by a lottery of rewards (only a few make it, but everyone has a chance), but also by a lottery of punishments (only a few are put away or killed, but it's better to play it safe, be quiet). The determination to get a few obscure Communists, or a few obscure Italian anarchists, only becomes comprehensible as part of such a system, a scheme only partly understood by those who carry it out, but with the accumulation of more than enough parts to make the plan whole. What is perhaps not seen at all by the jury, and only dimly by the prosecutor, is seen more clearly by Governor Fuller, the wealthy auto dealer, and Lowell, the textile millionaire president of Harvard.

Upton Sinclair wrote *Boston* in nine months, in what seems like a barely-controlled anger, right after the execution of Sacco and Vanzetti in August, 1927. He had become famous twenty years before, instantaneously, when his expose of the Chicago stockyards, the novel *The Jungle*, appeared serialized in the Socialist magazine *Appeal to Reason*, and then, within a few months of its publication as a book, became a national success and was reprinted in seventeen translations all over the world. *The*

Jungle influenced Bertolt Brecht's play *Saint Joan of the Stockyards*, was praised by George Bernard Shaw in England, and in America by the feminist Charlotte Perkins Gilman and the Socialist Eugene Debs. It became the prime example of "muckraking" literature for generations of Americans.

Sinclair went on from *The Jungle* to become one of the most productive and widely read American writers in the history of the country. Before his death in 1968, at the age of ninety, he had written ninety books and thousands of articles. His correspondence (collected at the Lilly Library of Indiana University) totaled 250,000 letters to and from people all over the world, famous and obscure.

Born in Baltimore of Southern parents, his father an itinerant, heavy-drinking salesman, his mother the proper, puritanical daughter of a minor railroad official, Sinclair grew up in vermin-infested boarding houses in Baltimore, and then, after the age of ten, in dingy rooms in Manhattan. He learned about class differences firsthand by observing the financial manipulations of a banker uncle. He was on his own at seventeen, already writing professionally. He went to City College and Columbia, taught himself French, German, and Italian, and, early on, read the anarchist poet Shelley.

He first turned to socialism in his early twenties, when he met Socialists, and began reading books like Kropotkin's *Mutual Aid*, Veblen's *Theory of the Leisure Class*, Edward Bellamy's utopian novel *Looking Backward*, and Jack London's *People of the Abyss*. His own writing was always incorrigibly political. His dissections of the educational system, the press, the arts, the politics of oil (his novel *Oil* was banned in Boston, oddly enough, for its mild sex passages rather than for its outrageous political viewpoint), were intended to bury capitalism under a barrage of facts, and to present socialism in a way that Americans could accept.

Sinclair was something of an activist too. He was arrested in New York in 1914 for picketing Rockefeller's office after the Ludlow Massacre (the burning to death of eleven children and two women in a miners' tent colony after a machine-gun attack by the Rockefeller-controlled National Guard). And in 1923 he was arrested for reading the First Amendment to striking IWW transport workers in San Pedro, California.

In 1922, after the trial of Sacco and Vanzetti, during the period of endless motions and appeals, Sinclair visited Vanzetti in Charlestown prison. Perhaps this was the beginning of that thinking process which led to *Boston.* Certainly, the portrait of Vanzetti in the novel is more poignant, more textured, than can be found anywhere in the literature on the case, except in the letters that Vanzetti and Sacco wrote from prison. I cannot resist quoting something Vanzetti (still trying to master the English language) wrote, which suggests as much about him as it does about Sacco:

> Sacco is a heart, a faith, a character, a man; a man lover of nature and mankind. A man who gave all, who sacrifice all to the cause of Liberty and to his love for mankind; money, rest, mundain ambition, his own wife, his children, himself and his own life...
>
> Oh, yes, I may be more witfull, as some have put it, I am a better babbler than he is, but many, many times in hearing his heartful voice ringing a faith sublime, in considering his supreme sacrifice, remembering his heroism I felt small small at the presence of his greatness and found myself compelled to fight back from my eyes the tears, quanch my heart trobling to my throat to not weep before him—this man called thief and assassin and doomed.

When, seven years after that visit to Vanzetti, Sinclair began to write *Boston,* just after the executions, he chose to tell the story through a sixty-year old grandmother. Perhaps he was impelled by his own experience with women. His first marriage was a failure. He seemed unable to give his wife, Meta Fuller, the passionate love she wanted, and they were divorced. It was Meta who read Charlotte Perkins Gilman's *Women and Economics,* and gave it to him, after which he went on to Bebel's *Women and Socialism* and the writings of Havelock Ellis. While this did not make him an ideal husband and father to their son, it made him conscious of the subjugation of women, and he later became a strong supporter of feminist programs, including birth control and pay for housewives.

Sinclair's heroine in *Boston* is Cornelia Thornwell, who deserts her Brahmin-banker family to live with poor Italians, work in a factory, walk a picket line, become a friend of Vanzetti. She becomes totally involved in the case. Such a heroine, improbable as she is, makes the book a pioneering literary work. Its feminist impulse is clear, through Cornelia, who walks a wide arc around her proper daughter to embrace her radical granddaughter, thinking, saying: "What was the reason women were always bound by fear? Because they were afraid! Why were they obedience? Because they obeyed!"

We are a bit uneasy with such a person—the kind of patronizing blue-blood-sympathizer-with-red-causes it is easy to poke fun at. But there is wisdom in the device, because through Cornelia's family connections, Sinclair can show us the Brahmins of Boston and America, their opulence as owners, their poverty as people, compared to the family of Beltrando Brini, with whom Cornelia lives.

Of course, there is simplification and romanticization, beneath which rests an undeniable truth about the effects of a capitalist culture on both its beneficiaries and its victims. In one of Sinclair's brilliant juxtapositions, he contrasts Nicola Sacco and Elbert H. Gary, chairman of the board of directors of the U.S. Steel Corporation. As Sacco and Vanzetti were awaiting execution, the press reported that Gary had died, and left a dying message for his loved ones, his last will and testament:

> I earnestly request my wife and children and descendants that they steadfastly decline to sign any bonds or obligations of any kind as surety for any other person, or persons; that they refuse to make any loans except on the basis of first-class, well-known securities, and that they invariably decline to invest in any untried or doubtful securities of property or enterprise or business.

As Sinclair puts it: "At this time, two anarchist wops, one of them an avowed atheist, the other a vague deist of the old-fashioned sort, were writing their last words to their beloved ones. Nicola Sacco wrote to his son, Dante:

> So, Son, instead of crying, be strong, so as to be able to comfort your mother...take her for a long walk in the quiet country, gathering wild flowers here and there, resting under the shade of trees, between the harmony of the vivid stream and the gentle tranquillity of the mother nature, and I am sure that she will enjoy this very much.... But remember always, Dante, in the play of happiness, don't you use all for yourself only...help the persecuted and the victim because they are your better friends.... In this struggle of life you will find more love and you will be loved."

Observing the Thornwell family up close, and the Brini family up close, Upton Sinclair shows us America in the way it does not want to be seen, as a class society, its politics as class politics, its justice as class justice. It is an old-fashioned view, obscured and complicated by the material and ideological possessions of middle-class America, and yet still fundamentally true.

In the midst of the Sacco-Vanzetti case, a wealthy man in Milton, south of Boston, shot and killed a man who was gathering firewood on his property. He spent eight days in jail, then was let out on bail, and was not prosecuted, the district attorney calling it "justifiable homicide." Upton Sinclair reports it in *Boston*, but it could be a news item from any period in American history, including our own.

When *Boston* came out in 1928, some reviewers, while admiring it as "propaganda," scorned it as art. But most praised it. The *New York Times* called it "a literary achievement...full of sharp observation and savage characterization...." The chairman of the Pulitzer Prize Committee of 1928 said later that *Boston* would have received the prize were it not for its "socialistic tendencies" and "special pleading." (When Sinclair did finally win a Pulitzer Prize in 1943, for the third of his eleven "Lanny Budd" novels, *Dragon's Teeth*, it was for a rather toothless novel about a heroic world wanderer, offspring of a munitions maker and a beauty queen, an art dealer, secret agent, sexual and political adventurer, a kind of left-of-center James Bond who waded through the mud of international politics with clean strides, a man not likely to consort with the likes of stockyard worker Jurgis Rudkus of *The Jungle*, or the fish peddler Vanzetti in *Boston*.)

Boston, along with *The Jungle*, is generally considered to be among Sinclair's best novels. He had not the literary gifts of a John Steinbeck, who combined verbal artistry with political passion. But he was a compelling story-teller, and he had his moments of real eloquence. Against so many contemporary novelists, bubbly with style, cynical about human possibility, pretentiously psychological, and ultimately empty, the power of Upon Sinclair's prose in *Boston*, the clarity of his viewpoint, seem refreshingly healthy.

George Bernard Shaw wrote Sinclair from England, praising his artistry in recreating historical fact:

> I have regarded you, not as a novelist, but as a historian; for it is my considered opinion, unshaken at 85, that records of fact are not history. They are only annals, which cannot become historical until the artist-poet-philosopher rescues them from the unintelligible chaos of their actual occurrence and arranges them in works of art.... When people ask me what has happened in my long lifetime I do not refer them to the newspaper files and to the authorities, but to your novels.

Boston does not fit orthodox library categories, which insist on the boundary between fiction and non-fiction. It is a history of the Sacco-Vanzetti case truer than the court transcript, more real than any non-fiction account, precisely because it goes beyond the immediate events of the case to bring the reader the historical furnace in which the case was forged, to the atmosphere in the country breathed in by all participants, despite the closed doors of the courtroom, judge's chambers, and jury room, poisoning the verdict. It puts the straight lines of neutral type in the law books under a microscope, where they show up as rows of trenches in the war of class against class.

It may be objected that it is a distortion of the facts to go outside the record of the case to the record of the system. But why should the historian who really seeks the truth about an event recapitulate the strictures of the courtroom, which focuses only on "the facts," scrupulously keeps out the "irrelevant," and then places in charge of determining the facts, and judging what is relevant, a black-robed agent of the system.

The greatness of *Boston*, in distinction to all the books arguing the guilt or innocence of Sacco and Vanzetti, is that it raises a far more important question: the guilt or innocence of the system of economics, politics, and culture which created factories like the Slater and Merrill shoe factory at South Braintree, millionaires like the Lowells and the Fullers, robbers like the Morelli gang (which may have done the job at South Braintree) and radicals like Sacco and Vanzetti, and lets them all loose, in a war to the death, where the rich control the armaments of bullet and law.

With such a view of the case, expectations of "justice" become as naive as expectations of winning at roulette, for in both cases, while there are exceptions, to keep the suckers coming, the structure of the game insures that everyone will be kept in place. If a case like that of Sacco and Vanzetti is seen, not as an objective weighing of evidence, but as an instance of the struggle between the classes, then Sacco's insistence from the beginning, waving aside all lawyers' promises and friends' hopes, makes profound sense: "They got us, they will kill us." So does his statement to the court, on sentencing: "I know the sentence will be between two classes, the oppressed class and the rich class.... That is why I am here today on this bench, for having been of the oppressed class."

That viewpoint seems dogmatic, simplistic. Not all court decisions are explained by it. But, lacking a theory to fit *all* cases, Sacco's simple, strong view is surely a better guide to understanding the legal system than one which assumes a contest among equals based on an objective search for truth.

Then on whom can the Saccos and Vanzettis of our time depend, when the judicial system, however frocked to disguise its shape, is made of the same stuff as the larger system to which it connects? Certainly not, Sinclair shows us through Cornelia Thornwell's shattered innocence, on judges, juries, higher courts, governors, committees of notables. Governor Fuller was polite but firm. The intellectual Lowell was calm but unyielding. The Massachusetts Supreme Court, the Justices of the U.S. Supreme Court, Holmes and Brandeis, reacted with coldness, the technicalities falling from their lips like icicles.

Nor could they count on the lawyers and committees for the defense, who depended on legal arguments, on the investigation of facts, always deluding themselves that more facts, better arguments, would win, not understanding that this was one of those moments in history when the ruling class closes ranks. At such moments, the liberal press retreats into cowardly cautiousness. And the customary niceties of free speech and assembly, so proudly paraded before the world as proof of America's goodness, are withdrawn, the permits canceled for meetings on the Boston Common, and the police called to club and arrest those who gather in defiance.

At such moments it does no good for an indefatigable investigator, the young lawyer Herbert Ehrmann, to follow up the confession of Sacco and Vanzetti's death-row partner, Madeires ("I hear by confess to being in the south Braintree shoe company crime and Sacco and Vanzetti was not in said crime. Celestine F. Madeires."), and to find a pile of astounding evidence pointing to the Morelli gang of Providence, Rhode Island.

Vanzetti had the answer. Unless a million Americans were organized, he and his friend Sacco would die. Not legal arguments, only mass action could save them. Not words, but struggles. Not appeals, but demands. Not petitions to the governor, but take-over of the factories. Not lubricating the machinery of a supposedly fair system, to make it work better, but a general strike to bring the machinery to a halt.

That never happened. Thousands demonstrated, marched, protested, not just in Union Square, Boston, Chicago, San Francisco, but in London, Paris, Buenos Aires, South Africa. It wasn't enough. In the

1960s, when a great national movement against the Vietnam war was created, involving millions of people, the vibrations shook some courts,
some juries, into acquittals for political defendants. But there was no such
mass movement for Sacco and Vanzetti.

Still, Vanzetti's idea held. If people struggled, organized, understood that it was not a court case, but an epic encounter, then, even if two
men died, something good would come out of it. As Vanzetti told a
reporter in the last days, foreseeing the effect: "This is our agony, and our
triumph." Indeed, Americans of every generation since that time have
learned, and some become more radical, by the recollection of the case of
Sacco and Vanzetti.

When Vanzetti was arrested, he had a leaflet in his pocket, advertising a meeting to take place in five days. It is a leaflet that could be distributed today, all over the world, as appropriate now as it was the day of
their arrest. It read:

> You have fought all the wars. You have worked for all the capitalists. You
> have wandered over all the countries. Have you harvested the fruits of your
> labors, the price of your victories? Does the past comfort you? Does the pre-
> sent smile on you? Does the future promise you anything? Have you found
> a piece of land where you can live like a human being and die like a human
> being? On these questions, on this argument and on this theme, the strug-
> gle for existence, Bartolomeo Vanzetti will speak.

That meeting did not take place. But Vanzetti did speak, and so
did Sacco, over the years of their imprisonment, in their letters, in their
legacy, in the literature carrying their message, their spirit forward. As in
Upton Sinclair's extraordinary book, *Boston*.

PART FIVE

HISTORY

1

Columbus and Western Civilization

In the year 1992, the celebration of Columbus Day was different from previous ones in two ways. First, this was the quincentennial, five hundred years after Columbus' landing in this hemisphere. Second, it was a celebration challenged all over the country by people—many of them native Americans but also others—who had "discovered" a Columbus not worth celebrating, and who were rethinking the traditional glorification of "Western civilization." I gave this talk at the University of Wisconsin in Madison in October of 1991. It was published the following year by the Open Magazine Pamphlet Series with the title "Christopher Columbus & The Myth of Human Progress."

George Orwell, who was a very wise man, wrote: "Who controls the past controls the future. And who controls the present controls the past." In other words, those who dominate our society are in a position to write our histories. And if they can do that, they can decide our futures. That is why the telling of the Columbus story is important.

Let me make a confession. I knew very little about Columbus until about 12 years ago, when I began writing my book *A People's History of the United States*. I had a Ph.D. in history from Columbia University—that is, I had the proper training of a historian, and what I knew about Columbus was pretty much what I had learned in elementary school.

But when I began to write my *People's History*, I decided I must learn about Columbus. I had already concluded that I did not want to write just another overview of American history—I knew my point of view would be different. I was going to write about the United States from the point of view of those people who had been largely neglected in the history books: the indigenous Americans, the black slaves, the women, the working people, whether native or immigrant.

I wanted to tell the story of the nation's industrial progress from the standpoint, not of Rockefeller and Carnegie and Vanderbilt, but of the people who worked in their mines, their oil fields, who lost their limbs or their lives building the railroads.

I wanted to tell the story of wars, not from the standpoint of generals and presidents, not from the standpoint of those military heroes whose statues you see all over this country, but through the eyes of the GIs, or through the eyes of "the enemy." Yes, why not look at the Mexican War, that great military triumph of the United States, from the viewpoint of the Mexicans?

And so, how must I tell the story of Columbus? I concluded, I must see him through the eyes of the people who were here when he arrived, the people he called "Indians" because he thought he was in Asia.

Well, they left no memoirs, no histories. Their culture was an oral culture, not a written one. Besides, they had been wiped out in a few decades after Columbus' arrival. So I was compelled to turn to the next best thing: the Spaniards who were on the scene at the time. First, Columbus himself. He had kept a journal.

His journal was revealing. He described the people who greeted him when he landed in the Bahamas—they were Arawak Indians, sometimes called Tainos—and told how they waded out into the sea to greet him and his men, who must have looked and sounded like people from another world, and brought them gifts of various kinds. He described them as peaceable, gentle, and said: "They do not bear arms, and do not know them for I showed them a sword—they took it by the edge and cut themselves."

Throughout his journal, over the next months, Columbus spoke of the native Americans with what seemed like admiring awe: "They are the best people in the world and above all the gentlest—without knowledge of what is evil—nor do they murder or steal...they love their neighbors as themselves and they have the sweetest talk in the world...always laughing."

And in a letter he wrote to one of his Spanish patrons, Columbus said: "They are very simple and honest and exceedingly liberal with all they have, none of them refusing anything he may possess when he is asked for it. They exhibit great love toward all others in preference to themselves." But then, in the midst of all this, in his journal, Columbus writes: "They would make fine servants. With fifty men we could subjugate them all and make them do whatever we want."

Yes, this was how Columbus saw the Indians—not as hospitable hosts, but as "servants," to "do whatever we want."

And what did Columbus want? This is not hard to determine. In the first two weeks of journal entries, there is one word that recurs seventy-five times: GOLD.

In the standard accounts of Columbus what is emphasized again and again is his religious feeling, his desire to convert the natives to Christianity, his reverence for the Bible. Yes, he was concerned about God. But more about Gold. Just one additional letter. His was a limited alphabet. Yes, all over the island of Hispaniola, where he, his brothers, his men, spent most of their time, he erected crosses. But also, all over the island, they built gallows—340 of them by the year 1500. Crosses and gallows—that deadly historic juxtaposition.

In his quest for gold, Columbus, seeing bits of gold among the Indians, concluded there were huge amounts of it. He ordered the natives to find a certain amount of gold within a certain period of time. And if they did not meet their quota, their arms were hacked off. The others were to learn from this and deliver the gold.

Samuel Eliot Morison, the Harvard historian who was Columbus' admiring biographer, acknowledged this. He wrote: "Whoever thought up this ghastly system, Columbus was responsible for it, as the only means of producing gold for export.... Those who fled to the mountains were hunted with hounds, and of those who escaped, starvation and disease took toll, while thousands of the poor creatures in desperation took cassava poison to end their miseries."

Morison continues: "So the policy and acts of Columbus for which he alone was responsible began the depopulation of the terrestrial paradise that was Hispaniola in 1492. Of the original natives, estimated by a modern ethnologist at 300,000 in number, one-third were killed off between 1494 and 1496. By 1508, an enumeration showed only 60,000 alive...in 1548 Oviedo (Morison is referring to Fernandez de Oviedo, the official Spanish historian of the conquest) doubted whether 500 Indians remained."

But Columbus could not obtain enough gold to send home to impress the King and Queen and his Spanish financiers, so he decided to send back to Spain another kind of loot: slaves. They rounded up about 1200 natives, selected 500, and these were sent, jammed together, on the voyage across the Atlantic. Two hundred died on the way, of cold, of sickness.

In Columbus' journal, an entry of September 1498 reads: "From here one might send, in the name of the Holy Trinity, as many slaves as could be sold..."

What the Spaniards did to the Indians is told in horrifying detail by Bartolomé de las Casas, whose writings give the most thorough account of the Spanish-Indian encounter. Las Casas was a Dominican priest who came to the New World a few years after Columbus, spent forty years on Hispaniola and nearby islands, and became the leading advocate in Spain for the rights of the natives. Las Casas, in his book *The Devastation of the Indies*, writes of the Arawaks: "...of all the infinite universe of humanity, these people are the most guileless, the most devoid of wickedness and duplicity...yet into this sheepfold...there came some Spaniards who immediately behaved like ravening beasts.... Their reason for killing and destroying...is that the Christians have an ultimate aim which is to acquire gold..."

The cruelties multiplied. Las Casas saw soldiers stabbing Indians for sport, dashing babies' heads on rocks. And when the Indians resisted, the Spaniards hunted them down, equipped for killing with horses, armor plate, lances, pikes, rifles, crossbows, and vicious dogs. Indians who took things belonging to the Spaniards—they were not accustomed to the concept of private ownership and gave freely of their own possessions—were beheaded, or burned at the stake.

Las Casas' testimony was corroborated by other eyewitnesses. A group of Dominican friars, addressing the Spanish monarchy in 1519, hoping for the Spanish government to intercede, told about unspeakable atrocities, children thrown to dogs to be devoured, new-born babies born to women prisoners flung into the jungle to die.

Forced labor in the mines and on the land led to much sickness and death. Many children died because their mothers, overworked and starved, had no milk for them. Las Casas, in Cuba, estimated that 7000 children died in *three months.*

The greatest toll was taken by sickness, because the Europeans brought with them diseases against which the natives had no immunity: typhoid, typhus, diphtheria, smallpox.

As in any military conquest, women came in for especially brutal treatment. One Italian nobleman named Cuneo recorded an early sexual encounter. The "Admiral" he refers to is Columbus, who, as part of his agreement with the Spanish monarchy, insisted he be made an Admiral. Cuneo wrote:

"...I captured a very beautiful Carib woman, whom the said Lord Admiral gave to me and with whom...I conceived desire to take pleasure. I wanted to put my desire into execution but she did not want it and treated me with her finger nails in such a manner that I wished I had never begun. But seeing that, I took a rope and thrashed her well.... Finally we came to an agreement."

There is other evidence which adds up to a picture of widespread rape of native women. Samuel Eliot Morison wrote: "In the Bahamas, Cuba and Hispaniola they found young and beautiful women, who everywhere were naked, in most places accessible, and presumably complaisant." Who presumes this? Morison, and so many others.

Morison saw the conquest as so many writers after him have done, as one of the great romantic adventures of world history. He seemed to get carried away by what appeared to him as a *masculine* conquest. He wrote:

"Never again may mortal men hope to recapture the amazement, the wonder, the delight of those October days in 1492, when the new world gracefully yielded her virginity to the conquering Castilians."

The language of Cuneo ("we came to an agreement"), and of Morison ("gracefully yielded") written almost five hundred years apart, surely suggests how persistent through modern history has been the mythology that rationalizes sexual brutality by seeing it as "complaisant."

So, I read Columbus' journal, I read Las Casas. I also read Hans Koning's pioneering work of our time—*Columbus: His Enterprise*, which, at the time I wrote my *People's History* was the only contemporary account I could find which departed from the standard treatment.

When my book appeared, I began to get letters from all over the country about it. Here was a book of 600 pages, starting with Columbus, ending with the 1970s, but most of the letters I got from readers were about one subject: Columbus. I could have interpreted this to mean that, since this was the very beginning of the book, that's all these people had read. But no, it seemed that the Columbus story was simply the part of my book that readers found most startling. Because every American, from elementary school on, learns the Columbus story, and learns it the same way: "In Fourteen Hundred and Ninety Two, Columbus Sailed the Ocean Blue."

How many of you have heard of Tigard, Oregon? Well, I didn't, until, about seven years ago, I began receiving, every semester, a bunch of letters, twenty or thirty, from students at one high school in Tigard, Oregon. It seems that their teacher was having them (knowing high schools, I almost said "forcing them") read my *People's History*. He was photocopying a number of chapters and giving them to the students. And then he had them write letters to me, with comments and questions. Roughly half of them thanked me for giving them data which they had never seen before. The others were angry, or wondered how I got such information, and how I had arrived at such outrageous conclusions.

One high school student named Bethany wrote: "Out of all the articles that I've read of yours I found 'Columbus, The Indians, and Human Progress' the most shocking." Another student named Brian, seventeen years old, wrote: "An example of the confusion I feel after reading your article concerns Columbus coming to America.... According to you, it seems he came for women, slaves, and gold. You say that Columbus physically abused the Indians that didn't help him find gold. You've said you have gained a lot of this information from Columbus' own journal. I am wondering if there is such a journal, and if so, why isn't it part of our history. Why isn't any of what you say in my history book, or in history books people have access to each day."

I pondered this letter. It could be interpreted to mean that the writer was indignant that no other history books had told him what I did.

Or, as was more likely, he was saying: "I don't believe a word of what you wrote! You made this up!"

I am not surprised at such reactions. It tells something about the claims of pluralism and diversity in American culture, the pride in our "free society," that generation after generation has learned exactly the same set of facts about Columbus, and finished their education with the same glaring omissions.

A school teacher in Portland, Oregon named Bill Bigelow has undertaken a crusade to change the way the Columbus story is taught all over America. He tells of how he sometimes starts a new class. He goes over to a girl sitting in the front row, and takes her purse. She says: "You took my purse!" Bigelow responds: "No, I discovered it."

Bill Bigelow did a study of recent children's books on Columbus. He found them remarkably alike in their repetition of the traditional point of view. A typical fifth grade biography of Columbus begins: "There once was a boy who loved the salty sea." Well! I can imagine a children's biography of Attila the Hun beginning with the sentence: "There once was a boy who loved horses."

Another children's book in Bigelow's study, this time for second graders: "The King and queen looked at the gold and the Indians. They listened in wonder to Columbus' stories of adventure. Then they all went to church to pray and sing. Tears of joy filled Columbus' eyes."

I once spoke about Columbus to a workshop of school teachers, and one of them suggested that school children were too young to hear of the horrors recounted by las Casas and others. Other teachers disagreed, said children's stories include plenty of violence, but the perpetrators are witches and monsters and "bad people," not national heroes who have holidays named after them.

Some of the teachers made suggestions on how the truth could be told in a way that would not frighten children unnecessarily, but that would avoid the falsification of history now taking place.

The arguments about children "not being ready to hear the truth" does not account for the fact that in American society, when the children grow up, they *still* are not told the truth. As I said earlier, right up through graduate school I was not presented with the information that would counter the myths told to me in the early grades. And it is clear that my experience is typical, judging form the shocked reactions to my book that

I have received from readers of all ages.

If you look in an *adult* book, the *Columbia Encyclopedia* (my edition was put together in 1950, but all the relevant information was available then, including Morison's biography), there is a long entry on Columbus (about 1,000 words) but you will find no mention of the atrocities committed by him and his men.

In the 1986 edition of the *Columbia History of the World*, there are several mentions of Columbus, but nothing about what he did to the natives. Several pages are devoted to "Spain and Portugal in America," in which the treatment of the native population is presented as a matter of controversy, among theologians at that time, and among historians today. You can get the flavor of this "balanced approach," containing a nugget of reality, by the following passage from that *History*:

"The determination of the Crown and the Church to Christianize the Indians, the need for labor to exploit the new lands, and the attempts of some Spaniards to protect the Indians, resulted in a very remarkable complex of customs, laws, and institutions which even today leads historians to contradictory conclusions about Spanish rule in America.... Academic disputes flourish on this debatable and in a sense insoluble question, but there is no doubt that cruelty, overwork and disease resulted in an appalling depopulation. There were, according to recent estimates, about 25 million Indians in Mexico in 1519, slightly more than 1 million in 1605."

Despite this scholarly language—"contradictory conclusions...academic disputes...insoluble question"—there is no real dispute about the facts of enslavement, forced labor, rape, murder, the taking of hostages, the ravages of diseases carried from Europe, and the wiping out of huge numbers of native people. The only dispute is over how much emphasis is to be placed on these facts, and how they carry over into the issues of our time.

For instance, Samuel Eliot Morison does spend some time detailing the treatment of the natives by Columbus and his men, and uses the word "genocide" to describe the overall effect of the "discovery." But he buries this in the midst of a long, admiring treatment of Columbus, and sums up his view in the concluding paragraph of his popular book *Christopher Columbus, Mariner*, as follows:

"He had his faults and his defects, but they were largely the defects of the qualities that made him great—his indomitable will, his superb faith in God and in his own mission as the Christ-bearer to lands beyond the seas, his stubborn persistence despite neglect, poverty and discouragement. But there was no flaw, no dark side to the most outstanding and essential of all his qualities—his seamanship."

Yes, his seamanship!

Let me make myself clear. I am not interested in either denouncing or exalting Columbus. It is too late for that. We are not writing a letter of recommendation for him to decide his qualifications for undertaking another voyage to another part of the universe. To me, the Columbus story is important for what it tells us about ourselves, about our time, about the decisions we have to make for our century, for the next century.

Why this great controversy today about Columbus and the celebration of the quincentennial? Why the indignation of native Americans and others about the glorification of that conqueror? Why the heated defense of Columbus by others? The intensity of the debate can only be because it is not about 1492, it is about 1992.

We can get a clue to this if we look back a hundred years to 1892, the year of the quadricentennial. There were great celebrations in Chicago and New York. In New York there were five days of parades, fireworks, military marches, naval pageants, a million visitors to the city, a memorial statue unveiled at a corner of Central Park, now to be known as Columbus Circle. A celebratory meeting took place at Carnegie Hall, addressed by Chauncey DePew.

You might not know the name of Chauncey DePew, unless you recently looked at Gustavus Myers' classic work, *A History of the Great American Fortunes*. In that book, Chauncey DePew is described as the front man for Cornelius Vanderbilt and his New York Central railroad. DePew traveled to Albany, the capital of New York State, with satchels of money and free railroad passes for members of the New York State legislature, and came away with subsidies and land grants for the New York Central.

DePew saw the Columbus festivities as a celebration of wealth and prosperity—you might say, as a self-celebration. He said that the quadricentennial event "marks the wealth and the civilization of a great people...it marks the things that belong to their comfort and their ease, their pleasure and their luxuries...and their power."

We might note that at the time he said this, there was much suffering among the working poor of America, huddled in city slums, their children sick and undernourished. The plight of people who worked on the land—which at this time was a considerable part of the population—was desperate, leading to the anger of the Farmers' Alliances and the rise of the People's (Populist) Party. And the following year, 1893 was a year of economic crisis and widespread misery.

DePew must have sensed, as he stood on the platform at Carnegie Hall, some murmurings of discontent at the smugness that accompanied the Columbus celebrations, for he said: "If there is anything I detest...it is that spirit of historical inquiry which doubts everything; that modern spirit which destroys all the illusions and all the heroes which have been the inspiration of patriotism through all the centuries."

So, to celebrate Columbus was to be patriotic. To doubt was to be unpatriotic. And what did "patriotism" mean to DePew? It meant the glorification of expansion and conquest—which Columbus represented, and which America represented. It was just six years after his speech that the United States, expelling Spain from Cuba, began its own long occupation (sporadically military, continuously political and economic) of Cuba, took Puerto Rico and Hawaii, and began its bloody war against the Filipinos to take over their country.

That "patriotism" which was tied to the celebration of Columbus, and the celebration of conquest, was reinforced in the second World War by the emergence of the United States as the superpower, all the old European empires now in decline. At that time, Henry Luce, the powerful president-maker and multi-millionaire, owner of *Time, Life,* and *Fortune* (not just the publications, but the *things!*) wrote that the twentieth century was turning into the "American Century," in which the United States would have its way in the world.

George Bush, accepting the presidential nomination in 1988, said: "This has been called the American Century because in it we were the dominant force for good in the world.... Now we are on the verge of a new century, and what country's name will it bear? I say it will be another American Century."

What arrogance! That the twenty-first century, when we should be getting away from the murderous jingoism of this century, should already be anticipated as an *American* century, or as any one nation's century. Bush must think of himself as a new Columbus, "discovering" and planting his nation's flag on new worlds, because he called for a U.S.

colony on the moon early in the next century. And forecast a mission to Mars in the year 2019.

The "patriotism" that Chauncey Depew invoked in celebrating Columbus was profoundly tied to the notion of the inferiority of the conquered peoples. Columbus' attacks on the Indians were justified by their status as sub-humans. The taking of Texas and much of Mexico by the United States just before the Civil War was done with the same racist rationale. Sam Houston, the first governor of Texas, proclaimed: "The Anglo-Saxon race must pervade the whole southern extremity of this vast continent. The Mexicans are no better than the Indians and I see no reason why we should not take their land."

At the start of the twentieth century, the violence of the new American expansionism into the Caribbean and the Pacific was accepted because we were dealing with lesser beings.

In the year 1900, Chauncey DePew, now a U.S. Senator, spoke again in Carnegie Hall, this time to support Theodore Roosevelt's candidacy for vice-president. Celebrating the conquest of the Philippines as a beginning of the American penetration of China and more, he proclaimed: "The guns of Dewey in Manila Bay were heard across Asia and Africa, they echoed through the palace at Peking and brought to the Oriental mind a new and potent force among western nations. We, in common with the countries of Europe, are striving to enter the limitless markets of the east.... These people respect nothing but power. I believe the Philippines will be enormous markets and sources of wealth."

Theodore Roosevelt, who appears endlessly on lists of our "great presidents," and whose face is one of the four colossal sculptures of American presidents (along with Washington, Jefferson, Lincoln) carved into Mount Rushmore in South Dakota, was the quintessential racist-imperialist. He was furious, back in 1893, when President Cleveland failed to annex Hawaii, telling the Naval War College it was "a crime against white civilization." In his book *The Strenuous Life*, Roosevelt wrote:

"Of course our whole national history has been one of expansion...that the barbarians recede or are conquered...is due solely to the power of the mighty civilized races which have not lost the fighting instinct."

An Army officer in the Philippines put it even more bluntly: "There is no use mincing words.... We exterminated the American

Indians and I guess most of us are proud of it...and we must have no scruples about exterminating this other race standing in the way of progress and enlightenment, if it is necessary..."

The official historian of the Indies in the early sixteenth century, Fernandez de Oviedo, did not deny what was done to natives by the *conquistadores*. He described "innumerable cruel deaths as countless as the stars." But this was acceptable, because "to use gunpowder against pagans is to offer incense to the Lord."

(One is reminded of President McKinley's decision to send the army and navy to take the Philippines, saying it was the duty of the United States to "Christianize and civilize" the Filipinos.)

Against las Casas' pleas for mercy to the Indians, the theologian Juan Gines de Sepulveda declared: "How can we doubt that these people, so uncivilized, so barbaric, so contaminated with so many sins and obscenities, have been justly conquered."

Sepulveda in the year 1531 visited his former college in Spain and was outraged by seeing the students there protesting Spain's war against Turkey. The students were saying: "All war...is contrary to the Catholic religion."

This led him to write a philosophical defense of the Spanish treatment of the Indians. He quoted Aristotle, who wrote in his *Politics* that some people were "slaves by nature," who "should be hunted down like wild beasts in order to bring them to the correct way of life."

Las Casas responded: "Let us send Aristotle packing, for we have in our favor the command of Christ: Thou shalt love thy neighbor as thyself."

The dehumanization of the "enemy" has been a necessary accompaniment to wars of conquest. It is easier to explain atrocities if they are committed against infidels, or people of an inferior race. Slavery and racial segregation in the United States, and European imperialism in Asia and Africa, were justified in this way.

The bombing of Vietnamese villages by the United States, the search and destroy missions, the My Lai massacre, were all made palatable to their perpetrators by the idea that the victims were not human. They were "gooks" or "Communists," and deserved what they received.

In the Gulf War, the dehumanization of the Iraqis consisted of not recognizing their existence. We were not bombing women, children, not bombing and shelling ordinary Iraqi young men in the act of flight and surrender. We were acting against a Hitler-like monster, Saddam Hussein, although the people we were killing were the Iraqi victims of this monster. When General Colin Powell was asked about Iraqi casualties he said that was "really not a matter I am terribly interested in."

The American people were led to accept the violence of the war in Iraq because the Iraqis were made invisible—because the United States only used "smart bombs." The major media ignored the enormous death toll in Iraq, ignored the report of the Harvard medical team that visited Iraq shortly after the war and found that tens of thousands of Iraqi children were dying because of the bombing of the water supply and the resultant epidemics of disease.

The celebrations of Columbus are declared to be celebrations not just of his maritime exploits but of "progress," of his arrival in the Bahamas as the beginning of that much-praised five hundred years of "Western civilization." But those concepts need to be re-examined. When Gandhi was once asked what he thought about Western civilization, he replied: "It's a good idea."

The point is not to deny the benefits of "progress" and "civilization"—advances in technology, knowledge, science, health, education, and standards of living. But there is a question to be asked: progress yes, but at what human cost?

Is progress simply to be measured in the statistics of industrial and technological change, without regard to the consequences of that "progress" for human beings? Would we accept a Russian justification of Stalin's rule, including the enormous toll in human suffering, on the ground that he made Russia a great industrial power?

I recall that in my high school classes in American history when we came to the period after the Civil War, roughly the years between that War and World War I, it was looked on as the Gilded Age, the period of the great Industrial Revolution, when the United States became an economic giant. I remember how thrilled we were to learn of the dramatic growth of the steel and oil industries, of the building of the great fortunes, of the criss-crossing of the country by the railroads.

We were not told of the human cost of this great industrial progress: how the huge production of cotton came from the labor of black slaves; how the textile industry was built up by the labor of young girls who went into the mills at twelve and died at twenty-five; how the railroads were constructed by Irish and Chinese immigrants who were literally worked to death, in the heat of summer and cold of winter; how working people, immigrants and native-born, had to go out on strike and be beaten by police and jailed by National Guardsmen before they could win the eight-hour day; how the children of the working-class, in the slums of the city, had to drink polluted water, and how they died early of malnutrition and disease. All this in the name of "progress."

And yes, there are huge benefits from industrialization, science, technology, medicine. But so far, in these five hundred years of Western civilization, of Western domination of the rest of the world, most of those benefits have gone to a small part of the human race. For billions of people in the Third World, they still face starvation, homelessness, disease, the early deaths of their children.

Did the Columbus expeditions mark the transition from savagery to civilization? What of the Indian civilizations which had been built up over thousands of years before Columbus came? Las Casas and others marveled at the spirit of sharing and generosity which marked the Indian societies, the communal buildings in which they lived, their aesthetic sensibilities, the egalitarianism among men and women.

The British colonists in North America were startled at the democracy of the Iroquois—the tribes who occupied much of New York and Pennsylvania. The American historian Gary Nash describes Iroquois culture: "No laws and ordinances, sheriffs and constables, judges and juries, or courts or jails—the apparatus of authority in European societies—were to be found in the northeast woodlands prior to European arrival. Yet boundaries of acceptable behavior were firmly set. Though priding themselves on the autonomous individual, the Iroquois maintained a strict sense of right and wrong..."

In the course of westward expansion, the new nation, the United States, stole the Indians' land, killed them when they resisted, destroyed their sources of food and shelter, pushed them into smaller and smaller sections of the country, went about the systematic destruction of Indian society. At the time of the Black Hawk War in the 1830s—one of hundreds of wars waged against the Indians of North America—Lewis Cass, the governor of the Michigan territory, referred to his taking of millions of acres from the Indians as "the progress of civilization." He said: "A barbarous people cannot live in contact with a civilized community."

We get a sense of how "barbarous" these Indians were when, in the 1880s, Congress prepared legislation to break up the communal lands in which Indians still lived, into small private possessions, what today some people would call, admiringly, "privatization." Senator Henry Dawes, author of this legislation, visited the Cherokee Nation, and described what he found: "...there was not a family in that whole nation that had not a home of its own. There was not a pauper in that nation, and the nation did not owe a dollar...it built its own schools and its hospitals. Yet the defect of the system was apparent. They have got as far as they can go, because they own their land in common...there is not enterprise to make your home any better than that of your neighbors. There is no selfishness, which is at the bottom of civilization."

That selfishness at the bottom of "civilization" is connected with what drove Columbus on, and what is much-praised today, as American political leaders and the media speak about how the West will do a great favor to the Soviet Union and Eastern Europe by introducing "the profit motive."

Granted, there may be certain ways in which the incentive of profit may be helpful in economic development, but that incentive, in the history of the "free market" in the West, has had horrendous consequences. It led, throughout the centuries of "Western Civilization," to a ruthless imperialism.

In Joseph Conrad's novel *Heart of Darkness*, written in the 1890s, after some time spent in the Upper Congo of Africa, he describes the work done by black men in chains on behalf of white men who were interested only in ivory. He writes: "The word 'ivory' rang in the air, was whispered, was sighed. You would think they were praying to it.... To tear treasure out of the bowels of the land was their desire, with no more moral purpose at the back of it than there is in burglars breaking into a safe."

The uncontrolled drive for profit has led to enormous human suffering, exploitation, slavery, cruelty in the workplace, dangerous working conditions, child labor, the destruction of land and forests, the poisoning of the air we breathe, the water we drink, the food we eat.

In his 1933 autobiography, Chief Luther Standing Bear wrote: "True the white man brought great change. But the varied fruits of his civilization, though highly colored and inviting, are sickening and deadening. And if it be the part of civilization to maim, rob, and thwart, then what is progress? I am going to venture that the man who sat on the ground in his tipi meditating on life and its meaning, accepting the kinship of all creatures, and acknowledging unity with the universe of things, was infusing into his being the true essence of civilization."

The present threats to the environment have caused a reconsideration among scientists and other scholars of the value of "progress" as it has been so far defined. In December of 1991, there was a two-day conference at MIT, in which fifty scientists and historians discussed the idea of progress in Western thought. Here is part of the report on that conference in the *Boston Globe*.

"In a world where resources are being squandered and the environment poisoned, participants in an MIT conference said yesterday, it is time for people to start thinking in terms of sustainability and stability rather than growth and progress.... Verbal fireworks and heated exchanges that sometimes grew into shouting matches punctuated the discussions among scholars of economics, religion, medicine, history and the sciences."

One of the participants, historian Leo Marx, said that working toward a more harmonious co-existence with nature is itself a kind of progress, but different than the traditional one in which people try to overpower nature.

So, to look back at Columbus in a critical way is to raise all these questions about progress, civilization, our relations with one another, our relationship to the natural world.

You probably have heard—as I have, quite often—that it is wrong for us to treat the Columbus story the way we do. What they say is: "You are taking Columbus out of context, looking at him with the eyes of the twentieth century. You must not superimpose the values of our time on events that took place 500 years ago. That is ahistorical."

I find this argument strange. Does it mean that cruelty, exploitation, greed, enslavement, violence against helpless people, are values peculiar to the fifteenth and sixteenth centuries? And that we in the twentieth century, are beyond that? Are there not certain human values which are common to the age of Columbus and to our own? Proof of that is that both in his time and in ours there were enslavers and exploiters; in both his time and ours there were those who protested against that, on behalf of human rights.

It is encouraging that, in this year of the quincentennial, there is a wave of protest, unprecedented in all the years of celebration of Columbus, all over the United States, and throughout the Americas. Much of this protest is being led by Indians, who are organizing conferences and meetings, who are engaging in acts of civil disobedience, who are trying to educate the American public about what really happened five hundred years ago, and what it tells us about the issues of our time.

There is a new generation of teachers in our schools, and many of them are insisting that the Columbus story be told from the point of view of the native Americans. In the fall of 1990 I was telephoned from Los Angeles by a talk-show host who wanted to discuss Columbus. Also on the line was a high school student in that city, named Blake Lindsey, who had insisted on addressing the Los Angeles City Council to oppose the traditional Columbus Day celebration. She told them of the genocide committed by the Spaniards against the Arawak Indians. The City council did not respond.

Someone called in on that talk show, introducing herself as a woman who had emigrated from Haiti. She said: "The girl is right—we have no Indians left—in our last uprising against the government the people knocked down the statue of Columbus and now it is in the basement of the city hall in Port-au-Prince." The caller finished by saying: "Why don't we build statues for the aborigines?"

Despite the textbooks still in use, more teachers are questioning, more students are questioning. Bill Bigelow reports on the reactions of his students after he introduces them to reading material which contradicts the traditional histories. One student wrote: "In 1492, Columbus sailed the ocean blue.... That story is about as complete as Swiss cheese."

Another wrote a critique of her American history textbook to the publisher, Allyn and Bacon, pointing to many important omissions in that text. She said: "I'll just pick one topic to keep it simple. How about Columbus?"

Another student: "It seemed to me as if the publishers had just printed up some glory story that was supposed to make us feel more patriotic about our country.... They want us to look at our country as great and powerful and forever right.... We're being fed lies."

When students discover that in the very first history they learn—the story of Columbus—they have not been told the whole truth, it leads to a healthy skepticism about all of their historical education. One of Bigelow's students, named Rebecca, wrote: "What does it matter who discovered America, really?... But the thought that I've been lied to all my life about this, and who knows what else, really makes me angry."

This new critical thinking in the schools and in the colleges seems to frighten those who have glorified what is called "Western civilization." Reagan's Secretary of Education, William Bennett, in his 1984 "Report on the Humanities in Higher Education," writes of Western civilization as "our common culture...its highest ideas and aspirations."

One of the most ferocious defenders of Western civilization is philosopher Allan Bloom, who wrote *The Closing of the American Mind* in a spirit of panic at what the social movements of the Sixties had done to change the educational atmosphere of American universities. He was frightened by the student demonstrations he saw at Cornell, which he saw as a terrible interference with education.

Bloom's idea of education was a small group of very smart students, in an elite university, studying Plato and Aristotle, and refusing to be disturbed in their contemplation by the noise outside their windows of students rallying against racism or protesting against the war in Vietnam.

As I read him, I was reminded of some of my colleagues, when I was teaching in a black college in Atlanta, Georgia at the time of the civil rights movement, who shook their heads in disapproval when our students left their classes to sit-in, to be arrested, in protest against racial segregation. These students were neglecting their education, they said. In fact, these students were learning more in a few weeks of participation in social struggle than they could learn in a year of going to class.

What a narrow, stunted understanding of education! It corresponds perfectly to the view of history which insists that Western civilization is the summit of human achievement. As Bloom wrote in his book: "...only in the Western nations, i.e. those influenced by Greek philosophy, is there some willingness to doubt the identification of the good with one's own way." Well, if this willingness to doubt is the hallmark of Greek philosophy, then Bloom and his fellow idolizers of Western civilization are ignorant of that philosophy.

If Western civilization is considered the high point of human progress, the United States is the best representative of this civilization. Here is Allan Bloom again: "This is the American moment in world history.... America tells one story: the unbroken, ineluctable progress of freedom and equality. From its first settlers and its political foundings on, there has been no dispute that freedom and equality are the essence of justice for us..."

Yes, tell black people and native Americans and the homeless and those without health insurance, and all the victims abroad of American foreign policy that America "tells one story...freedom and equality."

Western civilization is complex. It represents many things, some decent, some horrifying. We would have to pause before celebrating it uncritically when we note that David Duke, the Louisiana Ku Klux Klan member and ex-Nazi says that people have got him wrong. "The common strain in my thinking," he told a reporter, "is my love for Western civilization."

We who insist on looking critically at the Columbus story, and indeed at everything in our traditional histories, are often accused of insisting on Political Correctness, to the detriment of free speech. I find this odd. It is the guardians of the old stories, the orthodox histories, who refuse to widen the spectrum of ideas, to take in new books, new approaches, new information, new views of history. They, who claim to believe in "free markets" do not believe in a free marketplace of ideas, any more than they believe in a free marketplace of goods and services. In both material goods and in ideas, they want the market dominated by those who have always held power and wealth. They worry that if new ideas enter the marketplace, people may begin to rethink the social arrangements that have given us so much suffering, so much violence, so much war these last five hundred years of "civilization."

Of course we had all that before Columbus arrived in this hemisphere, but resources were puny, people were isolated from one another, and the possibilities were narrow. In recent centuries, however, the world has become amazingly small, our possibilities for creating a decent society have enormously magnified, and so the excuses for hunger, ignorance, violence, racism, no longer exist.

In rethinking our history, we are not just looking at the past, but at the present, and trying to look at it from the point of view of those who have been left out of the benefits of so-called civilization. It is a simple but profoundly important thing we are trying to accomplish, to look at the world from other points of view. We need to do that, as we come into the next century, if we want this coming century to be different, if we want it to be, not an American century, or a Western century, or a white century, or a male century, or any nation's, any group's century, but a century for the human race.

2

The Uses of Scholarship

We were sad to hear of the death in 1996 of Mario Savio, leader in the Sixties of the "Free Speech Movement" at the University of California in Berkeley. It reminded us that the movements of that decade provoked a re-examination of the role of the university and the position of the scholar in a world needing radical change. The following essay appeared in the *Saturday Review* of October 18, 1969, under the title "The Case for Radical Change." It appeared also as the opening chapter in my book *The Politics of History*, "Knowledge As A Form Of Power."

It is time that we scholars began to earn our keep in this world. Thanks to a gullible public, we have been honored, flattered, even paid, for producing the largest number of inconsequential studies in the history of civilization: tens of thousands of articles, books, monographs, millions of term papers; enough lectures to deafen the gods. Like politicians we have thrived on public innocence, with this difference: the politicians are paid for caring, when they really don't; we are paid for not caring, when we really do.

Occasionally, we emerge from the library stacks to sign a petition or deliver a speech, then return to produce even more of inconsequence. We are accustomed to keeping our social commitment extracurricular and our scholarly work safely neutral. We were the first to learn that awe and honor greet those who have flown off into space while people suffer on earth.

If this accusation seems harsh, read the titles of doctoral dissertations published in the past twenty years, and the pages of the leading scholarly journals for the same period, alongside the lists of war dead, the figures on per capita income in Latin America, the autobiography of Malcolm X. We publish while others perish.

The gap between the products of scholarly activity and the needs of a troubled world could be borne with some equanimity as long as the nation seemed to be solving its problems. And for most of our history, this seemed to be the case. We had a race question, but we "solved" it: by a war to end slavery, and by papering over the continued degradation of the black population with laws and rhetoric. Wealth was not distributed equitably, but the New Deal, and then war orders, kept that problem under control—or at least, out of sight. There was turmoil in the world, but we were always at the periphery; the European imperial powers did the nasty work, while we nibbled at the edges of their empires (except in Latin America where our firm control was disguised by a fatherly sounding Monroe Doctrine, and the pose of a Good Neighbor).

None of those solutions is working anymore. The Black Power revolt, the festering of cities beyond our control, the rebellion of students against the Vietnam war and the draft—all indicate that the United States has run out of time, space, and rhetoric. The liberal artifacts that represented our farthest reaches toward reform—the Fourteenth Amendment, New Deal welfare legislation, the U.N. Charter—are not enough. Revolutionary changes are required in social policy.

The trouble is, we don't know how to make such a revolution. There is no precedent for it in an advanced industrial society where power and wealth are highly concentrated in government, corporations, and the military, while the rest of us have pieces of that fragmented power political scientists are pleased to call "pluralism." We have voices, and even votes, but not the means—more crassly, the power—to turn either domestic or foreign policy in completely new directions.

That is why the knowledge industry (the universities, colleges, schools, representing directly $65-billion of the national spending each year) is so important. Knowledge is a form of power. True, force is the most direct form of power, and government has a monopoly on that (as Max Weber once pointed out). But in modern times, when social control rests on "the consent of the governed," force is kept in abeyance for emergencies, and everyday control is exercised by a set of rules, a fabric of values passed on from one generation to another by the priests and the teachers of the society. What we call the rise of democracy in the world means that force is replaced by deception (a blunt way of saying "education") as the chief method for keeping society as it is.

This makes knowledge important, because although it cannot confront force directly, it can counteract the deception that makes the government's force legitimate. And the knowledge industry, which directly reaches seven million young people in colleges and universities, thus becomes a vital and sensitive locus of power. That power can be used, as it was traditionally, to maintain the *status quo*, or (as is being demanded by the student rebels) to change it.

Those who command more obvious forms of power (political control and wealth) try also to commandeer knowledge. Industry entices some of the most agile minds for executive posts in business. Government lures others for more glamorous special jobs: physicists to work on H-bombs; biologists to work on what we might call, for want of a better name, the field of communicable disease; chemists to work on nerve gas (like that which killed 6,000 sheep in Utah); political scientists to work on counter-insurgency warfare; historians to sit in a room in the White House and wait for a phone call to let them know when history is being made, so they may record it. And sometimes one's field doesn't matter. War is interdisciplinary.

Most knowledge is not directly bought, however. It can also serve the purpose of social stability in another way—by being squandered on trivia. Thus, the university becomes a playpen in which the society invites its favored children to play—and gives them toys and prizes to keep them out of trouble. For instance, we might note an article in a leading journal of political science not long ago, dealing with the effects of *Hurricane*

Betsy on the mayoralty election in New Orleans. Or, a team of social psychologists (armed with a fat government grant) may move right into the ghetto (surely the scholar is getting relevant here) and discover two important facts from its extensive, sophisticated research: that black people in the ghetto are poor, and that they have family difficulties.

I am touching a sensitive nerve in the academy now: am I trying to obliterate all scholarship except the immediately relevant? No, it is a matter of proportion. The erection of new skyscraper office buildings is not offensive in itself, but it becomes lamentable alongside the continued existence of ghetto slums. It was not wrong for the Association of Asian Studies at its last annual meeting to discuss some problems of the Ming Dynasty and a battery of similarly remote topics, but *no* session of the dozens at the meeting dealt with Vietnam.

Aside from trivial or esoteric inquiry, knowledge is also dissipated on pretentious conceptualizing in the social sciences. A catch phrase can become a stimulus for endless academic discussion, and for the proliferation of debates that go nowhere into the real world, only round and round in ever smaller circles of scholarly discourse. Schemes and models and systems are invented that have the air of profundity and that advance careers, but hardly anything else.

We should not be surprised then at the volatile demonstrations for black studies programs, or for the creation of new student-run courses based on radical critiques of American society. Students demanding relevance in scholarship have been joined by professors dissenting at the annual ceremonials called scholarly meetings: at the American Philosophical Association, a resolution denouncing U.S. policy in Vietnam; at the American Political Science Association, a new caucus making radical changes in the program; at the American Historical Association, a successful campaign removing the 1968 meeting from Chicago to protest Mayor Daley's hooliganism; at the Modern Language Association, the election of a young, radical English teacher as president.

Still we are troubled, because the new urgency to use our heads for good purposes gets tangled in a cluster of beliefs so stuck, fungus-like, to the scholar, that even the most activist of us cannot cleanly extricate ourselves. These beliefs are roughly expressed by the phrases "disinterested scholarship," "dispassionate learning," "objective study," "scientific method"—all adding up to the fear that using our intelligence to further our moral ends is somehow improper. And so we mostly remain subservient to the beliefs of the profession although they violate our deepest feelings as human beings, although we suspect that the traditional neutrality of the scholar is a disservice to the very ideals we teach about as history, and a betrayal of the victims of an unneutral world.

It may, therefore, be worthwhile to examine the arguments for "disinterested, neutral, scientific, objective" scholarship. If there is to be a revolution in the uses of knowledge to correspond to the revolution in society, it will have to begin by challenging the rules that sustain the wasting of knowledge. Let me cite a number of them, and argue briefly for new approaches.

Rule 1: *Carry on "disinterested scholarship."* (In one hour's reading some weeks ago I came across three such exhortations, using just that phrase: in an essay by Walter Lippmann; in the Columbia University Commencement Address of Richard Hofstadter; in an article by Daniel Bell, appearing, ironically in a magazine called *The Public Interest.*) The call is naive, because there are powerful interests already at work in the academy, with varying degrees of self-consciousness.

There is the Establishment of political power and corporate wealth, whose interest is that the universities produce people who will fit into existing niches in the social structure rather than try to change the structure. We always knew our educational system "socialized" people, but we never worried about this, because we assumed our social norms were worth perpetuating. Now, and rightly, we are beginning to doubt this. There is the interest of the educational bureaucracy in maintaining itself: its endowment, its buildings, its positions (both honorific and material), its steady growth along orthodox lines. These larger interests are internalized in the motivations of the scholar: promotion, tenure, higher salaries, prestige—all of which are best secured by innovating in prescribed directions.

All of these interests operate, not through any conspiratorial decision but through the mechanism of a well-oiled system, just as the irrationality of the economic system operates not through any devilish plot but through the mechanism of the profit motive and the market, and as the same kinds of political decisions reproduce themselves in Congress year after year.

No one *intends* exactly what happens. They just follow the normal rules of the game. Similarly with education; hence the need to chal-

lenge these rules that quietly lead the scholar toward trivia, pretentious-
ness, orotundity, and the production of objects: books, degrees, buildings,
research projects, dead knowledge. (Emerson is still right: "*Things* are in
the saddle, and ride mankind.")

There is no question then of a "disinterested" university, only a
question about what kinds of interests the university will serve. There are
fundamental humanistic interests—above any particular class, party,
nation, ideology—that I believe the university should consciously serve. I
assume this is what we mean when we speak (however we act) of fostering certain "values" in education.

The university should unashamedly declare that its interest is in
eliminating war, poverty, race and national hatred, governmental restrictions on individual freedom, and in fostering a spirit of cooperation and
concern in the generation growing up. It should *not* serve the interests of
particular nations or parties or religions or political dogmas. Ironically,
the university has often served narrow governmental, military, or business
interests, and yet withheld support from larger, transcendental values, on
the ground that it needed to maintain neutrality.

Rule 2: *Be objective.* The myth of "objectivity" in teaching and
scholarship is based on a common confusion. If to be objective is to be
scrupulously careful about reporting accurately what one sees, then of
course this is laudable. But accuracy is only a prerequisite. Whether a
metalsmith uses reliable measuring instruments is a prerequisite for doing
good work, but does not answer the crucial question: will he now forge a
sword or a plowshare with his instruments? That the metalsmith has
determined in advance that he prefers a plowshare does not require him
to distort his measurements. That the scholar has decided he prefers peace
to war does not require him to distort his facts.

Too many scholars abjure a starting set of values, because they fail
to make the proper distinction between an ultimate set of values and the
instruments needed to obtain them. The values may well be subjective
(derived from human needs); but the instruments must be objective
(accurate). Our values should determine the questions we ask in scholarly inquiry, but not the answers.

Rule 3: *Stick to your discipline.* Specialization has become as
absurdly extreme in the educational world as in the medical world. One
no longer is a specialist in American government, but in Congress, or the

Presidency, or pressure groups: a historian is a "colonialist" or an "early national period" man. This is natural when education is divorced from the promotion of values. To work on a real problem (such as how to eliminate poverty in a nation producing $800-billion worth of wealth each year), one would have to follow that problem across many disciplinary lines without qualm, dealing with historical materials, economic theories, political problems. Specialization insures that one cannot follow a problem through from start to finish. It ensures the functioning in the academy of the system's dictum: divide and rule.

Another kind of scholarly segregation serves to keep those in the university from dealing with urgent social problems: that which divorces fact from theory. We learn the ideas of the great philosophers and poets in one part of our educational experience. In the other part, we prepare to take our place in the real occupational world. In political science, for instance, a political theorist discusses transcendental visions of the good society; someone else presents factual descriptions of present governments. But no one deals with both the *is* and the *ought*; if they did, they would have to deal with how to get from here to there, from the present reality to the poetic vision. Note how little work is done in political science on the tactics of social change. Both student and teacher deal with theory and reality in separate courses; the compartmentalization safely neutralizes them.

It is time to recall Rousseau: "We have physicists, geometricians, chemists, astronomers, poets, musicians, and painters in plenty, but we have no longer a citizen among us."

Rule 4: *To be "scientific" requires neutrality.* This is a misconception of how science works, both in fact and in purpose. Scientists *do* have values, but they decided on these so long ago that we have forgotten them; they aim to save human life, to extend human control over the environment for the happiness of men and women. This is the tacit assumption behind scientific work, and a physiologist would be astonished if someone suggested that he starts from a neutral position as regards life or death, health or sickness. Somehow the social scientists have not yet got around to accepting openly that their aim is to keep people alive, to distribute equitably the resources of the earth, to widen the areas of human freedom, and therefore to direct their efforts toward these ends.

The claim that social science is "different," because its instruments are tainted with subjectivity, ignores the new discoveries in the hard sciences: that the very fact of observation distorts the measurement of the physicist, and what he sees depends on his position in space. The physical sciences do not talk about certainty anymore, but rather about "probability"; while the probabilities may be higher for them than in the social sciences, both fields are dealing with elusive data.

Rule 5: *A scholar must, in order to be "rational," avoid "emotionalism."* (I know one man in Asian studies who was told by university administrators that the articles he wrote upon his return from Vietnam were too "emotional.") True, emotion can distort. But it can also enhance. If one of the functions of the scholar is accurate description, then it is impossible to describe a war both unemotionally and accurately at the same time. And if the special competence of the mind is in enabling us to perceive what is outside our own limited experience, that competence is furthered, that perception sharpened, by emotion. Even a large dose of emotionalism in the description of slavery would merely *begin* to convey accurately to a white college student what slavery was like for the black man.

Thus, exactly from the standpoint of what intellect is supposed to do for us—to extend the boundaries of our understanding—the "cool, rational, unemotional" approach fails. For too long, white Americans were emotionally separated from what the Negro suffered in this country by cold, and therefore inadequate, historical description. War and violence, divested of their brutality by the prosaic quality of the printed page, became tolerable to the young. (True, the poem and the novel were read in the English classes, but these were neatly separated from the history and government classes.) Reason, to be accurate, must be supplemented by emotion, as Reinhold Niebuhr once reminded us.

Refusing, then, to let ourselves be bound by traditional notions of disinterestedness, objectivity, scientific procedure, rationality—what kinds of work can scholars do, in deliberate unneutral pursuit of a more livable world? Am I urging Orwellian control of scholarly activities? Not at all. I am, rather suggesting that scholars, on their own, reconsider the rules by which they have worked, and begin to turn their intellectual energies to the urgent problems of our time.

Specifically, we might use our scholarly time and energy to sharpen the perceptions of the complacent by exposing those facts that any society tends to hide about itself: the facts about wealth and poverty, about tyranny in both communist and capitalist states, about lies told by politicians, the mass media, the church, popular leaders. We need to expose fallacious logic, spurious analogies, deceptive slogans, and those intoxicating symbols that drive people to murder (the flag, communism, capitalism, freedom). We need to dig beneath the abstractions so our fellow citizens can make judgments on the particular realities beneath political rhetoric. We need to expose inconsistencies and double standards. In short, we need to become the critics of the culture, rather than its apologists and perpetuators.

The university is especially gifted for such a task. Although obviously not remote from the pressures of business and military and politicians, it has just that margin of leeway, just that tradition of truth-telling (however violated in practice) that can enable it to become a spokesman for change.

This will require holding up before society forgotten visions, lost utopias, unfulfilled dreams—badly needed in this age of cynicism. Those outside the university who might act for change are deterred by pessimism. A bit of historical perspective, some recapitulation of the experience of social movements in other times, other places, while not wholly cheering, can at least suggest possibilities.

Along with inspirational visions, we will need specific schemes for accomplishing important purposes, which can then be laid before the groups that can use them. Let the economists work out a plan for free food, instead of advising the Federal Reserve Board on interest rates. Let the political scientists work out insurgency tactics for the poor, rather than counter-insurgency tactics for the military. Let the historians instruct us or inspire us, from the data of the past, rather than amusing us, boring us, or deceiving us. Let the scientists figure out and lay before the public plans on how to make autos safe, cities beautiful, air pure. Let all social scientists work on modes of change instead of merely describing the world that is, so that we can make the necessary revolutionary alterations with the least disorder.

I am not sure what a revolution in the academy will look like, any more than I know what a revolution in the society will look like. I doubt that it will take the form of some great cataclysmic event. More likely, it will be a process, with periods of tumult and of quiet, in which we will, here and there, by ones and twos and tens, create pockets of concern inside old institutions, transforming them from within. There is no great day of reckoning to work toward. Rather, we must begin *now* to liberate those patches of ground on which we stand—to "vote" for a new world (as Thoreau suggested) with our whole selves all the time, rather than in moments carefully selected by others.

Thus, we will be acting out the beliefs that always moved us as humans but rarely as scholars. To do that, we will need to defy the professional mythology that has kept us on the tracks of custom, our eyes averted (except for moments of charity) from the cruelty on all sides. We will be taking seriously for the first time the words of the great poets and philosophers whom we love to quote but not to emulate. We will be doing this, not in the interest of the rich and powerful, or in behalf of our own careers, but for those who have never had a chance to read poetry or study philosophy, who so far have had to strive alone just to stay warm in winter, to stay alive through the calls for war.

3

Historian
as Citizen

This piece appeared as an essay in the Sunday book review section of the *New York Times*, September 25, 1966. Although I had been educated in a very traditional way at New York University and Columbia University, and done a year of post-doctoral work at Harvard University, I had not been behaving like a traditional historian. That is, I had taken time out of scholarly work to participate in the Southern movement for civil rights, and, now living in Boston and teaching at Boston University, I was heavily involved in the movement against the war in Vietnam. This essay gave me an opportunity to think about the relationship between my two lives, as historian, as activist, and to turn from simply practicing what I called "history as private enterprise," to history as the work of a citizen.

When some historians march with Negroes in the South, and others demonstrate against Presidential foreign policy, one is led to wonder if we are witnessing a slow change in role for the historian.

509

Traditionally, he is a passive observer, one who looks for sequential patterns in the past as a guide to the future, or else describes historical events as unique and disorderly—but without participating himself in attempts to change the pattern or tidy the disorder.

In a world hungry for solutions, we ought to welcome the emergence of the historian—if this is really what we are seeing—as an activist-scholar, who thrusts himself and his works into the crazy mechanism of history, on behalf of values in which he deeply believes. This makes of him more than a scholar; it makes him a citizen in the ancient Athenian sense of the word.

The historian is one man among men, and how free is any man to change the world in which he lives? The world's great thinkers have been quite aware of the paradox of man as both created and creative, and acted accordingly. But thinking has become professionalized and "disciplined" in modern times, with a crushing effect on the propensity to act.

For historians, there is an additional trap: The more we work on the data of the past, the weightier the past seems. Events that have already taken place develop the look of having been *necessary*; indeed they were, but only at the instant they occurred, when further interference was impossible. This necessariness of the past tends to infect our thinking about the future, weighing down our disposition to act. Man is wounded by his history, and we then assume he must be transfixed by it.

History can work another way, however. If the present seems an irrevocable fact of nature, the past is most usable as a way of suggesting possibilities we would never otherwise consider; it can both warn and inspire. By probing the past we can counter myths which affect the way we act today. We can see that it is possible for an entire nation to be brainwashed; for an "advanced, educated" people to commit genocide; for a "progressive, democratic" nation to maintain slavery; for apparently powerless subordinates to defeat their rulers; for economic planning to be unaccompanied by restrictions on freedom; for oppressed to turn into oppressors; for "socialism" to be tyrannical; for a whole people to be led to war like sheep; for men to make incredible sacrifices on behalf of a cause.

Yet the historical experience of mankind does have limits; while it suggests some of the things that are possible, it has not at all exhausted the possibilities. Bounded in our imaginations, tyrannized by the past, we do not realize there is a universe of tricks still to be played. The past, in other words, suggests what can be, not what must be.

This is not at all to say that we are completely free at any moment in time. There is a remorselessly factual world which assails us at every turn, every decision. But because this world is *here* it exerts a disproportionate influence on our actions. The only way to compensate for this is to behave *as if* we are freer than we think. We can never—because the present is harsh and the future is shadow—weigh accurately how free we are, what our possibilities are at any moment. With such uncertainty, and recognizing the tendency toward overestimating the present, there is good reason for acting on the supposition of freedom.

Erik Erikson speaks in *Insight and Responsibility* about psychologists surprised by the strength of people, which seems to come, he says, from "unexpected encounters...and from opportunities beyond our theoretical anticipations."

Acting *as if* is a way of resolving the paradox of determinism and freedom, a way of overcoming the tension between past and future. It is risky to act as if we are free, but (unless one is content with things as they are) it is just as risky to act as if we are bound, and there is even less chance of reward. The leaps that man has made in social evolution came from those who acted *as if*; the four Negro youngsters in Greensboro who in 1960 walked into Woolworth's acted as if they would be served; Garrison and Phillips, against all apparent common sense, acted as if they would arouse a cold nation against slavery; England in 1940 acted as if it could repel a German invasion; Castro and his tiny group in the hills behaved as if they could take over Cuba.

Nietzsche in *The Use and Abuse of History* attacked the bullying nature of history and the sterility of academic historiography. His opening words were quoted from Goethe: "I hate everything that merely instructs me without increasing or directly quickening my activity." He called the formal detached-from-life history of his time "a costly and superfluous luxury of the understanding" while people "are still in want of the necessaries of life."

Later in this same essay, Nietzsche calls for man to free himself from the past. "People think nothing but this troublesome reality of ours is possible." And at another point he speaks of the "historically educated fanatic of the world-process" who "has nothing to do but to live on as he has lived, love what he has loved, hate what he has hated, and read the newspapers he has always read. The only sin is for him to live otherwise than he has lived."

This is the Existentialist call for Freedom, for Action, for the exercise of Responsibility by man. Too often these days the Existentialists are accused of a blind refusal to recognize the limits set by the world around them. Sartre, trying to reconcile Existentialism and Marxism, is attempting the impossible, critics have said. But Sartre does not fail to see the armies, the prisons, the blind judges, the deaf rulers, the passive masses. He talks the language of total Freedom because he knows that acting *as if* we are free is the only way to break the bind.

To see our responsibility to present and future, is a radically different approach to history, for the traditional concern of academic history, from the start of investigation to the finish, is with the past, with only a few words muttered from time to time to indicate that all this digging in the archives "will help to understand the present." This encirclement of the historian by the past has an ironic effect in the making of moral judgments.

The usual division among historians is between those who declare, as Herbert Butterfield does in *History and Human Relations*, that the historian must avoid moral judgments, and those, like Geoffrey Barraclough in *History in a Changing World*, who deplore the loss of moral absolutes in a wave of "historicism" and "relativism." What is ironic is the fact that when historians do make moral judgments they are *about the past*, and in a way that may actually weaken moral responsibility in the present.

Moral indignation over Nazism illustrates the point. When such judgment becomes focused on an individual, it buries itself with that person and sticks to no one else. It follows that Germans who obeyed orders during the war may now weep at a showing of *The Diary of Anne Frank*, blaming the whole thing on Adolf Hitler. (How often these days in Germany does one hear "if not for Adolf Hitler..."?) It is this *ad hominem* assignment of responsibility, this searching the wrong place for blame with a kind of moral astigmatism, which Hannah Arendt tried to call attention to in her dissection of the Eichmann case.

But is it any better to widen responsibility from the individual to the group? Suppose we blame "the Nazis." Now that the Nazi party is disbanded, now that anti-Semitism is once again diffuse, now that militarism is the property of the "democratic" Government of West Germany as well as the "socialist" Government of East Germany, doesn't that kind of specific attribution of blame merely deflect attention from the problems of today? If we widen it so as to include Germans and Germany, what effect does this have except to infinitesimally decrease the sale of Volkswagens, and to permit every other nation in the world but Germany to commit mayhem in a softer glow?

What we normally do then, in making moral judgments, is assign responsibility to a group which in some specific historic instance was guilty, instead of selecting the elements of wrong, out of time and place (except for dramatic effect), so that they can be applicable to everyone including ourselves. (Is this not why Brecht, Kafka, Orwell are so powerful?)

It is racism, nationalism, militarism (among other elements) which we find reprehensible in Nazism. To put it that way is alarming, because those elements are discoverable not just in the past, but now, and not just in Germany, but in all the great powers, including the United States.

I am suggesting that blame in history be based on the future and not the past. It is an old and useless game among historians to decide whether Caesar was good or bad. Napoleon progressive or reactionary, Roosevelt a reformer or a revolutionist. True, certain of these questions are pertinent to present concerns; for instance, was Socrates right in submitting to Athens? But in a recounting of past crimes, the proper question to ask is not "Who was guilty then?" unless it leads directly to: "What is our responsibility now?"

Erikson, in a section of his *Insight and Responsibility* entitled "Psychological Reality and Historical Actuality," speaks of Freud's concern because this patient Dora had confronted her family with some of their misdeeds. "Freud considered this forced confrontation an act of revenge not compatible with the kind of insight which he had tried to convey to the patient. If she now knew that those events had caused her to fall ill, it was her responsibility to gain health, not revenge, from her insight." What makes this story even more interesting is that there is a suggestion that Freud may himself have been guilty of the same thing, by being annoyed with what his patient had done, and discontinuing her treatment.

It is this irony in moral judgment which explains why we are surprised when someone like George Kennan opposes a "moralistic" approach to other countries. This approach, he says—correctly—looks backward rather than forward. It leads to fixed enmities and fixed friendships, both based on past conditions; it prohibits a flexibility in the future.

In politics, the practice is common to all sides. When the Soviet Union defines imperialism as a characteristic of capitalist nations, it is limiting the ability of its people to criticize undue influence exerted over another country by a socialist nation. When it defines corruption as a manifestation of "bourgeois" culture, it makes it more difficult to deal with such a phenomenon in its own society. When the United States defines the Soviet sphere as "totalitarian" and the West as "free," it becomes difficult for Americans to see totalitarian elements in our society, and liberal elements in Soviet society. Moralizing in this way, we can condemn the Russians in Hungary and absolve ourselves in Vietnam.

To *define* an evil in terms of a specific group when such an evil is not peculiar to that group but possible anywhere is to remove responsibility from ourselves. It is what we have always done in criminal law, which is based on revenge for past acts, rather than a desire to make constructive social changes. (Capital punishment notably, but also all imprisonment, illustrates this.) It is often said that the French are always prepared for the previous war. In the modern world, we are always ready to identify those responsible for the previous act of evil.

Both history and art should instruct us. The crucial thing is to reveal the relationship between evil and ourselves. This makes it enormously useful to show how Hitler could emerge out of a boy playing in the field. Or to show (as in *Lord of the Flies*) how innocent children can become monsters, or (as in Bergman's film *The Virgin Spring*) how a loving father can become a vengeful murderer or (as in *Who's Afraid of Virginia Woolf?*) how an "ordinary" man and wife can become vultures.

But to survey the atrocities in world history and to conclude (as the defense lawyer did in the film *Judgment at Nuremberg*) that "we are all guilty" leads us nowhere when it neglects to identify the elements of failure so that we can recognize them in the future. On the other hand, to end by punishing the specific persons who were indeed guilty is to leave us all free to act, unnoticed, in the same way. For when our day of judgment comes, it will be, like all the others, one disaster late.

If a work like *The Deputy* succeeds in having people ask not Why did the Pope remain silent? but, Why do people everywhere, at all times, and *now*, remain silent? then the play itself has broken the silence of the stage. And those of us who are deputies of that Muse, History, now need to break ours.

4

Secrecy, Archives, and the Public Interest

In 1970 I was invited to give a paper at the annual meeting of the Society of American Archivists in Washington D.C. My paper was entitled "The Archivist & The New Left," and was published a number of years later (1977) in a journal, *The Midwestern Archivist*. In introducing my article, the editor said: "Professor Howard Zinn shocked and offended many in his audience...[but] it was welcomed most enthusiastically by a relatively small group of mainly younger archivists who thereafter committed themselves to publicizing Zinn's views and persuading their colleagues of the validity of his criticisms of the archival profession. Largely as a consequence of Zinn's challenge, a small number of archivists in San Francisco the following year...founded ACT, an informal caucus dedicated to reform within both the Society of American Archivists and the archival profession."

L et me work my way in from the great circle of the world to us at the center by discussing, in turn, three things: the social role of the professional in modern times; the scholar in the United States today; and the archivist here and now.

I will start by quoting from a document—an insidious move to gain rapport with archivists, some might say, except that the document is a bit off the beaten track in archival work (a fact we might ponder later). It is the transcript of a trial that took place in Chicago in the fall of 1969, called affectionately "the Conspiracy Trial." I refer to it because the transcript occasionally touches on the problem of the professional person— whether a lawyer, historian, or archivist—and the relation between professing one's craft and professing one's humanity. On October 15, 1969, the day of the national Moratorium to protest the war in Vietnam, defense attorney William Kunstler wore a black armband in court to signify his support of the Moratorium and his protest against the war. The government's lawyer, Thomas Foran, called this to the attention of the judge, saying: "Your Honor, that's outrageous. This man is a mouthpiece. Look at him, wearing a band like his clients, your Honor."

The day before the Moratorium, Attorney Kunstler had asked the court to recess October 15 to observe the Moratorium. This dialogue between Kunstler and Judge Hoffman then followed:

> Mr. Kunstler:...And I think it is as important, your Honor, to protest more than some thirty thousand American deaths and Lord knows how many Vietnamese deaths that have occurred in that country as it is to mourn one man (Eisenhower) in the United States, and if courts can close for the death of one man who lived a full life, they ought to be closed for the deaths of thousands and millions of innocent people whose lives have been corrupted and rotted and perverted by this utter horror that goes on in your name and my name...
>
> The Court: Not in my name.
>
> Mr. Kunstler: It is in your name, too, in the name of the people of the United States.
>
> The Court: You just include yourself. Don't join me with you. Goodness. Don't you and I...
>
> Mr. Kunstler: You are me, your Honor, because every citizen...you are a citizen and I am a citizen.
>
> The Court: Only because you are a member of the bar of this court and I am obliged to hear you respectfully, as I have done.
>
> Mr. Kunstler: No, your Honor, you are more than that. You are a citizen of the United States.

The Court: Yes, I am.
Mr. Kunstler: And I am a citizen of the United States, and it is done in our
    name, in Judge Hoffman's name and William Kunstler's name.
The Court: That will be all, sir. I shall hear you no further.

Kunstler was trying to accomplish something very difficult, to get a judge to emerge from that comfortable corner which society had declared as his natural habitat, and to declare himself a citizen, even while on the bench, in his robes, plying his profession. Kunstler said a slaughter was taking place in Vietnam, and it was going on in the name of all citizens, and he wanted the Judge to recognize that fact not only in the evening at home after his robes were off, or at the country club on the weekend, but there, in his daily work, in his most vital hours, in the midst of his job of judging. Kunstler failed, but his attempt illustrates the tension all of us feel, if we have not been totally mesmerized by the grandeur of our position, the tension between our culture-decreed role as professionals and our existential needs as human beings.

Professionalism is a powerful form of social control. By professionalism I mean the almost total immersion in one's craft, being so absorbed in the day-to-day exercise of those skills, as to have little time, energy, or will to consider what part those skills play in the total social scheme. I say *almost-total* immersion, because if it were total, we would be suspicious of it. Being not quite total, we are tolerant of it, or at least sufficiently confused by the mixture to do nothing. It is something like Yossarian's jaundice, in *Catch 22*, where Joseph Heller writes:

> Yossarian was in the hospital with a pain in his liver that fell just short of
> being jaundice. If it became jaundice they could treat it. If it didn't become
> jaundice and went away they could discharge him. But this just being short
> of jaundice all the time confused them.

By social control I mean maintaining things as they are, preserving traditional arrangements, preventing any sharp change in how the society distributes wealth and power. Both in pre-modern and modern times, the basic combination for social control has remained the same: force and deception. Machiavelli, writing on the threshold of the modern era, drew upon the past to prescribe for the future that same combination: the power of the lion, the shrewdness of the fox. The modern era has magnified enormously both elements: it has concentrated force more efficiently than ever before and it has used more sophisticated techniques for deception. The printing press, heralding the spread of knowledge to large sections of the population, made large-scale deception both necessary and possible, and in the last four centuries we have progressed from the printing press to color television, from Machiavelli to Herman Kahn.

There were few professionals in the old days. Now they are everywhere, and their skills, their knowledge, could be a threat to the status quo. But their will to challenge the going order is constantly weakened by rewards of money and position. And they are so divided, so preoccupied with their particular specialties, as to spend most of their time smoothing, tightening their tiny piece of linkage in the social machine. This leaves very little time or energy to worry about whether the machine is designed for war or peace, for social need or individual profits, to help us or to poison us.

This specialization of modern times is pernicious enough for waiters, auto mechanics, and doctors, and the bulk of the workers in society, who contribute to the status quo without even knowing it, simply by keeping the vast machinery going without a hitch. But certain professionals serve the status quo in special ways. Weapons experts, or scientists in military research, may be enormously gifted in their own fields, yet so constricted in their role as citizens, as to turn over their frighteningly potent products without question or with very feeble questioning, to whatever uses the leaders of society decide. Remember the role of the humane genius, Robert Oppenheimer, in the decision to drop the atomic bomb on Hiroshima. Oppenheimer was a member of the Scientific Advisory Panel which recommended the dropping of the bomb in Hiroshima, thinking it was necessary to save lives. But Oppenheimer later commented (his testimony is in the files of the AEC):

> We didn't know beans about the military situation in Japan. We didn't know whether they could be caused to surrender by other means or whether the invasion was really inevitable.

Equally important for social control as the military scientists, are those professionals who are connected with the dissemination of knowledge in society: the teachers, the historians, the political scientists, the journalists, and yes, the archivists. Here too, professionalization leads to impotence, as everyone is given a little corner of the playground. And it is considered unprofessional to organize everyone in the yard to see if the playground director is violating various of the Ten Commandments as we play. We have all heard the cries of "don't politicize our profession" when someone asks joint action on the war in Vietnam. This has the effect of leaving only our spare time for political checking-up while those who make the political decisions in society—this being their profession—work at it full time.

The neat separation, keeping your nose to the professional grindstone, and leaving politics to your left-over moments, assumes that your profession is not inherently political. It is neutral. Teachers are objective and unbiased. Textbooks are eclectic and fair. The historian is even-handed and factual. The archivist keeps records, a scrupulously neutral job. And so it goes, as Kurt Vonnegut says.

However, if any of these specialists in the accumulation and dissemination of knowledge were to walk over to another part of the playpen, the one marked political sociology, they could read Karl Mannheim, who in *Ideology and Utopia*, points out (following Marx, of course, but it is more prudent to cite Mannheim) that knowledge has a social origin and social use. It comes out of a divided, embattled world, and is poured into such a world. It is not neutral either in origin or effect. It reflects the biases of a diverse social order, but with one important qualification: that those with the most power and wealth in society will dominate the field of knowledge, so that it serves their interests. The scholar may swear to his neutrality on the job, but whether he be physicist, historian, or archivist, his work will tend, in this theory, to maintain the existing social order by perpetuating its values, by legitimizing its priorities, by justifying its wars, perpetuating its prejudices, contributing to its xenophobia, and apologizing for its class order. Thus Aristotle, behind that enormous body of philosophical wisdom, justifies slavery, and Plato, underneath that dazzling set of dialogues, justifies obedience to the state, and Machiavelli, respected as one of the great intellectual figures of history, urges our concentration on means rather than ends.

Now maybe we have not been oblivious to this idea that the professional scholars in any society tend to buttress the existing social order and values of that society. But we have tended to attribute this to other societies, or other times or other professions. Not the United States. Now now. Not here. Not us. It was easy to detect the control of the German scholars or the Russian scholars, but much harder to recognize that the high school texts of our own country have fostered jingoism, war heroes, the Sambo approach to the black man, the vision of the Indian as savage, and the notion that white Western Civilization is the cultural, humanistic summit of man's time on earth.

We could see where scholars in Nazi Germany or Soviet Russian, by quietly doing their job, would be perpetuating an awful set of conditions; to keep *that* kind of social order intact, and we hoped intellectuals would rebel. The U.S. however, was a different matter; what was wrong here was not the social order itself, but problems at the margins of it. It was all right for intellectuals to keep this basically decent order intact by doing our jobs; and we could attack the problems at the margins by signing petitions and joining political campaigns after hours.

Events of the past decade, I would now argue, have begun to challenge that complacency, that part-time commitment to political involvement which assumes a basically just society, needing only marginal reforms. We have won those reforms. The U.S. is the great model in history of the reformist nation, and the past half-century has been labeled by one of our important historians as "The Age of Reform." We have had New Deal legislation to take care of our economic flaws, Civil Rights laws to take care of our racial problems, Supreme Court decisions to expand our rights in court, the Good Neighbor Policy, Marshall Plan, and Alliance for Progress to humanize our relations with other countries.

Yet, it is exactly at the crest of these reforms that the United States has found itself in a turbulent internal crisis in which a significant part of the younger generation has begun to question the legitimacy of the government, the values of the culture. How is it that after a barrage of Supreme Court decisions, Civil Rights laws, the confrontation between black and white in this country is at its most intense? How is it that after the New Freedom, the New Deal, the Fair Deal, the New Frontier, and the Great Society, the distribution of the immense resources of this society is at its most irrational, its most wasteful?

The problems of the United States are not peripheral and have not been met by our genius at reform. They are not the problems of excess, but of normalcy. Our racial problem is not the Ku Klux Klan or the South, but our fundamental liberal assumption that paternalism solves all. Our economic problem is not a depression but the normal functioning of the economy, dominated by corporate power and profit. Our problem with justice is not a corrupt judge or bribed jury but the ordinary day-to-day functioning of the police, the law, the courts, where property rights come before human rights. Our problem in foreign policy is not a particular mad adventure: the Spanish American War or the Vietnam War, but a continuous set of suppositions about our role in the world, involving missionary imperialism, and a belief in America's ability to solve complex social problems.

If all this is so, then the *normal* functioning of the scholar, the intellectual, the researcher, helps maintain those corrupt norms in the United States, just as the intellectual in Germany, Soviet Russia, or South Africa, by simply doing his small job, maintains what is normal in those societies. And if so, then what we always asked of scholars in those terrible places is required of us in the United States today: rebellion against the *norm*.

In the United States, however, the contribution of scholars to the status quo is more subtle and more complex than in more blatantly oppressive societies. Only a small number of scholars give direct service to the war. Most simply go about their scholarly business, their acts of commission subtle, their acts of omission gross. For instance, the historian's emphasis on presidents and laws only subtly perpetuates an elitist approach to politics; missing completely in Morison's *Oxford History of the American People* is the Ludlow Massacre of 1914. The political scientists' emphasis on electoral politics only subtly *suggests* that voting is the central problem in democratic control: you look in vain for extensive work on the politics of protest. The scholar's emphasis on Supreme Court decisions only subtly distorts the fact of constitutional rights; constitutional histories omit the reality of police power in determining how much free expression there really is on the streets.

The archivist, even more than the historian and the political scientist, tends to be scrupulous about his neutrality, and to see his job as a technical job, free from the nasty world of political interest: a job of collecting, sorting, preserving, making available, the records of the society. But I will stick by what I have said about other scholars, and argue that the archivist, in subtle ways, tends to perpetuate the political and economic status quo simply by going about his ordinary business. His supposed neutrality is, in other words, a fake. If so, the rebellion of the

archivist against his normal role is not, as so many scholars fear, the politicizing of a neutral craft, but the humanizing of an inevitably political
craft. Scholarship in society is inescapably political. Our choice is not
between being political or not. Our choice is to follow the politics of the
going order, that is, to do our job within the priorities and directions set
by the dominant forces of society, or else to promote those human values
of peace, equality, and justice, which our present society denies.

I would guess from my small experience—and I leave it up to you
to carry on the discussion from there—that the following points are true:

(1) That the existence, preservation, and availability of archives,
documents, records in our society are very much determined by the distribution of wealth and power. That is, the most powerful, the richest elements in society have the greatest capacity to find documents, preserve
them, and decide what is or is not available to the public. This means government, business, and the military are dominant.

(2) That one of the ways in which information is controlled and
democracy denied, is by the government withholding important documents from the public, or keeping secret their existence altogether, or cen-
soring them (how we must struggle to get data about the Gulf of Tonkin,
the Bay of Pigs, the bombing of Laos, CIA operations in Guatemala).
And that while the ostensible purpose of such secrecy is the physical security of the nation, the actual purpose is almost always the political security of those who run the nation. Ernest May writes in *A Case for Court
Historians*:

> The materials needed by historians would also contain much information
> which, on other than security grounds, government officials would prefer
> not to see released... Sec'y of State Rusk could conceivably have been
> embarrassed by revelations about advice he gave when Asst. Sec'y of State
> in the Truman Administration...

(3) That the collection of records, papers, and memoirs, as well as
oral history, is biased towards the important and powerful people of the
society, tending to ignore the impotent and obscure: we learn most about
the rich, not the poor; the successful, not the failures; the old, not the
young; the politically active, not the politically alienated; men, not
women; white, not black; free people rather than prisoners; civilians
rather than soldiers; officers rather than enlisted men. Someone writing

about Strom Thurmond will have no problem with material. But what if someone wants to write about the blind black jazz pianist, Art Tatum?

(4) That, despite the recent development of oral history, the written word still dominates, and this tends to emphasize the top layers, the most literate elements in the population.

(5) That the emphasis in the collection of records is towards individuals rather than movements, towards static interviews, rather than the dynamics of social interaction in demonstrations. For instance, where is the raw material—that *very* raw material—on the experience of demonstrators in Chicago at the hands of the police at the 1968 convention, which was used by the Walker Commission? I wonder, for instance, if Boston University, proud that it holds the papers of Martin Luther King, has recorded the experience of students who were clubbed by police at the Student Union last year?

(6) That the emphasis is on the past over the present, on the antiquarian over the contemporary; on the non-controversial over the controversial; the cold over the hot. What about the transcripts of trials? Shouldn't these be made easily available to the public? Not just important trials like the Chicago Conspiracy Trial I referred to, but the ordinary trials of ordinary persons, an important part of the record of our society. Even the extraordinary trials of extraordinary persons are not available, but perhaps they do not show our society at its best. The trial of the Catonsville 9 would be lost to us if Father Daniel Berrigan had not gone through the transcript and written a play based on it.

(7) That far more resources are devoted to the collection and preservation of what already exists as records, than to *recording* fresh data: I would guess that more energy and money is going for the collection and publication of the Papers of John Adams than for recording the experiences of soldiers on the battlefront in Vietnam. Where are the interviews of Seymour Hersh with those involved in the My Lai Massacre, or Fred Gardner's interviews with those involved in the Presidio Mutiny Trial in California, or Wallace Terry's interviews with black GI's in Vietnam? Where are the recorded experiences of the young Americans in Southeast Asia who quit the International Volunteer Service in protest against American policy there, or of the Foreign Service officers who have quietly left?

Let me point to some random pieces of evidence to illustrate these points I have made about the going bias in archival work. Recently,

I came across a list of letterpress publications sponsored, assisted, or endorsed by the National Historical Publications Commission of the General Services Administration. The papers of thirty-three Americans are being published. There is one black person on the list, and that is Booker T. Washington. What about Mother Jones, the labor organizer, or Bob Moses, the SNCC leader, or the papers of the man who lives down the street? I know that the very stress on collected papers is severely limiting, but there *are* papers of the leaders of protest movements. Of course there are problems: the papers of Big Bill Haywood were destroyed by the United States Government. But what of Eugene Debs or Clarence Darrow? I suppose it could be claimed that there is one important leader of a protest movement on the list: that is Jefferson Davis.

Another item of evidence: In an article by Amelia Fry and Willa Baum, oral historians at the University of California at Berkeley, the authors cite the lack of money as causing some oral history projects to erase important tapes. They note the feeling among some persons involved in oral history that "since preserving tapes is expensive and required special conditions, the decision should hinge on the affluence of the project and the relative importance of the person interviewed."

The Oral History Collection at Columbia University seems almost a caricature of the biases I have noted. It has long ignored the poor, the obscure, the radicals, the outcasts—it has ignored movements and living events. When I wrote from the South, in the midst of the civil rights movement, to the Columbia Oral History Collection to try to get them to tape what was happening at the time in Georgia, Alabama, Mississippi, I got a bureaucratic response which muttered about money and priorities and allocations, the upshot of which was: no. But the latest report of the Oral History Project gives doting attention to its Air Force Project, Navy Project, Marine Project. It is happy to have the reminiscences of General O'Donnell: how about the reminiscences of the various Yossarians in the Air Force? It has the Allan Nevins project, which consists of interviewing the friends of Allan Nevins. (Wouldn't it be more interesting to interview the enemies of Allan Nevins?) It will spend much time interviewing members of the Eisenhower Administration, based on a $120,000 grant from the National Archives. Has the Project interviewed Mrs. Fannie Lou Hamer of Ruleville, Mississippi, or Eldridge Cleaver or Dave Dellinger? Did it go to the Poor Peoples' March and interview the people camped

out there in the mud? Has it interviewed Vietnam veterans in the rehabilitation hospitals? Does it go into the ghetto around Columbia
University? Or is that job only for Kenneth Clark? For important contemporary interviews, one might do better to consult *Playboy Magazine*
than the Columbia Oral History Project.

Another item of evidence: In the American Historical Association
newsletter of April 1970, there is a report of the "Thirteenth Meeting of
the Advisory Committee on '*Foreign Relations of the United States,*' a series
of State Department documents issued by the year. The Advisory
Committee has representatives of the American Historical Association,
the American Political Science Association, and the Society of
International Law. One clause in the report reads: "In 1962 the Secretary
of State officially set the time lapse at 20 years; the committee cannot have
access to these Foreign Relations documents until twenty years have
elapsed. By what right, in a democracy requiring the enlightenment of the
public, does any bureaucrat make such decisions for us all? Yet this advisory committee of scholars is painfully obsequious before the might of
government: they complain that it takes as much as two years for the volumes of Foreign Relations to get clearance from Department of State, but
instead of challenging the whole concept of clearance, the committee only
asks humbly for the clearance procedure to move faster.

Note also that while the Foreign Relations staff must wait twenty years, the public at large must wait thirty years, and indeed the committee of scholars say they are "highly disturbed by the narrowing gap"
between the scholars' wait and the public's wait, and by the possibility of
"outside, *ad hoc* publication"—that is publication outside the official aegis
of the State Department and the committee of scholars. Such publication,
they warn, may beat the Foreign Relations series to the punch, and "provide inaccurate or partial accounts" which "may achieve a popular
impact." This could be offset, however, by quicker publication of the
Foreign Relations series, with the cooperation of the State Department.
We find in it another paragraph of outstanding timidity, in which the
committee expresses its concern that the open period may move back
beyond 30 years. Such a move, the committee says with measured syco-
phancy, would be "violative of the commendable record the Department
of State has maintained over the decades in making the foreign relations
documentation of the United States publicly and systematically avail-

able." In that paragraph the committee notes that other countries such as England are moving in the opposite direction, decreasing the years of closed records, and then it concludes: "The committee is not herewith advocating advancing the open period for full public access to diplomatic documentation, but it believes that everything should be done to prevent it from being set back in excess of thirty years."

Thus, the committee falls all over itself in gratitude that the public only has to wait thirty years. It doesn't want to rock the boat (which all hands aboard know is sinking) by asking for a shorter wait. Where is the bold, inquiring spirit of the scholar in a democratic state, demanding to see government documents as a right, not a privilege? No wonder, with such a government, and with such scholars, we so desperately need I.F. Stone.

What is the net effect of the kind of archival biases I have just described? To protect governmental authorities from close scrutiny, and therefore from the indignation, the anger that might result from a closer look at government policies. To glorify important people, powerful people, military, political, and business leaders, to keep obscure the lives of ordinary people in the society. To maintain such archival biases requires no malfeasance on the part of archivists, only passivity, only falling into the lines already set by the dominant trends of the profession.

I say *dominant* trends, because I know there are some good things being done in archival work, some pioneering efforts in recording events, in oral history with ordinary people, in black history, in labor history. But let's resist the characteristically American trick of passing off fundamental criticism by pointing to a few reforms. The Saigon regime reformed itself for twenty years before it finally fell. We are still passing civil rights laws, and poverty bills. Let us not once again be happy because like Yossarian, we don't quite have jaundice. We also are not quite cured. Like Yossairian, we are still in the hospital. Like him, we are in danger. And we will remain in danger until, like him, we rebel.

I have argued that the crisis of present-day America is not one of aberration, but of normalcy, that at issue are not marginal characteristics, but our central operating values: the profit system, racial paternalism, violence towards those outside our narrow pale. If this is so, then scholarly passivity, far from being neutral and disinterested, serves those operating values. What is required then is to wrench ourselves out of our passivity, to try to integrate our professional lives with our humanity.

I have only two proposals for archivists: One, that they engage in a campaign to open all government documents to the public. If there are rare exceptions, let the burden of proof be on those who claim them, not as now on the citizen who wants information. And two, that they take the trouble to compile a whole new world of documentary material, about the lives, desires, needs, of ordinary people. Both of these proposals are in keeping with the spirit of democracy, which demands that the population know what the government is doing, and that the condition, the grievances, the will of the underclasses become a force in the nation.

To refuse to be instruments of social control in an essentially undemocratic society, to begin to play some small part in the creation of a real democracy: these are worthy jobs for historians, for archivists, for us all.

5

Freedom
Schools

One of the remarkable achievements of the 1964 Mississippi Summer, when people came from all over the country to work with the civil rights movement, was the Freedom School. Thirty years later, it still stands, I think, as an extraordinary experiment in educational democracy. My wife Roslyn and I were in Mississippi that summer, and I volunteered to teach in one of the Freedom Schools in Jackson. I wrote this account for *The Nation*, November 23, 1964. It appeared under the title "Schools in Context: The Mississippi Idea."

The triple murder last summer in Mississippi probably would not have taken place if there had not been plans to set up a school at the Mount Zion Baptist Church near Philadelphia. It was the visit of three young civil rights workers to the burned-out school site which led them to arrest, and then death. That a school should frighten a band of Americans into committing murder is not totally credible; that those particular killers made a deliberate mental connection between their act and the establishment of a "Freedom School" in the area is unlikely. Yet education spells danger to certain people at certain times, and what happened in Mississippi last summer suggests a continued sensing of peril.

This article will be concerned, however, not so much with the danger the Freedom Schools represented to some in Mississippi but with the promise they opened for the rest of us, throughout America. For eight weeks, more than 2,000 Negro youngsters, averaging fifteen years of age but ranging from six to twenty-six and older, went to schools which violated all the rules and regulations of educational orthodoxy. They were taught by teachers who met no official qualifications; they assembled in church basements or on the streets or in the fields; they came and went without attendance records, grades or examinations.

It was an experiment that cannot be assessed in the usual terms of "success" and "failure," and it would be wrong to hail it with an enthusiasm which would then lead it to be judged by traditional criteria. But that venture of last summer in Mississippi deserves close attention by all Americans interested in the relationship between education and social change.

The idea, and the term "freedom school," were first brought before the civil rights movement by a slender Howard University student named Charles Cobb, who several years ago interrupted his studies to plunge into the Mississippi Delta as a field secretary for the Student Nonviolent Coordinating Committee. Cobb pursued his scheme with quiet, slow persistence, and when plans were laid last fall for a big "Mississippi Summer," with 1,000 or more volunteers to arrive in the state, Freedom Schools were on the agenda. Bob Moses, director of the Mississippi project, has a Masters degree from Harvard. He gave the idea close attention, and when Northern students were recruited during the spring many of them were told to be ready to teach.

The man who took charge of the summer Freedom School project for COFO (the Council of Federated Organizations: a union of SNCC, CORE and other civil rights groups in Mississippi) was Staughton Lynd, a young historian whose field, some might have noted warningly, is the American Revolution. He had spent three years in north Georgia in a rural cooperative community, and then three more years at Spelman College, a Negro women's college in Atlanta. He had just resigned from Spelman in protest against restrictions on the academic freedom of both students and faculty, and was then immediately hired by Yale University. From the orientation session at Oxford, Ohio, in early June to the end of August, Lynd was a dynamo of an administrator, driving into the remotest rural regions of Mississippi to keep the schools going.

At Oxford, the Freedom School teachers were warned about difficulties: "You'll arrive in Ruleville, in the Delta. It will be 100 degrees, and you'll be sweaty and dirty. You won't be able to bathe often or sleep well or eat good food. The first day of school, there may be four teachers and three students. And the local Negro minister will phone to say you can't use his church basement after all, because his life has been threatened. And the curriculum we've drawn up—Negro history and American government—may be something you know only a little about yourself. Well, you'll knock on doors all day in the hot sun to find students. You'll meet on someone's lawn under a tree. You'll tear up the curriculum and teach what you know."

They were also told to be prepared for violence, injury, even death. But they hardly expected it so soon. The first batch of teachers had just left the orientation session for Mississippi when word came that one of the summer volunteers (Andrew Goodman), a white community center director (Mickey Schwerner) and a local Meridian Negro youth (James Chaney) were missing. A publicity stunt, said Mississippi officials. But the SNCC veterans of Mississippi disagreed. "Man, those guys are dead," Jim Forman said.

The summer volunteers got into cars and into buses, and moved into Mississippi. Two hundred Freedom School teachers spread out over the state, from Biloxi in the Gulf Coast up into Ruleville in the Delta, and farther north to Holly Springs, covering twenty-five communities. Day by day, more and more Negro kids came around to the schools, and the expected enrollment of 1,000 rose to 1,500 then to 2,000.

One of the Jackson Freedom Schools opened in early August in a church basement just a short walk from the state COFO office on Lynch Street. Its combination of disorder and inspiration was very much like that of the other schools in the state. The "faculty" was more experienced than most: a young high school teacher of English from Vermont acted as "coordinator"—a combination of principal, janitor, recreation supervisor, and father confessor. Another youthful junior high school teacher of mathematics was from Brooklyn; there was one college professor of history who had taught for a number of years in a Southern Negro college; also, an enthusiastic young woman named Jimmy Miller, whose husband, Warren Miller, had written in *The Cool World* about young Harlem Negro kids. The teachers lived in spare rooms, or spare corners of rooms, in Negro houses of the neighborhood.

Two days before the school was set to open, in close to 100 degree heat, the teachers canvassed the neighborhood for students. Each asked one of the Negro youngsters hanging around the COFO office to go along with him, so as to establish from the start that these were friendly visitors walking up on the porches, knocking on the doors, asking: "Do y'all know about the Freedom School starting on Wednesday over at Pratt Memorial Church?" No, they mostly didn't, and so the information passed across the threshold: "It's for teen-age boys and girls, to learn about Negro history, and the Constitution, and the civil rights movement, and mathematics, and maybe French and Spanish, the way they don't get learning in the regular school." Kids on bicycles stopped, and one friend told another, and the word was passed on.

No one paid attention to details like age requirements, so that at the opening of school, sixty kids showed up, from six to nineteen; Jimmy Miller marched the six to ten children off to a corner, to read with them, and teach them freedom songs, and sound out French words whose English equivalents they had not yet discovered, and painstakingly correct their spelling.

With the older ones, fourteen to nineteen, any idea of going in an organized way through an outline of Negro history or American government was soon dropped. Beyond a core of seven or eight who came faithfully every morning at nine and stayed until mid-afternoon, there were a dozen others who came and went as they liked. So the history professor started each day from where the mood struck him, from some point on which he thought the students' recognition might be fastened just long enough to pull them onward.

One day, it was an editorial in the morning's *Clarion-Ledger*, charging that civil rights workers were teaching people to break the law. "What do you think about that editorial? Is it true? If you could write a letter to the editor about it, what would you say?...Here's paper and pencil, go ahead. We'll pick out one or two and *really* send them to the editor." This was not education for grades, not writing for teacher's approval, but for an immediate use; it was a learning surrounded with urgency. And the students responded with seriousness, picking apart the issues: Are we for the law? Is there a higher law? When is civil disobedience justified? Then the teacher explored with them the differences between statutory law, constitutional law, "natural" law.

On another day the teacher told his students about the annual fair he had visited the previous afternoon. It was held in Neshoba County where the bodies of the three murdered civil rights workers had just been discovered. A strain of tension and fear pervaded the crowds that day at the fair. Gov. Paul Johnson had said: "It is not Mississippi's obligation to enforce federal statutes." A representative of the John Birch Society had said: "I am for the Constitution, for freedom, for the open Bible." The students were asked: Do you disagree? Aren't you for the Constitution? For freedom? The discussion became heated. Distinctions were drawn, and became more and more refined, all by the students themselves, the teacher just listening: "Which Constitution does he mean, U.S. or Mississippi?...Maybe we're for different *parts* of the U.S. Constitution...Well, maybe we're for the same part, but we *interpret* it differently."

Teachers and students ate lunch together in the church basement, sang together, then separated into various activities. In a creative writing class, a teen-age girl named Lillie Mae Powell wrote a poem "The Negro Soldier":

One day while I was visiting a certain
City this is what I saw. A Negro
soldier with a broken arm who
was wounded in the war.

The wind was blowing from the
North; there was a drizzle of
Rain. He was looking from the
Last place; his arm was in a sling.

The Negro soldier didn't go
Home. He was looking to the east
And to the west. His broken arm
was in a sling.

The Jackson Freedom Schools faced only mild harassment. Early in the session, while canvassing for more students, two teachers—one a slim, blonde Skidmore undergraduate—were picked up by the police, held for several hours, then discharged. Violence spluttered around the COFO office in Jackson one ugly Saturday night: a young man building book shelves for a Freedom School bookmobile on the street across from the office was clubbed to the ground by a white man who fled in a car; a dance hall where teachers and students were spending the evening was sprayed with bullets by a passing car, and a Negro boy was wounded; crosses were burned. But by Mississippi standards, Jackson was peaceful.

In the rural areas of the state, the danger was greater. A church used as a Freedom School in the little town of Fluckstadt was burned to the ground (when the teachers arrived on the scene, fifteen youngsters were waiting under a tree for class to begin). A Northern doctor who spent the summer in Mississippi with the movement told of the two white girls who lived along in a hilltop house out in the country, 30 miles from Canton, and held a Freedom School there. In McComb, so dangerous that the Justice Department pleaded with the Mississippi project not to send anyone in there, a Freedom School was started by a Washington, D.C., speech teacher, a young Negro named Ralph Featherstone. Two days after the first contingent arrived, a bomb exploded in the midst of sleeping SNCC workers. But 100 children came regularly to attend the McComb Freedom School.

Violence took the headlines, but behind it a phenomenal thing was happening to Mississippi: 2,000 young people were having experiences that would—for some in a small way, for some drastically—change their lives.

The kind of teaching that was done in the Freedom Schools was, despite its departure from orthodoxy—or, more likely, because of it—just about the best kind there is. For the teachers were selected not by any mechanical set of requirements but on the basis of general intelligence, enthusiasm and the kind of social conscience that would drive them to spend a hot summer in Mississippi without pay. They taught, not out of textbooks, but out of life, trying to link the daily headlines with the best and deepest of man's intellectual tradition.

Their object was not to cram a prescribed amount of factual material into young minds, but to give them that first look into new worlds which would, some day if not immediately, lead them to books and people and ideas not found in the everyday lives of Mississippi Negroes. They didn't always succeed, but even their failures were warmed by the affection that sprang up everywhere between teachers and students, both aware that they talked with one another inside a common cradle of concern.

One afternoon in Jackson, a visiting folk singer brought the students of a Freedom School out into the sun-baked street back of the church, formed them into a huge circle, and taught them an Israeli dance chant imploring the heavens for rain to help the harvest. Older Negroes passed by, sat on porches, listened to their children utter strange words and dance this strange dance. The young ones seemed to understand; they were beginning, for the first time in their lives, to reach beyond their street, beyond their state, to join in some universal plea.

A Stanford University professor of English told how hard he had to work to make contact with these young boys and girls, so different from his regular students. But it came. He walked into class, put them at ease with some foolery, got them to talk about the events in the morning newspaper. Then: "Who would like to read a story?" One girl stubbornly had her back to the class. He asked her to read and she turned around. "She then read this story by Eudora Welty, 'The Worn Path,' and read it beautifully; it could have been a staged performance. And this was back of the church, the only place we had for my class, with the noise of traffic all around."

When the girl finished reading, the teacher asked the class: "Did you like the story?" There was a chorus: "Yes!" "Why?" They responded. He told them about subject and plot, about description and dialogue, how in general one analyzes a story. He asked how the story made them *feel*, and one said sad, and another said it made her laugh, and he asked how could a story do both at the same time, and spoke to them of *irony*. "God, how they understood!"

He bridged what they read and how they lived. He read to them from Ralph Ellison's *Invisible Man*. This was written, he said out of a Negro boy's personal experience. "Now I'll tell you a story of my personal experience." And he told of a wartime incident involving himself and Negro soldiers, in Charleston, South Carolina. And then, to the class: "Who else wants to tell a personal story?" The next day, one girl brought in a story which, he realized, was prose as good as that written by any

Stanford freshmen he had encountered. And so, literature was read and created at the same time.

In these classes, discussions of democracy, of the philosophy of nonviolence, were hardly academic. In one Jackson school the class met to elect delegates to a convention of all the Jackson Freedom Schools. An older fellow named Jimmy, age 24, had been hanging around the class for the past few days. He spoke breezily of having recently spent three years in jail for a knifing. The teacher suggested that Jimmy sit up at the desk and chair the meeting. He laughed and complied, "OK, now, I'll choose the delegates," he announced. There were objections from all over the room: "We've got to *elect* them"!

"What kind of resolutions are we going to propose to the convention?" a girl asked. One was suggested: "If any kid is treated brutally in school in Jackson, all the kids in the Jackson schools walk out; we'll have a chairman in each school; we won't act just on say-so; we'll get written affidavits and witnesses before we take action. It's something like a student union."

The teacher was curious: "Do students get beaten up in your schools?" A girl answered: her principal had beaten a boy until he bled.

Jimmy then told how he'd been beaten by a teacher when he was younger. And how he and some friends had then found the teacher alone and taken revenge. "We had a nice understanding after that." He hesitated. "But I don't know what I'd do now. You know this nonviolence we're talking about. If it happened now I might beat him. Or I might just laugh and go away. I was young then and full of hate. At that time, I see something I want. I take it. Now, I *ask*. It's the movement I guess...I want my son to come up different."

Role playing was used very often in the Freedom Schools. "Kids that age are natural actors," a teacher explained. "And it puts them in other people's shoes. We don't want to win easy arguments over straw foes. They have got to be tough thinkers, tough arguers." The teacher listed on the blackboard Barry Goldwater's reasons for voting against the civil rights bill: (1) It is unconstitutional. (2) No law will end prejudice ("We cannot pass a law that will make you like me or me like you."). (3) It can't be enforced. (4) It violates the idea of States' rights. The class went over the arguments, with one boy portraying Goldwater, and defending his points powerfully, another trying to break them down.

Outside on the street, in front of the building, an energetic, red-headed teacher was pointing to a blackboard propped up in the sun, the kids sitting in rows in the shade of the building. "OK, we can build any kind of community we want now. What will the rules be?" This was a hortatory kind of teaching, but a kind the schools fostered: constantly talking with students not just about what *is*, but about what *should be.*

A Harvard graduate in literature who had taught in Israel worked in a Vicksburg Freedom School.

> It was hard. Youngsters hung around the school, slept there. Every morning, they were like corpses on the floor. To start class, you had to clean them out. The school was cramped, noisy. We used role playing a lot. Kids would portray three generations of Negro families, and we learned history that way. We sat in a circle rather than the usual classroom format, to stress the equality of teacher and student. I read to them from Thomas Wolfe's *You Can't Go Home Again* and from Martin Luther King's *I Have a Dream*, then had them write speeches as if they were Senators urging passage of the civil rights bill. I tried to extend the idea of oppression beyond race. If you pick on a small kid with glasses and beat him up, aren't you acting the same as these white segregationists? I asked them.

One teacher spent a whole hour with his students discussing the word "skeptical." He told them: "This is a Freedom School and we should mean what we say. We should feel free to think as we want, question whomever we like, whether it's our parents, our ministers, our teachers, yes, me, right here. Don't take my word for things. Check up on them. Be *skeptical*." For these youngsters it was a new way of looking at the classroom. They told how in their high school in Jackson the rooms were wired so that at the flick of a switch the principal could listen in on any class in the school. Teachers were afraid to discuss controversial subjects.

The blonde girl from Skidmore College taught French to teenagers in her Freedom School. "I try to do the whole class in French, use pantomime a lot...I soon realized these kids had never had contact with a white person before; maybe that's the greatest thing about this whole experience. If nothing else is accomplished, it's been a *meeting*, for both student and teacher.... We have a Freedom Hour at eleven every morning. They run it themselves, make their own rules." She was asked if the Freedom Schools were not, in fact, *indoctrinating* the children. She paused. "Yes, I suppose so. But I can't think of anything better to indoctrinate them with. Freedom. Justice. The Golden Rule. Isn't there *some* core of belief a school should stand by?"

A green-eyed, attractive Radcliffe graduate, interpreter now for an international agency, whose field was Latin American history but who had not a day of teaching experience or education courses to her credit, went to work in a Freedom School:

> My kids were 9 to 13. I told them about the Spanish background of Negro slaves in the United States, about the Caribbean islands and the slave plantation system as it developed there, and compared that system with the one in the English colonies. I spoke to them about life in Brazil, about the multiracial societies in Latin America where people get along fine. I told them about the problems of kids their age in Venezuela, in Puerto Rico (where I've spent some time). Yes, it did something for them psychologically to know that there are people in the world worse off than they are!

Without a strict curriculum to follow, the schools capitalized on the unexpected. A class held out in the sun would take advantage of passers-by, draw them into discussion. One day, three Negro women came by who'd just been trying to register to vote and had been rebuffed. The teacher beckoned: "Come over here and tell my students what happened." And so the children learned about the registration procedure, about voting, about what to tell their parents about going down to register. One of the middle-aged women, her anger still fresh, told them they must become educated if they wanted to change things.

It was risky, teaching without an ordered curriculum. And because it was risky, the Radcliffe girl said, it led to treasures.

> I could experiment, do what I wanted, try things completely new, because I had no one to answer to, no reports to make. Nothing could happen to me or to these young people that would leave us worse off than before. And I could go off on tangents whenever I wanted, something I'd be afraid to do in a regular school setup. Wherever thoughts and discussion led, we followed. There was nothing we didn't dare turn to.

The road from study to action was short. Those who attended the schools began to come to mass rallies, to canvass for registration of voters, to question things around them for the first time. In Shaw County, "out in the rural," when the regular school began its session in August (Negro schools in the Delta open in August so that the children will be available for cotton picking in the fall), white Freedom School teachers were turned away from the regular school cafeteria, where some students had invited them to a lunch. The students then boycotted the school and flocked in large numbers to the local Freedom School.

The Freedom Schools' challenge to the social structure of Mississippi was obvious from the start. Its challenge to American education as a whole is more subtle. There is, to begin with, the provocative suggestion that an entire school system can be created in any community outside the official order, and critical of its suppositions. But beyond that, other questions were posed by the Mississippi experiment of last summer.

Can we, somehow, bring teachers and students together, not through the artificial sieve of certification and examination but on the basis of their common attraction to an exciting social goal? Can we solve the old educational problem of teaching children crucial values, while avoiding a blanket imposition of the teacher's ideas? Can this be done by honestly accepting as an educational goal that we want better human beings in the rising generation than we had in the last, and that this requires a forthright declaration that the educational process cherishes equality, justice, compassion and world brotherhood? Is it not possible to create a hunger for those goals through the fiercest argument about whether or not they *are* worthwhile? And cannot the schools have a running, no-ideas-barred exchange of views about alternative ways to those goals?

Is there, in the floating, prosperous, nervous American social order of the Sixties, a national equivalent to the excitement of the civil rights movement, one strong enough in its pull to create a motivation for learning that even the enticements of monetary success cannot match? Would it be possible to declare boldly that the aim of the schools is to find solutions for poverty, for injustice, for race and national hatred, and to turn all educational efforts into a national striving for those solutions?

Perhaps people can begin, here and there (not waiting for the government, but leading it) to set up other pilot ventures, imperfect but suggestive, like the one last summer in Mississippi. Education can, and should, be dangerous.

6

The New History

As I write this in 1996, the guardians of the "old history" are angry. Their heroes (Christopher Columbus, Andrew Jackson, Theodore Roosevelt, Woodrow Wilson, the giants of industry, and various military heroes) are increasingly being viewed as racists, militarists, and exploiters of labor. Indians, blacks, women, working people are getting more attention, their point of view listened to more closely. Twenty years ago, when I wrote the following article, a "new history" was just beginning to emerge, stimulated by the protest movements of the Sixties. This appeared in the *Boston Globe*, December 20, 1974, under the title "History Writing Changes."

There is a healthy change in the writing of history these days. We are hearing more from the bottom layers of society, so long submerged and silent under the volumes of memoirs produced by the political elite, and the histories written by intellectuals.

540

Out of the pages of a new book, *All God's Dangers*, an uneducated black man, Nate Shaw, speaks to us of his life, with enormous wisdom, with the rhythms of the southern earth in his language.

And we are listening now to those we thought dead. In Dee Brown's *Bury My Heart at Wounded Knee*, Chief Joseph challenges the intruder: "Perhaps you think the Creator sent you here to dispose of us as you see fit." And Red Cloud tells of the massacre of his people.

The graffiti has moved from the walls. It is a prison break. Tommy Trantino, a poet and artist in prison for life, starts his "Lock the Lock" with an unforgettable account of his first-grade encounter with the law: "The Lore of the Lamb."

Women, speaking out of the past, tell their hidden history in Eve Merriam's collection of memoirs, *Growing Up Female in America*. And the new Feminist Press publishes old-time treasures like "Life in the Iron Mills."

Working people talk honestly to Studs Terkel, who records their voices in *Hard Times* and *Working*.

Why are we now getting more history from below? Perhaps because of the tumult of social movements in America these past 15 years. Perhaps because we have less faith these days in the words of the famous. Now we are offended by Kissinger's definition of history, in his book *A World Restored*, in which he writes, "History is the memory of states."

To read the history of the Vietnam War from Kissinger's standpoint, the American troops were withdrawn and the truce was signed as a result of shrewd diplomacy (his own, of course) in Paris.

Such history would not only ignore the amazing resistance of the Vietnamese peasant to the most powerful military machine in the world. It would wipe out of our memories the huge movement against the war which grew in this country between 1965 and 1970. By 1968, half the draftees in northern California were failing to report for induction. One day in 1969, October 15, Moratorium Day, two million Americans gathered in thousands of places all over the country to protest the war. The movement spread into the armed forces, with GIs on patrol in Vietnam wearing black armbands of protest.

Mr. Nixon said the protesters had no effect on him. But the Pentagon Papers, not meant for public eyes, told the story: that in early 1968, the Johnson Administration was turned around in its escalation policy, not only by the Vietnamese spirit, but also by fear of the growing resistance to the war at home. And the Watergate record shows Mr. Nixon so undone by opposition that he became near-hysterical at the sight of one picketer near the White House.

It is good that we are getting more history from below. We have believed too long in our own helplessness, and the new history tells us how, sometimes, movements of people who don't seem to have much power can shake the rich and the powerful. Even out of their seats of power. Even into the prisoner's dock which they prepared for others.

7

"A University Should Not Be a Democracy"

When I first began teaching, I had a rather naïve idea that colleges and universities, however the world outside was dominated by money and power, were special havens for freedom of expression and democracy. It did not take long for me to be disabused of that idea. My first personal experience was at Spelman College in Atlanta, where my political activism offended the college president and—though I was a full professor, with tenure, and chair of the history department, presumably secure—he fired me, with forty-eight hours notice, for "insubordination," a charge which was undoubtedly true. The university, as in the title of Ellen Schrecker's book on McCarthyism in higher education, is "No Ivory Tower," but a battleground in which students, faculty, university workers have to struggle constantly for democratic rights. Boston University was a particularly intense site in that struggle. In this essay, I tried to put what happened there, under the presidency of John Silber, in the larger context of the attempt of the national establishment, after the exuberant democracy of the Sixties, to restore order and authority. This appeared in *The Progressive*, June 1980, under the title "A Showcase of Repression."

Think a bit about the history of these past twenty-five years in the United States—the years of the black revolt and the movements of women, prisoners, native Americans; the years of the great campaign against the Indochina war and the illumination of Watergate. It was in these twenty-five years that the Establishment began to lose control of the minds, the loyalties of the American people. And since about 1975, the Establishment has been working steadily, with some desperation, to reassert that control.

In those years of the movements, great numbers of Americans began to take democracy seriously, to think for themselves, to doubt the experts, to distrust the political leaders, and to lose faith in the military, the corporations, even the once-untouchable FBI and CIA. In mid-1975, the Harris poll, looking at the years since 1966, reported that public confidence in the military had dropped from 62 percent to 29 percent, in business from 55 percent to 18 percent, in the President and Congress from 42 percent to 13 percent. When the Survey Research Center of the University of Michigan posed the question, "Is the Government run by a few big interests looking out for themselves?" the answer in 1964 was "yes" from 53 percent of those polled.

Harvard political scientist Samuel Huntington reported to the Trilateral Commission—a group of Establishment intellectuals and political leaders from the United States, Europe, and Japan, assembled by David Rockefeller and Zbigniew Brzezinski in the early 1970s—on what he called "The Democratic Distemper." "The 1960s witnessed a dramatic upsurge of democratic fervor in America," Huntington observed, and that troubled him. He noted that in 1960 only 18 percent of the public believed the Government was spending too much on defense, but by 1969 this figure had jumped to 52 percent. He wrote:

> "The essence of the democratic surge of the 1960s was a general challenge to existing systems of authority, public and private. In one form or another, this challenge manifested itself in the family, the university, business, public and private associations, politics, the governmental bureaucracy, and the military services. People no longer felt the same obligation to obey

those whom they had previously considered superior to themselves in age, rank, status, expertise, character, or talents."

Huntington was worried: "The question necessarily arises, however, whether if a new threat to security should materialize in the future (as it inevitably will at some point), the Government will possess the authority to command the resources, as well as the sacrifices, which are necessary to meet that threat." We were beset, he wrote, by "an excess of democracy." He suggested "desirable limits to the extension of political democracy."

Let us imagine the nation's elite addressing itself to the problem posed by Huntington. If the proper respect for authority is to be regained, then surely the universities must do their job. It has usually been possible to count on them to fill the lower ranks of the Establishment with technical and professional people who, fairly well paid and engrossed in their own advancement, would serve as loyal guards for the system. But in the early 1960s, young black rebels came off the college campuses and formed the militant cutting edge of the black movement, and then the universities became the focal points of teach-ins and demonstrations against the war.

True, the loss of allegiance extended far beyond the campus, into the workplaces and homes of ordinary Americans, into the Army ranks where working-class GIs turned against the war. Still, with twelve million young people in college, the fear of a working-class-professional-class coalition for social change makes it especially important to educate for obedience. And the intensifying economic pressures of unemployment and inflation may suggest to the national elite that it is now easier, and also more necessary, to teach the teachers as well as the students the advisability of submitting to higher authority.

Thus, it may be part of some larger reordering of the nation's mind when the president of Boston University, John Silber, says on national television (CBS's *60 Minutes*, viewed by thirty million), "A university should not be a democracy.... The more democratic a university is, the lousier it is."

As soon as Silber became B.U.'s president in 1971, he began to act out his philosophy by destroying what is at the heart of humanistic education: the idea that students and faculty should have a decisive voice about the way education takes place. And he had an additional target: the idea that workers at the university should have some right to decide the conditions of their work.

Those of us who are involved in the intense, sometimes bizarre battles at Boston University have not had much time to step back and look for some grand national design into which we might fit. Furthermore, it seems immodest; we have not yet become accustomed to the fact that our campus, with its nondescript assortment of buildings straddling Commonwealth Avenue in the heart of the city, with its heterogeneous enrollment of 20,000 students, has begun to attract the attention of the country. It is as if a rare disease had broken out somewhere, and was being observed by everyone with much curiosity and a bit of apprehension.

John Silber, formerly a professor of philosophy at the University of Texas, had hardly settled into the presidential mansion—a twenty-room house, rent-free, only one of the many fringe benefits adding up to perhaps $100,000 a year which augment his $100,000 salary—when he embarked on the process the Germans call *Gleichschaltung*: "straightening things out." He quickly made it clear that he would not tolerate student interference with military recruiting at B.U. for the war in Vietnam. Early in 1972, his administration invited Marine recruiters to a campus building. When students sat down on the steps of that building, remaining there firmly but peaceably, he called the police. Arrests and beatings followed, and Silber said he was maintaining "an open university."

The university that was "open" to the Marine Corps turned out to be closed to the campus chapter of Students for a Democratic Society (SDS), which lost its charter and its right to meet on campus because a scuffle had taken place during an SDS demonstration. The logic was established: SDS was a violent organization, while the Marine Corps had a well-known record for pacifism.

A series of demonstrations followed, to which police were called again and again, and which they broke up with arrests and brutal beatings. The turmoil led to a huge assembly of the Faculty Senate, which voted overwhelmingly that Marine recruiting should be halted until faculty and students could discuss and vote on whether it should be resumed. Silber simply ignored the resolution. That summer, without the called-for campus discussion, he polled the faculty through the mail, not specifically asking about Marine recruiting, but rather about whether the faculty wanted an "open university." The answer, of course, was yes, and the recruiters were on campus to stay.

That fall, the students did vote, in an unprecedented turnout. A large majority rejected the policy of military recruiting on campus. Silber ignored them, too. Picketing students, he said, were "primates," and votes did not matter. "I would be much more impressed," he told the student newspaper, the *Daily Free Press*, "by a thoughtful document that was brought in by one single student than I would by a mindless referendum of 16,000." He would decide who was "thoughtful" and who was "mindless."

The centralization of power in Silber's hands, his contempt for faculty as well as students, his attempts to push tenured professors at the School of Theology into resigning, his repeated attacks on the tenure system—all this led to a burst of faculty unionization under the auspices of the American Association of University Professors (AAUP). Silber, confident of his oratorical powers, went to faculty meetings at the various colleges, arguing that a vote for unionization would mean the end of the "collegial" model and the introduction of the "industrial" model at Boston University. Nonetheless, the faculty voted by a clear majority for a union. In the next four years, the Silber administration spent huge sums of money before the National Labor Relations Board (NLRB) and in the courts, trying unsuccessfully to overturn that vote.

Silber's argument against the AAUP was that well-paid and articulate college professors don't need a union. But when other employees tried to act in concert to improve their situation, his administration did its best to beat them down. Workers at the Student Health Clinic were fired when they met to voice grievances. The NLRB, after lengthy hearings, ruled that the B.U. administration was guilty of unfair labor practices in firing seven employees and intimidating the rest.

In the spring of 1976, departmental budget cuts led to anger on all sides. Later, it was learned that while Silber was jacking up student tuition and telling the faculty there was no money for raises, he was putting several million dollars a year into "reserves" and listing these set-aside funds as "expenses" so that the budget barely showed a surplus.

There were calls for Silber's dismissal from ten of the fifteen deans, from faculties at various colleges in the university, from virtually every student organization, and finally from a Faculty Senate meeting. A committee of trustees, making its five-year evaluation of Silber, voted 7-

to-1 that his contract should not be renewed. But he worked furiously at lining up trustee votes, found powerful allies on the board, and persuaded them to keep him in the presidency.

As part of the campaign for control, Silber began to put the screws to campus newspapers that criticized him. Advertising was withdrawn from the *B.U. News* (which had been a pioneering critic of the Vietnam War under the editorship of Ray Mungo), causing it to close. A new student publication called *Exposure*, pitilessly anti-Silber (one of its headlines referred to him as: "Mediocre Philosopher, Expert Chiseler"), had its funds—allocated from student activities fees—cut off. A new policy was adopted: Campus newspapers that wanted funding from student activities fees must submit to prior review of their copy by faculty advisers. Programs at the campus radio station, WBUR, came under scrutiny of Silber's administrators, and one news director was fired when he refused to censor the tape of a speech by William Kunstler which contained a joke about John Silber.

It also became more and more clear that any faculty member who spoke out against Silber was in danger of being denied tenure or, if tenured, of being denied a pay raise. Again and again, departmental recommendations of raises for certain faculty who were outspoken critics of the Silber Administration were overruled. Early in Silber's administration, Professor Richard Newman, who had taught in the social sciences for nine years, resigned from the University, and told the *B.U. News* that budget cuts had eliminated almost half the faculty of his department, including "three or four of the best young teacher-scholars in the country." Newman said, "To disagree with the President is to be put on the Enemies List."

Students, faculty, and staff fought back. The *B.U. Exposure* raised outside money to keep publishing its stories of administration shenanigans. There was evidence that Silber was pushing law school applicants to the top of the list when financial contributions from their families were sought. "I am not ashamed to sell these indulgences," he told a meeting of the trustees, and somehow the *Exposure* got hold of the transcript. It was a joke, Silber explained. And later, when the *Exposure* reprinted an administration memorandum in which a wealthy trustee was described as having sought and received "pre-admission" to the law school for his two small grandchildren "for the twenty-first century," Silber said that was a joke, too—lots of jokes from an administration known for its utter lack of humor.

Clerical workers on campus, underpaid and harassed, began organizing a union and won an NLRB election. Librarians formed a union and won their election. The Silber administration refused to negotiate with them, as it had with the faculty union. When the buildings-and-grounds workers, long unionized, went on strike for a week in the fall of 1978, members of the other unions, along with students, formed large picket lines and held support rallies. They were getting ready for a big labor upsurge the following spring.

In April 1979, Boston University, whose employees were now probably the most organized of any private university in the country, became the most strike-ridden in the country. The administration, having exhausted its court appeals, had to enter into negotiations with the faculty union. It came to an agreement, under the faculty threat of an April strike deadline, then reneged on the agreement at the last moment.

The faculty called a strike that same evening. The next morning, the lines were up at twenty-one buildings. By noon, hundreds of picketing faculty were joined by clerical workers and librarians insisting that the administration negotiate with them on their own demands.

The Silber administration had not expected such a reaction. The strike quickly crippled the operations of the university. Of 800 faculty in the bargaining unit, at least 700 were observing the picket lines, and of these about 350 were picketing. It was a rare, perhaps unique event in the history of American higher education—professors and secretaries walking the picket lines together in a common strike.

After nine days, the administration and faculty agreed on a contract providing substantial wage increases and a grievance procedure, but leaving most decisions on tenure and other matters still in the hands of the president and trustees. The clerical workers and librarians were still on the picket lines. With varying degrees of anguish, most of the faculty, feeling bound by a no-sympathy-strike clause in the contact, went back to work, but about seventy refused to cross the picket lines and held their classes out of doors or off campus. In nine more days, with the clerical workers and librarians holding firm, the administration agreed to negotiate, and everyone went back to work.

However, by late summer, the bargaining between the clerical workers and the administration broke down. Faculty and students returning for the fall semester found picket lines in place. It took a week for the strike to be settled by a contract agreement.

A small number of faculty had refused to cross the clerical workers' picket lines and either held their classes elsewhere or had colleagues take their classes. Five of us—political scientist Murray Levin, journalist Caryl Rivers, historian Fritz Ringer (president of the faculty union during the spring strike), psychologist Andrew Dibner, and I—were warned that we had violated the no-sympathy-strike provision. We replied that we had acted as individuals, according to our consciences, in expressing our support for the clerical workers. The Silber administration announced it was proceeding against us under the contract (we were all tenured professors) utilizing a provision for the suspension or dismissal of tenured professors on grounds of "gross neglect of duty or other just cause."

The charges against the B.U. Five, as we came to be known, lent new urgency to the work of the Committee to Save B.U., formed by faculty and students to rid the campus of the Silber machine.

Last December 18, a record number of faculty crowded into the largest auditorium on campus and listened to colleagues detail the charges against the Silber administration—mismanagement, centralization of decision-making, discrimination against women, violations of civil liberties, abusive and insulting behavior towards faculty.

Managers, whether of a government or of an institution, must learn how to gauge the capacity for rebellion so that they can head it off with the proper mix of repressions and concessions. The Silber administration had misjudged, when it reneged on the union contract in the spring of 1979, the faculty's willingness and readiness to strike. It misjudged again when it went after the B.U. Five. The threat to fire tenured faculty for honoring their convictions (Silber was quoted in the press as saying that faculty who signed union contacts had surrendered their right of conscience) aroused immediate protest.

Salvador Luria, Nobel Laureate in biology at MIT and a veteran of the antiwar movement, began circulating a petition among faculty at MIT, Harvard, and other colleges and universities in the Boston area, calling for the charges against the Five to be dropped and for Silber to be fired. Five hundred faculty in the Boston area signed the petition within two weeks. Another petition, signed by Luria, Noam Chomsky, historian John

Womack of Harvard, and historian of science Everett Mendelsohn of Harvard, began circulating nationwide. The signatures came pouring in.

Alumni wrote letters to the B.U. trustees and the Boston newspapers. On campus, student groups called for the charges to be dropped and for Silber's removal.

The Massachusetts Community College Council, representing faculty at fifteen colleges, protested. A sociologist withdrew his request to be a visiting professor at B.U., citing the administration's action. The Massachusetts Sociological Association passed a resolution expressing its concern for "freedom of conscience." A visiting linguistics professor from Paris brought word back to France and a telegram came shortly after, signed by fifteen distinguished French academicians, declaring their support for the B.U. Five.

But the slick pro-Silber profile on *60 Minutes* drew letters of support from viewers around the country who saw Silber as the man who would make the dirty college kids clean up their rooms and whip the radical faculty into line.

This spring, Silber still seems to have a firm grasp on his Commonwealth Avenue fiefdom. The trustees have given no overt signs of disaffection. The faculty union is entangled in a hundred grievances in the slow machinery of the contract. B.U. students, just handed an outrageous 16 percent tuition increase, are only beginning to organize. The threat of punishment still keeps many faculty in line. Indeed, the Dean of the College of Liberal Arts has announced he is adding a new factor in determining merit raises: A faculty member's teaching performance and publications, however stellar, may be offset, he says, by "negative merit"— actions designed to "harm the University."

There are some signs, however, that the protests from all over the academic world are having an effect. In February, the administration, through the intercession of a committee appointed by the official Faculty Council, agreed to drop the charges against the B.U. Five, and to negotiate or arbitrate the question of punishment for faculty refusal to cross picket lines.

After six members of the Committee to Save B.U. appeared before the trustees, in an unprecedented contact with a board always remote from the faculty, it was learned that there were expressions of disaffection among the trustees, who have been Silber's last stronghold.

The board has welcomed Silber's enthusiasm for the banking and utilities interests they represent, as well as his friendliness toward the military. Silber has been a spokesman for nuclear power and against the evening out of utility rates to favor the small consumer. B.U. has an overseas program in which it services the American military with courses and degrees, and Silber has shown obvious deference to the Government's military needs in ROTC and recruiting.

Nevertheless, as faculty, secretaries, librarians, and buildings-and-grounds workers remain organized and determined to fight back, as students become increasingly resentful at being treated like peons in a banana republic, as protests from alumni and from the national academic community intensify, the trustees may have to reconsider. When risks become too great, the clubs of the Establishment sometimes decide to change to a form of control less crass and more conciliatory. To prevent more drastic upheaval, the board may replace Silber with its own version of a Gerald Ford or Jimmy Carter.

Back in 1976, John Silber wrote on the *op-ed* page of the *New York Times:*

> As Jefferson recognized, there is a natural aristocracy among men. The grounds of this are virtue and talent...Democracy freed from a counterfeit and ultimately destructive egalitarianism provides a society in which the wisest, the best, and the most dedicated assume positions of leadership.... As long as intelligence is better than stupidity, knowledge than ignorance, and virtue than vice, no university can be run except on an elitist basis.

That makes for a neat fit with the philosophy of Samuel Huntington and the Trilateral Commission as they react to the "excess of democracy" that sprang from the movements of the 1960s. The Establishment's need to reassert control over the universities expresses itself most blatantly in the authoritarianism of John Silber at Boston University, but there is some evidence of a national trend in higher education toward the punishment of dissent and toward more direct intervention by big business in the workings of the universities. Earlier this year, the *New York Times* reported that schools of business around the country—at Dartmouth, Duke, and Cornell, among others—now have "executives-in-residence," to match the more customary university practice of maintaining "artists-in-residence" and "writers-in-residence." And the American Council on Education has been urging colleges to recruit more aggressively and to increase their ties to business. Management and marketing consultants are now common presences on campuses, as are union-busting consultants and "security" advisers.

As the economic situation of the universities becomes more precarious and faculties shrink, it becomes easier to get rid of undesirables, whether political dissidents or just troublesome campus critics. If they are untenured, dismissal is a simple process. If they are tenured, some ingenuity is required. The files of the American Association of University Professors show, according to one member of the AAUP's committee on academic freedom, "a disturbing number of mean little cases this year." He said, "There seem to be many tenth-rate John Silbers around."

The AAUP refers to an increasing number of "indecencies." At Central Washington State University, a tenured professor of political science, Charles Stasny, was recently fired by the trustees for "insubordination" after he missed several classes because he attended a scholarly meeting in Israel. The administration had first approved his departure, then opposed it. At Nichols College, outside Worcester, Massachusetts, a non-tenured professor who questioned the leadership of the college president was summarily dismissed. At Philander Smith College in Little Rock, two tenured professors and one non-tenured faculty member were fired last June and told to leave the campus the same day; they had complained to student newspapers and the trustees about the lack of academic freedom on campus.

Whether at universities or an other workplaces, whether in the United States or in other countries, we seem to face the same challenge: The corporations and the military, shaken and frightened by the rebellious movements of recent decades, are trying to reassert their undisputed power. We have a responsibility not only to resist, but to build on the heritage of those movements, and to move toward the ideals of egalitarianism, community, and self-determination—whether at work, in the family, or in the schools—which have been the historic unfulfilled promise of the word *democracy*.

8

The Marines
and the
University

In early 1972 the war in Vietnam was going full blast. Boston University's new president, John Silber, invited the Marine Corps to come to the campus to recruit students for the Marines. Anti-war students and faculty decided to block the entrance to the building where the recruiting was to take place, and Silber called the police to arrest them. I was at home that week, sick with the flu, but when I heard from some of the participants what happened, I decided to write about the incident, especially to answer the argument, posed by Silber and others, that to interfere with Marine recruiting on campus was to violate civil liberties. My article was printed in the alternative newspaper, *The Boston Phoenix*, in early April, 1972, entitled "Silber, the University, and the Marines," and then was reprinted as a special supplement to the student newspaper, the *B.U. News*, as well as in several other publications.

What happened at Boston University on Monday, March 27, in front of the Placement Office, was a classic incident of what our textbooks call, without humor, "civilization." There were the young people (and a few older ones) protesting the violence of war, obstructively, nonviolently. There were the police, dispersing, clubbing, arresting them. There was the court intellectual patiently explaining to the world that the actions of the police were necessary to protect "freedom" or the "open" society or "respect for the law." (Our textbooks almost never report such incidents, which recur frequently in the history of civilization; they dwell on more romantic events—the Renaissance, the Reformation, the Bill of Rights, the rise of parliamentary democracy.)

The actors in the Boston University affair could not be better cast. The United States Marine Corps, whose business abroad is mass murder, played a benign employment agency. The Boston Tactical Police, whose business is brutality, played the role of protector of the community. And Boston University's President John Silber, whose business is obfuscation, played the role of educator.

There is not much to say about the Tactical Police Force; they look like and act like what they are. There is a bit more to say about the U.S. Marine Corps, especially because it is presented to us by Silber and the B.U. Public Relations Office (citing the words of a University Council statement of 1970) as one of several "legally constituted organizations from the field of education, government, social services and business" who offer "meaningful and satisfactory employment."

There is a good deal to say about John Silber, doing what some intellectuals have done throughout history—finding a comfortable protected niche which the going order is willing to finance, in return for filling the heads of the younger generation with the most important lessons that the order wants them to learn (never mind the courses on Kant, Spinoza, and Marx; on Tolstoy, Joyce, and Faulkner, on history and politics and sociology; they are out front, but secondary). That lesson, taught crassly in grade school and high school, more sophisticatedly in college, is: respect for authority. The headline in B.U.'s official administration newspaper, *Currents*, reads: "Disruptive Students Must Be Taught Respect For Law, Says Dr. Silber."

It is true that one crucial function of the schools is training peo-

ple to take the jobs that society has to offer—in business, government, or
the military—so that the assembly lines of profit and death, whether
blue-collar or intellectual, may be manned and the society kept going as
is. But the much more important function of organized education is to
teach the new generation that rule without which the leaders could not
possibly carry on wars, ravage the country's wealth, keep down rebels and
dissenters: the rule of obedience to legal authority. And no one can do
that more skillfully, more convincingly, than the professional intellectual.
A philosopher turned university president is best of all. If his arguments
don't work on the ignorant students—who sometimes prefer to look at
the world around them than to read Kant—then he can call in the police,
and after that momentary interruption (the billy club serving as exclama-
tion point to the rational argument) the discussion can continue, in a
more subdued atmosphere.

But let us spend a little time on the United States Marine Corps.
The rest of our discussion depends very much on who they are and what
they do. John Silber would rather not bring up the Marines; this is understandable because they are an embarrassing burden for anyone to bear.

Of all the branches of the military, the Marines are the purest specialists in invading and occupying other countries; they have been called
on again and again to do the dirty work of the American Empire. All
through the twentieth century, they have been the storm troops of United
States intervention in Latin America. It was under Woodrow Wilson, an
intellectual and university president, who entered the White House in
1913, that the Marines did some of their most ruthless work. In 1915,
they invaded Haiti to put down a rebellion against the brutal military dictatorship of Vilbrun Sam, and incidentally to do a favor for the National
City Bank of New York and other banking interests. The Haitians resisted, and the Marines killed 2,000 of them as part of a "pacification" program, after which Haiti came under American military and economic
control. The following year, Marines invaded the Dominican Republic to
help put down an insurrection there, and remained as an occupying force.

By 1924, the economic activities of half of the twenty Latin
American countries were being directed by the United States. "Law and
order" were necessary to allow the normal financial operations to continue without interruption. When rebellion broke out in 1926 in Nicaragua
(where from 1912 to 1925 a legation guard of American Marines had

stood watch in the Nicaraguan capital) "American fruit and lumber companies sent daily protests to the State Department," according to the Council on Foreign Relations. The following year, President Coolidge sent 5,000 Marines to put down the rebels.

More recently, in 1958, President Eisenhower sent 14,000 Marines into Lebanon (twice the size of the Lebanese army), and it must be said that oil was somewhere on his mind. And when a rebellion broke out in the Dominican Republic in 1965 against the military regime there, Lyndon Johnson sent the Marines. (On television one evening, the American public watched a Marine sergeant shooting in the back a man in Santo Domingo who was kicking garbage into the street). The dispatch of Marines had been urged several years before by Senator George Smathers, a close friend of the Kennedy-Johnson administrations and of business interests in Latin America, who said at the time: "Many Americans, having invested $250 million in the Dominican Republic, believe that Generalissimo Trujillo was the best guarantee of American interests in the country...open intervention must now be considered to protect their property and to prevent a communist coup."

In Vietnam, the Marines have participated in the general destruction of that country. They have shot civilians, burned villages, and contributed heavily to this country's shame. A dispatch to the *Washington Evening Star* (August 4, 1965) reported:

> This week Marines teamed with South Vietnamese troops to overrun the Viet Cong-dominated village of Chan Son, 10 miles south of Da Nang. Among 25 persons they killed were a woman and four children.
> "Two of the children died at the hands of a young Marine who tossed a grenade into a village air raid shelter.

William R. Corson, a Marine colonel in Vietnam, has written about the Marines' search-and-destroy missions:

> There have been many thousands of search-and-destroy missions in Vietnam since the spring of 1965. Each of these operations has its own sad story to tell in terms of the almost total disregard for their effect on the Vietnamese people. Search-and-destroy tactics against VC-controlled areas have degenerated into savagery...

Corson wrote of Marine and ARVN units forcing 13,000 Vietnamese, almost all old men, women, and children, from Trung

Luong, "Without a shot being fired, we had conspired with the ARVN to literally destroy the hopes, aspirations, and emotional stability of 13,000 human beings. This was not and is not war—it is genocide."

John Silber would like to avoid discussing the Marines. Philosophers are sometimes annoyed by the intrusion of facts into comfortably vague generalizations. He says "We're going to operate a free campus here, so that students who are interested in acquiring information on a variety of jobs may find that information available on this campus...I feel obligated to defend the open campus policy." One would think from the statement by Silber after the Placement Office events that students were protesting the recruitment of Fuller Brush salesmen, instead of men to burn huts, kill peasants, invade other countries. Silber wants us to forget that, and so he talks abstractly about the "open campus." But it is part of rational inquiry to examine the empirical content of concepts. Let's look at the "open campus":

The campus is not and never has been open, so the term is fraudulent. Not all organizations are given space to recruit; the very language of the University Council statement sets standards for recruiting—"legally constituted organizations" from certain fields; that provides a basis for exclusion. ("SDS has lost its privilege to schedule facilities on the Boston University campus." Dean Staton Curtis.) Not every professor is allowed to teach a course at Boston University; there are standards (academic and other kinds). Not all students are allowed to register; there are requirements (academic and financial). Not all courses are allowed to get credit; there are criteria set by the Academic Policy Committee. Not even all cars are allowed on the parking lot; there are fees and qualifications.

It is nonsense for the administration to pretend that we must let all organizations recruit or none; what is human intelligence for if not to make distinctions? Would the Placement Office schedule interviews for a company that announced its jobs open to "whites only"? Would the Housing Office list apartments by landlords who discriminated by race or religion? Indeed, the University does make distinctions, in dozens of ways, some justifiable, others not. But to speak blithely of an "open campus" is to distort the truth and to substitute slogans for rational thought.

There is enough historical experience with such slogans to make us suspicious. The term "free enterprise" used by the National Association of Manufacturers meant freedom for corporations at the expense of consumers. The term "freedom of contract" used by the Supreme Court in the early part of this century meant freedom for employers at the expense of women and children working sixty hours a week. The term "Open Door" used by President McKinley meant freedom for the United States to despoil China just as the other powers had done. And the term "open campus" used by John Silber means freedom for the Marines and Dow Chemical and Lockheed Aircraft (all "legally constituted organizations") to find the personnel to keep the war and the military-industrial machine going.

Here is Silber:

> We have made it perfectly clear that there is no immunity on this campus from the common and statutory law of the United States or the Commonwealth of Massachusetts. These laws are in effect, and Boston University will cooperate in enforcing these laws.

Is not respect for human life more important than respect for law? Why did not Silber say instead (telling the Marines to go elsewhere): "We have made it perfectly clear that there is no immunity on this campus from the laws of humanity, which say Thou Shall Not Kill." It is sad that a university president, presumably committed to rational inquiry, should make "respect for the law" his supreme value. It is a standard which shows ethical impoverishment and intellectual laziness.

The truth is that John Silber does not believe in an open campus. It is just that he wants to be the doorkeeper; he wants to set the standards for who may use the University. The pretense of an open campus is to avoid having to reveal his standards, because they are not easily defensible. They are not moral ones—not standards based on a concern for human beings—not when he opens the campus to the Marines. His standards are legal ones ("legally constituted organizations"). If you are lethal but legal, you will be welcome at Boston University; if you are nonviolent but illegal, the police will be called out to disperse you (violently). Silber's standard of legality is appropriate, not for the independent thinker in a democracy, but for the obsequious servant of the overbearing state.

Thus, the apparently absolute and attractive principle of the "open campus" is not what it seems. We cannot accept abstract principles without examining their specific content, without asking: what standards are being used, what distinctions are being made? Would we accept the principle of "open skies" without asking if this includes being open to planes carrying hydrogen bombs over populated cities? Would we accept "open riverways" without asking if this means being open to radioactive wastes, or "open streets" without asking if this means being open to cars driving sixty miles an hour past children playing?

The problem, which Silber either does not see or does not want to see, is that any valid principle (like "openness," or "freedom," or "security") when made an absolute, clashes with other principles equally valid. Somebody's liberty may clash with another person's security. Somebody's right to recruit personnel may clash with another person's right to live. As Zechariah Chafee put it, "Your right to swing your fist stops where my nose begins." To hold to any one principle like the "open campus" ignoring other values, is simplistic thinking; it also contains the seeds of fanaticism. John Silber, in the current B.U. situation, has shown elements of both.

A rational and human view would balance one ethical principle against others. This cannot be done in the abstract; it can only be done by looking into the factual content of a specific situation. If there is a "right to protest," and a "right to an open campus," there is no way of deciding a conflict between them *on ethical grounds*, without inquiring more closely: who is protesting and how and at what cost to human life and liberty; who is recruiting, and with what consequences for human beings? The one sure way of evading a decision on ethical grounds, and thus saving the job of investigating the facts, is to make the decision on *legal* grounds. This is what Silber has done. This avoidance of ethical issues is expected from policemen, but not from philosophers. To rest on the law, one need not inquire into the history and current behavior of the Marine Corps, into the shattered villages, the burned bodies of the Vietnamese people.

Even inside Silber's legalistic framework, however, empty as it is of human and moral content, there is a troublesome discrepancy. If he is so concerned with "respect for the law," how can he ignore the fact that the Marine Corps is recruiting for an illegal war, a war carried on outside the Constitution by the President and the military, in violation of a half-dozen international treaties signed by the United States? The only difference between the Marines recruiting and Murder, Inc. recruiting (aside from the scale of their violence) is that the lawlessness of the Marines is "legal" in the sense that the authorities, involved themselves in the same crimes, will not prosecute. What hypocrisy there is in the injunction "respect the law!"

When John Silber was asked at a press conference whether he would allow Nazis to recruit on campus, he evaded the issue by talking about the right of Nazis to *speak*. But the distinction between free speech and free action is a very important one. By muddying the distinction, Silber is able to transfer to actions like recruiting for war that immunity from regulation that we all want for free speech. But while there are gray areas between speech and action, recruiting is not in that area: the fact that it is accompanied by speech makes it no more an exercise in free speech than a meeting by corporate heads to fix prices, or the instructions of Captain Medina to move into the hamlet of My Lai.

Freedom of speech should be virtually absolute; this is not because it is not subject to the idea that competing values must be measured against one another for their human consequences, but because in the case of speech the measuring is easy. Free speech is in itself a valuable social good, and it is extremely rare that the exchange of ideas—no matter how wrong or even vicious certain ideas may be—creates such an immediate danger to any person's life or liberty as to warrant regulating it. (The Supreme Court, however, in its patriotic fervor, has often found immediate danger in radicals and pacifists passing out their literature.)

Speech is one thing. Activities which affect the health or liberty or lives of others, including the activities of business organizations and military organizations, are another matter. John Silber has talked much recently about "civilization and barbarism." But is not war the greatest barbarism? Would not a civilization worthy of the name, while absolutely respecting the free exchange of ideas, halt the aggressive violence of the military? Would not a decent university, while maintaining a campus open to all ideas, take a stand for human life against those who have violated it on such a frightful scale (the dead in Vietnam number over a million)?

Those words against the war which John Silber delivered at his inauguration remain empty so long as he does not act against the war when he has an opportunity to do so. How small a gesture, and yet what a lesson in defiance it would be for 15,000 B.U. students, if Silber would say to the Marines: "Do your dirty work elsewhere." Cannot a university president match the courage of the young men who have said to the military: we refuse to be inducted—or the courage of the men in the military who have said: we refuse to kill? Those young people, those GIs, acted illegally, but honorably. If John Silber seeks the safety that legality affords, he can have it, but only at the price of dishonor.

Silber: "...students must be taught...that the real issue is not ideology but respect for law." Is it possible that Silber does not know the chief social function of law has been, in the United States as elsewhere, to maintain the existing structure of privilege and property? Does he not know that the socialization of young people in obedience to law helps keep within the most narrow bounds any attempts to create a truly just society? Does he not know that "the law" cannot be sacred to anyone concerned with moral values, that it is not made by God but by fallible, interest-ridden legislators, and enforced by corrupt prosecutors and judges? Does he not know that the law weighs heaviest on the poor, the black, the social critics, and lightest on the corporate interests, the politically powerful? Does he not know that the police commit assault and battery repeatedly, and the President of the United States is responsible for the murder of hundreds of thousands of people? Does he not know that the law will never take the biggest lawbreakers to task because they are the ones who control the law, and they will use it instead against anti-war priests and nuns, black militants, and student protesters? Does he not understand that "respect for the law" as a supreme value is one of the chief characteristics of the totalitarian society?

Silber does not talk about the right of civil disobedience. He insists, however, that it stay within the rules laid down by the authorities (of which he is one) when the very spirit of civil disobedience is defiance of authority. He acts surprised when students blocking the Marine recruiters do not walk voluntarily to the police wagons. He seems not to understand that not every advocate of civil disobedience shares his limited definition of it. He invokes Socrates as one who insisted on going along with his own punishment because he felt a basic obligation to Athens. But, in the spirit of free inquiry, we may ask if Socrates was not, in those moments of debate with Crito, absurdly subservient to the power of the state. Should we model ourselves on Socrates (that is, on Plato, who put the words in Socrates' mouth) at his most jingoistic moment, saying about one's country that one must "obey in silence if it orders you to endure flogging or imprisonment, or it sends you to battle to be wounded or to die."

John Silber did not even seem to be embarrassed as he invoked the name of Martin Luther King, claiming that King "emphasized the importance of showing respect for lawfulness at the same time that he refused to abide by a specific law." That is a gross distortion. It is true that King went to jail rather than escaping, but it isn't at all clear that he did this out of any overall respect for "lawfulness" rather than out of tactical and dramatic motives, or simply out of lack of choice. I doubt that King would criticize Angela Davis or Daniel Berrigan, who carried their defiance of authority beyond that point of arrest, who refused to surrender to the government because they believed its activities did not deserve respect. It is true that King urged respect for his opponents and love for all fellow beings, but it is not true that he "emphasized...respect for lawfulness." I knew Martin Luther King, and was with him on occasions of civil disobedience, in Alabama and Georgia, and it is a disservice to his memory to twist his views so as to omit what was by far his chief emphasis: resistance to immoral authority.

Would Martin Luther King have equated the "violence" of sitting on the steps of the Placement Office (so much like the sit-ins of black students in segregated restaurants, which were also disruptive and illegal) with the violence of the government in war? When Silber said after the Placement office event, "We are not going to be intimidated by brute force and brute violence," he showed a shocking absence of that most essential quality of the intelligent, rational person: a sense of proportion. King was against violence, but he did have a sense of proportion. In his last years, he decided that he would not condemn the violence of black uprisings in the ghetto, before taking into account the record of violence by the United States government. Listen to him, speaking at Riverside Church in New York, April 4, 1967:

> ...I knew that I could never again raise my voice against the violence of the oppressed in the ghettos without having first spoken clearly to the greatest purveyor of violence in the world today—my own government.

How odd that a man whose own behavior that day at the Placement Office more closely resembled that of Birmingham's Bull Connor—replete with police dogs, hidden photographers, and club-wielding police—should invoke the name of Martin Luther King, who would have been there on the steps with the students.

The idea that one who commits civil disobedience must "willing-ly" accept punishment is an oft-repeated but fallacious notion. Silber repeatedly confuses "community" and "society" with government. He talks of "refusing to accept the penalties that go with violating the law" as showing "contempt for organized society." No, it is showing contempt for organized government, and that is justified when the government is behaving as badly as this one is. He talks of "the community...arresting and punishing them." It is not the community that arrests and punishes, but the legal authorities. The reason for showing contempt for govern-ment, for defying the law, is precisely because government and law show contempt for the lives and liberties of the community.

Silber talks of the "social contract" that we are supposed to have made with our government. Of course the government would like us to believe that such a contract exists, one binding us to obedience of the law and allowing the government to do as it pleases. It is as if Silber has not read, or has forgotten David Hume, back in the eighteenth century, who brought Locke back to earth and history by pointing out: "Almost all the govern-ments which exist at present, or of which there remains any record in his-tory, have been founded originally, either on usurpation or conquest, or both, without any pretense of a fair consent or voluntary subjection of the people." Silber talks as if we have some sort of obligation, based on a vol-untary agreement, to obey the leaders who have taken us again and again into war, who have allowed a few to monopolize the enormous wealth of this country. Hume, a conservative but honest man, told it like it is: "Is there anything discoverable in all these events but force and violence? Where is the mutual agreement or voluntary association so much talked of?"

What Silber calls "civilization," what he thinks we have a "social contract" to obey, is the state and its agents. What he calls "barbarism" is the courage of those who resist the state. "It is important that civilization not acquiesce to barbarism...civilization doesn't abdicate before the threat of barbarism; rather it calls the police." When antiwar protestors repre-sent "barbarism" and the Tactical Police represent "civilization," then we certainly need what Confucius suggested, a "rectification of names."

Here is Silber again (at the same press conference reported in the official *Currents*, from which the other quotations in this article are taken):

We had recourse to the police power of the state. Every civilized country in the world has found it necessary to rely on police power to protect itself against the use of force and violence by individual members of that community. When one calls upon the properly designated institution to exercise that force, it can certainly be an expression of civilization.

In Silber's inaugural address, on "The Pollution of Time," he deplored ignorance of history. But does he not know from history that the "civilized" countries have used massive violence against one another (Guernica, Dachau, Coventry, Dresden, Hiroshima, Nagasaki, Budapest, My Lai) and the most brutal force against movements of protest and resistance inside their borders? Does he not know from history that the "properly designated" institutions have engaged in a thousand times more force and violence than any individuals or any social movement of opposition?

If the word "civilization" can be given some positive moral content, it should mean the attempts of man to create a society in which the violence of war, and persecution by class or race or sex, are resisted and restrained, so that they can be ultimately eliminated. By such a definition, students blocking the recruiting of soldiers to kill Vietnamese peasants truly represent civilization; those who attack them, and those who order the attack, represent barbarism.

Does John Silber—bright, well-read, articulate, energetic—not understand these points about history, about nation-states, about the law, about morality, about war, about social protest? We are always surprised when educated people don't understand simple, clear concepts, but that is because the brightest people strain their perceptions through a mesh of interest, position, role. It didn't matter that McGeorge Bundy was "brilliant" from elementary school throughout graduate school and beyond; his vision was distorted by his position in the Establishment, his closeness to power, and he ended up supporting the most stupid, as well as the most immoral of policies in Vietnam.

Silber came to Boston University with strong ideas about academic "excellence," and enormous drive, determined to make the University "first-rate." But education is not a technological problem; it is more a matter of human relationships and moral concern. Academic excellence, in a context of amorality, does not have much meaning. Mussolini made the trains run on time; but the importance of that petered out on the sands of Ethiopia. Boston University cannot be a place of *moral* excellence, if it is run by a dictatorship, however efficient that dictatorship is.

What would a truly free campus be like? It would give absolute freedom to the exchange of ideas, of all kinds. It would insist on its own freedom from the power of government, of donors and trustees. It would not bow to law and authority; not to the authority of the President of the United States or to the authority of the President of the University. Its academic decisions would be made by faculty and students; staff and maintenance workers would share in decisions about the allocation of the university's money. The president and deans would carry out the decisions, as administrators constantly accountable to faculty, students and staff. The university's courses would be open to anyone, whether they could pay or not.

A truly free university would not celebrate obedience, for obedience is what has enabled governments to send young men by the millions to die in war. It would celebrate resistance and disobedience, because the world, so full of authoritarianism, so full of policemen, so racked with injustice and violence, needs rebels badly. It would admire not that technical intellectual efficiency which ignores the fate of human beings far away or near, but that combination of sense and sensibility one finds in good people everywhere, educated or not. It would understand that the most important thing about a university is not its programs or curricula or any of the accoutrements of the upward-striving educator, but its soul.

9

How Free Is Higher Education?

I was invited in 1991 to write this essay as part of a symposium on the university for the *Gannett Center Journal*, which came out of Columbia University. There had been going on for some time a hot national debate on "multi-culturalism," on freedom of speech in the university, on "political correctness." As a result of the movements of the Sixties, changes had taken place in American education, and some of these changes were causing a kind of hysteria among conservatives. I thought I would add my bit to the debate, based on my own experience in higher education.

E ducation has always inspired fear among those who want to keep the existing distributions of power and wealth as they are.

In my thirty years of teaching—in a small southern college, in a large northeastern university—I have often observed that fear. And I think I understand what it is based on. The educational environment is unique in our society: It is the only situation where an adult, looked up to as a mentor, is alone with a group of young people for a protracted and officially sanctioned period of time and can assign whatever reading he or she chooses, and discuss with these young people any subject under the sun. The subject may be defined by the curriculum, by the catalog course description, but this is a minor impediment to a bold and imaginative teacher, especially in literature, philosophy and the social sciences, where there are unlimited possibilities for free discussion of social and political issues.

That would seem to be an educational ideal, an arena for free discussion, assuming a diversity of viewpoints from a variety of teachers, of the most important issues of our time. Yet it is precisely that situation, in the classrooms of higher education, which frightens the guardians of the status quo.

They declare their admiration for such freedom in principle, and suggest that radicals are insufficiently grateful for its existence. But when teachers actually *use* this freedom, introducing new subjects, new readings, outrageous ideas, challenging authority, criticizing "Western civilization," amending the "canon" of great books as listed by certain educational authorities of the past, then the self-appointed guardians of "high culture" become enraged.

Early in my teaching career I decided that I would make the most of the special freedom that is possible in a classroom. I would introduce what I felt to be the most important, and therefore the most controversial, questions in my class.

When I was assigned, as a young professor at Spelman College, a college for black women in Atlanta, a course in "Constitutional Law," I changed the course title to "Civil Liberties" and departed from the canonized recital of Supreme Court cases. I did not ignore the most important of these cases, but I also talked with the students about social movements for justice and asked what role these movements played in changing the environment within which Supreme Court decisions were made.

When I taught American history, I ignored the canon of the traditional textbook, in which the heroic figures were mostly presidents, generals and industrialists. In those texts, wars were treated as problems in military strategy and not in morality; Christopher Columbus and Andrew Jackson and Theodore Roosevelt were treated as heroes in the march of democracy, with not a word from the objects of their violence.

I suggested that we approach Columbus and Jackson from the

perspective of their victims, that we look at the magnificent feat of the transcontinental railroad from the viewpoint of the Irish and Chinese laborers who, in building it, died by the thousands.

Was I committing that terrible sin which is arousing the anger of today's fundamentalists: "politicizing the curriculum"? Is there any rendition of constitutional law, any recounting of American history that can escape being *political*—that is, expressing a political point of view? To treat Theodore Roosevelt as a hero (which is usually not done overtly, but in an expression of quiet admiration)—is that less "political" than pointing to his role as an early imperialist, a forerunner of a long string of crude U.S. interventions in the Caribbean?

I have no doubt that I was taking a political stand when, in the early 1960s, I expressed respect for my students who missed classes to demonstrate in downtown Atlanta against racial segregation. In doing that, was I being more political than the fundamentalist Allan Bloom, at Cornell, who pointed with pride to the fact that the students in his seminar on Plato and Aristotle stuck to their studies and refused to participate in the social conflict outside the seminar room?

In my teaching I never concealed my political views: my detestation of war and militarism, my anger at radial inequality, my belief in a democratic socialism, in a rational and just distribution of world's wealth. To pretend to an "objectivity" that was neither possible nor desirable seemed to me dishonest.

I made it clear to my students at the start of each course that they would be getting *my* point of view on the subjects under discussion, that I would try to be fair to other points of view, that I would scrupulously uphold their right to disagree with me.

My students had a long experience of political indoctrination before they arrived in my class—in the family, in high school, in movies and television. They would hear viewpoints other than mine in other courses, and for the rest of their lives. I insisted on my right to enter my opinions in the marketplace of ideas, so long dominated by orthodoxy.

Surely the expression of "political views" (what is just, or unjust? what can citizens do?) is inevitable in education. It may be done overtly, honestly, or it may be there subtly. But it is always there, however the textbook, by its very bulk and dullness, pretends to neutrality, however noncommittal is the teacher.

It is inevitably there because all education involves *selection*—of events, of voices, of books—and any insistence on one list of great books or great figures or great events is a partial (in both senses of that term) rendering of our cultural heritage.

Therefore it seems to me that the existence of free expression in higher education must mean the opportunity for many points of view, many political biases, to be presented to students. This requires a true pluralism of readings, ideas, viewpoints—a genuinely free marketplace of thought and culture. Let both Shakespeare and Wole Soyinka, Bach and Leonard Bernstein, Dickens and W.E.B. Du Bois, John Stuart Mill and Zora Neale Hurston, Rembrandt and Picasso, Plato and Lao-tzu, Locke and Marx, Aeschylus and August Wilson, Jane Austen and Gabriel Garcia Márquez be available to students.

Such a free marketplace of ideas does not depend essentially on "the curriculum." How many words have been wasted moving those empty shells around the debating table! What is crucial is the content of those shells, which depends on who the teachers are and who the students are. A thoughtful teacher can take a course labeled "Western Civilization" and enlarge its content with an exciting global perspective. Another teacher can be given a course grandly called "World Civilization" and give the student an eclectic, limp recounting of dull events and meaningless dates.

That pluralism in thought that is required for truly free expression in higher education has never been realized. Its crucial elements—an ideologically diverse faculty, a heterogeneous student body (in class, race, sex—words that bring moans from the keepers of the "higher culture")—have always been under attack from outside and from inside the colleges and universities.

McCarthyism, in which the corporate nature of academic institutions revealed itself in the surrender of university administrators to government inquisitors (see Ellen Schrecker's book *No Ivory Tower: McCarthyism in the Universities* for the details), was only the most flagrant of the attacks on freedom of expression. More subtle, more persistent, has been the control of faculty appointments, contract renewals and tenure (inevitably with political considerations) by colleagues, but especially by administrators, who are the universities' links with the dominant forces of American society—the government, the corporations, the military.

Boston University, where I taught for many years, is not too far from typical, with its panoply of military and government connections—ROTC chapters for every military service, former government officials given special faculty posts, the board of trustees dominated by corporate executives, a president eager to curry favor with powerful politicos. Almost all colleges and universities are organized as administrative hierarchies in which a president and trustees, usually well connected to wealthy and important people in the outside world, make the critical decisions as to who may enjoy the freedom of the classroom to speak to the young people of the new generation.

Higher education, while enjoying some special privileges, is still part of the American system, which is an ingenious, sophisticated system of control. It is not totalitarian; what permits it to be called a democracy is that it allows apertures of liberty on the supposition that this will not endanger the basic contours of wealth and power in the society. It trusts that the very flexibility of a partially free system will assure its survival, even contribute to its strength.

Our government is so confident of its power that it can risk allowing some political choice to the people, who can vote for Democrats or Republicans but find huge obstacles of money and bureaucracy if they want an alternative. Our corporations are so wealthy that they can afford some distribution of wealth to a supportive middle class, but not to the 30 or 40 million people who live in the cellars of society.

The system can allow special space for free expression in its cultural institutions: the theater, the arts, the media. But the size of that space is controlled by money and power; the profit motive limits what is put on stage or screen; government officials dominate the informational role of the news media.

Yes, there is, indeed, a special freedom of expression in the academy. How can I at Boston University, or Noam Chomsky at MIT, or David Montgomery at Yale, deny that we have had more freedom in the university than we would have in business or other professions? But those who tolerate us know that our numbers are few, that our students, however excited by new ideas, go out into a world of economic pressures and exhortations to caution. And they know too that they can point to us as an example of the academy's openness to all ideas.

True, there is a tradition of academic freedom, but it is based on a peculiar unspoken contract. The student, in return for the economic security of a career and several years with some degree of free intellectual play, is expected upon graduation to become an obedient citizen, participating happily in the nation's limited pluralism (be a Republican or a Democrat, but please, nothing else).

The boundaries for free expression in the university, though broader than in the larger society, are still watched carefully. When that freedom is used, even by a small minority, to support social change considered dangerous by the guardians of the *status quo*, the alarm goes out: "The Communists are infiltrating our institutions"; "Marxists have taken over the curriculum"; "feminists and black militants are destroying classical education."

Their reaction approaches hysteria: "With a few notable exceptions, our most prestigious liberal arts colleges and universities have installed the entire radical menu at the center of their humanities curriculum," says Roger Kimball in his book *Tenured Radicals*. The shrillness of such alarms is never proportionate to the size of the radical threat. But the Establishment takes no chances. Thus J. Edgar Hoover and Joseph McCarthy saw imminent danger of communist control of the U.S. government; protectors of "the canon" see "tenured radicals" taking over higher education. The axes then get sharpened.

Yes, some of us radicals have somehow managed to get tenure. But far from dominating higher education, we remain a carefully watched minority. Some of us may continue to speak and write and teach as we like, but we have seen the axe fall countless times on colleagues less lucky. And who can deny the chilling effect this has had on other faculty, with or without tenure, who have censored themselves rather than risk a loss of promotion, a lower salary, a nonrenewal of contract, a denial of tenure?

Perhaps, after all, Boston University cannot be considered typical, having had for 20 years probably the most authoritarian, the most politically watchful university president in the country. But although it is hard to match John Silber as an educational tyrant, he can be considered (I base this on spending some time at other universities) not a departure from the norm, but an exaggeration of it.

Have we had freedom of expression at Boston University?

A handful of radical teachers, in a faculty of over a thousand, was enough to have John Silber go into fits over our presence on campus, just as certain observers of higher education are now getting apoplectic over what they see as radical dominance nationwide. These are ludicrous fantasies, but they lead to attacks on the freedom of expression of those faculty who manage to overcome that prudent self-control so prominent among academics. At Boston it must have been such fantasies that led Silber to determinedly destroy the faculty union, which was a minor threat to his control over faculty. He handled appointments and tenure with the very political criteria that his conservative educational companions so loudly decry. In at least seven cases that I know of, where the candidates were politically undesirable by Silber's standards, he ignored overwhelming faculty recommendations and refused them tenure.

Did I have freedom of expression in my classroom? I did, because I followed Aldous Huxley's advise: "Liberties are not given; they are taken." But it was obviously infuriating to John Silber that every semester 400 students signed up to take my courses, whether it was "Law and Justice in America" or "An Introduction to Political Theory." And so he did what is often done in the academy; he engaged in petty harassments—withholding salary raises, denying teaching assistants. He also threatened to fire me (and four other members of the union) when we held our classes on the street rather than cross the picket lines of striking secretaries.

The fundamentalists of politics—the Reagans and Bushes and Helmses—want to pull the strings of control tighter on the distribution of wealth and power and civil liberties. The fundamentalists of law, the Borks and Rehnquists, want to interpret the Constitution so as to put strict limits on the legal possibilities for social reform. The fundamentalists of education fear the possibilities inherent in the unique freedom of discussion that we find in higher education.

And so, under the guise of defending "the common culture" or "disinterested scholarship" or "Western civilization," they attack that freedom. They fear exactly what some of us hope for, that if students are given wider political choices in the classroom than they get in the polling booth or the workplace, they may become social rebels. They may join movements for racial or sexual equality, or against war, or, even more dangerous, work for what James Madison feared as he argued for a conservative Constitution: "an equal division of property." Let us hope so.

10

"Je Ne Suis Pas Marxiste"

For a long time I thought that there were important and useful ideas in Marxist philosophy and political economy that should be protected from the self-righteous cries on the right that "Marxism is dead," as well as from the arrogant assumptions of the commissars of various dictatorships that their monstrous regimes represented "Marxism." This piece was written for *Z Magazine*, June 1988, and reprinted in my book *Failure to Quit* (Common Courage Press, 1993).

Not long ago, someone referred to me publicly as a "Marxist professor." In fact, two people did. One was a spokesperson for "Accuracy in Academia," worried that there were "five thousand Marxist faculty members" in the United States (which diminished my importance, but also my loneliness). The other was a former student I encountered on a shuttle to New York, a fellow traveler. I felt a bit honored. A "Marxist" means a tough guy (making up for the pillowy connotation of "professor"), a person of formidable politics, someone not to be trifled with, someone who knows the difference between absolute and relative surplus value, and what is commodity fetishism, and refuses to buy it.

I was also a bit taken aback (a position which yoga practitioners understand well, and which is good for you about once a day). Did "Marxist" suggest that I kept a tiny statue of Lenin in my drawer and rubbed his head to discover what policy to follow to intensify the contradictions in the imperialist camp, or what songs to sing if we were sent away to such a camp?

Also, I remembered that famous statement of Marx: "Je ne suis pas Marxiste." I always wondered why Marx, an English-speaking German who had studied Greek for his doctoral dissertation, would make such an important statement in French. But I am confident that he did make it, and I think I know what brought it on. After Marx and his wife Jenny had moved to London, where they lost three of their six children to illness and lived in squalor for many years, they were often visited by a young German refugee named Pieper. This guy was a total "noodnik" (there are "noodniks" all along the political spectrum stationed ten feet apart, but there is a special Left Noodnik, hired by the police, to drive revolutionaries batty). Pieper (I swear, I did not make him up) hovered around Marx gasping with admiration, once offered to translate *Das Kapital* into English, which he could barely speak, and kept organizing Karl Marx Clubs, exasperating Marx more and more by insisting that every word Marx uttered was holy. And one day Marx caused Pieper to have a severe abdominal cramp when he said to him: "Thanks for inviting me to speak to your Karl Marx Club. But I can't. I'm not a Marxist."

That was a high point in Marx's life, and also a good starting point for considering Marx's ideas seriously without becoming a Pieper (or a Stalin, or a Kim II Sung, or any born-again Marxist who argues that every word in Volumes One, Two, and Three, and especially in the *Grundrisse*, is unquestionably true). Because it seems to me (risking that this may lead to my inclusion in the second edition of Norman Podhoretz's *Register of Marxists, Living or Dead*), Marx had some very useful thoughts.

For instance, we find in Marx's short but powerful *Theses on Feuerbach* the idea that philosophers, who always considered their job was to interpret the world, should now set about changing it, in their writings, and in their lives.

Marx set a good example himself. While history has treated him as a sedentary scholar, spending all his time in the library of the British Museum, Marx was a tireless activist all his life. He was expelled from Germany, from Belgium, from France, was arrested and put on trial in Cologne.

Exiled to London, he kept his ties with revolutionary movements all over the world. The poverty-ridden flats that he and Jenny Marx and their children occupied became busy centers of political activity, gathering places for political refugees from the continent.

True, many of his writings were impossibly abstract (especially those on political economy; my poor head at the age of nineteen swam, or rather drowned, with ground rent and differential rent, the falling rate of profit and the organic composition of capital). But he departed from that constantly to confront the events of his time, to write about the revolutions of 1848, the Paris Commune, rebellion in India, the Civil War in the United States.

The manuscripts he wrote at the age of twenty-five while an exile in Paris (where he hung out in cafes with Engels, Proudhon, Bakunin, Heine, Stirner), often dismissed by hard-line fundamentalists as "immature," contain some of his most profound ideas. His critique of capitalism in those *Economic and Philosophic Manuscripts* did not need any mathematical proofs of "surplus value." It simply stated (but did not state it simply) that the capitalist system violates whatever it means to be human. The industrial system Marx saw developing in Europe not only robbed them of the product of their work, it estranged working people from their own creative possibilities, from one another as human beings, from the beauties of nature, from their own true selves. They lived out their lives not according to their own inner needs, but according to the necessities of survival.

This estrangement from self and others, this alienation from all that was human, could not be overcome by an intellectual effort, by something in the mind. What was needed was a fundamental, revolutionary change in society, to create the conditions—a short workday, a rational use of the earth's natural wealth and people's natural talents, a just distribution of the fruits of human labor, a new social consciousness—for the flowering of human potential, for a leap into freedom as it had never been experienced in history.

Marx understood how difficult it was to achieve this, because, no matter how "revolutionary" we are, the weight of tradition, habit, the accumulated mis-education of generations, "weighs like a nightmare on the brain of the living."

Marx understood politics. He saw that behind political conflicts were questions of class: who gets what. Behind benign bubbles of togetherness (*We* the people...*our* country...*national* security), the powerful and the wealthy would legislate on their own behalf. He noted (in *The Eighteenth Brumaire*, a biting, brilliant analysis of the Napoleonic seizure of power after the 1848 Revolution in France) how a modern constitution could proclaim absolute rights, which were then limited by marginal notes (he might have been predicting the tortured constructions of the First Amendment in our own Constitution), reflecting the reality of domination by one class over another regardless of the written word.

He saw religion, not just negatively as "the opium of the people," but positively as "the sigh of the oppressed creature, the heart of a heartless world, the soul of soulless conditions." This helps us understand the mass appeal of the religious charlatans of the television screen, as well as the work of Liberation Theology in joining the soulfulness of religion to the energy of revolutionary movements in miserably poor countries.

Marx was often wrong, often dogmatic, often a "Marxist." He was sometimes too accepting of imperial domination as "progressive," a way of bringing capitalism faster to the third world, and therefore hastening, he thought, the road to socialism. (But he staunchly supported the rebellions of the Irish, the Poles, the Indians, the Chinese, against colonial control.)

He was too insistent that the industrial working class must be the agent of revolution, and that this must happen first in the advanced capitalist countries. He was unnecessarily dense in his economic analyses (too much education in German universities, maybe) when his clear, simple insight into exploitation was enough: that no matter how valuable were the things workers produced, those who controlled the economy could pay them as little as they liked, and enrich themselves with the difference.

Personally, Marx was sometimes charming, generous, self-sacrificing; at other times arrogant, obnoxious, abusive. He loved his wife and children, and they clearly adored him, but he also may have fathered the son of their German housekeeper, Lenchen.

The anarchist Bakunin, his rival in the International Workingmen's Association, said of Marx: "I very much admired him for his knowledge and for his passionate and earnest devotion to the cause of the proletariat. But...our temperaments did not harmonize. He called me a sentimental idealist, and he was right. I called him vain, treacherous, and morose, and I was right." Marx's daughter Eleanor, on the other hand, called her father "...the cheeriest, gayest soul that ever breathed, a man brimming over with humor..."

He epitomized his own warning, that people, however advanced in their thinking, were weighted down by the limitations of their time. Still, Marx gave us acute insights, inspiring visions. I can't imagine Marx being pleased with the "socialism" of the Soviet Union. He would have been a dissident in Moscow, I like to think. His idea of the "dictatorship of the proletariat" was the Paris Commune of 1871, where endless argument in the streets and halls of the city gave it the vitality of a grass-roots democracy, where overbearing officials could be immediately booted out of office by popular vote, where the wages of government leaders could not exceed that of ordinary workers, where the guillotine was destroyed as a symbol of capital punishment. Marx once wrote in the *New York Tribune* that he did not see how capital punishment could be justified "in a society glorying in its civilization."

Perhaps the most precious heritage of Marx's thought is his internationalism, his hostility to the national state, his insistence that ordinary people have no nation they must obey and give their lives for in war, that we are all linked to one another across the globe as human beings. This is not only a direct challenge to modern capitalist nationalism, with its ugly evocations of hatred for "the enemy" abroad, and its false creation of a common interest for all within certain artificial borders. It is also a rejection of the narrow nationalism of contemporary "Marxist" states, whether the Soviet Union, or China, or any of the others.

Marx had something important to say not only as a critic of capitalism, but as a warning to revolutionaries, who, he wrote in *The German Ideology*, had better revolutionize themselves if they intended to do that to society. He offered an antidote to the dogmatists, the hard-liners, the Piepers, the Stalins, the commissars, the "Marxists." He said: "Nothing human is alien to me."

That seems a good beginning for changing the world.

11

Jack London's *The Iron Heel*

I first encountered Jack London as a writer of adventure stories, when I was a teen-ager. After I became interested in political ideas, and learned that he was a Socialist and that he had written a political novel, *The Iron Heel*, I rushed to read it. Years later I was asked to write an introduction to a new edition of the book (Bantam, 1971), and this gave me an opportunity to review Jack London's life and to read the book once more.

Jack London climbed, sailed, stormed through forty years of life, all ending in the torment of sickness, and the calculated swallowing of a large dose of morphine tablets. Tired, he lowered himself into death, like the hero of his autobiographical novel, *Martin Eden*.

He had come out of the slums of San Francisco, the child of an unwed woman who held seances, and whose lover, a scholarly lecturer on astrology, denied he had fathered her son. By the time he was fifteen he had been a newsboy, worked in a cannery, begun to read hungrily the books of the Oakland Public Library, become a sailor and a fisherman, found a mistress, and was drinking heavily.

Before he was twenty-one, he had worked in a jute mill and laundry, hoboed the railroads to the East Coast, been clubbed by a policeman on the streets of New York, been arrested for vagrancy in Niagara Falls, watched men beaten and tortured in jail, joined the Socialist Party, pirated oysters in San Francisco Bay, read Flaubert, Tolstoy, Melville, and the Communist Manifesto, shot rapids and climbed mountains in the Klondike gold rush, preached socialism in the Alaskan gold camps in the winter of 1896, sailed 2,000 miles back through the Bering Sea, and sold his first adventure stories to magazines.

At thirty-one, he had written twenty books, married twice, run for mayor of Oakland on the Socialist ticket, covered the Russo-Japanese War, sailed to Hawaii and Polynesia, made huge sums of money, and spent every dollar. The books and stories that made him world-famous were of the sea, of dogs, of men in loving combat with the wilderness, the snows, the night.

Around 1906, Jack London set out on his great socialist novel, *The Iron Heel.* Also at this time, he wrote about his own past: "I was in the pit, the abyss, the human cesspool, the shambles and charnel-house of our civilization...I shall say only that the things I saw there gave me a terrible scare."

That terror, along with the vision of a socialist world and the brotherhood of man, he poured into the fantasy-realism of *The Iron Heel.* The imagination that had led people everywhere to devour his adventure stories now produced bizarre political conjurings: The First and Second Revolts, the Chicago Commune, The Mercenaries and the Frisco Reds, the Philomaths and the Valkyries, the Oligarchy, and the People of the Abyss.

If we take *The Iron Heel* as a premonition of the future—to bemuse us, fascinate us, frighten us—we will be deceived. It is the *present* that haunts a serious spinner of futuristic tales, and so it did Jack London. He uses the future to entice us out of the constricting corridors of here and now, far enough so that we can look back and see more clearly what is happening. He uses the love of Avis Cunningham for the remarkable Ernest Everhard to draw us into empathy with an undeniably arrogant but also undeniably attractive man who leads a socialist revolution in the United States.

But is Jack London's present also ours? Can the things he said about the United States in 1906 be applied to the nation in 1970? Have we not put behind us the wrongs of that older time, buried them under an avalanche of reforms and affluence? Have we not become a welfare state at home, a fearless defender of freedom abroad? In the Fifties, many Americans thought so.

At the start of the Seventies, however, there is a new mood. A fresh generation (of *radicals*, we begin to say, but there are too many of them to fit such a narrow definition) seems to have reached the conclusion that, aside from frills, tokens, gadgets, and rhetoric, all of which have proliferated in this century, the United States has not changed its basic characteristics: the rule of corporate wealth, the use of the big stick to bludgeon the discontented, both at home and abroad.

A formidable number of young people have lost their respect for the system, not because of books and lectures, but by observation and experience. As tiny children, they crawled under desks while sirens wailed in a preview of the atomic destruction of the earth. It seems now that they probably knew, with an intelligence far greater than that of teachers or parents or the country's leaders, how absurd it was to seek shelter under a wooden desk from the madness of governments armed with hydrogen bombs. By the time they grew up enough to read *Catch-22*, Yossarian's words shattered the cold war demonology of "them" and "us" and spoke to their childish wisdom: "The enemy is anybody who is going to get you killed, no matter which side he's on."

This generation watched on television as blacks were beaten bloody by Southern policemen while the FBI, sworn to uphold "law and order," stood by taking notes. They watched while blacks stealing shoes from store windows were shot dead by Northern policemen, who were then exonerated by the courts. In their living rooms they saw American soldiers ravage Vietnamese villages, bombing, shooting, setting fire to ancestral homes, laying waste an entire country, all in the name of freedom and peace. They saw the leaders of the country hurling the bodies of thousands of Americans into the Asian pyre in a lust of national righteousness.

And when these same young people went out onto the streets and campuses to protest, they too were clubbed, and some were killed, all in the name of stopping "violence." The America of 1970 is, perhaps, more shrewd at covering its deeds with slogans, than was the America of 1906. But the iron heel comes down as before.

In Jack London's time (1914), National Guardsmen fired into the tents of striking miners at Ludlow, Colorado, and killed twenty-five of them. In the spring of 1970, National Guardsmen fired into a crowd of striking students in Ohio and killed four of them. The killing in Colorado was justified by John D. Rockefeller, Jr., who owned the coal mines there, as the defense of "a great principle": the right to work in the mines. The killing in Ohio half a century later was justified also in the name of a principle: "law and order." No National Guardsmen were indicted in Colorado in 1914, but a strike leader was. No National Guardsmen were indicted in Ohio in 1970, but twenty-five demonstrators were.

In Jack London's time (1917, East St. Louis), a mob of civilians killed black men and women while the national government watched, claiming lack of jurisdiction. In our time (1964, Mississippi), two white and one black civil rights workers were killed by a mob including local law enforcement officers, while the national government stood by, claiming lack of jurisdiction.

Even those who live comfortably today in America live uncomfortably, on the crater's edge of violence: war, prisons, ghettos. The greatest violence comes not from protesters and revolutionaries but from governments. The greatest lawlessness is that of "law and order." Despite the tinsel of wealth and "progress" on all sides, what the workingman Ernest Everhard told the professor's daughter Avis Cunningham remains true: "Our boasted civilization is based upon blood, soaked in blood, and neither you nor I nor any of us can escape the scarlet stains."

The footnotes of *The Iron Heel*, supposedly written many centuries later to inform readers of what life was like in the early twentieth century, still cut deep to fundamental truths: "In those days, thievery was incredibly prevalent. Everybody stole property from everybody else. The lords of society stole legally, or else legalized their stealing, while the poorer classes stole illegally." In the America of 1970, petty thieves fill the jails-but Congress and the President approve tax legislation enabling the oil companies to legally steal millions of dollars from the public.

The corporation lawyer speaks bluntly to Avis: "What's right got to do with it? You see all those books. All my reading and studying of them has taught me that law is one thing and right is another thing." And

Avis' words to him might be addressed today to that whole army of professionals trained by a complex society: "Tell me, when one surrenders his personal feelings to his professional feelings, may not the action be defined as a sort of spiritual mayhem?"

Since Jack London's time, women have been given the right to vote, the election of senators has been transferred from the state legislatures to the public, and millions of blacks have joined the voting rolls. But the terse footnote in Chapter 5 of *The Iron Heel* still has the sound of truth: "Even as late as 1912 A.D., the great mass of the people still persisted in the belief that they ruled the country by virtue of their ballots. In reality, the country was ruled by what were called political machines."

Jack London's ultimate criticism of the capitalism of his day remains authentic: "In the face of the facts that modern man lives more wretchedly than the cave-man, and that his producing power is a thousand times greater than that of the cave-man, no other conclusion is possible than that the capitalist class has mismanaged...criminally and selfishly mismanaged." Perhaps the comparison with the cave-man is not too absurd, considering what proportion of the world is still sick, hungry, miserable, bombed-out; and how even the middle classes are trapped in an environment of polluted air, poisoned water, adulterated food, walled-off communities, unsatisfying jobs, adding up to both psychic and material insecurity. With our enormous wealth in the United States we have built highways, motor cars, motels, office buildings, guns, bombs, planes; we have wasted our resources on things either nonessential or dangerous, when these great resources—rationally, humanely used—could make life warm and human for all. London's point still holds: the profit of corporations, not the needs of people, decides what is done with the country's natural wealth.

Still fresh in the memory of 1906 was the take-over of the Philippines by the U.S. Army, all in the name of saving them from someone else's control, and the crushing of the Filipino rebels who opposed the American occupation. Someone says to Ernest Everhard in a passage remarkably prophetic for Vietnam: "Why, you spoke of sending the militia to the Philippines. That is unconstitutional. The Constitution especially states that the militia cannot be sent out of the country." And he replies: "What's the Constitution got to do with it?"

In the Fifties, the consciousness of the brutality of Stalin's socialism was so acute and the memory of Naziism so bitter, as to make *The*

Iron Heel seem more a commentary on those two societies than on what seemed the more benign, if flawed, American system. Today, we are more aware that *all* powerful states, including the United States, waste the resources of their countrymen, prey on smaller nations, use "law and order" to maintain power and privilege, and crush the dissenting few while pacifying the majority with promises, slogans, and symbols of progress.

Yet, with all these remarkable perceptions, *The Iron Heel* stopped short of understanding certain things which we, a half century later, can see a bit more clearly. Jack London's vision is still inviting: "Let us not destroy those wonderful machines that produce efficiently and cheaply. Let us control them. Let us profit by their efficiency and cheapness. Let us run them for ourselves. That, gentlemen, is socialism..."

We know now that this prescription is not enough, if the "us" becomes a bureaucratic party substituting for the capitalist state. We will have to develop an "us" in which the control of the machinery is local, held by the people who work at it, and yet where all who are affected by the production—the consumer, other producers—have ways of express-ing their desires. To establish cooperative control of production, combin-ing the advantages of centralized efficiency with local controls in a com-plex, technologically advanced society, is an art demanding thought and experimentation.

We suspect now, too, that Jack London's prescription for change—an armed revolution—which seemed so natural in 1906, is inadequate, given such sophisticated controls as we have today in the United States. London swung swiftly from faith in the ballot box, which many Socialists of his day shared, to disillusionment with that and belief in armed rebellion. Thus, Ernest Everhard rushes from one to the other: "And in the day that we sweep to victory at the ballot-box, and you refuse to turn over to us the government we have constitutionally and peaceful-ly captured, and you demand what we are going to do about it—in that day, I say, we shall answer you; and in roar of shell and shrapnel and in whine of machine guns shall our answer be couched."

In the modern, powerful, industrial state both these tactics—vot-ing and armed insurrection—are decoys. The ballot box, a tawdry token of democracy, enables shrewd, effective control in the mass society, by those on top. And armed revolution is so clearly suicidal against the power of the great national state, that we must suspect its advocates of being police agents—as in the abortive uprisings in *The Iron Heel.*

There is another emerging truth which Jack London ignored, to which this generation is especially sensitive: that the mode of revolution helps determine its future course. A "revolution" accomplished by the ballot box perpetuates the notion that real change can come about by manipulating papers, rather than by people struggling to change their personal lives, their immediate relationships, their communities, their work. Revolutions by force of arms carry forward into the new society that ruthlessness which London himself depicts, and too readily accepts, in *The Iron Heel.* Perhaps we have learned enough in the past half century to begin to think of a novel approach to revolution.

A new mode of revolution would go far beyond the ballot box. People everywhere would begin to live cooperatively, not in mass organizations which override individual feelings, but in small groups based on working together, resisting the state together. In such groups, new relationships of intimacy and cooperation, born of common struggles, could develop between black and white, male and female, old and young. All this, in the midst of an inhuman society, while fighting to change that society.

People would work as cultural and political guerrillas, mobile, imaginative, so embedded in the lower structures of the society, and in its crevices, in so many places, as to be invulnerable to the crude, massed power of the state. If crushed in one place, these affinity groups would rise again in ten other places, until there were so many changed minds, so many changed ways of living, that the revolution would not be defeated because it would be already here. The old structures, despite their wealth and arms, would flail ineffectually at such a revolution, and then begin to wither, because their sustenance—the labor that operates them, the minds that accept them—had turned to other things.

At the least, Jack London's *The Iron Heel* may cause us to think, not about some time long past, or some fantasy far ahead, but about now, here, ourselves.

12

Discovering
John Reed

The appearance in 1981 of a Hollywood movie, *Reds*, in which the main character is a Communist, the journalist John Reed, and is sympathetically portrayed, was startling. It was one of many pieces of evidence that the nation had moved a critical distance away from the Communist hysteria of the Fifties. The editors of the *Boston Globe* asked me, as a historian, to tell their readers about John Reed, and this piece appeared January 5, 1982.

Radicals are doubly exasperating. They not only refuse to conform to ideas of what true American patriots are like; they may not even fit common notions of what radicals are like. So with John Reed and Louise Bryant, who confounded and infuriated the guardians of cultural and political orthodoxy around the time of World War I. They are now being portrayed in Warren Beatty's grand movie, *Reds*, causing some critics to grumble about "communist chic" and "mod Marxism," in an unwitting replay of the barbs thrust at Reed and Bryant in their time.

It was bad enough that they and their remarkable friends—Max Eastman, Emma Goldman, Lincoln Steffens, Margaret Sanger—spoke out for sexual freedom in a country dominated by Christian righteousness, or opposed militarization in a time of jingoism and war, or advocated socialism when business and government were clubbing and shooting strikers, or welcomed what seemed to them the first proletarian revolution in history.

What was worse was that they refused to remain mere writers and intellectuals, assailing the system with words; they walked picket lines, loved freely, defied government committees, went to jail. They declared for revolution in their actions as well as their art, ignoring those cautions against commitment offered, in any generation, by the voyeurs of social movements.

John Reed could not be forgiven by the Establishment (nor even by some of its critics, like Walter Lippmann and Eugene O'Neill) for refusing to separate art and insurgency, for being not only rebellious in his prose but imaginative in his activism. He saw revolt as not mere fulmination, but fun, not just analysis but adventure. This caused some of his liberal friends to take him less seriously (Lippmann spoke of his "inordinate desire to be arrested"), not understanding that, to the power elite of the country, protest joined to imagination was dangerous, courage combined with wit was no joke. Grim rebels can be jailed, but the highest treason, for which there is no adequate punishment, is to make rebellion attractive.

Jack Reed, his friends called him. He was a poet all his life, from his comfortable childhood in Portland, Oregon, through Harvard College, peasant uprisings in Mexico, the strikes of silkworkers in New Jersey and coal miners in Colorado, the war fronts of Europe, the shouting, singing crowds of the Bolshevik revolution in Petrograd. But as his fellow editor of the *Masses*, Max Eastman, wrote: "Poetry to Reed was not only a matter of writing words but of living life." His many poems, in fact, were not memorable, but he rushed into the center of wars and revolutions, strikes and demonstrations, with the eye of a movie camera, before there was one, and the memory of a tape recorder, before that existed. He made history come alive for the readers of popular magazines and impoverished radical monthlies.

At Harvard between 1906 and 1910, Reed was an athlete (swimming and water polo), a prankster, a cheer leader, a writer for the

Lampoon, a student of the famous writing teacher they called Copey (Charles Townsend Copeland), at the same time, a protégé of the muckraker Lincoln Steffens. He was a mischievous critic of Harvard snobbery, though not a member of Walter Lippmann's Socialist Club. On graduation, he worked his way aboard a freighter to Europe—London, Paris, Madrid—then returned to join a cluster of Bohemian-radical writers living in Greenwich Village, where Steffens helped him get his first job doing rather routine editorial work for a literary political magazine called the *American*.

In New York in 1912, for anyone who looked around as sharply as John Reed, the contrasts of wealth and poverty stunned the senses. He began writing for the *Masses*, a new magazine edited by Max Eastman (brother of the socialist-feminist Crystal Eastman) and penned a manifesto: "Poems, stories, and drawings, rejected by the capitalist press on account of their excellence, will find a welcome in this magazine." The *Masses*, was alive, not a party organ, but a party, with anarchists and socialists, artists and writers, and undefinable rebels of all sorts in its pages: Carl Sandburg and Amy Lowell, William Carlos Williams, Upton Sinclair. And from abroad, Bertrand Russell, Gorky, Picasso.

The times trembled with class struggle. Reed went to Lawrence, Massachusetts, where women and children had walked out of the textile mills and were carrying on a heartrending, heroic strike with the help of the IWW (the revolutionary Industrial Workers of the World) and the Socialist Party. Reed met Bill Haywood, the IWW leader (in one description, "a great battered hulk of a man, with one eye gone, and an eminent look in the other"). From Haywood he learned of the strike of 25,000 silk workers across the Hudson River in Paterson, asking for an eight-hour day and being clubbed by the police. The press was not reporting any of this, so Reed went to Paterson. It was not in him to stand off and take notes. He walked the picket line, was arrested for refusing to move on, spent four days in jail.

When he wrote about this for the *Masses*, it was a new writing for him—angry, involved. He attended a mass meeting for the Paterson strikers, heard the young Irish radical Elizabeth Gurley Flynn speak of the power of folded arms, and Reed himself—never shy—led the crowd in singing the *Marseillaise* and the *Internationale*. He and Mabel Dodge, whose Fifth Avenue apartment was a center for art and politics (and who was soon to become his lover) got a wild, brilliant idea—to do a pageant on the strike in Madison Square Garden, with a thousand workers in the cast. Reed worked day and night on the script; the scenery was painted by John Sloan; and 15,000 people came and cheered.

In Mexico in 1914, Pancho Villa was leading a rebellion of peasants, and the *Metropolitan* asked Reed to go as its correspondent. Reed was soon in the thick of the Mexican Revolution, riding with Villa himself, sending back stories which were acclaimed by Walter Lippmann as "the finest reporting that's ever been done…. The variety of his impressions, the resources and color of his language seemed inexhaustible…and Villa's revolution, till then reported only as a nuisance, began to unfold itself into throngs of moving people in a gorgeous panorama of earth and sky." Reed's collection of articles, *Insurgent Mexico*, was not what is admired in journalism schools as "objective reporting." It was meant to help a revolution.

Reed had barely returned to New York, acclaimed now as a great journalist, when the shocking news of the Ludlow Massacre spread through the country. In Southern Colorado, striking miners had been machine-gunned and their families burned to death, attacked by National Guardsmen in the pay of the Rockefellers. He was soon on the scene, writing "The Colorado War."

Summer, 1914, he was in Provincetown, which was to become his refuge those next years, for swimming, writing, love-making (until 1916, a stormy affair with Mabel Dodge). That August, the war began in Europe. In an unpublished manuscript, Reed wrote: "And here are the nations, flying at each other's throats like dogs…and art, industry, commerce, individual liberty, life itself taxed to maintain monstrous machines of death."

Reed went home to Portland to see his mother, who never approved of his radical ideas. There, at the local IWW hall, he heard Emma Goldman speak. It was an experience. She was that generation's powerhouse of feminism and anarchism, her life itself proof that one could be a joyful, serious revolutionary.

The big periodicals of New York pressed him to cover the European war for them, and he agreed to go for the *Metropolitan*. At the same time he wrote an article for the *Masses*. It was a war for profit, he said. On the way to Europe, he was conscious of the rich on the first-class decks, and three thousand Italians kept like animals in the hold. He was soon in England, in Switzerland and Germany, and then, in France, walking through the fields of war: rain, mud, corpses. What depressed him most was the murderous patriotism seizing everyone on both sides, even some Socialists, like H.G. Wells in England.

When he returned to the States after four months, he found the radicals Upton Sinclair and John Dewey among the patriots. And Walter Lippmann too. Lippmann, now editor of the *New Republic*, wrote in December, 1914 a curious essay: "The Legendary John Reed." It defined the distance between himself and Reed. "By temperament he is not a professional writer or reporter. He is a person who enjoys himself." And then Lippmann, who clearly had pride in himself as "a professional writer," gave the ultimate dismissal: "Reed has no detachment and is proud of it."

It was true. Reed went back to the war in 1915, this time to Russia, to the burned and looted villages, to the mass killings of the Jews by the Tsar's soldiers, to Bucharest, Constantinople, Sofia, then Serbia and Greece. It was clear to him what patriotism meant: death by machine-gun fire or by famine, by smallpox, diphtheria, cholera, typhus. Back in America, he listened to the endless talk about military preparedness against "the enemy," and wrote for the *Masses* that the enemy for the American working man was the 2 percent of the population which owned 60 percent of the national wealth. "We advocate that the workingman prepare to defend himself against that enemy. This is our Preparedness."

Early in 1916, John Reed met Louise Bryant in Portland and they fell immediately in love. She left her husband and joined Reed in New York. It was the start of a passionate, poetic relationship. She was herself a writer and an anarchist of sorts. That summer Reed sought respite from the sounds of war on Provincetown's quiet beaches, with Bryant. There is a snapshot of her lying on the sands, nude and demure.

By April 1917, Woodrow Wilson was asking Congress to declare war on Germany, and John Reed wrote in the *Masses*. "War means an ugly mob-madness, crucifying the truth-tellers, choking the artists...It is not our war." He testified before Congress against conscription: "I do not believe in this war...I would not serve in it."

When Emma Goldman and Alexander Berkman were arrested under the Draft Act for "conspiracy to induce persons not to register," Reed was a witness in their defense. They were convicted and sent to prison. So were a thousand other Americans who opposed the war. Radical newspapers were banned, among them the *Masses*.

Reed was distressed by the way the working classes in Europe and America were supporting the war and forgetting the class struggle. Yet he continued to hope: "I cannot give up the idea that out of democracy will be born the new world—richer, braver, freer, more beautiful."

From Russia in 1917 came thunderous news. The Tsar, the old regime, were overthrown. A revolution was in progress. Here at last, Reed thought, was an entire population which refused to go on with the slaughter, turned on its own ruling class, and was setting about the creation of a new society, its outlines not yet clear, but its spirit intoxicating.

With Louise Bryant, he set sail for Finland and Petrograd. The revolution was bursting all around them, and they immersed themselves in its excitement: the mass meetings, the workers taking over factories, the soldiers declaring their opposition to the war, the Petrograd Soviet electing a Bolshevik majority. Then, on November 6 and 7, the swift, bloodless take-over of the railroad stations, telegraph, telephone, post office. And finally, workers and soldiers rushing ecstatically into the Winter Palace.

Racing from scene to scene, Reed took notes with incredible speed, gathered up every leaflet, poster and proclamation, and then, in early 1918, went back to the United States to write his story. On arrival, his notes were confiscated. He found himself under indictment with other editors of the *Masses* for opposing the war, but at the trial, where he and Eastman testified eloquently, boldly, about their beliefs, the jury could not reach a decision and the charges were dropped.

Now Reed was everywhere in the country, lecturing on the war, the Russian Revolution. At Tremont Temple in Boston he was heckled by Harvard students. In Indiana he met Eugene Debs, who would soon be sentenced to ten years for speaking against the war. In Chicago he attended the trial of Bill Haywood and a hundred other IWW leaders, who would get long prison sentences. That September, after he spoke to a rally of four thousand people, Reed was arrested for discouraging recruitment in the armed forces.

He finally got his Russian notes back, and in two months of furious writing produced *Ten Days That Shook the World*. It became the classic eyewitness account of the Bolkshevik Revolution, its words swarming over the pages with the sounds, as it seemed then, of a new world being born: "Up the Nevsky, in the sour twilight, crowds were battling for the latest papers...On every corner, in every open space, thick groups were clustered; arguing soldiers and students...The Petrograd Soviet was meeting continuously at Smolny, a centre of storm, delegates falling down asleep on the floor and rising again to take part in the debate, Trotsky, Kamenev, Volodarsky speaking six, eight, twelve hours a day..."

In 1919, the war was over, but Allied armies had invaded Russia, and the hysteria continued in the United States. The country that had made the word "revolution" glorious throughout the world now was frightened of it. Non-citizens were rounded up by the thousands, arrested, deported without trial. There were strikes all over the country, and clashes with police. Reed became involved in the formation of the Communist Workers Party, went to Russia as a delegate to the meetings of the Communist International. There he argued with party bureaucrats, wondered what was happening with the revolution, met Emma Goldman in Moscow, and listened to her cry out her disillusionment.

He continued to hope. He rushed from meeting to meeting, from a conference in Moscow to a mass meeting of Asians on the Black Sea. He was wearing himself out, and he fell sick, feverish, delirious. It was typhus. At thirty-three, in a Moscow hospital, at the height of his love affair with his wife and comrade Louise Bryant, and with the idea of revolution, he died.

John Reed's body was buried near the Kremlin wall as a hero. But in truth, his soul does not belong to any Establishment, there or here or anywhere. Strangely, in the year 1981, sixty years after his death, millions of Americans will learn of John Reed because of a motion picture. If even a tiny fraction of these are led thereby to think about war and injustice, art and commitment, about enlarging friendship beyond national boundaries for the possibility of a better world, that is a huge accomplishment for one brief, intensely-lived life.

PART SIX

MEANS AND ENDS

1

Violence
and
Human
Nature

A discussion on "human nature" seems inevitable in any discussion of war and its causes. And the belief in some innate human drive for war is very widespread. As someone involved constantly in arguments about the reasons for war, I could not simply dismiss, without examination, that belief. I turned to my own experience in World War II for clues, and also to survey what scientific evidence I could find on whether, indeed, there exists a "war instinct." This essay appeared in my book *Declarations of Independence* (HarperCollins, 1990).

I remember three different incidents of violence in three different parts of my life. In two of them I was an observer, in one a perpetrator.

In the fall of 1963 I was in Selma, Alabama, and saw two young black civil rights workers clubbed to the ground by state troopers and then attacked with electric prods, because they tried to bring food and water to black people standing in line waiting to register to vote.

As a twenty-two-year-old Air Force bombardier, I flew a bombing mission in the last weeks of World War II, which can only be considered an atrocity. It was the napalm bombing of a small French village, for purposes that had nothing to do with winning the war, leaving a wasteland of death and destruction five miles below our planes.

Years before that, while a teenager on the streets of Brooklyn, I watched a black man in an argument with an old Jewish man, a pushcart peddler who seemed to be his employer. It was an argument over money the black man claimed he was owed, and he seemed desperate, by turns pleading and threatening, but the older man remained adamant. Suddenly the black man picked up a board and hit the other over the head. The older man, blood trickling down his face, just kept pushing his cart down the street.

I have never been persuaded that such violence, whether of an angry black man or a hate-filled trooper or of a dutiful Air Force officer, was the result of some natural instinct. All of those incidents, as I thought about them later, were explainable by social circumstances. I am in total agreement with the statement of the nineteenth-century English philosopher John Stuart Mill: "Of all the vulgar modes of escaping from the consideration of the effect of social and moral influences upon the human mind, the most vulgar is that of attributing the diversities of conduct and character to inherent natural differences."

Yet, at an early point in any discussion of human violence, especially a discussion of the causes of war, someone will say, "It's human nature." There is ancient, weighty intellectual support for that common argument. Machiavelli, in *The Prince*, expresses confidently his own view of human nature, that human beings tend to be *bad*. This gives him a good reason, being "realistic," to urge laying aside moral scruples in dealing with people: "A man who wishes to make a profession of goodness in everything must necessarily come to grief among so many who are not good. Therefore it is necessary for a prince, who wishes to maintain himself, to learn how not to be good."

The seventeenth-century philosopher Thomas Hobbes said, "I put forth a general inclination of all mankind, a perpetual and restless desire for power after power, that ceaseth only in death." This view of human nature led Hobbes to favor any kind of government, however authoritarian, that would keep the peace by blocking what he thought was the natural inclination of people to do violence to one another. He talked about "the dissolute condition of masterless men" that required "a coercive power to tie their hands from rapine and revenge."

Beliefs about human nature thus become self-fulfilling prophecies. If you believe human beings are naturally violent and bad, you may be persuaded to think (although not *required* to think) that it is "realistic" to be that way yourself. But is it indeed realistic (meaning, "I regret this, but it's a *fact...*") to blame *war* on human nature?

In 1932, Albert Einstein, already world famous for his work in physics and mathematics, wrote a letter to another distinguished thinker, Sigmund Freud. Einstein was deeply troubled by the memory of World War I, which had ended only fourteen years before. Ten million men had died on the battlefields of Europe, for reasons that no one could logically explain. Like many others who had lived through that war, Einstein was horrified by the thought that human life could be destroyed on such a massive scale and worried that there might be another war. He considered that Freud, the world's leading psychologist, might throw light on the question Why do men make war?

"Dear Professor Freud," he wrote. "Is there any way of delivering mankind from the menace of war?" Einstein spoke of "that small but determined group, active in every nation, composed of individuals who...regard warfare, the manufacture and sale of arms, simply as an occasion to advance their personal interests and enlarge their personal authority." And then he asked, "How is it possible for this small clique to bend the will of the majority, who stand to lose and suffer by a state of war, to the service of their ambitions?"

Einstein volunteered an answer, "Because man has within him a lust for hatred and destruction." And then he put his final question to Freud, "Is it possible to control man's mental evolution so as to make him proof against the psychoses of hate and destructiveness?"

Freud responded, "You surmise that man has in him an active instinct for hatred and destruction, amenable to such stimulations. I entirely agree with you.... The most casual glance at world-history will show an unending series of conflicts between one community and another." Freud pointed to two fundamental instincts in human beings: the erotic, or love, instinct and its opposite, the destructive instinct. But the only hope he could hold for the erotic triumphing over the destructive was in the cultural development of the human race, including "a strengthening of the intellect, which tends to master our instinctive life."

Einstein had a different view of the value of intelligence in mastering the instincts. After pointing to "the psychoses of hate and destructiveness," Einstein concluded, "Experience proves that it is rather the so-called 'Intelligentsia' that is most apt to yield to these disastrous collective suggestions."

Here are two of the greatest minds of the century, helpless and frustrated before the persistence of war. Einstein, venturing that aggressive instincts are at the root of war, asks Freud, the expert on instincts, for help in coming to a solution. Note, however, that Einstein has jumped from "man has within him a lust" to "disastrous collective suggestions." Freud ignores this leap from instinct to culture and affirms that the "destructive instinct" is the crucial cause of war.

But what is Freud's evidence for the existence of such an instinct? There is something curious in his argument. He offers no proof from the field of his expertise, psychology. His evidence is in "the most casual glance at world-history."

Let's move the discussion forward, fifty years later, to a school of thought that did not exist in Freud's time, sociobiology. The leading spokesperson in this group is E.O. Wilson, a Harvard University professor and distinguished scientist. His book *Sociobiology* is an impressive treatise on the behavior of various species in the biological world that have social inclinations, like ants and bees.

In the last chapter of *Sociobiology*, Wilson turned to human beings, and this drew so much attention that he decided to write a whole book dealing with this subject: *On Human Nature*. In it there is a chapter on aggression. It starts off with the question: "Are human beings innately aggressive?" Two sentences later: "The answer to it is yes." (No hesitation here.) And the next sentence explains why: "Throughout history, warfare, representing only the most organized technique of aggression, has been endemic to every form of society, from hunter-gatherer bands to industrial states."

Here is a peculiar situation. The psychologist (Freud) finds his evidence for the aggressive instinct not in psychology but in history. The biologist (Wilson) finds his evidence not in biology but in history.

This suggests that the evidence from neither psychology nor biology is sufficient to back up the claim for an aggressive instinct, and so these important thinkers turn to history. In this respect, they are no different from the ordinary person, whose thinking follows the same logic: history is full of warfare; one cannot find an era free of it; this must mean that it comes out of something deep in human nature, something biological, a drive, an instinct for violent aggression.

This logic is widespread in modern thought, in all classes of people, whether highly educated or uneducated. And yet, it is almost certainly wrong. And furthermore, it's dangerous.

Wrong, because there is no real evidence for it. Not in genetics, not in zoology, not in psychology, not in anthropology, not in history, not even in the ordinary experience of soldiers in war. Dangerous because it deflects attention from the nonbiological causes of violence and war.

It turns out, however, that Wilson's firm assent to the idea that human beings are "innately aggressive" depends on his redefinitions of *innately* and *aggressive*. In *On Human Nature* he says, "Innateness refers to the measurable probability that a trait will develop in a specified set of environments.... By this criterion human beings have a marked hereditary predisposition to aggressive behavior." And the word *aggression* takes in a variety of human actions, only some of which are violent.

In other words, when Wilson speaks of people being "innately aggressive" he does not mean that we are all born with an irresistible drive to become violent—it depends on our environment. And even if we become aggressive, that need not take the form of violence. Indeed, Wilson says that "the more violent forms of human aggression are not the manifestations of inborn drives." We now have, he says, "a more subtle explanation based on the interaction of genetic potential and learning."

The phrase *genetic potential* gets us closer to a common ground between Wilson and his radical critics, who have attributed to him sometimes more extreme views about innate aggression that he really holds. That is, human beings certainly have, from the start (genetically) a *potential* for violence, but also a potential for peacefulness. That leaves us open to all sorts of possibilities, depending on the circumstances we find ourselves in and the circumstances we create for ourselves.

There is no known gene for aggression. Indeed, there is no known gene for any of the common forms of human behavior (I am allowing the possibility that a genetic defect of the brain might make a person violent, but the very fact that it is a defect means it is not a normal trait). The science of genetics, the study of that hereditary material carried in the forty-odd chromosomes in every human cell and transmitted from one generation to the next, knows a good deal about genes for physical characteristics, very little about genes for mental ability, and virtually nothing about genes for personality traits (violence, competitiveness, kindness, surliness, a sense of humor, etc.).

Wilson's colleague at Harvard, scientist Stephen Jay Gould, a specialist in evolution, says very flatly (in *Natural History Magazine*, 1976): "What is the direct evidence for genetic control of specific human social behavior? At the moment, the answer is none whatever."

The distinguished biologist P.W. Medawar puts it this way, "By far the most important characteristic of human beings is that we have and exercise moral judgment and are not at the mercy of our hormones and genes."

In the spring of 1986, an international conference of scientists in Seville, Spain, issued a statement on the question of human nature and violent aggression, concluding, "It is scientifically incorrect to say that war is caused by 'instinct' or any single motivation.... Modern war involves institutional use of personal characteristics such as obedience, suggestibility, and idealism.... We conclude that biology does not condemn humanity to war."

What about the evidence of psychology? This is not as "hard" a science as genetics. Geneticists can examine genes, even "splice" them into new forms. What psychologists do is look at the way people behave and think, test them, psychoanalyze them, conduct experiments to see how people react to different experiences, and try to come to reasonable conclusions about why people behave the way they do. There is nothing in the findings of psychologists to make any convincing argument for an instinct for the violent aggressiveness of war. That's why Freud, the founder of modern psychology, had to look for evidence of the destructive instinct in history.

There was a famous "Milgram experiment" at Yale in the 1960s, named after the psychologist who supervised it. A group of paid volunteers were told they were helping with an experiment dealing with the effects of punishment on learning. Each volunteer was seated in a position to observe someone taking a test, wearing electrodes connected to a control panel operated by the volunteer. The volunteer was told to monitor the test and, whenever a wrong answer was given, to pull a switch that would give a painful electrical jolt to the person taking the test, each wrong answer leading to a greater and greater electrical charge. There were thirty switches, with labels ranging from "Slight Shock" to "Danger—Severe Shock."

The volunteer was *not* told, however, that the person taking the test was an actor and that no real jolt was given. The actor would pretend to be in pain when the volunteer pulled the switch. When a volunteer became reluctant to continue causing pain, the experimenter in charge would say something like "The experiment requires that you continue." Under these conditions, two-thirds of the volunteers continued to pull the electrical switches on wrong answers, even when the subjects showed agonizing pain. One-third refused.

The experiment was tried with the volunteers at different distances from the subjects. When they were not physically close to the subject, about 35 percent of the volunteers defied authority even when they could not see or talk with the subject. But when they were right next to the subject, 70 percent refused the order.

The behavior of the people who were willing to inflict maximum pain can certainly be explained without recourse to "human nature." Their behavior was learned, not inborn. What they learned is what most people learn in modern culture, to follow orders, to do the job you are hired to do, to obey the experts in charge. In the experiment the supervisors, who had a certain standing and a certain legitimacy as directors of a "scientific" experiment, kept assuring the volunteers that they should go ahead, even if the subjects showed pain. When they were distant from the subjects, it was easier to obey the experimenters. But seeing or hearing the pain close up brought out some strong *natural* feeling of empathy, enough to disobey even the legitimate, confident, scientific supervisors of the experiment.

Some people interpreted the results of the experiment as showing an innate cruelty in human beings, but this was not the conclusion of Stanley Milgram, who directed the study. Milgram sums up his own views: "It is the extreme willingness of adults to go to almost any lengths on the command of an authority that constitutes the chief finding of the study.... This is, perhaps, the most fundamental lesson of our study: ordinary people, simply doing their jobs, and without any particular hostility on their part, can become agents in a terrible destructive process."

So it is a learned response—"always obey," "do your job"—and not a natural drive, that caused so many of the people to keep pulling the pain switches. What is remarkable in the Milgram experiment, given the power of "duty...obedience" taught to us from childhood, is not that so many obeyed, but that so many refused.

C.P. Snow, a British novelist and scientist, wrote in 1961,

> When you think of the long and gloomy history of man, you will find more hideous crimes have been committed in the name of obedience than have ever been committed in the name of rebellion. The German Officer Corps were brought up in the most rigorous code of obedience...in the name of obedience they were party to, and assisted in, the most wicked large scale actions in the history of the world.

What about the evidence from anthropology—that is, from the behavior of "primitive" people, who are supposed to be closest to the "natural" state and, therefore, give strong clues about "human nature"? There have been many studies of the personality traits of such people: African Bushmen, North American Indians, Malay tribes, the Stone Age Tasaday from the Philippines, etc.

The findings can be summed up easily: There is no single pattern of warlike or peaceable behavior; the variations are very great. In North America, the Plains Indians were warlike, the Cherokee of Georgia were peaceful.

Anthropologist Colin Turnbull conducted two different studies in which he lived for a while with native tribes. In *The Forest People*, he describes the Pygmies of the Ituri rain forest in central Africa, wonderfully gentle and peaceful people whose idea of punishing a wrongdoer was to send him out into the forest to sulk. When he observed the Mbuti tribe of Zaire, he found them cooperative and pacific. However, when Turnbull spent time with the Ik people of East Africa, whom he describes in *The Mountain People*, he found them ferocious and selfish.

The differences in behavior Turnbull found were explainable, not by genetics, not by the "nature" of these people, but by their environment, or their living conditions. The relatively easy life of the forest people fostered goodwill and generosity. The Ik, on the other hand, had been driven from their natural hunting grounds by the creation of a national game reserve into an isolated life of starvation in barren mountains. Their desperate attempt to survive brought out the aggressive destructiveness that Turnbull saw.

There have been many attempts to use the evidence of ethology (the study of the behavior of animals) to "prove" innate aggressiveness in human beings. We find Robert Ardrey using animal protection of their territory to argue for a "territorial imperative," which drives human beings to war against one another, or Desmond Morris, who uses the evidence of primates (*The Naked Ape*) to see human beings as deeply influenced by their evolutionary origins as tribal hunters.

But the study of animal behavior turns up all kinds of contradictory evidence. Baboons observed in a London zoo were found to be violent, but when studied on the plains of South Africa their behavior was peaceful. The difference was easily explainable by the fact that in the zoo baboons were strangers to one another, brought together by man. Even when baboons were aggressive, this consisted mostly of yelling and squabbling, not doing serious damage to one another.

We might note the work of Konrad Lorez, an important zoologist and a specialist in the study of birds who could not resist the temptation to turn to human behavior in his book, *On Aggression*. Lorenz is often cited to support the idea that aggressive instincts in human beings derive from evolutionary origins in animal behavior. But Lorenz was not that certain. Indeed, he said at one point that none of our so-called instincts are as dangerous as our "emotional allegiance to cultural values."

It is a big jump, in any case, from bees or ducks or even baboons to human beings. Such a jump does not take account of the critically different factor of the human brain, which enables learning and culture and which creates a whole range of possibilities—good and bad. Those wide possibilities are not available to creatures with limited intelligence whose behavior is held close to their genetic instincts (although even with them different environments bring different characteristics).

The psychologist Erik Erikson, moving away from Freud's emphasis on biological instinct and on impressions gained in infancy, has pointed to the fact that, unlike most animals, human beings have a long childhood, a period for learning and cultural influence. This creates the possibility for a much wider range of behaviors. Erikson says that our cultures have created "pseudospecies," that is, false categories of race and nation that obliterate our sense of ourselves as one species and thus encourage the hostility that turns violent.

Animals other than human beings do not make war. They do not engage in organized violence on behalf of some abstraction. That is a special gift of creatures with advanced brains and cultures. The animal commits violence for a specific, visible reason, the need for food and for self-defense.

Genetics, psychology, anthropology, and zoology—in none of these fields is there evidence of a human instinct for the kind of aggressive violence that characterizes war. But what about history, which Freud pointed to?

Who can deny the frequency of war in human history? But its persistence does not prove that its origin is in human nature. Are there not persistent facts about human society that can explain the constant eruption of war without recourse to those mysterious instincts that science, however hard it tries, cannot find in our genes? Is not one of those facts the existence of ruling elites in every culture, who become enamored of their own power and seek to extend it? Is not another of those facts the greed, not of the general population, but of powerful minorities in society who seek more raw materials or more markets or more land or more favorable places for investment? Is there not a persistent ideology of nationalism, especially in the modern world, a set of beliefs taught to each generation in which the Motherland or the Fatherland is an object of veneration and becomes a burning cause for which one becomes willing to kill the children of other Motherlands or Fatherlands?

Surely we do not need human nature to explain war; there are other explanations. But human nature is simple and easy. It requires very little thought. To analyze the social, economic, and cultural factors that throughout human history have led to so many wars—that is hard work. One can hardly blame people for avoiding it.

But we should take another look at the proposition that the persistence of war in history *proves* that war comes from human nature. The claim requires that wars be not only frequent, but perpetual, that they not be limited to some nations but be true of all. Because if wars are only intermittent—if there are periods of war and periods of peace and if there are nations that go to war and other nations that don't—then it is unreasonable to attribute war to something as universal as human nature.

Whenever someone says, "history proves..." and then cites a list of historical facts, we should beware. We can always select facts from history (there are lots to choose from) to prove almost anything about human behavior. Just as one can select from a person's life just those instances of mean and aggressive behavior to prove the person *naturally* mean and aggressive, one can also select from that same person's life only those instances of kind and affectionate behavior to prove him or her naturally nice.

Perhaps we should turn from these scholarly studies of history, genetics, anthropology, psychology, and zoology to the plain reality of war itself. We surely have a lot of experience with that in our time.

I remember reading John Hersey's novel, *The War Lover*. It interested me greatly, partly because I am an admirer of Hersey's writing, but even more because his subject was the crew of a Flying Fortress, the B17 heavy bomber in World War II. I had been a bombardier on such a crew in just that war. The novel's main character is a pilot who loves war. He also loves women. He is a braggart and a bully in regard to both. It turns out that his boasted sex exploits are a fraud and, in fact, he is impotent; it appears that his urge to bomb and kill is connected to that impotence.

When I finished reading the novel, I thought, Well, that may explain this piss-poor (a phrase left over from that war) fellow Hersey has picked as his subject and *his* lust for violence and death. But it doesn't explain war.

The men I knew in the air force—the pilots, navigators, bombardiers, and gunners on the crews flying over Europe, dropping bombs, and killing lots of people—were not lusting to kill, were not enthusiasts for violence, and were not war lovers. They—we—were engaged in large-scale killing, mostly of noncombatants, the women, children, and elderly people who happened to inhabit the neighborhoods of the cities that we bombed (officially, these were all "military targets"). But this did not come out of our *natures*, which were no different than when we were peacefully playing, studying, and living the lives of American boys back in Brooklyn, New York, or Aurora, Missouri.

The bloody deeds we did came out of a set of experiences not hard to figure out: We had been brought up to believe that our political leaders had good motives and could be trusted to do right in the world; we had learned that the world had good guys and bad guys, good countries and bad countries, and ours was good. We had been trained to fly planes, fire guns, operate bombsights, and to take pride in doing the job well. And we had been trained to follow orders, which there was no reason to question, because everyone on our side was good, and on the other side, bad. Besides, we didn't have to watch a little girl's legs get blown off by our bombs; we were 30,000 feet high and no human being on the ground was visible, no scream could be heard. Surely that is enough to explain how men can participate in war. We don't have to grope in the darkness of human nature.

Indeed, when you look at modern war, do you find men rushing into it with a ferocious desire to kill? Hardly. You find men (and some women) joining the armed forces in search of training, careers, companionship, glamour, and psychological and economic security. You find others being conscripted by law, under penalty of prison if they refuse. And all of them suddenly transported into a war, where the habit of following orders and the dinning into their ears of the rightness of their cause can overcome the fear of death or the moral scruples of murdering another human being.

Many observers of war, and former soldiers too, have spoken of the lures of war for men, its attractions and enticements, as if something in men's *nature* makes war desirable for them. J. Glenn Gray, who was in army intelligence and close to combat situations in the European theater during World War II, has a chapter in his book *The Warriors* called "The Enduring Appeals of Battle." He writes of the "powerful fascination" of war. He says, "The emotional environment of warfare has always been compelling.... Many men both hate and love combat." What are these "appeals" of war according to Gray? "The delight in seeing, the delight in comradeship, the delight in destruction."

He recalls the biblical phrase "the lust of the eye" to describe the sheer overpowering spectacle of war, the astounding scenes, the images, the vignettes—things never before experienced by young men who lived ordinary lives on ordinary farms or ordinary streets. That is certainly true. I had never seen the innards of a fifty-caliber machine gun; had never flown in an airplane miles high, in the night and close to the stars, overwhelmed by the beauty of that, and operated my bombsight and watched specks of fire flare like tiny torches on the ground below; and had never seen at close range the black puffs that were the explosions of antiaircraft shells, threatening my life. But that is not a love of war; it is an aesthetic need for visual and emotional excitement that comes, unrequested, with war and that can also be produced by other experiences.

Gray is also certainly right about the extraordinary comradeship of men in combat. But they don't *seek* combat because of that, any more than men in prison seek imprisonment because in prison they often forge human ties with fellow prisoners far stronger than any they have on the outside.

As for the "delight in destruction," I am skeptical about that. Granted, there is something visually exciting about explosions and something satisfying about hitting your target efficiently, as you were trained to do. But the delight that comes in a job well done would accompany any kind of job, not just destroying things.

All of the elements Gray and others have talked about as "the enduring appeals" of war are appeals not of violence or murder but of the concomitants of the war situation. It is sad that life is so drab, so unsatisfying for so many that combat gives them their first ecstatic pleasures, whether in "seeing" or companionship or work done well. It challenges us to find what the philosopher William James called "the moral equivalent of war," ways to make life outside of war vivid, affectionate, even thrilling.

Gray himself, although he tries to understand and explain those "enduring appeals," is offended by war. *The Warriors* recalls an entry in his own wartime journal, made December 8, 1944, which reflects not only his own feelings, but that of so many other veterans of war, that war *is* an affront to our nature as human beings. He wrote,

> Last night I lay awake and thought of all the inhumanity of it, the beastliness of the war.... I remembered all the brutal things I had seen since I came overseas, all the people rotting in jail, some of whom I had helped to put there.... I thought of Plato's phrase about the wise man caught in an evil time who refuses to participate in the crimes of his fellow citizens, but hides behind a wall until the storm is past. And this morning, when I rose, tired and distraught from bed, I knew that in order to survive this time I must love more. There is no other way.

When the U.S. government decided to enter World War I, it did not find an eager army of males, just waiting for an opportunity to vent their "natural" anger against the enemy, to indulge their "natural" inclination to kill. Indeed, there was a large protest movement against entrance into the war, leading Congress to pass punitive legislation for antiwar statements (2,000 people were prosecuted for criticizing the war). The government, besides conscripting men for service on threat of prison and jailing antiwar protesters, had to organize a propaganda campaign, sending 75,000 speakers to give 750,000 speeches in hundreds of towns and cities to persuade people of the rightness of the war.

Even with all that, there was resistance by young men to the draft. In New York City, ninety of the first hundred draftees claimed exemption. In Minnesota, the *Minneapolis Journal* reported, "Draft Opposition Fast Spreading in State." In Florida, two black farm workers went into the woods with a shotgun and mutilated themselves to avoid the draft; one blew off four fingers of his hand, the other shot off his arm below the elbow. A senator from Georgia reported "general and widespread opposition...to the enactment of the draft.... Mass meetings held in every part of the State protested against it." Ultimately, over 330,000 men were classified as draft evaders.

We have an enormous literature of war. Much of it was written by men who experienced combat: Erich Remarque and Ernest Hemingway on World War I; Norman Mailer, James Jones, Kurt Vonnegut, Joseph Heller, and Paul Fussell on World War II; Philip Caputo, Tim O'Brien, John DelVecchio, Bill Ehrhart, and Ron Kovic on Vietnam. The men they write about are not (with occasional exceptions) bloodthirsty killers, consumed by some ferocious instinct to maim and destroy other human beings. They connect across a whole century with the young scared kid in *Red Badge of Courage*; they experience fear more than hate, fatigue more than rage, and boredom more than vengefulness. If any of them turn into crazed killers for some moment or some hour, it is not hard to find the cause in the crazed circumstances of war, coming on top of the ordinary upbringing of a young man in a civilized country.

A GI named John Ketwig wrote a letter to his wife:

> After all those years of preparation in the schools, you walked out the door, and they told you it was your duty to kill the commies in South Vietnam. If you wouldn't volunteer, they would draft you, force you to do things against your will. Put you in jail. Cut your hair, take away your mod clothes, train you to kill. How could they do that? It was directly opposite

to everything your parents had been saying, the teachers had been saying, the clergymen had been saying. You questioned it, and your parents said they didn't want you to go, but better that than jail. The teacher said it was your duty. The clergy said you wouldn't want your mother to live in a communist country, so you'd best go fight them in Asia before they landed in California. You asked about 'Thou shalt not kill,' and they mumbled.

It was no instinct to kill that led John Ketwig into military duty, but the pressure of people around him, the indoctrination of his growing up. So it is not remarkable that he joined the military. What is remarkable is that a certain point he rebelled against it.

While two million men served in Vietnam at one time or another, another half million evaded the draft in some way. And of those who served, there were perhaps 100,000 deserters. About 34,000 GIs were court-martialed and imprisoned. If an instinct really was at work, it was not for war, but against it.

Once in the war, the tensions of combat on top of the training in obedience produced atrocities. In the My Lai Massacre we have an extreme example of the power of a culture in teaching obedience. In My Lai, a hamlet in South Vietnam, a company of U.S. soldiers landed by helicopter early one morning in March 1968, with orders to kill everybody there. In about one hour, although not a single shot was fired at them, they slaughtered about 400 Vietnamese, most of them old people, women, and children. Many of them were herded into ditches and then mowed down with automatic rifles.

One of the American soldiers, Charles Hutto, said later, "The impression I got was that we was to shoot everyone in the village.... An order came down to destroy all of the food, kill all the animals and kill all the people...then the village was burned.... I didn't agree with the killings but we were ordered to do it."

It is not at all surprising that men go to war, when they have been cajoled, bribed, propagandized, conscripted, threatened, and also not surprising that after rigorous training they obey orders, even to kill unarmed women and children. What is surprising is that some refuse.

At My Lai a number of soldiers would not kill when ordered to: Michael Bernhardt, Roy Wood, Robert Maples, a GI named Grzesik. Warrant Officer Hugh Thompson commanded a helicopter that flew over the scene and, when he saw what was happening, he landed the helicopter and rescued some of the women and children, ordering his crewmen to fire on GIs if they fired on the Vietnamese. Charles Hutto, who participated in the My Lai Massacre, said afterward.

> I was 19 years old, and I'd always been told to do what the grown-ups told me to do.... But now I'll tell my sons, if the government calls, to go, to serve their country, but to use their own judgment at times...to forget about authority...to use their own conscience. I wish somebody had told me that before I went to Vietnam. I didn't know. Now I don't think there should be even a thing called war...'cause it messes up a person's mind.

In British novelist George Orwell's essay, "Shooting an Elephant," he recalls his experience in Burma, when he was a minor official of the British Empire. An elephant ran loose, and he finally shot it to death, but notes he did this not out of any internal drive, not of malice, but because people around him expected him to do that, as part of his job. It was not in his "nature."

The American feminist and anarchist Emma Goldman, writing at the beginning of the twentieth century, before so much of the scientific discussion of the relationship between violence and human nature, said,

> Poor human nature, what horrible crimes have been committed in thy name! Every fool, from king to policeman, from the flathead parson to the visionless dabbler in science, presume to speak authoritatively of human nature. The greater the mental charlatan, the more definite his insistence on the wickedness and weaknesses of human nature. Yet how can any one speak of it today, with every soul a prison, with every heart fettered, wounded, and maimed?

Her point about "the visionless dabbler in science" was affirmed half a century later by Nobel Prize-winning biologist Salvadore E. Luria, who points to the misuse of science in attributing violent behavior to our genes. Moving away from genetic determinism and its mood of inevitability (as too often interpreted, the inevitability of war and death), Luria says that biologists have a nobler role for the future: to explore "the most intriguing feature—the creativity of the human spirit."

That creativity is revealed in human history, but it is a history that Machiavelli and a succession of scholarly pessimists ignore as they concentrate on the worst aspects of human behavior. There is another history, of the rejection of violence, the refusal to kill, and the yearning for community. It has shown itself throughout the past in acts of courage and sacrifice that defied all the immediate pressures of the environment.

This was true even in the unspeakable conditions of the German death camps in World War II, as Terence des Pres pointed out in his book *The Survivor*. He wrote, "The depth and durability of man's social nature may be gauged by the fact that conditions in the concentration camps were designed to turn prisoners against each other, but that in a multitude of ways, men and women persisted in social acts."

It is true that there is an infinite human capacity for violence. There is also an infinite potential for kindness. The unique ability of humans to *imagine* gives enormous power to idealism, an imagining of a better state of things not yet in existence. That power has been misused to send young men to war. But the power of idealism can also be used to attain justice, to end the massive violence of war.

Anyone who has participated in a social movement has seen the power of idealism to move people toward self-sacrifice and cooperation. I think of Sam Block, a young black Mississippian, very thin and with very bad eyes, taking black people to register to vote in the murderous atmosphere of Greenwood, Mississippi, in the early 1960s. Block was accosted by a sheriff (another civil rights worker, listening, recorded their conversation):

> SHERIFF: Nigger, where you from?
> BLOCK: I'm a native of Mississippi.
> SHERIFF: I know all the niggers here.
> BLOCK: Do you know any colored people?
> (The sheriff spat at him.)
> SHERIFF: I'll give you till tomorrow to get out of here.
> BLOCK: If you don't want to see me here, you better pack up and leave, because I'll be here.

History, so diligent at recording disasters, is largely silent on the enormous number of courageous acts by individuals challenging authority and defying death.

2

Non-
Violent
Direct
Action

The experience of the civil rights movement forced me to think about the process of social change—about the alternatives of violence and parliamentary reform, and about the principle that was at the heart of the Southern movement for equal rights—non-violent direct action. I presented this paper at the 1965 annual meeting of the American Orthopsychiatric Association in New York, and it was published in the *American Journal of Orthopsychiatry*, January, 1966.

In 1937 sociologist Robert S. Lynd wrote a little gem of a book entitled *Knowledge for What?* in which he attacked the divorce of scholarship from the problems of his day. The book has just been reissued 27 years later. In the interim the world has experienced Auschwitz and Hiroshima and Birmingham, yet the accusation in that book against the world of scholarship remains exactly as true in every line. Social scientists for the most part still are not focusing their research directly on the world's urgent problems. True, they are accumulating data on these problems, but too often they avoid moving too close to the presentation of solutions because at that point controversy enters. So the scholarly monographs and the social evils keep rising higher and higher in separate piles, parallel to one another with such Euclidian perfection that we begin to despair they ever will intersect.

I would like in this brief paper to at least initiate a discussion on the uses of power, not as an academic exercise, but in relation to what we see around us and to what we hear, which is more and more these days the sound of crowds in the streets.

The health of society, I assume, is dependent on a balance between people's expectations and the fulfillment of those expectations. Both the Buddhism of Gautama in the East and the Stoicism of Epictetus in the West in their emphasis on resignation as a means to happiness were fitted to the limits of a crude technology. Today the momentum of science has created worldwide waves of demand which *can* be fulfilled. Quiescence and resignation are no longer pertinent, and the clamor everywhere for change, though expressed in passion, is reasonable.

There is little question any more that change in our social institutions must come. Never before in history has there been such a consensus in objectives all over the world, nor such a variance of method in trying to achieve these objectives. Most men everywhere agree they want to end war, imperialism, racism, poverty, disease and tyranny. What they disagree about is whether these expectations can be fulfilled within the old frameworks of nationalism, representative government and the profit system. And running through the tension between agreement and disagreement are these questions: How much violence will be necessary to fulfill these expectations? What must we suffer to get the world we all want?

We have three traditional ways of satisfying the need for institutional change: war, revolution and gradual reform. We might define war as violence from without, revolution as violence from within and gradual reform as deferred violence. I would like to examine all three in the new light of the mid-twentieth century.

Assuming that change always involves a degree of dislocation and of social cost, man's problem is then how to achieve maximum desirable change at minimum cost. War at best has been a haphazard way of deciding this question, for the impetus of war piles up the dead with little regard for social consequence, so that even those wars fought against the most obvious of evils, such as the Civil War (with Negro slavery at stake) and World War II (with global slavery at stake), brought in the first case the uncontrolled gushing of what Edmund Wilson calls "patriotic gore" and in the second the needless bombings of Dresden and Hiroshima. At its worst, war has been mass slaughter without even the saving grace of a definable social goal. The Trojan War was the first and classic case, and that element of idiocy has persisted in all wars in varying degree.

Up to the hydrogen bomb, it was still possible to weigh cost and consequence. Now we can throw away the scales, for it should be clear to any rational and humane person that there is no piece of territory (not Berlin or Viet Nam or Hungary), there is no social system yet put into operation anywhere by man (not socialism or capitalism or whatever) which is worth the consequence of atomic war. If war ever in its shotgun way represented a method of achieving social progress, the illimitable scale of warfare today removes it forever as a justifiable method of social change. John U. Nef of the University of Chicago put it this way in his book *War and Human Progress*, which he wrote soon after World War II:

> The only justification for war is the defense of a culture worth defending, and the states of the modern world have less and less to defend beyond their material comforts, in spite of the claims of some to represent fresh concepts of civilization. The new weapons have made nonsense of defensive war. Peoples have been left without any means of defending except by destroying others, and the destruction is almost certain to be mutual.

What of revolution? Here the balance of achievement and cost is less haphazard, though still far from rational. The four great revolutions of modern times (the American, the French, the Russian and the Chinese) though all erratic in their movement towards social progress, in the end, I believe, justified the relatively small amount of violence required to fulfill them. But today, can we still look to revolutions as the chief means of social change, and as a useful means, whereby great change can be achieved at relatively small cost?

In some exceptional instances, yes. But, as a general rule, it seems to me that the conditions of the contemporary world have removed the feasibility of revolutions in the old sense. There are several reasons for this. One is that the power of weapons in the hands of the ruling elite makes popular uprisings, however great is the base of support, a very dubious undertaking. The other consideration, and probably more important, is that revolutions like wars no longer can be contained. They almost always involve one or more of the great nations of the world, and are either crushed by an outside power (as were the Hungarians in their revolt) or are prolonged to the point of frightful massacre (as the revolt in Viet Nam was met by the intervention of the French and then the Americans, and as the revolt in the Congo was stymied by Belgians and other forces). The Cuban revolution was an oddity; it was able to subsist because it brought into the picture not one but both the two leading world powers. There, even in success we can see the perils posed by revolution in the contemporary world, for the Cuban missile crisis almost set off a global disaster.

This removal of both war and revolution as methods of ushering in the inevitable changes would seem to leave us with the stock-in-trade of Western liberals: gradual reform. Here the United States is the prime example of peaceful accommodation, harmonizing gracefully with the requirements of change.

There is a double trouble with this pleasant solution: it does not square with the facts of the American past, and it does not fit the requirements of the American future. Let me explain what I mean.

It is remarkable how many persons, both in the United States and abroad, accept the legend that our country is the quintessential example of peaceful, progressive development as opposed to the violent change characteristic of other parts of the world. Yet the United States was born in violent revolution, and then solved its chief domestic problem not by reform but by one of the bloodiest wars in modern times. Its history has been punctuated with bursts of violence. Each outbreak was a reminder, quickly forgotten, that the changes we made through gradual reform were not fast enough or large enough to match the growing expectations of sections of the population: the slow steps made against slavery, for instance (the abolition of the slave trade as agreed to in Philadelphia in 1787, the Compromise of 1820 and the Compromise of 1850) were all failures, and the Civil War resulted.

Congress did not move fast enough to alleviate the pains of exploitation for the new industrial working class of the latter half of the nineteenth century, and so the period from 1877 to 1914 saw a series of labor explosions unmatched in their ferocity in any country in the world: the railroad insurrections of 1877, the Haymarket killings of 1886, the

Homestead strike of 1894, the textile strike at Lawrence in 1912 and the Ludlow Massacre in Colorado in 1914. What, if not the failure of American reformism, explains the growth of the Socialist Party to a million supporters in 1912, the emergence of the Industrial Workers of the World as a radical, militant labor union devoted to the abolition of the capitalist system? It took the hysteria of world war to help crush both these movements.

How successful was the reform of the Progressive Era of Theodore Roosevelt and Woodrow Wilson when the whole structure they built up to keep the economy intact (Federal Reserve System, Federal Trade Commission, antitrust legislation) collapsed in 1929, and ushered in another decade of violence (bonus marches and marches of the unemployed, of sit-down strikes and clashes between workingmen and police) and again ended not in prosperity but in war? Is it New Deal reform or war expenditures that keep today's economy from collapsing into another period of violent conflict? Can we really say that the history of our nation is of carefully phased reform measures, of peaceful evolution towards domestic prosperity and national peace?

And now, in this last decade, we suddenly have learned that what we thought was gradual progress towards ending race prejudice in the United States was not nearly sufficient. It has taken mass demonstrations in Montgomery, Alabama; mass arrests in Albany, Georgia; the violence of the Freedom Rides; the bombings in Birmingham, and the murders in Mississippi to make us aware of the failure of piecemeal reform to establish racial justice in America.

There are lessons in this, I believe, far beyond the race crisis in the United States, and I want to explore some of them. My point is that gradualism, even in that presumed mecca of reform, the U.S.A., never really has matched the push of events, and that today the momentum of world change has made it even less able to do so. Thus, *none* of the traditionally approved mechanisms for social change (not war, nor revolution, nor reform) is adequate for the kind of problems we face today in the United States and in the world. We need apparently some technique which is more energetic than parliamentary reform and yet not subject to the dangers which war and revolution pose in the atomic age.

This technique, I suggest, is that which has been used over the centuries by aggrieved groups in fitful, semi-conscious control of their own actions. With the Negro revolt in America, the technique has begun to take on the quality of a deliberate use of power to effect the most change with the least harm. I speak of non-violent direct action. This encompasses a great variety of methods, limited only by our imaginations: sit-ins, freedom rides and freedom walks, prayer pilgrimages, wade-ins, pray-ins, freedom ballots, freedom schools, and who knows what is on the horizon? Whatever the specific form, this technique has certain qualities: it disturbs the status quo, it intrudes on the complacency of the majority, it expresses the anger and the hurt of the aggrieved, it publicizes an injustice, it demonstrates the inadequacy of whatever reforms have been instituted up to that point, it creates tension and trouble and thus forces the holders of power to move faster than they otherwise would have to redress grievances.

The crucial problems of our time no longer can be left to simmer on the low flame of gradualism, only to explode. Poverty, for instance, will not be attacked on the scale which is required until the ease of the well off is punctured in some brusque way. And in this shrinking world, for how long can the United Sates contain its vast wealth inside the national membrane and spend billions on useless products while a million people starve in Calcutta? Once people begin to measure the distribution of wealth on global lines there may well be a clamor against the deformed concentration of it in one country of the world. Jet travel makes the world smaller than the Roman Empire. Then why shouldn't the parallel existence of America and India be as much as object of concern as the parallel existence in Rome of the opulence of emperors and the misery of slaves? And how else will horror be expressed under conditions of today except by some form of popular protest?

Consider another issue: with the possession of nuclear bombs proliferating in the world and with the mathematical probability of war by error increasing, can we depend on the normal parliamentary processes for concerned people to express to the powers of the world their revulsion against war? Should we not have an increasing number of those little bands of pacifists, from Bertrand Russell to the ones who sailed into the Pacific on the *Golden Rule*?

Also there is the problem of freedom for dissenters, which exists in East and West, North and South, in communist and capitalist countries, in the old nations and in the new nations. How else but by Poznan uprisings, by demonstrations and civil disobedience, can such freedom be maintained and extended?

For us in the United States, it is hard to accept the idea that the ordinary workings of the parliamentary system will not suffice in the world today. But recall that Jefferson himself, watching the Constitution being created, and thinking of Shay's Rebellion, spoke of the need for revolutions every twenty years. And Rousseau, at the very moment representative government was beginning to take hold, pointed to the inability of anyone to truly represent anyone else's interests. And Robert Michels, the Swiss sociologist, 150 years after Rousseau, showed us how an "iron law of oligarchy" operates within any government or any party to separate top from bottom and to make power-holders insensitive to the needs of the mass. No matter how democratic elections are, they represent only fleeting and widely separated moments of popular participation. In that long span between elections, people are passive and captive.

Thus, we face a dilemma: wars and revolutions today cannot be limited and are therefore very perilous. Yet parliamentary reform is inadequate. We need some intermediate device, powerful but restrained and explosive but controlled, to pressure and even to shock the decision-makers into making the kinds of changes in institutions which fit our world. Walter Millis, in an essay written for the Center for the Study of Democratic Institutions, has argued persuasively that the price we may have to pay for a world without war is a kind of intermittent guerrilla warfare, constantly bringing society into rough accord with popular demands. It turns out (and we have the experience of all bourgeois, socialist and national revolutions to support this) that *no* form of government, once in power, can be trusted to limit its own ambition, to extend freedom and to wither away. This means that it is up to the citizenry, those outside of power, to engage in permanent combat with the state, short of violent, escalatory revolution, but beyond the gentility of the ballot-box, to insure justice, freedom and well being, all those values which virtually the entire world has come to believe in.

This idea links the Negro uprising in America to the turmoil everywhere in the world. It also links present to past, for what I am suggesting is a more deliberate, more conscious, more organized use of those techniques of constructive dissent which man has used in spontaneity and in desperation throughout history.

Those of us reared in the tradition of liberal, gradualist reform, and cherishing tranquillity, may have to learn to sacrifice a little of these in order not to lose all of them. Such a course may not be easy, but it is not a bad substitute for the world as we have known it up to now, a world of simplistic and terrible solutions, where we oscillated constantly between two alternatives: the devastation of war or the injustice of peace.

3

The New Radicalism

By 1969 the civil rights movement and the anti-war movement had generated a huge amount of practical experience, without any obvious theoretical foundation. Priscilla Long thought it time to fill that gap. She assembled a set of essays in a book entitled *The New Left*, and it was put out by a small publisher in Boston, Porter Sargent. The introduction was written by historian and activist Staughton Lynd, and the very first essay was by someone generally acknowledged to be one of the intellectual mentors of the New Left, C. Wright Mills. The book included essays by Barbara Deming, Noam Chomsky, Daniel Berrigan, Paul Mattick, Percival and Paul Goodman. I wrote one called "Marxism and the New Left," which follows.

My intention in this paper is not to define the radicalism of the New Left but to redefine it. By a remarkable coincidence, that is, I believe, in the spirit of Marxism—to declare what something *is* by declaring what it should be. Marxism assumes that everything—including an idea—takes on a new meaning in each additional moment of time, in each unique historical situation. It tries to avoid academic scholasticism, which pretends to dutifully record, to describe—forgetting that to merely describe is to circumscribe. (The pretense of passive description is what Herbert Marcuse in *One-Dimensional Man* called *operationalism.*)

Marxism is not a fixed body of dogma, to be put into big black books or little red books, and memorized, but a set of specific propositions about the modern world which are both tough and tentative, plus a certain vague and yet exhilarating vision of the future, and, more fundamentally, an approach to life, to people, to ourselves, a certain way of thinking about thinking as well as about being. Most of all it is a way of thinking which is intended to promote action.

The New Left—that loose amalgam of civil rights activists, Black Power advocates, ghetto organizers, student rebels, Vietnam protesters—has been exciting because it has been acting. In that circle of encounter where the spirit of Marxism and the action of the New Left intersect, the New Left will take from Marxism—if it is wise—not all of its exact propositions about the world Marx and Engels lived in (a world which is partly the same today and partly different), but its approach. This approach demands a constant redefinition of theory in the light of immediate reality, and an insistence on *action* as a way of both testing and reworking theory.

One of the most quoted, and most ignored, in practice, of Marx's statements is the eleventh point of his *Theses on Feuerbach* (about 1845): "The philosophers have only interpreted the world in various ways; the point however is to change it." Since any body of ideas is part of the world, this suggests our job is not merely to interpret Marxism and the New Left, but to change them. Earlier in these *Theses*, Marx criticized Feuerbach's emphasis on "the theoretical attitude." He said: "Social life is essentially practical. All mysteries...find their rational solution in human practice."

In their best moments, thinking revolutionaries agree with this. When Mao Tse Tung was in Yenan, after the Long March, he gave his lecture "On Practice," where he talked of the primacy of experience in knowledge, of uniting perceptual knowledge with rational knowledge, rationalism with empiricism. He said: "The Marxist recognizes that in the absolute, total process of the development of the universe, the development of each concrete process is relative; hence in the great stream of absolute truth, man's knowledge of the concrete process at each given stage of development is only relatively true." That spirit is somehow different than what one encounters in the *Peking Review* these days, with its litany: Long Live Chairman Mao.

To try for a moment to act out the Marxist approach, look at the academic setting in which we live. We find that so much of what is called "intellectual history" is the aimless dredging up of what is and was, rather than a creative recollection of experience pointed at the betterment of human life. We are surrounded by solemn, pretentious argument about what Marx or Machiavelli or Rousseau really meant, about who was right and who was wrong—all of which is another way the pedant has of saying: "I am right and you are wrong." Too much of what passes for the theoretical discussion of public issues is really a personal duel for honor or privilege—with each discussant like the character in *Catch-22* who saw every event in the world as either a feather in his cap or a black eye—and this while men were dying all around him.

This scholasticism, oddly enough, has been typical both of the Old Left and of the academic journals, journals which would be horrified at being called Left or Right, and which indeed could hardly be accused of moving in any identifiable direction. Because the New Left is a successor to the Old Left in American history, and because it comes to a large extent out of the academic world (whether the Negro colleges of the South or the Berkeleys of the North), it is always being tempted by theoretical irrelevancies. Fortunately, the young people of today seem more nimble than their predecessors in avoiding this trap.

The contributions of the Old Left—and they were considerable—came not out of its ideological fetishism but out of its action. What gave it dynamism was not the classes on surplus value but the organization of the CIO, not the analysis of Stalin's views on the National and Colonial Question, but the fight for the Scottsboro boys, not the labored rationale for dictatorship of the proletariat, but the sacrifices of the Abraham Lincoln Battalion. I am not arguing here against theoretical discussion, or against long-range principles, or the analysis of sub-surface realities, but I am asserting that theory must be informed by observation and expressed in action. It must, in other words, be relevant.

A materialist approach—in the Marxian sense—makes suggestions rather than demands. One of these is that we look for the situational circumstances behind the behavior and thought of men, if we want to affect both. A dialectical approach—in the Marxian sense—suggests that we evaluate a situation not as fixed, but as in motion, and that our evaluation itself affects that motion. Dialectical materialism asks awareness that we are creatures of limited vision, in eyes and brain, and so must not assume that what we see or perceive is all—that conflicting tendencies often lie beneath the surface of any event.

These are not just academic observations: such an approach should make it easier for us to understand what is wrong when the government says to a penniless Negro in the Mississippi Delta, we have passed a bill and you are now free. Such an approach should help us to sense, in walking past the tenements of a city, temporarily quiet, the element of a violent insurrection. Marx's emphasis on the tyranny of economics can't tell us *how much* economic motivation there is behind any specific political act, but it can lead us to look for it. And so the New Left might go overboard in stressing economic interests in Southeast Asia as an explanation for escalation in Vietnam—but it might be devilishly right in noting the connection between U.S. economic interests in Latin American nations and the pro-American votes of these nations in the U.N.

Marxism, in other words, doesn't tell us *exactly* what we will find beneath the surface—it does suggest that we should look for—and it certainly insists that we look. A Marxist would have given Lysenko his microscope; but it was a Stalinist who told him—or created an atmosphere that told him—what he must find beneath it.

And if someone says this isn't dialectical materialism or Marxism—this is common sense, or rationalism, or pragmatism, or empiricism, or naturalism—why deny that, or argue? Who cares about credit? True, the Old Left didn't like to admit relations with any other ideology. It remained virginal and lonely. The New Left seems different.

There has been much talk about a Christian-Marxist dialogue—but if such a dialogue is to be useful perhaps it should begin with the idea that God is dead and Marx is dead, but Yossarian lives. This is only a way of saying: let's not spend our time arguing whether God exists or what Marx really meant, because while we argue, the world moves, while we publish, others perish, and the best use of our energy is to resist those who would send us—after so many missions of murder—on still one more.

A new radicalism should be anti-ideological, I believe, in the sense I have discussed. But it also should be—and here it has been inadequate—concerned with theory. I see three essential ingredients in such a theory. First we need a vision of what we are working toward—one based on transcendental human needs and not limited by the reality we are so far stuck with. Second, this theory should analyze the present reality, not through the prism of old, fixed categories, but rather with an awareness of the unique here and now and of the need to make the present irrationality intelligible to those around us. Finally, such a theory would explore—in the midst of action—effective techniques of social change for the particular circumstances we find at the moment.

Let me speak now about the first requirement of this theory, the vision of the future. Here the Marxian vision is useful. True, it is vague. But what better guard is there against dogmatism than vagueness? Uncertainty is not a virtue in depicting the facts of the moment; it may not only be tolerable, but desirable, in trying to portray the future.

I stress this as a Marxian vision, even though many non-Marxists have held the same vision—because while it's necessary to emphasize to the Left that it does not monopolize either compassion or insight, it is necessary to remind everyone else—the Christians, the Jews, the Buddhists, the Humanists, and anyone else—that they share certain aims with Marxism. No one of these groups is going to revolutionize the world by itself, and so all need to be reminded of a certain consensus of humanistic values that has developed in the modern world. Marxists and liberals at their best (and they have not usually been at their best) share this theoretical consensus, here and abroad. Indeed, one of the great contributions of the New Left has been to remind both Marxist countries and liberal capitalist countries how far is their behavior from the values they claim.

In *The Holy Family*, one of the early writings of Marx and Engels (about 1845) they say man needs to be "not negatively free to avoid this or that event" but "positively free to express his true individuality." They say this requires arranging the empirical world around us so that "man experiences and assimilates there what is really human, that he experiences himself as a man." Rather than punishing individuals for their crimes, we should "destroy the social conditions which engender crime, and give to each individual the scope which he needs in society in order to develop his life." This speaks to the so-called socialist countries of today which imprison writers who criticize the state. It also speaks to a country like the United States, which gives people the negative freedoms of the Bill of Rights, but distributes very unequally the scope in which people can develop their individuality, can exercise their freedom—so that some children can roam in little suburban mansions surrounded by gardens, and others are equally free to play in rat-infested tenements. While every one "has" freedom of speech, the corporation with a million dollars to spend on television time can speak to thirty million people, and the individual who can afford a soap box can speak to thirty people. What makes the New Left so critical of the wealthiest nation in the world is its acute consciousness that freedom means not only legal permission to occupy space, but the resources to make the most of this.

The New Left has not even begun to figure out how to explain this complex problem of freedom to all those people in the United States brought up on high school history books and American Legion essay contests. What can make the New Radicalism really new, and really pertinent to here and now, is to be able, without recourse to the stale slogans about "bourgeois freedom," to do justice to the degree of freedom that does exist for people in the United States—while noting that it *is* a matter of degree, that freedom in America is like wealth, plentiful, and very unequally distributed.

Let me turn to another element in the Marxian vision. There is still a widespread popular belief, heavily stressed on the *Reader's Digest* level, that Marxism believes in the supremacy of the state over the individual, while democracy believes the opposite. In fact, the existence of oppressively overbearing states in the world, which call themselves Marxist, reinforces this idea. But a true radicalism would remind people in both socialist and capitalist countries of Marx's and Engels' hope, expressed early in the *Manifesto*, that some day "the public power will lose its political character" and "we shall have an association in which the free development of each is the condition for the free development of all." This is not just a youthful aberration (there is a fad about the young romantic Marx and the old, practical Marx) because twenty-seven years later, Marx, in his *Critique of the Gotha Program*, says: "Freedom consists in converting the state from an organ superimposed upon society into one completely subordinate to it." Here also he says, on the subject of the state giving education to the people, "the state has need, on the contrary, of a very stern education by the people." And Engels, a year after Marx's death, in 1884, writes in his *Origin of the Family, Private Property and the State*:

> The society that will organize production on the basis of a free and equal association of the producers will put the whole machinery of state where it will then belong: into the musum of antiquities, by the side of the spinning wheel and the bronze ax.

Their attitude to the state is made even clearer and more specific in Marx's book on the *Civil War in France*, and Engels' *Introduction* to it, where, both of them point admiringly to the Paris Commune of early 1871. The Commune almost immediately abolished conscription and the standing army, declared universal suffrage and the right of citizens to recall their elected officials at any time, said all officials, high or low, should be paid the same wage as received by other workers, and publicly burned the guillotine.

The New Left is anti-authoritarian; it would—I expect—burn draft cards in any society. It is anarchistic not just in wanting the ultimate abolition of the state, but in its immediate requirement that authority and coercion be banished in every sphere of existence, that the end must be represented immediately in the means. Marx and Bakunin disagreed on this, but the New Left has the advantage over Marx of having an extra century of history to study. We see how a dictatorship of the proletariat can easily become a dictatorship over the proletariat, as Trotsky warned, as Rosa Luxemburg warned. The New Left should remind the socialist states as well as the capitalist states of Marx's letter of 1853 to the *New York Tribune* saying he didn't know how capital punishment could be justified "in a society glorying in its civilization."

In America, both liberalism and radicalism were beguiled into cheering for state power because under FDR it seemed beneficent: it enacted certain economic reforms, and it waged war against Hitler. The New Left, hopefully, will recognize that the state cannot be trusted, either to carry reforms far enough, or to drop bombs only on Nazi invaders and not on Asian peasants in their own country. It will therefore create con-stellations of power outside the state to pressure it into humane actions, to resist its inhumane actions, and to replace it in many functions by voluntary small groups seeking to maintain both individuality and co-operation. Black Power, in its best aspects, is such an endeavor.

The New Left in America needs to show people how the state, whether a proletarian dictatorship or a sophisticated welfare capitalism, constitutes a special interest of its own which deserves not unthinking loyalty, but criticism, resistance, and (even in its better moments) watchfulness. This New Left attitude toward the state expresses a more general attitude—against making instruments into absolutes or means into ends—against the deification of any party, any nation, any ideology, any method.

Now another point about the Marxian vision. Perhaps nowhere does Marx speak more directly to our mass society today, and therefore to the new radicals in mass society, than in his *Economic and Philosophical Manuscripts* of 1844. The estrangement of man described there is pertinent not only to the classical proletariat of his time but to all classes in every modern industrial society—and certainly to the young people of this generation in the Untied States. He talks of men producing things alien to themselves, which become monsters independent of them (look all around us, at our automobiles, our television sets, our skyscrapers, even our universities). People find no satisfaction in working. He points to the irony that in man's specifically human functions (working, creating) he feels like an animal, while only in his animal functions (eating, sex) does he feel like a human being. Our activity becomes not enjoyable in itself, but just means to keep alive. Activity *is* life—what else is life?—and yet it becomes in modern society only a means to life.

So, we become estranged from what we produce, from our own activity, from our fellow men, from nature (here Marxism must share credit with Taoism), and finally from ourselves—because we all find ourselves living another life, not the one we really want to live. The New Radicals of today are desperately conscious of this and try to escape it. They want to do work which is congenial to them—so they go to Mississippi or move into the ghetto—or they don't work at all rather than work at hateful or parasitic jobs. They often try to create relationships with one another which are not warped by the rules and demands of the world around them. The crucial cause of all these forms of estrangement is that people's activities are coerced rather than free, and so the young people today are defiant. Living differently is not easy, but the very act of attempting it is a free act.

From all this it is quite clear what Marx's values were; the free man, in his individuality, in his sociality, in his oneness with nature. The New Left is in accord here. Where it parts, I think, is in Marx's claim—although some attribute this to Engels (one of those academic disputes I spoke about) that this vision of unalienated man springs not from a wish, but from an observation—from a scientific plotting of a historical curve which moves inevitably in the direction of man's freedom.

Surely we don't have such confidence in inevitabilities these days—we've had too many surprises in this century. (Simone de Beauvoir says in her book *The Ethics of Antiquity* that there is no inevitable proletarian uprising—the movement may go in six different directions.) We are unabashed in declaring our subjective wants and desires—without needing a "scientific" basis for such wants. Here again, the discussion of whether ethical norms are grounded in empirical science is one of those academic discussions which lead us nowhere in actuality. Surely, most people agree on the gross necessities of life—food, sex, peace, freedom, love, dignity, self-realization. Our energy should be spent in working toward them, not in discussing their metaphysical meaning.

I suggested above that the second requirement of a pertinent theory is an analysis of the *particulars* of today's reality. One of Marx's great perceptions was that there is a material basis for man's alienation and unhappiness—the scarcity of goods which he and society need, producing conflict, exploitation, coercion. Thus, abundance is a prerequisite—thought not a guarantee—of man's freedom. In the United States, we face this paradox, that the state with the most enormous productive apparatus, indeed the only state in the world which has the technological capacity to have communism, and where a communist society would have the greatest chance of preserving the freedom of the individual (because the *socialist* societies are plagued by scarcity) gets apoplectic at the very mention of the word.

It is here in the United States that the slogan "to each according to his need" can have meaning. We have enough doctors and hospitals to give adequate medical care to whoever needs it, without rationing this according to wealth. We grow enough food in this country without insisting that people without money do with very little food. We can—if we want to—built enough homes in this country to eliminate slums. And so on. There is room for some scholarly work here: economists could sit down somewhere and work out a specific plan for free food in America, also for free college tuition and allowances. What the New Left needs to show, and in specific detail, is where the resources are in this country, what they *are* being used for, and what they *could* be used for.

The Marxian economic categories have long provided material for academic controversy—and I doubt that Marx intended this. But he was only human and perhaps he too succumbed to the temptations of the intellectual: his research, his curiosity, his passion for scheme-building and for scientific constructions ran away with him. I confess that I cannot see how his dense Volume II of *Das Kapital* on the "Circulation of Commodities" or his long expositions of absolute rent and differential rent are essential to revolutionary theory. Does it really matter if Böhm-Bawerk was right or wrong on the relationship between aggregate surplus value and aggregate prices of production?

Even so brilliant a theory as that of surplus-value—how relevant is it to social action? Has the militancy of workingmen in history required such an analysis to sustain it? Has such militancy been transformed into revolutionary consciousness anywhere by the comprehension of the distinction between the use value and exchange value of labor power? The Baran-Sweezy notion of a surplus (in *Monopoly Capital*) comprised of waste, military expenses, and unused capacity, is more fruitful, I think, as a theoretical prod to revolutionary action.

James Bevel is right when he says you can only organize large numbers of people around issues that are obvious or that can easily be made obvious. So instead of discussing the falling rate of profit, or the organic composition of capital, I would concentrate on what is readily observable—that this country has enormous resources which it wastes shamefully and distributes unjustly. A country that produces 200 billion dollars worth of goods and services a year, and this is not our full capacity, should not have ten million families living below the $3,000 a year level. All the Chamber of Commerce pronouncements, the fancy *Fortune Magazine* charts about our progress, the confident State of the Union Addresses, fall apart when you take a long walk through any major American city: through Harlem or Roxbury or Chicago's South Side.

The most useful Marxian statement about capitalist society is the largest one—that in an era when production is a complex, world-wide social process, and requires rationality, our system is incredibly irrational.

This is because corporate profit, not human need, governs what is produced and what is not produced. It is also because there is a huge vested interest—economic, military, political, psychological—in the production of present and future corpses, on which we spend seventy billion dollars a year. We spend about twenty billion dollars a year on public relations, advertising, promotion. We build too many cars, too many highways, too many office buildings, produce too many cigarettes, too much liquor, too many gadgets and not enough homes, schools, hospitals. Corporate profits after taxes amount to forty billion dollars a year—enough to raise every $3000 a year family to $7000 a year. The New Left, instead of getting involved in theoretical discussions about economic categories, needs to find ways to make clear to Americans how wasteful, irrational, and unjust is our economy.

With a vision of how man should live, with some perception of how men do live (and so many of us need to be *shown*), the most urgent theoretical problem for the New Left—and the one where traditional Marxism gives the least guidance—is: how do we change society? How do we redistribute the power in society in order to redistribute the wealth? How do we overcome those who are enjoying power and wealth and won't give it up? How do we stop the fanaticism of both civilian and military leaders who feel it is America's duty to establish its power, or its puppets, wherever possible in the world—and don't care how many people, Americans or others—they kill in the process?

The traditional Marxian idea of a revolution taking place because of a breakdown in the capitalist mechanism and an organized, class-conscious proletariat taking over, is hardly tenable today. Where socialist revolutions have taken place in the world, they have taken place mostly because war has weakened or destroyed the state and created a vacuum in which organized revolutionaries could take over. The traditional liberal idea of a gradual evolution towards freedom, peace, and democracy through parliamentary reform is also hardly tenable. We see that poverty and racism can be institutionalized, with only token steps taken to assuage their worst aspects; that by creating a contended, bloated middle class, by introducing state regulatory mechanisms in the economy, the *status quo* can be maintained. And furthermore, in foreign policy, it has become accepted that the President and a small group of advisers make foreign policy, while the mass communications industry creates a nation of sheep who give assent.

Certainly, in the United States, the traditional idea that the agent of social change will be the proletariat needs re-examination, when the best-organized of the workers are bribed into silence with suburban houses and automobiles, and drugged into compliance with mass entertainment. Perhaps unorganized workers—the bulk of the labor force—may play a part, but these consist of white collar workers, domestic workers, migratory and farm laborers, service industry workers, and various kinds of people who are the hardest to organize. Recent experience suggests that Negroes—and perhaps Negroes in the ghetto—may be the most powerful single force for social change in the United States. Marx envisioned the industrial proletariat as the revolutionary agent because it was in need, exploited, and brought face to face in the factory. The Negro is in need, exploited and brought together in the ghetto. And since Berkeley and the teach-ins, there is some evidence that students—especially as they are pushed more and more toward the mouth of the cannon—may be another important agent of change. Perhaps some peculiar combination, unpredictable at this moment, will be formed in a time of national crisis.

How will change come about? By tactics short of violent revolution, but far more militant than normal parliamentary procedure, it seems to me. Even the demonstrations of the civil rights movement were not enough to achieve more than tokens of change: a few laws, a few high appointments, and LBJ reciting "We Shall Overcome." Spontaneous uprisings in the ghetto are alarm signals, but do not produce change in themselves. It will take systematic, persistent organizing and education, in the ghettos, in the universities, plus co-ordinated actions of various kinds designed to shock society out of its lethargy.

The New Left's idea of parallel organizations, as a way of *demonstrating* what people should do, how people should live, has enormous possibilities: freedom schools, free universities, free cities—remember how these grew up in medieval times outside the feudal system—self-controlled communities. But also, free, active *pockets* of people inside the traditional cities, universities, corporations. In military combat, guerrilla warfare arose as an answer to overwhelmingly centralized military power. Perhaps we are in need of political guerrilla tactics in the face of mass society—in which enclaves of freedom are created here and there in the midst of the orthodox way of life, to become centers of protest, and examples to others. It is in techniques of organization, pressure, change, community-building—that the New Radicals need the most thought, and the most action. It may take an ingenious combination of energy and wit to carry through a new kind of revolution.

Action *is* preferably organized, thought-out action, but there should be room for whatever kinds of action any individual or group feels moved to undertake. In an era when it is so easy to feel helpless, we need the Existentialist emphasis on our freedom to act. The Marxist-Existentialist debate on freedom and determinism seems to me to be an empty one—an academic one. To stress our freedom is not the result of ignorance that we do have a history, that we do have an oppressive environment. But knowing of these pressures on us, we should be existentially aware that there is enormous indeterminacy in the combat between us and the obstacles all around. We never know exactly the depth or the shallowness of the resistance to our actions—until we act. We never know exactly what effect we will have. Our actions may lead to nothing except changing ourselves, and that is something. They may have a tiny cumulative effect, along with a thousand other actions. They may also explode.

What the fact of indeterminacy suggests is that we should not be preoccupied with prediction or with measuring immediate success—but rather should take the risk of acting. We are not totally free but our strength will be maximized if we act *as if* we are free. We are not passive observers, students, theorizers; our very thoughts, our statements, our speeches, our essays, throw a weight into a balance which cannot be assessed until we act. This Existentialist emphasis on the necessity for action—based on conscience, avoiding that cool and careful weighing of "the realities"—is one of the most refreshing characteristics of the New Radicalism in America.

Along with the Existentialist emphasis on freedom there is responsibility. To the extent that we feel free, we feel responsible. There is something about our time which makes it difficult for us not only to feel free but to feel responsibility. Contemporary life is complicated, and evil comes at the end of a long assembly line with a division of labor so intricate it is impossible to trace; everyone has responsibility and no one has responsibility. But if we are to feel our own freedom, we must feel our responsibility, not for anyone else's actions, but only for our own; not for the past and without any pledge to the future—but at this moment, now where we stand.

4

The Spirit of Rebellion

Writing a column to appear in the July 4, 1975 issue of the Boston Globe, I wanted to break away from the traditional celebrations of Independence Day, in which the spirit of that document, with its call for rebellion and revolution, was most often missing. The column appeared with the title "The Brooklyn Bridge and the Spirit of the Fourth."

In New York, a small army of policemen, laid off and angry, have been blocking the Brooklyn Bridge, and garbage workers are letting the refuse pile up in the streets. In Boston, some young people on Mission Hill are illegally occupying an abandoned house to protest the demolition of a neighborhood. And elderly people, on the edge of survival, are fighting Boston Edison's attempt to raise the price of electricity.

So it looks like a good Fourth of July, with a spirit of rebellion proper to the Declaration of Independence.

The Declaration, adopted 199 years ago today, says (although those in high office don't like to be reminded) that government is not sacred, that it is set up to give people an equal right to life, liberty, and the pursuit of happiness and that if it fails to do this, we have a right to "alter or abolish it."

The Declaration of Independence became an embarrassment to the Founding Fathers almost immediately. Some of George Washington's soldiers resented the rich in New York, Boston and Philadelphia, profiting from the war. When the Continental Congress in 1781 voted half pay for life to officers of the Revolution and nothing for enlisted men, there was mutiny in the New Jersey and Pennsylvania lines. Washington ordered two young mutineers shot "as an example." The shovelfuls of earth covering their bodies also smudged the words of the Declaration, five years old and already ignored, that "all men are created equal."

Black slaves in Boston took those words seriously, too, and, during the Revolution, petitioned the Massachusetts General Court for their freedom. But the Revolution was not fought for them.

It did not seem to be fought for the poor white farmers either, who, after serving in the war, now faced high taxes, and seizure of homes and livestock for nonpayment. In western Massachusetts, they organized, blocking the doors of courthouses to prevent foreclosures. This was Shay's Rebellion. The militia finally routed them, and the Founding Fathers hurried to Philadelphia to write the Constitution, to set up a government where such rebellions could be controlled.

Arguing for the Constitution, James Madison said it would hold back "a rage for paper money, for an abolition of debts, for an equal division of property, or for any other improper or wicked project..." The Constitution took the stirring phrase of the Declaration, "life, liberty and the pursuit of happiness" and changed it to "life, liberty and property." The Declaration was only a historic document. The Constitution became the law of the land.

Both documents were written by whites. Many of these were slaveholders. All were men. Women gathered in 1848 in Seneca Falls, New York, and adopted their own Declaration: "We hold these truths to be self-evident: that all men and women are created equal..."

The Constitution was written by the rich, who set up a government to protect their property. Gerald Ford is still doing it. They say he is a "good guy." He certainly has been good to big business. He has arranged for gasoline prices and heating bills to go up while the oil companies make enormous profits. He vetoed a bill to allow an interest rate for homeowners of 6 percent while the nation's ten biggest banks made $2 billion in profits last year.

Unemployment, food and rent are all rising; but $7 billion in tax breaks went to 160,000 very wealthy people last year, according to a congressional report.

No wonder the spirit of rebellion is growing. No wonder that even police, paid to be keepers of law and order and laid-off when they have served their purpose, are catching a bit of that spirit.

It is fitting for this Fourth of July, this anniversary of the Declaration of Independence.

5

Beyond
Voting

The political culture of the United States is dominated by voting. Every election year is accompanied by an enormous amount of attention, with the media and the politicians joining forces to try to persuade Americans that voting for one candidate or another is the most important act of citizenship. I decided to challenge that idea in this column, which appeared in the *Boston Globe* at the start of the election campaign of 1976.

G ossip is the opium of the American public. We lie back, close our eyes and happily inhale the stories about Roosevelt's and Kennedy's affairs, Lyndon Johnson's nude swims with unnamed partners and, now, Nixon's pathetic "final days" in office.

The latest fix is administered by reporters Woodward and Bernstein and the stuff is Nixon's sex life with Pat, Nixon drunk and weeping, Nixon cradled in the arms of Kissinger (who did it, we presume, for national security).

So we get high on trivia, and forget that, whether Presidents have been impotent or oversexed, drunk or sober, they have followed the same basic policies. Whether crooks or Boy Scouts, handsome or homely, agile or clumsy, they have taxed the poor, subsidized the rich, wasted the wealth of the nation on guns and bombs, ignored the decay of the cities, and done so little for the children of the ghettos and rural wastelands that these youth had to join the armed forces to survive—until they were sent overseas to die.

Harry Truman was blunt and Lyndon Johnson wily, but both sent armies to Asia to defend dictators and massacre the people we claimed to be helping. Eisenhower was dull and Kennedy witty, but both built up huge nuclear armaments at the expense of schools and health care. Nixon was corrupt and Ford straightforward, but both coldly cut benefits for the poor and gave favors to rich corporations.

The cult of personality in America is a powerful drug. It takes the energy of ordinary citizens which, combined, can be a powerful force, and depletes it in the spectator sport of voting. Our most cherished moment of democratic citizenship comes when we leave the house once in four years to choose between two mediocre white Anglo-Saxon males who have been trundled out by political caucuses, million dollar primaries and managed conventions for the rigged multiple choice test we call an election. Presidents come and go. But the FBI is always there, on the job, sometimes catching criminals, sometimes committing crimes itself, always checking on radicals as secret police do all over the world. Its latest confession: ninety-two burglaries, 1960-66.

Presidents come and go, but the military budget keeps rising. It was $74 billion in 1973, is over $100 billion now (the equivalent of $2000 in taxes for every family), and will reach $130 billion in 1980.

Presidents come and go, but the 200 top corporations keep increasing their control: 45 percent of all manufacturing in 1960, 60 percent by 1970.

No President in this century has stopped the trend. Not even FDR.

Yes, Roosevelt took steps to help poor people in the '30s. Minimum wages. Social security, WPA jobs. Relief. But that didn't change the basic nature of the capitalist system, whose highest priority has always been profits for the corporations and to hell with the rest.

Roosevelt was humane and wise, but, also, he had to react to signs of anger and rebellion in the country. He had seen the Bonus March of veterans to Washington under Hoover. In his first year, mass strikes—400,000 textile workers out in the South and New England. Longshoremen tied up the whole city of San Francisco. Teamsters took over Minneapolis. The unemployed were organizing, the bootleg miners taking over coalfields, tenants gathering in the cities to stop evictions.

Roosevelt was a sensitive man. But something big was happening in the country to sharpen his sensitivity.

1976: the multiple choice test is here again. Sure, there are better candidates and worse. But we will go a long way from spectator democracy to real democracy when we understand that the future of this country doesn't depend, mainly, on who is our next President. It depends on whether the American citizen, fed up with high taxes, high prices, unemployment, waste, war and corruption, will organize all over the country a clamor for change even greater than the labor uprisings of the '30s or the black rebellion of the '60s and shake this country out of old paths into new ones.

6

The Optimism of Uncertainty

The world "optimism," used here, makes me a little uneasy, because it suggests a blithe, slightly sappy whistler in the dark of our time. But I use it anyway, not because I am totally confident that the world will get better, but because I am certain that ONLY such confidence can prevent people from giving up the game before all the cards have been played. The metaphor is deliberate; it is a gamble. Not to play is to foreclose any chance of winning. To play, to act, is to create at least a possibility of changing the world. I wrote about this in a much longer piece requested by John Tirman of the Winston Foundation, and this essay appeared in my book *Failure to Quit* (Common Courage Press, 1993).

As this century draws to a close, a century packed with history, what leaps out from that history is its utter unpredictability.

This confounds us, because we are talking about exactly the period when human beings became so ingenious technologically that they could plan and predict the exact time of someone landing on the moon.

But who foresaw that, twenty-four years after the national Democratic Party Convention refused to seat blacks from Mississippi, a black militant would run for president, excite crowds, black and white, all over the country, and then dominate the Democratic Party Convention in Atlanta? Or (recalling Jesse Jackson's presentation of Rosa Parks to the Convention) who, on that day in Montgomery, Alabama, in 1955, when Rose Parks refused to move from the front of the bus, could have predicted that this would lead to a mass protest of black working people, and then would follow a chain of events that would shake the nation, startle the world, and transform the South?

But let's go back to the turn of the century. That a revolution should overthrow the Tsar of Russia, in that most sluggish of semi-feudal empires, not only startled the most advanced imperial powers, but took Lenin himself by surprise and sent him rushing by train to Petrograd.

Who could have predicted, not just the Russian Revolution, but Stalin's deformation of it, then Khrushchev's astounding exposure of Stalin, and recently Gorbachev's succession of surprises?

Or observe Germany after the first World War. There was a situation that fitted the Marxist model of social revolution most neatly—an advanced industrial society, with an educated, organized proletariat, a strong socialist-communist movement, a devastating economic crisis, and the still-fresh memory of a catastrophic war. Instead, the same conditions which might have brought revolution gave rise to that monstrous mutation, Nazism. Marxist scholars went into a dither of analysis to explain it.

I don't mean to pick on Marxists. But if they, probably the best equipped theoretically, the most committed and motivated to understand society, kept being bewildered, that suggests how impenetrable has been the mystery of social change in our time.

Who would have predicted the bizarre events of World War II— the Nazi-Soviet pact (those embarrassing photos of von Ribbentrop and Molotov shaking hands), and the German army rolling through Russia, causing colossal casualties, apparently invincible, and then being turned back at the gates of Leningrad, on the edge of Moscow, in the streets of Stalingrad, and then surrounded, decimated, and defeated, the strutting Hitler at the end huddled in his bunker, waiting to die?

And then the post-war world, taking a shape no one could have drawn in advance. The Chinese Communist Revolution, which Stalin himself had given little chance. And then the turns of that revolution: the break with the Soviet Union, the tumultuous and violent Cultural Revolution, and then another turnabout, with post-Mao China renouncing its most fervently-held ideas and institutions, making overtures to the West, cuddling up to capitalist enterprise, perplexing everyone.

No one foresaw the disintegration of the old Western empires happening so quickly after the war, or the odd array of societies that would be created in the newly independent nations, from the benign socialism of Nyerere's Tanzania to the madness of Idi Amin's Uganda.

Spain became an astonishment. A million died in the civil war which ended in victory for the Fascist Franco. I recall a veteran of the Abraham Lincoln Brigade telling me that he could not imagine Fascism being overthrown in Spain without another bloody war. After Franco was gone, and a parliamentary democracy, open to Socialists, Communists, anarchists, everyone, was established in Spain, that same man expressed his awe that it all happened without the fratricide so many thought was inevitable.

In other places too, deeply-entrenched regimes seemed to suddenly disintegrate—in Portugal, Argentina, the Philippines, Iran.

The end of World War II left two superpowers with their respective spheres of influence and control, vying for military and political power. The United States and the Soviet Union soon had 10,000 thermonuclear bombs each, enough to devastate the earth several times over. The international scene was dominated by their rivalry, and it was supposed that all affairs, in every nation, were affected by their looming presence.

Yet, the most striking fact about these superpowers in 1988 is that, despite their size, their wealth, their overwhelming accumulation of nuclear weapons, they have been unable to control events, even in those parts of the world considered to be their spheres of influence.

The Soviet Union, apparently successful in crushing revolts in Hungary and Czechoslovakia, has had to accommodate itself to the quick withdrawal of Yugoslavia from its orbit, the liberalization of Hungary in recent years, and the continued power of the Solidarity movement in Poland. Gorbachev's recent declarations about a new era in Soviet relations with the Warsaw Pact nations is a recognition of the inability of Soviet power to permanently suppress the desire for independence in neighboring countries.

The failure of the Soviet Union to have its way in Afghanistan, its decision to withdraw after almost a decade of ugly intervention, is the most striking evidence that even the possession of thermonuclear weapons does not guarantee domination over a determined population.

The United States has more and more faced the same reality.

It could send an army into Korea but could not win, and was forced to sign a compromise peace. It waged a full-scale war in Indochina, the most brutal bombardment of a tiny peninsula in world history, and yet was forced to withdraw. And in Latin America, after a long history of U.S. military intervention, with Yankee imperialism having its way again and again, this superpower, with all its wealth, all its weapons, found itself frustrated. It was unable to prevent a revolution in Cuba, and after succeeding in organizing a counter-revolution in Chile, could not prevent or overthrow a revolution in Nicaragua. For the first time, the nations of Latin America are refusing to do the bidding of *los norteamericanos.*

In the headlines every day, we see other instances of the failure of the presumably powerful over the presumably powerless: the inability of white South Africa to suppress the insurgency of the black majority; the inability of Israel, a nuclear power with formidable conventional arms, to contain the rebellion of Palestinians armed with stones in the West Bank and Gaza Strip.

This recitation of facts about twentieth century history, this evidence of unpredictability in human affairs, might be rather dull, except that it does lead us to some important conclusions.

The first is that the struggle for justice should never be abandoned because of the apparent overwhelming power of those who have the guns and the money and who seem invincible in their determination to hold on to it. That apparent power has, again and again, proved vulnerable to human qualities less measurable than bombs and dollars: moral fervor, determination, unity, organization, sacrifice, wit, ingenuity, courage, patience—whether by blacks in Alabama and South Africa, peasants in El Salvador, Nicaragua, and Vietnam, or workers and intellectuals in Poland, Hungary, and the Soviet Union itself. No cold calculation of the balance of power need deter people who are persuaded that their cause is just.

The second is that, in the face of the manifest unpredictability of social phenomena, all of history's excuses for war and preparation for war—self-defense, national security, freedom, justice, stopping aggression—can no longer be accepted. Nor can civil war be tolerated. Massive violence, whether in war or internal upheaval, cannot be justified by any end, however noble, *because no outcome is sure.* Indeed, the most certain characteristic of any upheaval, like war or revolution, is its uncertainty. Any humane and reasonable person must conclude that if the ends, however desirable, are uncertain, and the means are horrible and certain, those means must not be employed.

This is a persuasive argument, it seems to me, to direct at all those people, whether in the United States or elsewhere, who are still intoxicated by the analogy of World War II, who still distinguish between "just and unjust wars" (a universal belief shared by the Catholic Church, the capitalist West, and the Soviet Union), and who are willing to commit atrocities, whether on Hiroshima or in Budapest, for some good cause.

It is also an argument that needs to be examined seriously by those, who, in this world of vicious nationalism, terrible poverty, and the waste of enormous resources on militarism and war, understand the need for radical change. Such change is needed, yet it must be accomplished without massive violence. This is the great challenge to human ingenuity in our time. It is a challenge to blacks in South Africa, to Palestinians in the Occupied Territories (both of whom seem to understand it), as well as to Americans and Russians disgusted with their governments' robbery of national resources for profit and power.

The recognition of unpredictability is troubling. But all we have lost are our illusions about power and about violence. What we gain is an understanding that the means we use to struggle for justice, even for revolutionary change, must scrupulously observe human rights. The lives and liberties of ordinary people must not be sacrificed, either by government or by revolutionaries, certain that they know the end results of what they do, indifferent to their own ignorance.

7

Anarchism

That I could get a Ph.D. from a major American university without knowing anything about anarchism, surely one of the most important political philosophies of modern times, is a commentary on the narrowness of American education. I first became aware of anarchism when in 1968 I became friends with a fellow historian, Richard Drinnon, who had written a biography of the anarchist-feminist Emma Goldman, *Rebel in Paradise*. I read his book, then read Emma Goldman's autobiography *Living My Life*, and from that point on tried to learn as much as I could about anarchist thought and experience. For years, I taught a seminar on "Marxism and Anarchism" at Boston University. Herbert Read was famous in England not only as an art critic but as an anarchist, and his collection of essays, *Anarchy and Order*, was being published in its first American edition by Beacon Press in 1971. I wrote the following essay, entitled "The Art of Revolution," as an introduction to that volume.

The word *anarchy* unsettles most people in the Western world; it suggests disorder, violence, uncertainty. We have good reason for fearing those conditions, because we have been living with them for a long time, not in anarchist societies (there have never been any) but in exactly those societies most fearful of anarchy—the powerful nation-states of modern times.

At no time in human history has there been such social chaos. Fifty million dead in the Second World War. More than a million dead in Korea, a million in Vietnam, half a million in Indonesia, hundreds of thousands dead in Nigeria, and in Mozambique. A hundred violent political struggles all over the world in the twenty years following the second war to end all wars. Millions starving, or in prisons, or in mental institutions. Inner turmoil to the point of large-scale alienation, confusion, unhappiness. Outer turmoil symbolized by huge armies, stores of nerve gas, and stockpiles of hydrogen bombs. Wherever men, women and children are even a bit conscious of the world outside their local borders, they have been living with the ultimate uncertainty: whether or not the human race itself will survive into the next generation.

It is these conditions that the anarchists have wanted to end; to bring a kind of order to the world for the first time. We have never listened to them carefully, except through the hearing aids supplied by the guardians of disorder—the national government leaders, whether capitalist or socialist.

The order desired by anarchists is different from the order ("*Ordnung,*" the Germans called it; "*law and order,*" say the American politicians) of national governments. They want a voluntary forming of human relations, arising out of the needs of people. Such an order comes from within, and so is natural. People flow into easy arrangements, rather than being pushed and forced. It is like the form given by the artist, a form congenial, often pleasing, sometimes beautiful. It has the grace of a voluntary, confident act. Thus there is nothing surprising in Herbert Read, poet and philosopher of art, being an anarchist.

Read came to philosophical anarchism out of his special set of experiences: growing up in Yorkshire as the son of an English farmer, spending several years as a clerk in the industrial city of Leeds, going to the University there, writing poetry, entranced by art and literature—and then enduring the sounds and smells of war as a British Army Captain in World War I. For a while he was captivated, as were so many, by the Bolshevik Revolution, but the party dictatorship turned him firmly toward anarchism, which also seemed to fit more comfortably his wide-ranging interest in the arts: pottery, poetry, Wordsworth and Coleridge, art criticism, the philosophy of art.

He had written over forty books before he died in 1968, mostly on art and literature. In *Anarchy and Order*, published in England in 1954, he put together various essays he had written on anarchism, from his slim volume of 1938, *Poetry and Anarchism*, to his essay "Revolution and Reason," of 1953. This important book was never published in the United States, perhaps because America in the Fifties was not hospitable to anarchism, or to serious dissent of any kind. As we start the Seventies, the mood is different. Read offers us something that this generation seems to want and need: an aesthetic approach to politics.

The order of politics, as we have known it in the world, is an order imposed on society, neither desired by most people, nor directed to their needs. It is therefore chaotic and destructive. Politics grates on our sensibilities. It violates the elementary requirement of aesthetics—it is devoid of beauty. It is coercive, as if sound were forced into our ears at a decibel level such as to make us scream, and those responsible called this music. The "order" of modern life is a cacophony which has made us almost deaf to the gentler sounds of the universe.

It is fitting that in modern times, around the time of the French and American Revolutions, exactly when man became most proud of his achievements, the ideas of anarchism arose to challenge that pride. Western civilization has never been modest in describing its qualities as an enormous advance in human history: the larger unity of national states replacing tribe and manor; parliamentary government replacing the divine right of kings; steam and electricity substituting for manual labor; education and science dispelling ignorance and superstition; due process of law canceling arbitrary justice. Anarchism arose in the most splendid days of Western "civilization" because the promises of that civilization were almost immediately broken.

Nationalism, promising freedom from outside tyranny, and security from internal disorder, vastly magnified both the stimulus and the possibility for worldwide empires over subjected people, and bloody conflicts among such empires: imperialism and war were intensified to the edge of global suicide exactly in the period of the national state. Parliamentary government, promising popular participation in important decisions, became a facade (differently constructed in one-party and two-party states) for rule by elites of wealth and power in the midst of almost-frenzied scurrying to polls and plebiscites. Mass production did not end poverty and exploitation; indeed it made the persistence of want more unpardonable. The production and distribution of goods became more rational technically, more irrational morally. Education and literacy did not end the deception of the many by the few; they enabled deception to be replaced by self-deception, mystification to be internalized, and social control to be even more effective than ever before, because now it had a large measure of *self* control. Due process did not bring justice; it replaced the arbitrary, identifiable dispenser of injustice with the unidentifiable and impersonal. The "rule of law," replacing the "rule of men," was just a change in rulers.

In the midst of the American Revolution, Tom Paine, while calling for the establishment of an independent American government, had no illusions about even a new revolutionary government when he wrote, in *Common Sense*: "Society in every state is a blessing, but government even in its best state is but a necessary evil."

Anarchists almost immediately recognized that the fall of kings, and the rise of committees, assemblies, parliaments, did not bring democracy; that revolutions had the potential for liberation, but also for another form of despotism. Thus, Jacques Roux, a country priest in the French Revolution concerned with the lives of the peasants in his district, and then with the workingmen in the Gravilliers quarter of Paris, spoke in 1792 against "senatorial despotism," saying it was "as terrible as the scepter of kings" because it chains the people without their knowing it and brutalizes and subjugates them by laws they themselves are supposed to have made. In Peter Weiss's play, *Marat-Sade*, Roux, straitjacketed, breaks through the censorship of the play within the play and cries out:

> Who controls the markets
> Who locks up the granaries
> Who got the loot from the palaces
> Who sits tight on the estates

that were going to be divided between the poor

before he is quieted.

A friend of Roux, Jean Varlet, in an early anarchist manifesto of the French Revolution called *Explosion*, wrote:

> What a social monstrosity, what a masterpiece of Machiavellianism, this revolutionary government is in fact. For any reasoning being, Government and Revolution are incompatible, at least unless the people wishes to constitute the organs of power in permanent insurrection against themselves, which is too absurd to believe.

But it is exactly that which is "too absurd to believe" which the anarchists believe, because only an "absurd" perspective is revolutionary enough to see through the limits of revolution itself. Herbert Read, in a book with an appropriately absurd title, *To Hell With Culture* (he was seventy; this was 1963, five years before his death), wrote:

> What has been worth while in human history—the great achievements of physics and astronomy, of geographical discovery and of human healing, of philosophy and of art—has been the work of extremists—of those who believed in the absurd, dared the impossible...

The Russian Revolution promised even more—to eliminate that injustice carried into modern times by the American and French Revolutions. Anarchist criticism of that Revolution was summed up by Emma Goldman (*My Further Disillusionment in Russia*) as follows:

> It is at once the great failure and the great tragedy of the Russian Revolution that it attempted...to change only institutions and conditions while ignoring entirely the human and social values involved in the Revolution.... No revolution can ever succeed as a factor of liberation unless the *means* used to further it be identical in spirit and tendency with the *purposes* to be achieved. Revolution is the negation of the existing, a violent protest against man's inhumanity to man with all the thousand and one slaveries it involves. It is the destroyer of dominant values upon which a complex system of injustice, oppression, and wrong has been built up by ignorance and brutality. It is the herald of *new values*, ushering in a transformation of the basic relations of man to man, and of man to society.

The institution of capitalism, anarchists believe, is destructive, irrational, inhumane. It feeds ravenously on the immense resources of the earth, and then churns out (this is its achievement—it is an immense stu-

pid churn) huge quantities of products. Those products have only an accidental relationship to what is most needed by people, because the organizers and distributors of goods care not about human need; they are
great business enterprises motivated only by profit. Therefore, bombs,
guns, office buildings, and deodorants take priority over food, homes,
and recreation areas. Is there anything closer to "anarchy" (in the common
use of the word, meaning confusion) than the incredibly wild and wasteful economic system in America?

Anarchists believe the riches of the earth belong equally to all,
and should be distributed according to need, not through the intricate,
inhuman system of money and contracts which have so far channeled
most of these riches into a small group of wealthy people, and into a few
countries. (The United States, with six percent of the population, owns,
produces, and consumes fifty percent of the world's production.) They
would agree with the Story Teller in Bertholt Brecht's *The Caucasian
Chalk Circle*, in the final words of the play:

> Take note what men of old concluded:
> That what there is shall go to those who are good for it
> Thus: the children to the motherly, that they prosper
> The carts to good drivers, that they are well driven
> And the valley to the waterers, that it bring forth fruit.

It was on this principle that Gerard Winstanley, leader of the
Diggers in seventeenth century England, ignored the law of private ownership and led his followers to plant grain on unused land. Winstanley
wrote about his hope for the future:

> When this universal law of equity rises up in every man and woman, then
> none shall lay claim to any creature and say, This is mine, and that is yours,
> This is my work, that is yours. But every one shall put to their hands to till
> the earth and bring up cattle, and the blessing of the earth shall be com-
> mon to all; when a man hath need of any corn or cattle, take from the next
> storehouse he meets with. There shall be no buying or selling, no fairs or
> markets, but the whole earth shall be a common treasury for every man, for
> the earth is the Lord's...

Our problem is to make use of the magnificent technology of our
time, for human needs, without being victimized by a bureaucratic mechanism. The Soviet Union did show that national economic planning for
common goals, replacing the profit-driven chaos of capitalist production,

could produce remarkable results. It failed, however, to do what Herbert Read and other recent anarchists have suggested: to do away with the bureaucracy of large-scale industry, characteristic of both capitalism and socialism, and the consequent unhappiness of the workers who do not feel at ease with their work, with the products, with their fellow workers, with nature, with themselves. This problem could be solved, Read has suggested, by *workers' control* of their own jobs, without sacrificing the benefits of planning and coordination for the larger social good.

"Property is theft," Proudhon wrote in the mid-nineteenth century (he was the first to call himself an anarchist). Whether the resources of the earth and the energies of men are controlled by capitalist corporations or bureaucracies calling themselves "socialist," a great theft of men's life-work has occurred, as a kind of original sin which has led in human history to all sorts of trouble: exploitation, war, the establishment of colonies, the subjugation of women, attacks on property called "crime," and the cruel system of punishments which all "civilized societies" have erected, known as "justice."

Both the capitalist and the socialist bureaucracies of our time fail, anarchists say, on their greatest promise: to bring democracy. The essence of democracy is that people should control their own lives, by ones or twos or hundreds, depending on whether the decision being made affects one or two or a hundred. Instead, our lives are directed by a political-military-industrial complex in the United States, and a party hierarchy in the Soviet Union. In both situations there is the pretense of popular participation, by an elaborate scheme of voting for representatives who do not have real power (the difference between a one-party state and a two-party state being no more than one party—and that a smudged carbon copy of the other). The *vote* in modern societies is the currency of politics as *money* is the currency of economics; both mystify what is really taking place—control of the many by the few.

Anarchists believe the phrase "law *and* order" is one of the great deceptions of our age. Law does not bring order, certainly not the harmonious order of a cooperative society, which is the best meaning of that word. It brings, if anything, the order of the totalitarian state, or the prison, or the army, where fear and threat keep people in their assigned places. All law can do is artificially restrain people who are moved to acts of violence or theft or disobedience by a bad society. And the order brought by law is unstable, always on the brink of a fall, because coercion invites rebellion. Laws cannot, by their nature, create a good society; that will come from great numbers of people arranging resources and themselves voluntarily ("Mutual Aid," Kropotkin called it) so as to promote cooperation and happiness. And that will be the best order, when people do what they must, not because of law, but on their own.

What has modern civilization, with its "rule of law," its giant industrial enterprises, its "representative democracy," brought? Nuclear missiles already aimed and ready for the destruction of the world, and populations—literate, well-fed, and constantly voting—of a mind to accept this madness. Civilization has failed on two counts: it has perverted the natural resources of the earth, which have the capacity to make our lives joyful, and also the natural resources of people, which have the potential for genius and love.

Making the most of these possibilities requires the upbringing of new generations in an atmosphere of grace and art. Instead, we have been reared in politics. Herbert Read (in *Art and Alienation*) describes the stunted human being who emerges from this:

> If seeing and handling, touching and hearing and all the refinements of sensation that developed historically in the conquest of nature and the manipulation of material substances are not educed and trained from birth to maturity the result is a being that hardly deserves to be called human: a dull-eyed, bored and listless automaton whose one desire is for violence in some form or other—violent action, violent sounds, distractions of any kind that can penetrate to its deadened nerves. Its preferred distractions are: the sports stadium, the pin-table alleys, the dance-hall, the passive "viewing" of crime, farce and sadism of the television screen, gambling and drug addiction.

What a waste of the evolutionary process! It took a billion years to create human beings who could, if they chose, form the materials of the earth and themselves into arrangements congenial to man, woman, and the universe. Can we still choose to do so?

It seems that revolutionary changes are needed—in the sense of profound transformations of our work processes, or decision-making arrangements, our sex and family relations, our thought and culture—toward a humane society. But *this* kind of revolution—changing our minds as well as our institutions—cannot be accomplished by customary methods: neither by military action to overthrow governments, as some tradition-bound radicals suggest; nor by that slow process of electoral reform, which traditional liberals urge on us. The state of the world today reflects the limitations of both those methods.

Anarchists have always been accused of a special addiction to violence as a mode of revolutionary change. The accusation comes from governments which came into being through violence, which maintain themselves in power through violence, and which use violence constantly to keep down rebellion and to bully other nations. Some anarchists—like other revolutionaries throughout history, whether American, French, Russian, or Chinese—have emphasized violent uprising. Some have advocated, and tried, assassination and terror. In this they are like other revolutionaries—of whatever epoch or ideology. What makes anarchists unique among revolutionaries, however, is that most of them see revolution as a cultural, ideological, creative process, in which violence would be as incidental as the outcries of mother and baby in childbirth. It might be unavoidable—given the natural resistance to change—but something to be kept at a minimum while more important things happen.

Alexander Berkman, who as a young man attempted to assassinate an American industrialist, expressed his more mature reflections on violence and revolution in *The ABC of Anarchism:*

> What, really, is there to destroy?
> The wealth of the rich? Nay, that is something we want the whole of society to enjoy.
> The land, the fields, the coal mines, the railroads, factories, mills and shops? These we want not to destroy but to make useful to the entire people.
> The telegraphs, telephones, the means of communication and distribution—do we want to destroy them? No, we want them to serve the needs of all.
> What, then, is the social revolution to destroy? It is to take over things for the general benefit, not to destroy them. It is to reorganize conditions for the public welfare.

Revolution in its full sense cannot be achieved by force of arms. It must be prepared in the minds and behavior of men, even *before* institutions have radically changed. It is not an act, but a process. Berkman describes this:

> If your object is to secure liberty, you must learn to do without authority and compulsion. If you intend to live in peace and harmony with your fellow men, you and they should cultivate brotherhood and respect for each other.

If you want to work together with them for your mutual benefit, you must practice co-operation. The social revolution means much more than the reorganization of conditions only: it means the establishment of new human values and social relationships, a changed attitude of man to man, as of one free and independent to his equal; it means a different spirit in individual and collective life, and that spirit cannot be born overnight. It is a spirit to be cultivated, to be nurtured and reared, as the most delicate flower is, for indeed it is the flower of a new and beautiful existence.... We must learn to think differently before the revolution can come. That alone can bring the revolution.

The anarchist sees revolutionary change as something immediate, something we must do now, where we are, where we live, where we work. It means starting this moment to do away with authoritarian, cruel relationships—between men and women, between parents and children, between one kind of worker and another kind. Such revolutionary action cannot be crushed like an armed uprising. It takes place in everyday life, in the tiny crannies where the powerful but clumsy hands of state power cannot easily reach. It is not centralized and isolated, so that it can be wiped out by the rich, the police, the military. It takes place in a hundred thousand places at once, in families, on streets, in neighborhoods, in places of work. It is a revolution of the whole culture. Squelched in one place, it springs up in another, until it is everywhere.

Such a revolution is an art. That is, it requires the courage not only of resistance, but of imagination. Herbert Read, after pointing out that modern democracy encourages both complacency and complicity, speaks (in *Art and Alienation*) of the role of art:

Art, on the other hand, is eternally disturbing, permanently revolutionary. It is so because the artist, in the degree of his greatness, always confronts the unknown, and what he brings back from that confrontation is a novelty, a new symbol, a new vision of life, the outer image of inward things. His importance to society is not that he voices received opinions, or gives clear expression to the confused feelings of the masses: that is the function of the politician, the journalist, the demagogue. The artist is what the Germans call *ein Rüttler*, an upsetter of the established order.

This should not be interpreted as an arrogant distinction between the elite artist and the mass of people. It is, rather, a recognition that in modern society, as Herbert Marcuse has pointed out, there is enormous pressure to create a "one-dimensional mind" among masses of people, and this requires upsetting.

Herbert Read's attraction to both art and anarchy seems a fitting response to the twentieth century, and underscores the idea that revolution must be cultural as well as political. The title of his book *To Hell With Culture* might be misinterpreted if one did not read in it:

> Today we are bound hand and foot to the past. Because property is a sacred thing and land values a source of untold wealth, our houses must be crowded together and our streets must follow their ancient illogical meanderings.... Because everything we buy for use must be sold for profit, and because there must always be this profitable margin between cost and price, our pots and our pans, our furniture and our clothes, have the same shoddy consistency, the same competitive cheapness. The whole of our capitalist culture is one immense veneer: a surface of refinement hiding the cheapness and shoddiness of the heart of things.
>
> To hell with such a culture. To the rubbish-heap and furnace with it all! Let us celebrate the democratic revolution creatively. Let us build cities that are not too big, but spacious, with traffic flowing freely through their leafy avenues, with children playing safely in their green and flowery parks, with people living happily in bright efficient houses.... Let us balance agriculture and industry, town and country—let us do all these sensible and elementary things and *then* let us talk about culture.

The anarchist tries to deal with the complex relationship between changing institutions and changing culture. He knows that we must revolutionize culture starting now; and yet he knows this will be limited until there is a new way of living for large numbers of people. Read writes in the same essay: "You cannot impose a culture from the top—it must come from under. It grows out of the soil, out of the people, out of their daily life and work. It is a spontaneous expression of their joy in life, of their joy in work, and if this joy does not exist, the culture will not exist."

For revolutionaries, the aesthetic element—the approach of the artist—is essential in breaking out of the past, for we have seen in history how revolutions have been cramped or diverted because the men who made them were still encumbered by tradition. The warning of Marx, in *The Eighteenth Brumaire of Louis Bonaparte*, needs to be heeded by Marxists as well as by others seeking change:

> The tradition of all the dead generations weighs like a nightmare on the brain of the living. And just when they seem engaged in revolutionizing themselves and things, in creating something entirely new, precisely in such epochs of revolutionary crisis they anxiously conjure up the spirits of the past to their service and borrow from them names, battle slogans and cos-

tumes in order to present the new scene of world history in this time-honoured disguise and this borrowed language.

The art of revolution needs to go beyond what is called "reason," and what is called "science," because both reason and science are limited by the narrow experience of the past. To break those limits, to extend reason into the future, we need passion and instinct, coming out of those depths of human feeling which escape the bounds of a historical period. When Read spoke in London in 1961, before taking part in a mass act of civil disobedience in protest against Polaris nuclear submarines, he argued for breaking out of the limits of "reason" through action:

> This stalemate must be broken, but it will never be broken by rational argument. There are too many right reasons for wrong actions on both sides. It can be broken only by instinctive action. An act of disobedience is or should be collectively instinctive—a revolt of the instincts of man against the threat of mass destruction.
>
> Instincts are dangerous to play with, but that is why, in the present desperate situation, we must play with instincts...
>
> We must release the imagination of the people so that they become fully conscious of the fate that is threatening them, and we can best reach their imagination by our actions, by our fearlessness, by our willingness to sacrifice our comfort, our liberty, and even our lives, to the end that mankind shall be delivered from pain and suffering and universal death.

Anarchism seeks that blend of order and spontaneity in our lives which gives us harmony with ourselves, with others, with nature. It understands the need to change our political and economic arrangements to free ourselves for the enjoyment of life. And it knows that the change must begin now, in those everyday human relations over which we have the most control. Anarchism knows the need for sober thinking, but also for that action which clarifies otherwise academic and abstract thought.

Herbert Read, in "Chains of Freedom," writes that we need a "Black Market in culture, a determination to avoid the bankrupt academic institutions, the fixed values and standardized products of current art and literature; not to trade our spiritual goods through the recognized channels of Church, or State, or Press; rather to pass them 'under the counter.'" If so, one of the first items to be passed under the counter must surely be the literature that speaks, counter to all the falsifications, about the ideas and imaginings of anarchism.

8

Failure to
Quit

This essay (written for *Z Magazine* in 1990, and reprinted in my book *Failure to Quit*, was inspired (if you are willing to call this an inspired piece) by my students of the Eighties. I was teaching a spring and fall lecture course with four hundred students in each course (and yet with lots of discussion). I looked hard, listened closely, but did not find the apathy, the conservatism, the disregard for the plight of others, that everybody (right and left) was reporting about "the me generation."

I can understand pessimism, but I don't believe in it. It's not simply a matter of faith, but of historical evidence. Not overwhelming evidence, just enough to give hope, because for hope we don't need certainty, only possibility. Which (despite all those confident statements that "history shows..."and "history proves...") is all history can offer us.

When I hear so often that there is little hope for change from the present generation of young people, I think back to the despair that accompanied the onset of the Sixties.

Historians of the late Forties and Fifties (Richard Hofstadter, Louis Hartz) were writing ruefully about a liberal-conservative "consensus" that dominated the United States all through its history and that still prevailed, setting severe limits to change. Herbert Marcuse, at the start of the Sixties, saw American society, American thought, as "one-dimensional," with radical ideas absorbed and deflected, dissent repressed through "tolerance."

One could not read these men, socially conscious, desirous themselves of change yet despairing of it, without feeling a deep pessimism about the possibilities for change in the United States. As the year 1960 began, Princeton philosopher Walter Kaufmann lamented "the uncommitted generation" and wrote: "What distinguishes them is that they are not committed to any cause." Neither he nor Hofstadter, Hartz, Marcuse, nor anyone for that matter, could have predicted what would soon happen.

It was on the first of February in that first year of the new decade that four black students from North Carolina A & T College sat down at a "white" lunch counter in Greensboro, refused to move, and were arrested. In two weeks, sit-ins had spread to fifteen cities in five Southern states. By the year's end, 50,000 people had participated in demonstrations in a hundred cities, and 3,600 had been put in jail.

That was the start of the civil rights movement, which became an anti-war movement, a women's movement, a cultural upheaval, and in its course hundreds of thousands, no, millions of people became committed for a short time, or for a lifetime. It was unprecedented, unpredicted, and for at least fifteen years, uncontrollable. It would shake the country and startle the world, with consequences we are hardly aware of today.

True, those consequences did not include the end of war, exploitation, hunger, racism, military intervention, nationalism, sexism—only the end of legal racial segregation, the end of the war of Vietnam, the end of illegal abortions. It was just a beginning.

The uncommitted generation? I thought so too when, out of the Air Force, married, with two small children, finishing graduate work in history at Columbia University, I went South to teach in Atlanta, Georgia. My job was at Spelman College, where young black women, the daughters of railroad porters, teachers, ministers, maids, laborers, farmers, came to get their degrees. It was 1956. The atmosphere on that tree-lined, fragrant campus was sedate, quiet, careful, and only close attention to what was said and left unsaid revealed deep resentment just below the surface. By 1960, these same quiet students were sitting-in, demonstrating, picketing, going to jail. I learned that it was a serious mistake to interpret lack of action as lack of thought, lack of feeling. Rather, it was the absence of opportunities, openings, examples to emulate, groups to join—but when those appeared, the silence changed to uproar.

There is no such uproar today. There is an uncertain mixture of silence and commotion. The silence deserves attention. In 1984 there was a silent majority in this country that refused to vote for Reagan: 68 percent of the eligible voters (add the 21 percent who voted for Mondale with the 47 percent who didn't bother to vote). This leaves 32 percent who voted for Reagan, which was converted by a timid press and a gullible public into an "overwhelming mandate."

But there is more than silence.

There is a human carry-over from the Sixties. True, there are veterans of those movements who have been swallowed up by the gluttonous tigers of survival and "success" and live, happily or not, inside the bellies of those beasts, making do. But there are others, in the cages, yes, but holding off the carnivores with a chair and a prayer, stubbornly refusing to be eaten, looking for openings and opportunities, pushing the system to its limits while pointing beyond, keeping the spirit of resistance alive.

I think of two of my students at Spelman, among the many who were jailed during the Atlanta sit-ins: Marian Wright, going to Yale Law School, and to Mississippi with the Movement, now the tireless head of the Children's Defense Fund in Washington; Alice Walker, becoming a poet, a novelist, a feminist and political activist. I think of Carolyn Mugar, working with anti-war GIs in the Vietnam years, more recently a labor organizer in southern Massachusetts. Or Bernice Reagon, student leader and Freedom Singer in the Albany, Georgia Movement of 1961-62, now a folk historian at the Smithsonian, a formidable mind and voice, still a Freedom Singer ("Sweet Honey in the Rock"). And Staughton Lynd, historian, organizer of Freedom Schools in Mississippi, anti-war protester of the Sixties, now a labor lawyer in Ohio.

We all know such people, but it goes far beyond personal connections. There are thousands of local groups around the country—many more than existed in the Sixties—devoted to struggling for tenants' rights or women's rights, or environmental protection, or against the arms race, or to take care of the hungry and the homeless, or those in need of health care. There are now tens of thousands of professionals, many of them veterans of the movements of the Sixties, who bring unorthodox ideas and humane values into courtrooms, classrooms, hospitals.

Over 50,000 people have signed the Pledge of Resistance, committing themselves to protest against U.S. intervention in Central America. A small number, but it represents a large part of the nation, because survey after survey shows a majority of the country opposed to administration policy in Central America. Is it not reasonable to assume that a U.S. invasion of Nicaragua, so lusted after by the Reagan Administration, was forestalled, despite a timid Congress, by recognition that the public would not support such an action?

When activists commit civil disobedience to protest against the CIA or the arms race, or aid to the contras, the degree of their distance from the general sentiment can be measured, at least roughly, by how juries of ordinary citizens react. During the war in Vietnam, when religious pacifists entered draft boards illegally to destroy draft records as a way of protesting the war, juries became increasingly reluctant to convict, and near the end of the war we saw the dramatic acquittal of the Camden 28 by a jury which then threw a party for the defendants.

Acts of civil disobedience today, at a much earlier stage of U.S. intervention, are getting verdicts of acquittal when juries are permitted to listen to the defendants' reasons for their civil disobedience. In the spring of 1984, in Burlington, Vermont, the "Winooski 44" had occupied Senator Stafford's office to protest his support of aid to the contras. The jury heard many hours of testimony about conditions in Nicaragua, the role of the CIA, the nature of the contras, and voted for acquittal. One of the jurors, a local house painter, said: "I was honored to be on that jury. I felt a part of history."

In Minneapolis that same year, seven "trespassers" protesting at the Honeywell Corporation were acquitted. In 1985, men and women blocked the Great Lakes Training Station in Illinois, others blocked the South African Embassy in Chicago, nineteen people in the state of Washington halted trains carrying warheads, and all these won acquittals in court. Last year in western Massachusetts, where a protest against the CIA took place, there was another surprising acquittal. One of the jurors, Donna L. Moody, told a reporter: "All the expert testimony against the CIA was alarming. It was very educational."

Over the past six years, eighteen "Plowshares" actions, involving symbolic sabotage of nuclear weaponry, have resulted mostly in guilty verdicts. In the latest case, involving two Catholic priests and two others who broke into a naval air station near Philadelphia and damaged three aircraft, the judge refused the defense of "necessity" but allowed the jury to hear the defendants' reasons for their actions. The jury was unable to reach a verdict.

Several years ago, when Reagan announced the blockade of Nicaragua, 550 of us sat-in at the federal building in Boston to protest, and were arrested. It seemed too big a group of dissidents to deal with, and charges were dropped. When I received my letter, I saw for the first time what the official complaint against all of us was: "Failure to Quit." That is, surely, the critical fact about the continuing movement for human rights here and all over the world.

We hear many glib dismissals of today's college students as being totally preoccupied with money and self. In fact, there is much concern among students with their economic futures—evidence of the failure of the economic system to provide for the young, more than a sign of their indifference to social injustice. But the past few years have seen political actions on campuses all over the country. For 1986 alone, a partial list shows: 182 students, calling for divestment from South Africa, arrested at the University of Texas; a black-tie dinner for alumni at Harvard called off after a protest on South African holdings; charges dropped against 49 Wellesley protesters after half the campus boycotted classes in support; and more protests recorded at Yale, Wisconsin, Louisville, San Jose, Columbia.

But what about the others, the non-protesting students? Among the liberal arts students, business majors, and ROTC cadets who sit in my classes, there are super-patriots and enthusiasts of capitalism, but also others, whose thoughts deserve some attention:

Writing in his class journal, one ROTC student, whose father was a navy flier, his brother a navy commander: "This one class made me go out and read up on South Africa. What I learned made me sick. My entire semester has been a paradox. I go to your class and I see a Vietnam vet named Joe Bangert tell of his experiences in the war. I was enthralled by his talk...By the end of that hour and a half I hated the Vietnam war as much as he did. The only problem is that three hours after that class I am marching around in my uniform...and feeling great about it. Is there something wrong with me? Am I being hypocritical? Sometimes I don't know..."

Young woman in ROTC: "What really stuck in my mind was the ignorance some people displayed at the end of class. We were discussing welfare. Some students stated that people on welfare were lazy, that if they really wanted to, they could find jobs. Argg! These rich kids (or middle class or whatever) who have all they need and think they're so superior make me angry..."

The same student, after seeing the film *Hearts and Minds*: "General Westmoreland said 'Orientals don't value lives.' I was incredulous. And then they showed the little boy holding the picture of his father and he was crying and crying and crying...I must admit I started crying. What's worse was that I was wearing my Army uniform that day and I had to make a conscious effort not to disappear in my seat."

Young woman in the School of Management: "North broke the law, but will he be punished?... If he is let off the hook then all of America is punished. Every inner-city kid who is sent to jail for stealing food to feed his brothers and sisters is punished. Every elderly person who has to fight just to keep warm on a winter night will be punished.... The law is supposed to be on the common bond—the peace making body. Yet it only serves the function selectively—just when the people in control wish it to."

Surely history does not start anew with each decade. The roots of one era branch and flower in subsequent eras. Human beings, writings, invisible transmitters of all kinds, carry messages across the generations. I try to be pessimistic, to keep up with some of my friends. But I think back over the decades, and look around. And then, it seems to me that the future is not certain, but it is possible.

Suggestions
for Further
Reading

Some suggestions for further reading (I am not giving a formal listing of publishers, dates, and places because public libraries can easily locate books by title and/or author):

On Race:

I believe the most useful things to read on what Cornel West calls "race matters" (while making the point that race *matters*) are the writings of African-Americans themselves. My own first experience as a teenager, was with Richard Wright's *Native Son*, a startling introduction to the connection between two kinds of crime: those committed by black people out of desperation; those committed by a system of racial and class injustice. Years later, I read Richard Wright's *Black Boy*. That belongs to a group of books that takes you inside the growing-up experiences of black people, revealed in their autobiographical writings. You can go back to slave experiences, as in *The Autobiography of Frederick Douglass*, and then on to this century: W.E.B. Du Bois' *Souls of Black Folk*; Zora Neale Hurston's *Dust*

Tracks on a Road; Alice Walker's essays, *In Search of Our Mothers' Gardens*, Langston Hughes' *The Big Sea* and *I Wonder as I Wander*; and Malcolm X's *Autobiography*. Bringing it into the civil rights era, James Farmer's *Lay Bare the Heart*. African-American poetry should be read, not only that by Langston Hughes, but by Countee Cullen, Alice Walker, and others (Arna Bontemps' collection, *American Negro Poetry*, is excellent). There are the novels of Toni Morrison and Octavia Butler, the extraordinary stories and novels of Toni Cade Bambara, the plays of Leroi Jones and August Wilson.

There are many histories of the civil rights movement. I would recommend the oral histories collected by Henry Hampton and Steve Fayer (of the great television series *Eyes on the Prize*), *Voices of Freedom*, as well as those in Howell Raines' *My Soul is Rested*. Also, the interviews of their parents and grandparents done by Mississippi schoolchildren, *Minds Stayed on Freedom*. There is a wonderful photographic memoir by Danny Lyon, *Memories of the Southern Civil Rights Movement*.

Two splendid biographies stand out: David Levering Lewis' *W.E.B. Du Bois* (though it only goes up to 1919), and Martin Duberman's *Paul Robeson*. And a collection of documents ranging through American history, Gerda Lerner's *Black Women in White America*.

For a general history of African-Americans, there is an indispensable reference work: the three volumes of Herbert Aptheker's *A Documentary History of the Negro People in the U.S.* John Hope Franklin's *From Slavery to Freedom* is a classic.

For the history of Latino people, I would recommend the remarkable dual-language book, photos and text by Elizabeth Martinez, *500 Years of Chicano History*. And Ronald Takaki's multicultural history, *A Different Mirror*.

On Class:

Perhaps the first book I read that spoke to my own working class upbringing was by Upton Sinclair: *The Jungle*. Then, John Steinbeck's *The Grapes of Wrath*, which, years later, gave my students a better feel for the depression than any non-fiction account of the Thirties. Studs Terkel's *Hard Times* is a fascinating set of interviews with people who remember the depression years. When I began to study American history, I came across Charles Beard's *An Economic Interpretation of the Constitution*, which gave me a powerful insight into the class character of the American

Revolution. For that period, I would also recommend Gary Nash's *Class and Society in Early America*. There is a set of essays by American scholars, *The American Revolution*, edited by Alfred Young, which contributes to this approach.

Matthew Josephson's books, *The Robber Barons* and *The Politicos*, expose the close ties between corporate power and political power in the late nineteenth century. Douglas Dowd gives us a charming, radical economic history from 1919 to the 1990s in his memoir, *Blues for America*. One of the first books I read that gave me an idea of the rich complexity and drama of labor history, from the great railroad strikes of 1877 to the San Francisco general strike of 1934, was Samuel Yellen's *American Labor Struggles*.

Important to me, as I was becoming conscious of the crucial question of class, was to read Karl Marx's *The Communist Manifesto*, as well as the first volume of *Capital* (I did read the second and third volumes, but mercy requires that I not push them). Paul Baran and Paul Sweezy's *Monopoly Capital*, applies Marxian analysis to the United States after World War II.

Without presenting itself explicitly as a class analysis of American history, Richard Hofstadter's *The American Political Tradition* made clear how behind the sparring of the major political parties throughout the country's history there was a basic consensus around the capitalist system.

On War:

The first blow to my youthful awe of martial heroism came when I was eighteen or so and read Walter Millis' *The Road to War*, a devastating critique of our nation's entrance into World War I. But probably the most powerful influences that, for me, turned the glamour of war into unmitigated horror were novels: Henry Barbusse's *Under Fire*; Erich Maria Remarque's *All Quiet on the Western Front*; and even more, Dalton Trumbo's *Johnny Got His Gun*, all part of the revulsion that came after the first World War.

Despite my enthusiastic participation in World War II as an Air Force bombardier, it did not take long after the war to begin to reconsider the question of whether any war, even that "best of wars" (as I termed it, ironically, in one of my essays later) was justified. Probably the first piece of writing that turned me in that direction was John Hersey's

Hiroshima. Later, the novels *Catch-22* by Joseph Heller, and *Slaughterhouse Five* by Kurt Vonnegut, fit perfectly into my now-cynical view of that war.

My studies and teaching in American history, giving me a close look at U.S. foreign policy, persuaded me that our military interventions abroad, in Latin America, in the Pacific, were part of the empire-building among the Western nations, for reasons of political power and corporate profit. William Appleman Williams' *The Tragedy of American Diplomacy,* was an early influence. For books on Vietnam, I would recommend Marilyn Young's vibrant, powerful history, *The Vietnam Wars.* On U.S. foreign policy since the inception of the cold war, there is no better guide than the writings of Noam Chomsky. I will just mention a few of his books: *Necessary Illusions, Deterring Democracy,* and *Manufacturing Consent* (the latter written with Edward Herman).

For alternatives to war, there are a number of books by Gene Sharp, especially *The Politics of Non-Violent Direct Action.*

On Law:

I became aware of the injustice built into our legal system—against the poor, against blacks, against foreigners, against radicals—for the first time about the case of Sacco & Vanzetti. Indeed, it was a novel by Upton Sinclair, *Boston,* which introduced me to that dramatic moment in our history. Then I read a fascinating book by Louis Joughin and Edmund Morgan, *The Legacy of Sacco and Vanzetti.* I was introduced to the trial of the eight anarchists in the Haymarket Affair of 1886 by reading the novel by Howard Fast, *The American.* That led me to a book on the Haymarket events by Henry David, *The Haymarket Affair.* The name Clarence Darrow came up again and again in the trials of radicals and labor leaders, and I would recommend a collection of his addresses to the jury, *Clarence Darrow for the Defense.*

To get a picture of how American law, through the 19th century, began more and more to benefit the rich and powerful, one should read Harvard law professor Morton Hurwitz's *The Transformation of American Law.* On the trials of anti-war protesters in World War I, there is the classic by Zecchariah Chafee, *Free Speech in the United States.* A good survey of the anti-Communist hysteria of the cold war period is in David Caute's *The Great Fear.*

On issues of civil disobedience, there is the classic essay by Henry David Thoreau, *On Civil Disobedience*. Also, the writings of Tolstoy on this subject, when he had decided to stop writing novels and turn his attention to social issues, are collected in *On Civil Disobedience and Nonviolence*. I found philosophical grounding for ideas on civil disobedience in Albert Camus' *The Rebel*. Martin Luther King's *Letter from the Birmingham City Jail* is a passionate defense of civil disobedience.

On History:

I had not thought much about the social role of the historian until I read Robert Lynd's *Knowledge for What?* Alfred North Whitehead's *The Aims of Education* explores such questions too. Another thoughtful book about the problems of writing history (objectivity, morality, science, etc.) is the book by the British historian E.H. Carr, *What is History?*

In the early 20th century, an American writer, James Harvey Robinson, wrote a provocative book on this subject, *The New History*. There is an excellent collection of essays by Hans Meyerhoff, *The Philosophy of History in Our Time*. And a superb book by Peter Novick on the issue of objectivity among historians, *That Noble Dream*.

In the Sixties, Jesse Lemisch, a young radical historian, wrote a biting critique of the historical profession: *On Active Service in War and Peace*. There are certain historians who represent for me the ideal joining of impeccable research and social conscience. One is the British historian E.P. Thompson, who wrote *The Making of the English Working Class*. Another is an American, Richard Drinnon, as in his brilliant book about American expansionism, *Facing West*.

On Means and Ends:

I became interested in anarchist thought in the Sixties, when I read Richard Drinnon's biography of Emma Goldman, *Rebel in Paradise*. This led me to her own marvelous autobiography, *Living My Life*, and to her essays and speeches, collected in *Anarchism and Other Essays*. Her life-long friend Alexander Berkman, after spending fourteen years in prison for the attempted murder of the industrialist Henry Clay Frick, wrote the classic *Prison Memoirs of an Anarchist*. He also wrote one of the best short explanations of anarchism in his pamphlet-book *The ABC of Anarchism*. Selections from these books and from his letters can be found in the volume edited by Gene Fellner, *Life of an Anarchist.* The Russian anarchist-anthropologist Peter Kropotkin has had a group of his essays printed in *Revolutionary Pamphlets.*

George Orwell's *Homage to Catalonia* gives a fascinating account of what happened in Barcelona at the start of the Spanish Civil War when anarchists took over the city. This suggested a possible model of what a good society would be like, and I found an earlier possible model in the Paris Commune of 1871. There is a first person account of that remarkable event by Lissagaray, *History of the Commune of 1871,* and a later analysis by Frank Jellinek, *The Paris Commune of 1871.*

Staughton and Alice Lynd have put together an extraordinary collection, *Non-Violence in America,* which traces non-violent thought and action from the earliest days to the present. There is an older collection on this subject, international in scope, edited by Mulford Sibley, *The Quiet Battle.*

Also by Howard Zinn:

LaGuardia in Congress (Cornell University Press, 1959)

The Southern Mystique (Alfred Knopf, 1964)

SNCC: The New Abolitionists (Beacon Press, 1964)

New Deal Thought, ed. (Bobbs Merrill, 1965)

Vietnam: The Logic of Withdrawal (Beacon Press, 1967)

Disobedience and Democracy (Random House, 1968)

The Politics of History (Beacon Press, 1970)

The Pentagon Papers: Critical Essays, ed. with Noam Chomsky (Beacon Press, 1972)

Postwar America (Bobbs Merrill, 1973)

Justice in Everyday Life, ed. (William Morrow, 1974)

A People's History of the United States (Harper & Row, 1980)

The Twentieth Century: A People's History (HarperCollins, 1984)

Declarations of Independence: Cross-Examining American Ideology (HarperCollins, 1990)

Failure to Quit: Reflections of an Optimistic Historian (Common Courage Press, 1993)

You Can't Be Neutral on a Moving Train (Beacon Press, 1994)

HOWARD ZINN grew up in the immigrant slums of Brooklyn where he worked in shipyards in his late teens. He saw combat duty as an air force bombardier in World War II, and afterward received his doctorate in history from Columbia University and was a postdoctoral Fellow in East Asian Studies at Harvard University. His first book, *La Guardia in Congress*, was an Albert Beveridge Prize winner. In 1956, he moved with his wife and children to Atlanta to become chairman of the history department of Spelman College. His experiences there led to his second book, *The Southern Mystique*. As a participant-observer in the founding activities of the Student Nonviolent Coordinating Committee, he spent time in Georgia, Alabama, and Mississippi, and wrote *SNCC: The New Abolitionists*. As part of the American Heritage series, he edited *New Deal Thought*, an anthology. His fifth and six books, *Vietnam: The Logic of Withdrawal*, and *Disobedience and Democracy*, were written in the midst of his participation in intense antiwar activity. In 1968, he flew to Hanoi with Father Daniel Berrigan to receive the first three American fliers released by North Vietnam. Two years later came *The Politics of History*. In 1972 he edited, with Noam Chomsky, *The Pentagon Papers: Critical Essays*. In 1973 appeared *Postwar America*. In 1974 he edited *Justice in Everyday Life*. In 1980 came his epic masterpiece, *A People's History of the United States*, "a brilliant and moving history of the American people from the point of view of those who have been exploited politically and economically and whose plight has been largely omitted from most histories" (*Library Journal*). Recent books by Zinn include *Declarations of Independence: Cross-Examining American Ideology* and *You Can't Be*

Neutral on a Moving Train: A Personal History of Our Times. Professor emeritus of political science at Boston University, Zinn has also written three plays, *Emma, Daughter of Venus,* and *Marx in Soho.* He lives with his wife Roslyn in the Boston area, near their children and grandchildren.